FUNDAMENTALS of COMPUTERS in BUSINESS
A Systems Approach

FUNDAMENTALS of COMPUTERS in BUSINESS
A Systems Approach

Edward A. Tomeski
Fordham University and Barry College

with

Deborah S. Becker
George Stephenson
Dorothy E. Wood

Holden-Day, Inc. • San Francisco
London • Dusseldorf • Singapore • Sydney
Tokyo • New Delhi • Mexico

FUNDAMENTALS OF
COMPUTERS IN BUSINESS
A Systems Approach

500 Sansome Street, San Francisco, CA 94111

Library of Congress Catalog Card Number: 78-54208
ISBN: 0-8162-8733-3

Printed in the United States of America

234567890 809

Acquisition & Development Frederick H. Murphy
Production Supervision Michael Bass & Associates
Production Assistant Barbara Gordon
Editing Naomi Steinfeld
Proofreading Jane Ellen Long
Text & Cover Design S. Don Fujimoto & Associates
Creative Illustrations Dick Cole
Technical Illustrations Blakely Graphics
Layout John R. Kirschner and Associates
Typesetting Allservice Phototypesetting Company of Arizona
Printing Book Press

Dedicated to the
New Generation of Society,
who must cope with the
New Generation of Technology,
especially the Brodericks:
John Stanley,
Luke Joseph,
Mark Stephen,
Peter Gerard,
Thomas Edward,
& John William.

CONTENTS

PREFACE

This book has been written as an introductory course in computers and related subjects (e.g., data processing and information systems). It will be particularly useful to college and university faculty and students who are interested in the computer's role and use in business, government, and society. This book also can be useful within the context of training programs—for example, of business organizations, government offices, professional societies, technical institutes, and continuing education programs.

Fundamentals of Computers in Business is the result of my more than twenty years of practical experience (as a manager, a computer technician, and a consultant) as well as teaching and research experience at colleges and universities. While there are many computer books on the market, this book's particular qualities and strengths (which come from my wide experience in the field) can serve a significant segment of the market.

In particular, the focus is on:

1. *Readability.* Many computer books "turn off" students because of their overly technical emphasis and complex treatment of material. This textbook has been developed to facilitate the average student's understanding and interest.
2. *Pertinence.* Clear descriptions of the essentials of computers have been provided, taking care not to overwhelm the reader with details that pertain only indirectly to an introductory course about computers. Readability and pertinence have been attained without sacrificing the quality and integrity of the coverage of computer concepts and practices.

Some of the specific features of this book that make it appealing are:

- Use of the *systems approach.*
- Consideration of *management, organizational,* and *societal issues.*

- *Simplification of complex computer material,* while retaining the integrity of computer technology coverage.
- Presentation of *futuristic considerations,* including fourth- and fifth-generation computers, and forecasts to the year 2000 A.D.
- *Liberal use of pictures, diagrams, and graphics* to stimulate the learning and interest of television-oriented students.
- High degree of *organization* within chapters. Each chapter has: Objectives; Summary; Terms to Review; and Review Questions. In addition, exhibits are used to condense key material in the chapter.
- *Practical capsule cases and situations,* to illustrate points throughout the text.

The somewhat unique organizational scheme divides this book into six sections. Section I, Systems and Management Concepts, gives the reader a conceptual framework by introducing essential systems and management ideas that computer books lack all too often. Section II, Scope of Data Processing, introduces the student to data processing and computers in an enjoyable and challenging way. Section III, Computer Devices and Functions, covers necessary details about computer hardware. Section IV, Computer Professionals at Work, describes how computer technicians perform their tasks and interface with the computer. Section V, Management and Social Considerations, looks at various managerial-level issues (e.g., how to manage the computer, and how to get management information from the computer), as well as at issues that have broad societal implications (e.g., privacy and the computer). Finally, Section VI, Computer Trends, appraises the likely future of not only computers but also of those affected by computers.

The seventeen chapters of the book can easily be adapted to any academic calendar (e.g., regular-semester basis or quarter-semester basis).

I hope that the enormous amount of dedicated effort that has gone into the preparation of this book will contribute to a productive and pleasant learning experience for many people.

Edward Alexander Tomeski
Sea Girt, New Jersey and
Boca Raton, Florida

Acknowledgments

It has been correctly stated that we build on the shoulders of others.

I would like to give particular recognition to the invaluable contributions of three individuals. Professor George Stephenson reviewed Sections I, II, and III of the text, made valuable suggestions, and contributed original ideas. And Professor Deborah Shoen Becker reviewed and substantially improved parts of Section IV, and contributed to the material on software and computer programming. Dorothy E. Wood assisted with research for the original manuscript and provided creative material for the book.

The time in which to complete the manuscript was provided by the cooperation of Fordham University of New York City and Barry College of Miami, Florida. In particular, I would like to express my appreciation to Dr. Joseph F. X. McCarthy, Academic Vice President of Fordham University; Dr. M. Daniel Henry, Academic Vice President of Barry College; and Dr. R. W. Morell, Dean of the School of Business of Barry College. Sister M. Trinita Flood, O.P., President of Barry College, and Reverend James C. Finlay, S.J., President of Fordham University, were special sources of encouragement and support in my professional pursuits.

Mr. Frederick H. Murphy, President of Holden-Day, Inc., was responsive to my needs and encouraged both the initiation and progress of the project. Professor Elias Awad reviewed the original manuscript and offered many suggestions that enhanced the book greatly.

Mason P. Southworth, of International Business Machines Corporation's headquarters, was helpful in providing technical support and material for the book. Sister Beverly Bobola, O.P., gave expert advice on word processing in offices.

A number of the ideas used in this book arose as the result of my affiliation and work with management and computer professionals. Among these persons are: Dr. Harold Lazarus; Carl Heyel; Professor Sam Gaynor; Professor Donald D. Clarke;

Israel Diamond; George W. Elder; Gerald T. Montgomery; Robert Parker; Arthur H. Schneyman; Ed Halpern; Michael Cappi; Wiliam Brown, Jr.; Arch B. Johnston; Pierre-Michel Oury; Professor Marvin Reznikoff; Richard Westcott; and F. Walton Wanner.

Ms. Mary Viccica, Ms. Maria Teresa Rodriguez, and Ms. Rosalie Field provided secretarial support that, directly or indirectly, helped me complete the manuscript.

Dr. Aurea del Rosario was a special source of encouragement.

On a more personal basis, my mother, as always, provided a special environment, which has facilitated my research and writing.

To these persons—and to my students throughout the years—I owe much in the development and evolution of my thoughts.

Edward Alexander Tomeski

In these confused
and restless zones
in which present
blends with future
in a world of upheaval,
we stand
face to face
with all the grandeur,
the unprecedented grandeur,
of the phenomenon
of man.

TEILHARD DE CHARDIN

Our remedies
oft in ourselves
do lie,
Which we ascribe
to Heaven.

WILLIAM SHAKESPEARE

SECTION I

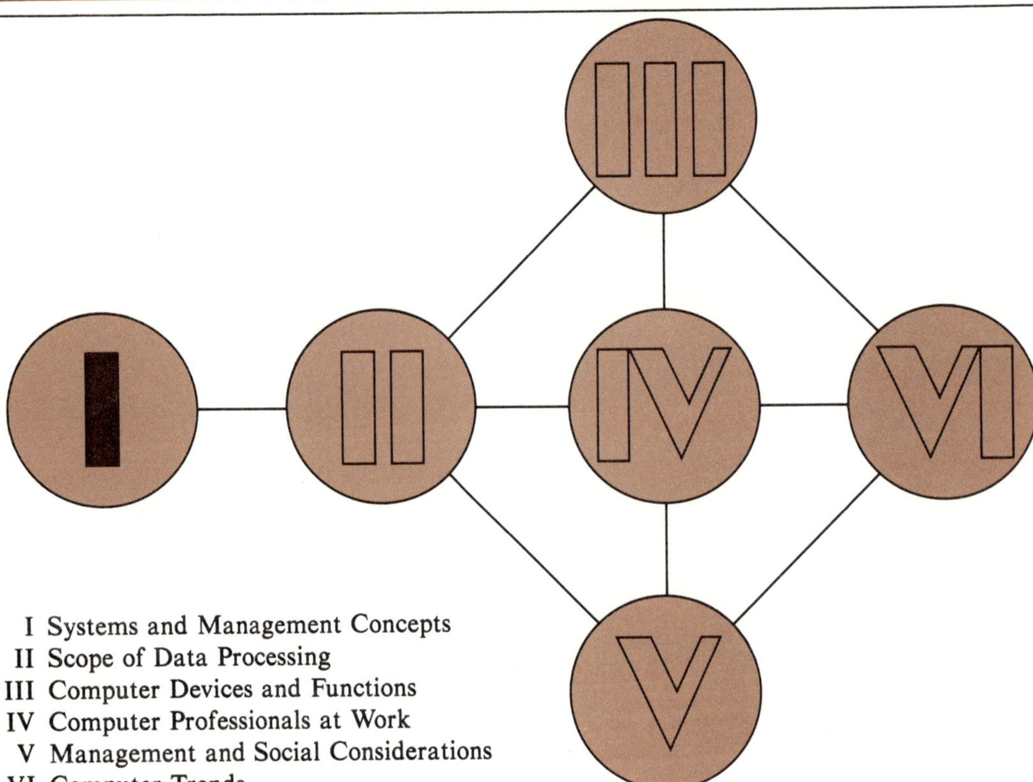

I Systems and Management Concepts
II Scope of Data Processing
III Computer Devices and Functions
IV Computer Professionals at Work
V Management and Social Considerations
VI Computer Trends

SYSTEMS AND MANAGEMENT CONCEPTS

. . . The systems approach . . . is . . . changing man's life, society, and his world view . . . and profoundly changing technology itself and its role.

PETER F. DRUCKER

One of the most potentially earth-shaking forces in our economy is the technology of information . . . we must decide on our information needs and how the computer can fill those needs. To do that, we must understand our operating processes, and the principles behind the processes.

PETER F. DRUCKER

"Can't see
the forest
for the trees"

CHAPTER 1

A SYSTEMS APPROACH TO BUSINESS

Objectives

The goal of this chapter is to broadly familiarize the reader with systems concepts, and to indicate how these concepts relate to society and business.

A SYSTEMS PHILOSOPHY

If computer professionals are to apply computer technology in a way that maximizes computer power, gains acceptance of those affected by the computer, and benefits the organization, then they need a systems philosophy.

A *system* is defined as an entity that is composed of *subsystems* and that has a common purpose and known boundaries. A nonsystems view is a myopic view: because it concentrates only on isolated subsystems, it fails to see relationships among subsystems.

The nonsystems philosophy is represented by the proverbial adage of the individual who sees the trees but is blind to the forest!

However, in a systems view, one would not only see the tree but also its place in the surrounding forest. In addition, one would realize those things needed to sustain the forest: fertile soil, rain, and sunshine. Other related matters might also be considered: a plan for farming the trees and reforestation; the appropriate use of the lumber cut from the trees; protection against forest fires and soil erosion; etc. In this sense, then, the single tree is seen as part of a system (see Exhibit 1–1).

But too often, computer technicians have focused on highly specialized aspects of computers and have failed to meaningfully relate their efforts to the broader needs of management, the organization, and society.*

SYSTEMS CONCEPTS

The word "system" is one of the most "in" words in professional circles. Among others, we hear and read about:

- Computer systems;
- Information systems;
- Scientific systems;

* Chapter 9 deals with the practical application of systems work in a computer environment.

Exhibit 1–1 A Systems View

- Solar system;
- Economic systems;
- International systems;
- Production systems;
- Political systems;
- Transportation systems;
- Military systems;
- Medical systems;
- Cardiovascular systems;
- Health systems;
- Cultural systems;
- Biological systems; and
- Education systems.

The widespread adoption of the word, if not the practice, suggests that systems concepts may be very important. We will consider some of the key systems concepts: general-systems theory, total system, integration of subsystems, adaptive systems, rational and human systems, and systems models (see Table 1–1). These concepts should give the reader at least an appreciation, if not a working familiarity, with systems approaches.

General-Systems Theory

The premise of the *general-systems theory* is that all things are related to all other things in the universe. Here is one general-systems classification:

- *Cells* are composed of atoms and molecules.
- *Organs* are composed of *cells* aggregated into tissues.
- *Organisms* (i.e., creatures) are made up of *organs*.
- *Groups* (e.g., families, teams, tribes) are collections of *organisms*.
- *Organizations* consist of *groups*.
- *Societies* are made of *organizations*, groups, and individuals (i.e., organisms).
- *Supernational systems* consist of a number of *societies* and national organizations.
- The *world system* encompasses all *supernational systems*, organizations, societies, etc.

From this we can see that there are connections between the smallest elements of life (e.g., atoms and molecules) and the broadest classification (e.g., all human beings comprising a world system).

The general-systems theory was developed to provide a unifying and integrating basis for the scientific disciplines (e.g., physics, chemistry, biology, and astronomy) to overcome the communications barriers that arose because of the increasing specialization and complexity of individual scientific disciplines. However, the general-systems theory applies to other activities, as well—including business and government.

Table 1–1
Key Systems Concepts

Concept	Description of Concept
System	Entity composed of subsystems and having a common purpose and known boundaries.
General-Systems Theory	Everything is related to everything else in the universe.
Total System	A comprehensive approach to system that is suited to the individual situation.
Integration of Subsystems	Appropriate linking together, or interfacing, of subsystems of a system.
Adaptive Systems	The dynamic nature of systems as they adjust to changing conditions in the environment.
Rational Systems	The use of rational approaches in the study of problems.
Human Systems	The recognition of the human factor, including emotions, needs, and values.
Systems Model	A universal model based on input, processing, and output.

The general-systems theory attempts to bring order and structure to chaos, segmentation, and complexity. At the same time, this theory takes into account the dynamics of change and the great uncertainty that exists in the universe.

The Total System*

It is impractical to relate every problem to all others in the universe. One must set some rational boundary to delimit the total system for any particular purpose; and often, time and economic factors govern how broadly one may consider the total system. Thus, the term *total system* is used as a matter of convenience. It identifies a series of interrelated subsystems that have a *common purpose* and known *boundaries*. For example:

> *For one purpose, one might consider the United Nations as a total system. Its subsystems would be the 150 or more member nations, representing the world population of in excess of four billion inhabitants. In this system, the United States is a subsystem of a larger system.*
>
> *For another purpose, the United States might be considered as a total system. It consists of fifty subsystems (i.e., the fifty states). The states can be considered to be*

* Semantics can pose a problem in this area. For purposes of this book, the terms "total system" and "system" will be used interchangeably. However, the word "total" does underscore the importance of a comprehensive approach to system.

composed of further subsystems: local governments such as counties, cities, towns, etc. Taken one step further, the local government units themselves are composed of subsystems (i.e., organizations, family households, and individuals).

The individual or organization that uses systems concepts must decide the scope of total system that is useful in a given circumstance. An overly broad definition of total system can make for an unwieldy situation; too narrow a definition can easily overlook opportunities and realities. In any case, the total-system concept means that any one subsystem can best be understood and improved by being viewed in relationship to all other subsystems within the total system.

However, one of the difficulties inherent in the total-system approach is that it involves intricacies of great magnitude, even in simple situations. For instance, if a system has only seven subsystems, we can say that it has forty-two relations (i.e., each of the seven subsystems is related to six other subsystems; thus 7×6). However, if we define the state of this system as the pattern produced in a network when each of these relations is either in being or not in being, there will be 2^{42} different relationships in the system. This is more than four million millions! This kind of scope indicates why the rigorous and exhaustive study of systems must have limitations, and why it remains as much art as science. Of course, in real life many of the options in systems are immediately obvious. Many, if not most, options are uneconomic, technically infeasible, or beyond the threshold of acceptance in the organization or society.

Beyond the sheer magnitude of relationships of subsystems is another problem—lack of perfect information. Rarely does one have available all the information one desires or requires to thoroughly analyze a total system, or indeed even one subsystem in a total system.

Despite the difficulties in dealing with a total system, the concept remains a useful one. It encourages broader approaches to problems and discourages narrow—and often shallow—approaches.

Integration of Subsystems

A total system has as one of its requirements the *integration* of its subsystems (see Exhibits 1–2 and 1–3). Integration refers to the appropriate linking together, or interfacing, of subsystems of the total system.

In addition to the technical difficulties involved in achieving such integration, there are organizational barriers. Traditional functions* of an organization (i.e., accounting and finance, marketing, manufacturing, and personnel) have resulted in specializations that discourage interfunctional (i.e., horizontal) integration. Each functional manager tends to protect his/her area of specialization from "outsiders." Even within a particular functional area (say, accounting and finance) it is difficult to

* Organizational functions differ among industries and organizations. For instance, while research and development may be a major function in technologically based companies, it may be a subfunction under manufacturing in other organizations; and still others may have no such function at all. Nonmanufacturing organizations organize somewhat differently. For instance, banks have major functions of checking and savings accounts, loans, and trusts.

Exhibit 1–2 Unintegrated Subsystems

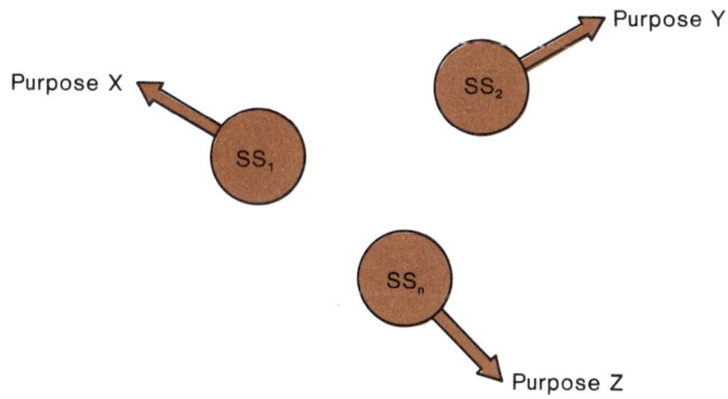

Exhibit 1–3 Integrated Subsystems

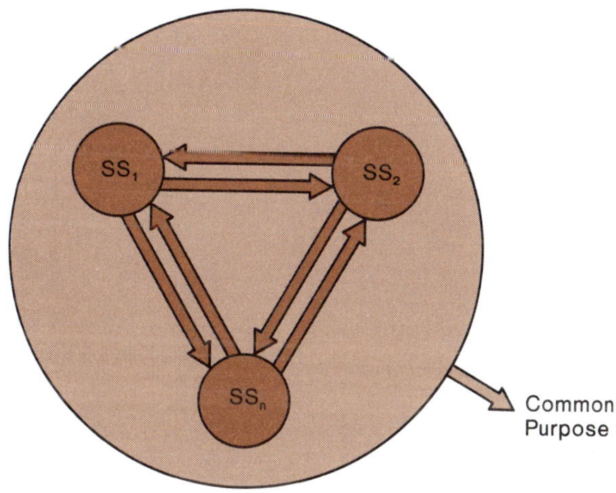

achieve vertical integration. Experience and studies indicate, for instance, that there are distortions in information, as it flows from top management down through various intermediary levels to employees; and inadequacies of information, as it flows upward from employees to management (see Exhibit 1–4).

Ideally, integrated subsystems can realign the *organizational structure.* Many different organizational structures have evolved over the years, reflecting an historical patchwork rather than a logical, realistic pattern of allocating organizational resources* (i.e., human, physical, and information resources). Frequently, in uninte-

* Organizational resources will be discussed in more detail in Chapter 2.

Exhibit 1–4 Conventional Organization Chart

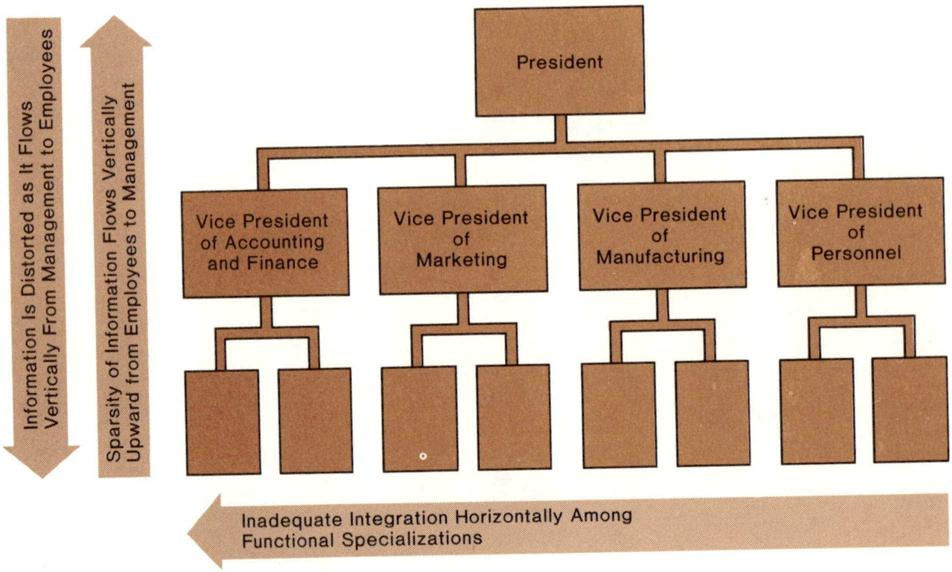

grated situations, the resources are allocated unwisely for purposes of reaching organizational goals. Information resources (e.g., reports) are frequently inadequate or out of phase with the physical- and human-resource elements.

A dramatic example of lack of integration is shown when a military force is pursuing a particular objective, and there is a breakdown in communications among elements of the force. If the air force bombs the wrong area, it may cause destruction of its own infantry comrades; it may ready the enemy for the invasion of the army, which had expected its air force to "soften up" the enemy positions; or it may require another bombing attempt at the correct target. In any case, the lack of integration has caused major problems.

The conventional organization chart is static and represents only formal relationships. A systems approach to organization (see Exhibit 1–5) attempts to indicate a more realistic view of interrelationships; this may include informal as well as formal relations. A person who depended on the formal depiction of the organization structure could be seriously misled, and consequently could assume a system that was out of phase with reality.

A total system, with integrated subsystems, can have a *synergistic* result (see Exhibit 1–6). This means that it can produce a positive effect greater than the sum of the individual parts.

Exhibit 1–5 A System View of Organizational Structure

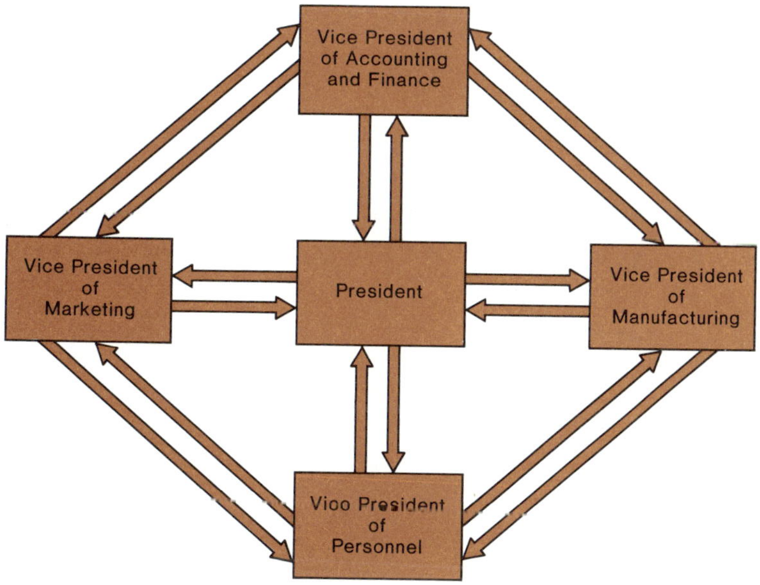

Bricks and mortar, which are unintegrated, can present an eyesore to a community. But when they are integrated by a creative architect and conscientious builder, the same material can result in a building that enriches the community both aesthetically and commercially.

The total-system approach means that one must continuously think in terms of the good of the entire organization, not just a particular unit of the organization (see Exhibit 1–7). It is not unusual for people to think in terms of their immediate environment and vested interest. But although a subsystem may function very efficiently independently, at the same time it may bankrupt the total system!

For example, a marketing department might take numerous sales orders for a new piece of equipment, and exceed its sales quota by a record amount. Looked at in isolation, the marketing department (a subsystem) has performed very effectively. However, suppose that the sales orders were for a piece of equipment that the manufacturing department (a subsystem) finds technically impossible to produce. The marketing department has caused harm to the total system (the organization) in the form of potential loss of sales, dissatisfied customers (who may take their business elsewhere), and considerable wasted effort and expense.

In sports, it is easy to think of an example of a team (i.e., system) with a group of superstars. Presumably, the goal of the team is to win. If the individual superstar

Exhibit 1–6 An Illustration of Synergism

Exhibit 1–7 Interdependency of Functions

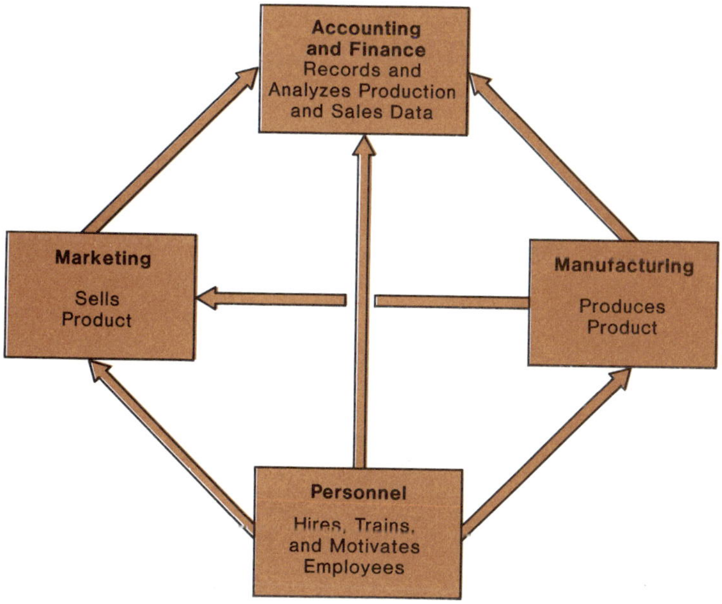

(i.e., subsystem) does his own thing, there is usually a lack of team play (e.g., lack of integration). Invariably, this results in performance below the team's capability, and a system that should be a winner becomes a loser.

Adaptive Systems

Some systems may be considered largely mechanistic, in that they operate as if governed by immutable laws of science. Such systems are called "deterministic." One example would be a guided missile sent into orbit, since an object in flight is governed by laws of nature, which have been verified scientifically (e.g., gravitation). However, most systems in business and government are highly dynamic; they have no predefined scientific rules that cover all possible occurrences. These dynamic systems are referred to as *adaptive*. In adaptive systems, human judgment tends to govern, rather than scientific laws.

Despite sophisticated analyses and careful planning, organizations that market women's fashions (i.e., clothes and cosmetics) are never certain of how the market will react to new products.

Politicians are keenly aware of the uncertainties of voter reactions to issues and politicians' stands on the issues. The ebb and flow of the fortunes of the Democratic and Republican parties are evidence of uncertainty in politics.

An adaptive system should not be approached as if it were closed or self-contained (see Exhibit 1–8). Rather, it should be viewed as a system that is open, and that not only is affected *by* its environment but also can itself *affect* its environment. Organizations tend to emphasize internal factors that are relatively controllable (e.g., the organization's manufacturing process), and to give little attention to external matters (e.g., competitor's strategies, government regulations, or population trends). A system must consider both internal and external factors realistically, if it is to function at high levels of performance. The executive or organization can no longer maintain a "public be damned!" or "What's good for General Motors is good for the nation!" attitude. Managers and organizations need to be sensitive to a growing variety of environmental factors and to the evolving changes in both laws and values. For example:

The equal employment opportunity and affirmative action laws have established new emphasis on equitable personnel policies and practices. These same practices, just a few years ago, were largely discretionary.

Increased public concern about such issues as environment (e.g., the quality of the air we breathe and the water we drink) and health have caused government and business organizations to rethink their goals and priorities, and have created opportunity for new enterprises and occupations to deal with these issues.

Rational and Human Systems

Traditionally, systems concepts have depended greatly on the scientific approach. This approach emphasizes rationality (i.e., reason, mathematics) as the basis for problem solving. Here is one such model, according to this approach:

- Identify the problem.
- Collect the key facts related to the problem.
- Discern the causes of the problem.
- Seek alternative solutions to the problem.
- Evaluate the alternative solutions, and identify the preferred alternative.
- Implement the solution, obtain feedback about its effectiveness, and make any required adjustments.

A *rational* approach to problem solving is needed to overcome the tendency to base problem-solving approaches on whim and fancy, bias and bigotry, or laziness and ignorance. The rational approach also helps reduce the degree of uncertainty in decision making in business and government.

Unfortunately, however, much so-called systems effort has severely neglected *human* factors, despite the fact that people, of course, are vital elements in systems (see

Exhibit 1-8 An Adaptive System

Exhibit 1–9 Rational and Human Systems

Exhibit 1–9). This neglect is probably the outgrowth of one of two extremist-rational views:

1. People are, to some extent, irrational and it is difficult to consider this in rational analysis; and/or
2. People are "cogs in the system" and they must adjust to the system.

One can picture the comedian Charlie Chaplin giving his classic rendition of a worker, who is merely an extension of an assembly line, trying to keep up with the inexorably faster pace of the tireless machines.

Since the strictly rational approach to systems has not been entirely satisfactory, people's considerations are consequently getting increased attention—even if these considerations do spoil those solutions that appear so ideally rational on paper (but seldom in practice).

Jobs traditionally were designed with efficiency and productivity in mind. This design was usually done by someone with an industrial-engineering background, who was fascinated by a stopwatch, and who considered workers somewhat as robots. Not infrequently, the results seemed to be efficiency and productivity increases. However, it was not unusual for other things to increase, also—for instance, alienation, absenteeism, turnover, and strikes. Only recently have a few organizations been considering job enrichment and other techniques that may make work more satisfying to workers.

Progressive systems-concepts call for a balanced approach toward both rational and human considerations. The age of human rights and human dignity require increased sensitivity to the impact of systems on individuals, groups, and society.

Systems Model

The *systems model* represents, in simplified form, a generalized view of how creatures, organizations, and computers operate (see Exhibit 1–10). A systems model consists of *input, processing,* and *output.* In addition, *objectives* must be set and *control* must be performed. Performance is measured by *feedback* signals (from input, processing, and output); these are compared with objectives.

Input. This symbol represents those things that are brought into the system for processing.

- For a *person,* input would be food, air, and water.
- For a *manufacturing organization,* input might be steel, oil (for energy), and human labor.
- For a *computer,* input might be data representing such things as sales and costs.

Exhibit 1–10 Systems Model

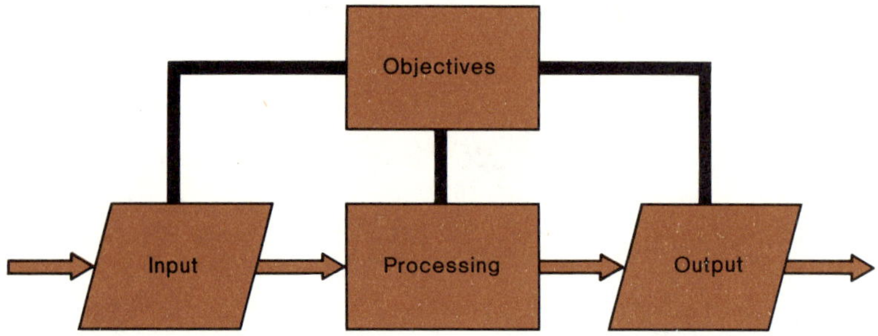

Legend: = Flow of Resources (e.g., human labor, physical material and money, information, etc.)

= Path of Feedback and Control

Processing. This step represents a transformation of the things that have entered the system as input. A series of processing operations takes place to complete the transformation.

- For a *person,* the processing includes the body's capacity for changing food, air, and water into the nutrients and other things needed by the organs, cells, etc.
- For the *manufacturing organization,* the processing might be the complex operations that turn steel, energy, labor, etc., into a product.
- For a *computer,* the processing might involve updating the organization's accounting records.

Output. Output represents a result of the processing.

- For the *individual,* output could be such things as maintaining health and sustaining life.
- For the *manufacturing company,* the output could be automobiles.
- For the *computer,* output might be an accounting report for management that indicates total sales, total costs, and so on, for the period.

Objectives, Feedback, and Control. Presumably, every individual and organization has objectives (even though these may range from rational to irrational, be formally expressed or merely subconscious thoughts). Whatever their nature or form, objectives are needed to give purpose to an entity and to provide a basis for measuring performance. Every person and organization asks the question: "How well am I doing?" Periodically, the person or organization receives feedback signals, which give information about the status and accomplishments of input, processing, and output. These signals may be explicit and quantified (e.g., 1,000 units have been processed) or subjective (e.g., I have eaten the food and I feel good and full of energy). In any case, the person or organization can compare the feedback signals with the objectives to determine whether the system is performing well or whether some corrective action is required. For example:

- If the person's objective is to lose weight, his/her feedback signals may alert him/her to stop eating midway in the eating process.
- If the organization's objective is to produce 1,500 units, but only 1,000 units are produced as output, an investigation might take place to determine why.

The computer can also be programmed to handle feedback signals to compare outcomes to objectives, and to carry out control. For instance:

- The computer might determine that total costs exceeded budget limits. This might be recorded on the output report for the attention of management.

The idea of systems models is an important one in the computer field, and it will be pursued at various points in this book.

SYSTEMS MODEL ANALOGY

In our everyday life, whether in business or school, we perform functions that closely resemble those described in the systems model (see Exhibit 1–11). The business person receives input in the form of paperwork, and he or she must process it. In performing the processing, the individual may need to refer to the organization's policy and procedures manuals to determine how things are to be done. That individual may also need to seek related data from a file cabinet (storage), or to use a desk calculator to perform certain computations. Invariably, the processing results in output, which may be a written message or an oral communication. As forthcoming chapters will show, the computer carries out functions that are quite similar to these.

Summary

Humans need to set a systems philosophy if they are to use computers intelligently. Many aspects of business can make use of a number of important systems concepts: general-systems theory, total system, integration of subsystems, adaptive systems, and rational and human systems. In addition, a systems model consisting of input, processing, and output can help us investigate and explain how people, organizations, and computers function.

Exhibit 1–11 Systems Model in Practice

Terms* to Learn

System
Subsystem
General-systems theory
Total system
Integration
Common purpose
Boundaries
Organizational structure
Adaptive system
Rational system
Human system
Systems model
Input
Processing
Output
Objectives
Feedback
Control
Synergism

Review Questions

1. Why is it important for a computer professional to develop a *systems philosophy?*
2. Define the term *system.*
3. Distinguish between *system* and *total system.* How are the two terms similar? How are they different?
4. Why is the term *system* such an "in" word in professional circles?
5. Discuss the system implications in *one* of the following: *solar system; economic system; political system; medical system;* or *educational system.*
6. Discuss the ideas behind the *general-systems theory.* Do you agree that everything in the universe is related to everything else? Does the theory have any practical use?
7. How does one set *boundaries* for a total system?
8. Give an example of *subsystems* and how they are integrated in a total system.
9. Discuss the limitation of conventional *organization charts* and *structures.* How might one overcome the limitation?
10. Why are traditional functions of an organization likely to be *unintegrated?* How might one achieve more complete integration?
11. Define what is meant by *synergism.*
12. Contrast *deterministic* and *adaptive* systems. Give an example of each.
13. Contrast *rational* and *human* systems. Is it possible to achieve a balance between the two?
14. Define and describe a *generalized-systems model.*
15. Discuss the application of *systems model* to a situation that you know.

* Some terms (e.g., input, processing, and output) are briefly introduced early in the text, but are defined more fully in future chapters. Therefore, some of the terms may be listed after several chapters. It is expected that the intervening material will help the reader refine and elaborate on the definition of previously learned terms.

A.D.A.
Corporation
CEMENT
Raw
Material

CHAPTER 2

MANAGING AN ORGANIZATION SYSTEM

Objectives

The purpose of this chapter is to demonstrate how the previously learned systems concepts can be used to study an organization and its management, as well as the use of computers.

THE NEED FOR SYSTEMS IN SOCIETY

Although systems concepts may be flawless theoretically, in actual practice they may face various barriers and limitations. Nevertheless, most thought leaders in various disciplines, including the computer field, endorse the idea and intention of systems concepts.

The systems-concepts approach has become increasingly relevant in our world because of the growing complexity of our society, the large size of many organizations, the relative shrinking of time and space, the explosion of information, the interdependency of organizations and people, and the diversity of ideals and goals. In other words, a systems framework seems needed to cope with the scope of the challenges and problems that face us. The following examples illustrate the kinds of realistic situations that require the use of systems concepts:

- Allocating the federal government's multi-billion-dollar budget for the numerous national defense and domestic programs.
- Managing an organization that may have hundreds of thousands of employees, tens of thousands of stockholders, perhaps as many as millions of customers, be operating in maybe one hundred different nations, and have a budget of several billion dollars.
- Determining an appropriate blend of public and private education facilities, taking into account such considerations as population trends, unemployment figures, and skills needed now and in the future.
- Planning for the best balance of transportation facilities (highways, railroads, rapid transit, etc.) for the present and future.
- Instituting environmental protection programs, while simultaneously assuring adequate energy for industry, government, homes, etc.

Problems such as these involve complex mixtures of technical, financial, economic, social, and political considerations. In creating a systems framework, the existing system must be analyzed carefully in terms of: purposes and objectives; available resources; operations; formal and informal organizational structure; constraints (such as laws); and social and other external influences, among other characteristics.

The design of a proposed system must, of course, consider how the new system will perform, compared with the existing system. Any change should result in demonstrable improvements, both for the organization and society. In designing a new system, it is particularly important to consider how other related systems will be affected. For example:

Industrial systems that formerly ignored their impact on ecological systems have greatly damaged national resources (e.g., wildlife and fresh water) and human systems (e.g., health of workers and citizens).

Chemical drugs that originally were intended to treat *one malady are now being discovered to be the possible* cause *of other damage to the human body.*

These experiences offer practical evidence to support the general-systems theory premise: everything is, in some way, related to everything else.

THE ORGANIZATION AS A SYSTEM

Studying an *organization as a system* can strengthen a computer professional's ability to understand how a computer can be used more effectively.

Exhibit 2–1 presents a model of the organization as a system. In this chapter, the content of this model will be explored in detail.

Objectives and Boundaries

An organization is considered to be an entity that has a stated purpose (i.e., objectives) and definite boundaries. For example:

A business enterprise may have the objectives of making ten million dollars in sales for the forthcoming year, one million dollars in profits, and a 20 percent rate of return on invested capital. Among its boundaries may be that its product line is electrical equipment, and that it operates in seventy-five different nations.

A government agency may have a purpose of rendering service and supplying information to citizens. Its boundaries may be set by its legal jurisdiction (i.e., a certain city in a particular state) and the budget that has been allotted to it (e.g., five million dollars to operate a hospital and health clinic).

Usually, the organization's top management sets the broad organizational objectives and boundaries, with guidance from the board of directors. These objectives and boundaries then become guidelines for subunits of the organization. An organization's objectives and boundaries are dynamic and are affected by the environment; consequently, the organizational system should be viewed as evolutionary rather than as static.

Exhibit 2–1 Model: The Organization as a System

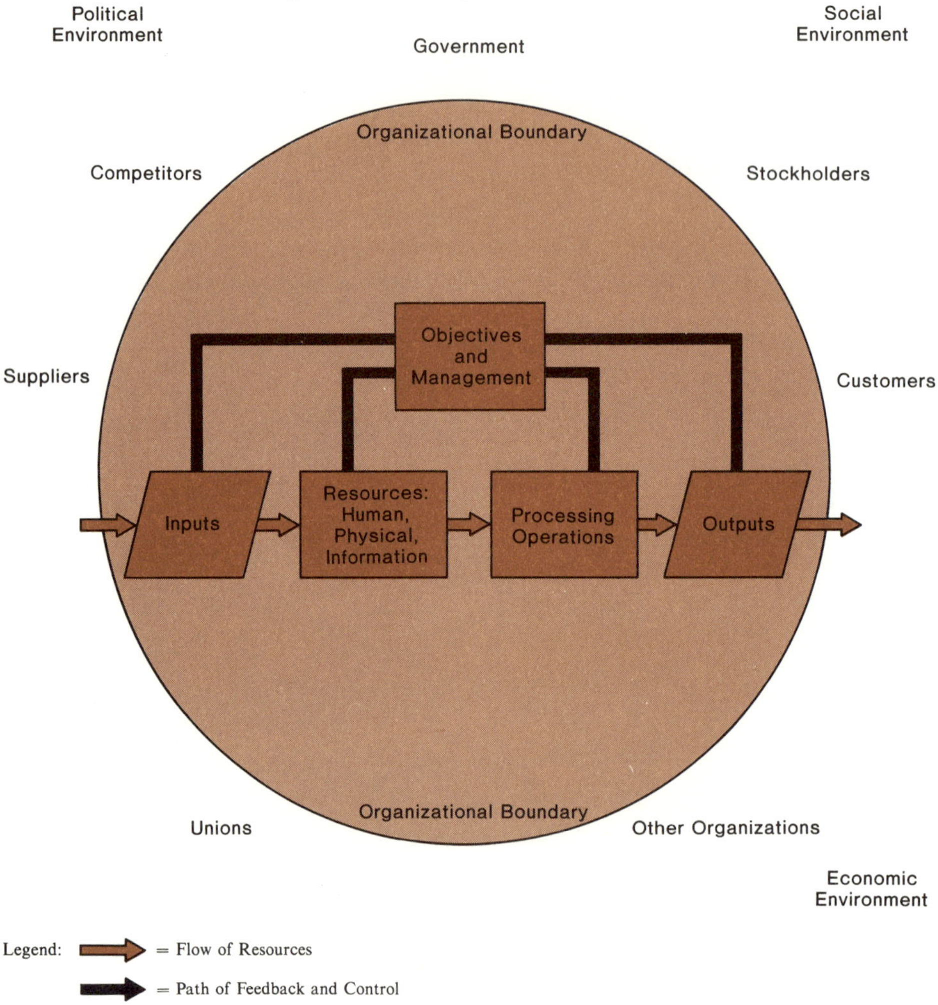

The objectives are set to provide the organization and management with direction, and to measure how effectively the organization is being run. By determining how each element is functioning (feedback), management can be responsive and control any element that is out of phase with established objectives.

An objective of the organization may be to operate its manufacturing plant at a minimum of 75 percent capacity. If, in a given month, operation falls to, say, 60 percent of capacity, management should be alerted. The reason for the decline should be determined, as well as what steps can be taken to correct the deviation from objective.

A good feedback system will alert management to out-of-control conditions as early as possible—not after the fact, when it may be too late to take corrective action.

Input and Resources

Each organization requires a suitable balance of *human, physical,* and *information* resources in order to operate (see Exhibit 2–2). The systems approach seeks the most appropriate quantity and quality of these organizational resource elements, and is concerned about how the elements are used in operation. In short, the objective is to use the resources in the best possible way, in order to facilitate the organization's stated purpose.

These resources may be available within the organization, or they may be obtained from external sources. In any case, the resources must be renewed periodically; we can call such additions "input." Thus, simply for our purposes, input constitutes the periodic new resources that are brought into the organization system.

Human Resources.* Human resources (people) represent the key element in any organization and often constitute the largest single cost† of operation. Human resources include managers, professional staff employees, office employees, and factory employees. Motivating human resources is particularly important, since highly motivated employees are important sources of creative ideas, improved productivity, and, ultimately, an effective organization. On the other hand, if employees are not positively motivated, it is very difficult for an organization to attain its desired levels of effectiveness.

Physical Resources. Physical resources encompass a host of things, including: plant and equipment; land; materials; supplies; money; and markets. These resources need to be utilized efficiently to reach the desired level of organizational effectiveness.

Information Resources. Information resources include the organization's records, files, and reports (see Exhibit 2–3). In a sense, the information is a recorded model of the organization's past history, its current status, and its future possibilities. The accounting records, statistical studies, and intelligence are also an important part of the resource. The information includes not only internal facts about the organization but also external facts (e.g., economic climate and competitive information). Of course, the information resources provide descriptive data about the other two

* The terms "human resources," "personnel," and "employees" are used interchangeably in this book. However, "human resources" appears to be the more progressive of the terms, and is gaining in acceptance over the longer-used "personnel" and "employees."

† However, some experts feel that human resources should be viewed as an asset (thus, human-asset accounting) rather than a cost.

Exhibit 2–2 Organizational Resources

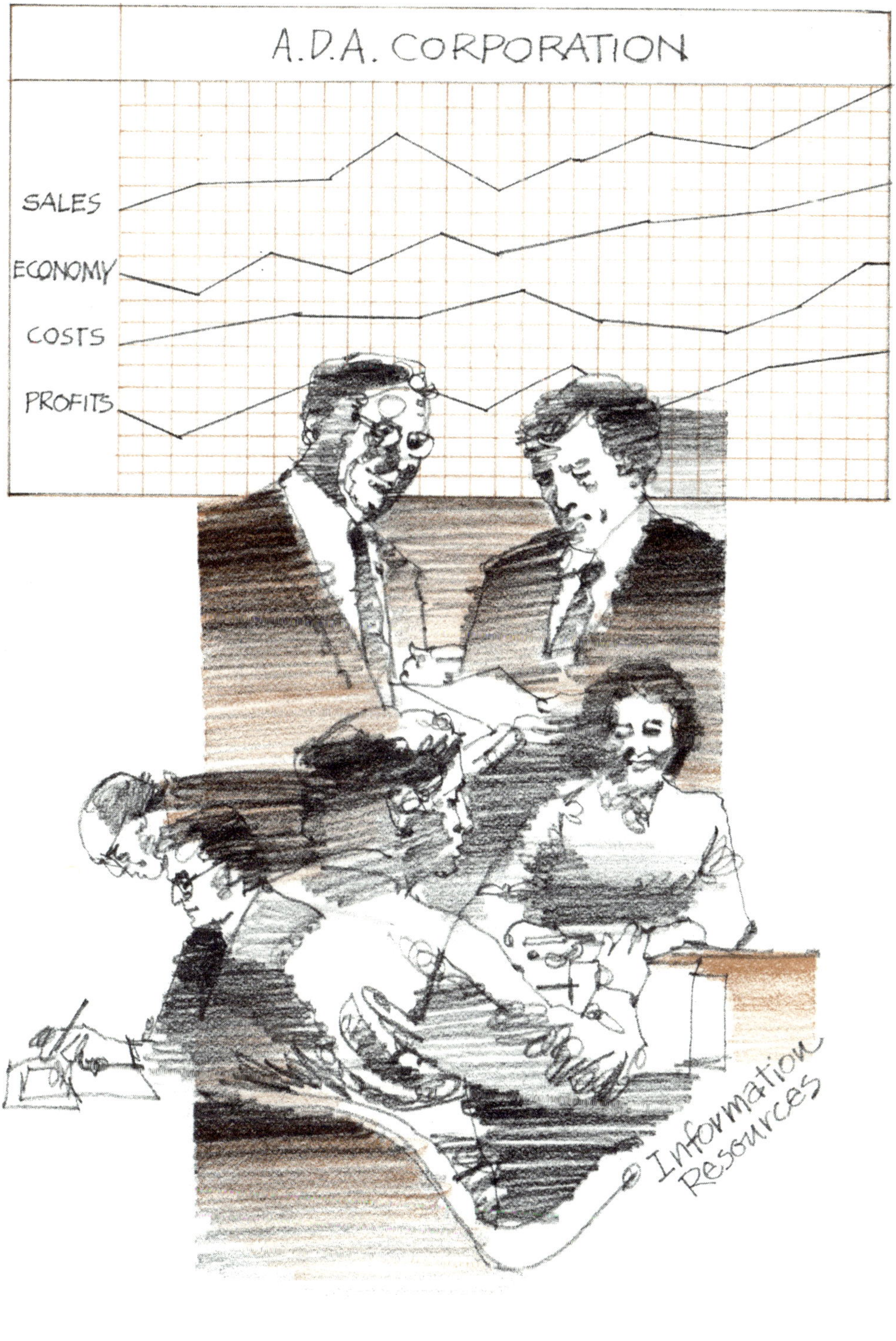

Exhibit 2–3 Information Resources

resources; for instance, they indicate the number and types of employees (human resources), and the value of assets (physical resources). The information resources are of most direct interest to computer professionals.

Processing Operations and Output

The three resources are interdependent—that is, they interplay in the actual *processing operations* of an organization, and the operations result in the generation of goods and services for the market (i.e., customers or clients).

> *An automotive company may employ thousands of employees with various skills (i.e., human resources), have millions of dollars in physical resources (e.g., factories, steel, and sales offices), and have elaborate accounting and management reports (i.e., information resources). All these resources are processed in some suitable combination in operations to produce the end product: automobiles.*

"Operations" thus means the actual work performed, whether that work includes operating a tool in a factory, preparing a report in an office, stocking the end product in a warehouse, selling the product to a customer, or counting the money received from a number of customers. In a manufacturing organization, operations means the total work effort that results in the transformation of resources into an end product for the market. In other types of organizations, the output (i.e., that which is generated by the system) is comparatively intangible; we call such organizations "service-type" organizations. For instance, a doctor (hopefully) makes a patient feel better; an entertainer gives fans enjoyment; a professor imparts knowledge to students.

An organization's processing operations are subject to change, particularly if higher levels of operational efficiency are to be attained, or new organizational objectives handled.

> *If an automotive company decided to produce transportation vehicles such as those depicted in the film "Star Wars," it would obviously require new and different resources (e.g., engineers familiar with exotic materials and air transportation as well as ground transportation; new sources of capital for new manufacturing facilities, or upgrading of existing ones; and new market information studies to determine the size of the customer potential).*

The output of the organizational system, whether it is a good or service, is intended to satisfy a demand (or need) in the market. Of course, there is a reciprocal result of satisfying a demand; that is, the organization is rewarded with payment for the good or service. This reward (usually money) comes to this organization as an input received from an external source (the market).

The general model suggests an overview that is useful in learning about systems concepts relative to organizations. In practice, of course, such a model must consider the unique differences and complex, specific characteristics that apply to any particular organization. For example, there are substantial differences between:

- A petroleum company's operations and those of a dress manufacturer.
- A department store chain with world-wide outlets in major cities and suburban areas, and a neighborhood shop in a small town.

Even direct competitors of somewhat comparable size (e.g., two food chains or two motel chains) usually have significant differences in operations.

Thus, while it is useful to understand a general model such as that presented in this discussion, it is also well to recall the old adage:

A wise person will recognize the commonalities in things that look different, but will also recognize the differences in things that look similar.

MANAGEMENT IN AN ORGANIZATION SYSTEM*

Management by Objectives (MBO)

A manager is the person who has the responsibility and authority to allocate the resources of the whole organization or a subunit of the organization. The manager's effectiveness is determined by the amount of resources that are used in relation to the results that are obtained from the resources. Each manager usually has some stated objective to be reached, and is evaluated on the basis of differences between actual performance and objectives. For example:

Two managers, A and B, are assumed to have similar areas of responsibility. Each has an objective to generate 20 percent rate of return, in a year, on the resources under the manager's direction. Let's assume that each has control over $500,000 in resources. At the end of the year, Manager A has generated $350,000 (a 70 percent rate of return) on the original resources. Manager B has generated $50,000 (only a 10 percent rate of return) on the original $500,000 in resources. Unless there is some special explanation for the difference, it seems clear that Manager A's performance has been excellent, while Manager B's performance has been marginal, at best. Furthermore, Manager B has not achieved the stated objective of a 20 percent rate of return.

Management Functions†

No matter what type and size organization the manager works for, every manager has certain generic functions to perform: planning, organizing, controlling, and actuating (see Exhibit 2–4). How well a manager carries out these functions will be determined by the *management-by-objectives* procedure just described.

* The organization and management concepts presented in this chapter apply, of course, to the operation of a computer department. Chapter 14 deals with specific guidelines for a well-run computer department.

† Different management authorities provide somewhat modified lists of functions.

Exhibit 2–4 Management Functions

Planning. *Planning* includes determining the likely future courses of action that will be needed to reach desired goals (i.e., objectives). The planning horizon may be short range (up to one year) or long range (frequently up to five years or more). The planning process is significant in that it provides direction for the organization's dynamic objectives and its shifting boundaries. Obviously, planning must consider both internal and external factors. Among the questions considered may be fundamental ones such as:

- What should our product or service be in the future?
- What is the likely size of the market for our product or service in the future?
- What resources (e.g., financing) will be needed to reach desired future objectives?

Organizing.* Organizing deals with the efficient and effective allocation and use of resources to achieve the organization's goals. Some types of considerations in *organizing* are:

- How centralized or decentralized shall our management be?
- How much responsibility and authority shall various employees be given?
- Where shall our organizational units be physically located (e.g., in what country? in what city?)?
- What types of skills and positions are needed in the units of the organization?

Controlling. *Controlling* refers to the approach the manager uses in order to keep informed about events that can determine the organization's possible success or failure. Obviously, the manager must have control over critical matters (i.e., a sudden change in sales trends) so that well-timed reactions can occur. Again, an *effective* control system usually depends on quick and accurate feedback from organizational units.

Actuating. *Actuating* involves the manager's capacity to get employees to carry out the tasks that must be performed. Leadership, an important facet of actuating, might come from the power inherent in the manager's formal position; or it might exist because of the employees' genuine esteem for the manager as a person. In most cases, leadership effectiveness probably results from a combination of the power of the position and the manager's individual personality and competence.

Management Actions

Each manager must take action in each of two broad categories: *decision making* and *communication.* Although these tasks often may require a group effort, frequently they are the manager's lone responsibility.

* Refer back to the discussion in Chapter 1 about organization charts and structure.

Decision Making. This is the manager's discretionary ability to select among available alternative courses of action. For instance, the manager must decide such fundamental things as:

- Which of several long-range plans to recommend.
- Which organization structure is best, under current circumstances.
- How elaborate a control and feedback mechanism is needed to protect against failure.
- How to actuate employees to be more productive.

Communication. In addition to actually making hard decisions, the manager must communicate these decisions clearly, so that employees will understand not only the decisions themselves but also their implications. The manager must also *coordinate* with peers (i.e., other managers), superiors (e.g., the president), and the public (e.g., stockholders and the press), when appropriate. Within this context, managers need good oral and writing skills. Often, good ideas fail to be productive—not because of intrinsic flaws, but simply because they have not been communicated to the target audiences clearly and attractively.

The reader should bear in mind that this model of the manager is intended only as a guideline. Each manager has an individual style of managing, which is influenced by such factors as his/her organization, education, and environment.

Table 2–1 is a matrix that attempts to summarize some of the ideas about the organization as a system, and the manager's role in such a system, that have been developed so far.

Table 2–1

A Matrix: Managerial Functions and Actions Related to the Organization System

Management Functions:		Planning		Organizing		Controlling		Actuating	
Management Actions:		Decision	Communication	Decision	Communication	Decision	Communication	Decision	Communication
Resources:	Objectives:								
Human	X	X	X	X	X	X	X	X	X
Physical	X	X	X	X	X	X	X		
Information	X	X	X	X	X	X	X		
Processing Operations	X	X	X	X	X	X	X		

Note: "X" identifies intersections that require managerial attention. Blanks identify intersections that are not too useful. Actuating usually refers to motivating people (i.e., human resources).

SYSTEMS CONCEPTS AND COMPUTERS

The systems concepts and, in particular, the systems model that was discussed previously are very relevant to computers. The computer, which fundamentally operates on the basis of input, processing, and output, is engineered to perform as a highly logical and powerful piece of equipment. However, people who work with computers must understand systems concepts in order to use this equipment effectively. The computer is most effective in organizations where:

- Management appreciates the organization as a system, and the appropriate roles of managers within such a system.
- Computer professionals use systems concepts in preparing work that is to be processed on the computer.

A well-designed computer system can help the organization to reach its objectives by:

- Improving the organization's information resources and, as a consequence, facilitating management's functions and actions.
- Identifying opportunities to improve the mix (quantity and quality) of the resources needed.
- Encouraging more efficient patterns for the organization's processing operations.
- Testing alternative opportunities that may result in new and beneficial organizational objectives.

Unfortunately, many, if not most, organizations have not approached the computer in a systems way. Such organizations have figuratively "thrown" work on the computer, and much of this work has been merely a hodgepodge of work that previously was done by manual and mechanical methods. In such instances, the computer may do things faster than people or slower machines, but it will also accentuate the old methods' flaws. It is true that the computer can process errors and nonsensical procedures much faster than alternative methods can! Little wonder that some organizations and people are disillusioned about computers.

Let us now consider the application of computers.

Parallel-Systems Models

The information system is used to provide the organization with a mechanism that reports on the conditions in the organization. Exhibit 2–5 shows us that the manufacturing system has certain inputs, processes, and outputs. Concurrently, the information system captures data about the manufacturing system, processes the data about manufacturing operations, and outputs information that reports on conditions in the manufacturing system.

Both the information system and the manufacturing system provide feedback to management so that a comparison with the original objectives can be made. For example:

Exhibit 2–5 Parallel Systems Models: Information and Manufacturing

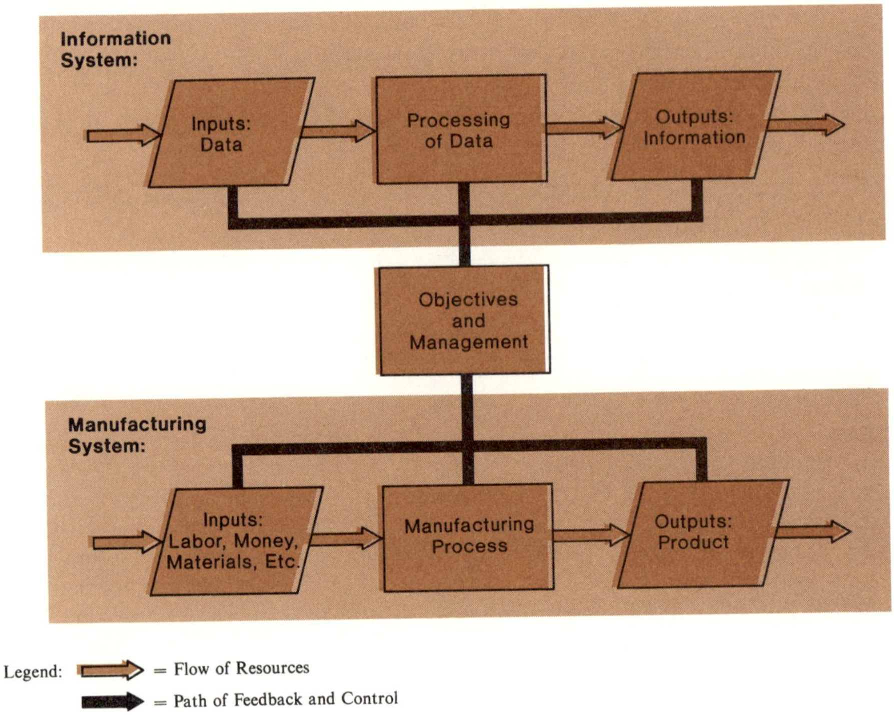

The organizational objectives for ADA Corporation may be to produce 1,000 widget units in a day for $1.00 or less per unit.

The input for the manufacturing system would be the materials (e.g., plastic, metal, screws) that go into producing widgets; the human resources needed (e.g., factory workers); etc. The manufacturing process would be the factory system that transforms the input into widgets. The output would be the finished widgets.

Concurrently, the information system would capture data reflecting the quantity and cost of materials, labor, etc., entering the manufacturing system; the performance during manufacturing; and the number of units that come out of the system. This data would be processed, and a report would be generated for management. This report would evaluate the performance of the manufacturing system and compare it to the objectives. If the report indicated that only 900 widgets were manufactured at a per unit cost of $1.10, management would want this feedback for at least control purposes. Management might also wish to take some corrective action.

Exhibit 2–6 Hierarchy of an Information System

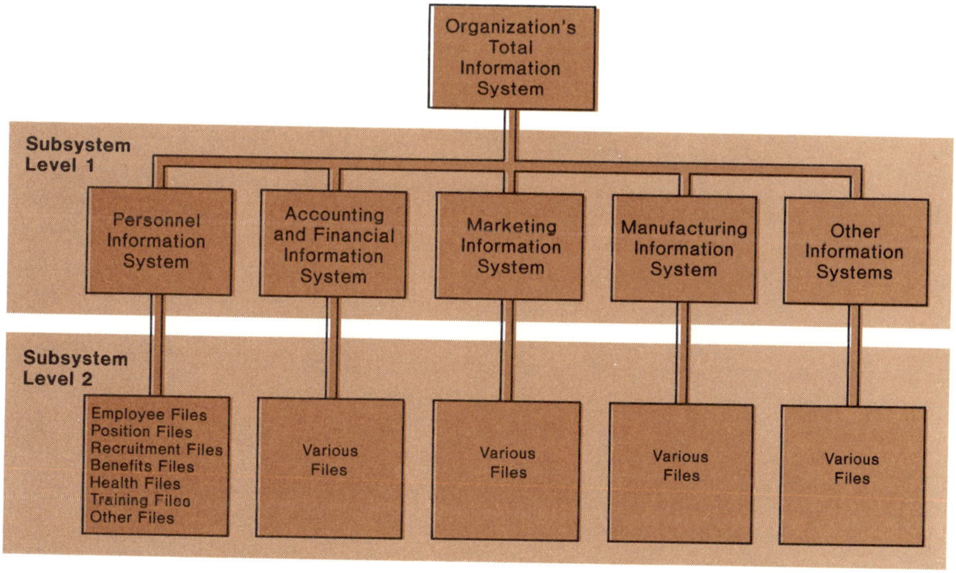

Note: All files are integrated and linked.

This example shows that an information system is intended as a reporting mechanism to inform management how well the organization is functioning.

Hierarchy of an Information System

Management-information systems will be detailed in Chapter 15, but here it is appropriate to briefly get perspective on the subject.

Information systems should be planned and integrated according to the systems concepts we've already explored. If this is not done, the information system will not be effective. Exhibit 2–6 illustrates that:

- A total-information system consists of a series of integrated and linked systems (subsystem level 1). In the example, each of the information systems for each function of the organization is, in effect, a subsystem of the total system.
- Each of the systems (subsystem level 1) is likely to have its own subsystems (subsystem level 2). However, only the subsystems for the personnel information system are listed in Exhibit 2–6.

Although increasing interest and effort are being directed towards integrated information systems, unfortunately, few organizations have yet achieved such completely integrated information systems. In practice, such an effort is enormously complex and costly; this is true particularly because organizations have evolved in a largely unsystematized way. Let us now consider a more specific example, dealing with a *personnel-information system.*

AN ILLUSTRATION: THE PERSONNEL APPLICATION

It has often been stated that people (human resources) are an organization's most valuable resource. Research and experience indicate that, too often, such statements are dealt with only as theoretical platitudes; in practice, organizations and managers often neglect human resources. High unemployment rates, high turnover rates, lack of confidence in our government and business institutions, declining productivity rate per employee, and increased crime by employees against organizations indicate the reality of this neglect.

It is interesting that, according to studies, the personnel application is often the one that is not computerized. Some subsystems (e.g., payroll, statistics needed for government reports) are frequently computerized; but few organizations have created a computerized total system for human resources.

Let's now consider two approaches to the computerization of the personnel application. The first ignores the systems concepts. The second incorporates a number of the systems concepts that are important for effective use of computers.

Negative-Systems Approach to Personnel Application

Frequently, particular existing phases of the personnel process are computerized in relative isolation from the rest of the process. Exhibit 2–7 illustrates such compartmentalization. Unfortunately, this approach impedes the attainment and coordination of common objectives. Moreover, it wastes considerable human effort—*data** are scattered through many *files* (e.g., employee records, position records, recruitment records, benefit records, etc.). Further, data are frequently overlapped and duplicated; and data that should coincide or relate often do not. In addition, the files frequently are not up to date. According to studies, organizations may have hundreds of separate and distinct personnel documents, and may record hundreds or thousands of different items of data on documents. Some of these items are reported repeatedly on different documents. As a result, the personnel staff finds it difficult to accurately and quickly search for data to provide answers; and because of the pressures of handling clerical work, the staff must neglect important personnel activities, including human contacts.

* Data are usually considered as relatively minute facts which require processing in order to be transformed into useful information. For example, sales data for a single transaction may have limited usefulness, but the manager may find sales data summarizing sales for an entire day to be valuable in determining which merchandise is selling and which is not. Chapter 8 explores data organization in depth.

Exhibit 2–7 Negative-Systems Approach to Personnel Application

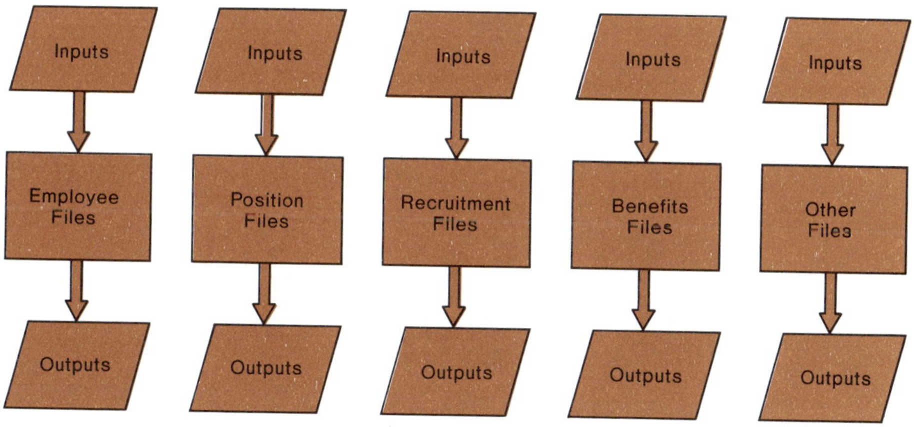

Systems Approach to Personnel Application

The opposite approach to computerization is to develop an overall plan for an integrated personnel system. As the plan proves economically and technically feasible, particular phases of the integrated system can be computerized in a planned sequence.

A model of a personnel information system is presented in Exhibit 2–8. Since this system is designed within an overall plan, it has a high degree of integration. There is a single stream of input data that flows into the system, and all computer programs* are available to direct the processing of input data and data files (*data bases*). A cluster of data bases are linked together for coordinated processing; a single input may simultaneously update several data-base files. In addition, related systems (such as the financial system) have clearly defined communication paths to and from the personnel system. Only authorized persons who can directly interrogate and use the system via a remote data-terminal have access to the system.

This approach entails integrating, by using the systems approach and the multiple files (including employee records, positions, recruitment, benefits, medical information, and training). It also attempts to keep up-to-date records so that inquiries may be answered with timely and accurate information. As a result, a great deal of duplication and inconsistencies in existing files should be eliminated.

In developing an effective computerized data system for personnel, certain minimum essentials must be met. A personnel data-base must be established that

* Computer programs can be considered as the instructions that tell the computer equipment what to do. Subsequent chapters will elaborate on the nature of computer programs; in particular, see Chapters 10 and 11.

Exhibit 2–8 Systems Approach to the Personnel Application

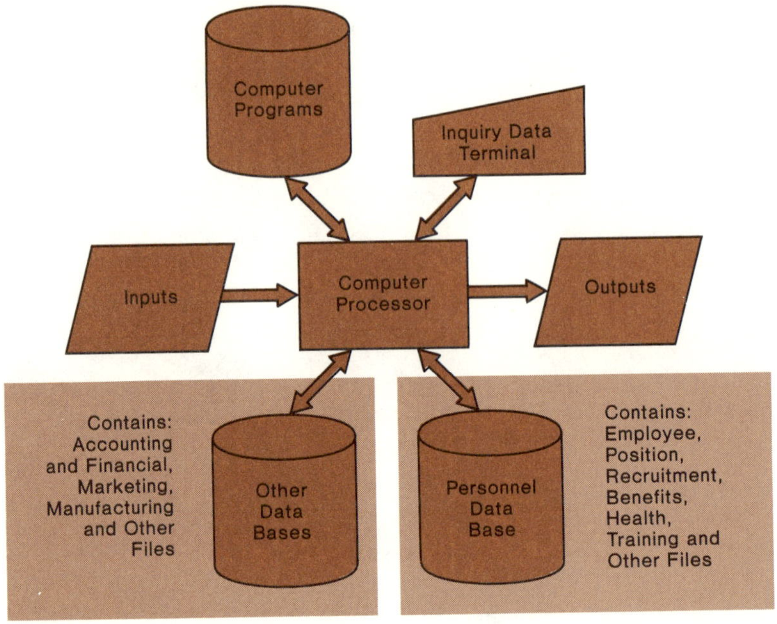

includes all data needs for making decisions and for fulfilling legal and other report requirements. For instance, the data must include such employee facts as: social security number; name; address; dependents; skills; education; marital status; and work assignments. Before being included in the data base, the data must be edited to ensure accuracy, nonredundancy, and consistency. Provision must be made for updating the data, so that they reflect a status that is current and useful to the users.

Since the data base usually entails consolidation and integration of formerly scattered and segmented files, it should provide information that is more pertinent and reliable than that in a negative-systems approach.

For the manager, *management by exception** can be programmed for such ongoing problems as: determining those employees for whom salary increases are overdue; determining those employees whose pay levels are inconsistent with their

* Management by exception refers to the idea that most managers do not have the time to review all information, and that only selective information should be called to their attention. The selective information usually involves matters that are at variance with some established standard (e.g., salespersons that are below quotas by 10 percent or more).

performance appraisals; identifying personnel or organizational units that have excessive lost time; and indicating manpower requisitions that have remained unfilled for excessive periods of time. In addition, management is now in the position to make studies that were difficult, if not impossible, to make before. For instance, employee bargaining groups may want to know the specific costs if vacation allowances are extended an additional week for certain employees. Or perhaps it may be desirable to identify all jobs that will be open in the next several years, due to retirements. And the identification of recruiting sources that will lead to reduced costs and an increased quality and quantity of candidates can be facilitated.

Eventually, an organization's computerized data-bank may be supplemented by interconnecting it with external or decentralized data banks. For example, it is possible to have computer communications with a cooperative, industry-wide data bank, or a network of public and private employment offices. Such a broad computer network may provide a basis for a rapid job-applicant matching system, consolidation of manpower data, and comprehensive salary surveys.

Summary

Systems approaches are valuable in dealing with complex problems and societal challenges at the international, national, or organizational level.

Systems concepts give us a powerful tool for studying and understanding the underlying structure and dynamics of organizations (e.g., businesses, government agencies, etc.), and provide insight about the role of management in organizations.

The computer professional must understand organizations and management clearly in order to use the computer in the most effective manner.

In short, a person who has a facility with systems thinking is able to cope with situations that may appear unfathomable to persons uninitiated in systems methods.

Terms to Learn

Organization as system
Human resource
Physical resource
Information resource
Processing operation
Management action
Decision making
Communication
Coordinate
Parallel systems

Management function
Management by objective (MBO)
Effectiveness
Planning
Organizing
Controlling
Actuating
Hierarchy of an information system
Personnel-information system
File
Data
Data base
Data record
Management by exception

Review Questions

1. Discuss *systems concepts* in relation to some important current situation (e.g., an environmental problem, a transportation problem, or a health problem). How can a systems approach help in understanding and resolving the problem?
2. Describe the model of the *organization as a system.*
3. Relate the model discussed in Question 2 to an *actual organization* with which you are familiar. You might consider using your local bank, department store, or college as the basis for your analysis. In particular, identify the organization's resources, processing operations, inputs, and outputs.
4. How would the *resources* of two organizations in different industries be dissimilar? You might consider contrasting an airline company with a steel company, or an insurance company with an electronics company.
5. Why are *information resources* of particular interest to a computer professional?
6. Define *management by objectives,* and give an example of it in use.
7. Define the *management functions,* and give an example of each in a practical context of a business.
8. What is the relation between *management functions* and *management actions?* Discuss the importance of decision making and communication in management effectiveness.
9. Discuss the relevance and possible use of the matrix in Table 2–1.
10. Describe the importance of *systems concepts* to the computer field.
11. Discuss the meaning of the *parallel systems models* presented in Exhibit 2–5.
12. How would you explain an *information hierarchy?*
13. Describe the weaknesses of the personnel application (presented in this chapter) that did not follow systems guidelines.

14. Describe the important features of the personnel application (presented in this chapter) that had been designed with systems concepts in mind. Contrast this answer with the one you gave in Question 13.
15. Define *management by exception,* and give an example of it in use.
16. Try to relate the following terms: *data, records, files, data base, information.**

* These terms will be developed in much more detail in subsequent chapters, especially Chapter 8.

SECTION II

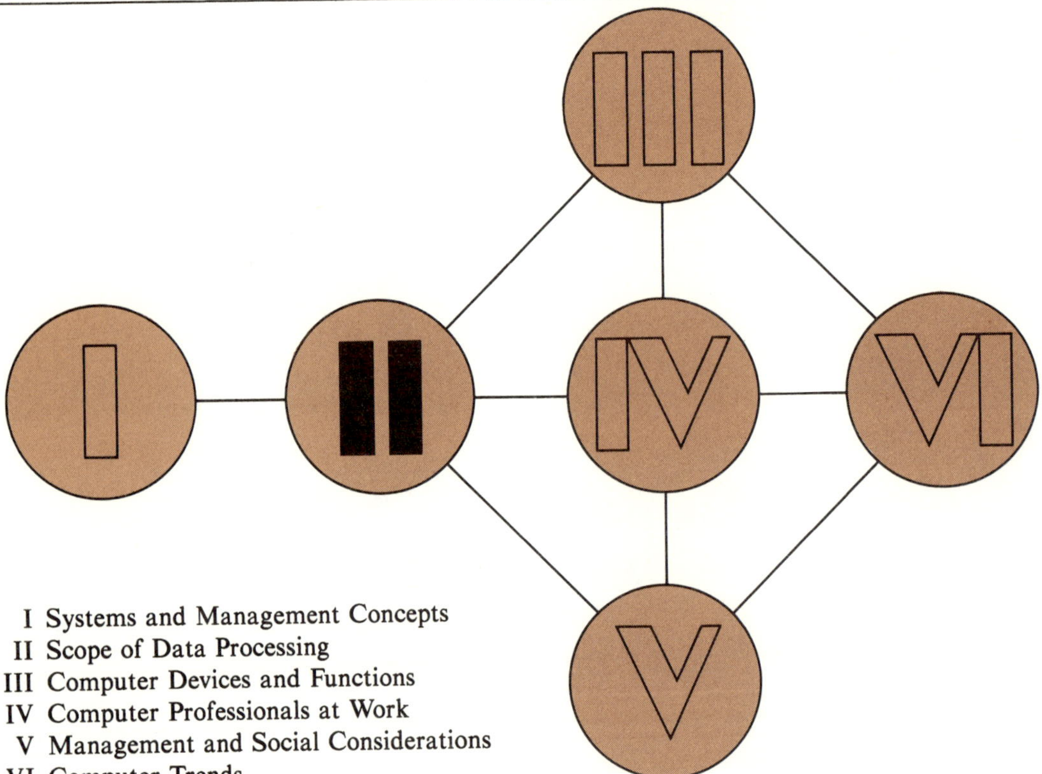
III
I
II
IV
VI
V
I Systems and Management Concepts
II Scope of Data Processing
III Computer Devices and Functions
IV Computer Professionals at Work
V Management and Social Considerations
VI Computer Trends

SCOPE OF DATA PROCESSING

We are now faced with a new ultimate weapon. This is the computer whose potential impact may surpass that of all of man's earlier devices. . . . In contrast to earlier devices, the computer requires no manual intercession after problem statement and data input.

ASHLEY MONTAGU AND SAMUEL S. SNYDER

An Adaptive
System

CHAPTER 3

DEVELOPMENTS IN DATA PROCESSING

Objectives

Chapter 3 discusses the nature of data processing and the place of computers in data processing. The material traces the evolution of data processing, particularly emphasizing the computer and its place in the business world.

The material in the chapter is presented under two topics:
Topic 1—Pre-Computer Era.
Topic 2—Computer Era.

TOPIC 1—PRE-COMPUTER ERA

BACKGROUND: SOCIETY AND TECHNOLOGY

Since human history and civilization first began, people have searched for tools to aid them. Wheels and rafts facilitated moving goods and people; spears and bows and arrows improved hunting and protection of the home; axes and hammers built shelters; and plows made it easier to work the land. Primitive humans used their fingers* and other simple methods to represent numbers. Markings, shells, stones, beads, and sticks were used to keep count of members of a family or tribe, of enemies, and of possessions. Although the eventual development of paper and writing instruments made it easier to record and transmit *data,* these innovations gave humans little aid in manipulating data. And the advent of formal bookkeeping and of taxation created a need for expanded recordkeeping.

The Industrial Revolution of the eighteenth century created many changes. Where work had once been performed in the home, now it was performed in larger units called factories. Power and machinery were harnessed to supplement or replace human toil. Sometimes, however, these changes occurred at the expense of human individuality and the environment; and there were dislocations that caused unemployment hardships.

In the nineteenth and twentieth centuries, the changes accelerated even further. The world population grew. So did large organizations, education, and modern military capabilities. Government services increased; technology advanced; and concurrently, social, economic, and technical developments occurred. During this period, the world was particularly affected by specific inventions, including: the automobile; the telephone; the airplane; the television; atomic energy; miracle drugs; and space ships.

* The act of using our ten fingers to count gave rise to our everyday mathematical reference to digits, and to our base-ten number system (0, 1, 2, 3, 4, 5, 6, 7, 8, 9). See Appendix A for further discussion.

These broad developments created a demand for improved *data-processing* systems to cope with the recordkeeping and analyses that the larger and more complex business organizations, governments, and other sectors of society required.

Accompanying the dynamic developments in technology was a concurrent growth, almost an explosion, in data-processing volume and complexity.

A better-educated population and work force will have the capacity to handle data of all kinds (e.g., newspapers, technical reports, and journals).

The growth of the scope of government has given rise to new laws, many of which require considerable reports from organizations and citizens and, conversely, reports from government to the public. The Internal Revenue Service and Office of Equal Employment Opportunity are examples.

Traditional accounting practices have become more intricate and elaborate. For instance, organizations that deal in international business may have to keep three or four different accounting sets (e.g., one set may satisfy the United States federal government; another may be for internal management; and another may reflect the accounting standards of the foreign nation in which the organization has an investment).

The massive movement towards a credit-based society, in which goods and services are charged rather than paid for in cash, has resulted in tremendous increases in paperwork (e.g., credit-card slips, periodic billing, and invoices).

These trends have placed such burdens on traditional data-processing methods that it now seems inconceivable that our economy could function without the vast data-processing power that computers provide.

Interestingly, while we are becoming aware of worldwide shortages and vanishing resources, we find that there are information excesses. Various sources indicate that about 75 percent of all the information available to mankind has been generated in the last two or three decades. Many millions of pieces of information are being generated each day, and at the current growth rate, the total amount is doubling about every ten years. It was, in fact, in response to such needs that the modern computer was invented.

Tools and other equipment enable people to greatly expand their normal capacities. For instance, without any aid, a person might be able to:

- Lift up to two hundred pounds;
- Walk or run several miles in an hour; and
- Perform up to about thirty calculations a minute.

But aided by tools and equipment, a person may be able to:

- Lift thousands of pounds;
- Travel at speeds of several hundred miles per hour; and
- Perform many thousands of computations per minute.

The modern computer is one of the most significant developments in history. Unlike other tools that extend people's abilities to do physical work, the computer is primarily designed to extend human mental capacities. Some computers can not only perform tasks millions of times faster than a human being,* but also perform thousands of times faster than the computers of just several years ago.

People seldom attempt to compete directly against the computer. Such a contest would be pointless, since in most cases the computer computes so much faster than human beings can. However, there are a few instances in which a computer has duplicated a set of calculations done by a human researcher. Isaac Asimov reports two such examples:

> *. . . Before the coming of the computer an English mathematician named William Shanks spent 15 years calculating the value of pi*† *and carried it to 707 decimal points (getting the last hundred-odd places wrong). More recently, a modern computer has carried out the calculation accurately to 10,000 decimal places, taking only a few days for the job.*
>
> *. . . The calculations required to work out the orbit of Mars took Kepler four years, according to his own report. Several years ago the calculations were repeated by computer in eight seconds.*

THE NATURE OF DATA ‡ PROCESSING

What Are Data?

As Chapter 2 mentioned, organizations generate data to keep a record of events and transactions that take place within the business. We are already familiar with some of these happenings. For instance, when we purchase merchandise in a department store by charging that purchase, a transaction has taken place. As a result, the sales clerk fills out a sales slip to record the relevant data (e.g., customer number, customer name, description of item sold, and dollar amount of the credit sale). In each functional area of every business, many such events and transactions occur; and data must be generated to record the facts about these events and transactions. Management needs data to get a picture of what is happening in the organization, as well as to fulfill some legal obligations (e.g., submitting reports to government, paying employees, and informing stockholders). Table 3–1 identifies some representative types of data in business organizations.

* It has been estimated it would take a person a full year to perform 1,000,000 calculations (i.e., add pairs of eight-digit numbers), say at a cost of at least $10,000. The same number of calculations can be performed by a computer for about 10 to 30 cents, and in well under one minute!

† Pi is, of course, the ratio of the circumference of a circle to its diameter, or about 3.1416. . . .

‡ "Data" is the plural of datum, the singular. However, in practice, the word data is often used for both.

Table 3–1

Some Representative Data Generation

Data Processing Functional Areas	Events or Transactions	Data Generation
Accounting and Finance	Payments on account. Receipts from customers.	Checks to be issued. Cash journal.
Marketing	Sale to customer. Monthly billing.	Sales slip. Bills and invoices.
Manufacturing	Planning production. Producing goods for inventory. Ordering materials and supplies.	Production schedules. Inventory records. Purchase order.
Personnel	Periodic payroll. Periodic transfers of funds to the government.	Payroll register and checks. Reports to the Internal Revenue Service and the Social Security Administration.

Data versus Information

The words "data" and "information" are closely related. For our purposes, "data" includes any fact that can be processed. For instance, data can be a single character, such as: 7. Or data can consist of a group of data, such as: 7, 13, 33, 1, 2, 17. Data may also consist of an intermix of types of data (e.g., numeric and alphabetic): 1, John Doe, 33, 17, Mary Smith, 99. However, all these data have little meaning or usefulness, because they are unorganized and insufficiently processed.

For instance, these data can be organized and processed (using certain assumptions) to reflect the following:

Employee Number	*Employee Name*	*Age*
1	John Doe	33
99	Mary Smith	17
Average Age		25 (50 ÷ 2)

Now the data have meaning and usefulness. We have transformed them by organizing and processing them. Such results can be considered as information. In our context, information consists of organized and processed data that have meaning and usefulness for the manager.

Exhibit 3–1 presents another comparison of data and information.

Exhibit 3–1 A Comparison of Data and Information

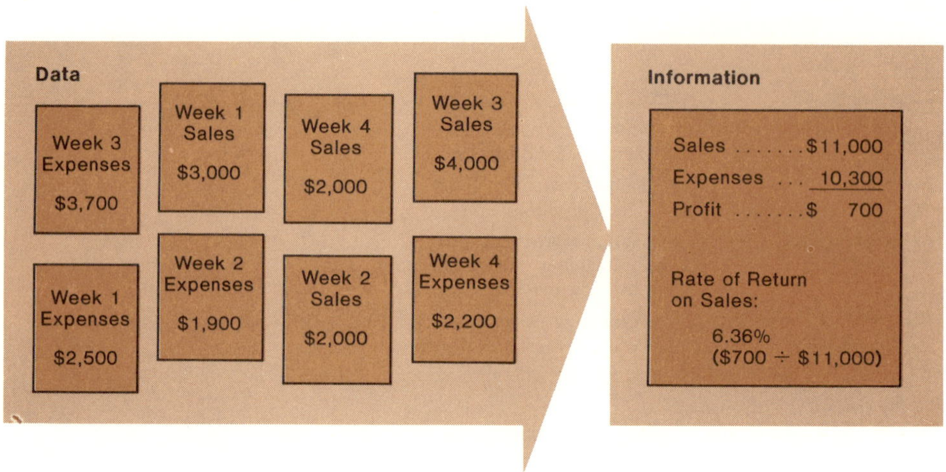

What Is Data Processing?

Data processing covers all the various methods that can be used to manipulate facts. The processing methods used may be *manual, mechanical,* or *electronic* (as with the electronic computer).

- A student who does his homework by solving algebra problems in a notebook is processing data.
- A secretary who is typing a business report is processing data.
- A computer that is solving a differential equation for an engineer is processing data.

In practice, many business applications require combined methods of processing. Thus, part of a payroll data-processing job may be done manually, part may be done with mechanical equipment, and the remainder may be done by computer (see Exhibit 3–2). For example:

> *It is not unusual for factory workers to manually record their hours worked (time in and time out) for the day. And one alternative requires them to manually put their time card in a time clock so that it can be stamped mechanically when they report for work and when they leave the factory for home. At the end of the week, it is usual for the factory workers' supervisor to review the time cards and to approve them by signing them; this authorizes the payroll department to prepare checks for*

Exhibit 3–2 Payroll Processing Methods

the employees. In a large factory, the employees' records may be maintained on a computer. The computer updates the employees' records, generates the payroll checks, and provides management with control information about the weekly payroll.

The actual steps in processing data usually include such things as:

- Reading the data.
- Recording the data.
- Editing the data.
- Sorting the data.
- Classifying the data.
- Performing calculations on the data.
- Recording the results of the calculations.
- Summarizing the data.
- Recording the results of the summarization.
- Distributing the data.
- Filing the data.
- Retrieving the data.
- Purging the data.

The above steps are not necessarily aligned in a particular order. They are merely meant to indicate the type of steps that may be included in data processing.

In order to clarify the relation between data-processing methods and steps in data processing, let us again look at the payroll application we just discussed.

Method	*Steps*
Manual insert by worker of card and mechanical stamping of card.	Record time on the time card.
Manual review by supervisor.	Edit and authorize the data on the time card.
Electronic computer.	Calculate payroll data and update employee payroll records. Generate payroll checks and reports for management.

In the above example, the computer does all the payroll calculations. However, suppose that the payroll were handled completely by people. What steps would be required to prepare the payroll? Some of them would be:

1. Read and analyze the employee's payroll record to determine whether the individual is an hourly employee (paid by the hour) or a salaried employee (paid a set amount each payroll period).
2. Analyze the data to determine whether the employee has any overtime hours for the work period.

Exhibit 3–3 An Example of a Payroll Register

ADA CORPORATION
PAYROLL REGISTER
FOR PERIOD ENDING 31 DECEMBER 19__

EMPLOYEE NAME	GROSS SALARY	DEDUCTIONS	NET SALARY
JOHN DOE	$ 300.00	$ 60.00	$ 240.00
MARY SMITH	325.00	70.00	255.00
A.B. WHITE	275.00	50.00	225.00
TOTALS	$7,500.00	$1,500.00	$6,000.00

3. Compute the employee's gross pay (regular pay plus any overtime pay). If the employee is an hourly worker, multiply the number of hours worked by the hourly rate of pay to determine pay.
4. Perform any deduction calculations (e.g., federal income tax or social security tax).
5. Compute the employee's net pay (gross pay less total deductions). This is the amount to be paid to the employee.
6. Record this payroll period's figures for the employee on the employee's year-to-date record. These data are needed for federal income tax reporting purposes, among others.

The above steps would be performed for each employee. Thereafter, a payroll register (see Exhibit 3–3) might be prepared, listing all employees with each one's payroll data (gross pay, deductions, net pay). This report would have summary totals, indicating the total dollar amounts for gross pay, deductions, and net pay. Of course, after the payroll was authorized, the employees would be paid (checks would be issued or cash distributed; or the pay could be credited to the employee's bank account).

While it's true that this book concentrates primarily on computer data processing, much data processing is done by manual and mechanical methods.

Generally, if work volume is very low, such work is handled manually or by means of simple mechanical aids (e.g., typewriter or pocket calculator). However, as the work volume increases, more sophisticated mechanical aids may be used (e.g., punched-card

Exhibit 3–4 Variety of Data-Processing Methods

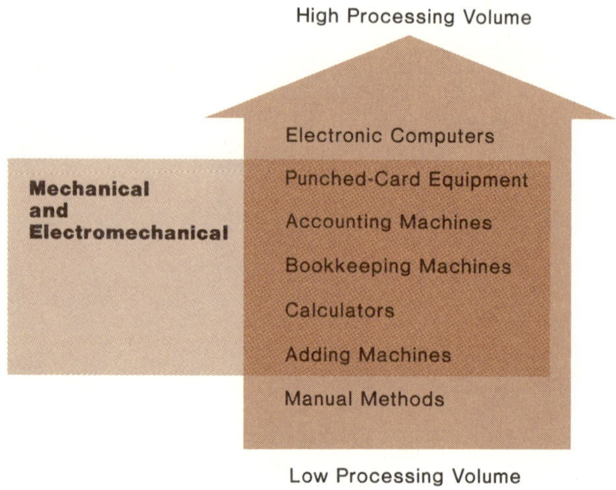

Exhibit 3–5 The Relative Cost Advantage of Using a Computer

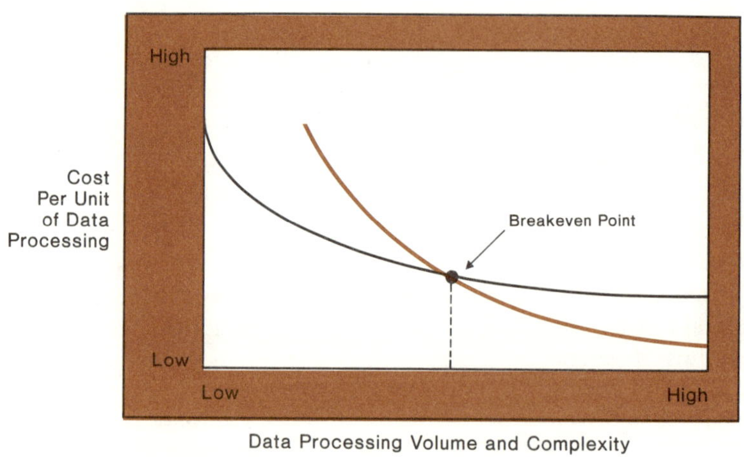

Legend: —— = Manual Method
—— = Computer Method

equipment). And in cases where the work volume is heavy, most organizations turn for help to the computer (see Exhibit 3–4).

Cost of Data Processing

The per unit cost of computer processing has decreased steadily. This is because of computer breakthroughs, which have increased processing speeds without being accompanied by comparable price increases. The per unit cost of manual processing, on the other hand, is increasing because of constantly increasing minimum-wage levels and inflation-induced salary increases, as well as because it is difficult to increase productivity in a strictly manual system. Smaller yet faster computers have become available and thus competitive with manual and mechanical methods, even at lower volumes of processing. Because of the initial fixed cost of the computer and the preparatory work for it, an organization must have a sufficient volume of data processing to justify using a computer. Exhibit 3–5 presents a chart showing that each organization will have a breakeven point at which the organization's data processing can be done more cheaply by computer than by noncomputer methods. The chart also indicates that, by using a computer, an organization has an opportunity to lower the per unit cost of data processing as volume increases (i.e., as the company grows). On the other hand, in a noncomputer system, as the volume of work increases there is likely to be little opportunity to reduce per unit costs, since the organization will constantly need to hire more employees to do the work.

HISTORICAL DEVELOPMENT OF DATA-PROCESSING AIDS

The modern computer was developed within the last three decades, but many prior developments contributed, even if indirectly, to its eventual emergence. We will identify just a few of the developments briefly.

Early Manual Methods and Devices

Any function, or use of a device, that depends strictly on human power can be considered a manual function. Such a function or device has a speed that is paced by the human being himself/herself.

The familiar abacus, one of the earliest counting devices (see Exhibit 3–6), was originated thousands of years ago. It is still used in some parts of the world (e.g., the Far East and Middle East).

In the fifteenth century, Luca Paciolo of Italy formalized double-entry bookkeeping methods which are the bases for modern accounting systems.

Exhibit 3–6 Abacus

Photograph courtesy of IBM Corporation

Early Calculating Machines

Early calculating machines were, by and large, invented by individuals whose theories were before their time: their machines either were difficult to build (because needed technology was not available), or they were built but never used widely.

Blaise Pascal, a seventeenth-century French philosopher and mathematician, and Gottfried von Leibnitz, a seventeenth-century German philosopher and mathematician, designed computational machines to aid in mathematical calculations.

Charles Babbage, an English professor of mathematics who lived in the eighteenth century, is sometimes referred to as the father of early computers (see Exhibit 3–7). His so-called "difference machine" and "analytical machine" (or engine) generally are credited as root sources of ideas that eventually culminated in the modern computers. Babbage's principal collaborator was another mathematician—Lady Lovelace, a daughter of poet Lord Byron.

Punched-Card Machines*

Punched-card machines proved to be both practical and popular as data-processing devices. The mechanical, then electromechanical, punched-card equipment led up to

* These machines are sometimes called electromechanical accounting machines (EAM) or unit-record machines (since the machines handle a single record as a unit, and then handle the next record, and so on).

Exhibit 3–7 Babbage Calculator

Photograph courtesy of IBM Corporation

the modern computer; and even today, such equipment occupies a role in data processing.

In the early nineteenth century, Joseph Marie Jacquard, a Frenchman, developed the first known automatic weaving loom that followed instructions that had been coded into punched cards.* At the end of the nineteenth century, Dr. Herman Hollerith,† an engineer, helped the United States Census Bureau to develop punched-card machines (see Exhibit 3–8) to speed up the processing of census data. The census data, stored as coded perforations on cards, could be manipulated rapidly (e.g., sorted into classifications) and counted (or "tabulated"). The Census Bureau was forced, out of

* See Chapters 6, 7, and 8 for more details about punched cards.

† It is interesting to note that Dr. Hollerith eventually formed his own company to manufacture and sell his punched-card equipment. This firm was one of those that were merged to form International Business Machines Corporation. James Powers, also with the U.S. Census Bureau, likewise formed a company to produce and market punched-card equipment. Powers' firm was acquired by Remington Rand Corporation, which later became part of the Sperry Rand Corporation.

Exhibit 3–8 Hollerith Punched-Card Devices

Photograph courtesy of IBM Corporation

necessity, to process its data faster. If punched-card equipment had not been made available for the 1890 census, it was anticipated that the data would not be totally processed until perhaps 1902–3, thus overlapping the 1900 census. The use of punched-card equipment spread to other organizations with large paperwork volume (such as insurance companies, banks, and government agencies).

Key-Driven Machines

There is a wide variety of key-driven machines. Some are driven strictly by human power; others are driven by a combination of electricity and human power.

Exhibit 3–9 MARK I Computer

Photograph courtesy of IBM Corporation

Late in the nineteenth century and early in the twentieth century, many key-driven machines were invented, primarily in the United States. Many of the modern versions of these machines are in use today. They include: the typewriter; the adding machine; the comptometer; and the calculator (which could subtract, multiply, and divide, as well as add).

After World War I, a number of bookkeeping, accounting, payroll, and billing machines were introduced. These machines combined some computational ability with the ability to retain (store) totals, and also to print data in several columns of an accounting record.

Early Computers

The early computers were generally built as one-of-a-kind devices for either universities or the government. Few individuals perceived that there would eventually be a substantial market for computers in the business world.

Howard Aiken of Harvard University, under research grants from International Business Machines Corporation (IBM) and the United States Navy Department, designed a computer named MARK (see Exhibit 3–9).* This mechanical computer was used for military planning purposes during World War II.

* Early computers were often given names, such as MARK, ENIAC, and EDVAC. These names were often contractions of more descriptive words; for example, ENIAC was derived from *E*lectronic *N*umerical *I*ntegrator *a*nd *C*alculator. As the number of different model computers grew, it was found more sensible to give computers a number identification (e.g., IBM 370) rather than a name.

As the name implies, the electronic computer operates extensively by electronic means, using a minimum of mechanical components. Eliminating physically moving parts increases the speed of processing in such computers. In the late 1930s, John V. Atanasoff, a professor of mathematics at Iowa State College, conceived of an electronic computer and built a model that was working by 1942. Later, J. Prosper Eckert (an electronic engineer) and John W. Mauchly (a physicist), of the Moore School of Engineering of the University of Pennsylvania, extended Atanasoff's work. Eckert and Mauchly built the ENIAC computer, which was in use for military-related calculations by 1945. By 1952, Eckert and Mauchly had EDVAC, an improved computer, in operation.

During this general period, several related important developments occurred. John von Neumann, a noted mathematician from the Institute for Advanced Study at Princeton University, conceived of a stored program,* which would replace the complicated, cumbersome, external-wired control panels and switches used on such computers as ENIAC. The first computer to incorporate von Neumann's idea was the EDSAC, which was operative around 1949 at the University of Cambridge, England. In addition, von Neumann made a second significant contribution; he argued that binary arithmetic† and not decimal arithmetic should be used by the computer. In 1948, Bell Telephone Laboratories scientists developed a new type of electronic amplifier, the first solid-state amplifier, which would eventually replace the vacuum tube—the *transistor.* Their invention increased the computer's speed and reliability.

By the early 1950s, computers began to be recognized as possibly having a place in the market. Remington Rand Corporation (now Sperry Rand Corporation) began to build the first computers for the general market (rather than the one-of-a-kind, under-special-contract kinds that had been built earlier). These early computers, called UNIVAC I, were first delivered to the U.S. Bureau of Census, and to General Electric Company's manufacturing facility in Louisville, Kentucky. UNIVAC gained nationwide attention (important publicity for the entire computer field) when it was used to predict the 1952 presidential election results. This publicity set the stage for the emergence of a computer industry in the United States and the world.

Summary

The computer is one of the most powerful and versatile inventions of human beings. Like all tools, it was developed to facilitate the work of people.

Data processing can be accomplished by elementary means, such as counting on one's fingers, or with aids such as the pocket calculator or the computer. In business, a variety of data-processing methods are frequently employed. However, there are common steps in any data-processing system, including: performing calculations; recording data; and summarizing data.

* Stored program concepts will be discussed in Chapter 5.

† Binary arithmetic will be discussed in Chapter 5 and Appendix A.

The modern computer was "born" in the 1940s. Some of the pioneers who are considered to have made notable contributions to the development of the computer include: Charles Babbage; Herman Hollerith; Howard Aiken; John V. Atanasoff; J. Prosper Eckert; John W. Mauchly; and John von Neumann.

Terms to Learn

Data
Information
Data processing
Manual data-processing
Mechanical data-processing
Computer (electronic) data-processing (CDP or EDP)
Punched-card machine
Transistor
Data-processing method
Data-processing step
Breakeven point
Cost per unit of data processing
Abacus
Blaise Pascal
Gottfried von Leibnitz
Charles Babbage
Herman Hollerith
Howard Aiken
John V. Atanasoff
J. Prosper Eckert
John W. Mauchly
John von Neumann
EDSAC
ENIAC
UNIVAC
MARK

Review Questions

1. Explain why *tools* have been important in the development of civilization.
2. Why is the *computer* particularly important to modern society?
3. Define *data processing*. Discuss the similarities and differences between these methods of data processing: *manual, mechanical,* and *computer.*
4. Describe the operation of a *data-processing system* with which you are familiar (e.g., cashing a check in a bank, registering for classes at college, or making a purchase at a department store). What methods are used? What steps are employed?
5. Why does *data-processing volume* have a strong influence on the method used to process data?
6. Explain why many businesses use a *composite system* of data processing (that is, they use a mixture of manual, mechanical, and computer methods).
7. Trace the early development of *data-processing aids* that predated the modern computer.
8. Discuss the contributions of the following persons to the field of data processing: Charles Babbage, Herman Hollerith, Howard Aiken, J. Prosper Eckert and John W. Mauchly, John V. Atanasoff, and John von Neumann.

Exhibit 3–10 First-Generation Computer: IBM 650

Photograph courtesy of IBM Corporation

TOPIC 2—COMPUTER ERA

THE COMPUTER GENERATIONS*

The period up to 1950 is considered the time during which the foundation for the computer industry was laid. By the time the 1950s began, organizations that manufactured and marketed computers had emerged, and the use of computers in business, government, hospitals, colleges, and other institutions had expanded dramatically. These developments can be traced most conveniently in terms of *computer generations* (see Table 3–2).

First Generation (1951–1958): Basic Applications

Since using organizations were just becoming initiated in the use of computers, most applications were very basic. For instance, payroll was almost invariably the first application that was put on the computer. However, payroll was a logical choice; its high degree of proceduralization and intelligibility made it receptive to programming.

* Computer professionals do not unanimously agree about what factors determine a computer generation, or about how many generations of computers there have been. However, the consensus seems to be that the real measure of a new generation of computers is a dramatic improvement in the cost/performance ratio. A new-generation computer tends to make the prior generation's computers obsolete.

In terms of the end user of the computer—that is, the organizations that use computers to process their data, in contrast with firms that manufacture and market computers—we can refer to the *first generation* of computers as one that involved basic applications.

During the 1951–58 period, IBM decided to follow Remington Rand in manufacturing and marketing computers. During this generation, representative computers were UNIVAC I, IBM 650 (see Exhibit 3–10), and IBM 701.

Computers built during this period were basically refinements of ENIAC, EDSAC, and EDVAC. In retrospect, we can characterize them as machines that were bulky in size, that required great amounts of air conditioning to dissipate the heat generated by their numerous vacuum tubes, and that needed high rates of maintenance

Table 3–2

Summary of Computer Generations

Generation	Examples of Computers*	Examples of Technological Characteristics	Status of User Focus
First Generation (1951–1958)	IBM 650 IBM 701 UNIVAC I	• Vacuum Tubes • Machine-language Programming	Basic Applications (e.g., Payroll)
Second Generation (1958–1964)	IBM 1401 IBM 1620 IBM 7000 Series	• Transistors • Magnetic Cores • Symbolic Programming Languages • Higher-Level Programming Languages • Magnetic Tape and Disk Storage	Widespread Applications (e.g., Accounting, Marketing, Manufacturing, etc.)
Third Generation (1964–1971)	IBM 360 Series	• Modularity and Compatibility • Solid-state Logic and Monolithic Integrated Circuits • Wide Variety of Input and Output Devices • Minicomputers • Additional Higher-Level Languages • Programming Packages	Integrating Applications (via Data Bases and Communications)
Fourth Generation (1971–1980)	IBM 370 IBM 3033	• Improved Circuitry • Microcomputers • Distributed Data Processing	Information Systems
Fifth Generation (1980s)	?	To be Determined	Manager's Aid

* IBM computers are often considered to be the de facto standard for the computer industry.

Exhibit 3–11 Second-Generation Computer: IBM 1401

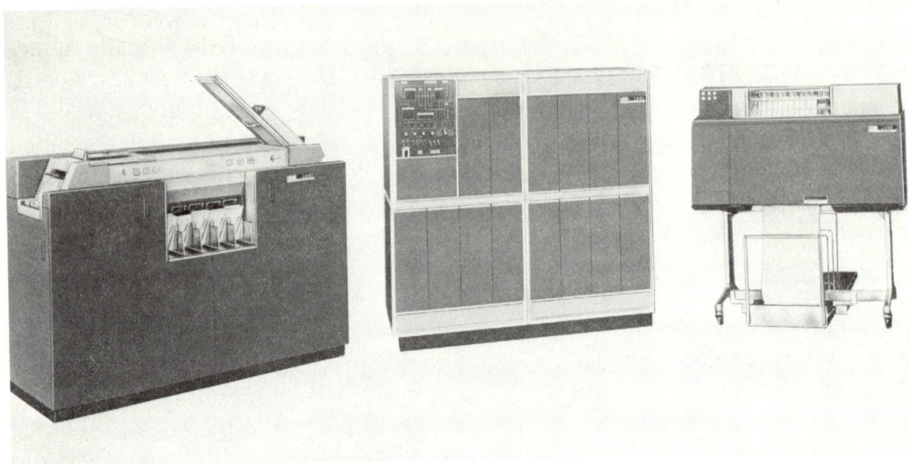

Photograph courtesy of IBM Corporation

and repair time to sustain reasonable equipment reliability. Initially, computers had to be programmed mainly in a machine language. This consisted of a difficult-to-remember numeric code, which was machine dependent (thus the term, "machine-level programming"); this meant that a program that was written for one specific computer model could not be used on a different model. People found computer programming laborious, and the programs lacked flexibility. If programmers wanted to use a new computer, they had to learn an entirely new programming language, and any existing computer programs slated for use had to be rewritten so that they could be processed on the new computer. Obviously, this was both time-consuming and costly.

But despite these limitations, business and government found computers comparatively advantageous, for some applications, over electromechanical punched-card machines and other key-driven machines. The most significant benefit was the relatively rapid data-processing speeds that were possible with computers. Also, the use of stored internal programs gave computers a potential versatility to handle complex problems that other business equipment could not handle.

Second Generation (1958–1964): Widespread Applications

Computers started to become a dominant growth industry in the United States economy. During the 1958–64 period, computer users, having gained confidence and experience during the first generation, began to apply computers in many different areas, including: billing; accounts receivable; sales statistics; inventory; purchasing;

accounts payable; cost accounting; and general ledger. This widespread use of computers indicated the euphoria that many organizations felt about computers. Unfortunately, many of the applications placed on the computer were not well planned or integrated. Often a hodgepodge of applications, lacking in good systems design, were computerized.

The most widely used *second-generation computers* were IBM's small- to medium-scale, business-oriented 1401 (see Exhibit 3–11), and its small, science-oriented 1620 computer. IBM's 7000 series dominated the large-scale computer market. In addition to IBM and Sperry Rand, other organizations began to manufacture and market computers. These companies included: Honeywell Corporation; Burroughs Corporation; National Cash Register Company; and Control Data Corporation. Radio Corporation of America and General Electric Company also entered the computer industry, but later they withdrew from it.

The second-generation computers had transistors instead of vacuum tubes—transistorized computers were faster, more compact, more reliable, and required less power and air conditioning. Also, they had an improved technique for internal storage: magnetic cores. These cores store data and instructions, and permit quick access to information in the computer's memory. An item could be located and made ready for internal processing in a few millionths of a second (microseconds), in contrast with the first-generation computers' internal speeds of a few thousandths of a second (milliseconds).* Magnetic tape, which can be processed much faster than punched cards, increasingly was used to obtain faster input to and output from the computer. Also, movement to improve direct-access storage devices, which would permit huge amounts of data to be constantly available to the computer, began. In such storage devices, the data could be reached directly. This accessibility provided an alternative to the sequential processing of data, which not only requires that data be externally gathered in batches and arranged in some logical sequence before being processed by the computer, but also requires processing of *all* data in a file, even if some are inactive.

In addition to programming computers in actual machine language, the option of using symbolic programming languages expanded. Such symbolic languages used mnemonic symbols,† which made the programming task easier for the human programmers. FLOWMATIC, developed by Dr. Grace Murray Hopper at the University of Pennsylvania, was a major breakthrough in the development of problem-oriented programming languages. The computer used a translator program, that also was written in machine language, to automatically convert the user's problem-oriented program into the tedious machine-language code. By 1959, the first widely adopted, standardized, problem-oriented language was developed: *FORTRAN* (FORmula TRANslator). This algebra-like language still remains in wide use. A program that is written in a problem-oriented (or higher-level programming) language such as

* It has been estimated that the blink of a human eye takes about 1/10th of a second, or 100,000 microseconds. Thus, in the 100,000 microseconds that elapse while a person blinks an eye, a fast, modern computer might be able to execute up to one million operations.

† As an example of a mnemonic code, the letter "A" might be used to signify that "addition" was to take place; "M" might indicate "multiplication;" and so on. This was an improvement over having to recall that "11" stood for addition and "16" stood for multiplication, which was the approach used in machine language.

Exhibit 3–12 Third-Generation Computer: IBM System/360 Model 40

Photograph courtesy of IBM Corporation

FORTRAN increases the computer's flexibility, since the program can be run on almost any computer. In addition to FORTRAN, many programming languages that are even more specialized have been developed.*

Third Generation (1964–1971): Integrating Applications

In the *third generation,* technology provided users with some of the tools they needed to start integrating the widespread, fragmented computer applications that had piled up during the second generation. In particular, the hardware and software needed for huge on-line data bases became available. And improved data terminals and communications equipment began to offer remotely located users more widespread access to a central computer.

* Software and programming are explored in Chapters 10 and 11.

Exhibit 3–13 Miniaturization of Circuits: Vacuum Tubes, Transistors, Solid Logic Technology Modules, Monolithic Integrated Circuits

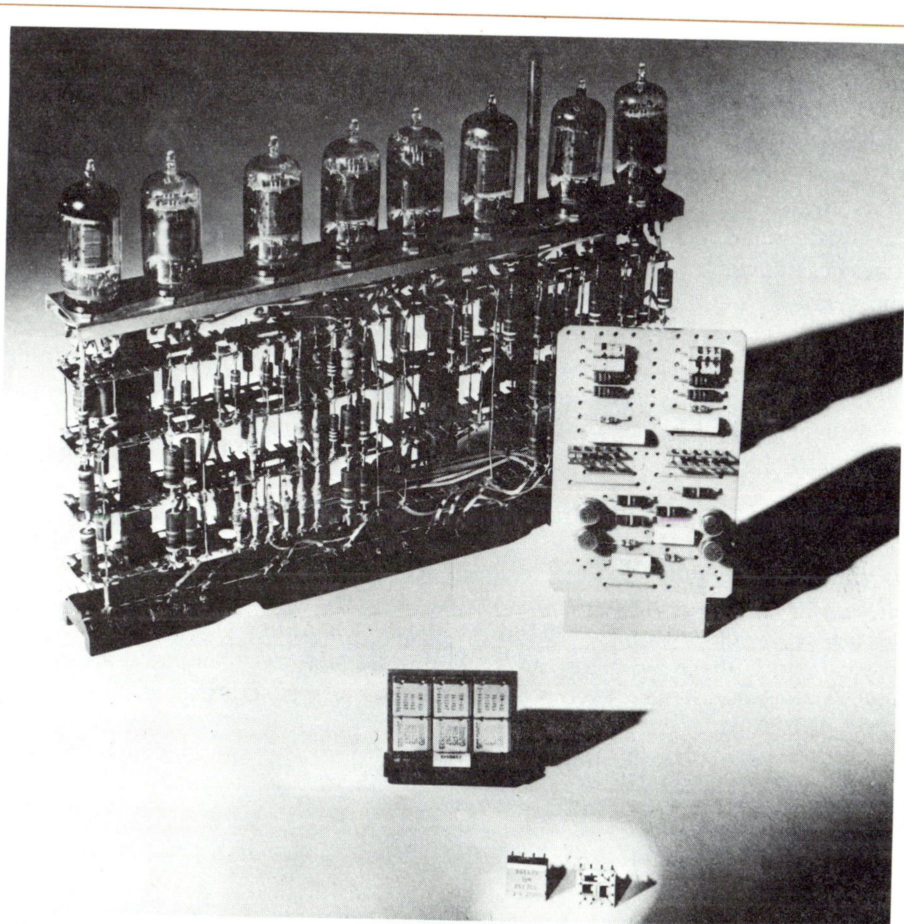

Photograph courtesy of IBM Corporation

The computer that set the standard for almost all other computers was the IBM 360 (see Exhibit 3–12). In fact, the 360 was a family of computers, ranging from small to large. All the 360 computers were modular; that is, any 360 computer could be expanded by adding optional equipment. Other computer manufacturers developed their own family of computers, some of which had compatibility features that allowed an IBM computer user to switch to a different vendor without having to make extensive changes in existing computer programs. Particularly in light of the costliness and time-consuming factor involved in changing or even upgrading computers, modularity and compatibility were indeed important developments.

Solid-state logic and monolithic integrated circuits, both of which are very miniaturized,* replaced transistors (see Exhibit 3–13). This new trend produced faster, more compact, and more reliable computers. A wide variety of improved-performance input and output devices appeared on the market, to keep up with the computer's tremendously increased speed.† Operating systems (master programs) became necessary to automatically direct and control the more sophisticated computer hardware and software.

During this period, minicomputers (some of which can fit on a desk) began to be significant in the computer industry. These compact, comparatively inexpensive computers greatly broadened the computer market, and they encouraged smaller units of organizations and small businesses to consider getting their own computer. New companies began manufacturing and marketing minicomputers; among them were Digital Equipment Corporation; Hewlett Packard Company; Texas Instruments Company; and Data General Company.

By the mid-1960s, there was wide support for a new, higher-level programming language called *COBOL* (COmmon Business Oriented Language).‡ This language has wide applicability for business data-processing applications. During this period, other higher-level programming languages and other program supports (e.g., packaged programs) accumulated.

Fourth Generation (1971–1980): Information Systems

There is some debate as to whether a *fourth generation* of computers has been spawned. Since future technological breakthroughs relative to computers are not likely to be as dramatic as they have been in the past, new generations will be harder to distinguish.

In the 1970s, organizations have increasingly used their computers to obtain information that helps them run their businesses and improve their organizational effectiveness. More and more, the computer is being viewed as an information machine. Chapter 2 explored information systems concepts briefly; in Chapter 15, these ideas will be discussed in more detail.

Computer manufacturers began delivering new lines of computers in the 1970s. One of these was the IBM 370 series, which is considered to be a refinement of the IBM 360 series. Technology has been responsible for still further improvements, regarding both speed and reliability, in circuit performance. In the late 1970s, the

* Compact vacuum-tube equipment contained an average of 6,000 components per cubic foot. It was possible to pack an average of about 100,000 transistors in a cubic foot. About 10 million integrated circuits can fit in a cubic foot of space.

† A powerful, fast computer must be fed enough data by input devices, or else the computer will be idle much of the time. Also, the computer must have rapid output devices so that it can disgorge results.

‡ The United States Defense Department established a policy that all computer vendors wishing to supply the department with computers would have to also have COBOL compilers available. This placed pressure on the computer manufacturers to develop such software, since the Defense Department is the largest single user of computers. Also, the American National Standards Institute (ANSI) endorsed COBOL as a standard for business applications. ANSI is a private organization that sets standards for industry—including the computer industry. As a result, COBOL is the widest-used programming language.

Exhibit 3–14 Fourth-Generation Computer: IBM System/370 Computer with an IBM 3033 Central Processor

Photograph courtesy of IBM Corporation

introduction of computers like the IBM 3033 announced even further improvements (see Exhibit 3–14). The IBM 3033 signals a truly new generation of computers that probably will emerge sometime in the early 1980s.

The expanded use of microcomputers,* which can be installed in any piece of equipment (e.g., automobiles, airplanes, and appliances), and minicomputers has given rise to distributed data-processing. This means that computer hardware and software are available and can be located and used at the point where the action is. This is somewhat the opposite of central data-processing. In the early days of computers, it was thought that data-processing work had to be sent to a central computer for processing. However, distributed data-processing makes computer power available at the data site.

Fifth Generation (1980s): Management Aid†

In the 1980s, we can expect that the computer will be used increasingly to aid the manager. A new generation of managers has been educated in an environment that views the computer as an everyday tool. In addition, organizations are reaching some degree of sophistication relative to computers; such organizations have talented computer professionals, data bases, and information systems. These ingredients are needed for an age that considers the computer as a management tool.

* Microcomputers are made by using a photographic process to reproduce on a small silicon wafer the numerous transistors, resistors, and diodes of conventional computers. The silicon wafer is then encased in ceramic. Next to oxygen, silicon, like sand, is the most abundant element on the earth. Thus, microcomputers can be made cheaply.

† See Chapter 15 for more details on this idea.

Exhibit 3–15 Developments in Computer Technology

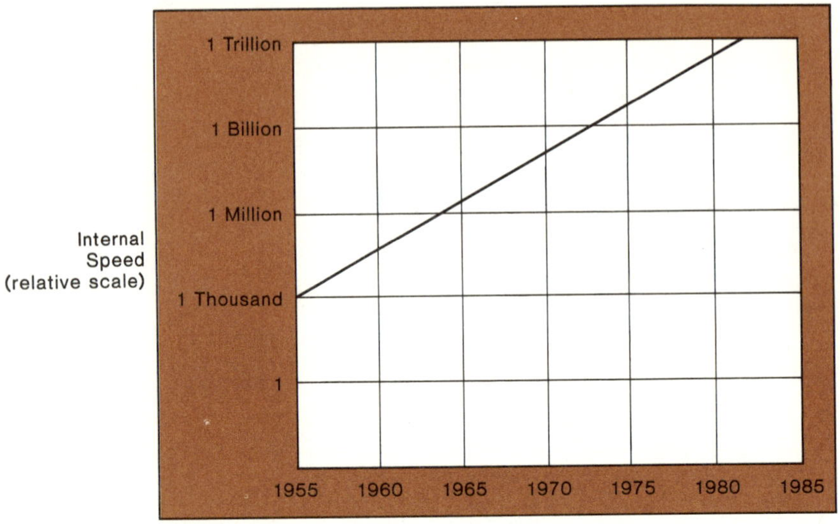

Under such circumstances, the manager will be able to use the computer for the management functions (i.e., planning, organizing, controlling, and actuating) and actions (i.e., decision making and communicating) that were discussed in Chapter 2.

We can anticipate, of course, that the computers* of the future will be even faster, more compact, and more reliable than ever before. Also, we predict significant simplifying approaches to computer programming; these will include not only English-like languages but also oral communication between humans and advanced computers.†

SIGNIFICANCE OF COMPUTER-TECHNOLOGY DEVELOPMENTS

The various developments that occurred during the generation of changes have had significant results (see Exhibit 3–15). The overall trends have been:

- Miniaturization of the computer.
- Rapidly increased processing speeds of the computer.

* Chapters 16 and 17 explore future computer trends in more detail.

† Such oral communication may resemble the conversations that took place between HAL computer and the two humans in the film, "2001: A Space Odyssey." By the way, HAL stands for *H*euristically-programmed *Al*gorithmic computer—which simply means that HAL can teach himself how to do new things, just as humans can.

- Significant improvement in the computer's reliability.
- Considerable expansion of the computer's capability.
- Reduced cost, per unit of processing, for the computer user.

First-generation computer speed* was expressed in *milliseconds* (thousandths of a second); second-generation speed was measured in *microseconds* (millionths of a second); third- and fourth-generation computers have operating speeds measured in *nanoseconds* (billionths of a second); and already there are models that are measured in *picoseconds* (trillionths of a second).†

In 1955, a computer might process 1,000 basic instructions for about thirty cents. By 1965, computers could process one million basic instructions for the same thirty cents. In the period from 1975 to 1980, computers are being created that, for about thirty cents, can process one billion basic instructions. This increase clearly suggests that, over time, the computer user has received more and more processing value from the computer.

To illustrate this point, see Table 3–3, which summarizes a specific example. The case involves a standard mix of about 1,700 computer operations‡ such as those that might be used in a typical business application like payroll. In the 1950s, such a mix of computer operations would have taken 375 seconds to carry out, and would have cost $14.54 in computer-related expenses. Now, that same mix of operations can be carried out in 5 seconds or less, at a cost of $.28 or less! Since the cost figures do not take

Table 3–3

A Comparative Analysis of Computer Costs

	1st Generation	2nd Generation	3rd Generation	4th Generation
Cost	$14.54	$2.48	$.59	$.28
Processing Time	375 Seconds	47 Seconds	37 Seconds	5 Seconds
Technology	Vacuum Tubes	Transistors	Solid Logic Technology	Monolithic Integrated Circuits
Programming Advances	Stored Program	Overlapping Input and Output	Operating System	Advanced Operating System

Note: The cost figures are not adjusted for inflation.
Adapted from a chart, courtesy of the International Business Machines Corporation.

* These rapid speeds are internal speeds; they occur within the computer's central processor, and they are not to be confused with actual production (e.g., number of checks or reports generated in a second).

† Such speeds are difficult for us to imagine. A spaceship traveling toward the moon at 100,000 miles per hour would move less than two inches in one microsecond! There are as many nanoseconds in one second as there are seconds in thirty years, or as many nanoseconds in a minute as there are minutes in 1,100 centuries! Electricity travels at about one foot per nanosecond, and this fact probably imposes an ultimate limit to internal computer speed.

‡ A computer operation (e.g., "read," "compute," "write") may consist of many basic instructions in binary form.

inflation and the reduced worth of current money into account, these reductions are even more impressive. Such figures clearly indicate why more and more organizations are turning to computers for data processing.*

THE COMPUTER INDUSTRY

Although the *computer industry* is one of the youngest in the U.S. economy, it has grown the fastest—now it ranks as one of the largest in the country. Some experts predict that within a few decades the computer industry will be the largest industry.

Exhibit 3–16 presents a graph showing the number of computers† (all manufactured by U.S. computer manufacturers) installed throughout the world.‡ For instance, it is interesting to note that:

- In 1953, only 50 computers were installed.
- By 1959 (the start of the second generation of computers), about 3,000 had been installed.
- In the 1960s, minicomputers started to become an important factor. By 1970, about 100,000 computers of all kinds had been installed. Five years later, when IBM 360s were being converted to IBM 370s, an estimated 300,000 or more computers were installed.
- The chart clearly shows that minicomputers are growing in number relatively faster than the traditional computers are. It is estimated that by the mid-1980s over 1,000,000 computers will be in use, and that half of them will be minicomputers.

While the United States remains by far the largest manufacturer of computers, computer companies also exist in a number of other nations, including England, Germany, Japan, France, Sweden, Italy, and the Soviet Union. Considerable capital is required to manufacture computers, and traditionally, only a few large organizations (e.g., International Business Machines Company, UNIVAC Division of Sperry Rand Corporation, Honeywell Corporation, and Burroughs Corporation) have dominated the market. However, the advent of minicomputers and microcomputers, which require less capital, has encouraged many smaller organizations to enter the computer manufacturing and marketing field.

The greatest number of computer users have been located first in the U.S., then in Western Europe, Japan, Canada, Australia, the Soviet Union, Mexico, Venezuela, Israel, Brazil, Saudi Arabia, and Iran. However, increasing advances in industrializa-

* The average value of computers installed has been falling steadily. For instance, the average computer purchase price in the 1950s was well over $1,000,000; in 1965, it was only about $300,000. In the early 1980s it should be about $100,000. Even more impressive is the fact that the $100,000 computer is many times more powerful than the early generation's $1,000,000 computer.

† Chapter 4 will more fully describe the characteristics of the different types of computers.

‡ These figures do not include microcomputers. The inclusion of such computers would further expand the growth picture by a significant amount.

Exhibit 3–16 Computers Installed

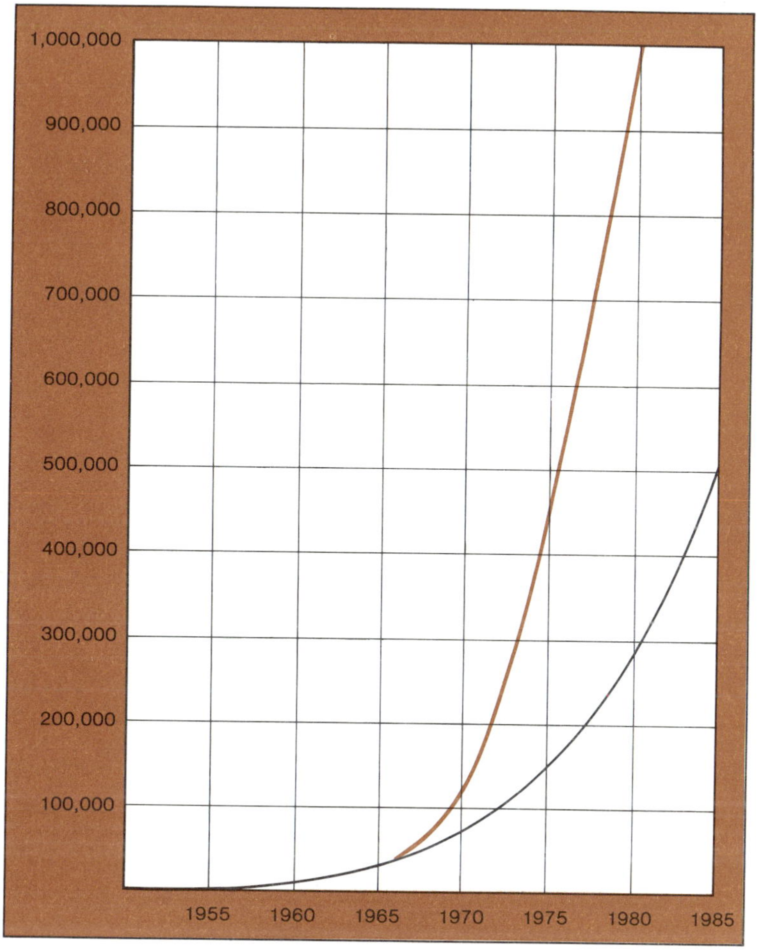

Legend: ——— = Number of computers, including minicomputers
——— = Number of computers, excluding minicomputers

tion and technology throughout the world will create a future for the computer in developing nations in such areas as Eastern Europe, Africa, South America, the Far East, and Middle East.

In addition to manufacturing and marketing computers, the computer industry also has many other related organizations—of which there are probably more than 5,000—with the following products and services: peripheral equipment that is support-

Exhibit 3–17 Revenues of Companies in the Computer Industry

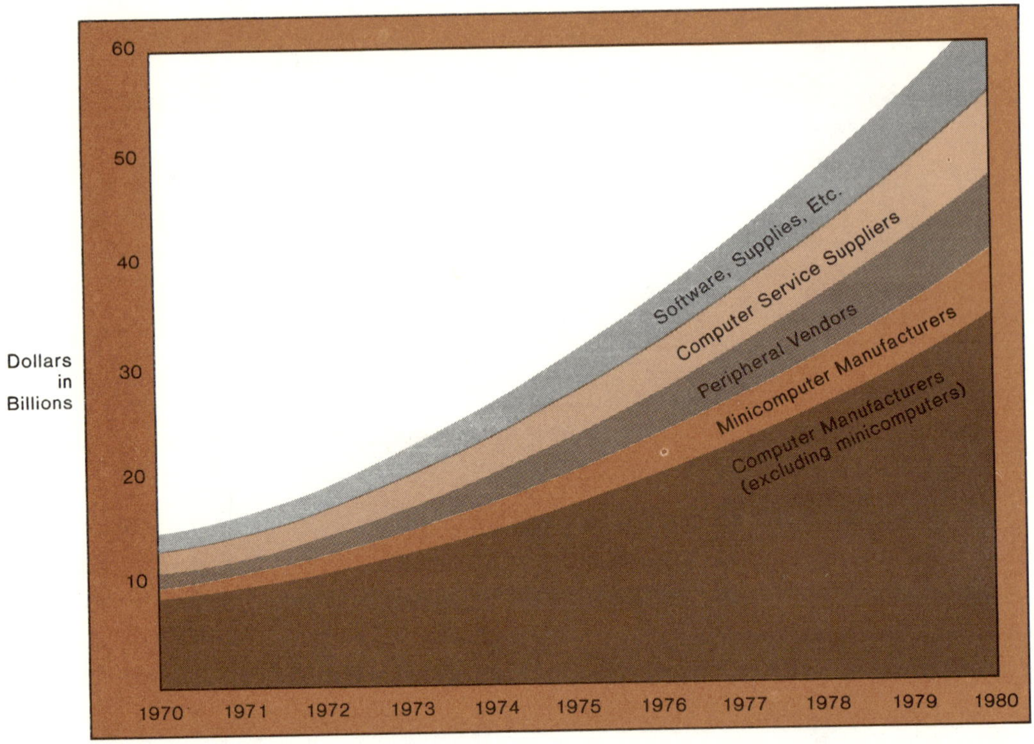

ive of the computer; computer service suppliers (e.g., service bureaus and consultants); and others, such as suppliers of software and paper.

Exhibit 3–17 indicates the growth and size of the U.S. computer industry. In the early 1970s, total revenue of companies in the computer business were around $20 billion. By 1980, total revenue tripled to $60 billion. Over the last two decades, the industry growth rate has averaged about thirty-five times that of the general economy. It is estimated that by 1985, revenues will be about $160 billion.*

The first retail computer store opened in 1975; and there also may be close to 1,000 retail outlets that sell relatively inexpensive computers to the computer hobbyist.

Another interesting aspect of the computer industry is the growth of occupations in computer-related work. This aspect will be discussed in Chapters 4 and 14.

* In 1970, computer-related spending was about 2 percent of the Gross National Product, or $100 per capita. In 1985, such spending is forecasted to be around 8 percent of the Gross National Product, or $670 per capita. In economic terms, this underscores the growing importance of the computer industry in our society.

RELATED DEVELOPMENTS: WORD PROCESSING AND MANUFACTURING AUTOMATION

While this book emphasizes the business use of the computer itself, two major related developments should be identified: *word processing* and *manufacturing automation.*

Word Processing

Despite the wide use of computers, about half of the U.S. employment force are classified as white-collar workers, and the percentage has been growing. Clerical workers (including secretaries and file clerks) comprise the largest single category of white-collar workers.

The number of secretaries in the United States has about doubled in the past ten years. Productivity levels in traditional offices tend not to keep pace with increases in salaries and related costs. In some organizations, maybe as high as 40 percent of costs can be connected to office-type work. Some of the studies of office costs indicate that a one-page letter that cost about $1.00 to prepare in the 1950s may cost about $5.00 by the end of the 1970s. These labor and cost pressures make labor-saving equipment for the office an attractive alternative; some word-processing offices report cost reductions of up to 50 percent or higher, compared to traditional office methods.

Exhibit 3–18 Word-Processing Equipment

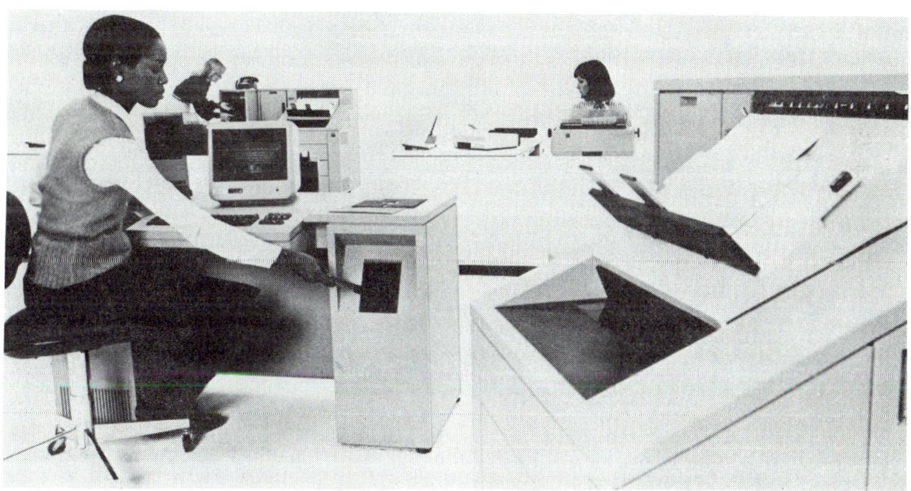

Photograph courtesy of IBM Corporation

Generally, word-processing equipment includes:

1. Automated typewriters with a memory capability that facilitates corrections and copy editing.
2. Computer-assisted editing and composing of documents, reports, and correspondence.
3. Electronic dictating and reproducing equipment.

Exhibit 3–18 shows some word-processing equipment. A visual display (television-like device) is used to guide the operator through each task. The system uses removable magnetic diskettes that can store up to 200,000 or more characters. The stored data can be easily changed, selected, sequenced, or reformatted to generate listings, reports, and documents. Data can be transmitted from some word-processing equipment to a computer.

There will be additional advances in this area, and the interface between word processing and computer processing seems to be an inevitable development. In publishing, for instance, computers are used to perform the complex calculations to quickly set up the print alignment for the articles in newspapers and the page format for magazines, journals, and books. Also, it has been reported that the Japanese have been experimenting with a dictating device that will tape a person's words; this device can then be switched to an automatic typewriter, which will type a document from the words contained on the tape. Wherever there is a large volume of reports or correspondence to type and/or to file and retrieve, word-processing equipment, in combination with computers, may be able to improve effectiveness.

Manufacturing Automation

Manufacturing automation has preceded modern computers. For many years, factories have used conveyor belts and devices to move the product being produced from work station to work station automatically. Special-purpose machines are also used that can at least partially operate independently of human intervention. Such machines have been preprogrammed to perform certain specific operations automatically. For instance, there are drills and presses that will carry out their functions with a minimum of human control and direction. Increasingly, robots are being used to perform hazardous tasks such as handling radioactive materials in laboratories.

An example of manufacturing automation is a modern petroleum refinery that takes crude petroleum and refines it into the numerous products used by organizations and individuals (e.g., gasoline, fuel oil, lubricants, and kerosene). Special-purpose computers and instruments make a large part of the multimillion-dollar refinery operation completely automated. The automation controls the flow of the petroleum products through the various stages of processing in the refinery; these controls automatically open and close valves, adjust temperatures, and measure various

Exhibit 3–19 Interface of Computer with Word-Processing Devices and Automation Equipment

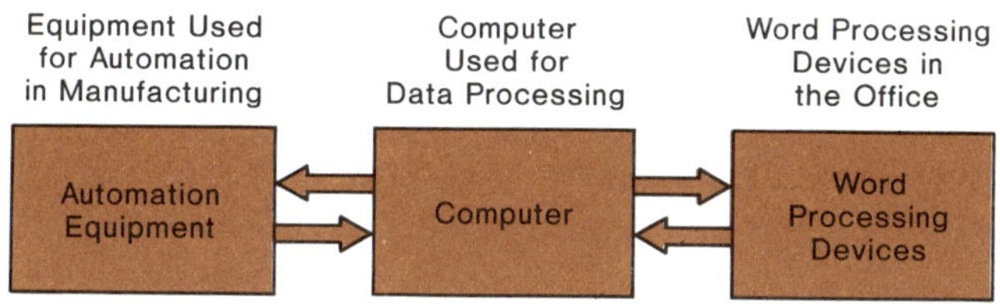

characteristics of the product. Relatively few human beings are needed to manage and operate the refinery complex.

In the future, we will probably see organizations' computers interfacing increasingly with both word processing in the office and automation in manufacturing plants (see Exhibit 3–19).

Summary

Since the early 1950s, computers have changed and grown dynamically. This book discusses five generations of computers (the fifth generation is the one of the future), and describes the significance and differences of each of these evolutionary periods. In terms of computer users, the use of computers has evolved, over time, through the following periods:

1. Basic applications;
2. Widespread applications;
3. Integrating applications;
4. Information systems; and
5. Manager's aid (the focus of the future generation).

In only about three decades, the computer industry has emerged as one of the largest industries, as well as the fastest-growing one, in the United States. The computer industry is also increasingly affecting other nations. This industry includes not only those organizations that produce computer equipment, but also other companies that offer related products, supplies, and services.

In the future, the interface of office word-processing and manufacturing automation with the computer that is used for data processing will constitute an increased focus of awareness.

Terms to Learn

Computer generation
First-generation computer
Second-generation computer
Third-generation computer
Fourth-generation computer
Fifth-generation computer
FORTRAN
COBOL
Solid-state logic and monolithic integrated circuit
Millisecond
Microsecond
Nanosecond
Picosecond
Computer industry
Word processing
Automation

Review Questions

1. Why is it convenient to think in terms of *computer generations?* How is a computer generation determined?
2. Discuss the *first generation* of computers and the user focus.
3. Discuss the *second generation* of computers and the user focus.
4. Discuss the *third generation* of computers and the user focus.
5. Discuss the *fourth generation* of computers and the user focus.
6. Discuss the *fifth generation* of computers and the user focus.
7. How have the technology developments, relative to computers, improved matters for computer users?

8. Discuss the *scope* of the computer industry, both from the standpoint of the manufacturers and suppliers and from that of the users. What has been the growth pattern of the computer industry?

9. Discuss the interface of the computer used for data processing with office *word-processing* and with *manufacturing automation.*

The Human Approach...
A+B-X=Y
... Vs. the Scientific Approach.

CHAPTER 4

AN OVERVIEW OF COMPUTER SYSTEMS

Objectives

This chapter provides an introduction to the technical features of computers. In particular, coverage includes: descriptions about the characteristics of computers; the elements of a computer system; the variety of different types of computers; and the advantages and limitations of computers.

The material in this chapter is presented under these topics:
Topic 1—Essentials of Computers.
Topic 2—Scope of Computers.
Topic 3—Computers in Use.

TOPIC 1—ESSENTIALS OF COMPUTERS

WHAT IS A COMPUTER?

The term "computer" could literally be used to identify any device that calculates. Initially, the computer was designed as a tool to manipulate numbers and solve arithmetic problems; this original use is understandable, since most of the early designers and users were mathematicians, scientists, and engineers. However, people began to realize that the computer could process symbols (e.g., alphabetic symbols) as well as numbers. Therefore, the literal interpretation of the word "computer" makes the word something of a misnomer, since the computer does more than just carry out addition, subtraction, multiplication, and division. Indeed, the computer can read input data, transfer or move data, store and retrieve data, test data by logical operations, and generate output results. In view of the fact that its functions are broader than just computing, the computer is sometimes more descriptively called an "electronic data processor" (EDP) or an "automatic data processor" (ADP).

The word "computer" has several different levels of meaning. Let us clarify these levels:

- In a very narrow sense, the computer is that piece of the *hardware** that performs the data processing. But more explicitly and correctly, this unit is the central processing unit (CPU). The CPU will be discussed in more detail later in this chapter.
- A broader view of the computer is: that which includes all *equipment* components that are interconnected to perform data processing. The equipment includes not only the CPU but also other devices that handle the input of data, the storage of

* The words "hardware" and "equipment" (as well as "devices" and "tools") are used interchangeably.

Exhibit 4–1 Characteristics of a Computer

A Computer

- Is Electronic
- Has Internal Storage
- Uses a Stored Program
- Can Perform Program Modification

data, and the output of results. Devices attached to the CPU are sometimes called "peripherals."

- A still more comprehensive view is the one that defines the computer as a system (thus, *computer system*). The computer system includes the hardware, the software, and the people who are integral to a computer's effective operation.

This book focuses primarily on the last definition—that the computer is part of a computer system.

General Characteristics of a Modern Computer

In general, computer professionals have established certain characteristics* that are used to determine whether a piece of equipment qualifies to be designated as a computer (see Exhibit 4–1). These characteristics are:

1. *Electronic*. A computer has electronic elements (circuits, transistors, etc.) that store and manipulate data and programs. Results are achieved through the movement of electric impulses rather than through the physical movement of internal parts. The computer operates with two-state logic (the binary system), which is based on two measurable states of electronic elements (i.e., "on" or "off").

   Why is the term "electronic" used instead of "electrical?" Every machine that uses electric current must have a means of controlling the flow of electricity. An electrical device employs moving mechanical parts to perform this function; that is why we often refer to this kind of device as "electromechanical." Its operations are relatively slow, because moving parts greatly reduce the overall speed of such devices. In a modern computer, the internal processing is electronic rather than electromechanical, because the flow of electricity is controlled by transistors and integrated circuits. These eliminate the need for the slower electromechanical

* Technical terms will be fully discussed later in this chapter, and at length in subsequent chapters.

devices. Technically, only the computer's central processing unit (CPU) is completely electronic. Other equipment connected to the computer's CPU are frequently electromechanical, including input devices, output devices, and secondary-storage devices.

2. *Internal Storage.* The computer has an internal storage (sometimes called *memory*) that is used for storing both the computer program (a series of instructions) and the data being processed.
3. *Stored Program.* The program of instructions, which stipulates the sequential operations that the computer is to carry out, is stored in the computer's internal storage in the same manner as data. The stored program's instructions must be determined, by humans, in advance of processing. Once the program is stored in the computer, the computer can carry out the instructions without human intervention. Engineered circuitry automatically interprets and executes the instructions. Different sets of instructions and/or data can be brought into the computer's storage and thus can change the processing being performed.
4. *Program Modification.* The computer can transform (by addition, subtraction, multiplication, and division) instructions as well as data. This ability to automatically modify a program, based upon some condition* arising during operations, can change the sequence or functions of instructions.

Types of Computers

There are several different types of computers (see Exhibit 4–2). These can be classified according to how the computer represents numbers; the computer's degree of specialization; and the type of applications that the computer handles best.

1. *Representation of Numbers*
   a. *Analog Computers.* This type of computer does not compute directly with numbers. Rather, it uses continuously varying physical magnitudes (e.g., temperature, voltage, pressure, or length) by which to represent numbers. Common examples of analog type of devices are the slide rule, the service-station gasoline pump, and the automobile speedometer.

      Analog computations are used primarily for scientific, engineering, and process-control purposes. They deal with quantities that are continuously variable; therefore, results can be read with only limited accuracy. For instance, the speedometer pointer might only be readable to the nearest mile per hour, and might appear to give a reading of 50 miles per hour—when in fact, at that particular point in time, the speed is actually 50.123 miles per hour.

   b. *Digital Computers.* This type of computer (which this book will discuss) operates on numbers directly, and handles them discretely and precisely, rather

* For instance, the condition may be the result of some logical decision (e.g., one number is greater than another number, a particular code is read, or a negative number is sensed).

Exhibit 4–2 Types of Computers

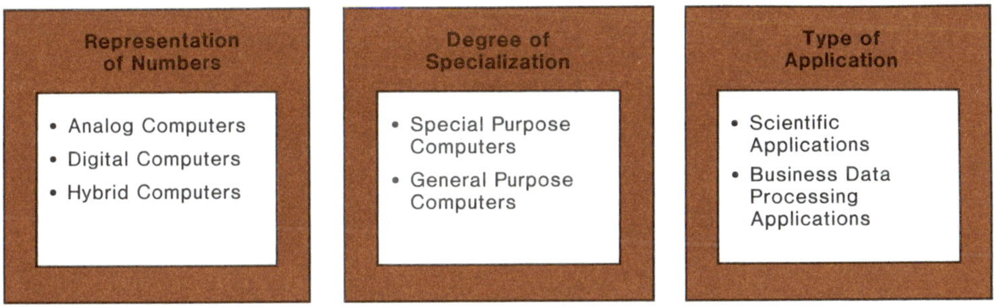

than approximately (unless an approximation is deliberately called for). Digital devices are based on counting in discrete units, while analog devices are based on measurement of continuous magnitudes.

Under ideal conditions, an analog computer may be accurate to within 0.1 percent of the correct value; however, digital computers can obtain whatever degree of accuracy is required.

Some computers (called *hybrids*) combine the features of both analog and digital computers.

2. *Degree of Specialization*
   a. *Special-Purpose Computers.* As the name implies, a special-purpose computer is designed to perform one task or several very specific tasks. The program is built into the machine permanently. Specialization causes the given task to be performed economically, quickly, and efficiently. However, the machine lacks versatility; it is inflexible and cannot be used to perform other work. For instance, special-purpose computers are used for solving navigational problems in sophisticated aircraft and ships, and such machines are exclusively dedicated to navigational uses. Automatic telephone switching circuits are another example.
   b. *General-Purpose Computers.* These computers (which will be discussed in this book) have the ability to handle a wide variety of different programs, and thus to solve many different problems. Because it is designed to do a wide variety of jobs rather than to perform a specific job, the general-purpose computer compromises certain aspects of speed and efficiency. However, the advantage of flexibility usually more than offsets these compromises. For instance, the general-purpose computer may handle an accounting problem one minute; an engineering problem the next minute; and so on.
3. *Type of Applications*
   a. *Scientific Applications.* Some computers are designed to handle scientific applications more effectively. Typically, such applications have a relatively

Exhibit 4–3 Elements of a Computer System

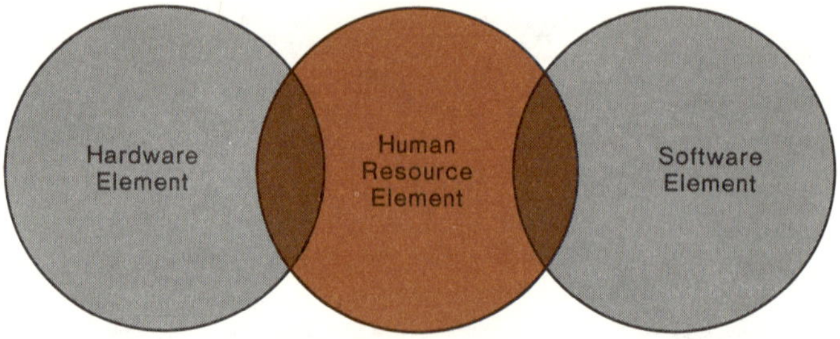

small volume of data, and hence of input and output requirements. Consequently, the speed with which these operations are performed is usually not too vital. However, since scientific problems most often involve a great deal of complex computation, the computer's computational speed is a critical consideration. Scientific results usually require only limited accuracy (say seven to ten significant digits), and this also has an effect on computer design.

b. *Business Data-Processing Applications.* Still other computers are designed to handle business data-processing applications (which this book will discuss) more effectively. These applications usually involve fairly large data files, and require faster input and output as well as large storage capabilities. Computational speed is not so important here, since arithmetic operations represent a relatively small part of the total job, and since the types of computations performed are simple. Particularly when dealing with monetary figures, business results often require absolute accuracy (e.g., accounting records, in order to balance, must be accurate to the penny, even in a total of a billion dollars); and this affects computer design.

   It is important to recognize that many modern computers can now effectively handle both scientific and business data-processing applications. However, the largest computers often are engineered with scientific applications in mind.

This book focuses primarily on digital, general-purpose computers that can handle business data-processing applications.

WHAT ARE THE ELEMENTS OF A COMPUTER SYSTEM?

In isolation, the computer would be unproductive; to use a computer productively, an assemblage of elements is required. Consequently, it is appropriate to refer to these elements as part of a total computer system (see Exhibit 4–3). The elements are interdependent, and the malfunctioning of any one can cause the entire total computer system to fail.

Human resources* are required to perform the planning, operations, and some of the controls external to the physical computer. Equipment (sometimes called hardware), including the physical computer and related peripheral machines, is integral to the system. Software (computer programs) is essential for the computer to carry out the desires of the human being.

Human Resources

Well over a million persons are estimated to be employed directly by computer-using organizations in computer-related occupations. The following occupations† are the primary classifications:

1. *Systems Analyst.* An employee who analyzes existing organizational structure, activities, procedures, and so forth; develops improved and new structures, activities, and procedures; and designs and guides implementation of improved and new systems.
2. *Management Scientist.* A highly skilled person who normally concentrates on problems requiring sophisticated mathematical skills, while performing tasks similar to those performed by the systems analyst.
3. *Computer Programmer.* An individual skilled in computer programming who converts the systems analyst's or management scientist's systems design into instructions that the computer can understand.
4. *Computer Operator.* A person trained to operate the various pieces of equipment that comprise the computer system.
5. *Data-Preparation Operator.* A person trained to operate a typewriter-like device that records programs and data, which are fed to a reading machine connected to the computer.
6. *Control Clerk.* A clerical worker who maintains human controls over input data and computer output in order to maximize the accuracy and integrity of the computer system's operations.

In addition, computer installations usually require various administrative and clerical employees. In a small computer installation, a few individuals may share all of the above-mentioned responsibilities. In large computer installations, the responsibilities are frequently even more specialized.

Also, many organizations have employees who are peripherally involved in data processing as adjuncts of their primary occupation; for example, engineers and scientists may use the computer for numerical analysis of research problems; teachers

* The staffing and organization of a computer department is discussed in greater detail in Chapter 14.

† Some of these positions are not mutually exclusive: that is, in some organizations, the same individual performs the functions of the systems analyst and programmer. Also, each occupation has levels—for example, senior, semisenior, junior.

Exhibit 4–4 A Computer System

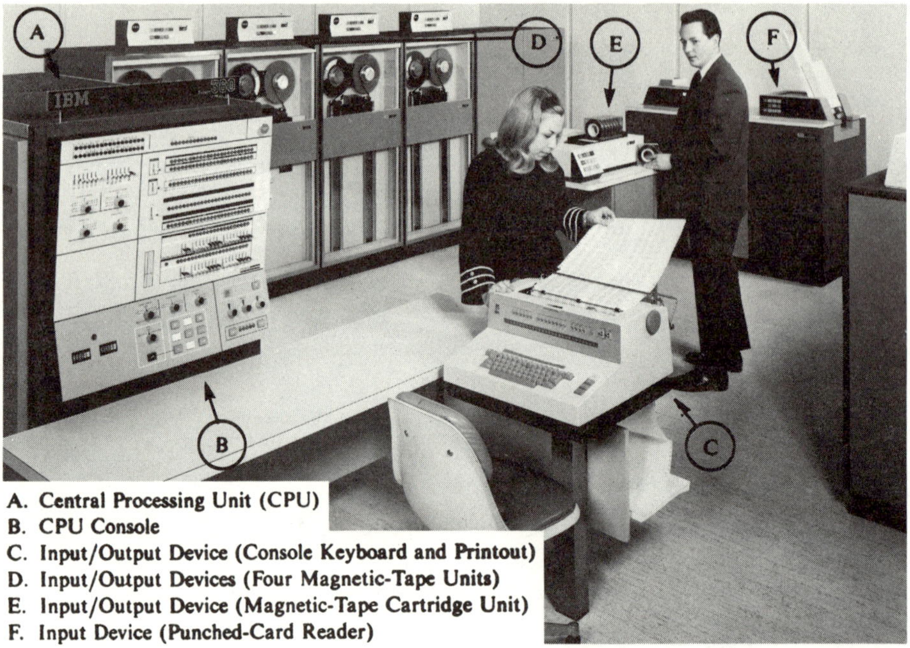

Photograph courtesy of IBM Corporation

may use the computer as an aid in instructing students; and stockbrokers may use a computerized quotation system to obtain the latest stock prices and related security analyses.

There are numerous independent computer consultants as well as computer specialists employed by management consulting firms and public accounting organizations. In addition, the manufacturers of computer products employ hundreds of thousands of computer-trained personnel in technical, marketing and other occupations.

Hardware*

The computer equipment includes the following functional machines: central processing unit (CPU); input devices; output devices; secondary-storage devices; and data-preparation devices (see Exhibit 4–4).

Equipment that is connected directly, via cable, to the CPU is "on-line." On the

* Chapters 5, 6, and 7 explore the hardware topic at greater length.

Exhibit 4–5 An Overview of Computer Equipment and Functions

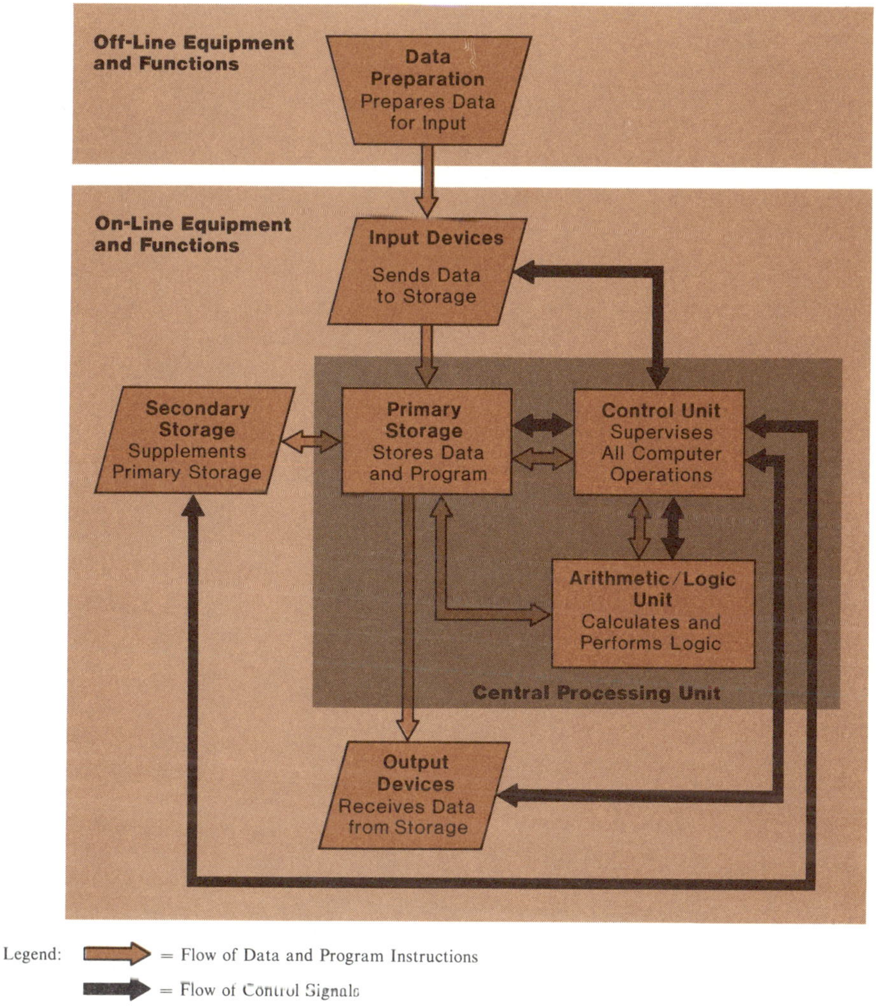

other hand, equipment that operates independently and is not cable-connected to the CPU is "off-line"—for example, data-preparation devices. All on-line equipment is under control of the CPU, which itself is under control of the software (computer programs) stored in the CPU's storage. The software directs the functions of the hardware.

1. *Central Processing Unit (CPU).* This unit is the "brain" or "heart" of the computer equipment (see Exhibit 4–5). The CPU is composed of primary or main storage

(memory);* the arithmetic/logic unit; and the control unit. Primary storage is like an electronic file; it holds the program(s) being used and data being processed. The arithmetic/logic unit performs computations and logical comparisons. The control unit acts as a monitor that directs the timing and flow of signals throughout the computer. It directs and coordinates all the operations of the computer, according to specifications set forth by the stored program. It interprets the instructions in the program and causes the computer's circuits to perform the proper operations at appropriate times. The CPU has a console that provides a means of communications between the human computer operator and the computer.

When the computer is manipulating data (e.g., performing arithmetical and logical operations), it is said to be "processing" the data.

2. *Input Devices*. There are a variety of on-line input devices. Some of the most common are: punched-card readers; punched-paper-tape readers; magnetic-tape units; magnetic-character readers; optical scanners; console keyboards; and remote data-terminals. These devices read the data that have been recorded on some medium (e.g., punched cards, paper tape, or magnetic tape) and transmit the data to the storage of the CPU. As an alternative, the data can be keyed in on a keyboard by an operator, and transmitted directly to the storage of the CPU. Programs are transmitted to the CPU in a similar way.

   When a computer receives input data, it is said to "read" the data; thus, "input" is synonymous with "reading."

3. *Output Devices*. There are a variety of on-line output devices, all of which are used to record the results of processing. If these results are to be used by people, the output device will probably be a high-speed printer, a cathode ray tube (CRT) similar to a television screen, or a graphic plotter. Output that is to be used for further machine processing may be generated by such output devices as punched-card punches, magnetic-tape units, and punched-paper-tape punches, among others. Output may also be transmitted to remote data-terminals.

   When the computer finishes processing data and is ready to present its results, it is said to be "writing" output; thus, "output" is synonymous with "writing."

4. *Secondary-Storage Devices*. These devices (sometimes referred to as "auxiliary" or "mass storage" or "memory") are optional supplements to primary storage. Secondary storage usually is used to hold programs and files of data that are not currently being used in the CPU. When it is time for the programs or data in secondary storage to be used, they are then moved into primary storage. Updated data or programs can be moved from the CPU's primary storage back to secondary storage.

   Punched cards are used for off-line storage; however, this type of file has definite limitations and must be introduced to the computer via an input device (i.e.

* Some authorities prefer to present main storage as a separate functional unit. In such instances, the CPU consists of the arithmetic/logic unit and the control unit. This book considers main storage as a part of the CPU.

punched-card reader), which is relatively slow. Magnetic-tape units and magnetic-disk units are examples of on-line secondary-storage devices; they are more efficient for providing large secondary-storage capacity that is on-line to the computer. Magnetic tapes and, in some cases, magnetic-disk packs may be removed from their units, thus providing off-line storage. Data recorded on magnetic media may be used as often as desired; when the data are no longer needed, new data can be written on top of the old data (much as new material can be recorded onto magnetic audio tape over the old).

Some devices—magnetic tape units, for instance—are classified as secondary-storage devices as well as input/output devices. This indicates their versatility.

Whether a device is classified as an input/output device or as a storage device can be a matter of fine distinction. A device that only reads or writes, such as a punched-card reader or a printer, is obviously either an input or an output device, respectively. On the other hand, a device such as a magnetic-tape unit or a magnetic-disk unit, which may be read from to provide input into main storage and *also* written on to provide output from main storage, may be classified variously at different times, depending on how it is being used in a particular program. If the device is only being read or written on, and if the particular tape reel or disk pack is mounted for this program run and removed afterwards, then it is either an input or output device. But if it is being both read from and written on in the course of the program, or if the tape reel or disk pack stays permanently on-line, then it also is performing a storage function.

5. *Data-Preparation Devices*. These devices are the links between the noncomputer world and the computer hardware. Data may enter the computer via a machine-readable medium, such as punched cards. Punched cards and other media (e.g., punched-paper tape) are prepared by machine operators, using such off-line data-preparation devices as a key punch machine.*

   In some cases, the machine-readable medium occurs as an automatic byproduct when a clerk prepares a source document (such as a bill) by using a machine such as a bookkeeping machine or an accounting machine.

   Punched cards may also be processed off-line by various electromechanical devices prior to being processed by the computer. Such off-line punched-card devices include sorters, collators, interpreters, and reproducers.

   There is a trend toward entering data directly into the computer. This means that the data is sent from on-line data terminals directly to the computer at the time the original transaction is generated, thus eliminating the need to create any physical medium (such as a punched card). Direct entry also includes reading magnetic and optical characters from original documents.

   The original preparation of computer programs for entry into a computer follows a process similar to the data-preparation process.

* Procedures for key punching are presented in Appendix B.

Software*

There are two broad categories of software: systems programs and applications programs.

1. *Systems Programs.* These programs are general in nature. Used in jobs common to most computer installations, they are operating aids that are usually obtained from computer manufacturers or computer consultants (e.g., software houses). Systems programs handle the following kinds of general functions: translating a higher-level language program into the computer's machine language; scheduling jobs through the computer; sorting data files; and other functions. The systems programs make the computer even more automatic; and since the manufacturer writes the programs and also provides all users of its computers with copies (sometimes for a fee), the users do not have to write similar programs themselves.
2. *Applications Programs.* An applications program is written by the programming staff of a computer-using organization (as differentiated from the computer manufacturer). The program usually solves a particular application or problem that is unique to that organization. Examples of such programs are: payroll; general accounting; sales statistics; and inventory. Although numerous organizations may need similar applications programs (such as payroll), different organizations often require different programs for similar applications. This makes standardization somewhat difficult. However, more and more prewritten applications programs are available from various sources. These programs can eliminate the user's need to write its own program. Sometimes such a program needs only minor modifications in order to suit an organization's specific needs. These prewritten programs (sometimes called "packages" or "canned programs") can be bought or rented from consultants, software houses, computer manufacturers, universities, and other computer-using organizations.

Programming Languages. A wide variety of computer-programming languages are available. The programmer must be familiar with one or more of them in order to write a computer program. Each programming language has very specific standards and rules of use, which the programmer must know and adhere to when developing a program. There are two broad categories of programming languages: machine-level languages and higher-level languages.

1. *Machine-Level Languages.* Each particular computer model has a machine language, which is based on the internal engineering architecture of the equipment, and which is developed and provided to users by the computer manufacturer. Simply, a machine-level language is the language of the computer—the only language the computer understands without translation. If such a language is used in writing a program (say a user's payroll program), the programmer must be

* Software is discussed at greater length in Chapters 10 and 11.

familiar with the specific machine-level language as well as with the details of the computer equipment to be used. Programs written in machine-level language can only be used on the computer model for which that language was written. Such languages are said to be machine-oriented.

Writing programs in machine language is not only difficult for humans to do, but is also subject to error. In an attempt to facilitate human programming and to eliminate human error, assembly language, which is very close to machine language, was designed. But since the computer understands only machine language, the computer must translate assembly language before it can use it as a program. Therefore, assembly language is considered a higher-level language than machine language; but since it is both machine-dependent (varying from one model computer to another) and close to machine language, it may be classified as a machine-level language.

2. *Higher-Level Languages.* More universal languages are available that are relatively machine-independent and therefore are considered to be higher-level than machine-level languages. These problem-oriented (sometimes called procedure-oriented) languages permit programs to be written without requiring the programmer to be intimately familiar with the architecture of the equipment to be used. Since such languages are somewhat similar, in some respects, to normal English and/or algebra, they are easier for people to use than machine-level languages. Normally, a program written in a higher-level language like this can be used on almost any available computer. Higher-level languages include FORTRAN and COBOL. Such languages must, of course, be translated by a computer program* into machine language before the computer can use the corresponding programs.

Software Development. People (programmers) prepare programs, and programs are necessary to tell the computer what operations to perform. The program must be inside the computer (in computer primary storage) to direct its actions at the time the data are to be processed.

The process of developing a computer program begins when the person with a problem collaborates with a systems analyst to bring the problem into focus. This involves carefully defining what information is needed, and what the best way of getting this information is.

The systems analyst provides the computer programmer with specifications to guide the writing of the program. The programmer uses these specifications to write the computer program. In order to write the program, the programmer must have a working knowledge of the programming language that is to be used, and to some extent, he/she may require some knowledge of the computer equipment to be used in processing the application.

The programmer prepares the instructions of the program in some higher-level language; has the computer translate this "source program" into machine language;

* The program performing the translation is called a "compiler." See Chapter 10 for details.

tests the resulting machine-language "object" program; detects and eliminates errors (debugs the program); and makes sure that the program conforms to the original systems specifications. To be processed by the computer program, data must also be in the proper form for processing by the computer. Once the program has been tested fully and once it satisfies the user, it is ready for scheduling as a routine operation in the computer department. However, programs are subject to updating for new procedures, as they occur; this updating process is known as "program maintenance."

Summary

A computer has several distinguishing technical characteristics: it is electronic; it has internal storage; it has a stored program(s); and its program(s) can be automatically modified.

There are several different types of computers. This book concentrates on computers that are digital, general purpose, and used for business data-processing applications.

The computer is viewed as part of a system (i.e., a computer system). The computer equipment must be accompanied by computer professionals (human resources) and software (computer programs) if it is to be used effectively.

Terms to Learn

Hardware
Equipment
Computer
Computer system
Peripherals
Electronic
Internal storage
Memory
Stored program
Program
Program modification
Analog computer
Digital computer
Hybrid computer
Special-purpose computer
General-purpose computer
Scientific application
Business data-processing application
Central processing unit (CPU)
Primary storage
Control unit of CPU
Arithmetic/logic unit
Input device
Output device
On-line
Off-line
Secondary-storage device
Data-preparation device
Software
Systems program
Application program
Programming language
Machine-level language
Higher-level language
Software development

Review Questions

1. What is a *computer?* What are its characteristics?
2. Contrast an *analog computer* with a *digital computer.*
3. Contrast a *special-purpose computer* with a *general-purpose computer.*
4. How do *scientific applications* differ from *business data-processing applications?*
5. Why does this text focus on computers that are digital, general purpose and used for business data-processing applications?
6. What are the three main *elements* of a computer system?
7. Why is it important to concentrate on a computer *system* rather than on only the computer itself?
8. Describe in your own words how a computer *operates.*
9. Describe the functions of the *central processing unit.*
10. Describe the functions of *input devices* and *output devices.*
11. Describe the functions of *secondary-storage devices.*
12. What are *data-preparation devices* used for?
13. Define what is meant by the term *software.*
14. Compare *systems programs* with *applications programs.*
15. Discuss the relevance of *programming languages,* and of *machine-level languages* and *higher-level languages.*
16. What is meant by *software development?* Who does the development?

TOPIC 2—SCOPE OF COMPUTERS

CLASSIFICATION OF MODERN COMPUTERS

A wide variety of computers is available to users. These computers can vary in cost, features, speed, complexity, and other characteristics.

One arbitrary but useful method of classifying computers is to group them into five classifications: *microcomputers; minicomputers; small-size computers; medium-size computers;* and *large-size computers* (see Table 4–1). These classifications are not rigid, and there is no universal agreement about which characteristics qualify a computer for a particular classification. In fact, modern computers increasingly are using a modular-design approach, which means that within certain engineered limits, a given computer model can be expanded in terms of storage capacity, number of input/output devices, or other features. Consequently, arbitrary classifications are becoming less significant. However, they are useful for gaining a simplified overview of the wide range of computers.

Table 4–1
Classification of Modern Computers

Classification	Purchase Cost*	Comments
Microcomputers	$500 and up	Can be used as a personal computer at home or in a neighborhood store.
Minicomputers	Up to $60,000	Suitable for small organizations or for decentralized units of larger firms.
Small-Size Computers	Up to $250,000	Minicomputer users can expand to small-size computers. Also, such computers are used as supplements for larger computers.
Medium-Size Computers	Up to $1,000,000	Most large organizations have one or more of these. Require high volume of data and/or computation, and large staff of computer professionals.
Large-Size Computers	Up to $10,000,000 or more	Used only by very large organizations with enormous data volume and/or computational needs. Must be supported with large and sophisticated staff of computer professionals.

* To determine rental cost per month, an approximate figure can be obtained by dividing by fifty months. Micro and minicomputers typically are purchased, not leased or rented.

First, let us consider the widely used hand-held or pocket *calculator.*

Calculators

In recent years, the number of electronic calculators in use (see Exhibit 4–6) has grown tremendously. How do these differ from electronic computers? First, most calculators have limited and permanently wired-in programs. In contrast, a computer can use a wide variety of programs; also, when needed, a program can be brought into the computer's storage.

Second, the computer can execute a long string of instructions on massive data files automatically; most calculators, on the other hand, require the user to key-in each instruction as it is used and to enter data comparatively slowly via a keyboard.

Third, the computer has a wide variety of input and output devices available; the calculator depends on the data keyed-in by the user instead. In sum, the calculator is useful for computing a limited range of arithmetic problems and limited quantities of data used by an individual, but it cannot cope with the more complex problems and large quantities of data used by most organizations.

However, in future years, the distinction between such calculators and computers will probably blur. Even today, there are a few higher-priced programmable calculators that allow interchangeable programs to be entered into the calculator.

Exhibit 4–6 A Calculator

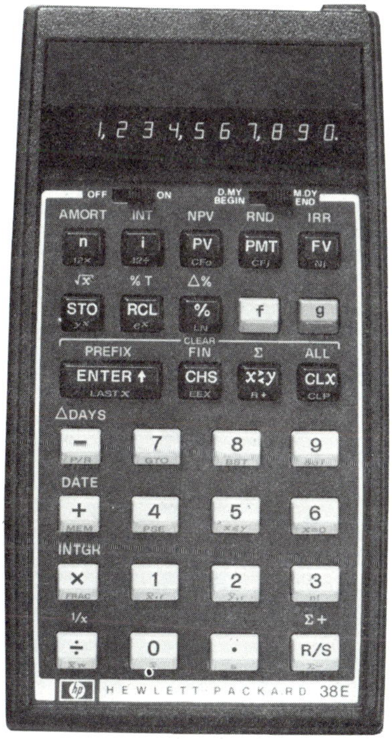

Photograph courtesy of Hewlett-Packard Corporation

Microcomputers*

As the name implies, a microcomputer is a tiny computer. Its small size and low cost make it appropriate for a variety of uses, including as a personal computer in the home. Its development in the 1970s was a continuation in the evolution of smaller and less expensive computers. Since such a computer may cost about $500, it is within the cost range of even the neighborhood store.

* Microprocessors, or a computer on a chip, carry this miniaturization even one step further. Such a processor can be held in the palm of a person's hand. The microprocessor is usually a component in another piece of equipment, and the specific functions to be performed are programmed into the microprocessor. They can be used for telephones, postal scales, games, traffic lights, blood analyzers, sewing machines, supermarket checkout counters, and security alarms, among other applications. A microprocessor may cost as little as $20.

Exhibit 4–7 A Desk-Top Minicomputer

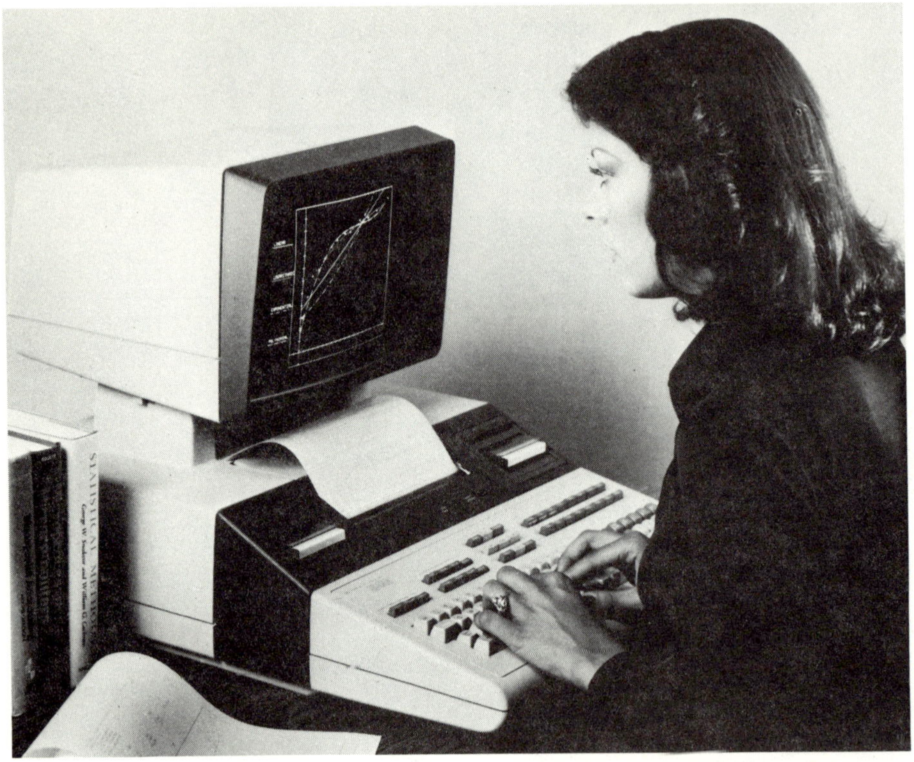

Photograph courtesy of Hewlett-Packard Corporation

Minicomputers

Mini-size computers are compact in size. Some fit on a desk top (see Exhibit 4–7), and a few are built to be portable (see Exhibit 4–8). They are relatively inexpensive and usually sell for under $60,000; many are available for under $20,000. To maintain low prices, the internal storage capacity of minicomputers is usually limited.

The teletype and typewriter keyboard devices are common input/output devices because they are low in cost. They are, however, comparatively slow, restricting the volume of data that can pass through the computer in a given period of time. Many minicomputers may be connected to a wider range of faster input/output devices and secondary-storage devices; and although this increases their capacity to handle more data in a given period of time, it also increases their cost.

Exhibit 4–8 A Minicomputer: PDP 11/60

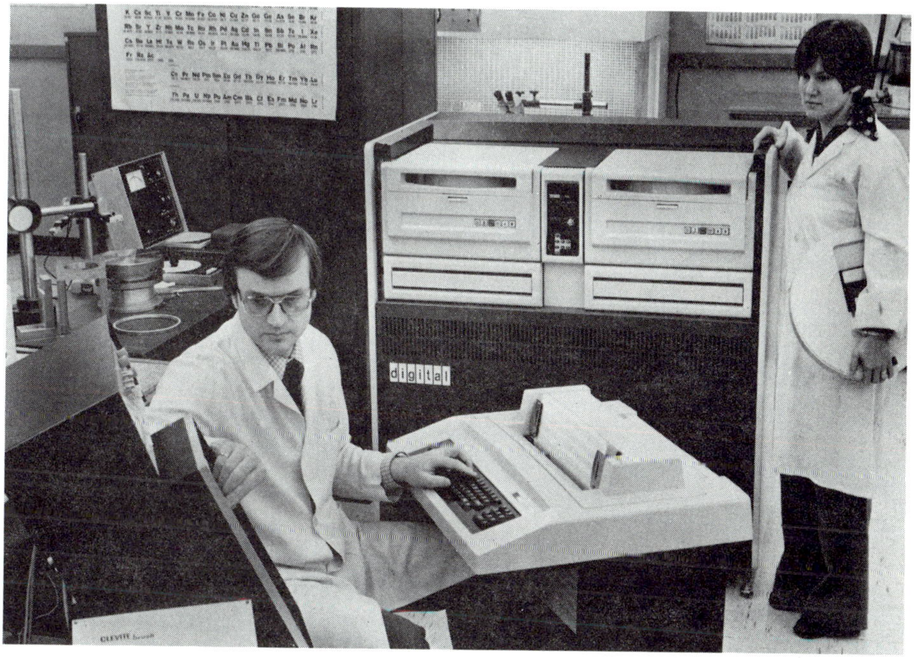

Photograph courtesy of Digital Equipment Corporation

The minicomputer can be applied: in a small organization that cannot afford a more expensive computer; as a remote computer that handles some of the work for a larger computer; or as part of a decentralized network of minicomputers that replaces a large central computer.

Small-Size Computers

Typically, the operating speeds and data-handling capabilities of small computers (see Exhibit 4–9) are considerably less than those of medium-size and large-size computers. The small-size computers lease for under $5,000 a month or can be purchased for under $250,000; the actual price depends on the options selected by the user. As with minicomputers, the small-size computers also have limited internal storage, to keep prices down. Because of their greater overall efficiency, the use of tapes and magnetic disks, instead of punched cards, as file-storage media on small computers is increasing.

Organizations with a volume of data that taxes the capability of punched-card

Exhibit 4–9 A Small-Size Computer: VAX 11-780

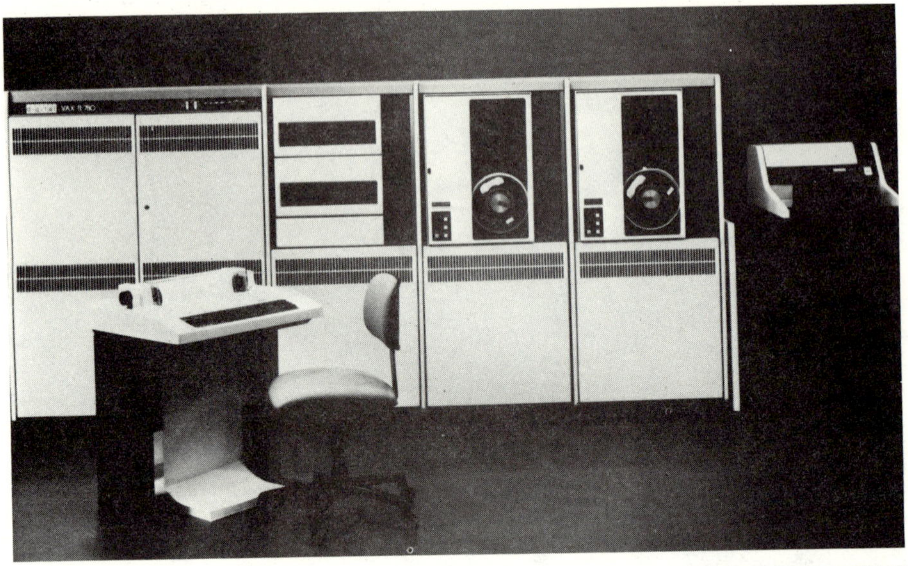

Photograph courtesy of Digital Equipment Corporation

equipment or minicomputers often upgrade to a small-size computer. Even in large organizations, sometimes it is desirable to supplement a medium-size or large-size computer with one or more small-size computers, which may be located in subunits of the organizations. They are often used to handle particular jobs that do not require the power of the more sophisticated computers.

Medium-Size Computers*

A medium-size computer is considerably more powerful than a small-size computer. Therefore it is able to handle more complex applications and to work more rapidly. To some extent, most medium-size computers are magnetic-tape- and magnetic-disk-oriented. These computers lease for from $5,000 to about $20,000 a month; purchase prices range approximately from $250,000 to $1,000,000. Internal storage capacities are normally in the range of 264,000 storage locations or more. Frequently, these intermediate computers can handle data-communications links and remote devices.

Medium-size computers usually require substantial staffs of systems analysts and

* Exhibits 3–12 and 3–14 presented in Chapter 3, showing IBM 360 and IBM 370 systems, illustrate medium-size and large-size computers, respectively.

Exhibit 4–10 Relative Costs of Computer Processing

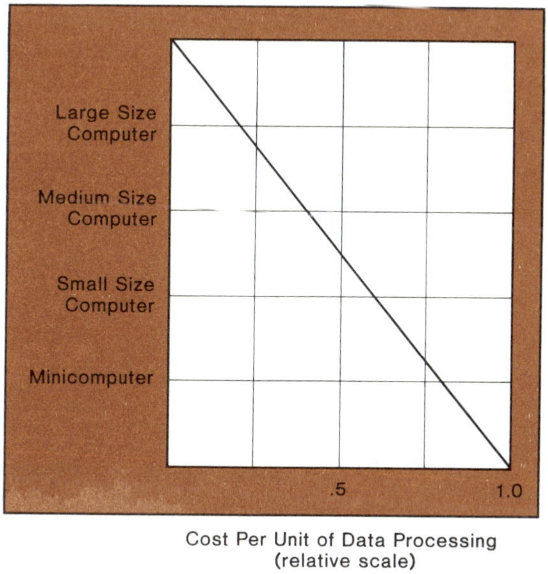

programmers. Most of these computers are installed in organizations that have large data-processing and computational needs.

Large-Size Computers*

The large-size computer offers both very fast operating speed and large storage capacity. It is not unusual for such a computer to have a high-speed storage unit with millions of storage locations. Many input/output devices can be connected to such a computer, including smaller computers that do preliminary processing for the larger computer. Large-size computers can efficiently handle several different applications at the same time. Normally, they rent for over $20,000 a month; some rent for as much as $250,000 or more a month. The purchase price for such a computer starts at about $1,000,000; a few cost more than $10,000,000. The upper end of this range is sometimes classified as super-size computers.

While these large computers are very expensive, they are also very powerful. This means that the per unit cost of data processing is very low. Generally speaking, the more expensive the computer, the more powerful it is. The result is lower per unit costs (see Exhibit 4–10).

* Exhibits 3–12 and 3–14 presented in Chapter 3, showing IBM 360 and IBM 370 systems, illustrate medium-size and large-size computers, respectively.

Only large organizations can afford such equipment or have the volume of work to keep such powerful computers busy. The federal government departments (e.g., the Department of Defense and the Atomic Energy Commission), industrial enterprises with substantial research efforts, and research universities are among the few types of organizations that use such computers.

A complex computational job that might take a minicomputer many weeks to do may be solved in minutes or seconds on a large-size computer.

MODULARITY AND COMPATIBILITY

As Chapter 3 mentioned, there has been a trend towards computers that are modular and compatible. In brief, here is an explanation of these terms.

Modularity

One might say that earlier computers had fixed engineering features. If a user's workload began to tax a computer, the user had to get a larger computer. In the early days of modern computers, this involved not only extensive conversion problems but also sometimes the almost complete rewriting of all accumulated applications programs. Third-generation computers began to emphasize computers that were modular; this meant that the user's computer could be expanded in capability by adding additional hardware features (e.g., by increasing internal storage and input and output units). It also meant that each computer manufacturer moved towards having a family of computers. Thus, if a user did reach the limits of, say, a small-size computer's ability to expand, he/she could replace that computer with a medium-size computer in the same family line. Again, the conversion problem was minimal, because a family of computers has similar engineering design.

Compatibility

IBM computers have been the de facto standards of the computer industry, because of its dominant position in the computer market. Recognizing the realities of the situation, a number of IBM's competitors also have developed families of computers—which, in some cases, are highly compatible with IBM computers. This means that a present user of IBM computers can switch to a competitor (such as Honeywell) and anticipate that the new computer will have some type of technical compatibility feature (which may be hardware and/or software) that will permit programs originally written for the IBM computer to work on the competitor's computer.

Modularity and compatibility have been valuable trends for computer users; and while conversion problems have not been eliminated, they have been at least eased for the users.

Summary

Computers can be classified according to their cost, which is at least an approximate index of relative computer power. The five classes discussed here are: microcomputers; minicomputers; small-size computers; medium-size computers; and large-size computers. Sometimes another class is added: supercomputers.

Most modern computers are modular and compatible. Modularity permits the user to expand, within a given computer line, as need for more computer power arises. Compatibility enables the user to switch from one manufacturer's computer to another manufacturer's computer. Both modularity and compatibility ease the burdens on the user as the computer needs of the organization change.

Terms to Learn

Calculator
Microcomputer
Minicomputer
Small-size computer
Medium-size computer
Large-size computer
Modularity
Compatibility

Review Questions

1. Discuss the *classifications* of computers.
2. How does an organization determine which classification of computer is proper for it?
3. Why is there such enormous growth in the numbers of *microcomputers* and *minicomputers?*
4. Why are there relatively few *large-size computers?*
5. Contrast the *cost* of a minicomputer with the cost of a large-size computer. Also contrast the relative *power* of the computers.
6. How does a *pocket calculator* differ from a *computer?* In what ways are they similar?
7. What is the significance of the *per unit cost* of data processing?
8. Discuss the significance of *modularity* and *compatibility* to the computer user.

Exhibit 4–11 Simple Stand-Alone Computer Configuration

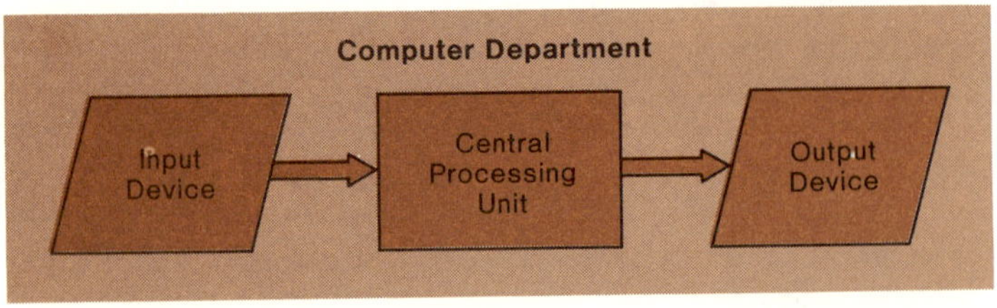

TOPIC 3—COMPUTERS IN USE

VARIETY OF COMPUTER CONFIGURATIONS

Each computer is engineered to permit a latitude of different configurations, depending on the user's need (somewhat like the array of options available when one is purchasing an automobile). Generally, the user can: order a computer with a different mix of input and output devices; select the size of primary storage; select secondary storage, as needed; and order only the software that matches the organization's computer-processing needs.

Simple Stand-Alone Computer Configuration

Exhibit 4–11 shows a simple stand-alone computer configuration that doesn't have a communication* link with any remote data-terminal or other computer.

Sophisticated Stand-Alone Computer Configuration

Exhibit 4–12 shows this configuration with many additional options added. This makes it a more sophisticated configuration.

Computer-Communication Network

Exhibit 4–13 suggests how complex configurations can become in a computer-communication network that involves remote data-terminals and computers that are connected to a central computer.

The configurations presented merely indicate some of the options available to the computer user and are not exhaustive.

* The words "communication" and "transmission" are closely related, and are used interchangeably in this discussion.

Exhibit 4–12 Sophisticated Stand-Alone Computer Configuration

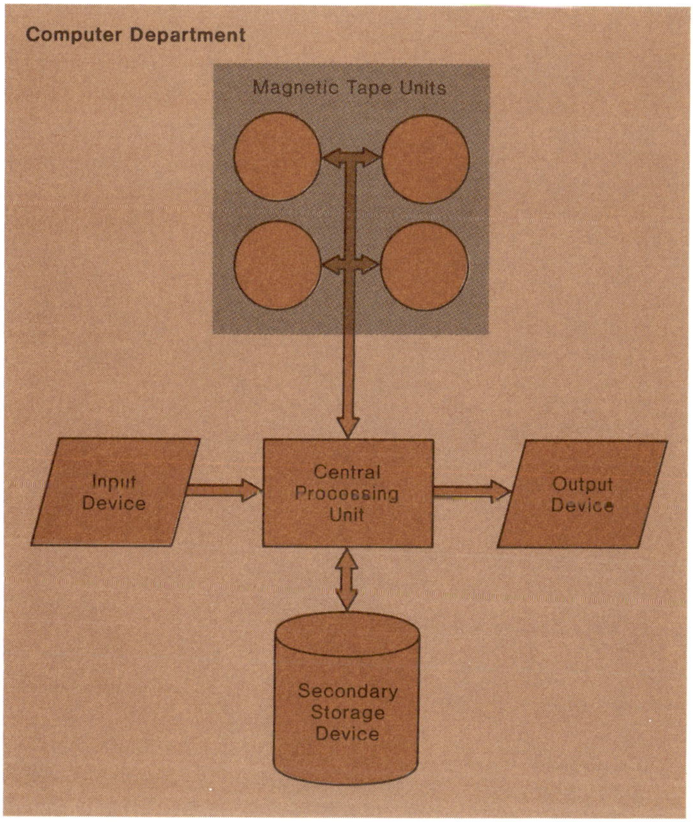

Distributed Data-Processing Concept

The emergence of small-size computers and minicomputers has helped reduce the emphasis on centralized data-processing. Under this system, all units of the organization had to send or transmit their work to the central computer department for computer processing. The central computer department then sent or transmitted results back to the units of the organization.

But now, organizations have the option of placing reasonably powerful and inexpensive computers in the organization's decentralized work units—in short, of putting computer power in the actual location of the transactions. The decentralized unit's computer may be able to perform all of the needed data processing, or it may do only part of the data processing and transmit selected data to a larger computer,*

* The central computer, in a distributed data-processing approach, is sometimes called the "host computer." In another approach, there is no central host computer; instead there is a ring of computers (usually minicomputers), which often have the capability of transmitting data among themselves.

Exhibit 4–13 Computer Communication Network

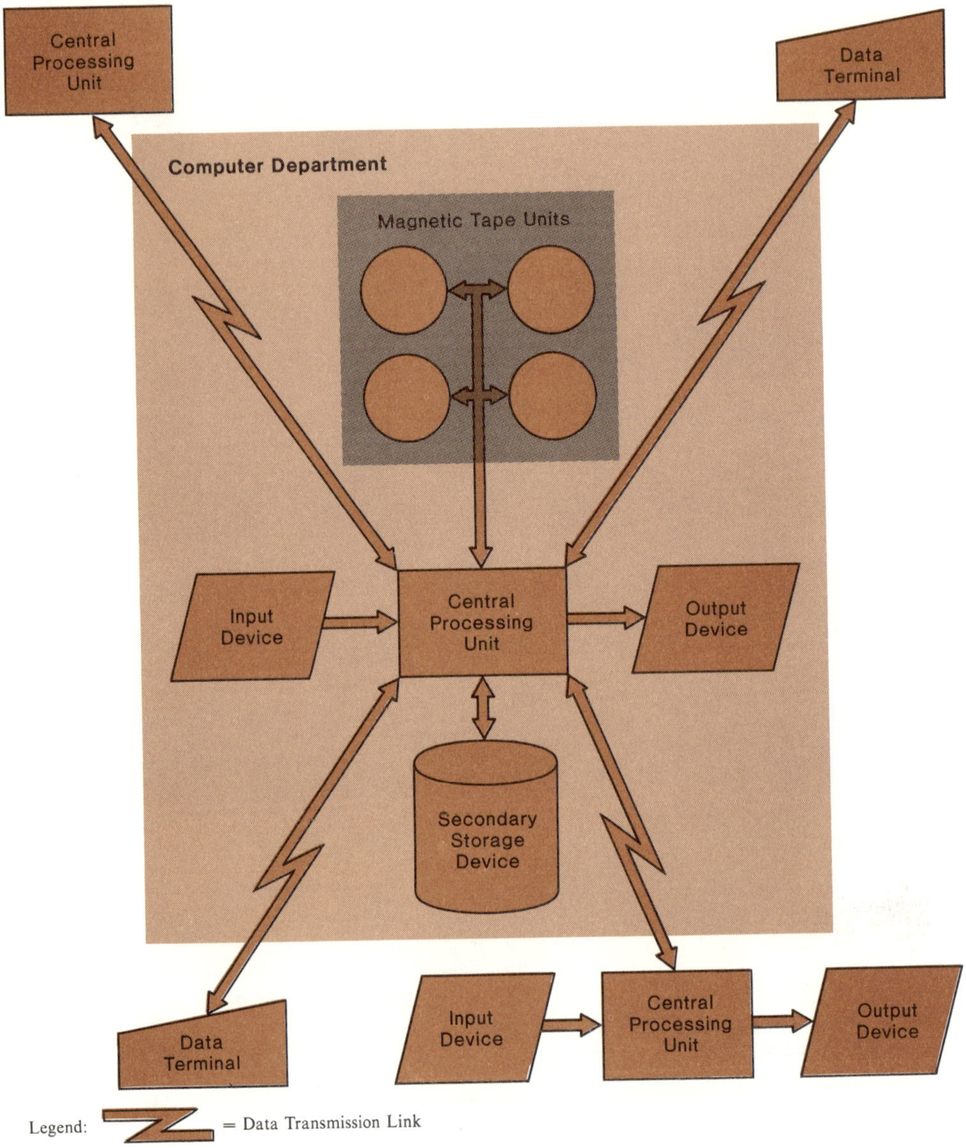

located elsewhere in the organization (e.g., headquarters office), for further processing.

Exhibit 4–14 illustrates the nature of distributed data-processing.

Exhibit 4–14 Distributed Data-Processing Concept

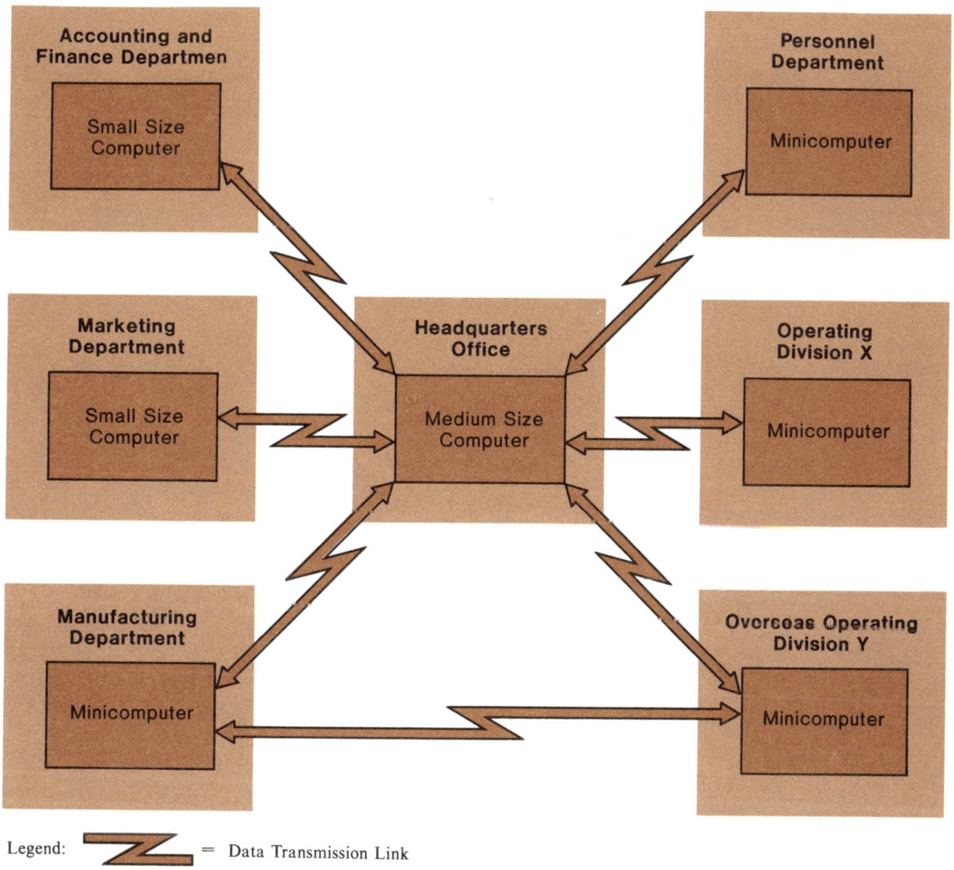

DATA COMMUNICATIONS*

What Is Data Transmission?

Many organizations have multiple users of computers; some of these users are geographically remote from the organization's headquarters offices. Even within an office building, there may be hundreds or thousands of employees who use a particular computer. Users have several options to choose from in communicating data to and in receiving data from the computer. These include the following:

* The terms "data communication," "data transmission," and "teleprocessing" are used interchangeably.

Exhibit 4–15 An Example of Off-Line Data Transmission

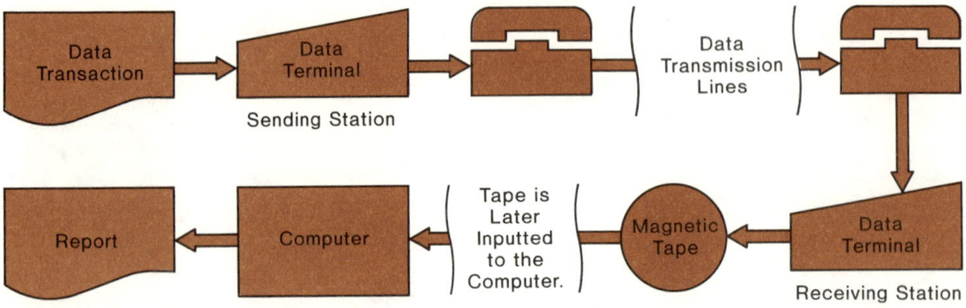

Exhibit 4–16 An Example of On-Line Data Transmission

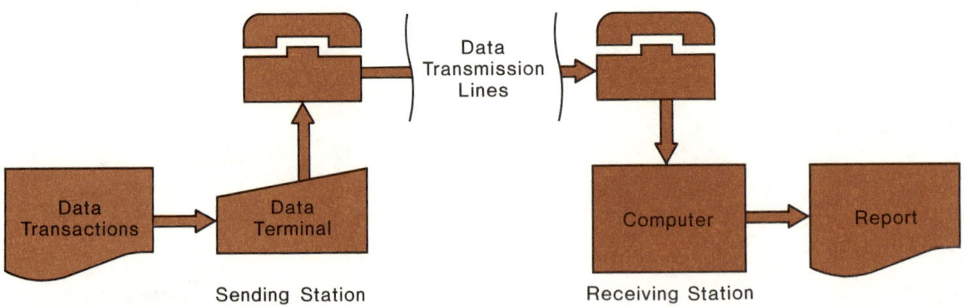

- People may have to depend on mail delivery or messenger service to bring data to and from the computer. This usually involves delays and dependency on intermediaries. Also, the cost of such delivery service has risen rapidly.
- Each unit of the organization can be supplied with its own computer. However, it is not frequently economically feasible to do this for all units.
- Data may be transmitted, via communications links, between remote locations and the computer. Just as the telephone and telegraph services have speeded up oral and written messages between people, so data transmission can speed up the flow of data messages.

Data transmission may take place from a data terminal in one location to a data terminal in another location. In this case, both data terminals can be off-line to the computer (see Exhibit 4–15). Or data transmission may be transmitted on-line to a computer (see Exhibit 4–16) from a remote data-terminal or from another computer.

Traditionally, the relatively high cost of data transmission and the frequency of errors in transmitting have constrained the multiplication of such systems. However, in recent years, improved economic and technical factors have made such systems increasingly appealing.

Communication Services*

Normally, an organization that wishes to transmit data uses one of the common carrier services to carry the messages from station to station. Following is a brief description of these services.

Narrowband Services. Usually, this service is used where data volume is relatively low; the transmission rates usually range from 45 to 300 bits† per second. Examples of this are the telephone companies' teletypewriter exchange service (TWX) and Western Union's telex service.

Voiceband Services. Voiceband services use ordinary telephone lines to send data messages. Transmission rates vary from 300 to 4,800 bits per second, and higher.

Wideband Services. Wideband services provide data transmission rates from several thousand to several million bits per second. These services are limited to high-volume users. Such services generally use coaxial cable or microwave communication. Space satellites, a more exotic development, have been employed to rapidly transmit data from any part of the world to another part of the world.

Transmission Modes

Data transmission may occur in one of three modes (see Exhibit 4–17):

Simplex. Data is transmitted in one direction, only; the sending station cannot receive data.

Half Duplex. Data can be transmitted back and forth between two stations, but data can only go in one of the directions at any one point in time.

Duplex. Data can be transmitted simultaneously between two stations. Both stations can send and receive data at any point in time.

* Communication services may be either *leased* or *dialed up*. A leased communication channel, which gives the user exclusive use of the channel, is used where there are continuing data-transmission needs. The dial-up variety requires the person to dial the computer (and, of course, the line may be busy); thus, this alternative is appropriate when there are periodic data to transmit.

The equipment elements in data transmission are: the computer; data terminal(s); a communication control unit (CCU); and a data set (or modem). The CCU communicates between the CPU and the data set. The data set converts computer and data terminal signals (which are in direct current [DC]) to appropriate communication tones needed by communication carriers. The process of converting a DC signal to tones for transmission is called *modulation*, while converting tones back to a DC signal is called *demodulation* (the word *modem* is derived from these two words).

A connection point on the communication control unit for a communication line is known as a *port*.

† In the communications field, a transmission rate is often expressed in terms of a *baud* rating. One baud corresponds to one bit per second. Chapter 5 will explain the significance of bits.

Exhibit 4–17 Data-Transmission Modes

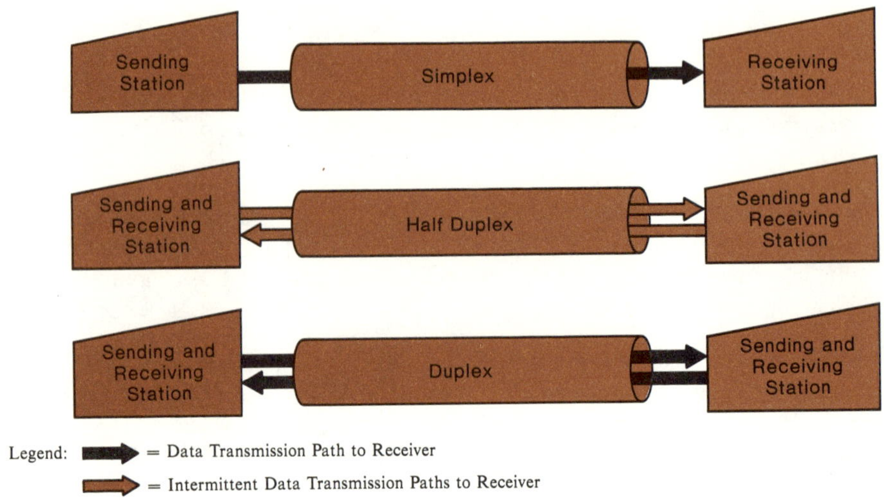

Message Switching

Some organizations with a heavy volume of data to transmit use a special computer for the purpose of data message switching. The computer receives all transmitted data; stores it; and, when an outgoing communications line is available, forwards it to the receiving point.

REAL-TIME COMPUTERS

A real-time computer is one that can perform data processing in rapid response to user needs. Such a system usually performs relevant data processing at almost the same moment that an event or transaction is taking place. For instance, while a customer is inquiring about a particular plane flight, the computer is searching its storage for the answer; when that customer purchases his/her ticket, the computer simultaneously generates the data for the transaction and updates the seat reservation inventory record stored in the computer.

In real-time processing,* there is minimal time lag between an event or transaction and the related data-processing. This is distinguished from periodic data-processing updating, in which days, weeks, or even months can go by between the time an event or transaction occurs and the point at which data processing actually takes place. One example of periodic data-processing is the preparation of monthly accounting statements: a transaction that takes place on the first day of the month may be left

* Invariably, real-time systems use data transmission in the ways we've already discussed.

unprocessed (batched) until all transactions for the month are available. It is not unusual for accounting statements only to be available several weeks after the end of a month (e.g., January accounting statements may not be processed and available until mid-February).

Because real-time computers involve costly and sophisticated hardware, data transmission, and programming, an organization must carefully compare the value of quick information with the additional cost of obtaining it. Some businesses may not really need real-time systems; others, such as the airline industry, may find them essential.

TIME-SHARING COMPUTERS

The time-sharing computer is one type of real-time computer. It accommodates the needs of the many users who access the computer through data terminals.* The user can operate a data terminal (which performs the input and output functions) without having any knowledge of the computer hardware and programming. The data terminal is connected to the computer by communication line; often, the remote user thinks of the data terminal as the equivalent of a computer. Ideally, time sharing gives the users rapid service, even if many users are simultaneously using data terminals connected to the same computer. All users think that the computer is promptly responding to their individual needs.

The user may either access programs and data that already are in computer storage, or, using the data terminal, enter new programs and data to the computer for manipulation. Usually, the user keys in input on a keyboard, and receives output in the form of a printout or a display on a cathode ray tube (television-like screen).

A time-sharing computer has to be able to handle many input/output data terminals that operate at relatively low rates of speed (since input occurs at the speed of the human operator who is keying in data).

This system is sometimes referred to as the "conversational mode," since it permits the user to first state a problem and then to have a dialogue with the computer. This conversation or dialogue helps the user probe a file to find answers to questions that initially may be vague and/or poorly defined.

ADVANTAGES AND LIMITATIONS OF COMPUTERS

Advantages of Computers

Some of the advantages of using a computer are:

1. *Speed.* The most obvious advantage of using a computer is speed. The computer can perform calculations and data processing more quickly than alternative methods

* Time sharing usually involves polling, which is a technique that periodically checks each data terminal to find if there are any data to be transmitted. Procedures for using a time-sharing data terminal are explained in Appendix C.

can. Work that might take humans months or even years to complete manually may be accomplished in hours, or at most days, by computer. For example, some computers can do hundreds of thousands or even millions of arithmetic operations per second.

2. *Accuracy.* If the computer is properly programmed and provided with accurate data, it will do the intended work with a very high degree of accuracy. The computer does exactly what the program tells it to do. In addition, the computer does not get bored or fatigued, thus avoiding the errors humans might well make under the same circumstances.
3. *Reliability.* The computer can work almost twenty-four hours a day (with a little time out for equipment check-out and maintenance) every day of the year, and still operate reliably. Modern electronic computers perform at high levels of reliability, and equipment failures are very few.
4. *Retention.* The computer can store and search massive files of data and programs. The content of the files does not fade or get lost, and it can be used time and time again.
5. *Economy.* The advantages of speed and accuracy can often be translated into dollar savings realized. Usually, the per unit cost of processing data or doing computations by computer is considerably lower than by alternative means (i.e., manual or mechanical methods). There are also other advantages—for instance, more prompt billing can result in improved cash collections. Accurate records can reduce the frequency of bad decisions that were made because of unreliable or unavailable information.

   Just as the industrial revolution resulted in lower costs per unit for manufactured products, the computer revolution is resulting in lower cost per unit for information.
6. *Wide Applicability.* A computer can be used to solve a wide variety of problems that arise in science and business. The boundaries of what the computer can accomplish are limited only by the ability and imagination of its users.

Limitations of Computers

Some of the current limitations of computers are:

1. *Dependence on People.** The computer can only execute the precise instructions that human beings provide. It cannot independently engage in original or creative thinking. Some computers have been programmed to play a respectable game of

* It can be argued that this dependence is, in fact, advantageous—few of us would want a society that was completely under control of an "intelligent" computer that was independent of human beings.

chess, develop art work, and even compose music. But all the planning begins with the people who develop the systems and do the programming.

2. *Time-Consuming Systems and Programming Work.* The computer is unproductive until it is given the program that tells it what operations to perform. The development of a systems design and computer program can be both time-consuming and costly. Some efforts take many years of human effort, as well as hundreds of thousands of dollars.
3. *Disruptiveness.* A computer that is introduced into an organization or to do a particular job can be disruptive to that organization and to the people in the unit. Frequently, the computer procedures require far-reaching changes in organizational structure, work assignments, types of employees, and procedures. The result can be reduced morale, alienation, confusion, chaos, and even sabotage.
4. *Robot-Like Processing.* The computer performs as instructed; and if the instructions and/or data are in error, the computer will commit those errors tirelessly and obediently. In essence, the computer is a low-grade moron, capable of doing only what it is told to do, and doing that meticulously—even if its instructions are nonsensical.

Summary

Users have available a wide range of possible computer configurations, ranging from a simple stand-alone computer to complex computer-communication networks involving several computers and numerous I/O devices.

Of particular interest is the growing use of distributed data-processing, which is partly reversing the former trend of central data-processing.

Also, modern computers frequently are using data communications links to transmit data up to many thousands of miles.

Time-sharing computers and real-time computers are interesting approaches to computer use. In time sharing, many users who are not necessarily knowledgeable about computers can nevertheless use a computer and obtain quick response from it. Real time involves rapid computer processing that minimizes any delay from the point when an event takes place to the instant results are gotten from the computer.

An objective look at computers will reveal a number of impressive strengths, as well as some drawbacks.

Terms to Learn

Computer configuration
Stand-alone computer

Computer-communication network
Distributed data-processing
Host processor
Data transmission
Data communication
Teleprocessing
Remote device
Communication service
Transmission mode
Message switching
Time-sharing computer
Polling
Conversational mode
Real-time computer
Response time
Baud
Bandwidth
Narrow bandwidth
Voice bandwidth
Wide bandwidth
Centralized data-processing
Communications control unit (CCU)
Modem
Data set
Dial-up service
Leased line
Demodulation
Modulation
Duplex
Half duplex
Simplex
Port

Review Questions

1. How does an organization develop a *computer configuration* that suits its particular needs?
2. What is the difference between a *stand-alone computer* and a *computer-communication network?*

3. What is the *distributed data-processing* concept? How is it related to a *computer-communication network?*
4. What is *data transmission*, and why is it growing in importance?
5. Discuss the differences between the three categories of *communication services* for data transmission.
6. Define the three modes of *data transmission.*
7. Contrast *time-sharing computers* with *real-time computers.* How are they similar and how are they different?
8. If you were recommending a computer to your organization, what *advantages* and *disadvantages* would you be alert to in making a judgment?

SECTION III

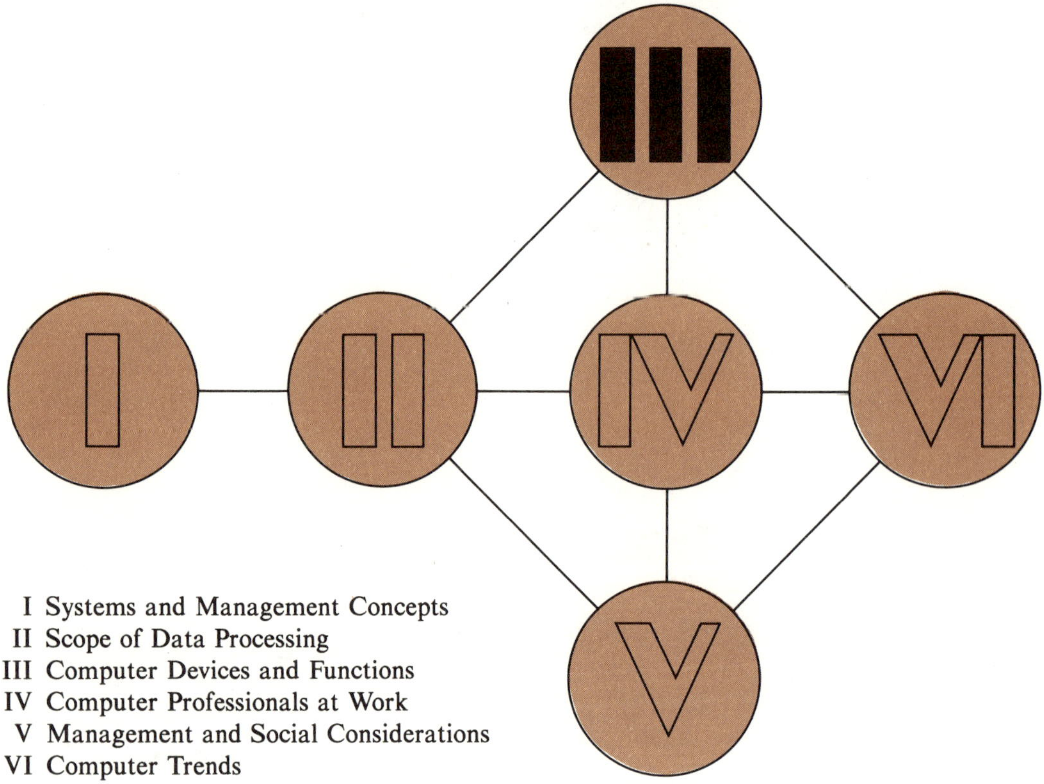
III
I
II
IV
VI
V
I Systems and Management Concepts
II Scope of Data Processing
III Computer Devices and Functions
IV Computer Professionals at Work
V Management and Social Considerations
VI Computer Trends

COMPUTER DEVICES AND FUNCTIONS

The computer burst upon the scene around 1950. With its unprecedented power for analysis and dissemination of extremely varied kinds of data in unbelievable quantities and at mind-staggering speeds, it has become a major force behind the latest acceleration in knowledge-acquisition. Combined with other increasingly powerful analytical tools for observing the invisible universe around us, it has raised the rate of knowledge-acquisition to dumbfounding speeds.

ALVIN TOFFLER

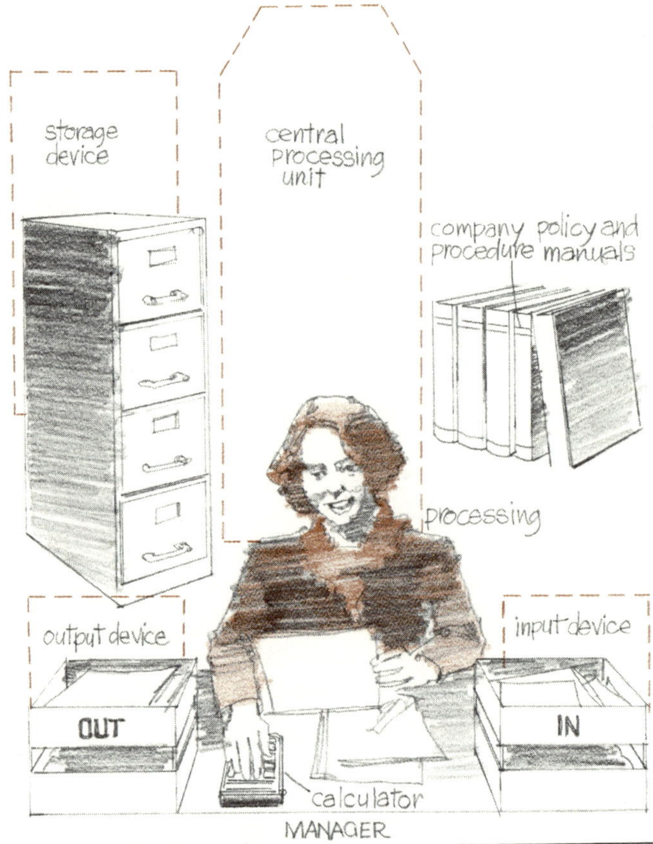
storage device
central processing unit
company policy and procedure manuals
processing
output device
input device
OUT
IN
calculator
MANAGER

CHAPTER 5

STORAGE AND THE CENTRAL PROCESSING UNIT

Objectives

Chapter 5 clarifies the internal codes used by the CPU, the characteristics of storage, and how the CPU actually functions.

The material in Chapter 5 is presented under the following topics:
Topic 1—Internal Computer Codes.
Topic 2—Facts About Storage.
Topic 3—The CPU's Functions.

TOPIC 1—INTERNAL COMPUTER CODES

WHAT IS DATA REPRESENTATION?*

Human communication uses symbols; these consist of the ten decimal numbers (0 through 9), a set of twenty-six alphabetic characters (A through Z), and a series of special characters (e.g., $, %, ¢, and +, among others). The human being can use a direct-entry device to enter data messages into the computer (e.g., by depressing keys on a keyboard), or an input device that reads data recorded on machine-readable media (e.g., punched cards).†

Internally within the CPU, a special computer code represents numbers and other characters (see Exhibit 5–1). The output can occur in a form that is readable by humans (e.g., a printed report or a message on a CRT) or in a media form that is machine readable (e.g., magnetic tape), which will be used in further stages of computer processing.

Thus, the input medium, the CPU processing, and the output medium usually involve special codes that represent the data that humans use. The equipment's engineering design sets these special machine codes, which are used to make computer processing more efficient and accurate.

Fortunately, since the equipment can generate and convert these special codes automatically, when required, people do not have to undergo the laborious task of learning the codes and working with them directly.

BINARY REPRESENTATION

The early calculating machines (e.g., Pascal's) used a wheel divided into ten equal sectors to represent the ten digits 0 through 9. Each decimal position required one

* Data representation is explained in more detail in Appendix A.

† The codes used by input and output media are discussed in Chapter 6.

Exhibit 5–1 Codes Used in Computer Systems

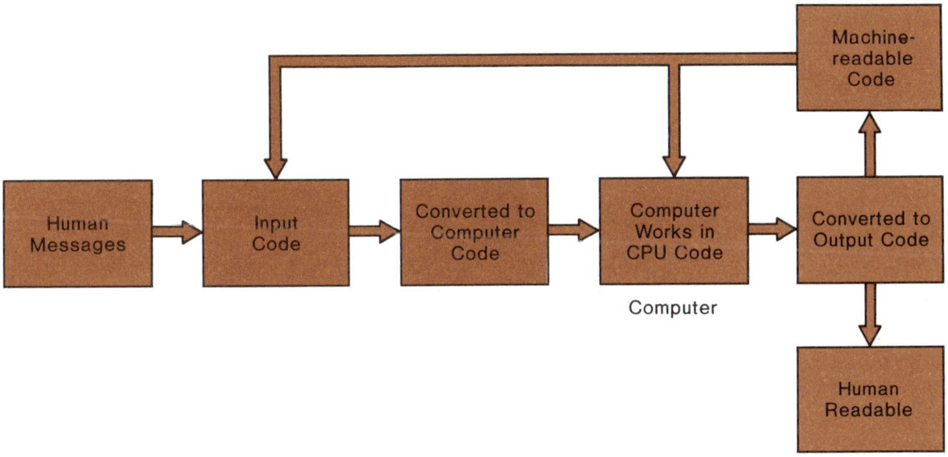

wheel (physical device), and that wheel could take on any one of ten positions (states) depending on whether the digit to be represented in that position was 0, 1, 2, . . . , or 9.

When, to represent data, we pass from mechanical physical devices like wheels to electromechanical, electric, electronic, and magnetic devices in order to get the speed that we require in a modern computer, we come up against a basic problem: these latter devices do not possess ten states that are stable (i.e., that do not drift from one state to another), easily distinguishable from one another, and unvarying over time (until the device fails). These devices generally have only two states that fit the above requirements. For example, a light bulb is either on or off. Using a rheostat, one could obtain different degrees of brightness, which could be considered as distinct states; but these could not be easily distinguished and would vary as the light bulb aged. Similarly, a transistor is either conducting or not; the fact that it might be conducting different amounts cannot be normally used. An electromechanical relay is either open or closed. Magnetism has two possible directions, and a magnetic device is magnetized in one direction or the other. We can even carry this analysis to the idea of representing data by holes in cards: we either have a hole in a certain position or we do not. One might try to get more states by varying the size or shape of the holes, but if the holes are to be sensed rapidly by means of completing electric circuits through the holes, only the presence or absence of a hole in a certain position can be rapidly detected. Therefore, we can use only two states: hole or no-hole (see Exhibit 5–2).

This leads us to the conclusion that if we are to get high speeds, we must use physical devices that have only two states. These two states are usually represented by the symbols 0 and 1. Which symbol is associated with which actual physical state of a physical device is a design feature that need not concern us further here.

In the everyday world, we make use of many more than two symbols to represent data. We normally use the ten decimal digits, the twenty-six alphabetic letters

Exhibit 5–2 Computer Components Operating in Binary

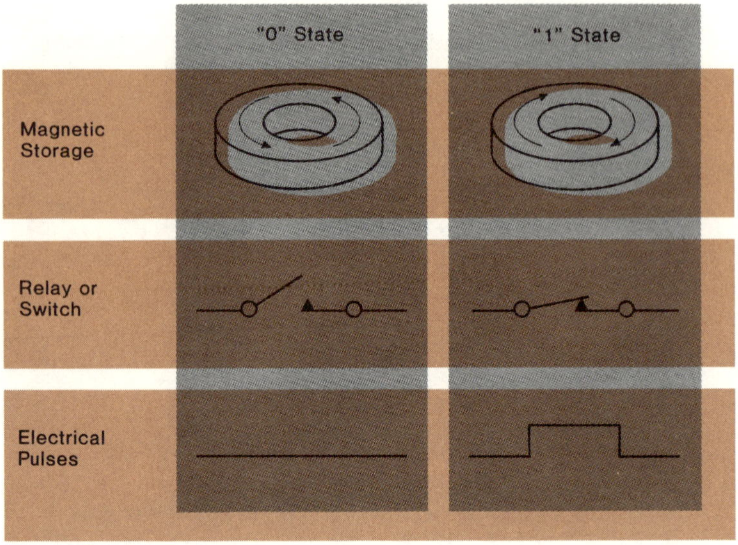

(including upper- and lower-case), and a series of special characters* for various purposes, including punctuation. But in the world of computers, we represent data by using only two symbols (which then may be represented by physical devices that have two states); and this representation is known as *binary representation.*

There are two principal ways of representing data by means of only two symbols (binary representation):

1. Pure binary (used for numbers only).
2. Binary coded system.

CPU CODES

The CPU uses a binary system in storing and handling data (see Exhibit 5–3). Binary simply means that all data are represented by a series of only two symbols: "1" and "0."† Since the CPU only has to recognize 1s and 0s, its job is simplified. If it had to deal with our conventional symbols (i.e., twenty-six different alphabetical characters,

* Among special characters, one is easily overlooked—the "blank." The position and number of blanks in a sequence of characters is important not only for esthetic reasons, but also for the meaning for the sequence of characters. Take a simple example: recording the month, day, and year. What would 12580 mean? Does it mean 12 5 80 (twelfth month, fifth day of 1980) or does it mean 1 25 80 (first month, twenty-fifth day of 1980)? Another example is that of a name—say JBASH. Is the name J BASH or is it J B ASH? In a string of numbers (98704532 . . .) if we run them together they lose meaning and integrity; 98 70 45 32 . . . mean something totally different than if they have no blanks.

† Sometimes the numeric 0 is slashed (Ø) to distinguish it from the alphabetic O.

Exhibit 5–3 A Comparison: Computer Arithmetic and Human Arithmetic

ten different digits, and many different special symbols), the CPU would need much more complex and costly circuits.

Computers use several variations of the binary system; some can switch from one binary system to another, under program control. We will discuss both the pure binary code and the binary coded system known as *EBCDIC* (Extended Binary Coded Decimal Interchange Code).

Pure Binary

This code is used only for mathematical applications; it is not intended to handle alphabetic data. Since the binary system only uses two symbols (1, 0), it is called a *base-two system.* This means that starting from the low-order position (right-most), successive positions represent successively higher powers of the base two as we move to the left (or higher-order positions). To illustrate this latter point, consider the following:*

Exponential Value	2^{31}	. . .	2^3	2^2	2^1	2^0
Integer Value	1073741824	. . .	8	4	2	1

The binary numbers "1" and "0" are frequently referred to as "1 bit" and "0 bit." The word *bit* is a contraction of *bi*nary digi*t*. To represent a quantity, each bit (either 0 or 1) is multiplied by its respective bit positional value; the products are then added together, giving the decimal equivalent of the binary number. For example, if we had a binary number 0110, it could be converted to decimal by the following means:

2^3	2^2	2^1	2^0
8	4	2	1
0	1	1	0

$0 \times 1 = 0$
$1 \times 2 = 2$
$1 \times 4 = 4$
$0 \times 8 = \underline{0}$
$\underline{6}$

If we wished to record the decimal value of 17 in binary, it would be as follows:

2^4	2^3	2^2	2^1	2^0
16	8	4	2	1
1	0	0	0	1

$1 \times 1 = 1$
$1 \times 16 = \underline{16}$
$\underline{17}$

* In this example, we used 2^{31} as the upper limit, since a popular computer uses a 32-bit code for pure binary. Since the 32nd bit is used for sign (plus or minus) the exponent 31 is used in the illustration.

Remainder Method. The previously described method of determining the combination of positional values that produces the required binary number is awkward to use when dealing with larger numbers. In such cases, the remainder method is an alternative way to convert a decimal to binary. The decimal is divided by two, and the quotient and all succeeding quotients are in turn divided by two. The division is repeated until a quotient of 0 is obtained. The equivalent binary number is composed of the remainders; the first remainder is the right-most or least significant digit, and the final remainder is the left-most, or most significant digit. For example, let's convert the decimal 38* to binary:

Divisor	*Quotient*	*Remainder*
2	0	1
2	1	0
2	2	0
2	4	1
2	9	1
2	19	0
2	38	▲

Resultant binary number, read from top to bottom $(100110)_2$

When the divide operation produces a result of zero, then the process is terminated. Of course, the calculation can be proved as follows:

2^5	2^4	2^3	2^2	2^1	2^0
32	16	8	4	2	1
1	0	0	1	1	0

$0 \times 1 = 0$
$1 \times 2 = 2$
$1 \times 4 = 4$
$0 \times 8 = 0$
$0 \times 16 = 0$
$1 \times 32 = 32$
$(38)_{10}$

* In our everyday arithmetic we assume all our numbers are in our normal decimal form (base 10). However, take the number 100110. Is it a binary number? Or is it a decimal number? Obviously, there is a wide difference between the numbers, since a binary 100110 is equivalent to a decimal 38. We would certainly prefer to have 100,110 dollars than 38 dollars! Technically, we can overcome this problem by the use of subscripts. Thus, $(100110)_2$ would clearly indicate a base-two number, while $(100110)_{10}$ would mean that the figure is in base ten.

Table 5–1
Three Binary Codes Used in Computers

Character	BCD Representation		EBCDIC Representation		ASCII Representation	
	Zone Bits	Numeric Bits	Zone Bits	Numeric Bits	Zone Bits	Numeric Bits
0	00	1010	1111	0000	0101	0000
1	00	0001	1111	0001	0101	0001
2	00	0010	1111	0010	0101	0010
3	00	0011	1111	0011	0101	0011
4	00	0100	1111	0100	0101	0100
5	00	0101	1111	0101	0101	0101
6	00	0110	1111	0110	0101	0110
7	00	0111	1111	0111	0101	0111
8	00	1000	1111	1000	0101	1000
9	00	1001	1111	1001	0101	1001
A	11	0001	1100	0001	1010	0001
B	11	0010	1100	0010	1010	0010
C	11	0011	1100	0011	1010	0011
D	11	0100	1100	0100	1010	0100
E	11	0101	1100	0101	1010	0101
F	11	0110	1100	0110	1010	0110
G	11	0111	1100	0111	1010	0111
H	11	1000	1100	1000	1010	1000
I	11	1001	1100	1001	1010	1001
J	10	0001	1101	0001	1010	1010
K	10	0010	1101	0010	1010	1011
L	10	0011	1101	0011	1010	1100
M	10	0100	1101	0100	1010	1101
N	10	0101	1101	0101	1010	1110
O	10	0110	1101	0110	1010	1111
P	10	0111	1101	0111	1011	0000
Q	10	1000	1101	1000	1011	0001
R	10	1001	1101	1001	1011	0010
S	01	0010	1110	0010	1011	0011
T	01	0011	1110	0011	1011	0100
U	01	0100	1110	0100	1011	0101
V	01	0101	1110	0101	1011	0110
W	01	0110	1110	0110	1011	0111
X	01	0111	1110	0111	1011	1000
Y	01	1000	1110	1000	1011	1001
Z	01	1001	1110	1001	1011	1010

Notes: Only the codes for numbers and the alphabet are presented. For purposes of clarity and condensation, codes for special characters, etc., have not been presented.

BCD stands for Binary Coded Decimal; EBCDIC stands for Extended Binary Coded Decimal Interchange Code; ASCII stands for American Standard Code for Information Interchange. The BCD system, formerly widely used in CPUs, needed only six bits to represent a character but could not provide for as many different configurations of characters as an eight-bit code.

Binary-Coded System

There are several different versions of the binary-coded system; we will concentrate on the eight-bit EBCDIC, since it is so widely used.* Since this code can be used to handle all types of data (numeric, alphabetic, and special symbols), it, rather than the pure binary system discussed above, is invariably used for business data-processing.

Table 5–1 depicts the EBCDIC code configurations for the decimal digits and our alphabetic characters. The chart also contrasts EBCDIC with two other binary codes—BCD and ASCII—but they will not be discussed here. Since certain media (e.g., some punched cards and magnetic tape) use BCD to represent data, BCD will be referred to in Chapter 6, when input and output media are discussed.

Each EBCDIC character is represented by a unique string of 1s and 0s; each string consists of eight bits (each group of eight bits is referred to as a *byte*). The four left-hand bits are referred to as "zone" bits; they identify the group classification of a character (for instance, all numbers have zone bits of 1111). The four right-hand bits are referred to as "numeric" bits. The EBCDIC representation can be summarized as follows:

Characters	*Zone Bits*	*Numeric Bits*
0 through 9	1111	0000 through 1001
A through I	1100	0001 through 1001
J through R	1101	0001 through 1001
S through Z	1110	0010 through 1001

The numeric part of the EBCDIC representation is derived from the positional value of base-two mathematics† (discussed under "pure binary code"). This can be seen by studying the following:

	Numeric Bits Positional Value			
Character	*8*	*4*	*2*	*1*
0	0	0	0	0
1	0	0	0	1
2	0	0	1	0
3	0	0	1	1
4	0	1	0	0
5	0	1	0	1
6	0	1	1	0
7	0	1	1	1
8	1	0	0	0
9	1	0	0	1

* An 8-bit code permits 256 unique codes (2^8), which is more than enough for our twenty-six alphabetic characters, ten decimal digits, and commonly used special symbols.

† Our everyday arithmetic is the decimal system that is called base ten because it uses ten different digits (i.e., 0, 1, 2, 3, 4, 5, 6, 7, 8, 9).

If the number thirty-seven were recorded in EBCDIC, it would require a total of sixteen bits and would appear as follows:

Zone Bits	Numeric Bits	Zone Bits	Numeric Bits
1 1 1 1	0 0 1 1	1 1 1 1	0 1 1 1

The zone bits (1111) tell the CPU that it is handling numeric data; and the computer can easily determine the value of the numeric bits as follows:

8	4	2	1	8	4	2	1
0	0	1	1	0	1	1	1

= 3   = 7

= 37

In another example, assume that the number 529 is stored in EBCDIC. It would appear as follows:

Zone Bits	Numeric Bits	Zone Bits	Numeric Bits	Zone Bits	Numeric Bits
1 1 1 1	0 1 0 1	1 1 1 1	0 0 1 0	1 1 1 1	1 0 0 1

= 5   = 2   = 9   = 529

A total of twenty-four bits was required to store the number 529.

When dealing with numeric data, it is possible to strip away the zone bits to store two digits in a byte. This is called the *packed decimal format.** In the packed format, 529 would be stored as follows:

0 1 0 1	0 0 1 0	1 0 0 1	1 1 1 1	
= 5	= 2	= 9	= +	= 529+

The low-order bits (1111) are used for sign position.† By using the packed-decimal format, only sixteen bits, rather than twenty-four, are required to store the number 529. When using numeric data, the use of the packed-decimal format can save considerable storage space.

If the computer were handling alphabetic data (let's say the name DEW), it would require a total of twenty-four bits. DEW would appear as follows:

* The unpacked EBCDIC representation is also referred to as *zoned decimal.*

† A negative (−) number would have a bit configuration of 1101 in the low-order positions. In the unpacked format, the low-order zone bits are used to indicate the sign (plus or minus).

Table 5–2

A Comparison of Binary Representation

Character	Pure Binary Representation	EBCDIC Representation			
		Zone Bits	Numeric Bits	Zone Bits	Numeric Bits
31	1 1 1 1 1	1111	0011	1111	0001
9	1 0 0 1			1111	1001
17	1 0 0 0 1	1111	0001	1111	0111
A	*			1100	0001

* Not applicable.

Zone Bits	Numeric Bits	Zone Bits	Numeric Bits	Zone Bits	Numeric Bits
1 1 0 0	0 1 0 0	1 1 0 0	0 1 0 1	1 1 1 0	0 1 1 0
= D		= E		= W	

Let's take another example. Suppose that we had a mix of numeric and alphabetic data—for instance, 7 Lane.* It would appear as follows:

Zone Bits	Numeric Bits	Zone Bits	Numeric Bits	Zone Bits	Numeric Bits	Zone Bits	Numeric Bits	Zone Bits	Numeric Bits
1 1 1 1	0 1 1 1	1 1 0 1	0 0 1 1	1 1 0 0	0 0 0 1	1 1 0 1	0 1 0 1	1 1 0 0	0 1 0 1
= 7		= L		= A		= N		= E	

Special symbols are handled similarly in EBCDIC. For instance, the dollar sign ($) symbol is represented by a unique group of eight bits, as follows:

Zone Bits	Numeric Bits
0 1 0 1	1 0 1 1

Table 5–2 presents some examples of binary representation that compare pure binary and EBCDIC.

* There is no blank between "7" and "Lane" in storage. Such editing usually takes place at the output stage of processing. To leave blanks in storage would waste considerable space in memory.

Parity-Check Bit

When calculating and performing certain internal computer operations, it frequently is necessary to move data from one storage location to another. To ensure that the data that initially were read into storage have been moved correctly, an internal engineered self-checking feature is normally a part of computer design. This checking feature is called a *parity check*. A parity check functions by means of an additional bit (a ninth bit in EBCDIC) associated with each byte.* When data are read into the CPU, a parity-check bit is activated (i.e., becomes a "1" bit) if required to maintain an odd number of bits. Computers using this method are called "odd-parity-check machines."† To illustrate this point, consider the alphabetic characters "A" and "J." They would appear as follows:

A =

Parity-Check Bit	Zone Bits	Numeric Bits
0	1 1 0 0	0 0 0 1

J =

Parity-Check Bit	Zone Bits	Numeric Bits
1	1 1 0 1	0 0 0 1

Without counting the parity-check bit, the character "A" is composed of three "1" bits, while the character "J" is composed of four "1" bits. Since the character "A" is already represented by an odd number of "1" bits, the parity-check bit is not needed (it remains set to "0"). However, the character "J" is represented by four "1" bits, which is, of course, an even number of "1" bits. Therefore, the parity-check bit is automatically activated (it is set to "1"); hence, the character "J" is now represented by an odd number of bits (five "1" bits). Both characters "A" and "J" now conform to the rule that each character must be represented by an odd number of "1" bits.‡

* Technically, one can say that EBCDIC is an eight-bit code (if one excludes the parity check bit) or a nine-bit code (if one includes the parity-check bit).

† There are other computers that operate under an even-parity-check basis. In such machines, each character must be represented by an even number of "1" bits.

‡ Suppose that, in an odd-parity-checking computer, a malfunction causes an extra bit to be added or dropped. This will give a character an even number of bits, which will be recognized by the computer as an error condition. However, suppose that the malfunction causes two extra bits to be added or dropped. In this case, odd parity will be maintained, even though there is an error. The likelihood of such a happening is, fortunately, remote. The chance of a single parity-bit error has been estimated as one in one billion; the chance of two errors affecting a particular character is one in 1,000,000,000,000,000,000! In a computer with one microsecond access, the probable frequency of double errors (which may go undetected) is one per thirty thousand years!

Summary

Internally, the CPU operates by using a special code—a binary code. All data and instructions that enter the CPU are automatically converted to binary code, and are handled in the coded form in the CPU. There are several variations of binary code.

Terms to Learn

Data representation
Character
Code conversion
Computer code
Pure binary
EBCDIC
ASCII
BCD
Binary digit (Bit)
Binary 1
Binary 0
Zone bit
Numeric bit
Byte
Base two
Base ten
Positional value
Zoned decimal format
Packed decimal format
Parity check

Review Questions

1. Contrast the *decimal (base-ten) system* with the *binary (base-two) system.*
2. Why does the CPU process data in the form of *binary* rather than in our *normal symbols* (decimal, our alphabet, special symbols)?
3. How does the decimal 24 appear in pure binary?
4. What is the decimal equivalent of the pure binary number 110001?
5. Why is pure binary used for mathematical problems?
6. How does *EBCDIC* differ from pure binary?
7. Why is EBCDIC used for *business data-processing applications?*
8. How would the decimal number 124 be recorded in *EBCDIC?* In *zoned decimal format?* In *packed decimal format?*
9. Convert the packed decimal binary number 0011 1000 0001 1111 to a decimal equivalence.
10. How would your given name be recorded in EBCDIC?
11. Discuss parity checking.

TOPIC 2—FACTS ABOUT STORAGE

WHAT IS STORAGE?

Computer storage is similar to a manually maintained file cabinet. In such a file cabinet, records are maintained in some predetermined order (e.g., alphabetically, or numerically by some code such as account number) so that they may be retrieved easily and used when desired.

Computer storage consists of any compilation of data or programs maintained in some logical way on machine-readable media or stored in retentive devices.

Computer storage is often compared not only to an ordinary filing cabinet, but also to a group of numbered mailboxes in a post office (see Exhibit 5–4). Each post office box is identified and located by a unique number. In that way, the postal clerk knows where to deposit mail, and the recipient knows the specific place to obtain his/her mail. Similarly, computer storage has an addressing structure* that directs the computer to specific boxes (called locations) in storage so that data can be placed in or retrieved from those locations.

A computer's storage capacity is an important dimension of its capability. An analogy can help us comprehend the vast storage capacity of various devices. A double-spaced typed page, for instance, contains about 200 words, which are composed of about 1,000 individual symbols called characters. A typical filing cabinet can store about 100 pages per file-drawer-inch. Assuming 20-inch drawers and 5 drawers per cabinet, we can determine the following:

- 1 typed page = 1,000 characters
- 1 file-drawer-inch = 100,000 characters
- 1 file drawer = 2,000,000 characters
- 1 file cabinet = 10,000,000 characters
- 100 file cabinets = 1,000,000,000 characters

There are computer storage devices that can hold equivalent volumes of data. The data that are stored in such computer storage normally are maintained in a more orderly method than is the paper that gets jammed into file cabinets.

Along with a computer's capacity to store data, another important characteristic is the time required to retrieve the data. This time is referred to as the "average access time" that typically is required to locate and obtain any data item from a storage device. In primary storage, the access time is typically one millionth of a second, or even faster! In secondary storage, the access time may be only a thousandth of a second; this is less time than it takes to blink an eye!

Regarding cost: in the 1970s, it cost an estimated $25 per month to store a million characters of data in a direct-access storage device. By the 1980s, this cost will be reduced to 50 cents!

* Certain types of computer storage (e.g., magnetic tape and punched cards) are nonaddressable.

Exhibit 5–4 Addressing Structure: Post Office Boxes and Computer Storage

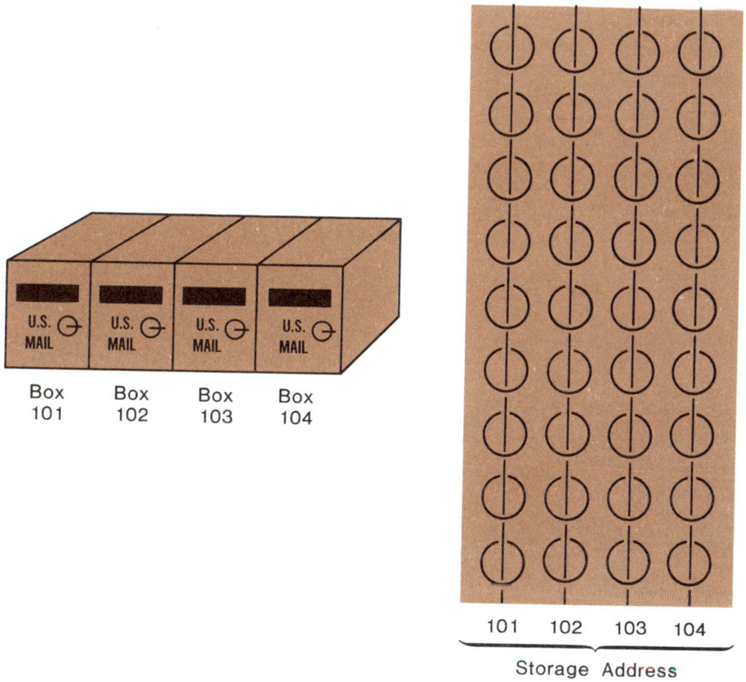

HIERARCHY OF STORAGE

In the computer's CPU, storage is arranged in an orderly way—from the smallest storage location to the largest. One must understand this hierarchy and its related terminology in order to identify the various storage levels.

1. A *bit* (binary digit) is a location that can hold an electronic or magnetic charge equal to a binary 1 or binary 0.
2. A *byte* is a location of eight bits (nine, if the parity check bit is included), which can hold a single character (a decimal digit, an alphabetic character, or a special symbol) in binary form. In packed format, a byte can hold the equivalent of two decimal digits.
3. A *computer word* is a location that holds a number of bits. The size of a computer word varies, depending on different manufacturers and computer models. For instance, in one widely used computer series, the word size is equivalent to thirty-two bits or four bytes. Other computers have different-size computer words, gener

ally, they range in size from sixteen to sixty-four bits. In some computers, programming makes it possible to use double words (i.e., a thirty-two-bit word can be expanded to sixty-four bits).

4. *Primary storage* (composed of bits, bytes, and words) is the CPU's internal storage unit. The size of primary storage varies, according to computer manufacturers and computer models. Table 5–3 indicates the range of primary storage offered by five different models produced by a single computer manufacturer. In this example, a small computer might have as little as 4K of memory capacity,* which can be expanded to 8K, 12K, or 16K by adding on additional modules. The large computer can be ordered with primary storage whose capacity is in the range of 128K up to 1,024K.

Table 5–3

Representative Range of Primary Storage Capacities

	Small ◄——		Computer		——► Large
Primary Storage Capacity (K = 1024 Bytes)	Model A	Model B	Model C	Model D	Model E
4K	X				
8K	X	X			
12K	X				
16K	X	X	X		
24K		X			
32K		X	X		
64K		X	X	X	
128K			X	X	X
256K			X	X	X
512K				X	X
768K					X
1024K					X

5. Various kinds of *secondary storage* are used to supplement primary storage. Usually, secondary storage is somewhat slower than primary storage; but it often has much more total storage capacity and is less expensive (per unit of storage) than primary storage. However, primary storage handles data much more rapidly than most

* K is derived from "kilo," which means 1,000. In the IBM computer line, K is equivalent to 1,024 storage locations (or bytes). Thus, for instance, 32K actually stands for 32,678 separately addressable storage locations, each of which can hold one byte of data. Often, in general discussions, only the thousands are used; thus while one may say 32,000 (or 32K), it is understood that 32K means 32,678.

secondary storage. Some secondary-storage devices are permanently on-line with the CPU; others hold files that are not constantly on-line to the CPU. (Thus, such files are sometimes off-line and not readily available to the CPU.) Secondary-storage devices can store upwards of hundreds of millions of bytes of data. Magnetic-disk and magnetic-tape storage are among the secondary-storage devices that are used most widely with modern computers.

Table 5–4, summarizing the hierarchy of storage, assumes a hypothetical computer that has a total on-line storage of 1,114,112 bytes. The hierarchy of storage should be viewed as building blocks: bits make up bytes; bytes make up words; words collectively form primary storage; and primary and secondary storage together provide total on-line storage capacity.

Table 5–4
An Example of Storage Hierarchy

Storage Level	Storage Capacity
Total On-Line Storage	1088K (1,114,112 Bytes)
Secondary Storage (On-Line)	1024K (1,048,576 Bytes)
Primary Storage	64K (65,536 Bytes)
Computer Word	Four Bytes
Byte	Eight Bits (or Nine, with Parity-Check Bit)
Bit	One Binary 0 or 1

K = 1024 bytes.

ADDRESSING STRUCTURE

Primary storage and certain secondary storage devices (e.g., magnetic disk units and magnetic drums) store data and instructions in addressable locations. Other types of secondary-storage units (e.g., magnetic-tape units, punched-card devices) do not store data and instructions in addressable locations.

In addressable storage, each location has an address associated with it. Depending on the computer, the location may be a group of bits that represent one character (e.g., eight bits in EBCDIC code) or it may be a string of bits (e.g., thirty-two bits) that represent a number in pure binary form. The address associated with each storage location permits the CPU to reference that location directly.

To put data into or remove data from the location, either the programmer or the program must know the location's address.

Exhibit 5–5 A Comparison of Fixed- and Variable-Length Words

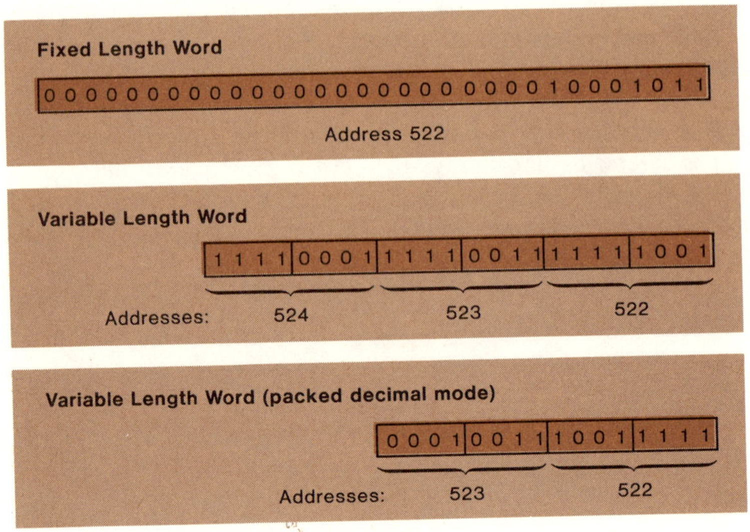

Variable-Length Word Storage*

In some computers, a single character can be referred to if the address of the location in which it is stored is stated. Machines whose circuitry is designed to process data serially as single characters are said to be "character-addressable." When a character-addressable computer is instructed to read from a specific location, it reads any number of succeeding locations or characters, depending on the particular instruction or on a code that is provided. In effect, the computer operates on *variable-length* words. This is particularly advantageous for business applications (e.g., in handling variable data such as names and addresses). EBCDIC (discussed earlier in the chapter) operates in this way.

Fixed-Length Word Storage

In computers that are not character-addressable, each address refers to a fixed number of locations (e.g., thirty-two bits) that can hold a fixed number of binary digits. Each group of digits is treated as a single unit of data. In effect, the computer operates on

* In a variable-length-word machine, a storage location is accessed by specifying only one address, which indicates the beginning of the data. Since storage locations vary in length, one of two methods is used to indicate the end of the data: 1. A special code (called a word mark) is placed in the location of the left-most character of the stored data; or 2. A program instruction specifies the number of characters of the word to be processed and its left-most starting address.

*fixed-length words.** As previously indicated, the choice of word size is made when the computer is designed and engineered. All operations are performed in parallel, to accommodate the standard-size word of the particular computer. Such computers are said to be "word-addressable." This is usually especially advantageous for mathematical and scientific applications when pure binary arithmetic is most efficient.

To illustrate these two methods of storage structure, let us assume that the number 139 is stored in storage (see Exhibit 5–5). In a fixed-length word (we will assume a fixed thirty-two bits per word), there would be twenty-four unused high-order bits, and then "10001011" (the pure binary equivalent of 139). Obviously, the fixed-length word wastes storage space when relatively small numbers are stored. The entire thirty-two bits would be addressed in its entirety; in the example, we assume that the address is 522. In a variable-length-word machine, assuming the use of EBCDIC, three adjacent eight-bit storage locations can hold the coded binary equivalent of 139. The assumed addresses for the data are 522, 523, and 524. Moreover, the number 139 could conceivably be stored in packed-decimal form, which means that the data could be stored in sixteen consecutive bits.

The Address and Content of Address

There is an important distinction between the address and the content of the address. The "address" identifies the location where data is stored. The "content of the addressable location" is the data stored there. For instance, if the value of 7 is stored in a location with an address of 309, it is important to recognize that 7 is the data stored—and not 309!

In most computers, no particular area of storage is reserved for either programs or data. There are no built-in physical boundaries in storage; rather, storage is used at the discretion of the programmer or under software determination. A specific area of storage (i.e., a series of addressable locations) may first be used to store data for one operation, and later used to store the program's instructions for a different operation.

Instructions usually are grouped together in ascending sequence and stored in sequential locations, according to the logical order in which the instructions are normally to be executed. Unless altered by a special instruction, the instructions will be carried out in sequence.

Nondestructive Read-Out and Destructive Read-In

Regarding the way in which things are stored and retrieved, the computer significantly differs from a mailbox (to hark back to the mailbox analogy). When the contents of the mailbox are removed, the box is emptied; but when the contents of a storage location are retrieved by the computer, the contents remain in the location. Addressable storage

* In some widely used computers, the programmer can address either each character (variable-word length) or a word (fixed-word length) by using an appropriate set of instructions. This permits the CPU's storage to be used most efficiently, according to the specific nature of each programmed application.

Exhibit 5–6 Examples of Nondestructive Read-Out and Destructive Read-In

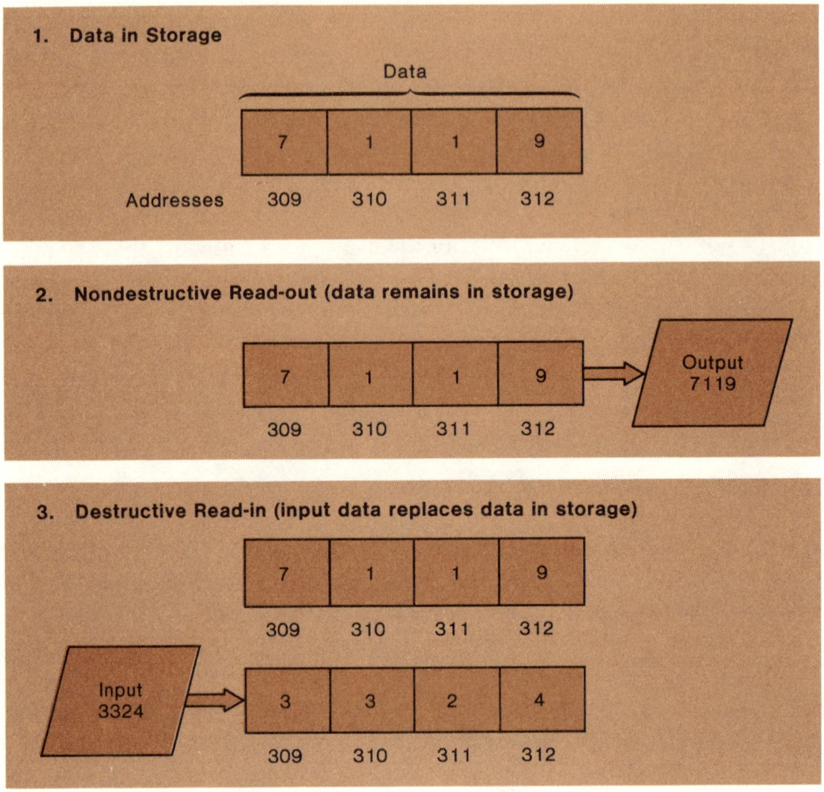

has *nondestructive read-out;* that is, data can be read out of addressable storage any number of times, without destroying the data. On the other hand, when a new letter is inserted into a mailbox, the previous contents remain undisturbed (unless someone removes them manually). But when the computer stores (or reads in) new data in a location, the previous contents are replaced by the new data. Addressable storage has *destructive read-in,* since data, as it enters a location, electronically erases anything that previously was stored in that location.

In Exhibit 5–6, the number "7119" is stored in addresses 309 through 312, and it can be outputted any number of times. However, when a new number (assume the number "3324") is brought into addresses 309 through 312, it automatically replaces the previously stored data (i.e., "7119").

Exhibit 5–7 Types of Computer Storage

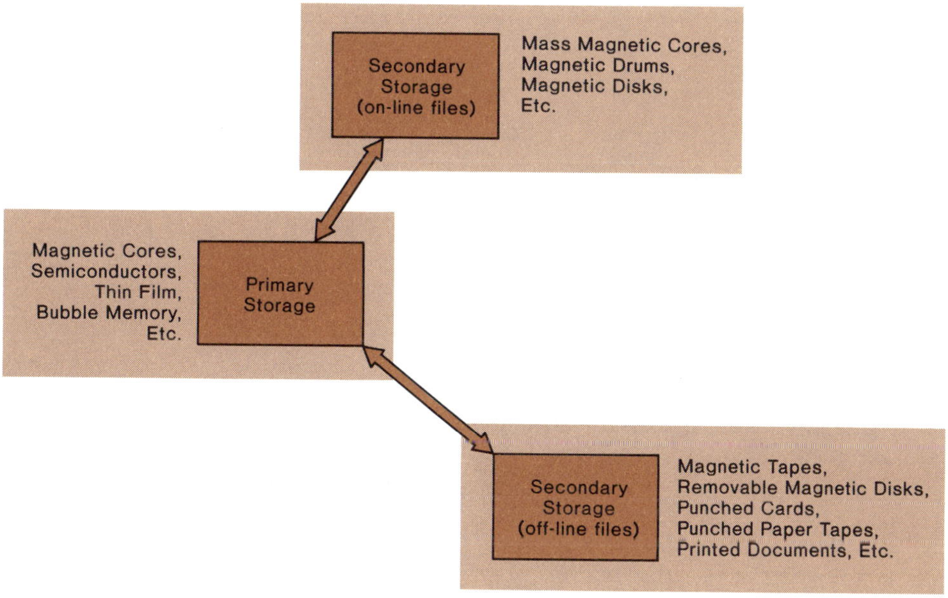

PRIMARY STORAGE

The principal storage unit of a computer is called *primary storage.** It can be either built into the CPU, or housed in a separate unit (if the latter, it is still an essential component of the CPU's functions).

All data or instructions that enter or leave the CPU must pass through primary storage. Further, primary storage must hold all instructions and data that currently are being processed by the CPU.† Compared with secondary storage, primary storage usually is limited in capacity because of the relatively high cost (per unit of storage) of the fast primary storage. Instructions and data that are not currently being processed usually are relegated to secondary-storage devices so that they don't tie up primary storage. When instructions and data are required in primary storage, they are trans-

* Primary storage (or memory) is sometimes referred to as "main storage," "internal storage," and "high-speed storage." Some references treat primary storage as a separate unit, on-line with the CPU. However, this book treats primary storage as an integral part of the CPU itself.

† If a computer's primary storage has a total of, say, 8,096 bytes of storage, the first byte is assigned address 0, the second byte is assigned address 1, and so on up to 8,095.

Exhibit 5–8 The Use of Primary Storage

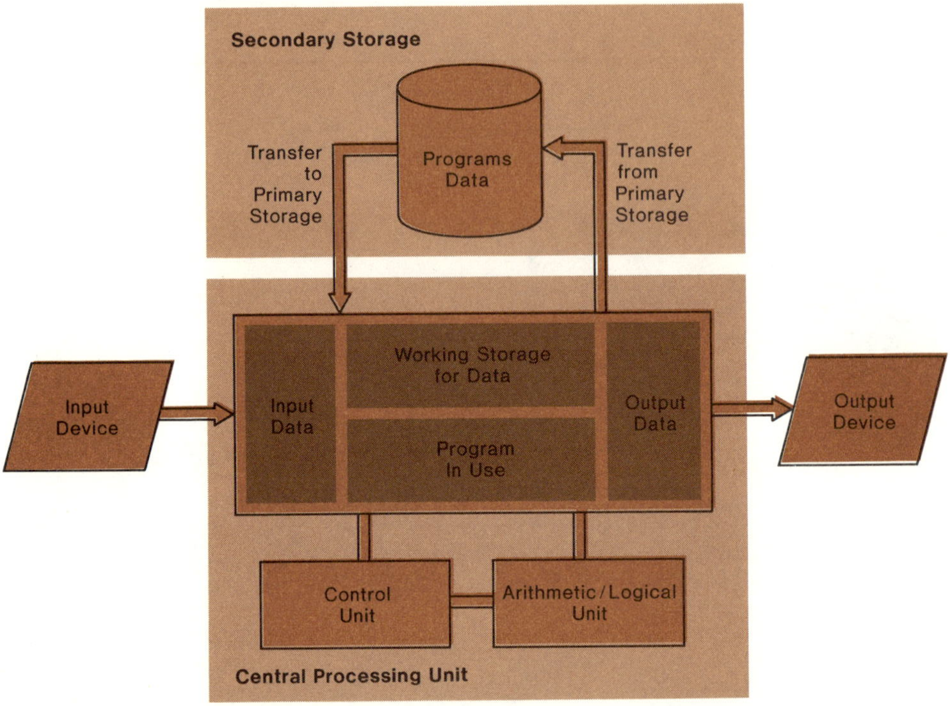

ferred from input devices or secondary-storage devices to primary storage. When the instructions and data in primary storage are no longer needed for current processing, they are normally transferred to output devices or secondary-storage devices (see Exhibit 5–7).

In order for the computer to operate, it must have both data and a program (a series of instructions) in storage. Both data and programs can enter the computer via an input device or a secondary-storage device. First, the program (usually in media code) is read by the input device or retrieved from secondary storage. Then electrical signals (representing the program) are sent to primary storage. Then the data (usually in media code) are read by the input device or retrieved from secondary storage; and electrical signals (representing the data) are sent to primary storage. The computer program must be in primary storage before the data enter primary storage. As the data enter primary storage, they can be processed, according to the program's instructions. Exhibit 5–8 illustrates how areas of primary storage would be established for: the program in use; input data; the data being worked on (called working storage); and the preparation of the output data so that they can be transferred out of the CPU.

Exhibit 5–9 EBCDIC and Primary Storage

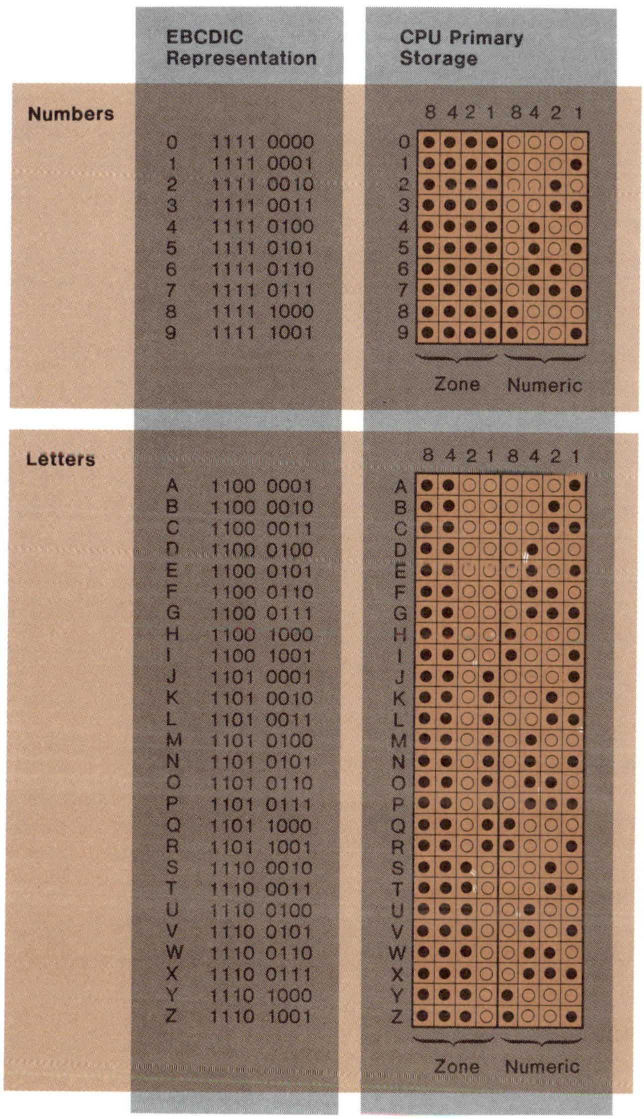

Legend: ● = "On" Bit (binary 1)
○ = "Off" Bit (binary 0)

Composition of Primary Storage

Historically, computers of the recent past have used magnetic cores as primary storage. However, new types of primary storage have been introduced; one of the more advanced approaches is the use of "semiconductor memory." This memory system is produced in modules; each module consists of two silicon (monolithic integrated circuit) chips. Other developments in storage include: thin-film memory; cryogenic memory; electro-optical memory; laser holographic memory; and bubble memory. There is no need to become conversant with the technical properties or peculiar ways in which each exotic memory unit operates. The important thing to remember is that they are all extremely rapid and reliably retentive.

When data enter primary storage, they are sent to specific addressable locations. "On" and "off" conditions—which are the equivalent of binary 1s and binary 0s—let the CPU know which data are stored in each address. Exhibit 5–9 illustrates how EBCDIC is actually represented inside primary storage. The darkened bits are used to signify an "on" condition (a binary 1), while the white bits are used to signify an "off" condition (a binary 0).

To give a specific example,* suppose that a person, using a direct-entry keyboard, sent the following message to the CPU: "2951 ALEX." That input data would be converted to binary form and stored in primary storage. Exhibit 5–10 shows how that data would be recorded in memory.

Since many computers can store data either in pure binary representation (if numbers are involved) or in EBCDIC representation, it is appropriate to consider how the use of storage differs in these cases. Exhibit 5–11 shows how the number "1103" would be stored in a thirty-two-bit pure binary word; it is obvious that such a small number does not use very much of the word's capacity. This exhibit also indicates how the number "1103" would be stored in four eight-bit bytes in EBCDIC representation.

The maximum number that can be recorded in a thirty-two-bit word in pure binary is 2,147,483,647. This assumes that all bits are "on" and that the sign position is plus.† In EBCDIC packed-decimal format, the maximum number that can be recorded in thirty-two bits is 9,999,999. In EBCDIC zoned-decimal format, the maximum number that can be recorded in thirty-two bits is 9,999 (see Exhibit 5–12). This illustration underscores pure binary's ability to cope more efficiently with large numbers, and EBCDIC's weakness in handling such numbers.

Virtual Storage

It seems that the computer's primary storage is never large enough. Programmers frequently find that the primary storage cannot handle their programs' instructions. Three alternatives have arisen to deal with this problem.

* In the examples presented, the parity-check bit is assumed but not shown.

† If the thirty-second bit is not "on" (0), the figure is a positive one; if the bit is "on" (1), the figure is a negative one.

Exhibit 5–10 Data in Primary Storage

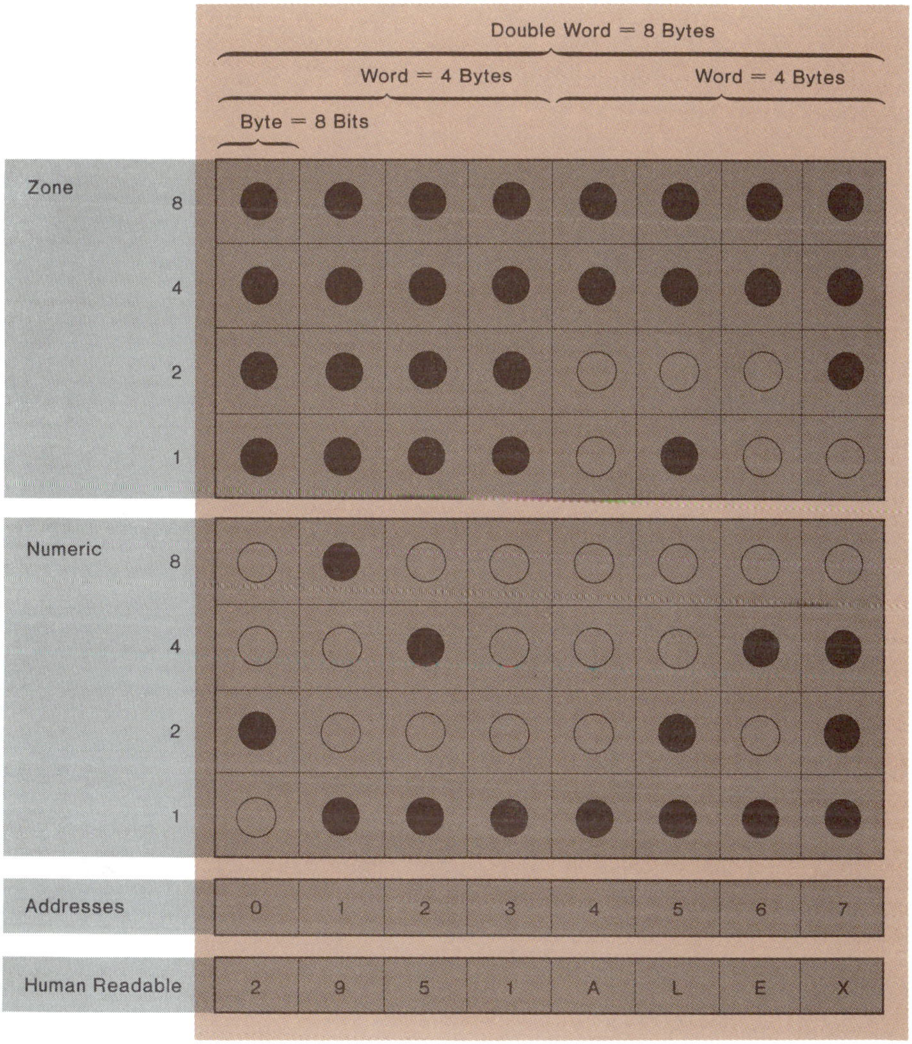

1. Convince the organization to obtain a larger primary-storage unit.
2. Subdivide the program into several smaller programs. This might make the output of the first program the input to the second program, and so on.
3. Divide the program into sections. As each section is loaded into primary storage and the required processing is completed, the next section is brought into primary

Exhibit 5–11 A Comparison of Pure Binary and EBCDIC Representation

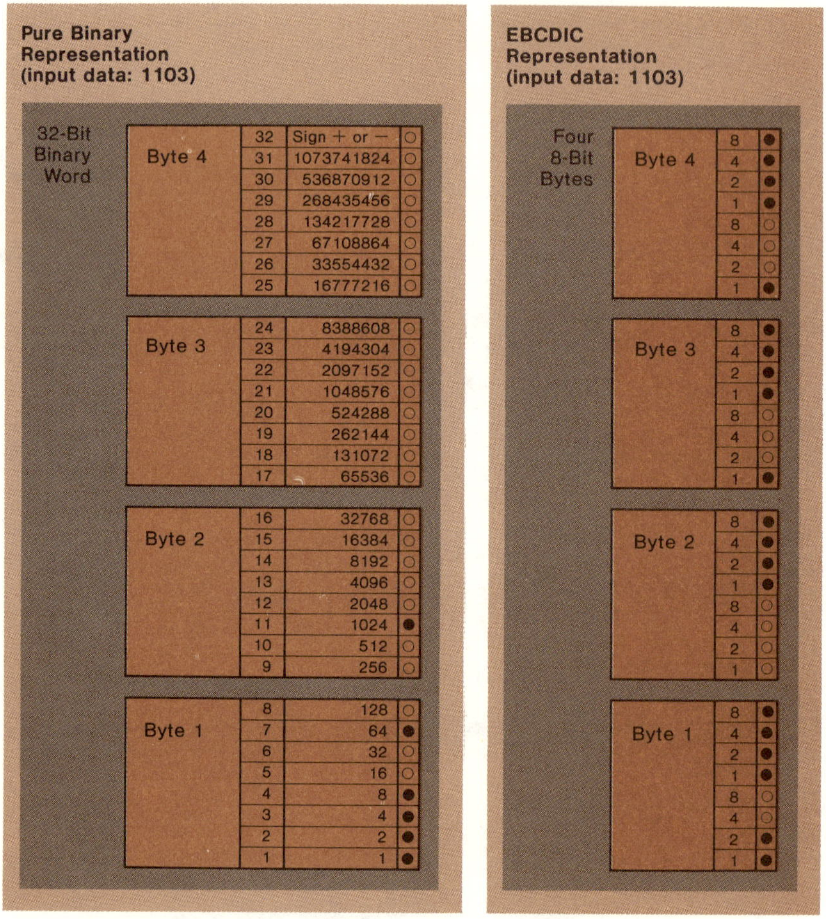

storage. This is known as an overlay system, referring to the fact that instructions within storage are destroyed when new instructions are placed over them.

Alternative 1 obviously involves greater cost for increased storage. Alternatives 2 and 3 get along with existing storage, but they require increased processing time, since the program is processed in sequential pieces.

Virtual storage allows the programmer to use secondary storage to store programs that require more primary storage than is available. Parts of the program, in use, are brought from secondary storage to primary storage as they are needed. These

Exhibit 5–12 Comparison of Storage Methods' Capacities

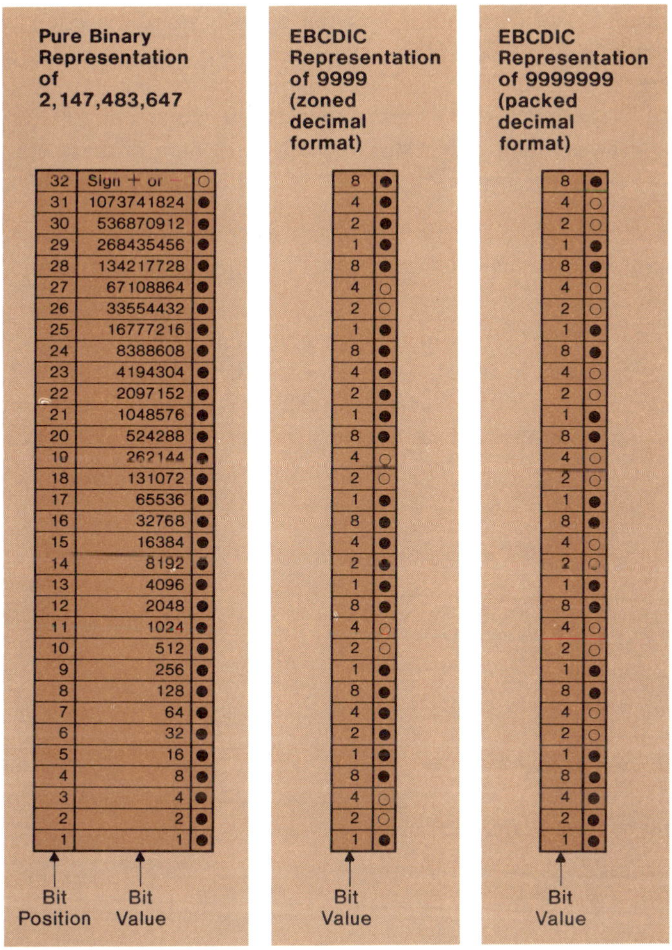

Note: The number 2,147,483,647 can be obtained by adding the bit value for each bit.

parts of the program are referred to as "pages." Only those program pages that are currently to be used are needed in primary storage. When a page is no longer needed, the primary storage space that it occupies can be reused for some other purpose.

Virtual storage relieves the programmer of having to divide his/her program to fit into an inadequately sized primary storage. In combination, the software and hardware features that the computer manufacturer provides support the virtual-storage technique and greatly expand primary storage's apparent capacity.

SECONDARY STORAGE

Secondary storage* supplements the functions of primary storage. While primary storage is mandatory for any computer, secondary storage usually is an optional attachment. Normally, primary storage is the built-in storage section of the CPU; secondary storage is usually a separate piece of hardware that is cable-connected to the CPU. Secondary storage generally is slower and less costly (per unit of storage) than primary storage. Also, because it is less expensive, it is not unusual for secondary-storage devices to have much larger storage capacities than primary storage.

Secondary-storage devices belong to one of two broad classifications:

1. Devices, attached to the CPU, whose files are continuously maintained on-line. Such fixed-storage devices include magnetic cores, magnetic drums, and fixed magnetic disks.
2. Devices, attached to the CPU, whose files are not continuously on-line. Such storage devices include magnetic tapes, removable magnetic disks, punched cards, and punched-paper tapes. The files used by such devices are normally processed by computer, removed for physical storage, and then replaced on the storage devices by other files.

A Comparative Example

Table 5–5 illustrates and compares some of the features of a few secondary-storage and primary-storage methods.

From the chart, a number of conclusions are clear:

1. Primary storage is much more expensive than secondary storage, which explains why it is used principally for holding programs and data in current use, rather than for semipermanent or permanent storage purposes.
2. The cost of storage, in secondary-storage devices, is relatively inexpensive.
3. The average access time† to locate data, and the transfer rates of data, are very rapid for primary-storage devices.
4. Secondary-storage devices have a wide range of performance (access times and transfer rates). Punched cards are relatively slow; magnetic tape has medium-range performance; and some magnetic-disk devices are rapid.

* Secondary storage can also be considered as a form of input and/or output device. Although this will be explored in Chapter 7, since secondary storage supplements the CPU's primary storage the topic was introduced in this chapter. Secondary storage is sometimes also referred to as "auxiliary storage," "external storage," "low-speed storage," and "mass storage."

† "Access time" is the average time it takes to locate a specific record in a particular storage device. "Transfer rate" refers to the amount of data that can be transferred (moved) in a second.

A small-volume job with no time pressures might be handled economically by punched-cards-storage methods. A large-volume job, requiring semipermanent storage of data and reasonably quick results, might best be handled by magnetic tape or magnetic disk. A very important, urgent job for which cost was not a consideration might be stored in magnetic cores.

In short, specific application needs should be matched with the appropriate storage method.

Secondary-storage devices often have the capacity to store millions or even billions of characters of data. Files of data and programs can be called in from secondary storage by the control unit, and moved into primary storage. Conversely, the data and programs in primary storage can be transferred to secondary-storage devices.

Some of the secondary-storage devices are also considered to be input/output devices. These include punched-card devices, magnetic-tape devices, and magnetic-disk devices. These devices will be discussed at greater length in Chapter 7.

As we mentioned previously, some secondary-storage devices have addressable storage (similar to primary storage's magnetic cores), while other secondary-storage devices do not. Magnetic drums and magnetic disks have addressable storage; magnetic tape and punched cards do not.

Magnetic cores, magnetic disks, and magnetic drums are direct-access devices—

Table 5–5

A Comparative View of Some Storage Approaches

Type of Storage	Approximate Access Time to Locate a Record	Approximate Data Transfer Rate (Characters Per Second)	Estimated Cost to Store 1000 Characters Per Year
Secondary Storage			
Punched Cards	Minutes to Hours	Up to 1,600	Pennies to Nickels
Magnetic Tape	Minutes	Up to 320,000	Nickels to Dimes
Magnetic Disk	Several Milliseconds	Up to 800,000	Dimes to Quarters
Primary Storage			
Magnetic Core	Several Microseconds	Up to 4,000,000	$100, But Dropping
Semiconductor: Monolithic Integrated Circuits	Several Microseconds	Up to 8,000,000	$200, But Dropping

Notes: Magnetic core is sometimes used for secondary storage.

Based on the above figures, semiconductor memory could transfer the equivalent of almost seven 500-page books in a second!

that is, a particular record can be located without searching through an entire file.* This is important in applications in which transactions must be processed immediately, as they occur, to update the status of a file, or where frequent inquiries are made to individual records. Such direct accessing would not be possible without addressable storage locations.

On the other hand, nonaddressable storage (such as magnetic tape and punched cards) processes data in strictly sequential order. That is, to locate a desired record, the file of magnetic tape and/or punched cards must be processed from beginning to end—even if only one record is needed in a large file.

One of the advantages of removable storage (e.g., magnetic tapes, some magnetic disks, and punched cards) is that such off-line external files have virtually no limitation as far as storage size is concerned. For instance, some organizations have many thousands of magnetic-tape reels containing data files. They are usually kept in external storage (off-line from the computer); when a tape reel is to be processed, it is taken from external storage and manually inserted on a magnetic tape device for processing. Once the magnetic tape is loaded into a magnetic-tape device, it is considered to be part of on-line secondary storage.

Files and programs that are used frequently are generally stored on-line in secondary storage. Files and programs that are used relatively infrequently probably should not clutter on-line secondary storage, and are best stored off-line until they are needed for processing.

Summary

The computer has the capability to retain data in storage (memory). The basic unit of storage is the bit, which can hold either a binary 1 or a binary 0. Eight bits make one byte. Each computer has a primary storage that holds the instructions, and data that are currently being manipulated or processed. Most computers also have secondary storage, which supplements primary storage. Primary storage is addressable, which means that the computer can keep track of data stored in any of the addresses; if needed, such data can be retrieved easily and quickly.

Terms to Learn

Storage
Address
Location
Addressable storage
Word-addressable
External storage
Data transfer rate
Alphabetic data

* If desired, direct-access devices can process data files in sequential order.

Nonaddressable storage
Computer word
Storage capacity
Primary storage
Semiconductor memory
K
Variable word-length
Fixed word-length
Access time
Character-addressable
Numeric data
Special symbols
Code
Symbol
Decimal
Nondestructive read-out
Destructive read-in
Virtual storage
Direct-access device

Review Questions

1. Define *bit, byte,* and *computer word.*
2. Discuss the relationship of *primary storage* and *secondary storage.*
3. What is meant by *12K* of primary storage?
4. Contrast a computer with *variable word-length storage* with one with *fixed word-length storage.*
5. Differentiate between the *address* of a storage location and the *data* in the storage location. Give an example.
6. What is meant by *nondestructive read-out* and *destructive read-in?* What is the significance of these characteristics?
7. Define *virtual storage.*

TOPIC 3—THE CPU'S FUNCTIONS

WHAT DOES THE CPU* DO?

The CPU controls and supervises the entire computer system, handles the arithmetic and logical operations, and provides primary storage for data and programs.

The control unit of the CPU directs and coordinates all operations called for by the program (instructions). The control unit decodes each instruction and then activates the appropriate circuits necessary for input and output devices to perform, for data to be moved to and from storage, and for data to be routed to and from the

* The CPU is sometimes referred to as the *main frame.*

arithmetic/logical unit. The action of the control unit causes the entire computer system to operate in an automatic, integrated manner. Some of the specific functions that the control unit directs are: starting and stopping an input or output device; moving a data record from secondary storage to primary storage; moving data to the arithmetic/logical unit for computational purposes; and routing data from storage to an output device.

The arithmetic/logical unit contains the circuitry to perform arithmetic and logical operations. The arithmetic unit calculates, shifts numbers, sets the algebraic sign of results, rounds figures, and so on. The logical unit carries out the decision-making operations (e.g., comparing two numbers to determine which is the larger one), usually to change the sequence of instruction execution.

Instruction Set

Each computer is engineered with the capacity to carry out certain operations when a specific instruction's operation code (called *opcode* for short) is decoded by the CPU's control unit.

For instance, one particular computer has available an instruction set of 95 operation codes for business-type instructions, and 44 for scientific-type instructions. The entire instruction set consists of 139 different operation codes that tell the computer which of the engineered operations to execute.

Many of the operation codes are of interest only to the technical programmer. However, certain operation codes are required for any computer. These include:

1. *Reading* (or input). There must be an operation code that will instruct the computer to transfer data from input devices/secondary-storage units to primary storage.

Table 5–6
Some Examples of Instructions

Operation	BASIC Language Instruction	FORTRAN Language Instruction
Read (Input)	READ J, K	READ (d,f) J, K
Calculation (Process)	L = J + K	L = J + K
Branching and Logical Steps (Decision)	IF L >= 100 THEN 999	IF (L.GE.100) GO TO 999
Movement (Process)	LET M = L	M = L
Writing (Output)	PRINT L	WRITE (d,f) L
Termination	END	END

Note: In FORTRAN, each read and write instruction (statement) must specify a device (I/O) unit number (substitute for "d" in the instruction) and a format (f) statement that describes the data's characteristics. For purposes of clarity, at this point the format statement is not shown.

2. *Calculations.* Various operation codes are needed to tell the computer which arithmetic functions to carry out on particular data. Calculations are processing operations.
3. *Branching and Logical Steps* (or decision). The computer must have the capacity to determine conditions, based upon logical tests (e.g., which of two numbers is larger?), and to provide alternative routines on the basis of that determination.
4. *Movement of Data.* Operation codes must be available to allow for movement of data within primary storage and between primary and secondary storage. Data movements are processing operations.
5. *Writing* (or output). There must be an operation code that will instruct the computer to transfer data from primary storage to output devices/secondary-storage units.
6. *Termination.* This operation code tells the computer to cease operations.

Table 5–6 illustrates how such elementary operations might appear in two programming languages, BASIC and FORTRAN.* You will note that there is considerable similarity between the two languages.

The J and K after READ merely indicate that the computer will input two data fields,† which are assigned variable names J and K.

The calculation equation indicates that J and K should be added and that the result should be placed in a symbolic storage address called L.

The decision step involves testing the value of the variable L to determine whether it is greater than or equal to the absolute numeric amount 100. If L equals 100 or more, the computer is instructed to branch to instruction number 999. If L is less than 100, the computer will continue with the next sequential instruction. (In BASIC >= means "greater than or equal to," while in FORTRAN ".GE." has the same meaning.)

The movement operation merely indicates how a value (represented by the variable L) can be moved and stored in a second location (represented by the label M). Now the data would be stored in two storage locations (L and M).

The output instruction causes the computer to print out the value of the sum (L).

The termination operation causes the computer to stop processing the particular job.

It is very important to recognize that variable names‡ (such as J, K, L, and M) are used in programming to identify both data fields and symbolic addresses in storage. The computer itself automatically assigns absolute addresses,§ but the human being can work with the symbolic addresses. These are much more convenient for people; the

* Chapters 10 and 11 will elaborate on these and other programming languages.

† A field is a group of characters that represent some specific data. For instance, an employee record might contain an employee-number field, a rate-of-pay field, a department-number field, etc. These ideas about data organization are explored in Chapter 8.

‡ This is not too different from algebraic equations (e.g., A + B = X). When we wish to solve the equation, we then substitute actual numeric values (data e.g., 10 + 7 = 17)

§ An absolute address is one that is built into the logic of the circuits by the computer engineers (e.g., address 0000, 0001, 0002, etc.).

computer performs the arduous task of keeping track of actual addresses where actual data is stored. Thus, when we say we are inputting J, we are saying that some data will be read in substitution of J, and that the computer will assign a storage location for the data and keep track of where they are stored.

Let us assume that, in our illustration, J has a value of 10 and K has a value of 7. Table 5–7 traces how the data will be affected by the various instructions presented in Table 5–6. In simple form, this indicates how instructions affect data in storage.

Later in this chapter, an example of a program containing such instructions will be analyzed and explained in greater detail.

Machine Cycles

All computer operations take place in fixed intervals of time. These intervals are measured by regular pulses that are emitted by an electronic clock at frequencies as high as several million per second. A fixed number of pulses determines the time of each basic machine cycle. In computer usage, time references are stated in terms of milliseconds, microseconds, and nanoseconds.

Table 5–7

How Instructions Affect Data in Storage

Assume J = 10 and K = 7

	Variables				
Operation	J	K	L	M	Comments
Read (Input)	10	7			At this point L and M are blank.
Calculation (Process)	10	7	17		J and K are added and the sum is placed in L.
Branching and Logical Steps (Decision)	10	7	17		Since the value of L is less than 100, the computer will go to the next sequential instruction.
Movement (Process)	10	7	17	17	The value in L is moved to M. It is now in both locations.
Writing (Output)	10	7	17	17	The value in L, which is 17, is printed out.
Termination	10	7	17	17	Processing is terminated, but note that all the data remain in their respective storage locations.

Note: Refer to instructions in Table 5–6.

- .1 = 1/10 second, or 100 milliseconds
- .001 = 1/1,000 second, or 1 millisecond (ms)
- .000001 = 1/1,000,000 second, or 1 microsecond (μsec)
- .000000001 = 1/1,000,000,000 second, or 1 nanosecond (ns)

In some supercomputers, there is even a faster machine-cycle measure of time; it is called a picosecond, which stands for one trillionth of a second.

There are two distinct machine cycles: instruction time, when the control unit fetches an instruction from primary storage and interprets it; and execution time, when the control unit fetches the data and the actual processing is performed in the arithmetic/logic unit.

Within a machine cycle, the computer can perform a specific operation or group of operations. The number of operations required to execute a single instruction depends on the instruction. For instance, all things being equal, fewer operations are required to add two figures than to multiply the same two figures. Various operations are combined to execute each instruction.

Instructions usually consist of at least two parts: an *operation** and an *operand*. The operation tells the computer what function to perform. For example: read data from the input device; add two numbers; or, move data from secondary storage to primary storage. The operand can be the address of data or an instruction in storage, or it can identify the address of an input/output device. It also can specify a control function, such as shifting a quantity in storage, or rewinding a reel of tape. To illustrate the structure of an instruction, consider the following:

Operation	Operand A	Operand B
ADD	764	313

This instruction can be interpreted to mean: perform the addition function by adding the value stored in address 764 and the value stored in address 313.

To receive, interpret, and execute instructions, the CPU must operate in a prescribed sequence, which is determined by the specific instruction and is carried out during a fixed interval of timed pulses.

Registers and Counters†

A computer frequently has several storage locations that have been set aside for special purposes. In contrast, most primary storage is for general purposes: any data or instructions can be stored anywhere in primary storage. Various registers and counters are examples of special-purpose storage locations.

Registers are named according to their function. For example:

1. An *instruction register* is used to hold the complete instruction taken from storage.

* The operation is sometimes referred to as the *opcode* (operation code) or the command.

† In different computers, registers and counters differ in number and function.

2. An *instruction address register* contains the location in primary storage that holds the instruction.
3. An *operand address register* holds the address of a storage location containing data, or it can identify a device in the computer system.
4. An *operation register* contains an operation code that indicates the function the computer should execute.

Registers differ in size, capacity, and use.

The counter is used to increment and decrement a value. For instance, such a counter may be used to signal the instruction address register to automatically proceed to the next instruction after an instruction has been executed.

Instruction Cycle

The initial machine cycle required to execute an instruction is called an *instruction cycle*. The time required for this cycle is referred to as instruction time (or *I-time*). During I-time, the following operations take place:

1. The instruction is taken from primary storage and moved to the instruction register. The control unit is able to fetch the proper instruction because the instruction address register always holds the address (or location in storage) of the pertinent instruction.
2. The operand part of the instruction is decoded in the operand address register; therefore, the control unit knows the address, in storage, of the pertinent data to be processed.
3. The operation part of the instruction is decoded in the operation register. The control unit's circuits know what specific operations are to be performed for each operation code that is used.
4. The location of the next instruction is set in motion, as a counter automatically increments the instruction address register. (Recall that instructions normally are stored in sequence in storage.)

At the start of a computer run, an instruction address register normally is set to the address of the first program instruction. This instruction is brought from storage, and while it is being executed the instruction counter automatically advances (steps) the instruction address register to the location that corresponds to the space occupied by the next stored instruction. By the time one instruction has been executed, the address register has located the next instruction in program sequence. The stepping action of the counter is automatic. In other words, when the CPU is directed to a series of instructions, it executes them one after another until instructed to do otherwise. The normal stepping of the instruction counter can also be reset back to the beginning of the program (the address of the first instruction) so that the entire program can be repeated for another incoming-data record. This ability to break the sequence in which instructions are carried out, by looping back to a different part of the program, establishes the computer's ability to operate automatically and to adapt to different conditions in data.

Execution Cycle

I-time usually is followed by one or more machine cycles that occur during execution time (or *E-time*). The number of *execution cycles* required depends on the instruction that is to be executed. The E-time cycle starts by removing from storage the data that the operation address register has located. The operation code (opcode) part of the instruction tells the control unit what specific operations are to be performed on the data; and during E-time, those operations (e.g., read, compute, compare, write) are carried out. If the operand address register identifies a device, rather than data in storage, then the control unit gives proper directions to that device.

During E-time, two operations related to data storage are part of the execution cycle: access time and transfer time.

1. *Access time* is defined as the time interval between a request for the transfer of data to or from a storage device and the completion of this operation. It is the sum of waiting time (if any) and transfer time.

   In devices with mechanical movement (e.g., magnetic-tape units, magnetic-disk units, or magnetic drums), there is a normal delay or waiting time before data can be transferred.

2. *Transfer time* is the time required for movement of data, once movement begins. Often this is stated in terms of transfer rates (e.g., characters per second). For devices with mechanical movement, the transfer rate depends on recording density (characters per inch) and mechanical speed (e.g., inches per second of movement, for magnetic tape; or revolutions per second, for magnetic disks and magnetic drums).

THE COMPUTER IN OPERATION

Assume the following facts about a data processing application (a purposely simplified example):* a single punched card is to be read by an input device. The punched card contains two fields of data (called J and K). The computer is to add the data contained in the two fields. The sum of the two fields is to be written out by an output device.

Refer to Exhibit 5–13. The first step is the loading of the program (consisting of four instructions† on punched cards) into primary storage. We will assume that the four cards constituting the program are read by the input device, and that each instruction‡ is stored in a separate addressable location in the storage unit. The first

* This simplified example is a version of the program that was presented earlier in this chapter.

† The instructions, while resembling widely used actual programming languages, are stylized to present this example in an uncluttered, simple way. Chapter 11 goes into the specifics of actual programming.

‡ Although we learned that it is possible to address each character, we will assume for this example that an address is the location of a group of relevant characters (i.e., an instruction or a data field).

Exhibit 5–13 Loading a Program and Data into Storage

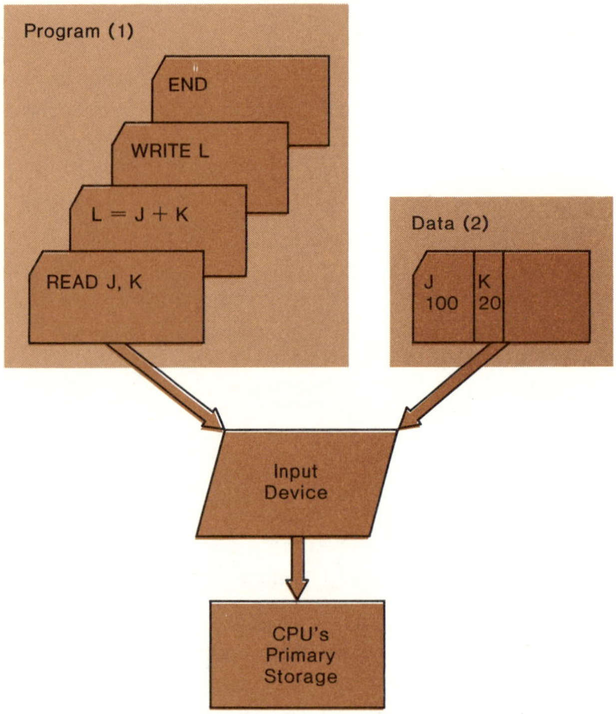

instruction is stored in the location with the address 00; the second instruction is stored in address 01; the third and fourth instructions are stored in addresses 02 and 03, respectively. At this point, the instruction address register is set to the first instruction's address (in this case 00).

Refer to Exhibit 5–14. At this juncture, the computer's primary storage and registers would appear as indicated in Exhibit 5–14. Of course, the data would actually be stored in binary code, as we explained earlier.

Now the I-time cycle begins. The instruction in location 00 is sent to the instruction register, and the counter automatically increments the instruction address register by 1. Thus, the instruction address register is set to 01 (identifying the address of the next instruction). The operation register decodes the opcode (READ), and the operand address register indicates the data to be read as variables "J" and "K."

Refer to Exhibit 5–15. At this point, the execution cycle (E-time) begins. The control unit directs the circuitry to carry out the specified operation (i.e., "READ"), and the operand indicates that two data values, "J" and "K," are involved. The control unit engages the input device, which senses the pattern of perforations in the punched card. The electrical equivalent of what is punched in the card (in our example, "100" in

Exhibit 5–14 A Program Loaded into Primary Storage

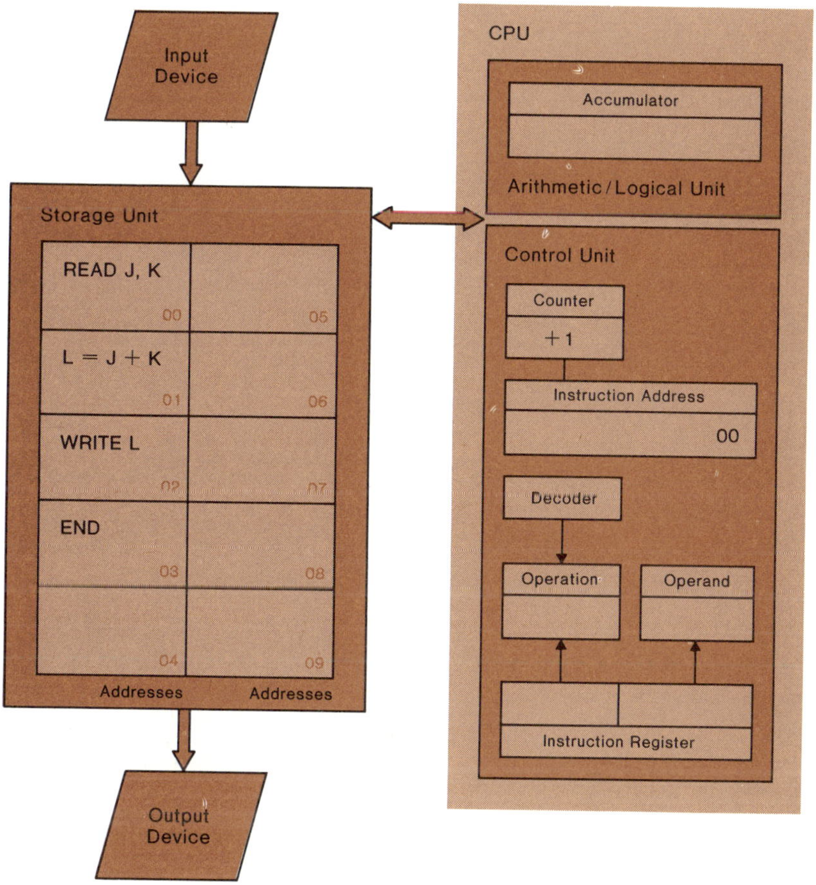

variable "J" and "20" in variable "K") is sent to primary storage. When the program gives variable names (such as "J" and "K") to the operands, the computer's own software automatically assigns specific storage location addresses to the data. Let us assume that variable "J" is assigned the address of 05 in storage, and that variable "K" is assigned the address of 06 in storage. Thus, the value of 100 will be stored in address 05, and the value of 20 will be stored in address 06. After the reading takes place, the actual punched card will be moved to a stacker of the input device, and the next data card to be read will be moved to the reading position of the input device.

Refer to Exhibit 5–16. Now, the next I-time takes place. The instruction in address 01 is brought to the instruction register (replacing the previous contents of the register). The counter increments the instruction address to 02, setting it for the next instruction's address. The opcode and operand registers are decoded. The E-time cycle

Exhibit 5–15 Transferring Data from an Input Device to Primary Storage

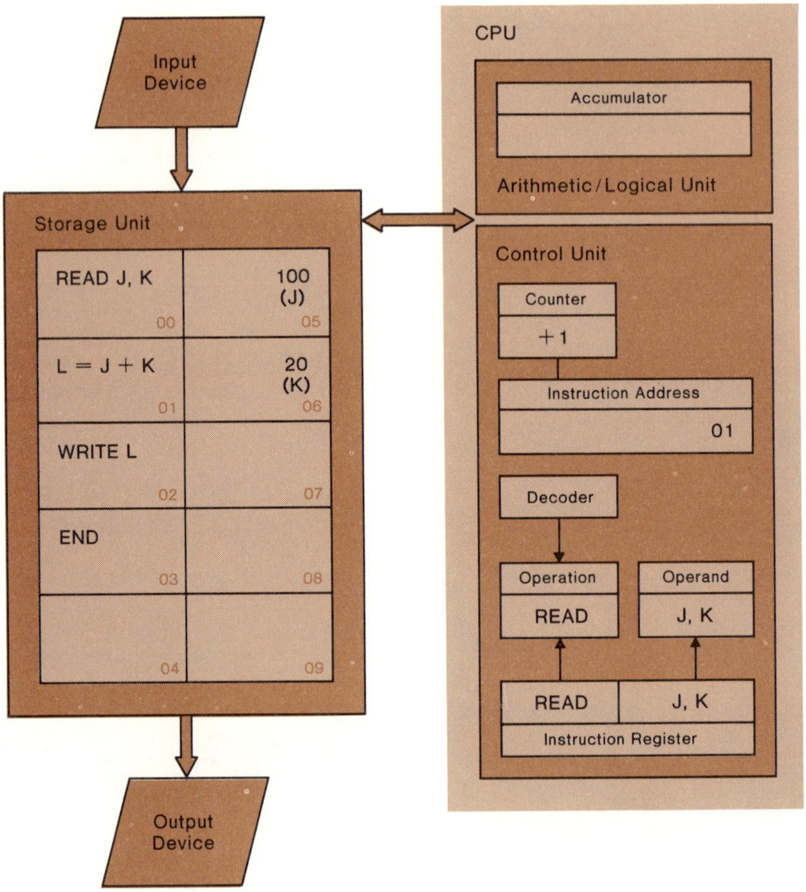

takes place. The instruction (L = J + K) activates the adder in the arithmetic/logical unit. The data in the locations labelled "J" and "K" (addresses 05 and 06, respectively) are moved to the arithmetic unit. Here, addition takes place, resulting in the sum "L" (the actual numbers involved in the addition would be 100 + 20 = 120). The computer's software would assign a storage address for "L" (let us assume address 07), and the sum (120) would be moved from the arithmetic unit to address 07 in storage. Note that the contents of addresses 05 and 06 would not be disturbed by the operations.

Refer to Exhibit 5–17. Next, the instruction in address 02 is brought to the instruction address; then the instruction address register is stepped up by 1. The operation code (WRITE L) and operand are decoded, and the control unit activates the output unit to accept data ("L") from primary storage, and to write it as output. The value 120 will be printed.

Exhibit 5–16 Computing and Storing Results in the CPU

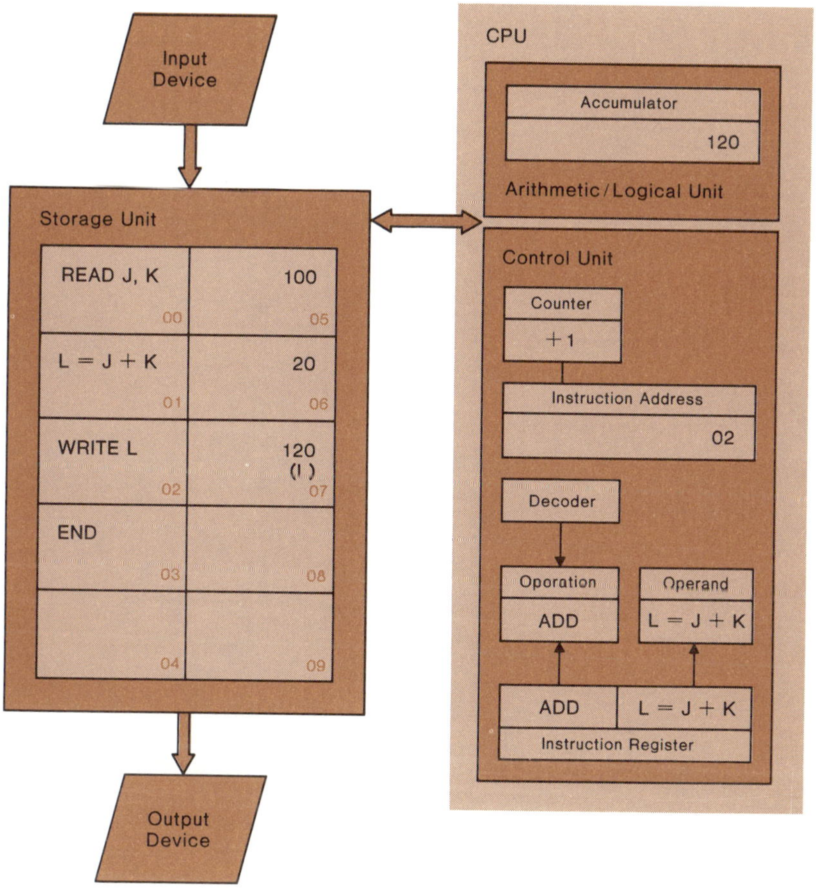

Refer to Exhibit 5–18. When the last instruction (from address 03) is decoded, it will cause the CPU to stop processing for this program. Internally in primary storage, certain information remains stored (the instructions, and the values for "J," "K," and "L"). In order to prevent subsequent data-processing jobs from using information that has been left over from previous jobs, storage and registers can be reset to blank or zero automatically, by means of several methods, before a new application is run on the computer. Also, when new data enter any storage location or register, they automatically electronically erase whatever data remained from prior processing.

Exhibit 5–17 Output of Results

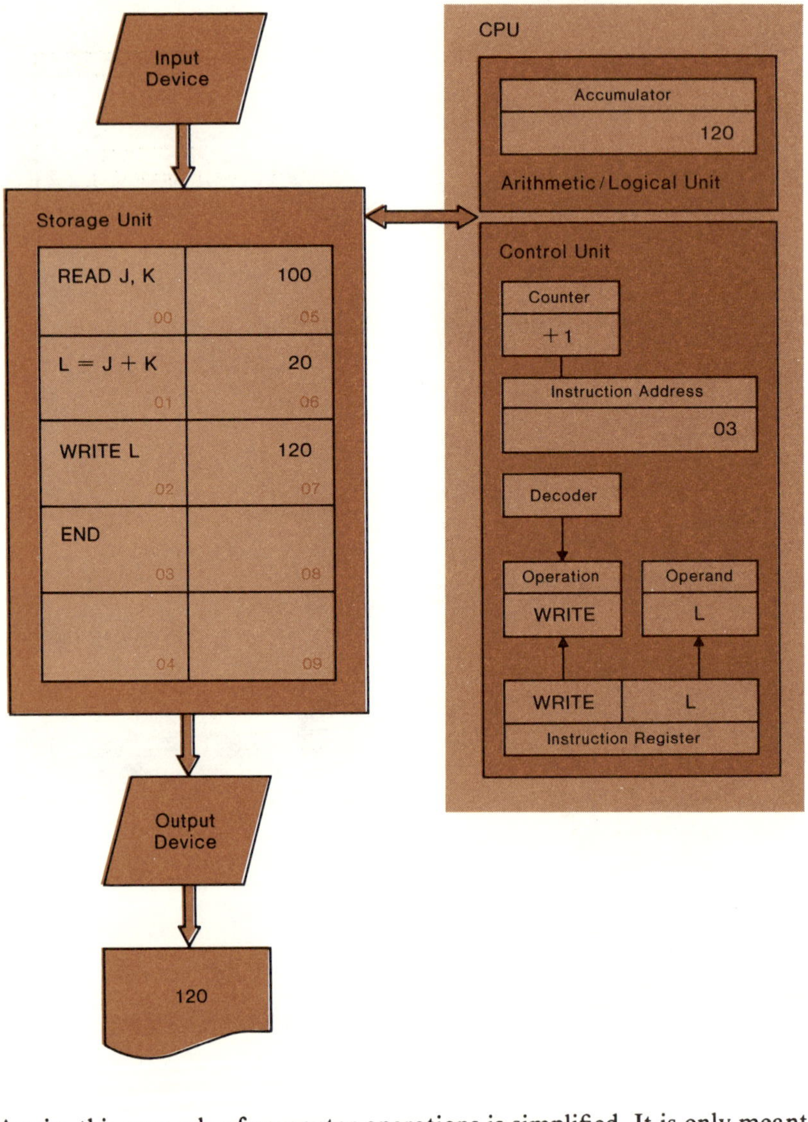

Again, this example of computer operations is simplified. It is only meant to give the reader who lacks a computer background a general appreciation of such operations. In actual computer operations, the applications are much more complex and voluminous, of course, than the trivial, single-computation application presented here. Also, computer operations do not stop after one job is done; rather, as soon as one job is completed, the computer automatically moves on to the next, and so on.

Exhibit 5–18 Halting Computer Operations

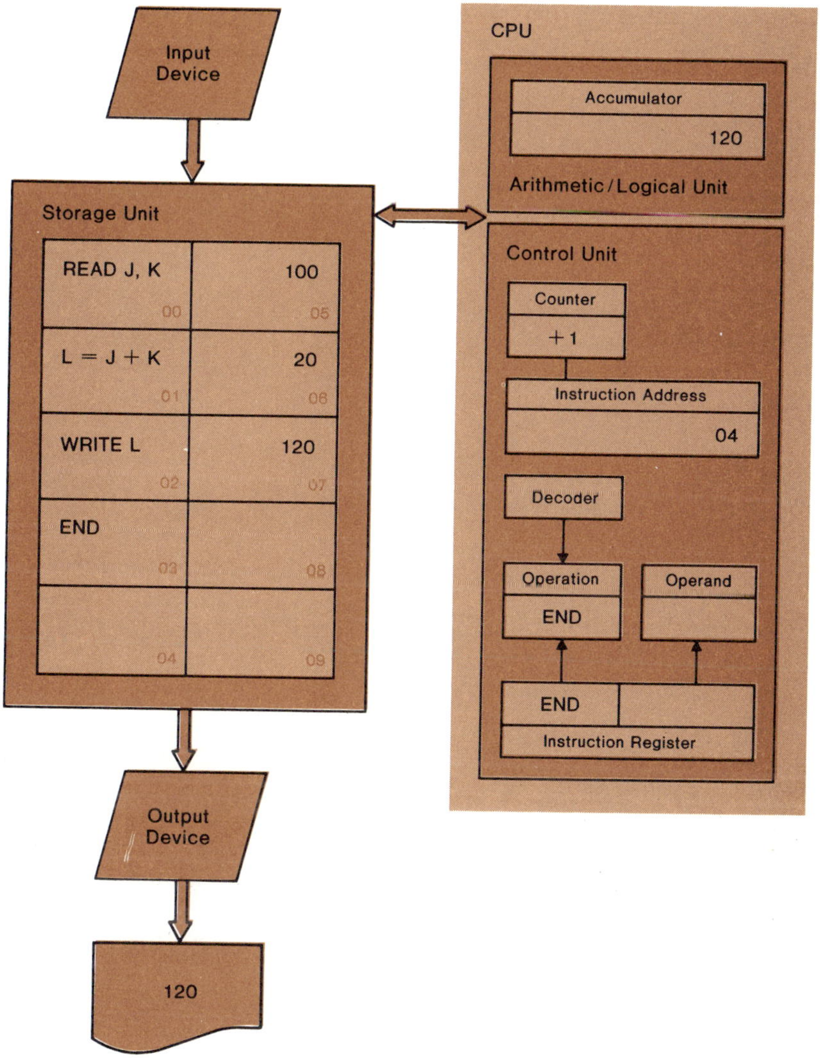

Summary

The CPU must have a program (instructions) and data in primary storage before the computer can produce meaningful results. The CPU operates in a very structured and methodical way. The example given in the previous pages is a purposely simplified abstraction of how the computer actually works.

Terms to Learn

Main frame
Instruction set
Machine cycle
Variable name
Symbolic address
Absolute address
Control unit of CPU
Arithmetic/logic unit
Accumulator
Instruction address register
Instruction register
Register
Counter
Cycle
Instruction cycle
Execution cycle
I-time
E-time
Operation
Opcode
Electronically erase
Cycle time
Read
Calculate
Branch
Move
Write
Terminate
Field

Review Questions

1. What is an *instruction set?* Give examples.
2. Define *machine cycles*, *I-time*, and *E-time*.

3. Give an example of the *operation code* and *operands* of an instruction.
4. In your own words, describe how the computer operates. How does the CPU interpret a *program,* and how does it *process* data?
5. What is in primary storage after the CPU reaches the end of a particular job?

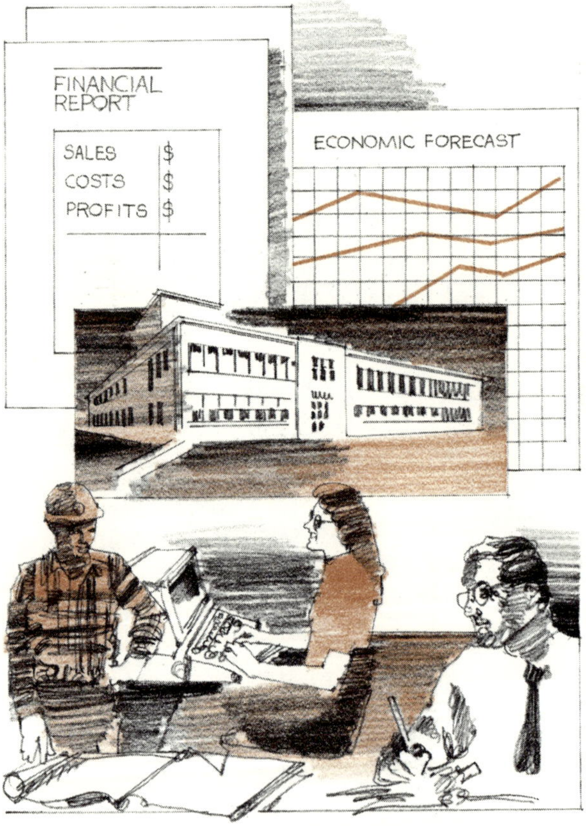
FINANCIAL
REPORT
SALES $
COSTS $
PROFITS $
ECONOMIC FORECAST

CHAPTER 6

INPUT AND OUTPUT MEDIA

Objectives

A considerable amount of data are transported to and from the computer by machine-readable media. Perhaps the most familiar of the media to the layperson is the punched card. Human beings use media to convey their messages to the computer; conversely, the computer sends its messages, for human use, on media. Since media can be considered an important link between people and computers, Chapter 6 will explore input and output media as they relate to human beings.

WHAT ARE RECORDING MEDIA?*

No matter how powerful the computer is, it is useless unless it is fed data and programs. Such input can be communicated to the computer in a number of alternative ways (see Exhibit 6–1):

1. Data (or programs) can be transferred from secondary storage to the computer. This is a very rapid method of getting data to the CPU.
2. Some documents (e.g., checks and many utility bills) are machine-readable and can be sent directly to an on-line input device for feeding to the CPU.
3. If a document is not machine-readable in its native state, an operator can use a typewriter-like keyboard that is connected to the computer and can key in the data that should be transmitted to the CPU. This is known as "direct entry." Since the speed is determined by the person who is keying in the data, it is relatively slow.
4. When documents are not machine-readable, a keying-in process that is off-line to the computer can convert them into machine-readable media (e.g., punched cards). Subsequently, the machine-readable media is forwarded to be read by an input device connected to the CPU.

Communication of data to and from the CPU is accomplished by input and output devices (discussed in Chapter 7) that are cable-connected to the computer's central processing unit. Except when direct-entry keying in is involved, all data-transfer methods use some type of media (e.g., punched cards, magnetic disk, or machine-readable source documents) (see Exhibit 6–2). The media are the substances (paper, cards, or tapes) that physically transport and store the data that are used by the computer.

The media use some type of coding structure, since the computer cannot effec-

* "Media" is the plural; "medium" is the singular. In practice, media is often used for both.

Exhibit 6–1 Alternative Methods of Sending Data to the Computer

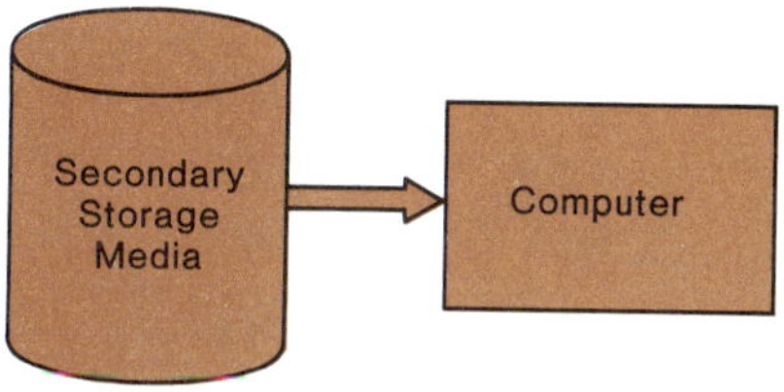

1. Transferring Data From Secondary Storage

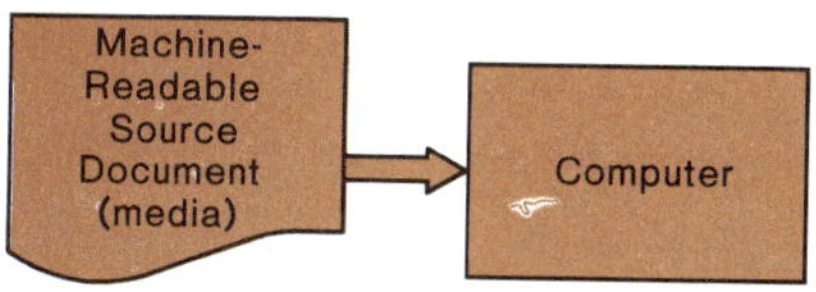

2. Inputting Data From Machine-Readable Source Documents

3. Direct Entry (on-line) Input Via a Keyboard

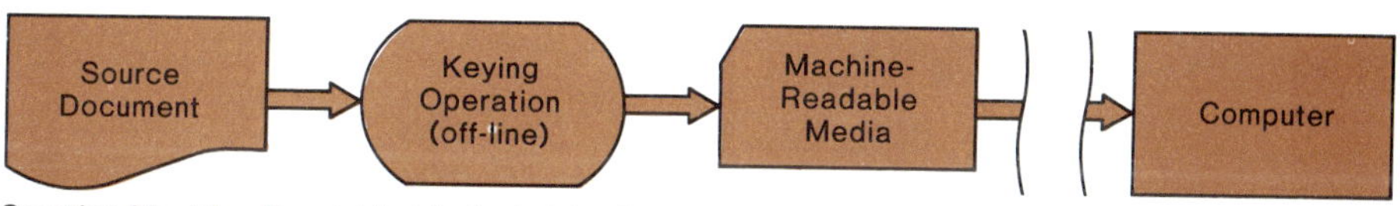

4. Creating Machine-Readable Media (off-line) For Subsequent Inputting to the Computer

tively handle normal methods of communication by human beings. That is, computers do not understand the spoken messages or the handwriting of people. Some limited advances have been made in this area, and a few computer applications exist, in which the computer can handle stylized oral or handwritten messages directly. As we will see, some media use binary-type coding (such as that discussed in Chapter 5) in communicating data to the computer. Some media codes are both readable by the computer and intelligible to humans; other media codes are difficult for humans to understand; while in still other cases they are not even visible to human eyes. The entire purpose of using machine-readable media and codes is to put data messages into a form that can be efficiently communicated to the computer.

The computer's output can occur in a form that can both be read by and useful to people (e.g., a printed report or display on a television-like screen). Or computer

Exhibit 6–2 Some Examples of Data-Recording Media

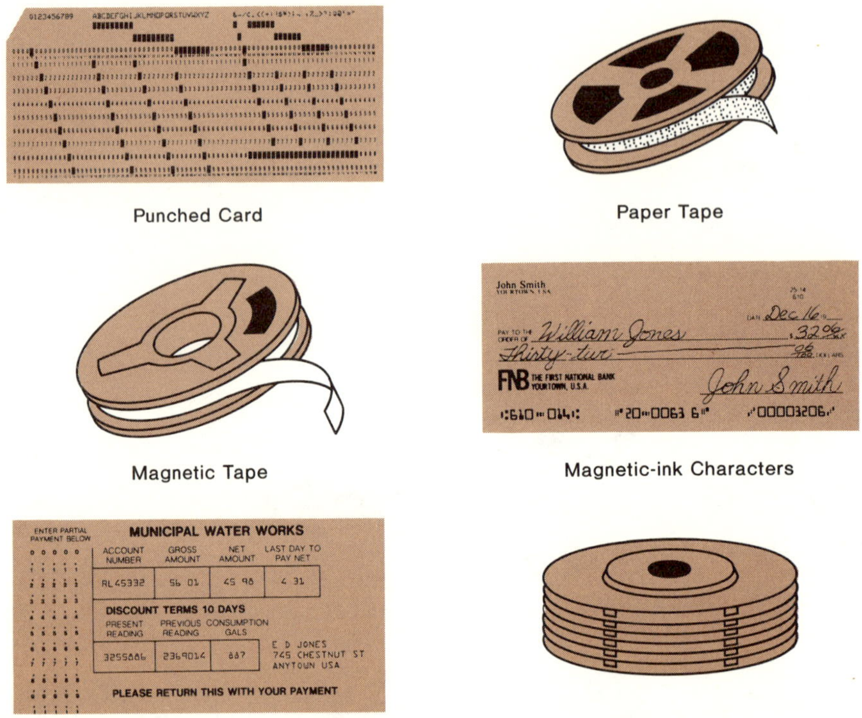

Punched Card

Paper Tape

Magnetic Tape

Magnetic-ink Characters

Optically Readable Characters

Magnetic Disk

output can be in machine-readable form (e.g., magnetic tape), which can be used in subsequent computer processing.

Some of the more frequently used media are discussed now (see also Table 6–1).

PUNCHED-CARD MEDIA

The punched card is one of the most widely used media. It can either carry data as input of the CPU, or record data as output from the CPU.

Eighty-Column Punch Card

Exhibit 6–3 shows a standard punched card.* The card area is divided into eighty columns and twelve rows. On punched cards, a column is a vertical area (from top to

* Punched cards have different sizes and capacities, depending on the machines used and application involved. For instance, one punched card can hold ninety characters of data, whereas the standard card holds a maximum of eighty characters. In addition, a ninety-six-column punched card has been introduced; this is used primarily for small-business computer applications.

Exhibit 6–3 Punched-Card Medium: Eighty-Column Card

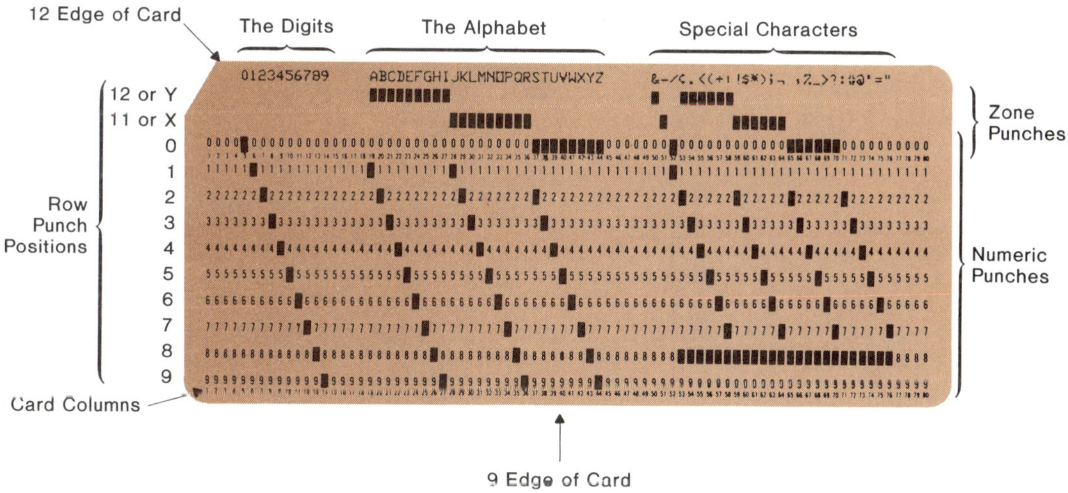

bottom of the card), and a row is a horizontal area. Each row is divided into small areas, called "punching positions," where holes may be punched. In each row there are eighty punching positions in a line.

Table 6–1
Summary of Media

Medium	Comments
Punched card	Low-volume input and output medium, and off-line storage.
Punched-paper tape	Low-volume input and output medium, and used in data transmission.
Magnetic tape	High-volume input and output medium, and large sequential file storage.
Magnetic disk	High-volume input and output medium, and large direct-access file storage.
Magnetic-ink character recognition	Direct reading of source documents as input.
Optical character recognition	Direct reading of source documents as input. Also, possible use of turn-around documents.
Printout	Relatively low-speed output.
Cathode ray tube	Visual display of output. Slow keyboard entry of input data and inquiry capability.
Microfilm	Miniaturization of printout data for improved off-line filing and retrievability.

Exhibit 6–4 Punched-Card Code for Alphabet

Letter	Zone Row Punched		Numeric Row Punched
A	12	and	1
B	12	and	2
C	12	and	3
D	12	and	4
E	12	and	5
F	12	and	6
G	12	and	7
H	12	and	8
I	12	and	9
J	11	and	1
K	11	and	2
L	11	and	3
M	11	and	4
N	11	and	5
O	11	and	6
P	11	and	7
Q	11	and	8
R	11	and	9
S	0	and	2
T	0	and	3
U	0	and	4
V	0	and	5
W	0	and	6
X	0	and	7
Y	0	and	8
Z	0	and	9

Each column on a punched card can be used to represent only one character. A character, of course, is any single number, alphabetic character, or special symbol. The largest number of characters that can be punched in a single card is eighty.

In Exhibit 6–3, the twenty-six letters of the alphabet, the ten numerals, and special symbols have been printed across the top of the punched card. Each character has been printed above the column in which it is punched. For instance, the letter "A" is punched in column 5. The number 9 is punched in column 45.

The coding system shown in Exhibit 6–3 is sometimes called the *punched-card*

Exhibit 6–5 Punched-Card Medium: Ninety-Six-Column Card

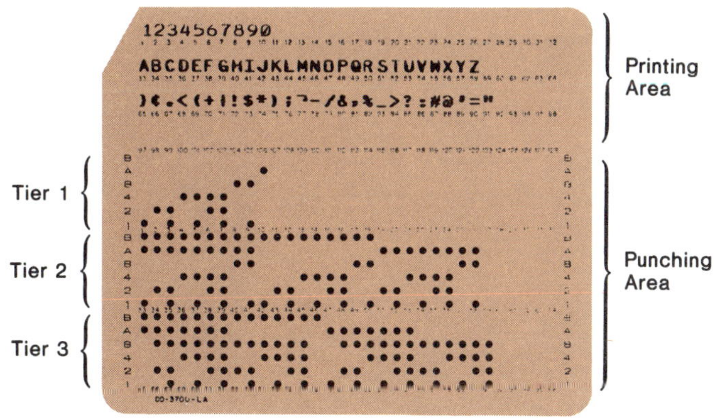

code or *Hollerith code* (after Herman Hollerith, the developer of punched-card machines).

A punched hole is simply called a "punch." The row that contains it is identified by its number. For example, a hole punched in one of the positions in the 12 row is called a "12-punch." A hole punched in one of the positions in the 9 row is called a "9-punch." A 1-punch is a hole punched in one of the positions in the 1 row.

The number of punching positions in a column is the same as the number of rows on the card; each column on a card contains twelve punching positions.

The 0 through 9 rows on a punched card are identified by numbers printed on the punching positions. The 12 and 11 rows do not have numbers printed in the punching positions.

A punch in one of the rows numbered 0 through 9 is called a "numeric punch."

The top three rows of a card are used for zone punches; they are the 12 row, the 11 row, and the 0 row. The 0 row is used for both zone punches and numeric punches, as required.

The punched-card coding system uses one single punch in a column to code a numeric character.

Each alphabetic character is represented by the combination of one zone punch and one numeric punch (see Exhibit 6–4).* The letters A through I are formed by the 12 punch and the digit punches 1 through 9; the letters J through R are formed by the 11 punch and the digit punches 1 through 9; and the letters S through Z are formed by the 0 punch and the digit punches 2 through 9.

When used in the coding for an alphabetic character, a punch in the 0 row is considered a zone punch.

* The code used in punched cards can be called binary. The existence of a hole is equivalent to an "on" condition (binary 1), and the absence of a hole is equivalent to an "off" condition (binary 0). From this perspective, the previous chapter's discussion of the binary system comes into play.

Exhibit 6–6 The Ninety-Six-Column Card in Use

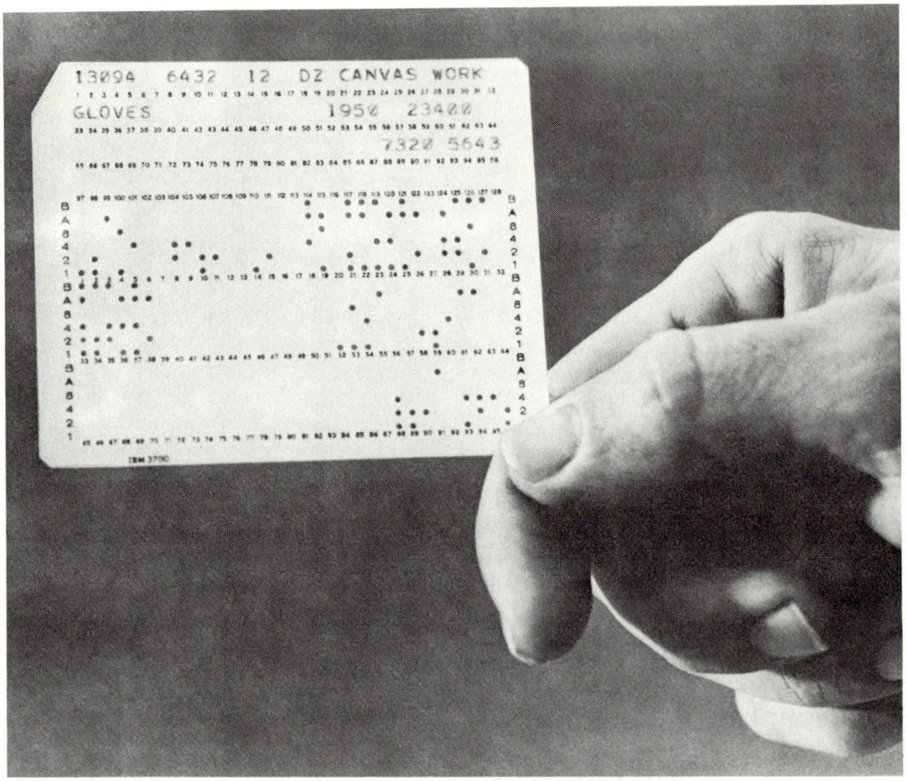

Photograph courtesy of IBM Corporation

Special characters are such characters as ":", ";", ",", "*", "$", "%", etc. Special characters are represented by one punch, two punches, or three punches. For instance, the ampersand (&) is represented by a 12 punch only; the asterisk (*) is represented by an 11, a 4, and an 8 punch. Each different character is represented by a unique combination of one, two, or three punches.

Ninety-Six-Column Punch Card

Exhibits 6–5 and 6–6 show the so-called midget card that is used in one computer manufacturer's smaller computer line. The ninety-six-column card is less than half the size of the standard eighty-column card.

The ninety-six columns are stacked in three tiers, each consisting of thirty-two columns of data. The first tier contains columns 1 through 32; the second tier contains columns 33 through 64; and the third tier contains columns 65 through 96. At the top of the card there is space for four lines (or 128 characters) of printing. In the illustration, the digits 1 through 9 and 0* are punched and printed in columns 1 through 10; the letters of the alphabet are punched and printed in columns 33 through 58; and special characters are punched and printed in columns 65 through 91.

The code structure that is used for the ninety-six-column punched card is 6-bit BCD (binary coded decimal) representation (refer back to Table 5–1 in Chapter 5). For numbers and the alphabet, the code is:

Characters	*Zone Bits*		*Numeric Bits*
	B	*A*	
1 through 9	0	0	0001 through 1001
0	0	1	0000
A through I	1	1	0001 through 1001
J through R	1	0	0001 through 1001
S through Z	0	1	0010 through 1001

Perforations (punched holes) in the ninety-six-column card represent the equivalent of the binary "1;" and an absence of perforations represents the binary "0."

PUNCHED-PAPER-TAPE MEDIA

Paper tape can carry data as input to the CPU, or it can be used to record data that is output from the CPU.

Exhibit 6–7 shows data that have been coded in a strip of eight-channel paper tape. A *channel* is a horizontal area, running lengthwise on the paper tape, which can contain a hole. Characters are represented on paper tape by distinctive patterns of punched holes. For instance, the coding for the character "A" is a pattern of three holes; each of these holes is punched in a different channel. The small holes between the 4 channel and the 8 channel are engaged by a drive sprocket, which moves the tape through a machine. These sprocket holes are not sensed when a character is read.

Besides the eight-channel paper tape, there is a five-channel paper tape (see Exhibit 6–8). This type of paper tape has been used for many years to transmit and receive teletype messages. Since a character is represented by a maximum of five holes, the code used to represent a character is somewhat different from that used by the eight-channel tape. For instance, even though some numbers and letters of the alphabet are represented by identical punch patterns, a machine reading from paper tape can tell the difference by means of a letter/figure/shift code. Any characters following a letter code (all channels punched) are read as letters, while the characters following a figure code (channels 1, 2, 4, and 5 punched) are read as numerals or special characters.

* The zero (0) is recorded on the ninety-six-column card as 01 0000; but in the BCD representation for the CPU (as presented in Chapter 5), it is recorded as 00 1010. This is the lone difference between the code used for the ninety-six-column card and the listing shown in Table 5–1 (Chapter 5).

Exhibit 6–7 Punched-Paper Tape (Eight Channels)

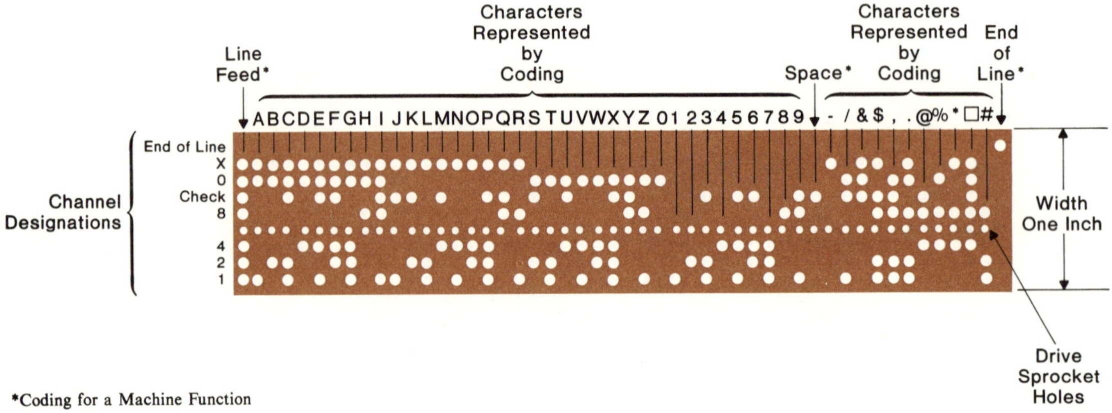

*Coding for a Machine Function

Many years ago, the five-channel paper tape originally was developed so that telegraph wire circuits could transmit messages. Today, it is still used for this purpose: both five-channel paper tape and eight-channel paper tape are used to transmit data from remote locations to computer facilities.

Paper tape is a continuous medium (i.e., a string of data records on a continuous reel of paper tape), in contrast to a discontinuous medium, such as punched cards.

MAGNETIC-TAPE MEDIA

Magnetic tape* consists of plastic material, one side of which is covered with a magnetic coating (see Exhibit 6–9). The tape is similar to that used on a conventional tape recorder. A widely used standard for computer magnetic tape is ½ inch wide and 2,400 feet long. Magnetic tape can carry data as input to the CPU, or it can be used to record data that is output from the CPU. Magnetic media like magnetic tape have advantages over other types of media (e.g., punched cards). For instance, magnetic tape is reusable. When data on a tape are no longer needed, new data can be recorded over the old; the new data recordings automatically erase and replace the old data. Of course, the physical perforations in punched cards or paper tape cause the media to be unusable once the punched data have outlived their usefulness.

Small spots on the tape, located in the magnetic coating, can be individually magnetized (see Exhibit 6–10). A bit is a magnetized spot on magnetic tape, and the word "bit" is a contraction of the words "*bi*nary digi*t*."

* All magnetic storage has the features mentioned in Chapter 5: nondestructive read-out and destructive read-in.

Exhibit 6–8 Punched-Paper Tape (Five Channels)

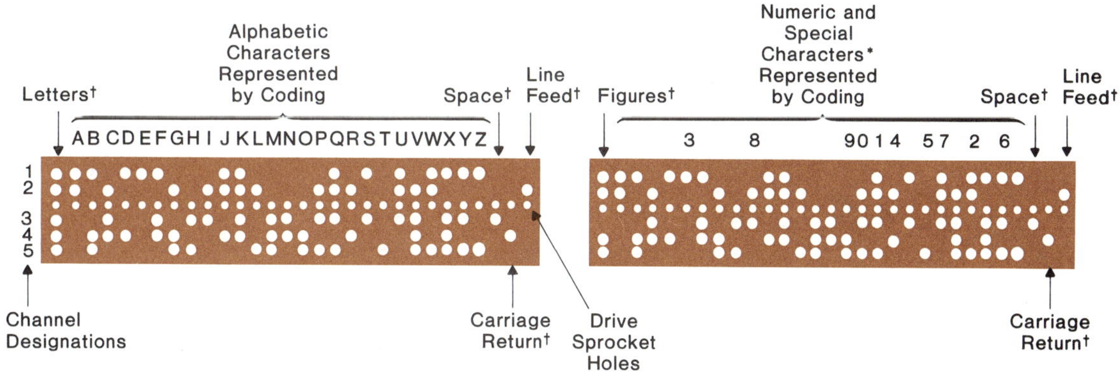

*The unlabeled punch patterns on the strip at the right are used to cope special characters or functions as required.

†Coding for Machine Functions

For illustration purposes, Exhibit 6–10 shows the bits on magnetic tape as small black circles. However, bits are not visible on the actual tape. Just by looking at a piece of magnetic tape, you cannot tell whether bits have been recorded on it. If a bit has not been recorded in a particular spot of magnetic tape, this means that the particular spot has not been magnetized.

Bits are arranged on magnetic tape in columns and tracks similar to the columns and rows of a punched card. A *column* goes across the width of the tape, while a *track* goes along its length. Thus, each track (sometimes called a channel) runs from one end of a reel of tape to the other end.

Several types of magnetic tape are in use. The two most widely used tapes have either seven tracks or nine tracks. Exhibit 6–10 shows an example of a seven-track tape. The coding structure is that of BCD representation (see Table 5–1 in Chapter 5),

Exhibit 6–9 Magnetic-Tape Medium

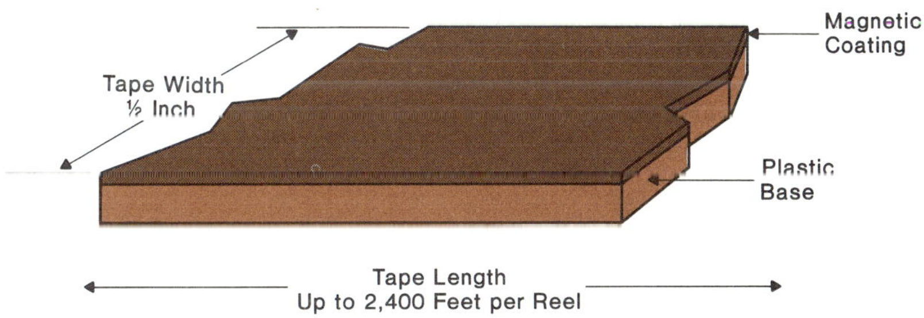

Exhibit 6–10 A Comparison of Seven-Track and Nine-Track Tape

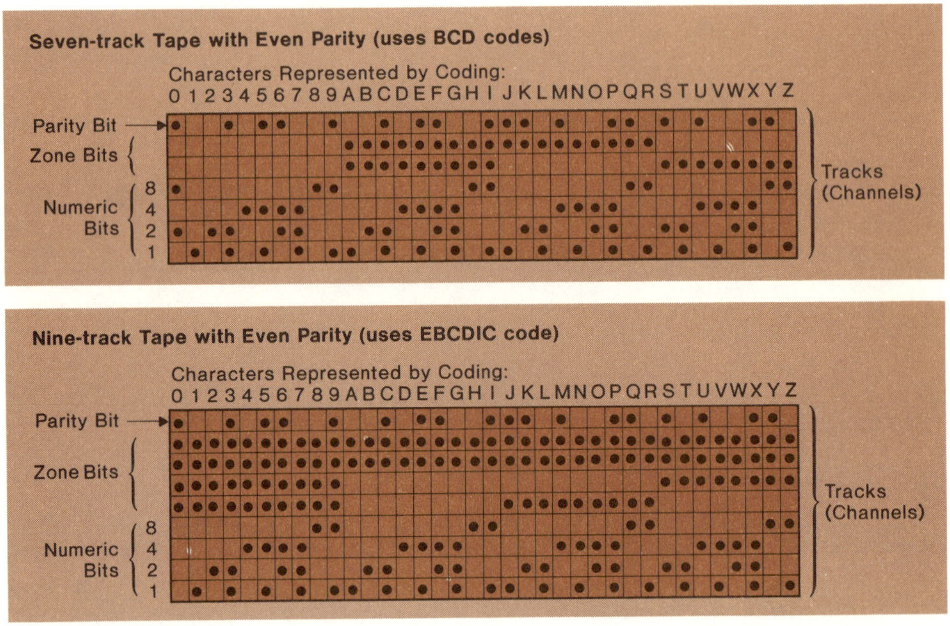

Note: The channels of the nine track tape are actually arranged somewhat differently from the above version, which is presented only for better understanding.

which is also used in recording data on the ninety-six-column punched card. However, there is one difference: the magnetic tape has a channel for checking parity. The parity-check bit (discussed in Chapter 5 in relation to computer storage) ensures that a bit won't erroneously be added or dropped during processing.*

The nine-track magnetic tape (see Exhibit 6–10) uses the coding structure of EBCDIC. As mentioned in Chapter 5, EBCDIC has eight bits for each character, plus a ninth bit for parity-checking purposes.

Exhibit 6–11 shows the actual arrangement of the channels for nine-track tape. The computer manufacturers decided on the repositioning to increase the reliability of the tape. The most frequently used channels are located near the center of the tape; the less frequently used channels are located along the outer part of the tape. This arrangement is helpful, because tiny debris fragments and microscopic cracks—which can create unwanted noise on the tape—occur most frequently along the tape's outer edges. In the illustration, the word "cat" is depicted in conventional EBCDIC code, along with how it would appear on the repositioned channels of a nine-track tape.

* The magnetic tape illustrated uses odd-parity checking, which is consistent with our discussion in Chapter 5. However, some systems employ even-parity checking.

Exhibit 6–11 Actual Channel Arrangement of Nine-Track Tape

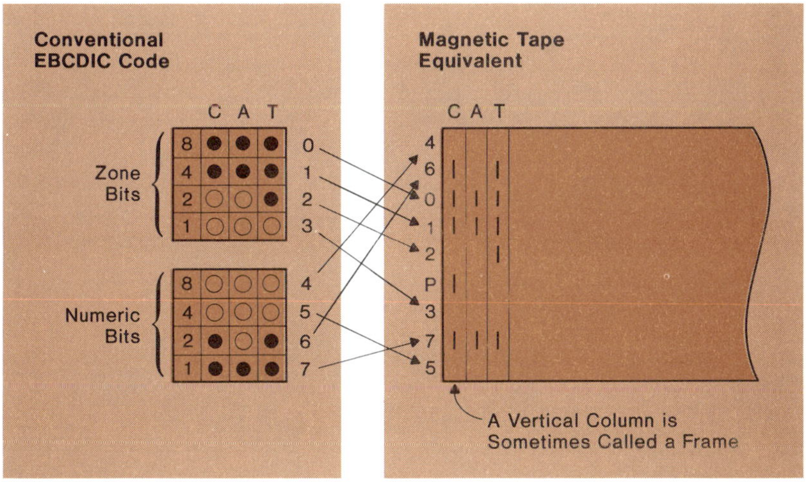

Magnetic tape is a continuous medium (therefore similar to punched-paper tape) that is held either on magnetic-tape reels or in tape cassettes or cartridges (see Exhibits 6–12 and 6–13).

Data are recorded on magnetic tape at different recording densities, depending on the specific computer and magnetic-tape device being used. Among the more frequently used densities (in characters per inch) are 200, 556, 800, and 1600. Recently, a density of 6,250 characters per inch was announced. The following calculation is used to figure the maximum capacity of a reel of tape: length of the tape multiplied by the density. Assume a standard tape of 2,400 feet and a recording density of 800 characters per inch. The tape's maximum capacity would be 23,040,000 characters of data (2,400 feet times 12 inches times 800 characters per inch). This is roughly equivalent to the amount of data that can be recorded on 300,000 fully punched cards. A reel of tape can be carried in one's hands; 300,000 punched cards would have to be moved by a pickup truck!*

Because writing automatically destroys any previous data on magnetic tape, a file-protection device is used to prevent accidental erasure of data (see Exhibit 6–14). This device is a plastic ring that fits into a round groove that is molded in the tape reel. When the ring is in place, either reading or writing can occur.† When the ring is removed, writing is suppressed; only reading can take place. Therefore, the ring is removed whenever tapes are to be saved for future reference or use.

* In actual practice, a tape's capacity is reduced by gaps that must be left between records. This situation will be discussed in Chapter 8.

† In the computer field there is the saying, "no ring—no write."

Exhibit 6–12 Reel of Magnetic Tape

Photograph courtesy of IBM Corporation

Exhibit 6–13 Magnetic-Tape Cartridge

Photograph courtesy of IBM Corporation

Exhibit 6–14 Magnetic Tape File-Protection Device

MAGNETIC-DISK MEDIA

The magnetic disk resembles a phonograph record in appearance; it is metal-coated and can retain magnetic recordings that represent data. Each disk has a number of tracks on its surface (in some cases, both upper and lower surfaces are used). Exhibit 6–15 shows a disk surface with 200 tracks, although some disks have fewer or more tracks. Notice that tracks are identified from 000 (for the outermost track) to 199 (for the innermost track). Some disks' surfaces are segmented into sectors that are individually addressable. A sector usually contains one record or one unit of data.

Data are recorded on a magnetic disk in the form of magnetized spots on the tracks (see Exhibit 6–16). The recording resembles magnetic tape. The nondestructive read-out feature and destructive read-in feature of magnetized storage also apply to magnetic disks.

A variety of disks are available. Some disks are permanently affixed to the magnetic-disk device and cannot be removed. Others (disk packs) not only are removable from the magnetic-disk device (see Exhibit 6–17) but also can be replaced by another disk pack. Depending on the manufacturer and model, there is also some variation as to the data-recording densities, number of tracks, and number of disks for any particular magnetic-disk device.

Demand for low-cost, direct-access storage has given rise to the so-called floppy disk or diskette (see Exhibit 6–18), which is like a phonograph record enclosed in a plastic jacket. The floppy disk has found particular application with minicomputers and data-entry processing.

To get a feeling for a disk unit's capacity to store data,* let's now consider a widely used magnetic-disk unit. This particular unit has 6 disks, with 12 recording surfaces; however, the upper surface of the top disk and the lower surface of the bottom

* As with magnetic tape, the disk's capacity is reduced by necessary space gaps. This will be discussed in Chapter 8.

Exhibit 6–15 Example of a Magnetic-Disk Surface

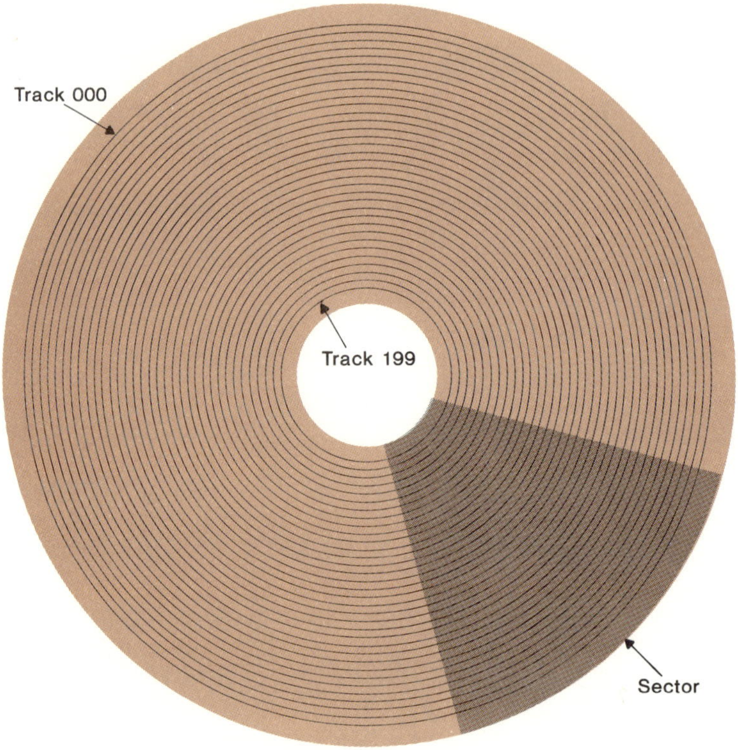

disk are not used for data (since they can be scratched). Each of the 10 surfaces has 200 tracks. Each track can hold 3,625 characters.* Thus, the entire disk unit can hold a total of 7,250,000 characters (10 disk surfaces times 200 tracks times 3,625). Other disk units can hold several hundreds of millions of characters. But generally, although the disk can hold a large amount of data, it is not quite as compact as magnetic tape.

DOCUMENT MEDIA

Two major types of media permit humans and machines to read data: documents printed in magnetic ink, and documents printed with optical characters.

* Although the tracks get smaller as they get closer to the center of the disk, each track holds the same amount of data because the density of recording is greater on the tracks near the center.

Exhibit 6–16 EBCDIC Coded Data on Magnetic Disk

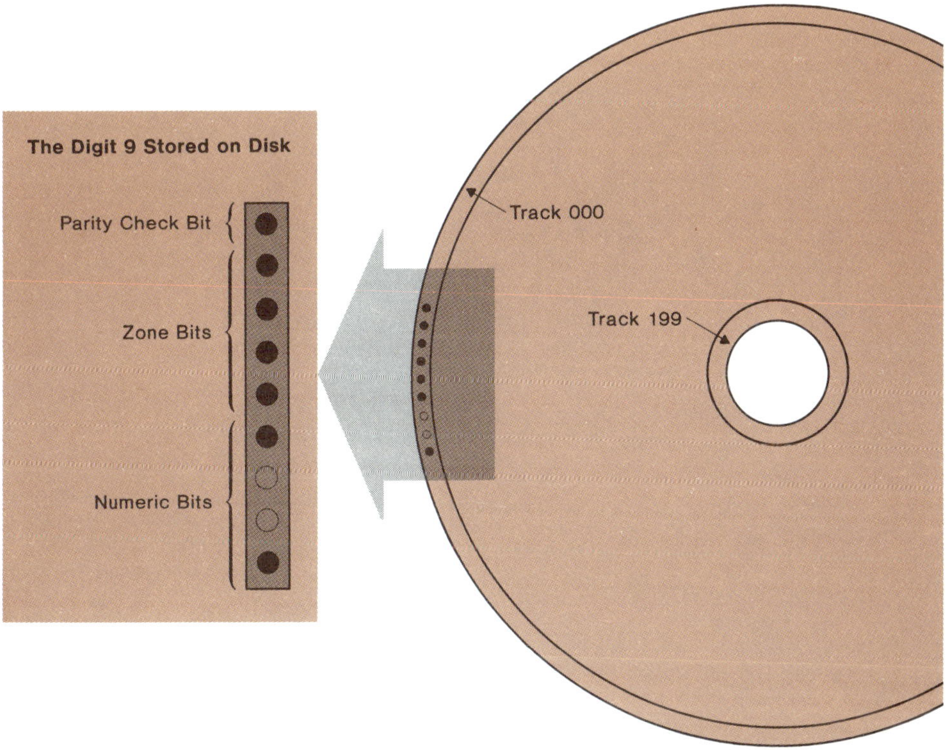

Magnetic-Ink Character Recognition (MICR)

MICR is based on data that are recorded in stylized print form with special magnetized ink, so that machines can process the recordings. This method is primarily used in the banking industry, and most checks are now processed under the MICR approach. The data printed across the bottom of a bank check are recorded in MICR form; the characters represent the bank on which the check is drawn, the customer's account number and the dollar amount of the check. Only numbers and special characters are used in the MICR character set (see Exhibit 6–19).

The checks themselves are prepared off-line. When they are originally printed by a printing press, the MICR about the bank identification number, as well as the data

Exhibit 6–17 Magnetic-Disk Pack

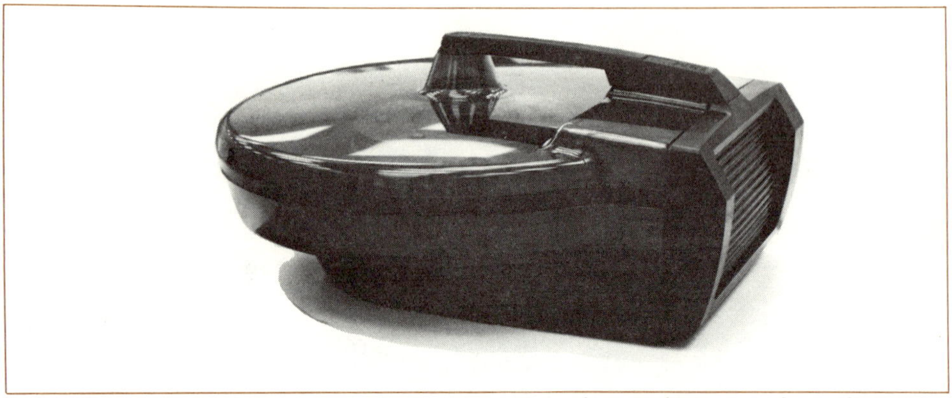

Photograph courtesy of IBM Corporation

Exhibit 6–18 Floppy Disk (Diskette)

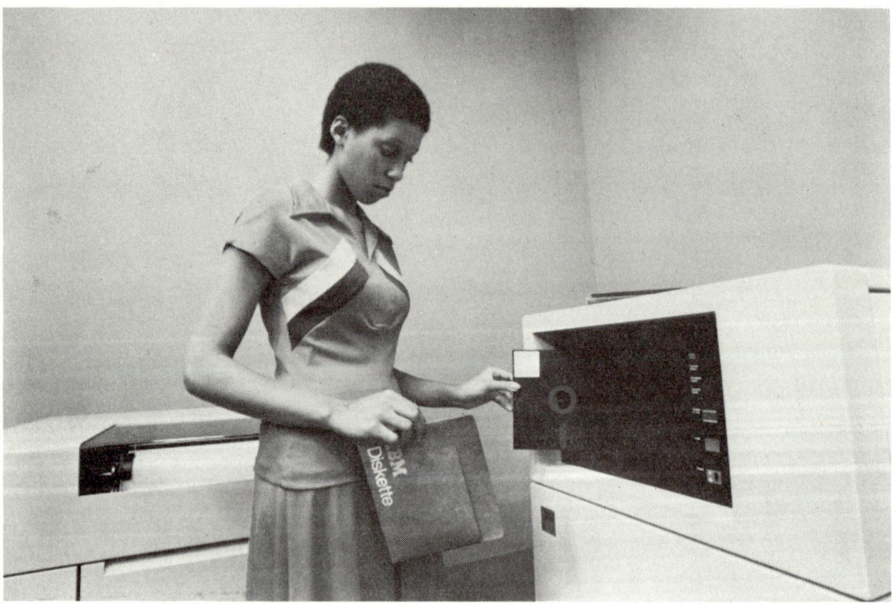

Photograph courtesy of IBM Corporation

Exhibit 6–19 Magnetic-Ink Character Set

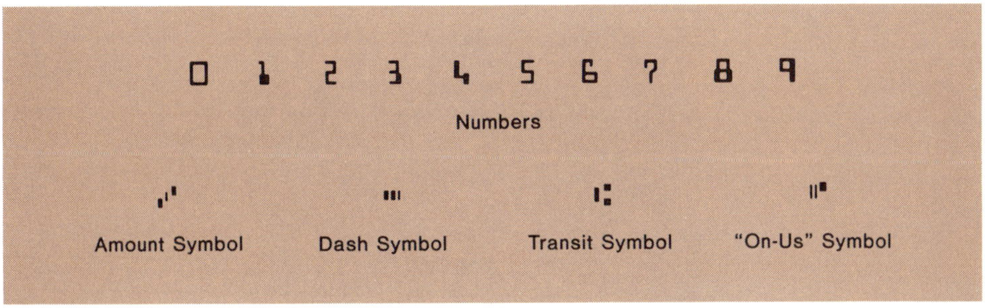

Exhibit 6–20 Sample Check with MICR Encoding

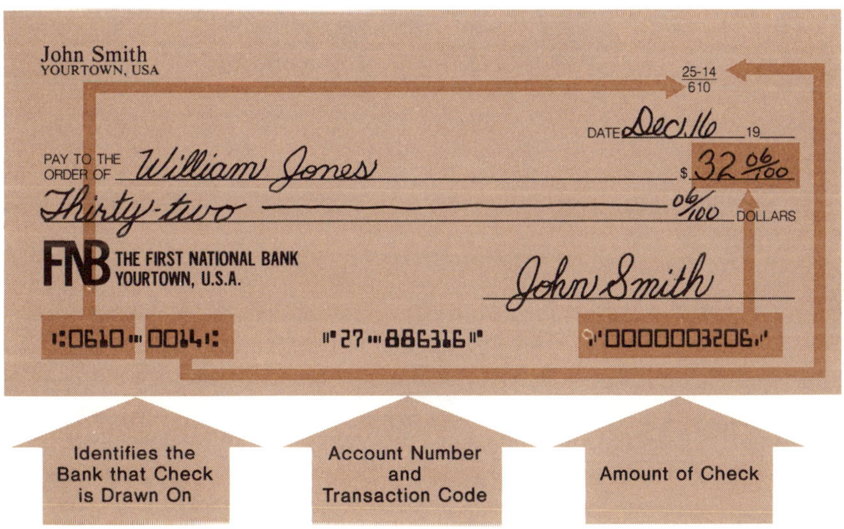

about the customer's bank account number, are printed simultaneously (see Exhibit 6–20). The checks then are turned over to the proper bank customer for use. Once the checks have been cashed or deposited in a bank, an operator uses an off-line encoding machine to encode, in magnetic ink, the dollar amount on the check's bottom-right side.

MICR data are used for input purposes. Unlike other media (e.g., punched cards and magnetic tape), MICR cannot be used for output purposes.

Exhibit 6–21 OCR Character Set

Optical Character Recognition (OCR)

OCR is a process in which printed documents are scanned by photoelectric methods; the pattern of light reflected from the document reveals to the machine the specific characters that are recorded. OCR recording is done with ordinary ink or pencil, in contrast to the special magnetized ink that MICR requires. Also, the OCR characters have a somewhat different configuration than the MICR characters do. Alphabetic, numeric, and special characters can be printed in the OCR character set (see Exhibit 6–21).

Large-volume billing applications (e.g., the bills of utility companies [see Exhibit 6–22], credit-card organizations, and magazine subscription outfits) increasingly are being adapted to OCR methods. The customer paying the bill returns the bill, which has OCR data (e.g., customer number and dollar amount of the bill) recorded on it, along with payment. Thus, the billing organization's bill (or the part returned by the customer) becomes input for recording cash payments received from the customer. This procedure, sometimes referred to as the use of "turn-around documents," has the advantage of minimizing or eliminating the keying process when cash receipts are received from customers.

Exhibit 6–22 Sample Utility Bill with OCR Data

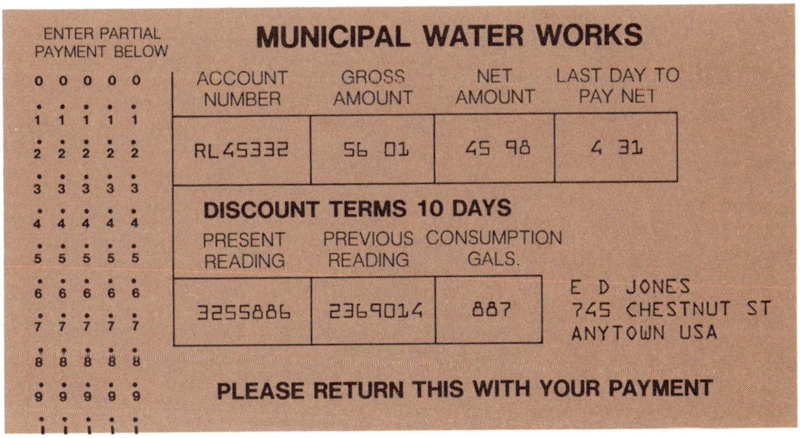
ENTER PARTIAL PAYMENT BELOW

0 0 0 0 0
1 1 1 1 1
2 2 2 2 2
3 3 3 3 3
4 4 4 4 4
5 5 5 5 5
6 6 6 6 6
7 7 7 7 7
8 8 8 8 8
9 9 9 9 9

MUNICIPAL WATER WORKS

ACCOUNT NUMBER	GROSS AMOUNT	NET AMOUNT	LAST DAY TO PAY NET
RL45332	56 01	45 98	4 31

DISCOUNT TERMS 10 DAYS

PRESENT READING	PREVIOUS READING	CONSUMPTION GALS.
3255886	2369014	887

E D JONES
745 CHESTNUT ST
ANYTOWN USA

PLEASE RETURN THIS WITH YOUR PAYMENT

OCR is also employed in the area of test scoring (see Exhibit 6–23).* It is particularly suited for recording answers to multiple-choice and true-or-false types of questions. The individual taking the test merely marks the appropriate boxes in pencil on the examination form to indicate the selected answer. Thereafter, a machine can automatically determine the number of correct answers by sensing whether the pencil markings are in the proper locations.

OCR characters can be sent as input to the CPU. Also, printers can be used to generate OCR output.

PRINTED MEDIA

Almost every data-processing application requires certain processed data to be available in the form of conventional printed output that people can use (see Exhibit 6–24). The output device that produces the printed medium is known as a "printer." It is similar to a very rapid typewriter.

The standard punched card can contain a maximum of 80 characters of data. The most frequently used printers can have 132 characters (including blanks) on each line (although some printers can only print 100 characters per line, while others can print 144 or more characters per line).

Printed output are sometimes referred to as *continuous forms*, since they usually

* This process is sometimes referred to as "mark sense recording."

Exhibit 6–23 A Test Score Sheet with Optical Marks

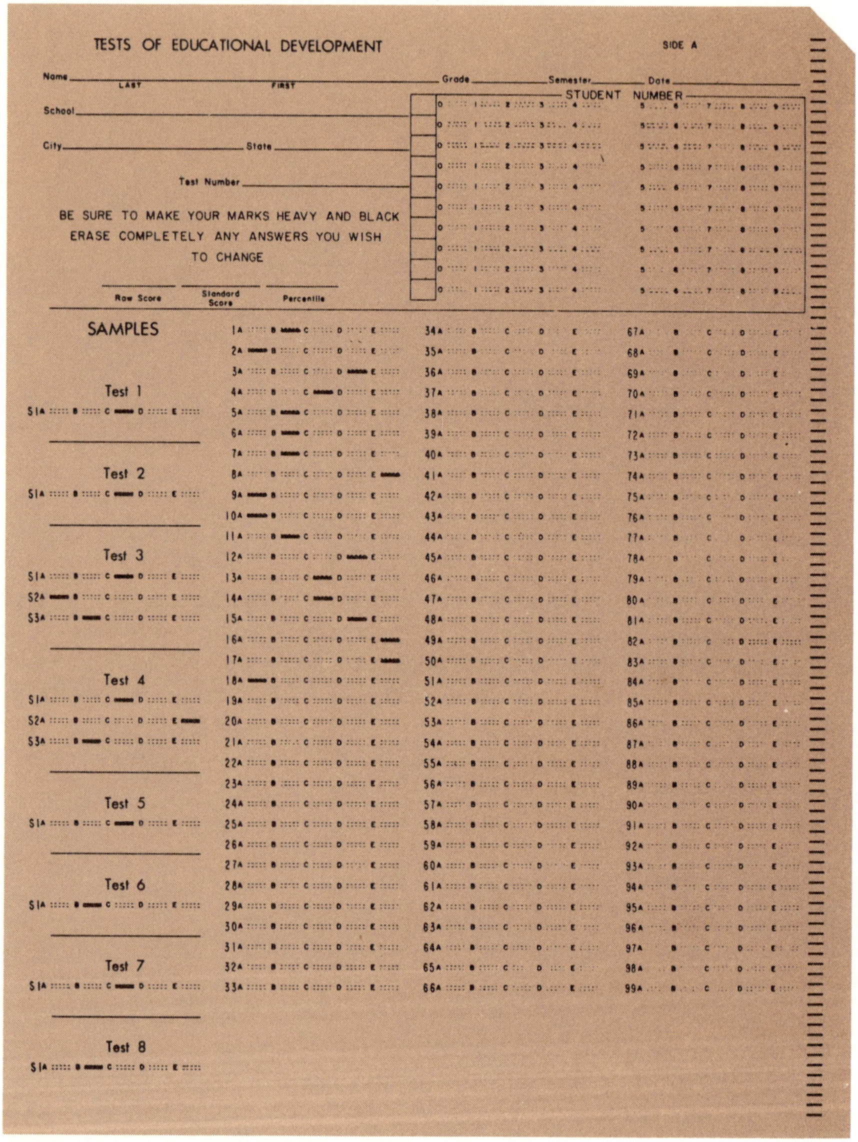

are connected, separated only by perforations (see Exhibit 6–25). These forms are fed into the printer as one continuous form to maintain maximum printing speeds and so that forms do not require constant alignment.

Exhibit 6–24 Simplified View of Typical Printed Medium

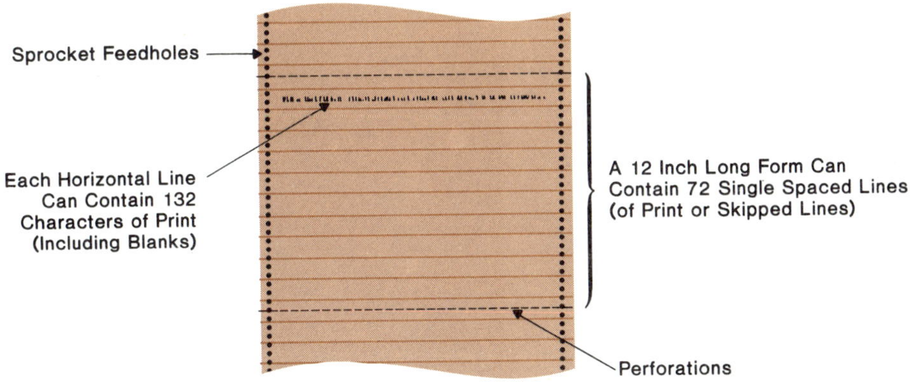

Standard continuous forms are available with up to five-part paper (original plus four carbon copies). Most standard stock continuous forms are twelve inches long. Since usually six lines of data are printed per inch, most continuous forms may contain up to seventy-two lines of data. However, because of top and bottom margins, and because many printouts utilize double or even triple spacing, most printed output have fewer than seventy-two lines of data.

Printed media may be on plain lined or unlined sheets, or on special preprinted forms (e.g., on the continuous forms, an organization's logo normally is preprinted by a printing press).

While most computer printers use continuous forms, there are printers that will handle printing on cut forms (that is, discontinuous forms).

The printer can print OCR characters* as well as conventional type. The advantage of OCR characters is that the printed output can be used as subsequent input in further processing steps.

CATHODE-RAY-TUBE (CRT) MEDIA

Visual display devices permit the computer user to view a cathode ray tube (CRT) (similar to a television screen) in order to see data that otherwise would be printed on paper. The CRT (see Exhibit 6–26) can also present other visual material, such as tables, charts, and graphs. Up to about 2,000 characters of data can be displayed on a screen at any one time.

* While printed output can be in OCR characters, printed output cannot be in MICR characters. MICR characters require very precise tolerances, which are not readily available on printers connected to computers. All MICR printing takes place off-line on printing presses and encoders.

Exhibit 6–25 Continuous Printed Forms

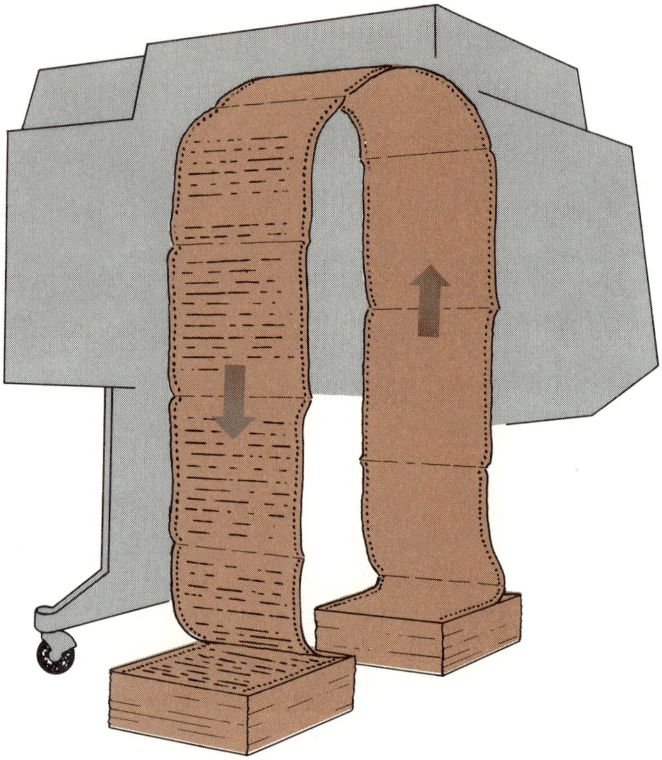

Some CRTs have an optional printout feature. The CRT user who wants something that appears on the screen to be available in printed form can make use of this printout feature.

MICROFILM MEDIA

Microfilm—a miniature photographed record or document—has been in existence for many years as a noncomputerized storage medium. In recent years, the computer field has recognized the virtues of microfilm, especially its particular applicability in situations where great volumes of printed output must be kept in files. Replacing printed output with microfilm allows a considerable compaction of storage requirements, and an easier search through the records for particular data. Micro-image forms tend to be reduced from their original size by 1/24 to 1/42. The microfilm recording may either be on rolled film on reels, or on cards containing individual microfilm

Exhibit 6–26 Cathode-Ray-Tube Display

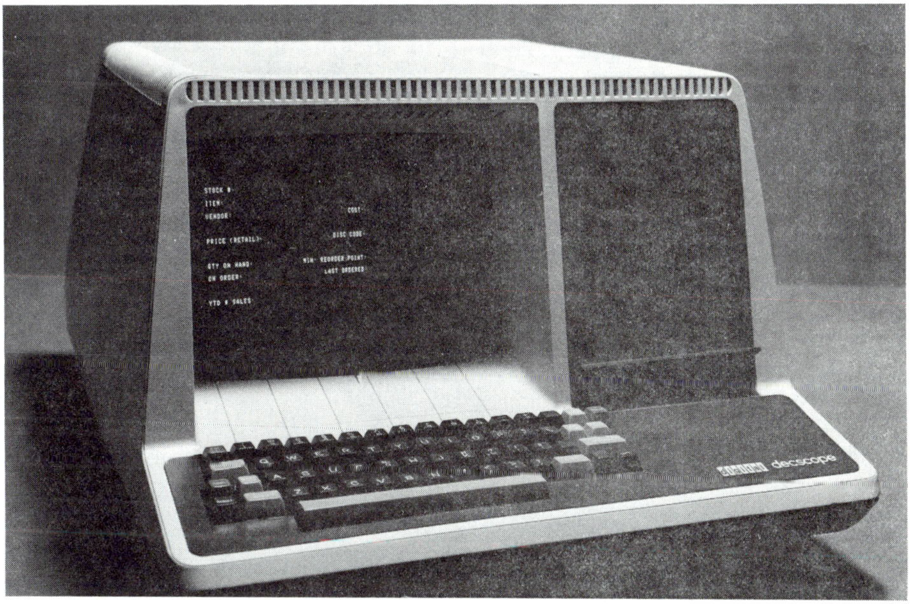

Photograph courtesy of Digital Equipment Corporation

records. Certain microfilm systems also allow such data records to be searched by computer; in such cases, the microfilm can also be used as input.

Summary

Media are the substances that carry data to and from the computer. The data on media are read by the input devices or secondary storage devices that send the data to the CPU. The CPU transmits data to output devices or secondary-storage devices that record the data on media.

There is a variety of media. The specific medium used depends on such factors as: the capability of the specific computer used; the input/outout devices and secondary-storage devices available; and the nature of the computer application to be processed.

Some media, such as magnetic tape, can handle large volumes of data quickly and efficiently. Others, such as punched cards, are not as suitable for handling large volumes of data. Still others, such as MICR, have relatively restricted applications (MICR applies primarily within the banking industry, for check-processing).

The various types of media use different coding patterns and formats.

Terms to Learn

Media
Medium
Machine-readable
Punched card
Hollerith code
Punched-card row
Punched-card column
Zone-punching position
Numeric-punching position
Punched-paper tape
Channel
Magnetic tape
Density
Track
Reel
Cartridge
Cassette
Tape ring
Storage protection
Magnetic disk
Disk pack
Diskette
Floppy disk
Sector
Magnetic-ink character recognition (MICR)
Optical character recognition (OCR)
Continuous form
Cathode ray tube (CRT)
Microfilm

Review Questions

1. Define *media,* and identify some specific examples.
2. Why are *machine-readable* media so important?
3. Describe how data are recorded on an eighty-column punched card. How would your year of birth be recorded in the card? How would your first name be recorded in the card? Describe how the same data would be recorded on the ninety-six-column punched card.
4. How does *punched-paper tape* differ from *punched cards?*
5. Describe *magnetic tape.* Contrast seven-track and nine-track tape.
6. Why is magnetic tape preferable to punched cards for large-volume data files?
7. What is nondestructive read-out and destructive read-in?
8. How are data coded on magnetic tape? What relationship does the code pattern have to the binary system?
9. Describe a *magnetic disk.* How does it differ from magnetic tape?
10. Describe a *magnetic-ink character-recognition document.* What is the main use of MICR?
11. Describe an *optical character-recognition document.* Identify several uses of OCR.
12. How does MICR differ from OCR?

13. Describe *computer-printed media,* and some of the standards that apply. What are *continuous forms?*
14. How is the *cathode ray tube* superior to printed media? What are its limitations, compared with the printed media?
15. What are *microfilm media,* and how might they be helpful in an office with extensive files for clerical use?

A.D.A. CORPORATION
SALES
ECONOMY
COSTS
PROFITS
© Information Resources

CHAPTER 7

INPUT AND OUTPUT DEVICES

Objectives

This chapter presents a survey of the various input and output hardware that communicate to and from the CPU. It also discusses the interface of the I/O devices with the functions of the CPU.

The material is presented under the following topics:
Topic 1—Interface of CPU and I/O Devices.
Topic 2--Description of Peripherals.
Topic 3—Other Devices.

TOPIC 1—INTERFACE OF CPU AND I/O DEVICES

WHAT ARE INPUT AND OUTPUT DEVICES?

Definition of Input and Output Devices*

As Chapter 6 mentioned, all data going to the computer's CPU come from input devices or secondary-storage devices, and all data coming from the computer's CPU are directed to output devices or secondary-storage devices. Simply, then, an *input* device is a piece of equipment that sends data messages to the computer's CPU, and an *output* device is a piece of equipment that receives data and information messages from the computer's CPU (see Exhibit 7–1).

It is important to distinguish between the input and output devices discussed here, and the input and output media discussed in Chapter 6. *Media* (e.g., punched cards and magnetic tape) are the substances on which data are physically recorded. The input *devices* can read the data recorded on the media and can send electrical signals that represent the data to the CPU. The output devices receive electrical signals from the CPU and record (or write) appropriate messages on media. Equipment that is also classified as secondary storage (e.g., magnetic-tape devices) fulfills input and output functions, in addition to the storage function.

There is a wide variety of input and output devices (see Table 7–1). Some are strictly input devices; some are strictly output devices; and others can serve as either input or output devices. Still other I/O devices can function as on-line secondary-storage devices (supplementing primary storage).

Most input and output devices have indicator lights as well as operating keys and switches. These lights show a unit's status: "on," "off," "ready," "selected," and so on.

* In addition to the traditional computer manufacturers (e.g., IBM and Honeywell), many other organizations concentrate on manufacture and marketing peripherals (i.e., input and output devices). Some of these organizations are: Mohawk Data Sciences; MSI Data; Computing Machinery; Inforex; and Datapoint.

The lights help the operator see the status of each piece of equipment visually. The operator uses the operating keys and switches primarily to start and stop data-processing operations manually (on-line devices can also be activated or halted by stored program instructions). The specific functions and uses of the various indicator lights, keys, and switches are explained in the operations manuals that the manufacturers of the respective devices supply.

Exhibit 7–1 Some Examples of Input and Output Devices

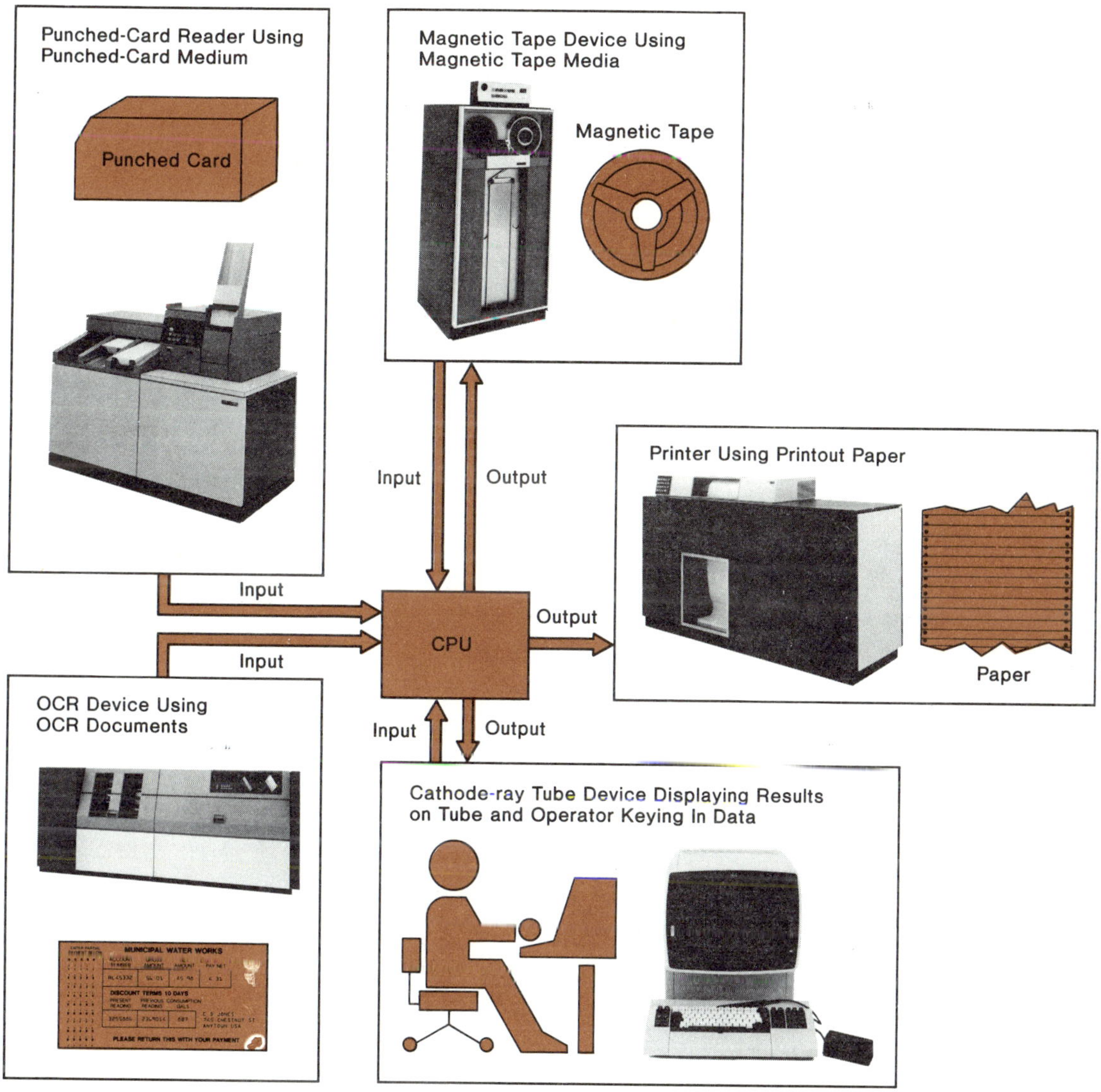

How the I/O Devices Work

Most input/output devices are automatic: once started, they continue to operate until some positive indicator stops their operation. Instructions in the stored program select the required device; direct it to read or write; indicate the storage location into which data will be entered or from which data will be taken; and indicate when processing is completed.

Basically, all input and output devices work the same way. Exhibit 7–2 illustrates the fundamental phases in the flow of input data to the CPU and the output of results. An input device reads the input medium (or, alternatively, an operator depresses keys on a keyboard). The code pattern, representing data, that is recorded on the medium is converted to electrical signals. These signals are sent, via a cable, from the input device to the CPU. The physical input medium itself remains in the input device. The electrical signals carried by the cable are sent to appropriate locations in the CPU's primary storage. The CPU carries out its tasks of data manipulation under direction of a stored program. When appropriate, the CPU sends output electrical signals through a cable

Table 7–1

Some Examples of Input and Output Devices

Device	Medium Used	Functions of Device		
		Input	Output	On-Line Secondary Storage
Punched-Card Readers	Punched Cards	X		
Punched-Card Punches	Punched Cards		X	
Punched-Paper-Tape Readers	Punched-Paper Tape	X		
Punched-Paper-Tape Punches	Punched-Paper Tape		X	
Magnetic-Tape Devices	Magnetic Tape	X	X	X
Magnetic-Disk Devices	Magnetic Disks	X	X	X
Magnetic-Ink Character-Recognition Devices	MICR Documents	X		
Optical Character-Recognition Devices	OCR Documents	X		
Printing Devices	Printout Paper		X	
Cathode-Ray-Tube Devices	Display on CRT	X	X	
Microfilm Devices	Microfilm	X	X	
Data Terminal Devices	Various*	X	X	
Console Devices	Various*	X	X	

* Typically, data-terminal devices involve the use of a keyboard for the input function. Some terminals have a printout or a CRT for output; still others have other types of output media generated. Console devices normally involve a console typewriter for input and output; various dials and switches for communicating with the computer; and console lights that can display CPU output to the operator.

that connects with an output device. The electrical signals represent the output data (or results) that are generated by the CPU or that were passed earlier from an input device to the CPU. The electrical signals actuate an output device, which converts the signals to an appropriate output code pattern so that data are recorded on an output medium contained in the output device. All input and output data must enter or leave the CPU's primary storage.

Input and output devices that are cable-connected to the CPU and that communicate directly with the CPU are said to be *on-line*. Devices that are not cable-connected to the CPU and that do not communicate directly with the CPU are said to be *off-line*. However, some I/O devices may be on-line for some operations, while for other operations the same devices may perform off-line without tying up the CPU.

Comparison of I/O Devices

Although all input and output devices serve the same basic functions of communicating data to and from the CPU, their varieties represent a diverse capability. Some

Exhibit 7–2 Flow of Data to and from the CPU

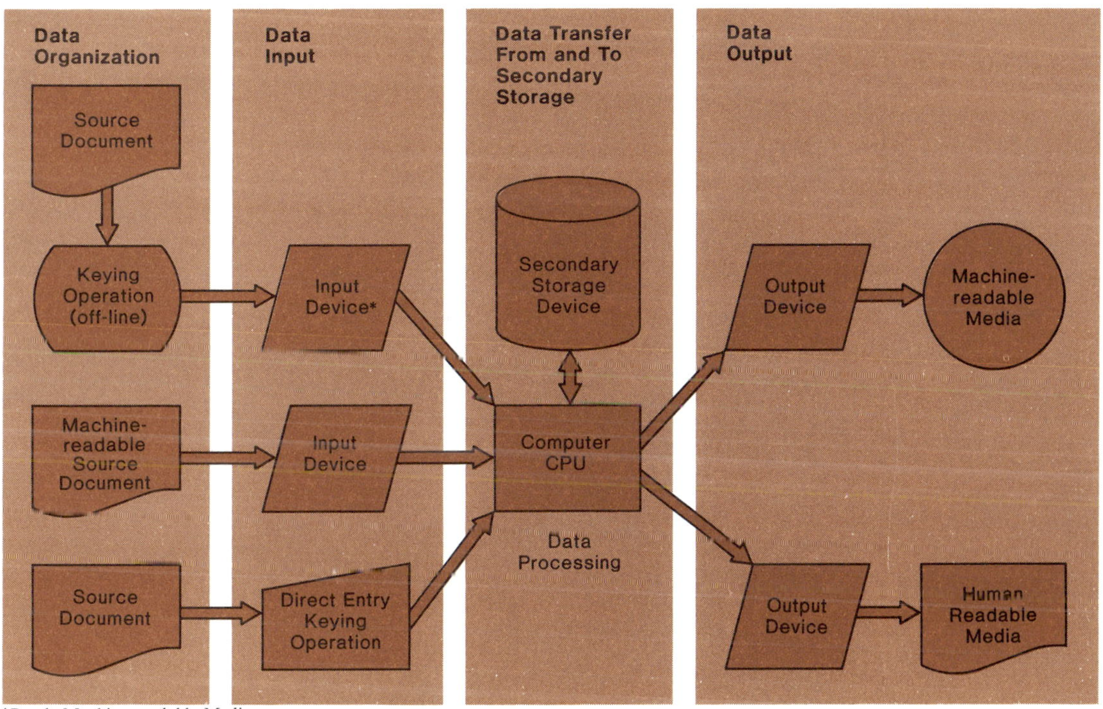

*Reads Machine-readable Media

devices can handle data at very rapid speeds; others are slow-speed machines. Generally, the higher the rated speed of a device, the more expensive it is.

The user needs to determine which input and output devices are appropriate to the organization's data-processing applications and economics.

Table 7–2 shows representative speeds of some of the input and output devices. Even a single type of device (e.g., a punched-card reader) may come in several models, each having a different rated speed. The analysis in the exhibit separates those devices that are for secondary-storage purposes (also serving for I/O purposes) from those that are strictly input and output devices. This separation is done because the storage devices can transfer data at high rates of speed; in that sense, they are different from the strictly I/O devices.

The CPU of most computers is very fast (performing operations in terms of mil-

Table 7–2
Some Representative Speeds of Input and Output Devices

I/O Device	Unit of Measurement	Typical Rates of Speed		
		Low	Medium	High
Punched-Card Readers	Cards per Minute	300	600	1,200
Punched-Card Punches	Cards per Minute	100	300	500
Punched-Paper-Tape Readers	Characters per Second	350	500	1,000
Punched-Paper-Tape Punches	Characters per Second	20	100	150
Magnetic-Ink Character-Recognition Devices	Documents per Minute	750	1,200	1,600
Optical Character-Recognition Devices	Documents per Minute	100	200	400
Printing Devices	Lines of Print per Minute	300	600	2,000
Cathode-Ray-Tube Devices	Characters per Second	250	1,000	10,000
Console/Data Terminal Devices' Printout	Characters per Second	6	8	16

Secondary Storage Device	Range of Transfer Rates* (Thousands of Characters per Second)
Magnetic-Tape Devices	15 to 320
Magnetic-Disk Devices	100 to 800
Magnetic-Drum Devices	275 to 1,000
Magnetic-Core Devices	250 to 4,000

* Transfer rates mean the amount of data that can be transferred, per second, from secondary storage to the CPU's primary storage.

Exhibit 7–3 A Comparison of I/O Configurations

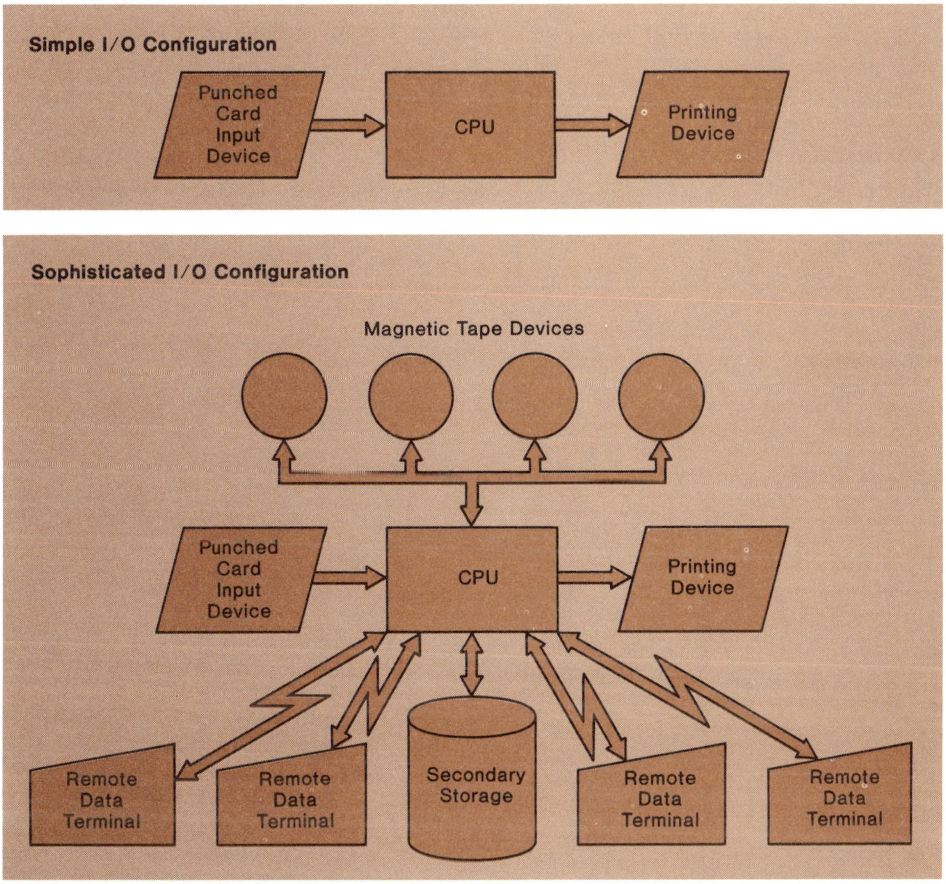

lionths or billionths of a second), while I/O devices are comparatively slow. The user needs to select a balance of I/O devices that will keep the CPU productively busy. Otherwise, the expensive CPU will be underutilized. The "throughput" (work gotten through the computer) can be maximized if the input and output devices can keep pace with the CPU. This can be accomplished by several means, one of which is to have a sufficient number of I/O devices, with appropriate speeds, on-line to the computer. Generally, the smaller the computer (in terms of power), the fewer the I/O devices it can service and the slower the speed of these devices. The larger the computer (in terms of power), the greater the number of I/O devices it can service and the higher the speed of these devices (see Exhibit 7–3). However, there are exceptions to this generalization; for instance, a powerful time-sharing computer may service many very slow data terminals. The time-sharing computer is kept busy by having it service several dozen or even maybe one hundred data terminals.

Assume that a simple computer system has one input device that can transfer data at 15,000 characters per second, but that has a relatively slow output device that can produce an average of 500 characters per second. Since the entire system is slowed down or governed by the slowest link in the system, the input device and CPU will be used inefficiently and, in essence, will be waiting on the output device to do its job.*

A Comparative Example. To illustrate the dramatic differences in the data-processing handling capacities of I/O devices, let's compare data read to the CPU from magnetic tape and punched cards (see Table 7–3).

Table 7–3

A Comparison of Magnetic-Tape and Punched-Card Processing

	Magnetic-Tape Processing	Punched-Card Processing
Recording Density	1,600 Characters per Inch	80 Characters per Card
Media Passing Speed	200 Inches per Second	1,200 Cards per Minute
Characters Transferred per Second	$1,600 \times 200 = 320,000$	$80 \times 1,200 \div 60 = 1,600$
Capacity	Up to 10 million or more characters per reel.	125,000 punched cards (80 columns) would be required for 10 million characters. This would be a deck more than 70 feet in length.
Convenience	Handling and security are easier with a reel of tape.	A mass of punched cards involve handling and security problems.
Cost of Medium	A reel of tape costs less than $25, and is reusable.	125,000 punched cards at about $1 per 1,000 would cost $125, and do not have the reusable characteristic.

Note: These calculations are merely illustrative, since there are a variety of different types of magnetic tape and magnetic tape units, and punched-card systems.

To ascertain punched-card reading, assume a fast punched-card reader that reads data at the rate of 1,200 punched cards per minute. This means that 20 cards can be read in a second (1,200 divided by 60 seconds). Since a standard punched card can hold a maximum of 80 characters, we multiply 20 cards per second by 80 characters and discover that 1,600 characters can be transferred (or read) per second.

To find the magnetic-tape reading rate, assume a rapid magnetic-tape unit that reads tape at the rate of 200 inches per second. Further, assume a recording density of

* When the CPU is delayed by slow I/O devices, the computer system is said to be "I/O bound." When the CPU does not service the I/O devices in a timely way, the computer system is said to be "CPU bound."

1,600 characters per inch. With this information, we can calculate that the tape unit can transfer 320,000 characters per second (200 inches per second multiplied by 1,600 characters per inch).

The above comparison means that the magnetic-tape unit can transfer data 200 times more rapidly than the punched-card reader (320,000 characters per second versus 1,600 characters per second)! Another way of saying this is that it would take a punched-card reader 200 hours (or about 8 days) to do the work that it would take a magnetic-tape unit only 1 hour to do!*

The above example underscores the importance of carefully analyzing the appropriate I/O units for a CPU and of deciding which I/O units to use for a particular job.

I/O CONTROL UNITS, CHANNELS, AND BUFFERS

Technically speaking, input and output devices are not directly connected to the CPU. Rather, they are cable-connected to I/O control units, which themselves are cable-connected to I/O channels through which data pass to and from the CPU's primary storage (see Exhibit 7–4).

Normally, a stored program instruction initiates an input or output device operation. The instruction is transmitted to the I/O channel, which relays it to the proper I/O control unit, which in turn activates the proper I/O device.

The I/O control units and channels carry out functions that, in earlier computers, were handled by the CPU's control unit. These functions help improve the computer's overall productivity.

I/O Control Units

As its name implies, the I/O control unit performs certain control functions over input and output devices. Sometimes the I/O control unit is built into the input or output device; in other cases, the control unit is a separate piece of equipment that may be used to govern several input or output devices.

The I/O control unit's functions include:

1. Code conversion during input and output operations. The input medium's code (e.g., punched-card code) is converted to the proper CPU code (e.g., EBCDIC). The output from the CPU is converted from the CPU code to the appropriate output medium's code (e.g., normal language for the printer).
2. Checking the validity of data. For instance, if the input medium has a parity checking code, the I/O control unit will test the data's validity.
3. Data buffering (discussed later).

* To give another example of relative speeds, assume that a textbook has 500 pages; an average page has about 500 words, or about 2,500 characters. Thus, in total, the book has about 1,250,000 characters. It takes many, many hours for a human being to read such a book. A punched-card device could read the equivalent data in about 13 minutes, while a magnetic-tape device could read the data in as few as 4 seconds!

Exhibit 7–4 I/O Control Units and Channels

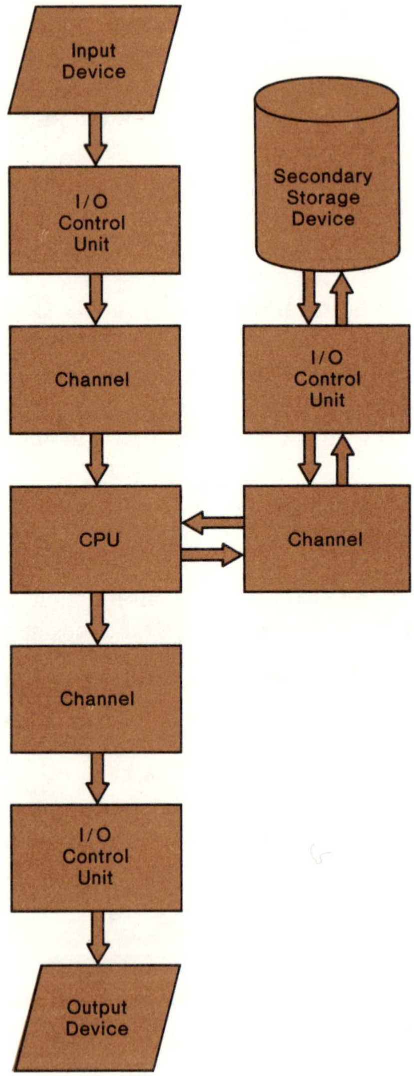

If more than one device is governed by an I/O control unit, additional functions of the control unit are to:

1. Determine the priority of the I/O devices; and
2. Signal the appropriate I/O device when it is to operate.

The individual I/O control unit is specifically designed for its particular I/O device or group of devices. By equipping each I/O device or group of similar devices with a specialized controller, the CPU can transmit standard codes and instructions no matter which I/O device is ultimately used, or what its own code or operating speed is. Thus there may be one control unit for punched-card equipment, another control unit for magnetic-tape units, still another for magnetic-disk units, one for printers, and so on.

An Example of Code Conversion. Letters and special characters in Hollerith standard punched-card code utilize a zone (12, 11, or 0 zone) in combination with numeric punches. Table 7–4 illustrates the EBCDIC that corresponds to the punched-card code.

When an input device reads a punched card, the Hollerith code is converted automatically to EBCDIC code and is stored in a storage position in primary storage. For instance, the letter "A" in punched-card code consists of a 12 zone punch and a 1 numeric punch. When stored in primary storage of the CPU, the letter "A" would be stored as follows:

Zone Bits				Numeric Bits			
1	1	0	0	0	0	0	1

To further illustrate the transfer of data from an input-medium code to the CPU code, let's consider a punched card that has the number 17 punched in columns 79 and 80 of the card (see Exhibit 7–5). The data in the punched card are sensed by the punched-card reader, and electrical signals are then sent through cable to the CPU. Before entering the CPU, the Hollerith code is converted to EBCDIC code, which is stored in the proper addressable location in primary storage.

I/O Channels*

A channel is a piece of equipment that usually is located between main storage and the I/O control unit(s) that it monitors. Sometimes it is contained within the physical frame that houses the CPU, or it may be a separate piece of equipment that is cable-connected to the CPU. A channel is like a small computer. It executes a channel program's I/O channel commands, just as the CPU executes the instructions of a user's stored program. The primary purpose of a channel is to direct input and output operations.

* There are two types of channels: 1. The *selector* channel, which transmits all data of one record from an input device to main storage, or all data in one area of storage to an output device. This type of transfer is called *burst mode*. Selector channels are usually attached to I/O control units of devices that transfer data at high speeds (e.g., magnetic-tape units, magnetic-disk units). Generally, one control unit is interfaced with one selector channel at any one time; and 2. The *multiplexor* channel, which usually operates in byte mode. Only one byte of data is transferred to or from main storage in one operation. Such channels usually are interfaced with I/O control units that service relatively slow I/O devices (e.g., punched-card readers and punches; printers). Generally, several I/O devices and their control units are attached to one multiplexor at any one time. The channel can accept or receive data from one device, then another, and so on (see Exhibit 7–6).

Table 7–4

A Comparison of EBCDIC and Hollerith Punched-Card Codes

	EBCDIC		Hollerith Punches
Character	Zone Bits	Numeric Bits	
A	1100	0001	12-1
B	1100	0010	12-2
C	1100	0011	12-3
D	1100	0100	12-4
E	1100	0101	12-5
F	1100	0110	12-6
G	1100	0111	12-7
H	1100	1000	12-8
I	1100	1001	12-9
J	1101	0001	11-1
K	1101	0010	11-2
L	1101	0011	11-3
M	1101	0100	11-4
N	1101	0101	11-5
O	1101	0110	11-6
P	1101	0111	11-7
Q	1101	1000	11-8
R	1101	1001	11-9
S	1110	0010	0-2
T	1110	0011	0-3
U	1110	0100	0-4
V	1110	0101	0-5
W	1110	0110	0-6
X	1110	0111	0-7
Y	1110	1000	0-8
Z	1110	1001	0-9
0	1111	0000	0
1	1111	0001	1
2	1111	0010	2
3	1111	0011	3
4	1111	0100	4
5	1111	0101	5
6	1111	0110	6
7	1111	0111	7
8	1111	1000	8
9	1111	1001	9

When an input/output operation is to be performed, the CPU identifies the required channel by referring to a table set up in main storage. The storage location of the first instruction in the channel program to be executed is forwarded to the CPU, which then is free to continue its processing. The channel carries out its own program, transferring data to or from main storage independently. A channel is free to

Exhibit 7–5 Conversion of I/O Codes to CPU Codes

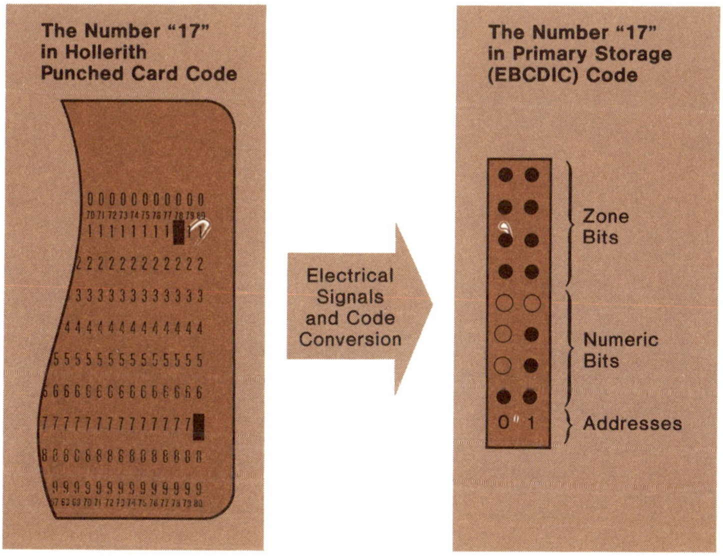

execute other commands as soon as it has told a control unit what to do and what device to do it with.

Thus, a channel is constantly juggling various input/output operations to make the most efficient use of computer time; not only does it overlap different inputs and outputs but it also manages to do so without tying up the CPU.

As soon as a particular input/output operation is completed, the control unit signals the channel. The channel, in turn, signals the CPU. This signal (referred to as an "input/output interrupt") means, in effect, "My particular job is done. As soon as convenient, use the data I have given you (if it was an input operation) or give me any additional data you have (if it was an output operation)."

This automatic-interrupt capability must be built into the computer components. The commands to the channels and the orders to I/O control units are also preprogrammed into the system. The ordinary user need only write his/her program; it will then be executed automatically, at appropriate times.

Buffers and Overlapping

Data transfer and processing within the CPU occur at extremely fast speeds. However, the data-transfer speeds of most I/O devices and secondary-storage devices are considerably slower than those of the CPU. The relative slowness of the I/O devices is in part because many of the devices have parts that physically move (unlike the CPU, I/O devices are not completely electronic), and some operate with media that must be

Exhibit 7–6 Selector and Multiplexor Channels

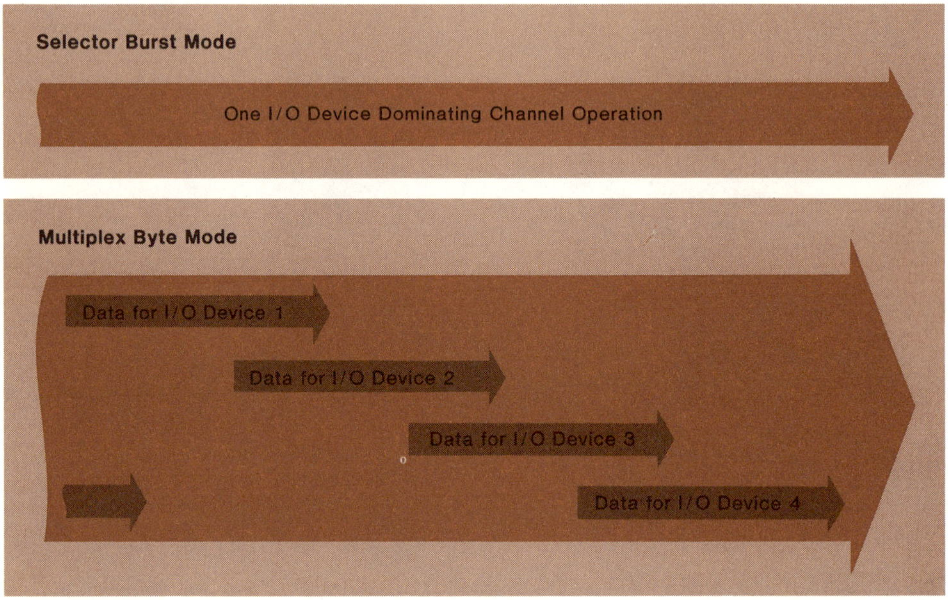

physically transported by a mechanical mechanism (e.g., the movement of punched cards and magnetic tapes).

To improve the balance between the speed of the CPU and the speed of the input/output devices, computers use *buffers*. A buffer is a temporary but fast storage area (similar to main storage) for data that are being transferred to and from I/O devices. A buffer that is external to the CPU is usually part of the I/O control unit. Other buffers are internal, since they are part of the CPU's main storage.

Data are transferred from input devices to the buffer, or from the CPU's primary storage to the buffer. The data in the buffer can be accumulated while the CPU does other internal processing. The transfer of data from the buffer to main storage is accomplished in a fraction of the time that would be required if the data were read directly into main storage from relatively slow input devices. Likewise, output data are assembled rapidly in a buffer while the CPU is performing various operations. While the CPU is free to continue other operations, the data can be sent to the output devices. When the buffer is filled with data and ready for transfer, it signals the CPU (if it is sending data to primary storage) or the appropriate output device (if data are being released for output). These buffered data-transfers are accomplished automatically; the user programmer does not have to instruct the buffer to do its job.

The buffers allow the flow of data to be more rapid, both from and to the CPU's primary storage. Also, it frees the CPU to continue its processing during the input and

Exhibit 7–7 Nonoverlapped and Overlapped Processing

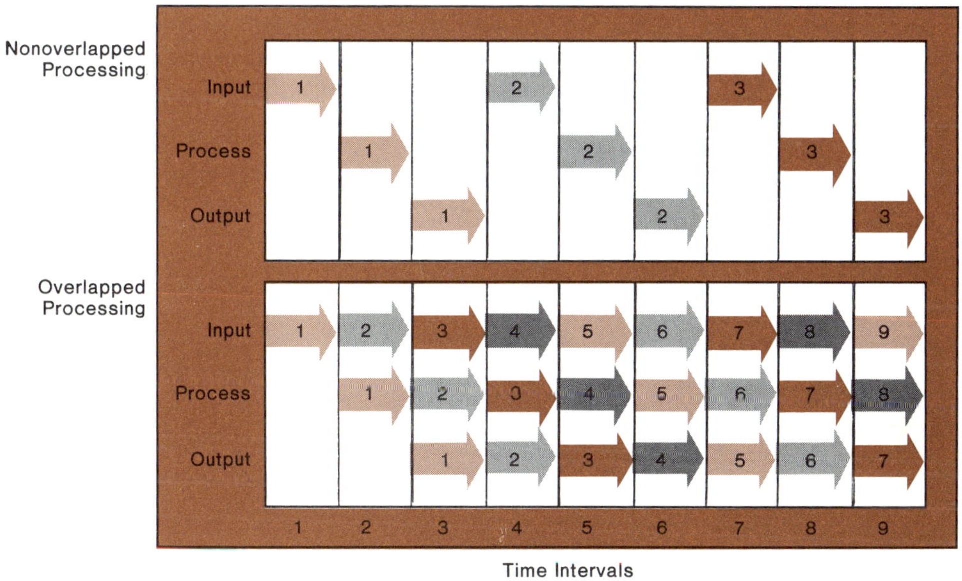

Note: While the above chart suggests the nature of overlap, the length of the time intervals for input, processing and output are not intended to convey the idea that, in practice, the three operations always have equal time requirements. In actual operations, process time intervals are normally shorter than input and output time intervals.

output operations. This creates *overlapped* operations (i.e., when several operations occur at the same time) (see Exhibit 7–7). If a computer is not overlapped in processing, the computer will be relatively unproductive, and the CPU may be idle up to 99 percent of the time. By overlapping processing, the computer can be more productive and the CPU will be used much more effectively.*

Summary

I/O units are vital in a computer system, since they feed the CPU and receive the results generated by the CPU. The interface between I/O devices and the CPU is made more efficient through the use of I/O control units, channels, and buffers. The objective is to obtain effective and high throughput of work in the computer system. The computer system should be neither I/O-bound nor CPU-bound.

* A more advanced version of overlapping, which is called *multiprogramming,* is discussed in Chapter 10. Multiprogramming involves having two or more different programs in primary storage; concurrent execution of the programs permits more efficient use of computer time.

Terms to Learn

Input device
Output device
I/O
Direct entry
Data entry
Transfer rate
Rate of speed
Control unit of I/O
Channel of I/O
Multiplexor channel
Selector channel
Burst mode
Byte mode
Buffer
CPU-bound
I/O-bound
Overlapping

Review Questions

1. Define *input* and *output devices.*
2. Describe clearly the distinction between *media* and *I/O devices,* and explain how and why media are used by some I/O devices.
3. Which I/O devices do not use media? How can they function without media?
4. Describe the flow of data from *input devices* to the *CPU,* and the flow of data from the *CPU* to *output devices.*
5. Which devices are strictly *input* units? Which are strictly *output* devices? Which serve as *both* input and output devices?
6. Explain why some I/O units are also considered to be *on-line secondary-storage units.*
7. What governs the type, and how many I/O devices are connected to a particular CPU?
8. Contrast the speed of a *magnetic-tape device* with that of a *punched-card device.* When would it be best to use the magnetic-tape device, and when the punched-card device?

9. Define *I/O channels, control units,* and *buffers.* Describe what functions they perform.
10. Why is *overlapping* important?

TOPIC 2—DESCRIPTION OF PERIPHERALS

TYPES OF I/O DEVICES*

Some of the more frequently used I/O devices are:

Punched-Card Devices

Punched-card devices process data that have been recorded on punched-card media.

Card reading and card punching are two distinct functions, and are performed by two separate devices (see Exhibits 7–8 and 7–9). However, sometimes these two devices are physically housed in one piece of equipment. In such cases the device is called a "card read-punch."

Card reading is the input function. Two types of reading mechanisms are available: reading brushes and photoelectric cells (see Exhibit 7–10). In the brush-type reader, cards are mechanically moved from a read input hopper to reading brushes. The reading brushes electrically sense the presence or absence of holes in each position of the card. The data in the card are converted to electrical impulses, which are sent on to the CPU. After a card is read, it is moved mechanically to a card stacker. The photoelectric-type card reader performs the same basic functions as the brush-type reader; the difference is in the method of sensing the perforations in the cards. Photoelectric cells are activated by the presence of light. As a punched card is passed over a light source in the card reader, the light that passes through the punched holes activates photoelectric cells (one cell for each punching position in the card).

Card punching is the output function. The card punch mechanically moves blank cards, one at a time, from the punch input hopper, under a punching mechanism that punches data sent by the CPU in the form of electrical pulses. After a card has been punched, it is moved to the output stacker.

A human operator loads cards into the punch input hopper and read input hopper and removes processed cards from the output stackers.

Punched-Paper-Tape Devices

Paper-tape devices process data that have been recorded on paper-tape media. Tape reading and tape punching are two distinct functions, which are performed by two

* While the term "device" refers to input and output equipment, some of the equipment is also referred to as units (that is, magnetic-tape units, magnetic-disk units, etc.). Thus, the words "devices" and "units," when used to refer to I/O equipment, are used interchangeably. Collectively, I/O devices are sometimes referred to as *peripherals.*

Exhibit 7–8 Punched-Card Reader Device

Photograph courtesy of IBM Corporation

Exhibit 7–9 Punched-Card Punch Device

Photograph courtesy of IBM Corporation

Exhibit 7–10 Card-Reading Brushes and Photoelectric Cells

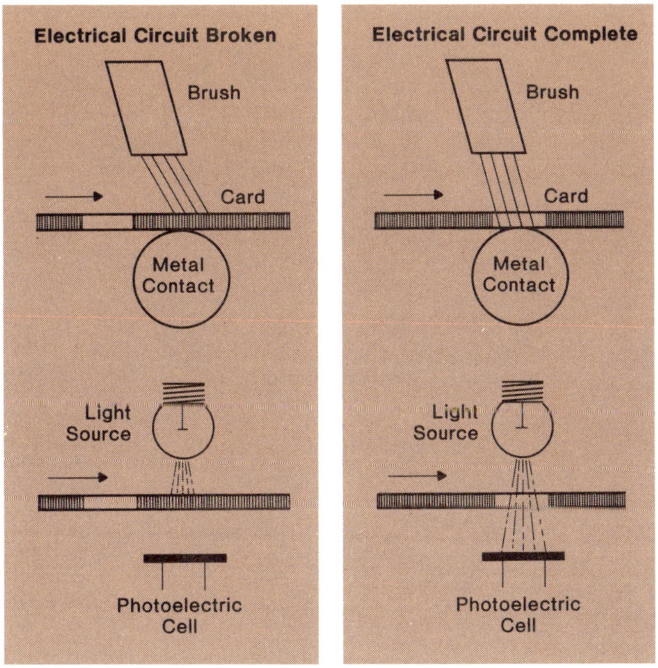

Exhibit 7–11 Punched-Paper-Tape Reader Device

Photograph courtesy of IBM Corporation

Exhibit 7–12 Punched-Paper-Tape Punch Device

Photograph courtesy of IBM Corporation

separate devices (see Exhibits 7–11 and 7–12). However, sometimes these two devices are physically housed in one piece of equipment. In such cases the device is called a "tape read-punch."

Magnetic-Tape Devices*

A magnetic-tape unit can be used for either input or output purposes (see Exhibits 7–13 and 7–14). Data can be read from a magnetic tape or written on a magnetic tape, and the data can be sent to or from the CPU's storage.

Before a tape unit can read or write, however, it must be prepared for operation. Two tape reels are mounted on the unit, and the tape is threaded through a tape-transport mechanism; the mechanism has a read/write assembly with heads that can either sense (read) magnetized recordings on the tape or record (write) magnetized recordings on the tape.

During operation, the tape moves from one reel (e.g., reel A) through the left vacuum-column across the read/write head, and through the right vacuum-column to a take-up reel (e.g., reel B). The loop in each vacuum column provides slack to prevent high-speed starts and stops from snapping the tape. Tape may be rewound or backspaced to the beginning of the reel.

* Magnetic devices (such as magnetic-tape units, magnetic-disk units, and magnetic-core units) use media that have the nondestructive read-out and destructive read-in features that were discussed in Chapter 5.

Most magnetic tape (as mentioned in Chapter 6) comes in recording densities (characters per inch) of 200, 556, 800 and 1,600; a new density has been introduced of 6,250. Some typical speeds of passing magnetic tape by tape drives are 36, 75, 112.5, and 200 inches per second.

Exhibit 7–13 Magnetic-Tape Unit

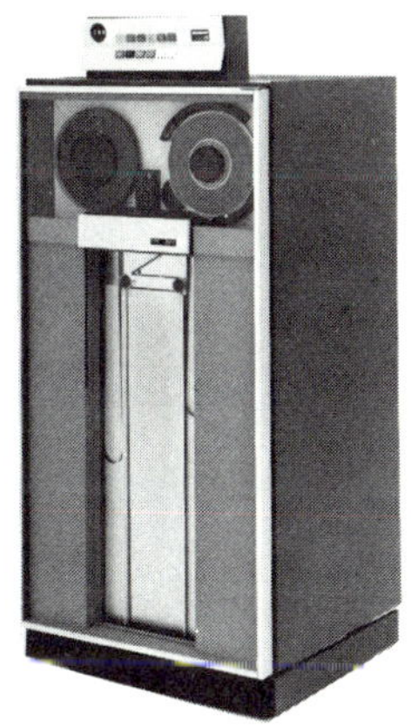

Photograph courtesy of IBM Corporation

Exhibit 7–14 Schematic of Magnetic-Tape Unit

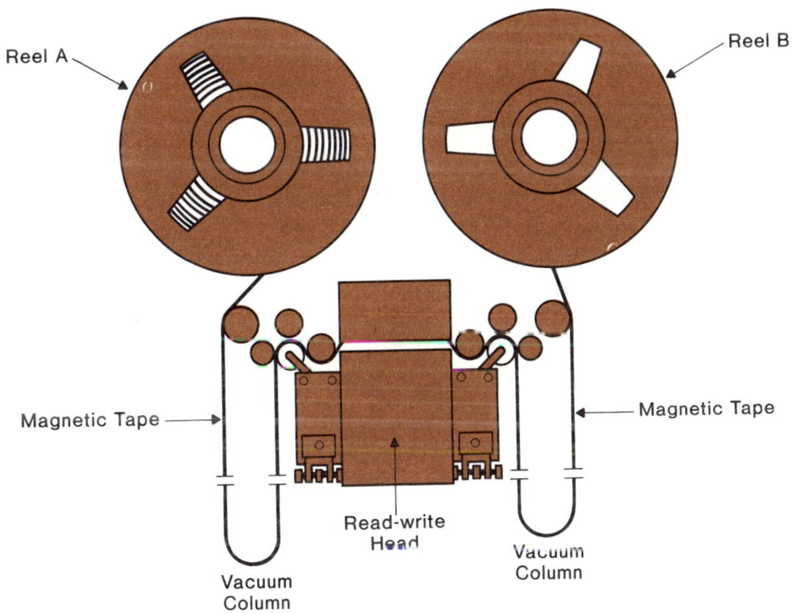

Exhibit 7–15 Magnetic-Tape-Cartridge Unit

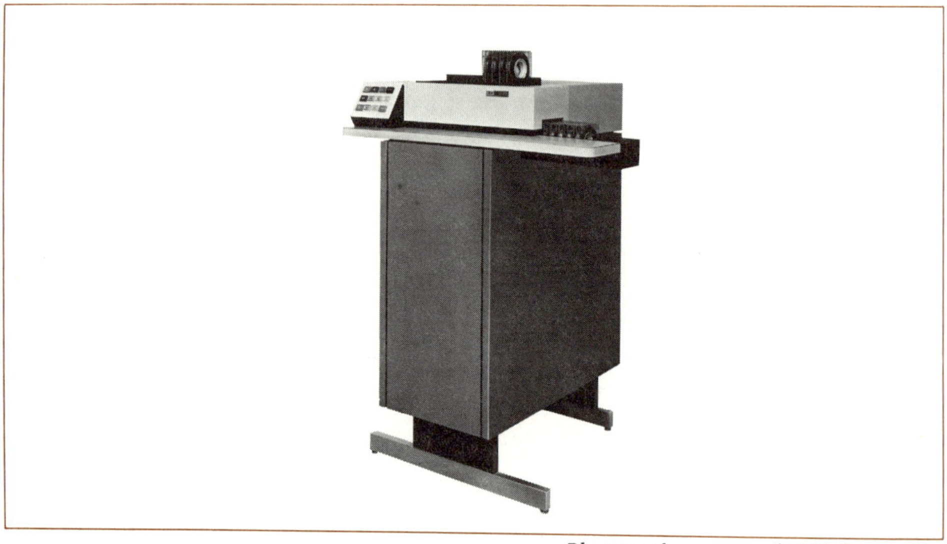

Photograph courtesy of IBM Corporation

Most tape drives provide data validation,* most commonly by means of parity checking. If equipment malfunction causes a bit to be dropped or erroneously added, the device notes a parity error, and the operator is alerted. Thus the tape drive can verify that the data transmitted are valid.

The use of magnetic-tape cartridges is increasing; Exhibit 7–15 shows a device that handles such cartridges.

Magnetic-Disk Devices

A magnetic-disk device is a piece of equipment that houses and can handle magnetic disks. Data on disks can be sent to the CPU's main storage, and the CPU can send data to be stored on magnetic disks.

Exhibit 7–16 depicts a set of six disk units.† The disks, housed in a disk unit, are mounted one above the other on a common shaft; the shaft rotates the group of disks at a constant speed (see Exhibit 7–17). There are six disks on a shaft, and (as Chapter 6 explained) there are a total of ten used surfaces (surfaces 0 though 9). Each surface is serviced (for read or write purposes) by a read/write head. In a typical disk unit, all the

* Besides vertical parity checking, longitudinal (horizontal) checks are used in some systems. This further maintains the accuracy of data on tape.

† As mentioned in Chapter 6, a variety of different magnetic-disk units are available. Although the example in this discussion is used widely, it is presented here only to illustrate concepts.

Exhibit 7–16 Set of Six Magnetic-Disk Units

Photograph courtesy of IBM Corporation

Exhibit 7–17 Schematic of Magnetic-Disk Unit

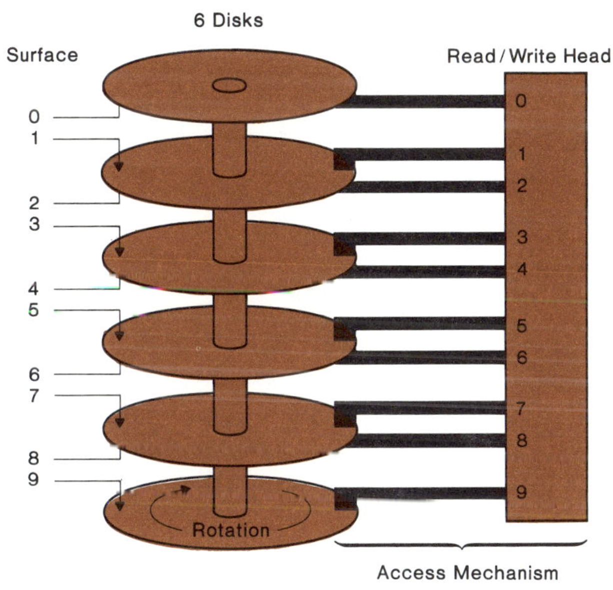

Exhibit 7–18 Schematic of Disk Cylinder

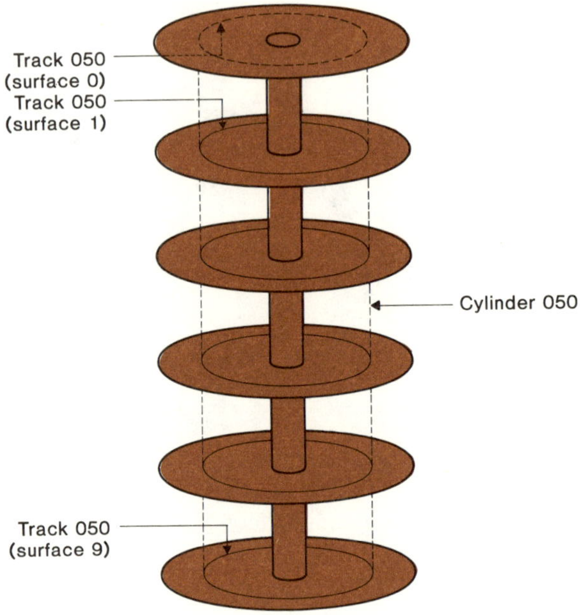

ten read/write heads simultaneously move in and out, seeking the track containing the appropriate data. If, for instance, the access mechanism were positioned at track 1, all ten read/write heads could read or write on track 1 of all ten surfaces. Collectively, all common tracks are referred to as a "cylinder."* If data have been completely read from track 1 on disk surface 0, the most efficient next step would be to read or write on another track 1 (say disk surface 1), since the access arms would not have to move at all.

Exhibit 7–18 is a schematic of a cylinder. In the illustration, all the track 50s on the ten disk surfaces comprise the cylinder. If a disk unit has ten disk surfaces, each having 200 tracks, then there would be 200 cylinders. If we assume (as we did in Chapter 6) that each track can store 3,625 characters, then a cylinder can hold 36,250 characters (10 tracks times 3,625 characters). The total capacity of the disk unit would be 7,250,000 characters (200 cylinders times 36,250 characters). Other disk-unit models can store hundreds of millions of characters.

The speed at which a magnetic disk operates in accessing data is measured in milliseconds. The time is determined primarily by how long it takes to move the read/write head to the proper track (obviously, a move from track 0 to track 199 will

* Some disk units have a single read/write head that services all disks in a unit; others have independent read/write heads that do not move in unison. In such cases, the cylinder concept doesn't apply.

Exhibit 7–19 Magnetic-Drum Device

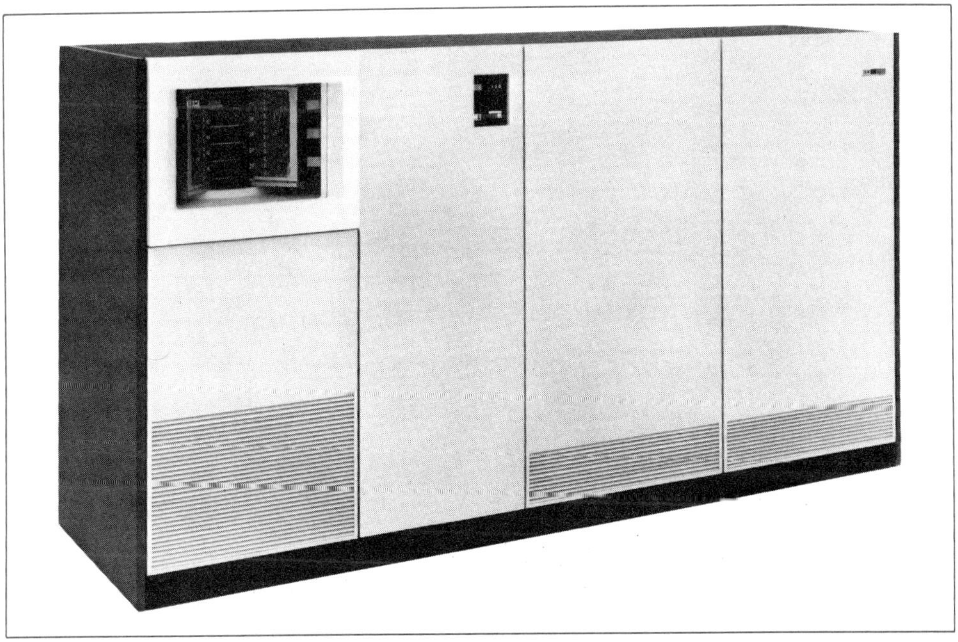

Photograph courtesy of IBM Corporation

take more time than a move from track 0 to track 1 will), and by the latency or rotational delay. This latter time is related to locating the appropriate data on a track as the disks rotate on the shaft. After the read/write head has been positioned over the required record, the data transfer speed becomes the point of primary interest.

Magnetic-Drum Devices

A drum* is mounted vertically on a shaft (see Exhibit 7–19), and the data are recorded on the drum's outer surface as magnetized spots. Data are recorded around the drum in specific, addressable locations that are in bands or tracks around the drum. The drum has fixed read/write heads for each track. Data are transferred to and from the drum as the surface of the drum rotates past the fixed head.

The drum is a constant-speed rotating cylinder. The magnetized recordings on the drum can be read repeatedly as the drum rotates. Each time new data are read into an area (addressable location), the old data are automatically erased from that location.

* Although some authorities consider the magnetic drum to be a type of medium, this book does not— the magnetic drum is usually a fixed, integral part of the device (that is, it is engineered to be a physical component of the magnetic-drum device itself).

Exhibit 7–20 Example of Magnetic Drum

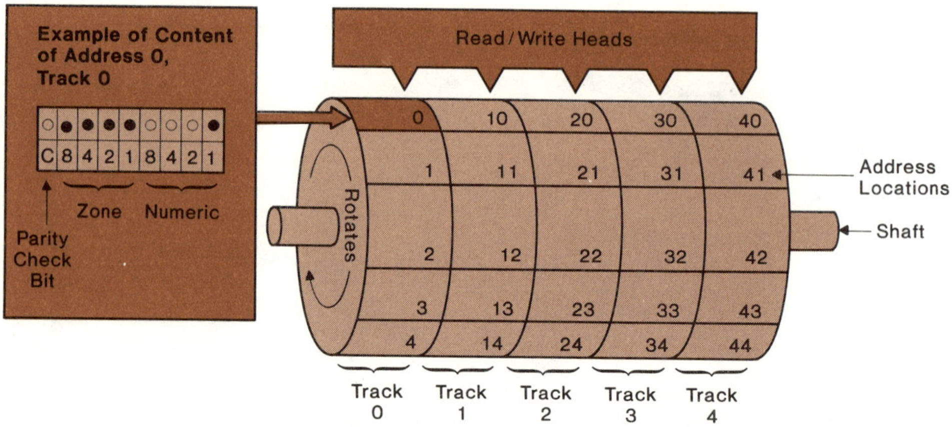

A specific number of storage locations are addressable on each drum; the capacity of a drum varies, depending upon the model used.

Exhibit 7–20 presents a simplified example of a drum that has five tracks (0 through 4) and fifty storage locations (addresses 0 through 49). (Since the picture only displays the front of the drum, one must imagine that half the storage locations are on the back of the drum.) Data are stored on the drum in magnetized spots, representing binary code (similar to how data are stored in magnetic cores).

The size, storage capacity, and other features of magnetic drums differ from model to model.

Magnetic-Core Devices

During the development of the second- and early third-generation computers, magnetic-core devices usually comprised primary storage. However, the primary storage units of newer computers make use of more advanced technology (e.g., monolithic integrated circuits).

However, magnetic cores remain one of the fastest and most dependable types of storage (see Exhibit 7–21). Since they can be used for rapid secondary storage, they can be used for input and output purposes.

The coding structure and method of operation of cores are similar to those of primary storage (refer back to Chapter 5). A magnetic core is a tiny, circle-shaped, ferrite ring. It can, as its name indicates, be magnetized. Each core is equivalent to a bit. When magnetized in one direction, it is assumed to hold a binary “1”; when magnetized in the opposite direction, the core is assumed to hold a binary “0.” Cores are set in the form of planes and are stacked to form a basic module.

Exhibit 7–21 Magnetic-Core Device

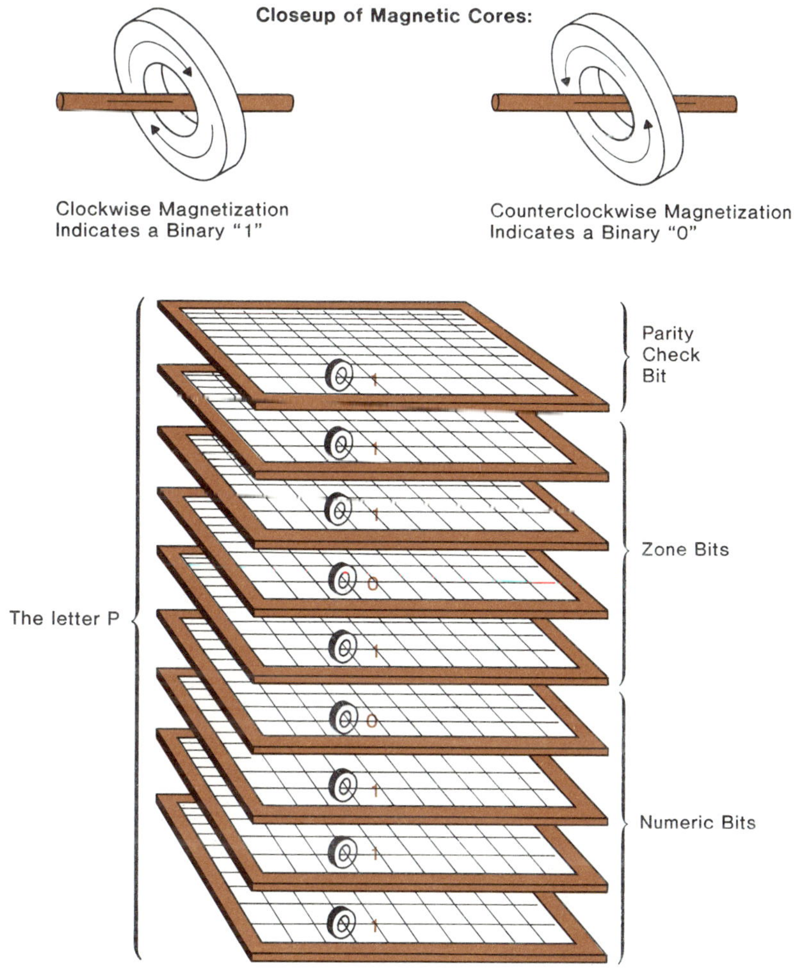

Mass secondary-storage units are available that can store millions of bytes of data. Since the cores are integral, engineered parts of the device itself, no media are involved.

Document-Handling Devices

1. *Magnetic-Ink Character-Recognition (MICR) Devices.* MICR reader-sorter devices (see Exhibit 7–22) interpret the characters at the bottom of checks; sort the checks by account number or bank number into output pockets; and can transfer the

Exhibit 7–22 Magnetic-Ink Character-Recognition Device

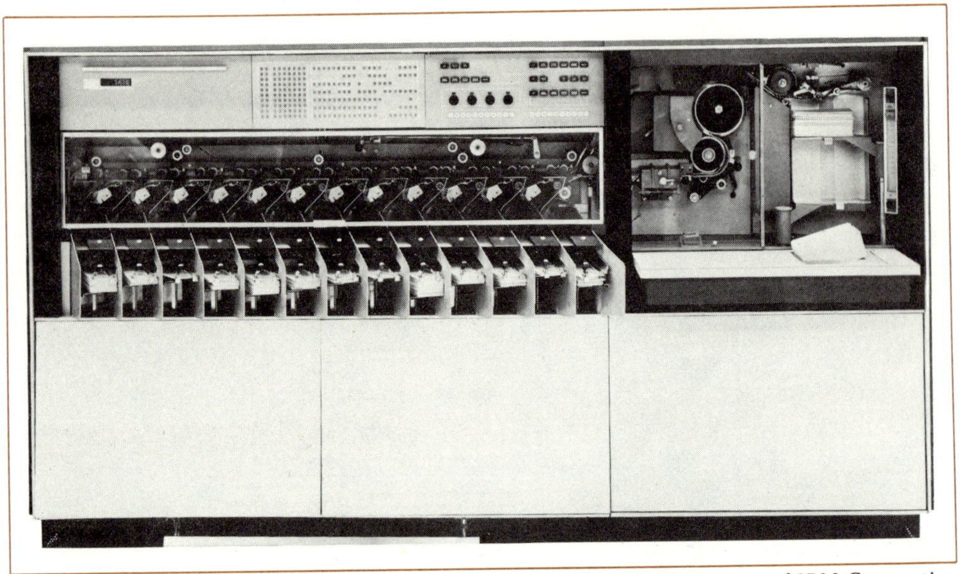

Photograph courtesy of IBM Corporation

data read to the CPU. Deposit slips can also be similarly processed. The use of such a device permits checks to be sorted automatically, while bank customers' accounts simultaneously are updated.

2. *Optical Character-Recognition (OCR) Devices.* OCR (see Exhibit 7–23) is a process in which printed or handwritten documents are scanned by photoelectric methods; the pattern of light reflected from the document reveals to the OCR device the specific characters that are recorded. The OCR reader-sorter devices interpret the characters (which usually are recorded in designated locations on the paper medium); can sort the documents into output pockets; and can transfer the data read to the CPU, where further processing can take place (e.g., a customer's account can be updated or a test can be scored).

Printing Devices

The general public is most familiar with the computer output that is produced on printers (see Exhibit 7–24). Such output includes bills, checks, invoices, management reports, statistical analyses, and mailing labels.

The two basic methods of printing are "impact" and "nonimpact." The impact method of printing is performed by pressing a typeface against paper and inked ribbon,

Exhibit 7–23 Optical Character-Recognition Device

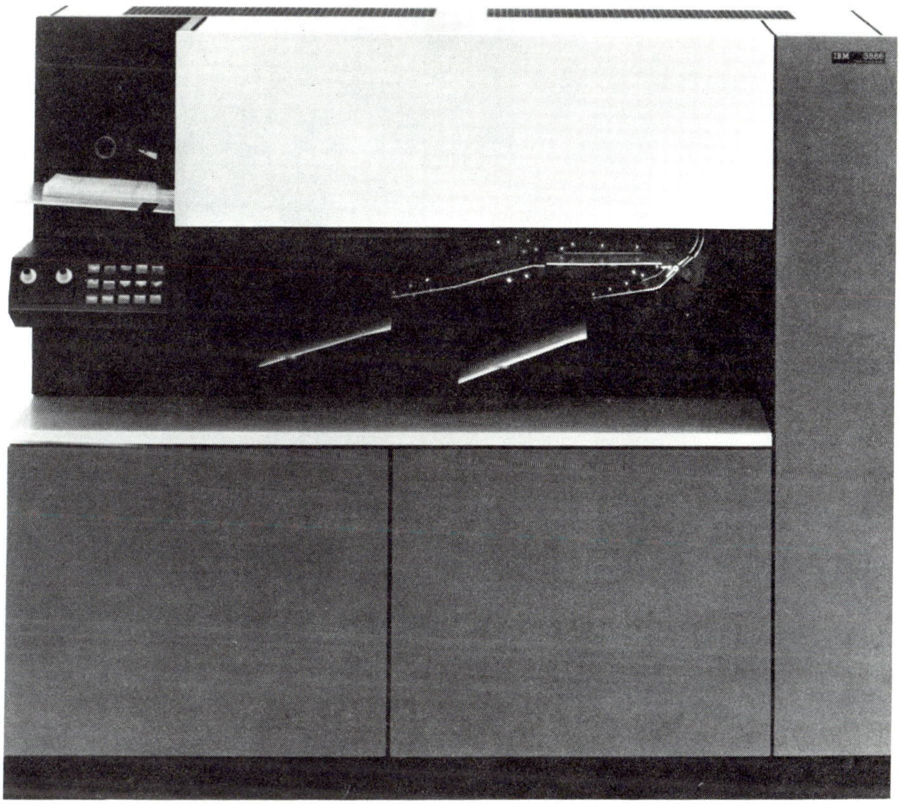

Photograph courtesy of IBM Corporation

as with typewriters. Nonimpact (or electrostatic) printers generally form images by means of electrical or chemical processes.

There are two basic types of printers: "character printers" and "line printers." Character printers are slow in speed, since they print 1 character at a time; typically, speeds range from 10 to 120 characters per second. A line printer prints an entire line (usually, up to 132 characters) at a time; printing speeds range from 300 to 2,000 lines of print per minute.

Some printers print on continuous forms, while others can print on discontinuous forms (see Chapter 6, "Input and Output Media"). Printers are available with different print fonts (e.g., some can print only upper-case letters; others can print both upper- and lower-case letters) and different sets of special symbols.

Exhibit 7–24 Printer Device

Photograph courtesy of IBM Corporation

Cathode-Ray-Tube (CRT) Devices

The CRT (see Exhibit 7–25) is a television-like device that can display data on a screen. Using a keyboard, an operator initiates a request for data, and the data are transferred from the CPU's storage to the CRT, where the displayed data can be retained as long as needed. The size of the display screen and the density of the recording determine how much data can be displayed at any one time. The operator can also use the CRT's keyboard to enter data into the CPU's storage. Some CRTs also allow data to be entered with a light pen; an operator uses this pen to record a message or picture on the screen, from which it is transmitted directly to the CPU's storage. Data can be displayed before they are sent to the CPU.* This enables the operator to visually check the data's accuracy, correct, erase, backspace, reenter, or clear an entire (or partial) input message before it is released for storage in the CPU.

A CRT can contain over one million display points, each of which is illuminated, in turn, by a beam that moves at great speed across the screen of the CRT. To create a constant and continuous image on the tube, the beam sweeps the screen many times per second.

* Some CRTs have a printout option. This makes a selective hard copy of anything viewed on the display screen.

Exhibit 7–25 Cathode-Ray-Tube Device

Photograph courtesy of Digital Equipment Corporation

Microfilm Devices

Computer output microfilm (COM) devices have been developed so that a computer may produce human-readable output. While the microfilm recorder may be on-line, more typically the output takes the form of magnetic tape. Then, the magnetic tape is converted, off-line, to microfilm (which is produced by the microfilm recorder). When microfilm records are needed, an off-line microfilm reader can be used to locate the records and to display them visually. Printed copies of the microfilm images can be enlarged.

Although they are not widely used, there are also computer devices that can input the data from microfilm to the CPU. Such devices are referred to as "computer input microfilm" (CIM).

Voice-Response Devices

Computers now have some limited capability to give English voice-responses* in reply to inquiries transmitted to the CPU. All the spoken words needed to respond to possible

* Chapter 6's discussion of media did not cover the voice-response device because it is debatable whether the voice or spoken words constitute a type of medium.

Exhibit 7–26 Retail Point-of-Sale Device

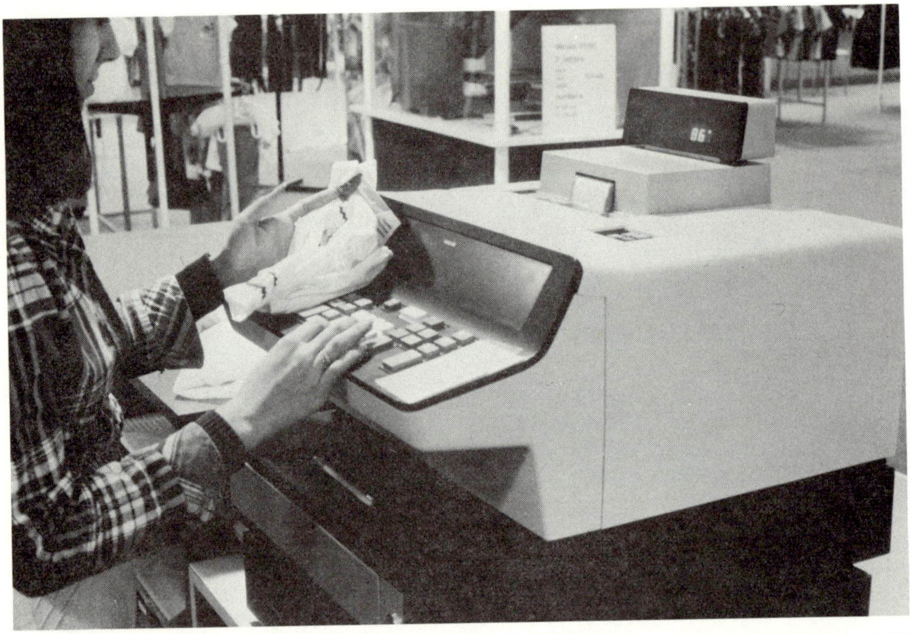

Photograph courtesy of IBM Corporation

inquiries are prestored, in the form of electrical signals, on a storage device (usually a magnetic drum). Each word is given a code. When inquiries are received, the CPU composes a reply message in coded form, which is then transmitted to an audio-response device, which assembles the words in the proper sequence and transmits the message to the inquirer. At present, the vocabulary of such computer systems is quite limited.

Data-Terminal Devices

This category covers many different types of hardware. Most data terminals are located out of the area that houses the computer; in fact, the data terminal often is located some distance (maybe thousands of miles) from the computer (refer to the discussion of data transmission in Chapter 4).

Out of the wide variety that are available to users, we will consider a few representative data terminals.

Point-of-Sale Devices. These devices, often referred to as POS, increasingly are being used in department stores and food-chain markets (see Exhibits 7–26 and 7–27). The

Exhibit 7–27 Supermarket Point-of-Sale Device

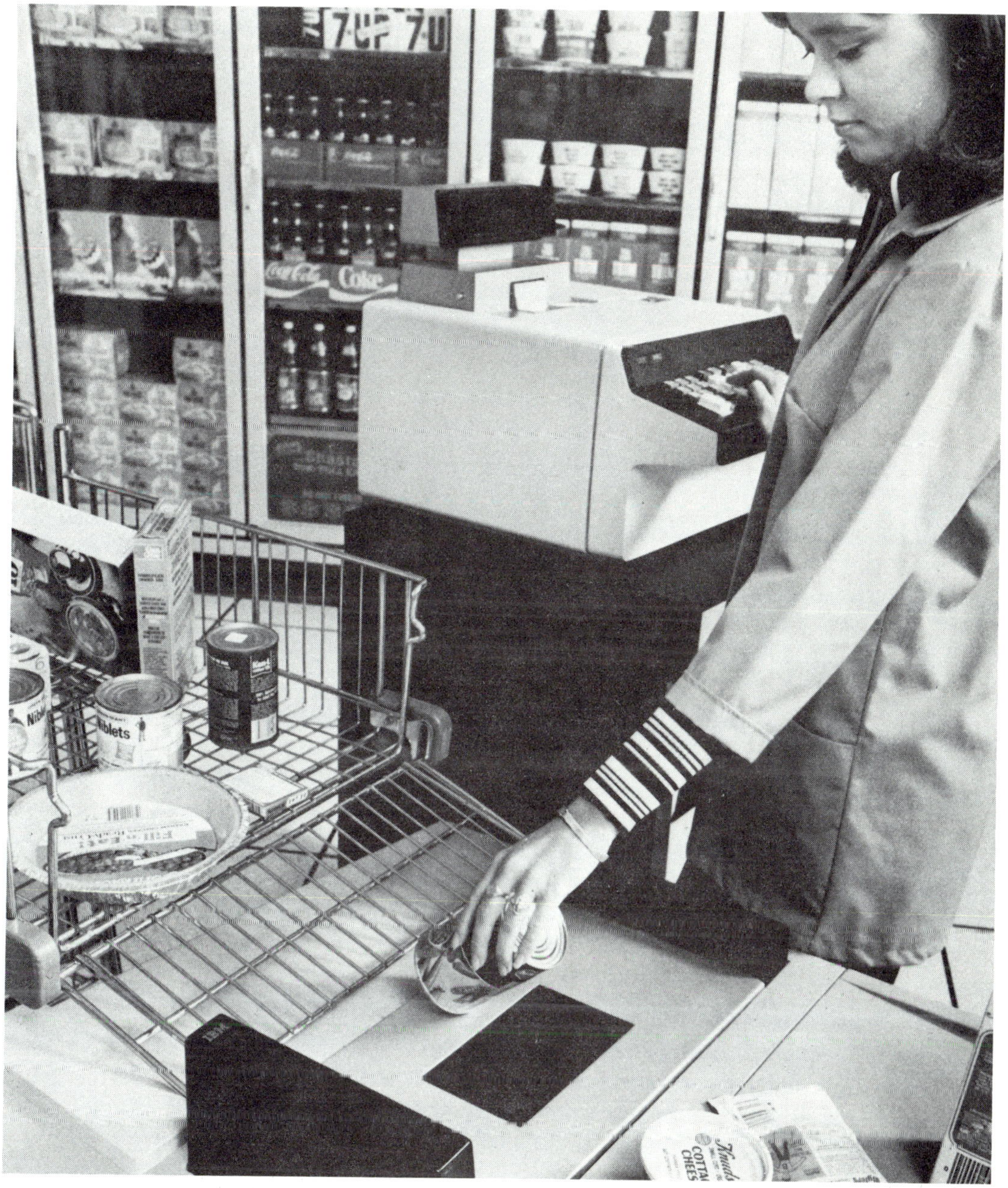

Photograph courtesy of IBM Corporation

Exhibit 7–28 Data-Collection-Terminal Device

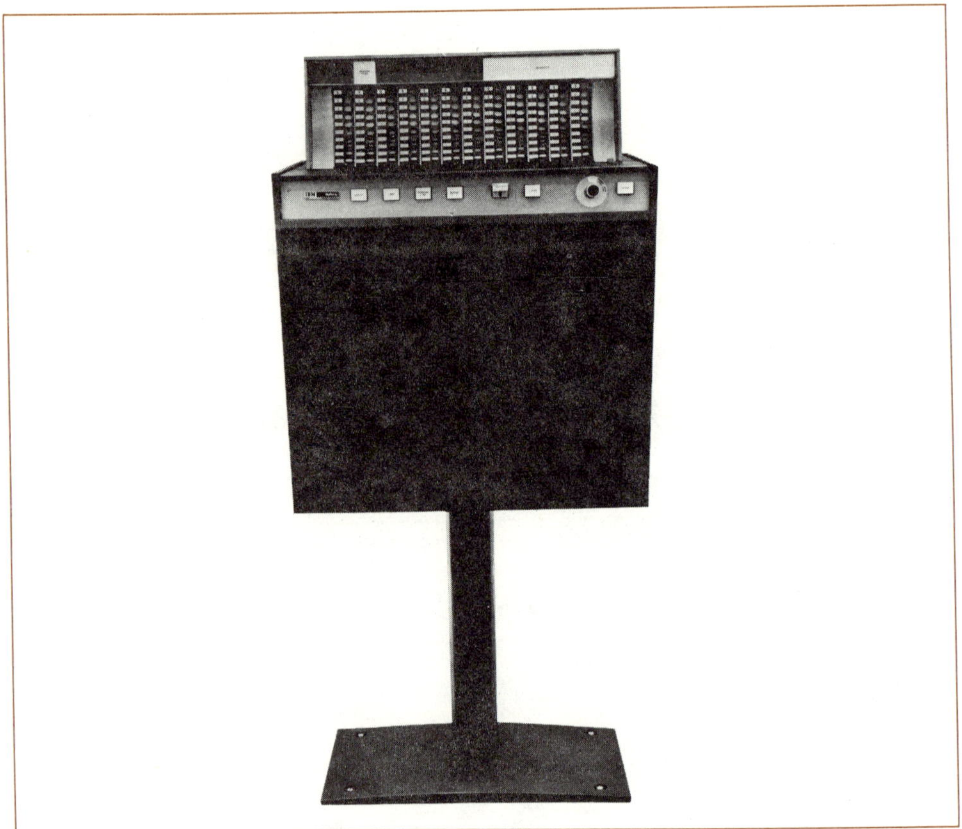

Photograph courtesy of IBM Corporation

most sophisticated versions can read the bar codes* on a product label (containing product identification and related data) and automatically trigger a tape of the customer's purchases. Concurrently, the terminal can communicate with the enterprise's computer to ascertain the most current unit cost of the item, and to record sales and inventory-change information.

Data-Collection Devices. These terminals (see Exhibit 7–28) are used most frequently in manufacturing operations to record data; for example, about when a job is started, what materials are used for the job, and when the job is completed. In this way, the organization's computer can monitor the entire manufacturing process, and can compare it with the plans and schedules to ascertain any variances.

* These are known as *U*niversal *P*roduct *C*odes (UPC).

Exhibit 7–29 Bank Data-Terminal Device

Photograph courtesy of IBM Corporation

Bank Data-Terminal Devices. Many banks are installing automatic tellers (see Exhibit 7–29) that enable customers to use banking services at any time, even when the bank is closed. For instance, with a password credit-card-type identification, a customer can obtain cash from his/her account late at night or on a holiday. The computer checks the password, determines the status of the account, and authorizes the data terminal to dispense (or reject) the requested amount of money. The more traditional bank terminal requires a human bank teller. The insertion of a savings-account book into the terminal will update the customer's record, both in the savings-account book and in the bank's computer records. For instance, the computer automatically computes interest on the account and records the amount.

Other Data-Terminal Devices. Even the telephone instrument can be used as a data terminal by dialing the computer and then using the touch-tone phone keyboard to input data (a digital subset must be attached to the telephone if it is to handle data rather than oral communications).

There are remote job-entry (RJE) terminals that can read punched cards and send the data to a central computer. Some of these terminals can receive data and information from the central computer and print it on a printer, at the remote location.

Exhibit 7–30 Direct-Entry Keying-In Device

Photograph courtesy of IBM Corporation

There are also so-called "intelligent" terminals, which can perform limited computer functions at the remote point before sending the processed data to a more powerful computer for further processing. The more powerful computer can also send data and information to the intelligent terminal.

Of course, because of its visual display feature, the cathode-ray-tube terminal is one of the most popular terminal devices.

Direct-Entry Input Devices

Closely related to data terminals is the direct-entry input device (see Exhibit 7–30). Such an on-line station permits an operator to key in data and have them sent directly to the computer. Often, such devices have a display screen that permits the operator to check the accuracy of the keyed-in data so that the transmission of inaccurate data to the computer is minimized.

Computer Console Devices

Every computer has a console with a control panel (see Exhibit 7–31). The operator uses this to monitor and control the computer's activities. The console may be mounted on the cabinet containing the CPU, or it may be a separate piece of equipment that is cable-connected to the CPU.

The console control panel contains indicator lights that display the contents of the

Exhibit 7–31 Computer Console

Photograph courtesy of IBM Corporation

CPU's various storage areas. These displays generally are presented in binary-based notation, such as hexadecimal or octal. During program execution, of course, these lights change far too rapidly for anyone to read them. However, when the computer halts, the displayed contents may help determine what has happened in the CPU.

The console also contains other indicator lights. These reveal such things as: power-on or -off; parity-error indication; and error conditions in input or output equipment. In addition, the console contains various keys and switches for entering instructions to the CPU manually.

Most computer consoles have a low-volume I/O device such as a typewriter- or cathode-ray-tube data terminal (see Exhibit 7–32). With this device, the operator can enter messages into the CPU, or the computer may be programmed to output certain messages (e.g., to the operator) on the device.

Summary

There is a wide variety of input and output devices, employing a diversity of media, that are used to communicate data messages to the computer, and to transmit messages from the computer to output devices and to people.

Exhibit 7–32 Computer Console and CRT

Photograph courtesy of IBM Corporation

The preceding pages presented some representative descriptions of input and output devices. However, the realistic situation is much more complex, since input and output devices are manufactured by many different companies, whose equipment have differing features and costs.

The computer user needs to balance the type and number of input and output units with the power and capability of the organization's central processor, the applications to be processed on the system, and cost/benefit considerations.

Terms to Learn

Peripheral devices
Punched-card device
Paper-tape device
Magnetic-tape device
Magnetic-disk device
Magnetic-drum device
Magnetic-core device
Access time
Latency
Optical character-recognition (OCR) device
Printing device
Cathode-ray-tube (CRT) device
Microfilm device
Voice-response device
Data-terminal device
Remote job entry (RJE)
Intelligent terminal

Rotational delay
Read/write head
Document-handling device
Magnetic-ink character-recognition (MICR) device
Computer console device
On-line device
Point-of-sale (POS) device
Universal product code (UPC)
Direct-entry input device

Review Questions

1. Describe the functions of the *punched-card reader* and *punch*.
2. How does the *magnetic-tape unit* operate?
3. Discuss *magnetic-disk devices* and contrast their operation with *magnetic-tape units*. Contrast both of them with *magnetic cores*.
4. What is the significant advantage of *magnetic methods* (tape, disk, cores, drums) over *other methods?*
5. What commonalities do the following devices have: *printers, cathode ray tubes,* and *microfilm devices?*
6. Identify some uses of *remote data-terminals* that you have had experience with as a student, a consumer, and a citizen.
7. How does the *computer console* function as an I/O device, and for what purposes?

TOPIC 3—OTHER DEVICES

OFF-LINE DEVICES

The devices discussed so far have been those that are cable-connected (on-line) to the computer and that usually work in that mode.

However, there are other devices that always (or almost always) process data off-line from the main computer. Such off-line processing takes place because it is either not economic or not technically feasible to perform the functions directly on the computer. Some of the off-line devices that are important in a computer department are discussed briefly here.

Data-Preparation Devices

Many data-preparation devices operate off-line from the CPU. These are used to convert source documents, which usually are typed or handwritten, into some type of machine-readable medium, which subsequently can be fed to an on-line input device,

Exhibit 7–33 Key-Punch Machine

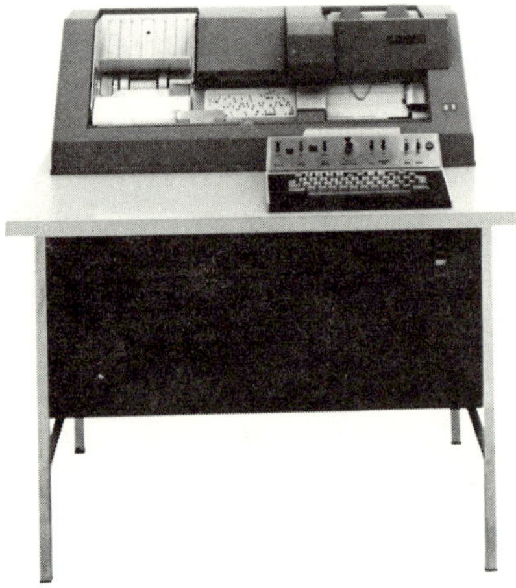

Photograph courtesy of IBM Corporation

and thence to the CPU. Most of the data-preparation devices are mechanical or electromechanical and are at least partially directed and activated by a human operator. A few of the data-preparation devices include:

1. A card punch* (key punch machine), which perforates blank cards as an operator depresses keys on a typewriter-like keyboard (see Exhibit 7–33).
2. Keying in directly to magnetic tape and magnetic disk is an approach that offers an alternative to the card-punching process. The operator depresses keys on the keyboard and this action records magnetized spots on magnetic tape or magnetic-disk media. Some of these devices use a small computer to monitor and control the recording process.
3. A byproduct punched-paper tape, which can be obtained when a bookkeeping machine, an accounting machine, a cash register, or almost any other machine is activated.
4. OCR documents can be generated by cash registers or almost any other machine.
5. A magnetic-ink inscriber, which, when an operator depresses keys on a typewriter-like keyboard, can encode MICR characters at the bottom of checks. The enscriber's primary use is to encode the check's dollar amount at the bank where the

* Procedures for key punching are presented in Appendix B.

Also, a decollating machine is useful in removing carbon paper from multiple copies of continuous forms.

Summary

Often, it is not feasible to do all data processing on the main computer. Some work is better done, from both economic and technical standpoints, by off-line devices like those mentioned in this section of the chapter.

Terms to Learn

Off-line device
Key punch
Data-preparation device
Auxiliary device
Electromechanical punched-card equipment
Control panel
Burster
Decollator
Key-to-disk device
Key-to-tape device

Review Questions

1. Discuss why it is sometimes better to process some work *off-line* rather than *on-line*. Identify some off-line devices.
2. Contrast *data-preparation devices* with *direct-entry devices*.

SECTION IV

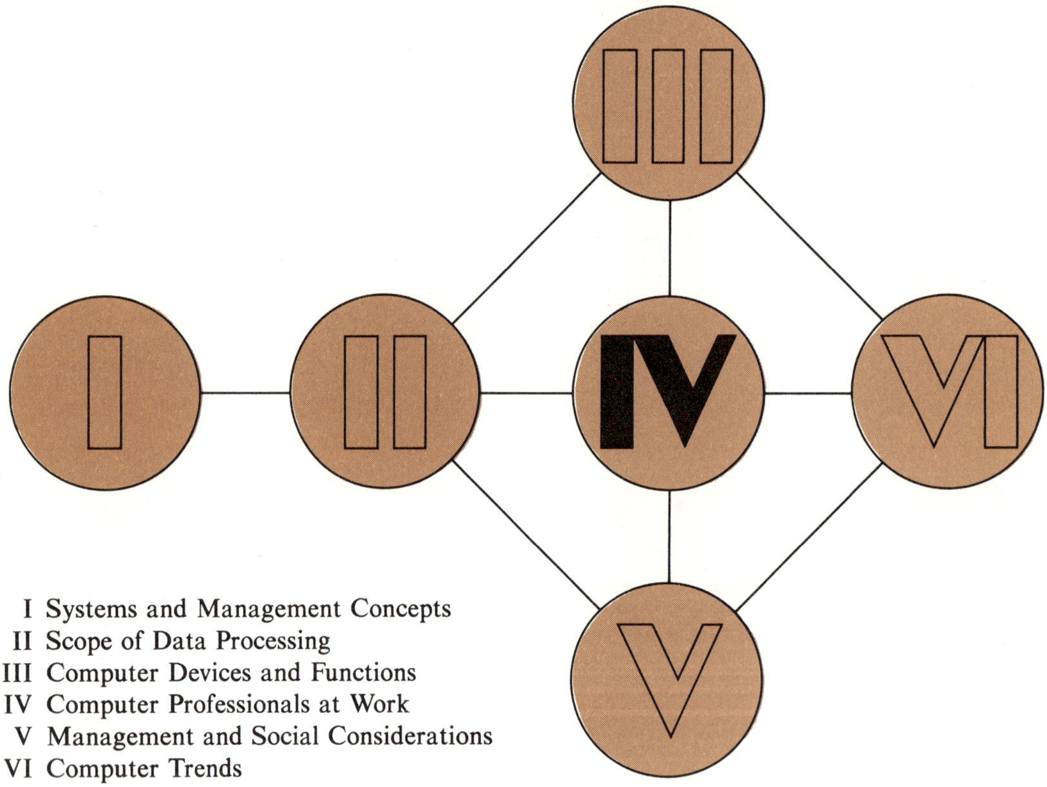

I Systems and Management Concepts
II Scope of Data Processing
III Computer Devices and Functions
IV Computer Professionals at Work
V Management and Social Considerations
VI Computer Trends

COMPUTER PROFESSIONALS AT WORK

The modern age [1810] has a false sense of superiority because of the great mass of data at its disposal; but the valid criterion of distinction is rather the extent that man knows how to perform and master the material at his command.

WOLFGANG VON GOETHE

The brain must be extraordinarily cleverly packaged and "wired," with such a small total information content and so low a processing rate, to be able to do so many significant tasks so much better than the best computer.

CARL SAGAN

1990 GOALS
SALES:
PROFITS:
PLANNING
ORGANIZING
ED
BILL
MARY
JOE
MIKE
PHIL
DON
QUOTA ACTUAL
JOE 100 110
120
CONTROLLING
ACTUATING

CHAPTER 8

DATA ORGANIZATION

Objectives

Chapter 8 emphasizes the importance of a disciplined approach to data organization. A planned and systematized approach is not only an essential ingredient of an effective computer system; it is fundamental to the work of the computer professional.

Two topics are emphasized:
Topic 1—Data Organization Guidelines.
Topic 2—Data Organization in Use.

TOPIC 1—DATA ORGANIZATION GUIDELINES

WHAT IS DATA ORGANIZATION?

Designing applications for a computer requires that fastidious care be taken in establishing the specifications for both data to be processed by the computer, and the program that is to instruct the computer. This chapter studies various aspects of data organization. The preparation of programs will be discussed later, in Chapters 10 and 11.

An unorganized approach to data would cause chaos in a data-processing system, whether it was a manual, a mechanical, or an electronic computer system. We have all experienced the frustration that occurs when you can't find a misplaced file or piece of correspondence. Magnify that frustration more than a hundred times, and you get some idea of the havoc that can be caused by unorganized data.

If you had 1,000 student files, how would you arrange them so that you could locate any one when you wished to do so? To answer this question, you have to know how you would be searching for a particular file (e.g., would you be searching for the student name? the student's identification number?). Obviously, the files might be arranged either alphabetically, by name, or numerically, by student number. Also, if the classification were meaningful, the files could be grouped (e.g., seniors, juniors, sophomores, freshmen).

In a computer system, data must be organized so that the computer can know (through programming techniques) the nature and location of the data it must process. Planning the organization of data is one of the responsibilities of systems analysts, systems designers, and computer programmers. Among other things, these people must determine the best organization for: input data; data stored in files; data stored in primary and secondary storage; and output data. While on the surface this may seem to be a relatively simple task, in fact, as enterprises establish data bases, it is an increasingly complex matter.

HIERARCHY OF DATA

Data must be approached on an organized basis if it is to be useful. In data processing, the hierarchy of data is ordered from the smallest element to the most comprehensive. The hierarchy of data is described below:

1. A *character* is any single number, alphabetic letter, or special symbol.
2. A *data field** is an area that can hold one or more characters that, together, represent a specific data element (e.g., the name field, the dollar-amount field, the quantity field).
3. A *data record* consists of a group of related data fields (e.g., employee's record, customer's record, or inventory record).
4. A *data file* is a compilation of related data records maintained in some prearranged order (e.g., an employees' file might consist of 1,000 individual employees' data records, and the records might be arranged in file by employee number).
5. A *data base* (or data bank) usually consists of several related and integrated data files.

Exhibit 8–1 illustrates the relationship among fields, records, and files. A highly organized approach to data such as this is required in systems and programming work.

PHYSICAL AND LOGICAL FILES, RECORDS, AND FIELDS

A *physical file* is a physical unit, such as a reel of magnetic tape or a magnetic disk. A *logical file* is a complete set of records, for a specific area or purpose, that may occupy a fraction of, all of, or more than one physical file. For example, an employee master file is a logical file, containing a record for each employee; it may require less than one reel of magnetic tape, exactly one reel, or more than one reel of tape.

Similarly, a *logical record* consists of those fields or data items chosen to describe some entity. A logical record may extend over part or all of a physical record, such as a punched card, or may require two or more physical records. For instance, each individual employee's records may require three punched cards (e.g., one for the employee's name and address, one for personnel data about the employee, and one for payroll data).

* The data field is sometimes called a "data item."

Exhibit 8–1 Relationships in Data Hierarchy

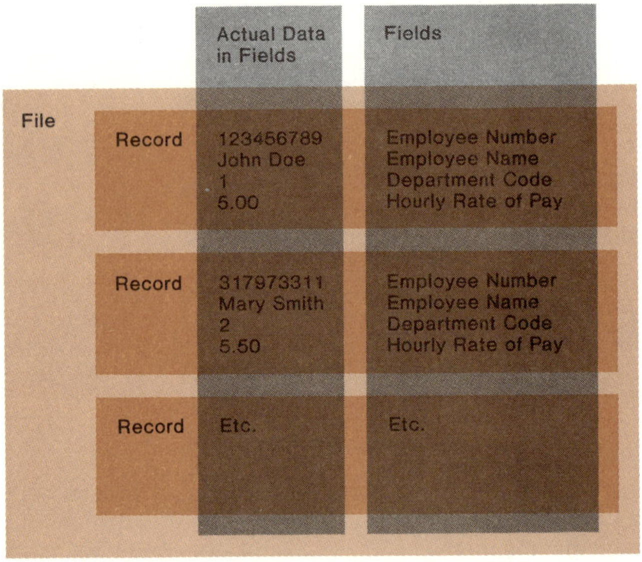

A *data field* (or item) may be composed of two or more lower-level items. For example,* the data item DATE may be formed from three items: MONTH, DAY, and YEAR. The structure is as follows:

DATE

MONTH DAY YEAR

When the item DATE is specified, the entire date is referenced. When YEAR, or MONTH, or DAY is specified, only the specified portions are referenced. These three subfields are referred to as "elementary items" because they are not subdivided into still more elementary items.

Variable vs. Fixed Field-Lengths

A data item may vary in length from one record to another. For example, an item called EMPLOYEE-NAME could be expected to vary from one employee to the next. This means that fields can be designed in either of two ways: in fixed item-size or in variable item-size. A field that is fixed in length must be wide enough to accommodate the largest data anticipated.

* In the example, "DATE" is a group item, while the others ("MONTH," "DAY," and "YEAR") are elementary items.

Exhibit 8–2 Variable vs. Fixed Field-Lengths

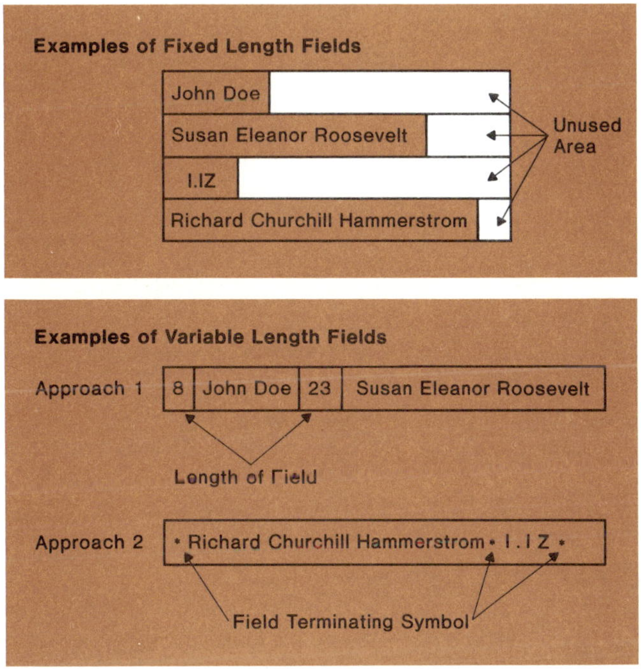

For a variable-length field,* the length of the item must be specified in one of two ways: either a subfield containing the length of the item is placed at the beginning of the field, or a special symbol is placed at the end of the field. Exhibit 8–2 illustrates these approaches and indicates that fixed-length fields can result in wasted area.

Variable vs. Fixed Record-Lengths

Within a file, the number of fields in each record may vary. For example, an employee record file contains a record for each employee. Among the data items, the record may contain a field for each position held by the employee within the company. Some employees will have many such entries; others may have only one.

This type of situation leads to the possibility of fixed- or variable-length records. If the record size is fixed, sufficient fields must be reserved to accommodate all anticipated employee data. Unused data items are filled with blanks or some other fill

* Variable-length fields cannot be used with punched-card media, since all card fields are of fixed length.
In Chapter 5 we discussed variable-length and fixed-length words in connection with storage and addressing concepts.

character, as determined by the programming language used. If the record size is variable, a data item identifies the number of fields that are present in each record.

Here is one way in which the variable-length-record approach is used for two records from a personnel file. The first employee (Doe) has had only one previous position with the company; the position code is #264. The second employee (Smith) has held four prior positions (position codes 78, 92, 110, and 116).

Employee Number	*Name*	*Current Position Number*	*Department Code*	*Number of Previous Positions*	*Position Numbers*			
123456789	Doe	378	1	1	264			
317973311	Smith	117	2	4	78	92	110	116

The "Number of Previous Positions" field controls the number of spaces, for position numbers, that should be set aside for each individual employee record.

The fixed-field-size and fixed-record-size approach is simpler to program and generally requires less CPU execution time than the variable approach does. However, it tends to require more storage. If either can be used, the systems analyst or programmer should estimate the relative costs of both alternatives and select the more efficient one.

KEY FIELDS AND CODES

Usually, each data record is assigned one or more identifying numbers and codes. These fields are referred to as *key fields.** They are used to facilitate the processing and maintenance of data records. Since the computer can handle numbers more efficiently than handle alphabetic characters, numbers usually are employed to signify key fields and codes. The nature of the job determines the specific identifying numbers and codes used for a particular application.

For example, let's consider three different data files.

1. In an *employee* file, each record undoubtedly is identified by an employee number. In addition, each employee record may contain a numeric code that identifies the department in which the person works (e.g., Code 1 may signify the accounting department; Code 2 may identify the manufacturing plant; and Code 3 may identify the sales department).
2. In a *customer's* file, each record contains a customer number and also, perhaps, a numeric code signifying the customer's credit rating (e.g., Code 1 may identify an excellent credit risk; Code 2 may identify a good credit risk; and Code 3 may identify a fair risk).
3. In an *inventory* file, each record contains an inventory number to distinguish each different type of item in inventory. In addition, there may be a numeric code,

* Sometimes key fields are called "control fields."

specifying where the inventory is stored (e.g., Code 1 may identify the New York warehouse; Code 2 may stand for the Chicago warehouse; and Code 3 may identify the Los Angeles warehouse).

Such key fields and codes permit a file to be logically arranged (and, when needed, to be rearranged). The codes are also useful in grouping like items together. For instance, an employee file may be maintained in employee-number sequence, as indicated below:

Employee Number	*Name*	*Department Code*	*Hourly Rate of Pay*
123456789	John Doe	1	5.00
317973311	Mary Smith	2	5.50
713023987	Ruth Brown	1	4.00
867900931	Robert Hope	3	6.00
979834899	James Gilmore	2	4.50

In other circumstances, it may be desirable to have the file rearranged in department-code sequence, as follows:

123456789	John Doe	1	5.00
713023987	Ruth Brown	1	4.00
317973311	Mary Smith	2	5.50
979834899	James Gilmore	2	4.50
867900931	Robert Hope	3	6.00

There are various ways in which to assign numbers and codes to data records. The most straightforward approach is to give a sequential number in the order in which the numbers are assigned. For instance, employee numbers may be assigned to employees in sequential order—the next person hired is given the next available number. However, some organizations try to assign numbers that will maintain the file in some alphabetic order. Others may want the employee number to connote other facts, as well; for instance, the first two digits may identify the employee's job-classification code.

Sometimes considerable planning is required to decide on the best identifying-number and code structure. The structure must at least provide sufficient unique numbers to satisfy all data records and all conditions that require a unique number.

PUNCHED-CARD RECORDS

A punched card is frequently referred to as a *unit record*. This means that only one specific data record is placed on any one punched card (i.e., even if there is space, two separate data records are not put on a single punched card). The nature of the application determines what fields are required and how many columns must be allotted to each field. It is essential that the width assigned to any field must be

Exhibit 8–3 Layout of Employee Punched Card

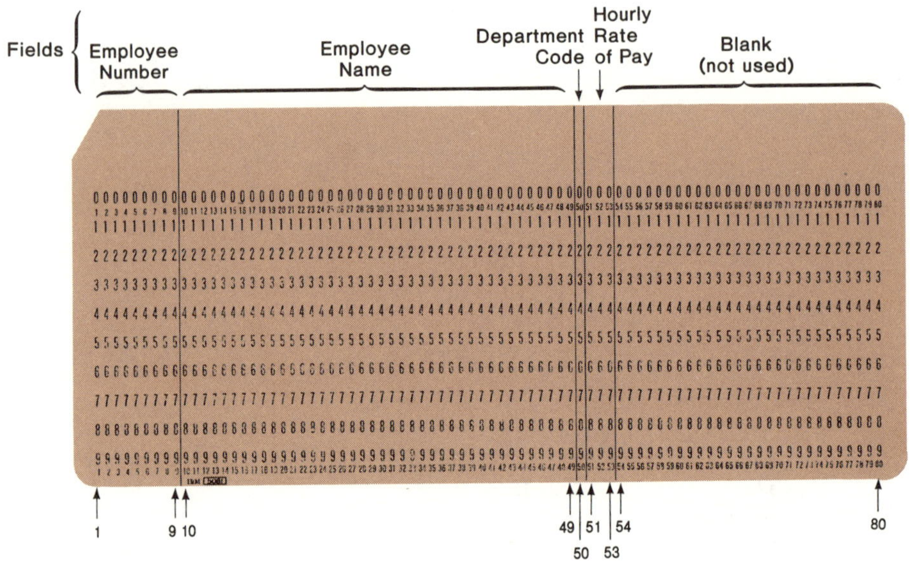

sufficient to handle the largest unit of data that will ever be stored in that particular field.

Exhibit 8–3 illustrates a punched-card record. If there were two hundred employees in the organization, there would be two hundred punched cards (or unit records), assuming that one card apiece was sufficient to record all the data about an employee. The specific data for each employee would be punched in his/her record. In all the records, columns 54 through 80 would be blank, since they were not assigned as fields. All the related data-records (or the two hundred punched cards) would collectively be considered the data file (employee file).

The employee-number field (columns 1 through 9) is, of course, a numeric field. The employee-name field (columns 10 through 49) is an alphabetic field. Obviously, employees will have different-length names (some will be relatively short—e.g., John Doe—while others may fill the entire field). The unused portion of the field is left blank; thus, for John Doe,* columns 18 through 49 would be left blank. Also, alphabetic and alphameric † fields are normally *left-hand justified;* this means that

* The name John Doe is seven characters wide; adding to this the space between given and surname makes a total of eight digits. Thus, the name requires the space in columns 10 through 17.

† Alphameric fields are those that can contain *both* alphabetic and numeric characters.

data are recorded starting from the left-most column in the field. In this particular example, the recording of any name always begins in column 10. The department-code field is a one-digit numeric field, and it occupies column 50. The hourly-rate-of-pay field is, of course, a numeric field, and it occupies columns 51, 52, and 53. The decimal point is not recorded in the record, since it is taken care of via programming technique. Since the field has three columns, it can hold a maximum rate of pay of 9.99 (excluding the decimal point). Numeric fields, contrary to alphabetic and alphameric fields, are *right-hand justified.* That is, the lowest-order part of a numeric number is recorded in the field's right-most column; the rest of the number is recorded from right to left in the field. Unused portions of a numeric field are either left blank or filled in with high-order zeroes.

It is important to justify data in fields properly. For example, suppose that the employee record contains a two-column-wide field for recording the number of dependents. Assume that John Doe has three dependents and Mary Smith has one dependent.

Right Way to Justify Numeric Data		*Wrong Way to Justify Numeric Data*		*Why Wrong?*
Columns		Columns		
54	55	54	55	
	3	3		Would be interpreted as 30 dependents.
0	1	1		Would be interpreted as 10 dependents.

If the computer is told that the field has two digits in it, it has no way of recognizing that the "3" and "1" in column 54 really should be recorded in column 55. The computer will automatically assume that the figures are "30" and "10," which will cause improper data-processing and, thus, incorrect results. This example illustrates the importance of recording data in the proper column of a field; improperly justified numeric data, used in computations, can result in completely wrong answers.

If alphabetic fields are justified incorrectly, the results will be displayed differently from the way in which we have become accustomed to seeing printed material. For example, assume the following alphameric data:

Card Columns	*How Printed If Correctly Left-Hand Justified*	*How Printed If Incorrectly Justified*
1–20	Joe Smith	Joe Smith
21–40	1357 Lark Street	1357 Lark Street
41–60	Any City, Florida	Any City, Florida

On the surface, the way in which the alphabetic fields are justified may seem a minor point. Yet it is essential to justify data properly in order to achieve accurate end results and adhere to proper business procedures and practices.

Exhibit 8–4 Master and Transaction Files

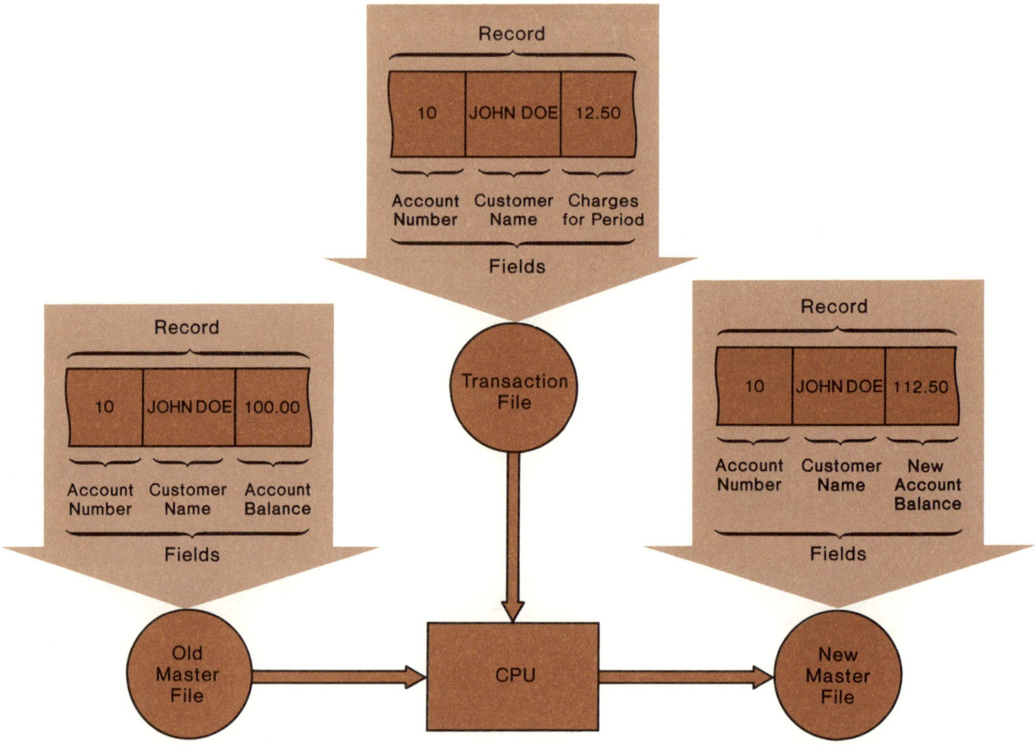

DATA FILES

Data files are most frequently maintained on punched cards, magnetic tape, or direct-access devices (e.g., magnetic disks and drums). Punched-card files are useful in small computer installations, or in initially recording and collecting data (especially when small volumes of data are involved). However, most large-volume data files are maintained on either magnetic tape or direct-access devices, such as disks. These files can be processed and searched much more rapidly than punched-card files can. Frequently, files initially are created on punched cards, and then are transferred by machine to magnetic tape or disk.

The arrangement of the records on a file depends on the intended use. Key fields and codes can be used to arrange the data in the desired pattern. The rearrangement of the files can be accomplished off-line or on-line, depending on the medium used and how much time and money are available. For instance, punched-card files are sorted off-line before they are processed by the computer. Magnetic-tape files can be rearranged (sorted) on-line or off-line. Magnetic-disk files normally are rearranged on-line.

Master Files

A *master file* (see Exhibit 8–4) is usually a permanent-type file containing some data that are fairly constant, and other data that are updated periodically. An example of a master file is a customer file, which has a data record for each customer. In the data record are some fairly constant data fields, such as: customer number; customer name; and customer address. Also, some data in the data record are subject to periodic updating. Such data fields include the dollar amount due from the customer, and payments from the customer during the month.

Transaction Files

A *transaction file* (again, see Exhibit 8–4) is usually a temporary file that holds data used to update master files. A sales file is an example of a transaction file; it has a data record of all sales to each customer who has made credit-charge purchases during a certain period. The computer processes the transaction file; this file is then used to update the customers' accounts, which are maintained in the master file (e.g., the customer's balance due, as reflected in the master file, plus the new sales, as indicated in the transaction file, equals the customer's new balance due).

Summary

If we are to use a computer efficiently, it is essential that data be organized logically.

Data organization alternatives are governed by such things as: the nature of the application, and the kinds of computers and software that are available.

Detailed planning is required to logically organize the several levels of data: data fields, data records, data files, and data bases.

Terms to Learn

Data organization
Data hierarchy
Character
Data field
Data record
Data file
Data base
Physical and logical file
Physical and logical record
Physical and logical field

Group item
Elementary item
Variable record-length
Fixed record-length
Variable field-length
Fixed field-length
Unit record
Key field
Key code
Punched-card-unit record
Left-hand justified
Right-hand justified
Low-order position
High-order position
Significant digit
Master file
Transaction file

Review Questions

1. What is *data organization,* and why is it important in computer work?
2. Give an example of a *data organization problem* in your school work, job, or home.
3. Explain the elements of the *data hierarchy.*
4. Contrast a *physical file* with a *logical file,* a *physical record* with a *logical record,* and a *physical field* with a *logical field.*
5. What are *variable* and *fixed field-lengths?* What are the advantages and disadvantages of each?
6. What are *variable* and *fixed record-lengths?* What are the advantages and disadvantages of each?
7. Define *key fields* and *key codes.* Give an example of how they might be used in an inventory application.
8. Assume that you were recording student data in punched cards. Describe how you would *organize* the following data: student number; student name; date of birth; sex code. How many columns would you allocate to each field? How would you justify the data in each field?
9. What is a *master file?* What is a *transaction file?* How are these two types of files related?

TOPIC 2—DATA ORGANIZATION IN USE

FILE ORGANIZATION

There are several methods of organizing data files (see Table 8–1). The choice depends on the computer equipment and software available, the application, and cost. The basic methods of file organization are *sequential access* and *direct access.*

Table 8–1
Methods of Data Processing

Transaction Data	Master-File Organization	When Applicable
Batched and Sequenced	Sequential	• No On-Line Inquiries • High Activity Rate • No Need for Constantly Up-to-Date Master Files
Random	Direct Access	• Need for On-Line Inquiries and Responses • Some Need for Up-to-Date Master Records • No Control Over the Flow of Transaction Data
Random and Real-Time	Direct Access	• Need for On-Line Inquiries and Responses • Need for Constantly Up-to-Date Master Files • No Control Over the Flow of Transaction Data

Sequential File Organization

In a sequential file, records are arranged in ascending- or descending-sequence order, according to a key field (e.g., employee number). To locate a specific record in the file, start at a given reference point (often the beginning of the file) and search each record in sequence until the desired record is located (see Exhibit 8–5). Assume that data record 999 is being sought. In order to reach that record, read the previous 998 records until the desired record is finally reached and made available for use by the computer. Since sequential files such as punched cards and magnetic tape are not addressable,

Exhibit 8–5 Searching for a Record in a Sequential File

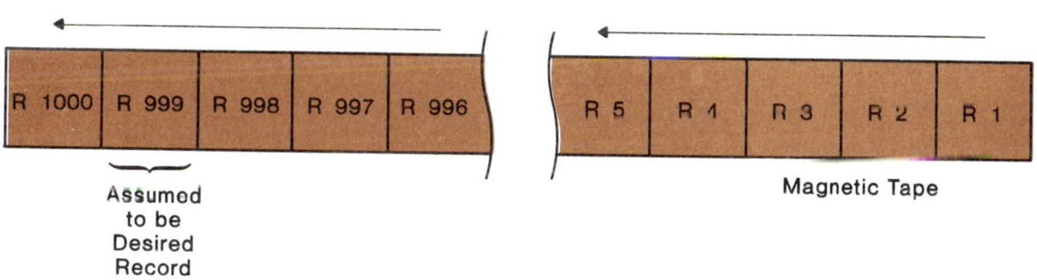

Exhibit 8-6 A Comparison of Unblocked and Blocked Records

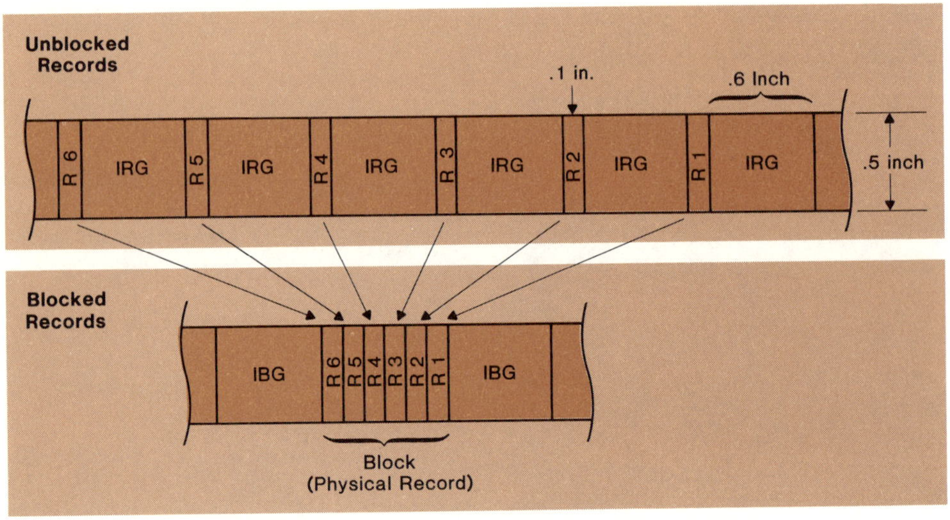

search each record in sequence and test a key field in the record (e.g., account number) until the target record is finally found.

Sequential files are frequently maintained on magnetic tape, although, in smaller computer systems, punched cards are sometimes used. In some applications, it is most efficient to batch transactions and process them sequentially at periodic intervals. Because of this reason, and because magnetic tape is a relatively inexpensive file medium, the sequential-file organization is used widely.

Direct-access devices such as magnetic disks may also be used for sequential storage and processing.

Interrecord Gap and Blocking. To provide separate records on magnetic tape, an "interrecord gap" (IRG)—an unused segment of tape—exists between records. This gap permits the tape to stop and remain in position to read the next record. On nine-track tape, the usual length of the interrecord gap is six tenths (0.6) of an inch. Since this length can waste tape, it is wise to block records, if feasible. "Blocking" means grouping a series of individual records that are separated by gaps (see Exhibit 8–6). For instance, a blocking factor of six might be used; that is, six records will be treated as a block. The space between blocks is called an "interblock gap" (IBG). An individual block of data between two interblock gaps is called a *physical record,* while the individual records within the block are called *logical records.*

As the illustration shows, when gaps on the tape are reduced, more of the tape can be used for actual data. If records are *un*blocked, the IRG (blank areas) can take up more of the tape space than the actual data do!

As Chapter 6 mentioned, a magnetic tape has great storage capacity. For

Exhibit 8–7 A Magnetic Tape Showing Labels and Tapemarks

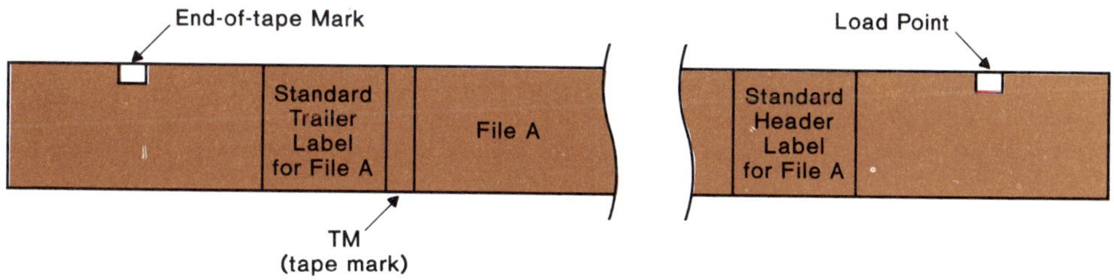

instance, a 2,400-foot tape with recording density of 800 characters per inch could theoretically hold up to 23,040,000 characters of data. However, the blank gaps on the tape, which do not hold data, must be provided for. Assume that there are 80 character records, which are held in .1 of an inch of tape of the 800 density-type. The IRG is .6 of an inch, or equivalent to the space that could be occupied by 480 characters. Since the IRG is six times the width of the actual data record (if the entire tape is used) 1/7 of the tape contains actual data and 6/7 of the tape is blank gaps! Thus, the tape will have approximately 3,291,428 characters of data (1/7 of 23,040,000). The remainder of the tape will be blank; this is the equivalent of 19,748,572 characters (6/7 of 23,040,000). Since we assume a data record is 80 characters, about 41,143 records can be held on a reel of tape (3,291,428 divided by 80).

Now assume that the records are blocked by groups of six records. Since the blocked records are 480 characters (6 times 80 characters each), and since (as we previously determined) an IBG is .6 of an inch (the equivalent of 480 characters), one half of the tape contains actual data and the other half has blank gaps. There are 11,520,000 characters of data on a reel of tape (one half of 23,040,000); since a data record is 80 characters, about 144,000 records can be held on a reel of tape (11,520,000 divided by 80).

When the records are blocked, the magnetic tape can hold 144,000 records (instead of the 41,143 it can hold under unblocked conditions).

Labels and Tapemarks. Each file on tape has an identification label, which contains such information as the file's name, its date of origin, and its date of expiration. For example, a payroll file may be labelled: "Payroll Master File, 1979, Expiration Date 1/1983." This is called a "header" label, and it serve two purposes:

1. It tells us that we are processing the correct file—that is, the Payroll Master File and not the General Leader File; and
2. It protects existing files from being destroyed.

The header label is separated from the data blocks by a special character known as a "tapemark" (see Exhibit 8–7).

Exhibit 8–8 A Batch Sequential Data-Processing Application

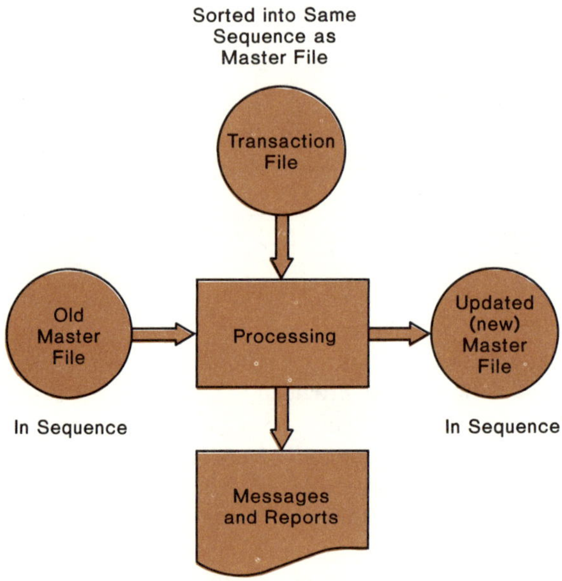

Note: The computer reads each record, updates the master record (if there is a transaction affecting it), and writes the record on the updated tape.

The end of a file is also marked by a tapemark, which follows the last data record. A trailer label containing information such as the number of records in the file follows the tapemark. Such information is valuable because it reveals whether a record has been inadvertently omitted during processing.

When data are recorded on tape, the beginning of the area to be used is indicated by a reflective spot. This "load point" is composed of aluminum foil, visible to the naked eye, and sensitive to the mechanism of the tape drive. A similar indicator called the "end-of-tape mark" exists at the end of the tape.

Batch Processing. With a sequential-file organization, transactions that are to be processed against a master file are accumulated in batches (see Exhibit 8–8). For example, employee daily time-records might be accumulated throughout the month. Before the monthly payroll is to be prepared, the transactions (daily time-records) are sorted into the same sequence as the employee master file (presumably in employee-number order). The master file* is updated by means of the data on the sorted transaction file; the result is that the master file will reflect new earnings to date. At

* The master file usually contains data (e.g., hourly rate of pay, income tax category) not available on the transaction file. Each time a magnetic-tape master file is updated, a new master file is generated.

this point, the payroll can be prepared. This type of processing is referred to as "sequential-file updating."

Sequential-file organization is impractical or inefficient for on-line systems where the status of a particular account must be inquired about, and/or where records must be currently updated. For example, in an airline reservation system, an agent at a remote terminal must frequently determine the availability of seating for a particular flight, and must be able to post transactions such as reservations or cancellations immediately. In a sequential-file organization, the agent would have to search through large segments of files each time he or she needed a specific record. This would greatly slow down the information process, eventually paralyzing the airline industry.

The advantages of sequential-file organization are relatively low-cost file media (usually magnetic tape), and efficient processing when transactions can be batched and the activity rate is relatively high. The disadvantages of sequential-file organization are that: transactions must be sorted into the same sequence as the master file's before processing can take place; the entire file must be processed, no matter how low the activity rate;* and this type of organization cannot handle on-line updating of records.

Direct-Access File Organization

A direct-access storage device such as magnetic disk can be used for sequential-file processing (see Exhibit 8–9). In this case, the disk is used as if it were magnetic tape. However, unlike tape processing, the file does not have to be copied during updating; those disk records that must be updated can be changed on the existing record. While sequential-file processing is feasible, it does not use the disk's direct-access capability.

In contrast with sequential-access files (in which individual records are not directly addressable), each location in a direct-access file is addressable. Thus, transactions need not be sorted before direct-access files are updated. The act of processing transactions in the order in which they occur (without sorting them) is called *random processing*. If such transactions are processed immediately when the related event takes place (e.g., a sale to a customer), the transaction is said to be in *real time*.† One example of such processing is the on-line airline reservation system. Obviously, the airline does not have any way of knowing (or controlling) which customers will be making reservations, or what flights will be requested. Since the data are received randomly and must be processed immediately, a sequential-file organization would not be useful here.

A direct-access file is maintained on storage devices such as magnetic disks, magnetic drums, and magnetic cores. What is significant about such direct-access

* For an example, a high activity-rate (or ratio) might involve 10,000 records in a payroll application, where almost 100 percent of the records must be processed each payroll period. A low activity rate (or ratio) might involve updating a slow-moving inventory application, where perhaps only 10 percent or fewer of the items are active in a given period of time. The payroll application could be handled efficiently by a sequential-file approach; the inventory application is probably best handled by a direct-access-file approach.

† Real-time processing was discussed in Chapter 4.

Exhibit 8–9 Direct-Access Device Used for Sequential Files

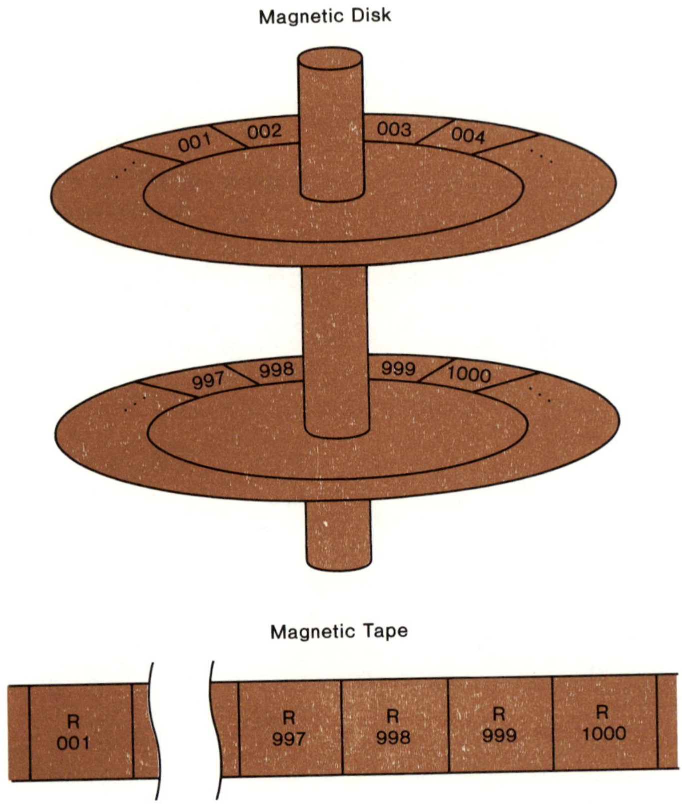

storage devices is that the complete file does not have to be searched in order to store and retrieve individual records.

Exhibit 8–10 illustrates how disk addresses and data records are arranged on a track of a magnetic disk (note the use of gaps—blank areas—between various elements).* The need to have a stored physical address and blank areas reduces the storage space that is otherwise available for data. Each record is preceded by a disk address, which indicates the record's unique position on the track. The disk address allows direct access to the record. To locate a specific record on a direct-access file, use a "record key" or "identifier" to ascertain the proper address. There are several different ways to determine a record's address; each has certain advantages and disadvantages. One of the most widely accepted addressing methods for direct access devices is the use of a table or index (indexed sequential-file organization).

* As with magnetic tape, data records can be blocked on disks, thus reducing the gaps. Also as with magnetic tape, most disks have some type of parity checking to assure accuracy of data.

Exhibit 8–10 Example of Addresses and Data Records on Disk

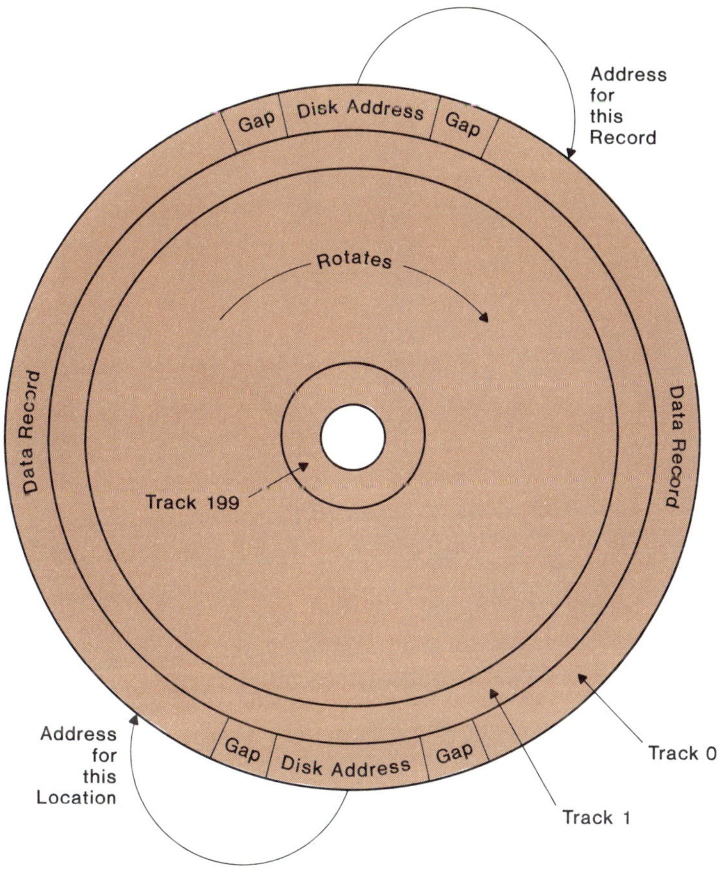

Indexed Sequential-File Organization. To refresh our knowledge of the material covered in Chapters 6 and 7, let's again go over some features of disk storage. Let's assume a disk unit with certain characteristics:

- 6 disks have 12 disk surfaces, 2 of which are not usable.
- Each disk surface has 200 tracks (identified as 000 to 199), and each track can hold up to 3,625 characters of data.
- A cylinder consists of all common tracks. Thus, there are 200 cylinders, and each cylinder can hold 36,250 characters (10 tracks times 3,625).
- The entire disk unit can hold 7,250,000 characters (10 disk surfaces times 200 tracks times 3,625 or, as an alternative way of computing, 200 cylinders times 36,250).

Exhibit 8–11 Example of Cylinder Index and Track Index

Cylinder Index

Record Key	Cylinder Location of Data Record
*	C0
1500	C1
3000	C2
4500	C3
6000	C4
7500	C5
.	.
.	.
.	.
300000	C199

Track Index (for cylinder 3)

Record Key	Track Location of Data Record
*	T0
3170	T1
3340	T2
3510	T3
3680	T4
3850	T5
4020	T6
4190	T7
4360	T8
4500	T9

*Reserved for Storing Index

Note: The record key indicates the highest number record key on the respective cylinder or track.

To access any specific data within the disk unit, we need to know which cylinder is pertinent and which track of the cylinder holds the data.

In a typical indexed sequential file, two indexes are kept; a cylinder index and a track index. The cylinder index is used to find the cylinder in which the record (or data) is located, while the track index indicates which specific track contains the data record.

Exhibit 8–11 suggests a type of index that might be used for a large inventory file having up to 300,000 record keys.* Records would be stored in sequential order on the disk and could be processed sequentially, if appropriate. More likely, however, such a file would be processed by direct access in answer to inquiries such as: "What is the status of inventory number (record key) 3317?" It would be senseless to search the enormous file in sequence to locate only a single record or a few records.

Note that in Exhibit 8–11, a record key is affiliated with each of the 200 cylinders. The record key represents the highest-number record key in the respective cylinder. For instance, all records up to 1500 are in cylinder 1; all records from 1501 through 3000 are in cylinder 2; and so on. The same principle applies for the track index. All

* The example deals with a single application, having 300,000 record keys, that uses all the storage in a disk unit; in actual practice, however, it is not unusual for several applications to be stored in a disk unit.

records up to 3170 are stored on track 1; all records from 3171 through 3340 are on track 2; and so on. Suppose that we were searching for record 3317. The computer could determine, by searching the cylinder index, that record key 3317 is stored in cylinder 3. Then, by searching the track index, it could determine that record key 3317 will be found on track 2. (Obviously, this is much more rapid than searching through the file in sequence.) Once the computer has determined the track number, it can find a specific record (in this case 3317) by searching for a key equal in the stored record (in other words, it will search for a matching 3317 stored in the data record itself). The cylinder index tells the disk's access mechanism which cylinder to search; the track index specifies which of the tracks is pertinent.*

This method is like an index in a book. Such an index contains subjects (keys) and their corresponding pages (addresses). The reader can use the index to locate and access a specific topic without having to read the book from the beginning until he/she reaches the desired topic.

The strength of the indexed sequential-file organization is its versatility—its ability to be used either in the sequential mode or direct-access mode. However, the index can take up considerable disk space, and it takes some time for the index to be searched when direct accessing is required. Therefore, when sequential file processing is not important, alternative methods of disk file organization, which adhere strictly to direct-access organization, may be worth considering. Following is a discussion of these alternatives.

Random-Access File Organization. In a direct-access file, individual records are located in the file by a record key or identifier without use of an index. There are two basic ways to accomplish this:

1. *Direct Relations.* In this alternative, the record key is the same as the storage address. For example, record 123 would be stored in disk address 123.† The direct-relation method is the fastest and most straightforward way of locating records. However, it is seldom practical to number records according to their storage location (just think of the problem that would occur as new records were added or deleted). Also, this approach tends to waste storage space. For example, consider an organization with 20,000 employees whose employee numbers range from 1 to 30,000 (the extra numbers are for possible expansion as well as for employees who have left the organization). The employee records could be stored in locations 1 to 30,000, using the direct-relation approach. However, only two-thirds of the storage locations would be used. For these reasons, the direct-relation method is used only in the few instances where it is practical to have the same record key as the storage address.
2. *Randomizing.* In this method, the record key is operated on mathematically, yielding a number that is used as the address of the record. This method is

* When an indexed sequential file is created, the records are written on disk; and as this is happening, the cylinder and track indexes are created and recorded on the outer track (which we refer to as track 0).

† Disk address 123 might actually stand for disk surface 1, track (cylinder) 23.

sometimes called "key transformation." A number of different techniques for transforming the record key are available.

One method used to ascertain the storage address is to divide the record key by the number of the storage addresses to be used and to use the remainder as the address for the record. Let's assume that there are 5 records to be stored in 11 locations (addresses 0 to 10). Assume that the keys for the 5 records are as follows: 3, 17, 33, 51, and 98. The addresses would be determined as follows:

$$\begin{aligned} 3 \div 11 &= 0 \text{ with 3 remaining} \\ 17 \div 11 &= 1 \text{ with 6 remaining} \\ 33 \div 11 &= 3 \text{ with 0 remaining} \\ 51 \div 11 &= 4 \text{ with 7 remaining} \\ 98 \div 11 &= 8 \text{ with 10 remaining} \end{aligned}$$

Thus, the records will be stored in addresses 3, 6, 0, 7, and 10, respectively. Storage would appear as follows:

	33			3			17	51			98
Addresses	0	1	2	3	4	5	6	7	8	9	10

However, a problem exists if another record generates the same address as one of the above. For instance, suppose that the next record key was 99. It would generate an address of 0 ($99 \div 11 = 9$ with 0 remaining). However, address 0 already has data stored there (record key 33).* This problem is solved through use of pointers. Simply, a pointer in address 0 would send computer control to the proper address for the synonym record key. An illustration of this follows.

Pointer	1										
Record	33	99		3			17	51			98
Addresses	0	1	2	3	4	5	6	7	8	9	10

The pointer in address 0 indicates that the synonym record 99 should be located in address 1. The problem of possible synonyms and the complexity of the mathematics involved in key transformation are shortcomings that sometimes limit the use of randomization.

Direct-Access Processing. In processing a transaction against a direct-access file (see Exhibit 8–12), the record to be altered is copied from direct-access storage, updated, and then written back—usually in the same location, which destroys the location's previous contents. If there was an error in updating, it's too late—the pre-update record is no longer available. In sequential-file updating, on the other hand, the old

* Record keys that generate the same storage address already used are called "synonyms."

Exhibit 8–12 A Direct-Access Data-Processing Application

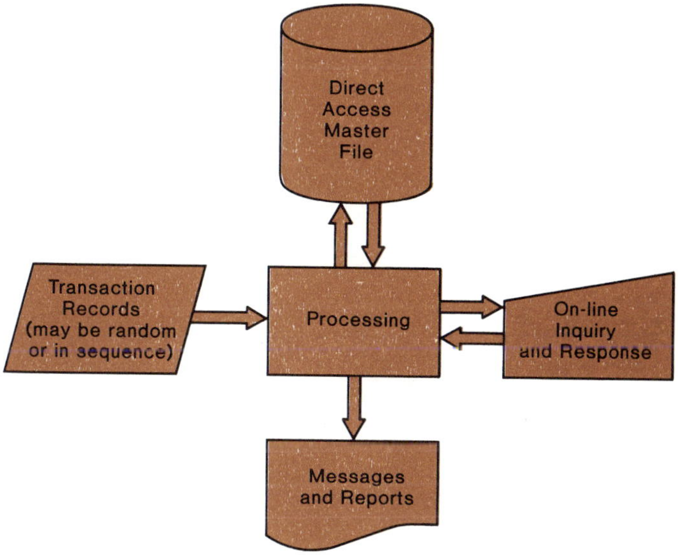

Note: The computer reads each transaction, locates the particular master record to be updated, does the updating, and writes the record back on file.

master-file is intact after the file-updating run. Since the direct-access file risks error in updating, special precautions must be taken to safeguard the file. These include: the computer's careful editing of all input transactions; the retention of transaction data for some time; periodic "dumps" (or printouts) of storage; and other security provisions.

Many of the modern data-processing approaches (e.g., data base, real-time processing, time sharing) require the use of direct-access-file organization. Generally, sequential-file organization does not satisfy the needs of such approaches.*

The advantages of the direct-access-file organization are that: transactions need not be sorted; on-line inquiries and updating are handled; and several files can be processed and updated concurrently.

The disadvantages of the direct-access-file organization are that: file devices, such as magnetic disks, are relatively expensive; processing is slower and less efficient than batch-sequential processing for high activity-rates; and special precautions are needed to safeguard the direct-access files.

Comparison of Sequential and Direct-Access Methods. Exhibit 8–13 contrasts sequential-file organization and processing, and direct-access-file organization and process-

* Despite the apparent advantages of direct-access processing, it has been estimated that about 80 percent of all data processing is still sequential and batch-oriented.

Exhibit 8–13 A Comparison of Sequential and Direct-Access Methods

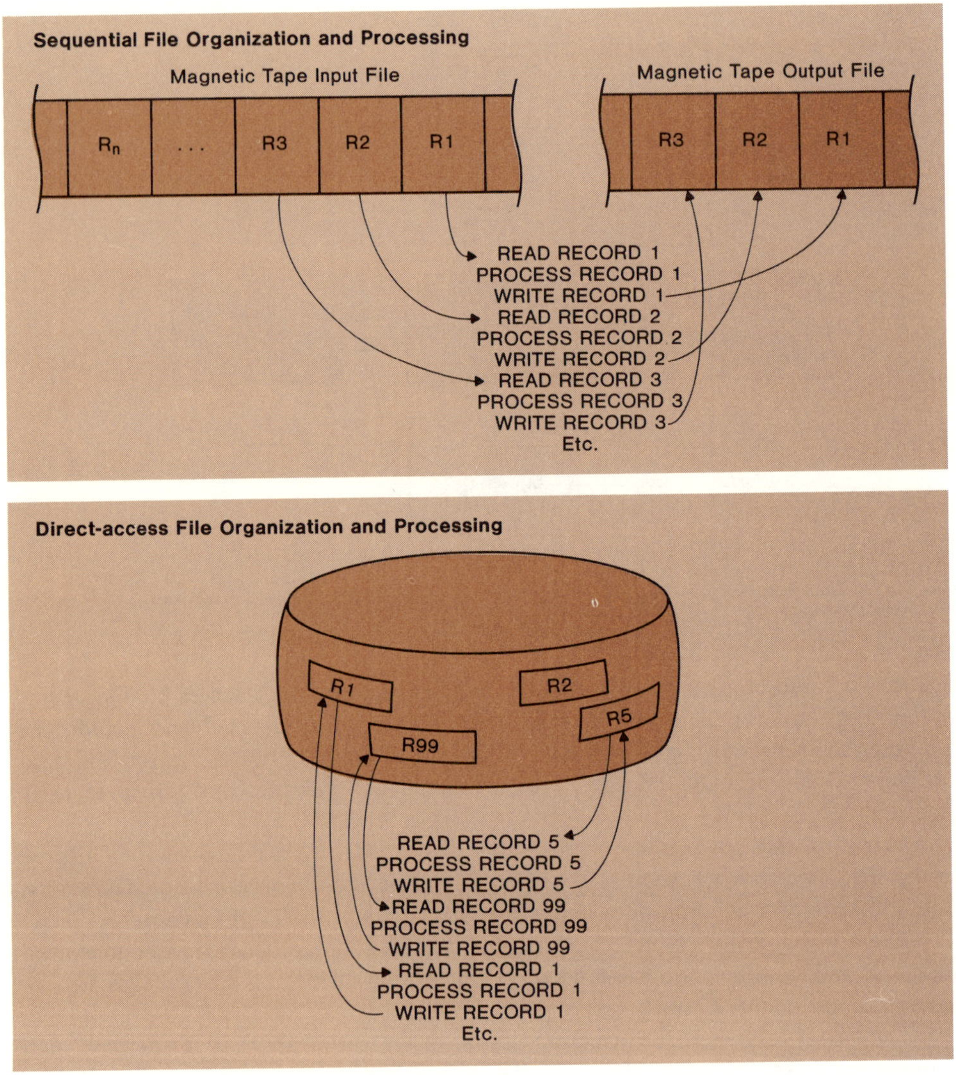

ing. In sequential methods, the records are arranged on magnetic tape in ascending sequence. First, record 1 is read, processed, and written; next, record 2 is read, processed, and written; and each consecutive record is handled in this manner. Also, an original record is read from one tape and then processed by the CPU; but the updated record is written on a second tape.

In direct-access methods, the records may or may not be arranged in sequence, and processing does not have to follow any sequence (it may, in fact, be random). If necessary, record 5 can be handled first, followed by record 99, followed by record 1, and so forth. Direct-access methods make it possible to return the processed record directly to its original location. Unlike sequential methods that use magnetic tape, direct-access methods do not require that a new output file be created.

Among the techniques used to organize data in storage more efficiently, so that they may be accessed when needed, are *tables, arrays,* and *lists.*

ADDRESSING TECHNIQUES

Tables

Tables are used to improve the efficiency of data organization of direct-access files. A simple table may be defined as a set of "paired entries." The first entry in each pair is called the "argument." The table is searched until the desired argument is located. The value read out of the table is its "function."

Tables frequently are used in data-processing applications. In particular, tables stored in computer memory are used as an index to locate records in a direct-access file. Suppose, for example, that a company has personnel records for 200 employees stored on 7 tracks of a magnetic disk. An internally stored table could be used to locate records, as follows:

Track Number	*Employee Number*
1	1 to 30
2	31 to 60
3	61 to 90
4	91 to 120
5	121 to 150
6	151 to 180
7	181 to 200

Such a table makes it easy to find the proper track number to obtain data about a particular employee, thus eliminating the need to search through several tracks before locating the desired record.*

Arrays

A special form of table is one in which the argument is simply the position of the data in the table. For example, here is a table showing the gross sales for a store during a particular work week:

* Note that tables are used in the previously discussed indexed sequential-file organization.

Day	*Gross Sales*
1	$ 50.00
2	200.00
3	250.00
4	150.00
5	400.00
6	350.00

Tables in which data are stored by position in this manner are called *arrays*. Thus, an array is an ordered set of data, for which the argument is one of the integers, one, two, three, and so on.

The computer memory need not store the array argument. The computer need store only the data itself, plus the location of the first data-element. The location of any other element may then be determined by addition. For example, if sales for day one is stored at computer storage address 1001, then sales for day four is normally stored at address 1001 plus 3, or 1004.

There are more complex two- and three-dimensional arrays that greatly extend the power of this technique.

Lists

Another important form of data structure is the *list*. In a list organization, logical records are connected by means of "pointers" (or "links").* A pointer is a field in a record that gives the address of another record, which is logically related to the first.

To illustrate a simple list structure, suppose that a company maintains a customer file on a direct-access device. Each customer record contains the customer number (which is the key field) and other related data.

At any point in time, there may be several outstanding invoices for a particular customer. Assume that a record of each invoice is maintained in a second direct-access file, called the "invoice" file. When an order is billed to the customer, a new invoice is added to this file; when the customer pays an invoice amount, the invoice is deleted from the file.

The system must be structured so that at any time the company can determine the outstanding invoices for a particular customer. Such a list is shown here:

Customer File

Address	*Customer No.*	*Customer Information*	*Pointer*
200	1		352
201	2		
202	3		
203	4		

* Such pointers or links are also referred to as "chaining."

Invoice File

Address	*Invoice No.*	*Invoice Information*	*Pointer*
350	500		
351	503		
352	527		355
353	516		
354	509		
355	514		X

In this example, customer number 1's record has a pointer (or address) of 352 that "points to" the location of the first invoice for that customer in the invoice file. The first invoice-record (in address 352), in turn, contains a pointer that "points to" the location of the second invoice for that customer; the second invoice-record is stored in address 355. The last invoice in file for the customer contains a special symbol (X) in the pointer field.

List organization is an efficient method of linking related data-records that may be stored in different storage locations.

DATA BASE

Historically, the approach to data processing has been fragmented. The total data-processing requirements for an organization have been split into a series of applications, with a separate file(s) for each application. Although this has been somewhat satisfactory for each application, it has led to a proliferation of files, some with similar data. For example, a payroll file and a personnel file invariably contain much common data for each employee. If they are maintained as separate files, delays in updating one file or the other when changes occur may create conflicting information within the files. Also, it is sometimes difficult to obtain a coordinated response to an inquiry that affects several applications that have separate files.

As a result, more integrated approaches to data processing have been emphasized.* In terms of data organization this focus has led to the concept of a data base.† A data base is an integrated set of files, tables, arrays, and other data structures (see Exhibit 8–14). Separate files may exist in a data base, but they are linked together (by list organizations) to help the entire organization get the information it needs. Data bases require large storage capacities, as well as sophisticated software called data-base management systems (DBMS).

* Recall that Chapters 1 and 2 explored integrated systems concepts.

† Vast data bases are available, for a fee, to users. For instance, the U.S. Government provides magnetic tapes containing data about statistics collected in periodic census polls. Firms such as Standard and Poor's sell magnetic tapes containing a wealth of data about business organizations.

Exhibit 8–14 Trend Towards Data-Base Management

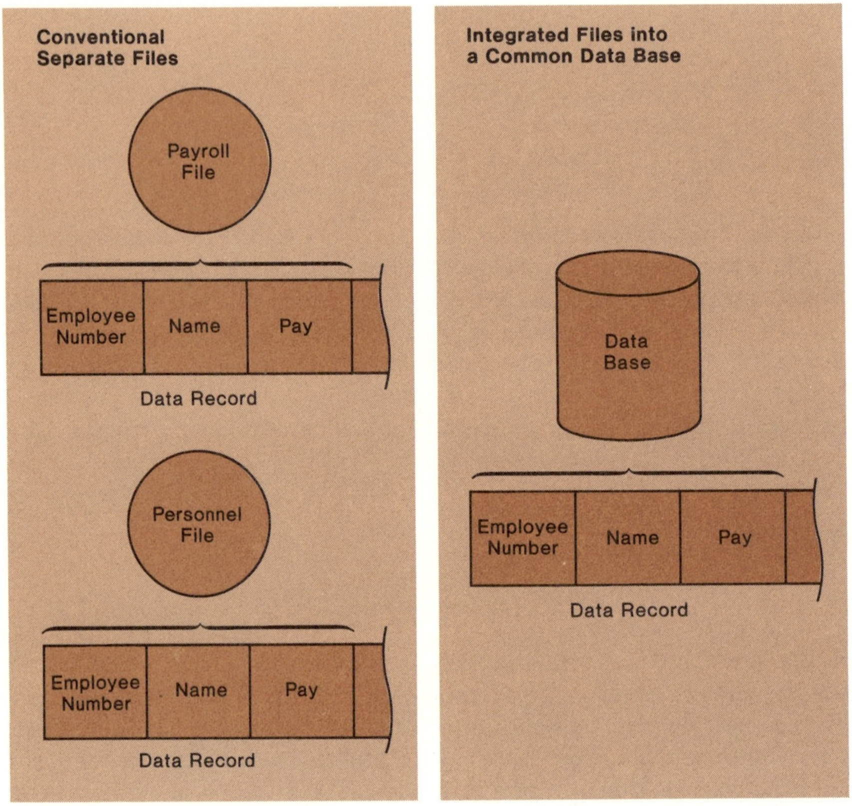

DATA MANIPULATION

Data manipulation consists of: *classifying, merging, sorting,* and *moving and editing* data. These functions, along with computation and logical operations, are widely used in data processing and influence the approach to data organization.

Classifying

Classifying is the grouping of data into categories or classes. For example, the following (alphabetized) list shows employee names and job classifications:

Name	*Job Classification*
Ruth Brown	Accounting Clerk
Richard Furth	Salesman
Robert Hope	Accounting Clerk
Elizabeth Masters	Personnel Specialist
Joseph Vickers	Salesman

Such a list can be reclassified to group employees by job classification:

Job Classification	*Name*
Accounting Clerks	
	Ruth Brown
	Robert Hope
Salesmen	
	Richard Furth
	Joseph Vickers
Personnel Specialist	
	Elizabeth Masters

Sorting

Sorting is the arranging of a list (or file) of data into a desired sequence. For example, consider the following lists of inventory numbers, where the first list is in random order and the second list is in ascending sequence.

Random List	*Sorted List*
849	101
101	222
532	275
980	532
222	789
789	849
275	980

Sorting is basic to the sequential processing method, since transaction files are sorted into the same sequence as master files before file updating is performed. In most applications, an ascending numerical sequence is used, but sometimes a descending numerical sequence is used; and in other applications, an ascending alphabetic sequence is used.

A computer sorts by manipulating magnetic-tape or -disk files. If transaction records are on punched cards, they can be sorted off-line by punched-card equipment, or they can be converted to magnetic tape or disk for sorting on-line. Since sort-routine programs are already available (usually, they are furnished by the computer manufacturer), individual users do not have to write them. To use the packaged sort-routine, the record key-field on which the file is to be sorted, the record length, and other file characteristics are specified.

There are two phases in tape sorts. First, records are sorted into initial strings; second, the strings are progressively merged into longer strings, until the entire file is sequenced. A "string" is a group of records that have been sorted.

Merging

Merging (or collating) is the combining of two or more sorted files into a single file in the same sequence. For instance, an organization might have two warehouses that store inventory. In this simplified example, the list of inventory numbers of Warehouse 1 and Warehouse 2 are merged.

Warehouse 1 Inventory Numbers	*Warehouse 2 Inventory Numbers*	*Merged Inventory Numbers*
132	101	101
275	222	132
458	275	222
789	532	275
932	789	275
	849	458
	980	532
		789
		789
		849
		932
		980

Merging is often used to consolidate two or more transaction files into a single file, in preparation for updating a master file.

Moving and Editing

Moving and editing operations are used primarily to structure data into desired output formats. For example, in the process of assembling output records, data items are moved from input or working-storage areas of computer memory to output areas. Editing operations primarily display information in a human-readable fashion, which includes the suppression of leading zeroes and the insertion of such editing symbols as commas, dollar signs, and decimal points. Here is an example:

Unedited Data Inside the Computer

0007634599

Edited Data as Displayed to User

$ 76,345.99

Even if the computer can effectively work with unedited data, such data cannot be deciphered by humans unless the computer goes through an editing routine before displaying the output.

Summary

There are numerous technical considerations that must be taken into account when organizing data, including: use of sequential or direct-access files; use of variable- or fixed-length fields and records; codes to be assigned to key fields; addressing scheme to be used; and data manipulation required.

Data organization is one of the several analysis tasks that ultimately determine how well the company will utilize the computer. Sloppy approaches to data organization can result in ineffective computer applications.

Terms to Learn

Sequential file organization
Direct-access file organization
Blocking
Interrecord gap (IRG)
Interblock gap (IBG)
Cylinder
Key
Indexed sequential-file organization
Direct-relation addressing
Randomize (transformation) addressing
Pointer
Link
Synonym

Access mechanism
Access method
Addressing technique
Table
Array
List
Random processing
Real-time processing
Batch processing
Data-base management system (DBMS)
Data manipulation
Classifying
Merging
Sorting
Moving
Editing

Review Questions

1. Define *sequential file organization.*
2. Assume a magnetic-tape file with recording density of 800 characters per inch. If each data record is 160 characters, how many records could be stored on a 2,400-foot reel of tape? Calculate based on
   a. Unblocked records; and
   b. Blocking by groups of 5 records.
3. Define *direct-access file organization.*
4. Under what conditions would direct-access file organization be preferred over sequential file organization?
5. What is meant by *random processing?* Contrast random processing with *batch processing.*
6. What is meant by *real-time processing?*
7. Discuss the following addressing approaches for direct-access organization: *index sequential, direct relation,* and *randomize.*

8. Describe the following techniques: *tables, arrays,* and *lists.*
9. What are the characteristics of a *data base?*
10. Discuss the data manipulation steps of: *classifying, sorting, merging,* and *moving and editing.*

COMPUTER
PAYROLL REPORT
ADA CORPORATION
TOTAL PAYROLL
PAYROLL RECORDS STORAGE
TIME CARDS
TIME CARDS
SUPERVISOR

CHAPTER 9

SYSTEMS ANALYSIS, DESIGN, AND APPLICATIONS

Objectives

Chapter 9 sketches the techniques that systems people use. These people are responsible for appraising existing systems and developing new and improved systems. This work must be done before the computer is programmed or the computer application is processed. An array of typical systems applications is also identified in this chapter.

Topics covered in the chapter are:
Topic 1—Systems Guidelines.
Topic 2—Systems Techniques.
Topic 3—Systems Structure.

TOPIC 1—SYSTEMS GUIDELINES

WHAT ARE SYSTEMS ANALYSIS AND DESIGN?

***Systems** analysis* and *design work* involve studying a problem area and constructing an improved way of handling it. Of course, such systems work can involve manual and mechanical methods, as well as electronic computers.

The systems work must be accomplished before the computer is programmed, and before the computer can process an application.

Conduct of a Systems Study

A *systems study* is established to: appraise a problem area; determine what the real problems are; develop alternative ways to solve the problem; evaluate the alternatives; and identify the preferred alternative. If the recommendation is approved, then the detailed design of the improved system begins to be implemented.

Systems studies should be conducted in an integrated manner (see Chapters 1 and 2); this means that they should proceed within the context of the organization's overall goals and best interest. For instance, any specific systems study should consider the interrelationship with other systems (e.g., a payroll system will certainly have an impact on a personnel system, as well as on the organization's accounting system). Therefore, it is helpful for people engaged in systems work to have a broad knowledge of the organization, including its policies, procedures, operations, and personnel. Frequently, systems studies are conducted by a task force, whose membership provide breadth and depth. Often, a blend of backgrounds are included (e.g., systems analysts, computer programmers, representatives from the affected departments, and consultants).

Exhibit 9–1 Major Steps in Computerizing an Application

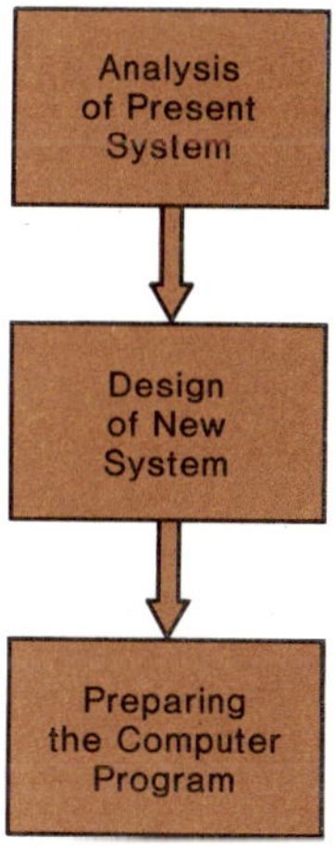

Comments

Identification of problem, and analysis of existing system. Determine possible approaches to improving system.

Select best alternative system and prepare systems specifications including: output requirements, files, input requirements, etc.

Prepare detailed computer program flowchart and write the program. Test and debug the program. Prepare files and input. Document the entire system. Place the program in actual operation. Perform any program maintenance, as becomes required.

The study team frequently has to coordinate with management on a regular basis, to ensure that the study team's direction and progress are meaningful. Since systems changes affect the organization's structure, the work process, the procedures, and the employees' morale, management should be involved in each systems project. Systems studies should be subject to careful planning and project management, covering target dates, allocation of resources to the project, and periodic reports on progress status. Moreover, the systems analyst and study team must justify their recommendations by means of both tangible factors (costs and benefits) and intangible factors (which are difficult to quantify—e.g., the effect of change on morale). One-time costs and benefits, as well as recurring costs and benefits, should be considered.

Exhibit 9–1 indicates the major planning steps involved in computerizing an application. This chapter primarily discusses the first two steps: analysis of the present system, and design of the new system. A subsequent chapter will deal with the details of preparing the computer program.*

ANALYSIS OF THE PRESENT SYSTEM

Systems analysis work begins with identifying a problem that relates to some deficiency in the existing system. For instance, the payroll system may be making calculation errors, drawing checks improperly, and processing payroll checks late. To learn

* In addition, Chapters 13 and 14 discuss material about the systems work required when a computer is evaluated and installed, and managerial approaches to directing systems projects.

about the existing system, the systems analyst gathers facts—by observing, by using questionnaires, by conversing with and interviewing knowledgeable persons, or by participating in the actual doing of the work. Part of the fact-gathering process involves collecting such salient details as: forms used; statistics regarding work load; nature of the data used; peaks and valleys of work flow; procedures followed in performing the work; employees' job descriptions in the area being studied; and relevant costs of the present system.

After the facts have been gathered,* the system analyst studies the material collected, so that he/she can develop a model (e.g., mathematical, pictorial, or written narrative) that represents the existing system. Most frequently, the model is represented in a systems flowchart, which is accompanied by a narrative description that elaborates on the pictorial content. In addition to developing a model of the existing system, the systems analyst needs to appraise its strengths and weaknesses. Studying the existing system lets the analyst understand the problem area in a practical sense, and also suggests possible improvements that can be made.

DESIGN OF THE NEW SYSTEM

Based upon the findings obtained by studying the existing system and other constraints (e.g., computer hardware and software availability), the systems analyst begins to envision the overall design of a new system that improves upon the present system's deficiencies. Often, members of the systems task force come up with a new systems design that initially takes the form of words, general systems flowcharts, and broad pictorial representations.

In designing a new system, the major consideration is the requirements of the end user. For instance, if a new payroll system is being developed, the systems analyst probably should not begin the design work until the requirements of the employees and executives responsible for the payroll, the auditors who verify the payroll, and so on are determined. The users' output requirements can largely determine the approach to be taken in designing the system. Of course, the systems analyst is expected to offer the users ideas and recommendations; frequently, users are unaware of a computer's capabilities and limitations.

In addition to considering the user requirements, the systems analyst must consider much more detailed specifications that he/she must give the computer programmer. In this sense, the systems analyst forms the communication link between the users and the computer; he/she must be able to effectively communicate with persons who are not knowledgeable about computers, as well as with other individuals who are computer technicians.

* This phase can take merely a few hours or days for a simple system, but for a complex system it could take man-years.

Output Specifications

In designing a system, a good place to start is in determining the answer to the question, "What output does the user require from the system?" Output must be intelligible not only to the analyst but, more importantly, to the individuals who will actually use the output.

The following illustrates the specific concerns of the systems analyst:

1. What medium should be used for output (e.g., printed report? CRT display picture?)?
2. What should the content of the output be (e.g., which specific data fields, and what are the maximum widths of each field of data)?
3. What should the format of the output be (i.e., how shall it appear, physically)?
4. Which data will be preprinted* on forms (assuming that the output is to be a printed report) by a printing press, and which will be generated by the computer?
5. How often is the output required, and in what volumes?
6. When (what specific dates and times) is the output required?
7. What should the distribution of the output be?
8. What controls (e.g., accuracy checks, privacy protection) are required?

Armed with the above insights, the systems analyst creates images (layouts) of how the output will appear, and then coordinates with others to obtain viewpoints and approvals (e.g., from users). If the output is sufficiently complicated, a forms-design expert may be required. For instance, there are many qualities of paper and inks that can substantially affect the cost of any planned output; since sometimes tens of thousands or hundreds of thousands of copies of a form are involved, it is desirable to obtain expert advice.

The output specifications provide the systems analyst with substantial clues about required file specifications and input specifications, as well as about processing requirements.

File Specifications

The analyst must design the various data files (primarily master files) that eventually will be able to generate the output requirements. In doing this, the analyst must consider complex technical factors,† some of which include:

* Frequently, the constant headings (e.g., the name and address of the organization) are preprinted on forms by a printing press. Such printing is usually aesthetically more attractive than that available from high-speed printers attached to computers.

† Some of these factors were discussed in Chapter 8, "Data Organization."

1. What medium (e.g., magnetic tape? magnetic disk?) will be used for the files?
2. Should the files be arranged for sequential or direct-access processing?
3. Which specific data-fields are required in the file, and what are each field's characteristics (width, numeric or alphameric, etc.)?
4. How might the files be processed, and what key fields are required to facilitate such processing?
5. What will be the frequency of use of the files?
6. What will be the volume of records maintained in the files?
7. Must the files be maintained on-line for inquiry purposes?
8. How will the files be updated?
9. How will the files be controlled?

The systems analyst, considering questions like these, probes for facts and specifies which particular files he/she envisions for the system.

Input Specifications

Input specifications must be developed for those data (e.g., transaction data, file-maintenance data) that are required to update master files. Among the questions that must be taken into account are:

1. Where will the source data be obtained (e.g., which department will supply it?)?
2. What source documents, if any, will transmit the data to the computer department?
3. Will a medium (e.g., punched cards) be used to record the input data (and if so, which?); or will the data be sent into the computer by direct entry?
4. Will the data be fed to the computer in sequential order, or randomly?
5. Which specific data fields are required for the input data records, and what are each field's characteristics (width, numeric or alphameric, etc.)?
6. How will the input data be processed, and what key fields are required to facilitate such processing?
7. What will be the volume of input data?
8. What files will be updated by the input data?
9. How will the input data be controlled?

Usually, the analyst will have to design a series of input forms (e.g., source documents, punched cards) to be used for input purposes.

Processing Specifications

In addition to designing the output, files, and input, the analyst must identify what specific processing is desired of the computer. This requires answers to such questions as:

1. Which specific files and/or input data are required to achieve the desired end result?
2. At what point in processing will the files and/or input data be read into the computer?
3. What specific fields of the files and/or input data will be used for processing purposes?
4. Which key fields will determine what processing steps are to be carried out with a record?
5. Which computations are to be performed, and with which data?
6. Which logical steps are to be performed, and with which data?
7. Are there exceptions (special situations) that must be taken into account?
8. What provisions have to be made for possible problems (e.g., erroneous data) discovered during processing?
9. What kind of updating of files is required, and/or what output is to be generated?
10. What is the volume and/or size of the processing job, and how long is it likely to take?
11. Approximately what size primary storage and secondary storage will be needed to perform the processing?

Frequently, the processing specifications are represented in *flowchart* form (a pictorial representation that shows the major steps and sequence of data processing). *Decision tables* also may be used to supplement the flowchart; the tables define actions to be taken when certain prespecified conditions have been fulfilled. Both flowcharts and decision tables will be discussed later in this chapter.

Other Specifications

The analyst specifies other related requirements; for instance, clerical procedures, off-line processing, file retention schedules, and program maintenance requirements.

In addition, the systems analyst must thoroughly understand hardware and software technical considerations, since they will affect the system's design. On one hand, the existing hardware and software constrain the analyst's setting of design specifications; on the other hand, the analyst must be able to justify changes relative to available hardware (e.g., expanding primary or secondary storage) and software (e.g., obtaining a more powerful software package) when such changes are needed and can be backed up by cost/benefit analysis.

All these types of systems-design specifications are required before a computer program should be written. The analyst gives the programmer the requirements specifications, which then guide the programmer's programming effort.

Aside from these types of technical considerations, the systems analyst must be acutely aware of the social considerations (e.g., the impact on employees of changing to the new system) and the overall economic considerations (costs and benefits for the organization, compared to the existing system).

Summary

The tasks of the systems professional are enumerated in this part of the book. It is important to carefully understand the problem area and to analyze the existing system to ascertain its deficiencies and what improvements are needed. The design of a new system involves a host of complex considerations about such things as output, files, input, and processing. In addition, social and economic considerations must be taken into account.

Terms to Learn

Systems analysis
Problem definition
Systems design
Systems analyst
Systems designer
Systems study
Output specification
File specification
Input specification
Processing specification

Review Questions

1. What is the purpose of a *systems study,* and what steps are involved in its conduct?
2. What is involved in *systems analysis work?*
3. What is involved in *systems design work?*
4. Why do systems analysis and design *precede* any computer programming work?
5. In designing a new system, what *types of specifications* must be established for output, files, input, and processing?

6. Take a simple application (e.g., payroll or student grade records) and identify some of the *output specifications, file specifications, input specifications,* and *processing specifications.*
7. Discuss the following statement: "While the technical aspects of systems analysis and design are important to a successful computer application, the economic and social considerations are even more important."

TOPIC 2—SYSTEMS TECHNIQUES

FLOWCHARTS AND DECISION TABLES

One of the most useful techniques in systems analysis, systems design, and programming logic is the flowchart.

A flowchart uses various standard symbols, interconnected by lines and arrowheads, to present a coherent, pictorial representation of the steps in a system.

There are two types of flowcharts. The *systems flowchart,* prepared by the systems analyst, is the more general chart; it does not focus on the details of computer logic. The *program flowchart,* used by the programmer, focuses on the computer's logic in analyzing the application.

While it is possible to write a computer program without a flowchart, it is best to first depict any complex application as a flowchart, before writing the computer program. The flowchart forces the individual to discipline his/her thinking and to identify each operation in logical sequence; and often, it reveals situations that otherwise would probably have been overlooked. If a flowchart is available, a computer program is likelier to be written more quickly and to operate more effectively than if it hadn't used a flowchart as a guideline.

A plastic template facilitates the drawing of flowcharts. Exhibit 9–2 shows the various symbols that are used in flowcharting. Although some flowcharting symbols have been standardized, two different people may develop somewhat different flowcharts in solving a particular problem—and both may have come up with reasonable solutions.

Systems Flowchart

The systems flowchart gives a general overview of a system, and deals with noncomputer as well as computer processing. However, the systems flowchart does not go into detail about the specific, minute computer-processing steps as the program flowchart does. For instance, a systems flowchart may use only a few symbols to summarize computer processing, while the supporting program flowchart may use hundreds or even thousands of symbols to painstakingly detail the individual computer operations

Exhibit 9–2 Symbols Used in Flowcharting

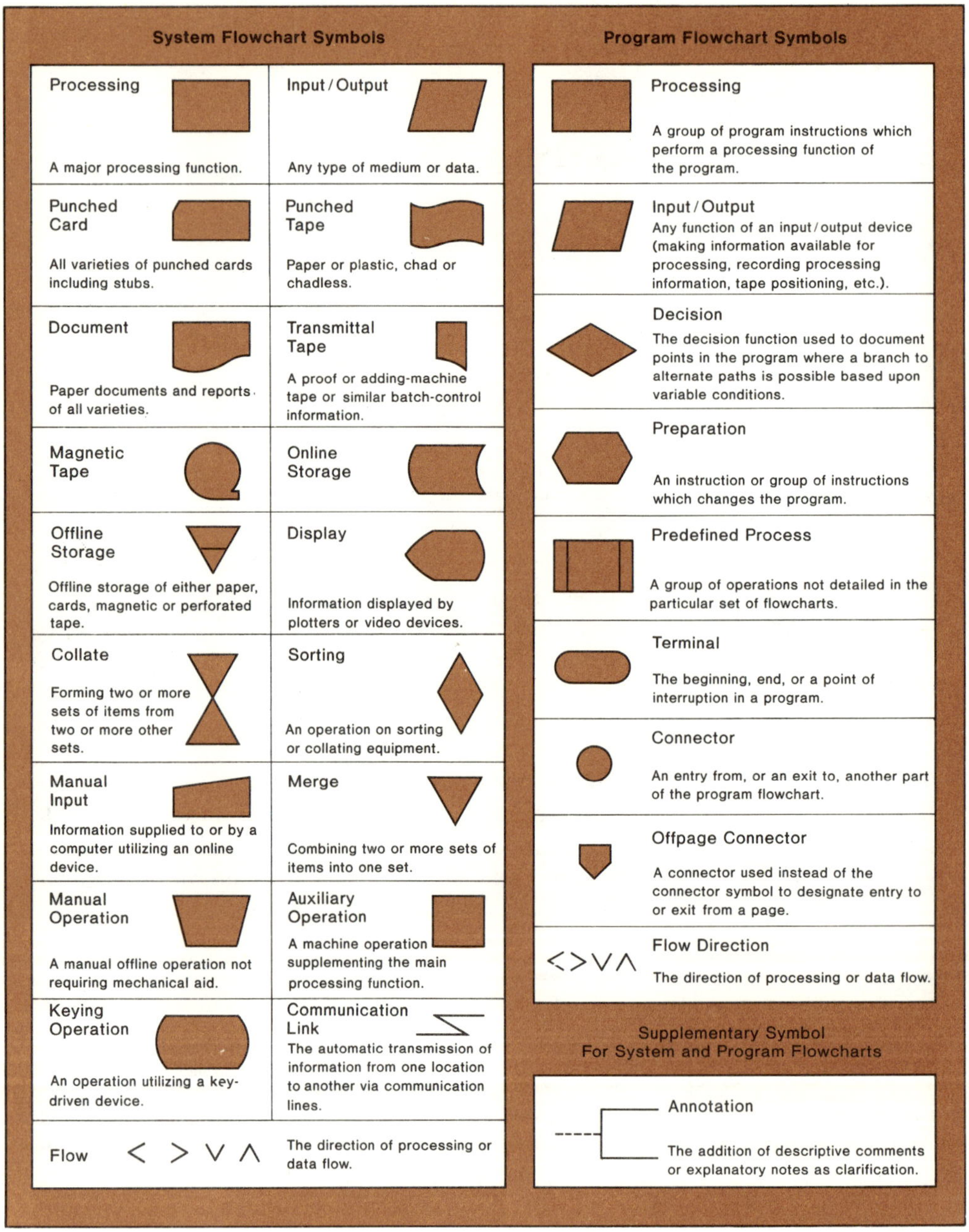

Exhibit 9–3 General Structure of a Systems Flowchart

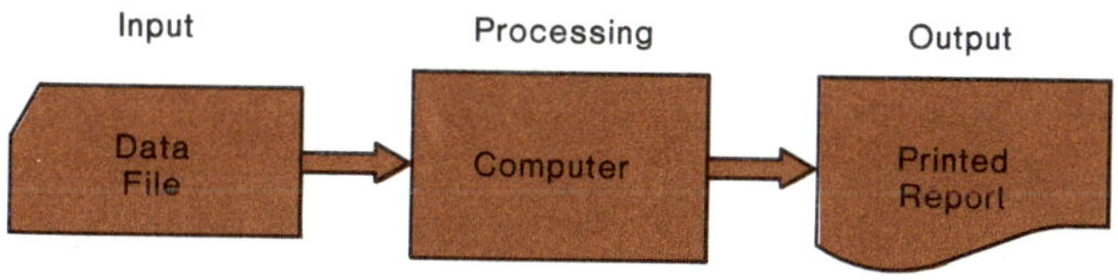

needed to accomplish the job. The systems flowchart serves as a broad roadmap for the systems analyst and computer programmer. A general example of a systems flowchart is presented in Exhibit 9–3. Additional examples of systems flowcharts will be presented later in this chapter under "Specific Applications."

Program Flowchart

The program flowchart is a very specific, detailed, pictorial representation of computer operations. The program flowchart may contain many dozens, hundreds, or even thousands of symbols that may have been summarized in a few symbols on a systems flowchart. The computer programmer uses the program flowchart as a blueprint to guide the actual writing of the computer program.

A program flowchart can be developed with the use of the following symbols (see also Exhibit 9–4):

1. The *rectangle,* which represents computer-processing operations such as arithmetic functions.
2. The *parallelogram,* which is used to indicate either input or output functions (sometimes referred to as "reading" and "writing").
3. The *diamond symbol,* which is used for a step that requires a logical decision (e.g., is one number larger than another number?).
4. The *oblong,* which is used for terminal purposes; that is, the beginning or interruption of a program.
5. The *small circle,* which is referred to as a "connector." The connector is used to link one part of a flowchart with another part of the flowchart.
6. *Lines* with arrowheads are used to connect symbols and to indicate the flow of computer control.

A few other symbols are available to clarify or elaborate on the flowchart.

There are several flowchart guidelines that are widely accepted and that facilitate standardized charting technique. They are:

1. Use the appropriate standard flowcharting symbols.

Exhibit 9–4 General Use of Flowcharting Symbols

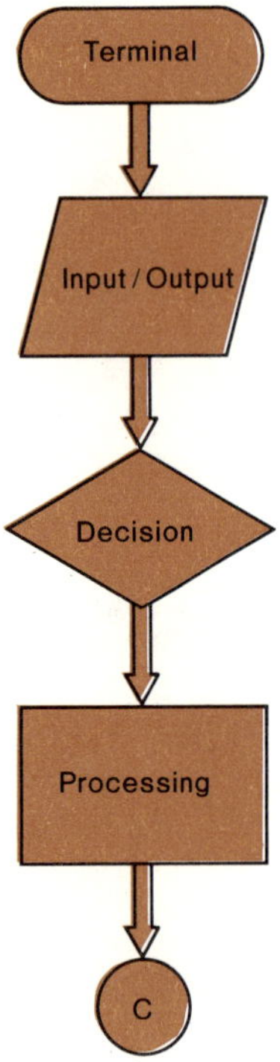

The beginning, End, or Point of Interruption in a Program

Any Input / Output Function, Such as Punched Card Reading or Printing

Any Program Branch Point that is Based on the Value of a Variable or Constant

Any Group of Instructions that Performs a Processing Function, Such as Arithmetic

An Entry or Exit Point that Interconnects with a Distant Point in the Program
(C for connector)

2. Develop a general systems flowchart prior to preparing a detailed program flowchart.
3. Flowchart from the top to bottom of a page, and from the left to the right.
4. Avoid intersections of lines used to depict the flow of logic. Overlapping lines can create confusion in the chart.
5. Use connectors to reduce the number of flow lines. Connectors are particularly helpful when a flowchart is several pages long, and where several loops are needed in the logic of the flowchart.

The use of a template encourages a neat and orderly development of the flowchart, which facilitates logical analysis and understanding—always objectives of systems work.

The general structure that is common to program flowcharts is presented in Exhibits 9–5 and 9–6. Translated into words, input data is read into the CPU; the processor performs certain processing operations on the data; and at least some of the data are transmitted as output. Since it would be senseless, in most cases, to read and

Exhibit 9–5 A Program Flowchart Without a Loop

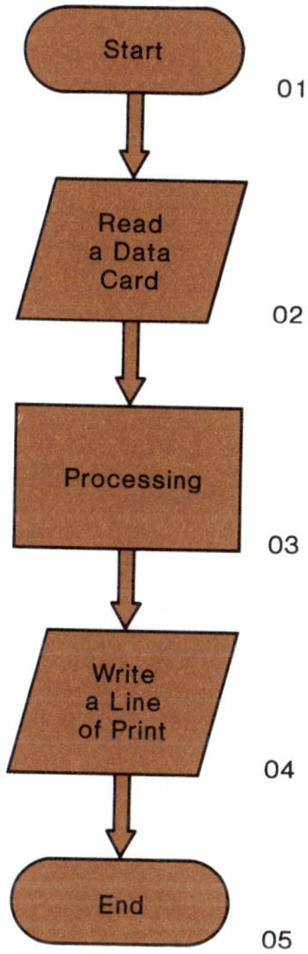

Note: It is helpful to number the flowchart symbols to facilitate reference to a particular symbol.

process only a single-input record, most data-processing jobs consist of large data-files that must be processed; and each record (or selected records) must be processed by means of the same general procedure. The computer is used most effectively when large amounts of data are processed without interruption by the same program. It would be time-consuming and costly to process one record and have the computer halt or stop, then to process a second record and have another halt, and so on. The objective is to have the computer operate as automatically as possible, without interruption.

Exhibit 9–5 illustrates a flowchart that provides for the processing of one input data record. This flowchart depicts the computer processing a single input and then writing a single line of print on a document.

Exhibit 9–6 illustrates a slightly modified flowchart that can process an entire file of data, rather than just one record. The difference between the two charts is that there is a loop in Exhibit 9–6 that lets the computer keep carrying out the programmed procedure for all input data records. Notice that Exhibit 9–7 presents another useful flowchart technique. Suppose that there is an intermix of different types of data cards

Exhibit 9–6 A Program Flowchart With a Loop

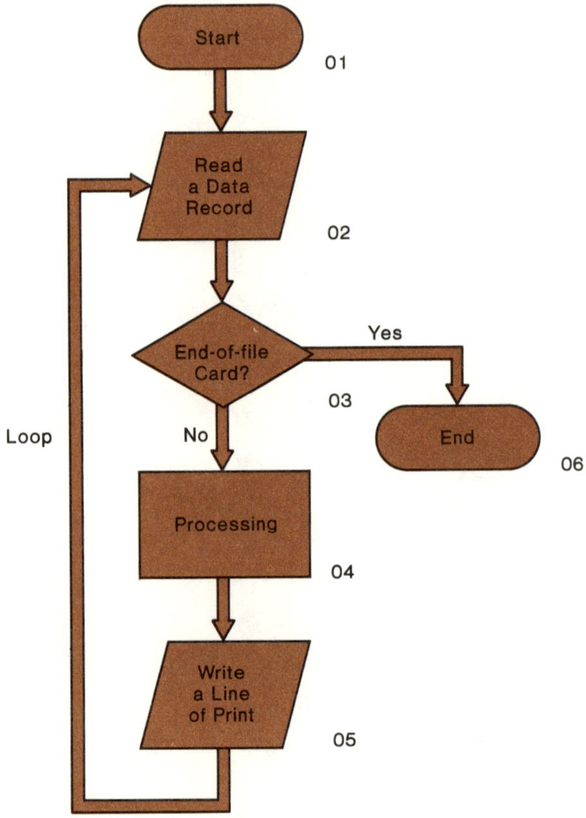

Note: When there is a single path (such as in the loop above), it is called an "unconditional branch." When there are two or more paths, depending on a condition, such a decision point results in a conditional branch.

in a file to be processed. For example, assume that there are two types of personnel cards—one for male employees and the other for female employees. In each data card, this would require a code to distinguish males from females. Code 1 in a specific field (say column 80 of a punched card) could signify a male employee, and code 2 in the field could mean a female employee. At step 04, a decision symbol permits the directing of computer logic in different paths, depending on the results of the decision test. If the data record is a type code 1, it will follow that particular routine; if the data record is a type code 2, it will follow the other routine. This type of testing provides the computer with the powerful option of handling virtually unlimited different conditions—even if they exist in the same data file.

Up to this point, we have discussed flowcharts in a very conceptual and general

Exhibit 9–7 A Program Flowchart Testing for Different Conditions

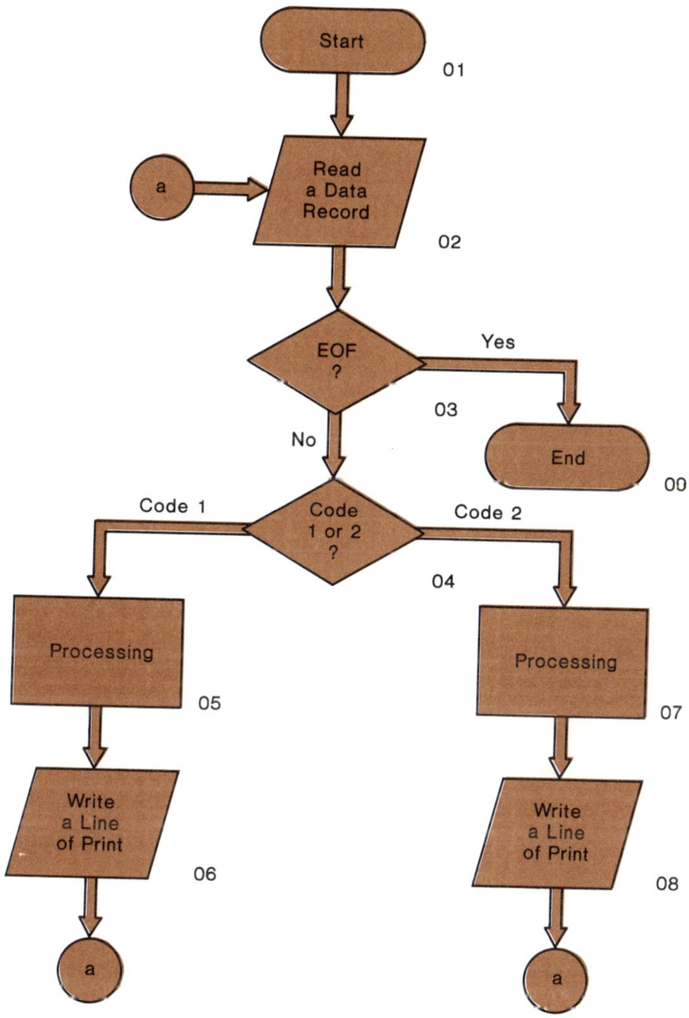

way. Now let's consider how a flowchart might be used in practice, in connection with an application.

Example of Program Flowchart Use

Let's take a simple, practical example to illustrate how flowcharting may be applied. Suppose that we wish to compute the arithmetic mean (simple average) for a group of figures. Algebraically, the solution to the problem could be stated as:

$$A = \text{Sum of Data}_n \div N$$

A stands for average; n indicates an indeterminate amount of data that must be summed; and N stands for the number of data items. How would we do this manually? Assume certain data, such as: 10, 20, 30, 10, 40. We would simply add the numbers to get the sum (110), and then divide by the number of items (5). The answer would be 22 (110 divided by 5).

Of course, since such a simple problem can be solved manually, it would be senseless to process it by computer. However, imagine that there were several thousand data items, that such computations had to be done quickly and accurately, and that larger figures were sometimes involved. In such cases, it is likely that the computer would be very helpful. Once a program has been developed, it can be used time and time again to solve the average computational problem, thus freeing humans for more productive work.

Exhibit 9–8 presents a program flowchart showing the logic of solving the above problem in computer terms. The flowchart is presented based on a number of assumptions. First, there will be one data field (item) in each record; this data field is referred to by the variable name DITEM. Second, the accumulation of the numeric values of the data (DITEM) will be stored in a symbolic address with the name SUM. The divisor (number of data items) will be called COUNT. Last, the result we are looking for will be called by the variable name AVG (standing for average).

Next, let us assume some limited amount of actual data so that we may see how the flowchart works.

	DITEM
Data Record #1	50
Data Record #2	20
Data Record #3	10
Data Record #4	60
Data Record #5	30
Data Record #6	00

Assume that each data record is processed in sequence through the flowchart.

Symbols 1, 2, and 3 on the flowchart can be considered to be preliminary steps.* The computer starts and two storage locations having the symbolic addresses of SUM and COUNT are initialized to zero. These steps are necessary to erase any data that may have been left in those storage locations by a previous job. We will come back to the point shortly.

Symbol 4 causes the individual data record to be read that would bring DITEM into storage for processing (recall that DITEM also represents a symbolic storage address).

* Such preliminary steps are sometimes called "housekeeping steps."

Exhibit 9–8 A Program Flowchart to Determine Arithmetic Mean

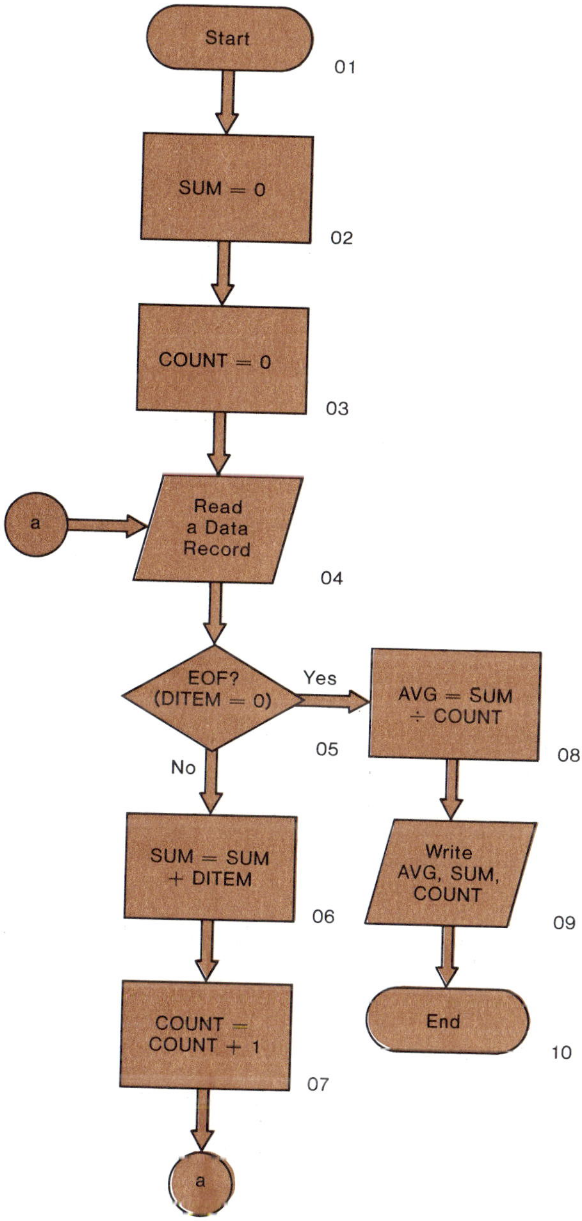

Note: Computer programs for the above flowchart are presented in Chapter 11.

Symbol 5 tests whether all the data have been processed. If the computer does not receive some positive indication that it is through processing, it could stay in an endless loop, waiting for more data. Our way of indicating that the job is done is to place a dummy data record (#6) at the end of the data file; note that it has zeros in the DITEM field. When that record is eventually read, the computer can be alerted that it has processed all the data records for the job. If end of file (EOF) has not been reached, the branch is to the next step (Symbol 6).

Symbol 6 causes the computer to accumulate the values of the data and store them in storage location SUM.

Symbol 7 results in an accumulation of "1" for each data record that is processed. The accumulation is stored in the location COUNT.

After each data record is processed, the connector (a) sends control back to read another data record. The computer will stay in the loop until the dummy card (end of file) is read; when EOF is sensed, the branch will be to the end-of-file routine.

Symbol 8, which is part of the EOF routine, causes the SUM to be divided by the COUNT to derive the AVG.

Symbol 9 asks the computer to output the result.

Symbol 10 tells the computer that it has completed the particular job.

How would the data records have appeared in the CPU? Let's look at how the storage locations and the accumulator* would have appeared after each data record, in our example, was processed:

Status of CPU After Each Data Record Is Processed

Data Record	*Accumulator*	*DITEM*	*SUM*	*COUNT*†	*AVG*
#1	0 + 50 = 50	50	50	1	
#2	50 + 20 = 70	20	70	2	
#3	70 + 10 = 80	10	80	3	
#4	80 + 60 = 140	60	140	4	
#5	140 + 30 = 170	30	170	5	
#6	170 ÷ 5 = 34	00	170	5	34

The last line indicates the status of the CPU at the point of termination.

As a point of clarification, suppose that we omitted Symbols 2 and 3 from the flowchart, and did not zero out locations SUM and COUNT. Further, suppose that the value of 100 remained in the location SUM from a prior job. This would have resulted in an erroneous computation, since the value in SUM, at the end of our job, would have been 270 and not 170. The average would have been printed as 54 (270 ÷ 5) instead of 34! This underscores the importance of zeroing out all storage locations that are to be used for accumulation purposes. It is not essential to zero out other storage areas (e.g.,

* The accumulator is, of course, part of the CPU's arithmetic/logic unit.

† The accumulator would also, of course, cause the one-digit counting to take place each time through the loop. The above example only shows the accumulator's handling of the summation of DITEM and calculation of the AVG.

Exhibit 9–9 Four Quadrants of a Decision Table

Condition Stub	Condition Entry
Action Stub	Action Entry

areas into which we read data) since, as you will recall, reading data into a storage location automatically erases whatever data may be stored there. This destructive read-in feature has been mentioned in prior parts of this book.

Decision Tables

A *decision table* is a tabular analysis that can supplement certain flowcharts, particularly in problems with complex decision logic.

A decision table is divided into quadrants (see Exhibit 9–9).

1. The *upper-left quadrant* (called the "condition stub") sets forth the existing conditions, in question form.
2. The *lower-left quadrant* (called the "action stub") outlines, in narrative form, the action to be taken to meet each of the conditions.
3. The *upper-right quadrant* (called the "condition entry") answers the questions asked in the condition-stub quadrant. Answers are represented by a "Y" to signify "yes" and "N" to signify "no," or a blank to show that the condition involved has not been tested.
4. The *lower-right quadrant* (called the "action entry") indicates, by a check mark or by an "X," the appropriate action resulting from the answers to the conditions entered in the condition-entry quadrant.

Let's use a very simple example (the arithmetic mean problem flowcharted in Exhibit 9–8) to illustrate a decision table (see Table 9–1). In actual practice, a decision table is used only in considerably more complicated situations that have several conditions and actions.

Table 9–1

A Simplified Example of a Decision Table

Is It an End-of-File Record?	N	Y
Add Value in DITEM to Previous Total in SUM	X	
Add "1" to COUNT	X	
Loop Back to Read the Next Data Card	X	
Divide SUM by COUNT		X
Write the Results: SUM, COUNT		X
End Processing		X

Now let's look at a somewhat more sophisticated example of a decision table (see Table 9–2).* The condition stub indicates the two factors that determine the award of a letter grade to a student; the numeric grade average, and the extent of unexcused absences from class. The action stub signifies the possible actions that can or should be taken. The condition entry indicates the various alternatives that may be encountered (that is, combinations of a numeric grade and extent of unexcused absences). The action entry specifies the action to be taken for the various condition entries encountered.

The decision table focuses on the logical decisions in a problem. The construction of an accompanying flowchart for an actual application is likely to involve more computer operations, since a flowchart identifies input, output, processing steps, logical operations, and the sequence of operations. Since the flowchart views a data-processing application more comprehensively, the decision table can supplement (but not replace) the flowchart.

Summary

Among the techniques available to the systems professional are flowcharting and decision tables. These two techniques are among the most useful and the most widely adopted. Facility in using the techniques enhances the quality of systems analysis and design. Systems techniques are intended to bring about logical and objective systems effort.

* In Table 9–2, certain factors need to be more specific. For instance, grade classifications are mutually exclusive: 60 to 69.9, 70 to 79.9, etc. Also, what constitutes excessive unexcused absences (e.g., two cuts, three cuts) needs to be specified.

Table 9–2

A More Sophisticated Example of a Decision Table

	Condition Entry									
IF (Condition Stub)	1	2	3	4	5	6	7	8	9	10
Grade Average Is 90 to 100?	Y	Y	N	N	N	N	N	N	N	N
Grade Average Is 80 to 90?			Y	Y	N	N	N	N	N	N
Grade Average Is 70 to 80?					Y	Y	N	N	N	N
Grade Average Is 60 to 70?							Y	Y	N	N
Grade Average Is below 60?									Y	Y
Excessive Unexcused Absences?	N	Y	N	Y	N	Y	N	Y	N	Y
THEN (Action Stub)										
Award a Grade of A	X									
Award a Grade of B		X	X							
Award a Grade of C				X	X					
Award a Grade of D						X	X			
Award a Grade of F										
Consider Student for Special Award	X							X	X	X
Invite Student to Consultation on Weak Performance								X	X	X
	Action Entry									

Legend:
Y = Yes. N = No.
Blank = Irrelevant.
X = Action to Be Taken.

Terms to Learn

Systems flowchart
Program flowchart
Flowchart symbol
Loop
Branch
Conditional branch
Unconditional branch
End-of-file (EOF) condition
Decision table
Action stub
Action entry
Condition entry
Condition stub
Housekeeping
Initialize
Terminal symbol
Input/output symbol
Decision symbol
Processing symbol
Connector symbol

Review Questions

1. What is a *flowchart,* and of what value is it to the computer professional?
2. Distinguish a *systems flowchart* from a *program flowchart.*
3. Identify the *guidelines* for good flowcharting.
4. Assume that there is a single file of data cards, and that each card contains data about one student. Each card contains a sex-code field (i.e., 1 = female, 2 = male). Draw a program flowchart that would read the data cards, test on sex code, count the number of female students, count the number of male students, and print out separate totals for the two categories of students. Be sure to include a loop provision in the chart.
5. What are the similarities and differences between *flowcharts* and *decision tables?*
6. Suggest a simple application for a decision table, and try to develop the table.
7. Do research to determine the "rules" for the social security deductions in a payroll application. Discuss the "rules" in class, and then develop a flowchart and decision table to present the logic of the "rules."

TOPIC 3—SYSTEMS STRUCTURE

SYSTEMS APPLICATIONS

General Applications

The computer processes a wide diversity of applications. These days there is hardly an industry or a medium- or large-sized organization in which the computer does not play a prominent data-processing role; and increasingly, even smaller organizations are finding applications for the computer.

Some representative users of the computer include:*

1. *Federal Government*. The United States Government uses computers to: process income tax returns; maintain social security records; perform logistical analyses for the military; monitor outer space probes; and perform many other uses.
2. *Local Government*. States, counties, and cities use computers to: maintain property-tax records; handle motor-vehicle registration records; process traffic violations; and maintain criminal records.
3. *Hospitals*. Medical facilities use computers to: maintain records about patients; perform medical diagnoses; monitor patients' vital signals (e.g., heartbeat, respiration); and perform other applications.
4. *Schools*. Educational institutions are using computers to: maintain records on students; keep track of library collections; help teach students; and perform in many other administrative and research areas.
5. *Museums*. Museums and other cultural units are employing them to keep inventories of art, music, natural specimens, etc.
6. *Sports Teams*. Computers have been utilized to track and appraise potential players, to analyze opponents' strengths and weaknesses, and to more accurately determine results and winners in such events as track and swimming.
7. *Political Parties*. Political parties have been using computers to keep track of supporters and donations, as well as to analyze alternative political strategies and the likely outcomes of elections.
8. *Media*. Magazines and journals use the computer to maintain large subscriber mailing lists. Newspapers employ the computer to facilitate accurate and rapid typesetting, and some maintain computerized indexes of news events. Television stations are using the computer to more accurately forecast weather- and election-related news.

* One study indicated that the industries that use the computer most extensively are as follows, in ranked order: manufacturing; data-processing service bureaus; federal government; banking; state and local government; education; wholesale and retail sales; insurance; and utilities.

9. *Retailing.* Large department chains and stores use the computer to keep records about customers' charge accounts as well as the status of merchandise inventory.
10. *Transportation.* Airlines and railroads keep updated, computer-maintained records of seat availability. This lets them quickly and accurately inform travellers whether space to particular destinations on particular dates is available. Also, large aircraft and ships use computational aids in navigation.
11. *Hotels and Theaters.* Various types of enterprises employ computers to keep track of room/seat availability.
12. *Banks.* Most checking and savings accounts' records are computerized to some degree, as are many other financial records.
13. *Insurance Companies.* Insurance companies use computers to calculate complex mathematical and statistical tables that are related to risks and premium rates, as well as to maintain considerable policy record-keeping.
14. *Legal.* Various legal offices are placing the complex laws and court decisions into computers so that legal searches can be made more quickly and accurately.
15. *Engineering.* Engineering experts use the computer to facilitate the design of structures (e.g., highways, bridges, buildings, dams, and ships).
16. *Research.* Scientists use the computer to perform sophisticated calculations that cannot otherwise be performed (e.g., nuclear research and astronomical calculations).
17. *Industrial Organizations.* Business firms use the computer in practically every area, including: accounting and finance; marketing; manufacturing; and personnel.
18. *Process Control.* Some enterprises, such as electrical-generating utilities and oil refineries, use the computer to significantly control their operations (e.g., monitor furnaces, turbines, generators, and valves).

Specific Applications*

In almost every type of business, several specific applications are common: payroll, accounting, sales, and inventory.

While most businesses have these computer applications,† the nature of an

* The specific applications presented in this chapter are intended to be illustrative. While they are somewhat typical of applications in most organizations, they are not comprehensive in scope or detail.

† Within organizations, certain functions use the computer more than other functions. One study indicated the following relative use:

	Early 1970s	*Late 1970s*
Accounting, finance, and administration	47%	36%
Marketing and distribution	23%	27%
Manufacturing	19%	24%
Research and engineering	11%	13%

Exhibit 9–10 Systems Flowchart of Payroll Application

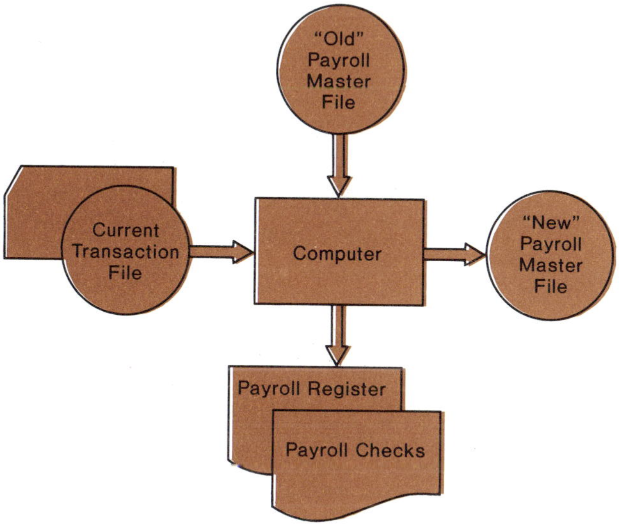

organization's industry (e.g., automotive, chemical, or retailing) and of its own internal policies and procedures inevitably puts the stamp of individuality on its system designs, compared with those of other organizations (even firms within the same industry).

Nevertheless, it is helpful to briefly consider some of the characteristics often found in such specific computer applications. Systems flowcharts are used to depict overviews of the applications.

1. *Payroll Application.* An organization must maintain a master file of employees to be periodically paid (e.g., weekly or monthly payrolls) (see Exhibit 9–10). The individual employee's master record contains such data as: employee number; social security number (which is sometimes used as the employee number); employee name and address; marital status; exemptions for income-tax purposes; salary or hourly rate of pay; year-to-date earnings; year-to-date income tax withholding; and year-to-date social security deductions.

   Before the payroll can be generated, certain transactions must be processed. These include inputting hours worked (for hourly workers), and changes to master records (e.g., new employees, terminated employees, salary increases, changes to number of exemptions). The transaction file is used to update the master file, once the updating has been completed, the master file can be used to generate the current payroll. Frequently, a payroll register is first generated by computer. After the register has been verified and approved, the computer subsequently generates the

Exhibit 9–11 An Example of a Payroll Register

ADA CORPORATION
PAYROLL REGISTER
FOR THE PERIOD ENDING 31 DECEMBER 19__

EMPLOYEE NUMBER	EMPLOYEE NAME	GROSS SALARY	DEDUCTIONS	NET SALARY
123456789	JOHN DOE	$ 300.00	$ 60.00	$ 240.00
211793451	MARY SMITH	325.00	70.00	255.00
453091832	A. B. WHITE	275.00	50.00	225.00
TOTALS		$7,500.00	$1,500.00	$6,000.00

payroll checks with attached payroll stubs, which give the employees a record of their earnings for the current period and year to date (see Exhibit 9–11).

Since there are usually few random inquiries about payroll records, such files can be maintained in sequential files (e.g., magnetic tape).

2. *Accounting Application.* Every organization maintains accounting records (e.g., general ledger, accounts-receivables ledgers, and various journals), since they are needed to report information to the government, owners of the business, and management (see Exhibit 9–12). Accounting's end objective is to generate financial statements—primarily the income statement and the balance sheet (which shows assets, liabilities, and net worth). In accounting, all entries are either debits or credits. All accounts need to be classified. For instance:

Account Classification	*Chart of Account Numbers*
Income Accounts	100 to 199
Expense Accounts	200 to 299
Asset Accounts	300 to 399
Liability Accounts	400 to 499
Net-Worth Accounts	500 to 599

Once the accounts are classified and assigned account numbers, a computer program can be developed to routinely handle debit and credit entries. A credit transaction increases income accounts, liability accounts, and net-worth accounts,

Exhibit 9–12 Systems Flowchart of Accounting Application

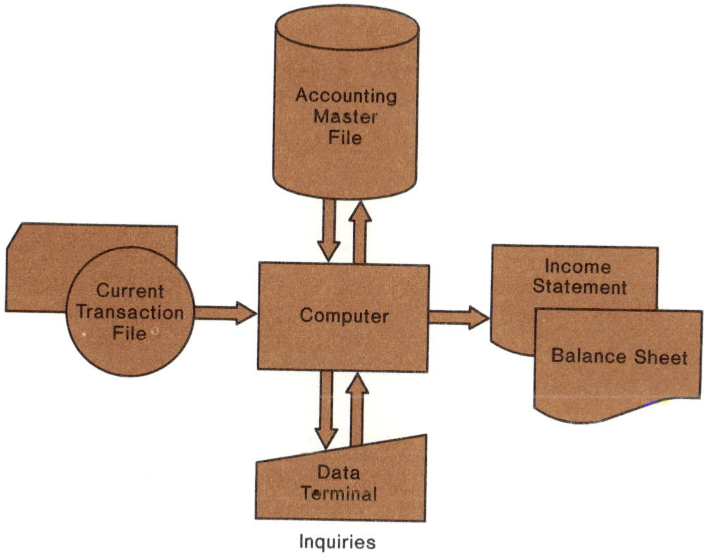

while debits decrease them. A debit transaction increases expense accounts and asset accounts, while credits decrease them. In accounting, the rigid rules are very susceptible to computer-programming techniques; which explains why one of the first applications to be computerized involves accounting records.

Each account record in a master file usually contains a field for account number and a field for the balance of the account (either a debit or credit amount). The debit or credit may be signified by a special code, or specific fields may be set aside for the debit amount and the credit amount, respectively.

Periodically, transaction files are entered with debits and credits to be posted against specific account numbers. After all transactions have been posted up to and including the last day of the month, the balance in each individual account is determined (taking the appropriate net between debits and credits or vice versa, depending on the class of account).

Thereafter, the updated master file can be processed by following highly stylized rules of accounting. The income and expense accounts are used to generate the monthly income-statement (profit or loss from operations—see Exhibit 9–13); the asset, liability, and net-worth accounts are used to generate the balance sheet (reflecting any change in the net worth since the last reporting period)

Traditionally, since accounting records have been largely reported on a monthly basis, many such records have been maintained in sequential files (e.g., on magnetic tape). However, some accounting records (such as accounts-receivables ledgers) may involve considerable inquiries during the period; consequently, some

Exhibit 9–13 An Example of a Simple Income Statement

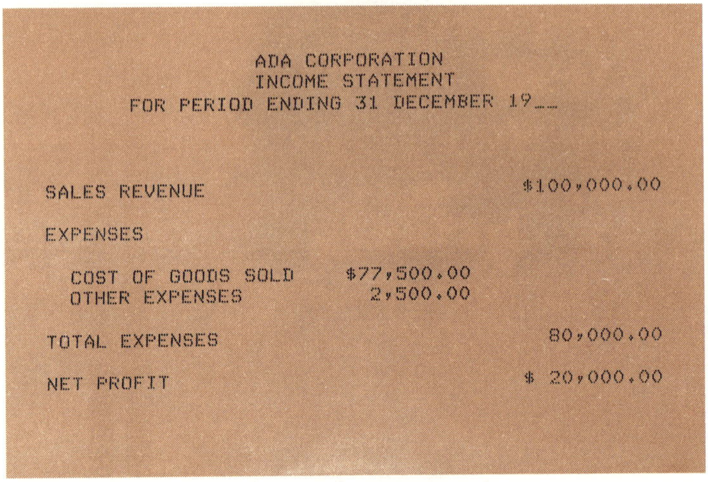

ADA CORPORATION
INCOME STATEMENT
FOR PERIOD ENDING 31 DECEMBER 19__

SALES REVENUE		$100,000.00
EXPENSES		
COST OF GOODS SOLD	$77,500.00	
OTHER EXPENSES	2,500.00	
TOTAL EXPENSES		80,000.00
NET PROFIT		$ 20,000.00

organizations are placing some or all of their accounting records on direct-access storage files.

3. *Sales Application.* Organizations that have any volume of transactions with customers seriously consider computerizing the processing (see Exhibit 9–14).

   Typically, sales transactions involve the following types of data: customer account number (if the sale is being charged); identification of product sold to customer; quantity of product sold to customer; unit price of the product sold to the customer; and total of sale (obviously, the customer may have purchased more than one type of product).

   Sales can be for either cash or credit (charge). Cash sales and credit sales must be reflected in the organization's sales statistics (e.g., the quantity of each product sold in each location of the organization). On the other hand, only the credit sales data are needed for updating the accounts-receivables master records (moneys owed by customers to the organization for products not yet paid for). The customer's accounts-receivable master record normally contains such data fields as: customer account number; name and address; previous unpaid balance; details of products purchased during the month; and details of payments paid on account during the month. The accounts-receivable record is used periodically (usually monthly) for billing customers. The billing process then generates additional transactions: cash payments, which must enter the system to reduce the outstanding amounts in the accounts-receivable master records.

   As a sales transaction enters the computer system, it can be used to update the customer's accounts-receivable record and to simultaneously update the organiza-

Exhibit 9–14 Systems Flowchart of Sales Application

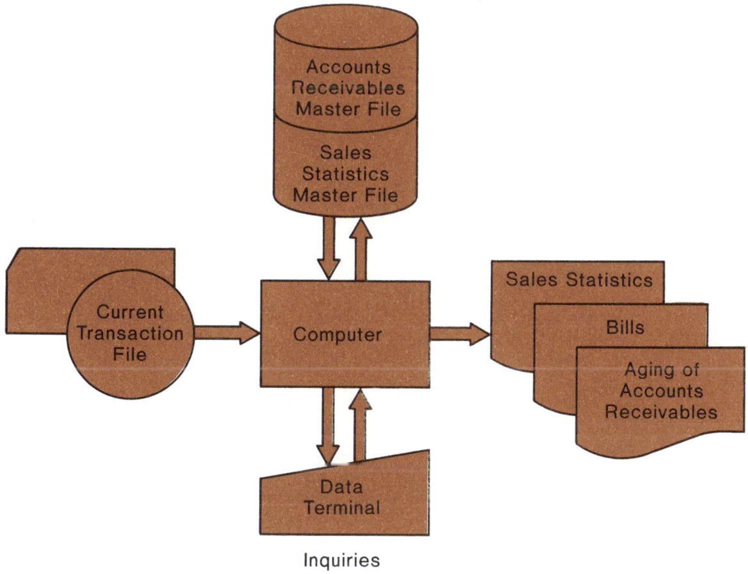

tion's sales-statistics master file. The updated accounts-receivables master file (see Exhibit 9–15) can be used to generate reports that indicate the status of past-due accounts and the effectiveness of collecting moneys due. The updated sales-statistics master file can be used to generate reports that indicate which products are selling well and which departments are performing well in selling their goods.

Increasingly, records such as sales statistics and accounts receivables are being maintained on direct-access storage devices that allow management to get frequent reports on sales trends and collection effectiveness.

4. *Inventory Application.* Many organizations consider their inventory records to be the biggest payoff application for computerization (see Exhibit 9–16). Some organizations (e.g., retailers, manufacturers) have so much of their resources tied up in inventories that any improvement in inventory handling can pay handsome returns to the organization. For instance, a well-designed inventory system may help to:
   a. Identify which inventory is excessive, and permit cost-saving reductions in the future.
   b. Statistically indicate which inventory levels are inadequate and must be increased, lest loss of customer business occur because of out-of-stock conditions.
   c. Suggest purchasing strategies for replenishing inventory at lower costs (e.g., pooling needs from several warehouses and thus obtaining higher-quantity discounts from suppliers).

Exhibit 9–15 An Example of Accounts-Receivable Analysis

ADA CORPORATION
ACCOUNTS RECEIVABLES
FOR THE PERIOD ENDING 31 DECEMBER 19__

CUSTOMER NUMBER	CUSTOMER NAME	TOTAL DUE	CURRENT BALANCES	OVER 30 DAYS PAST DUE	OVER 60 DAYS PAST DUE	90 DAYS OR MORE PAST DUE
15	C.C. ZIP CO.	$ 1,000	$ 500	$ 300	$ 200	
27	U. ONLY CORP.	2,500	2,500			
33	DIP COMPANY	50				$ 50
TOTALS		$25,000	$20,000	$3,000	$1,500	$500

Exhibit 9–16 Systems Flowchart of Inventory Application

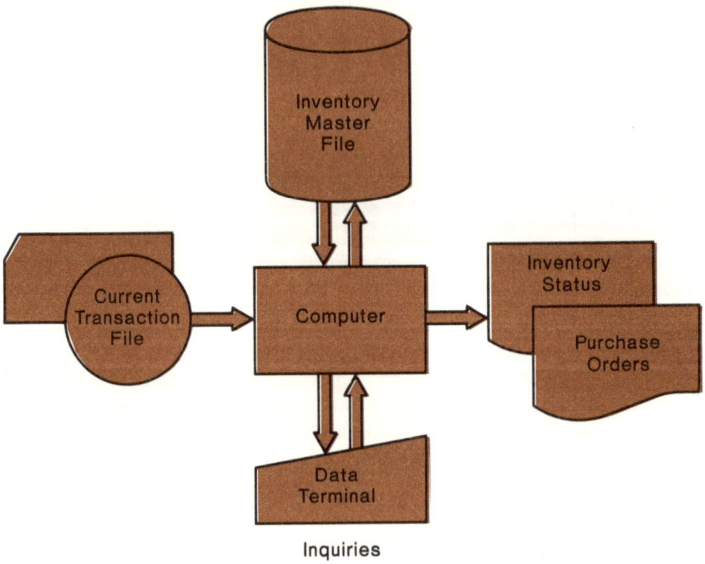

Exhibit 9–17 An Example of an Inventory Status Report

ADA CORPORATION
INVENTORY STATUS
FOR THE PERIOD ENDING 31 DECEMBER 19__

INVENTORY NUMBER	INVENTORY DESCRIPTION	TOTAL UNITS ON HAND	TOTAL UNITS ON ORDER	REORDER POINT*	
123	WIDGETS-TYPE A	100	25	90	
217	THINGAMAJIGS	50	0	25	
378	WATCHAMACALLITS	250	0	250	REORDER
956	WIDGETS-TYPE B	30	0	10	

* The reorder point is that point at which inventory is reordered in order to keep a sufficient supply on hand to satisfy customer demand. For instance, there are 125 units of Widgets-Type A on hand or on order; when 35 units are sold, the reorder point of 90 will be reached. At that time, the organization will order more Widgets-Type A. The quantity to reorder depends on a number of factors, including inventory turnover in a given period, expected customer demand in the future, carrying cost of warehousing the inventory, quantity discounts for buying in large quantities, and possible increases in per unit costs in the future. The "best" reorder quantity is sometimes referred to as the economic order quantity (EOQ), which is often expressed in the form of a mathematical equation.

Inventory transactions identify inventory (or product) number, quantity and unit cost of additions or withdrawals from inventory, etc. The master record must contain such data fields as: inventory (or product) number; total quantity of item on hand; average unit cost; quantity of items on order but not yet delivered; and some indication of past history of usage of the inventory item.

The transactions are used to update the inventory master (see Exhibit 9–17). As a result, the updated master records can be used to determine which inventory items must be replenished, what quantity should be ordered, and so on.

Since inventory records are vital to answering customer inquiries ("Do you have x number of Product Y on hand?"), many inventory systems are maintained on direct-access files.

These specific systems applications are presented in very broad terms, merely to suggest some parameters of a few widely computerized applications. Of course, before the computer can handle such systems applications, the detailed computer programming must be accomplished. The next two chapters cover the nature of software and the programming task.

Summary

The systems professional must not only have technical ability, but also be able to identify the applications opportunities available where the computer can bring benefit to the organization. There is a broad array of proven computer applications; these are good foundations for developing more imaginative and unique applications.

Terms to Learn

System application
Payroll application
Accounting application
Sales application
Inventory application

Review Questions

1. Discuss the use of computers in several *different types of organizations* (e.g., department stores, colleges and universities, restaurants, hotels and motels, city government, and hospitals).
2. Discuss computer applications in a *particular functional area of business:* accounting and finance, marketing, manufacturing, personnel, etc. What benefits can be derived from such computer applications contrasted to the work being done by noncomputer methods?

The computer uses binary math.
1010
+111
10001
10
+7
17
People use decimal math.

CHAPTER 10

INTRODUCTION TO SOFTWARE

Objectives

Chapter 10 offers an overview of the software that complements the computer hardware. Types of programming languages, as well as systems programs, are dealt with. Software must be understood in order to more keenly appreciate the writing of a computer program.

Topics in Chapter 10 are:
Topic 1—Essentials of Software.
Topic 2—Special Issues About Software.

TOPIC 1—ESSENTIALS OF SOFTWARE

WHAT IS SOFTWARE?

In Chapter 4, the nature of *software* was mentioned briefly. In this chapter, software is discussed in greater detail.

There are two broad categories of software: "systems programs"* and "applications programs"† (see Exhibit 10–1). Systems programs are support programs that are general in nature and that facilitate the computer's efficient operation. The computer manufacturer itself develops some of the main systems-programs and makes them available to all users of their computers. Many of the systems programs are quite sophisticated, and most user organizations are not in the position to write such programs themselves.

Applications programs, on the other hand, are written by user organizations for their own particular applications (e.g., payroll, accounting, or inventory). This chapter deals primarily with systems programs. Chapter 11 will focus mainly on the applications-programming phase.

Software can be broadly defined as the instructions that direct the computer hard-

* Systems software should not be confused with the content of Chapter 9. Systems software are programs, while systems analysis and design are those human tasks that precede any programming effort.

† Applications software can be expensive. Even a relatively common application, such as the creation of a 20,000-instruction payroll package, may cost around $160,000. Systems software can be even more expensive; it is reported that it costs a computer manufacturer tens of millions of dollars to develop an operating system (operating systems are explained later in this chapter).

One estimate is that up to $100 billion may be invested world-wide in applications software. This amount exceeds the value of the installed computer hardware around the world!

Exhibit 10–1 Relation of Systems Software and Applications Software

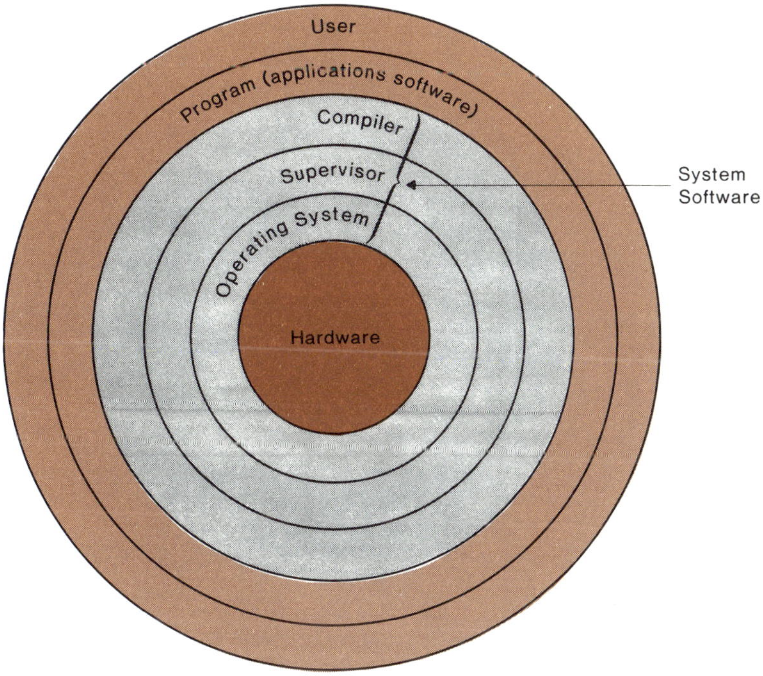

ware to carry out certain desired operations so that some specified result is achieved (e.g., generating a payroll or updating accounts receivables). These instructions are written in a specialized language.* For the purposes of this book, all programs are referred to by the term "software." While computer equipment has vast potential in its circuits, storage units, registers, etc., the computer must remain unproductive until the appropriate software is fed into its memory. Thus, software† is what enables people to direct the computer to carry out specific tasks.

* It is estimated that there are more than one hundred programming languages. About fifteen languages are still widely used and implemented; others are used for specialized purposes or with special computers; and still others are largely obsolete. A study indicated that the widest-used languages, for business applications, are (in ranked order): COBOL, Assembler Language, FORTRAN, PL/1, RPG, BASIC, and APL.

† Besides the software available from the computer manufacturers or developed by the user, there are software houses that sell or lease software to users. Some of these software houses are: Management Information Service; Applied Data Research; University Computing; Boole & Babbage; Informatics; Management Science America; and Information Science.

Exhibit 10–2 Use of a Machine-Language Program

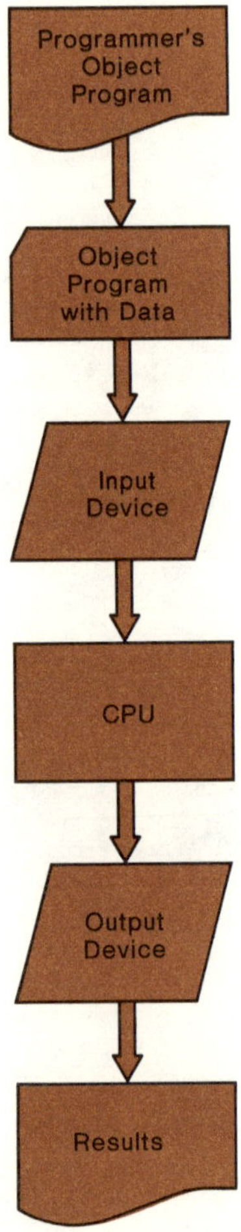

MACHINE-LEVEL PROGRAMMING LANGUAGES

All programs, whether they are systems programs or applications programs, must ultimately be translated into machine language—and each particular computer has its own native language.

This native, or machine, language is designed, along with the computer equipment, by the computer manufacturer. The computer's circuits are designed and built to understand the messages conveyed by the particular machine language. Virtually every computer manufacturer, and indeed each different model computer, has differ-

Exhibit 10–3 An Example of a Machine-Language Instruction

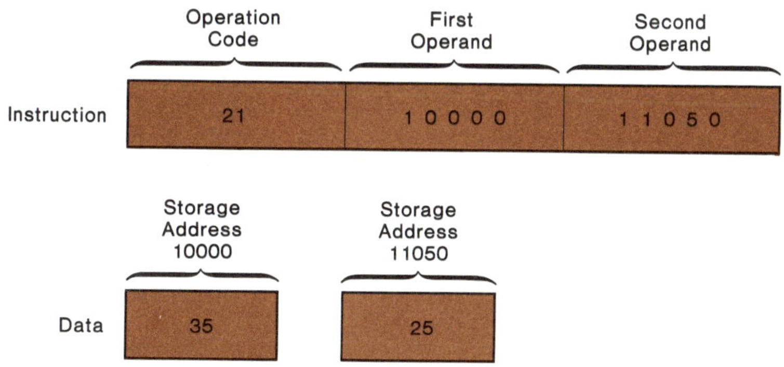

ent *machine-level languages*. This means that a program written in machine language for computer X will not work on computer Y—and indeed will probably not work on any other computer (except one that is identical to computer X).

The most direct way for a person to program the computer is to code instructions in machine language. To use machine language to write a program, the programmer must understand exactly how each instruction works and must assign locations in storage for data and instructions. The programmer must write an instruction to indicate each operation that is to be performed. Therefore, there is a one-to-one relationship between the instructions that the programmer codes and the computer operations. In machine language, the complete list of instructions is known as the "program." A machine-level language program (sometimes referred to as an "object" program) can be executed by a computer without its first being subjected to a translating process to make it machine-usable (see Exhibit 10–2).

In general, most programmers find the machine-language approach to programming time-consuming, tedious, conducive to human error, and relatively expensive (particularly in the program-preparation and -debugging stages). But there are two basic advantages to using machine language. A program written in this language tends to utilize the computer's storage more efficiently and may take less time to process on a computer than a comparable program written in a higher-level programming language would take. (Higher-level languages will be discussed later.) However, for most user purposes, the disadvantages of machine language outweigh its advantages, and today few user-applications programs are written in machine language. On the other hand, most systems programs, particularly those written by the computer manufacturer, are written directly in machine-level language by highly skilled programmers. This makes sense, since such systems programs often are intended to be resident and on-line in computer storage.

Exhibit 10–3 illustrates a typical machine-language instruction. In the example, assume that operation code "21" indicates to the computer's circuits that it is to perform an addition operation. The first and second operands identify the locations of the two data elements to be added. When the instruction is executed, the computer generates the sum of the data stored in addresses 10000 and 11050, thus deriving a result of 60 (35 + 25).

As far as the computer is concerned, the only thing that distinguishes instructions from data is when each is brought into the CPU. Of course, instructions must be stored in areas of storage that are not occupied by data, and vice versa. If data are brought to the CPU during instruction time (I-Time), the CPU will attempt to decode them as an instruction. And if a program instruction is taken to the CPU arithmetic and logical section during E-time, it will be treated as if it were data.

ASSEMBLY-LEVEL PROGRAMMING LANGUAGES

The most frequently used symbolic-type language is termed *assembly.* It is called assembly language because a machine-language program is "assembled" when a program that is written in assembly language is translated. Each assembler language is unique and can only be used with one computer model. One of the widest-used assembly languages is IBM's BAL (Basic Assembler Language).

Writing programs in assembly language is an advancement over writing programs in machine language, because it permits symbols,* rather than only numbers, to be used in writing instructions. Although the programmer still needs to know how the computer will execute each opcode, the computer assigns storage locations for data and instructions automatically, in the translating step. The programmer assigns a *label* (or symbolic address) to each data item and uses the label when referring to the data item (e.g., in an operand of an instruction). For example:

	Operation Code	*First Operand*	*Second Operand*
Machine-level instruction	21	10000	11050
Assembly-level instruction	A	REG	OVT

Obviously, it is easier for humans to recognize that "A" (rather than "21") stands for "add," and to associate "REG" (rather than 10000) with "regular pay," and "OVT" (rather than 11050) with "overtime pay."

When the assembly-type programming language is used, a translator, commonly called an *assembler,* is used. The assembler (or translating program) is a systems program that the computer manufacturer usually provides, and that must be in the computer's primary storage. The programmer's application program is written in assembler language (referred to as the *source program*). This is then read into the computer. The assembler automatically translates the source program, one instruction at a time, into machine-level instructions. This machine-language version is referred to

* Sometimes this is referred to as the use of "mnemonics." This involves the use of symbols to assist human memory.

Exhibit 10–4 Use of Assembly-Language Program

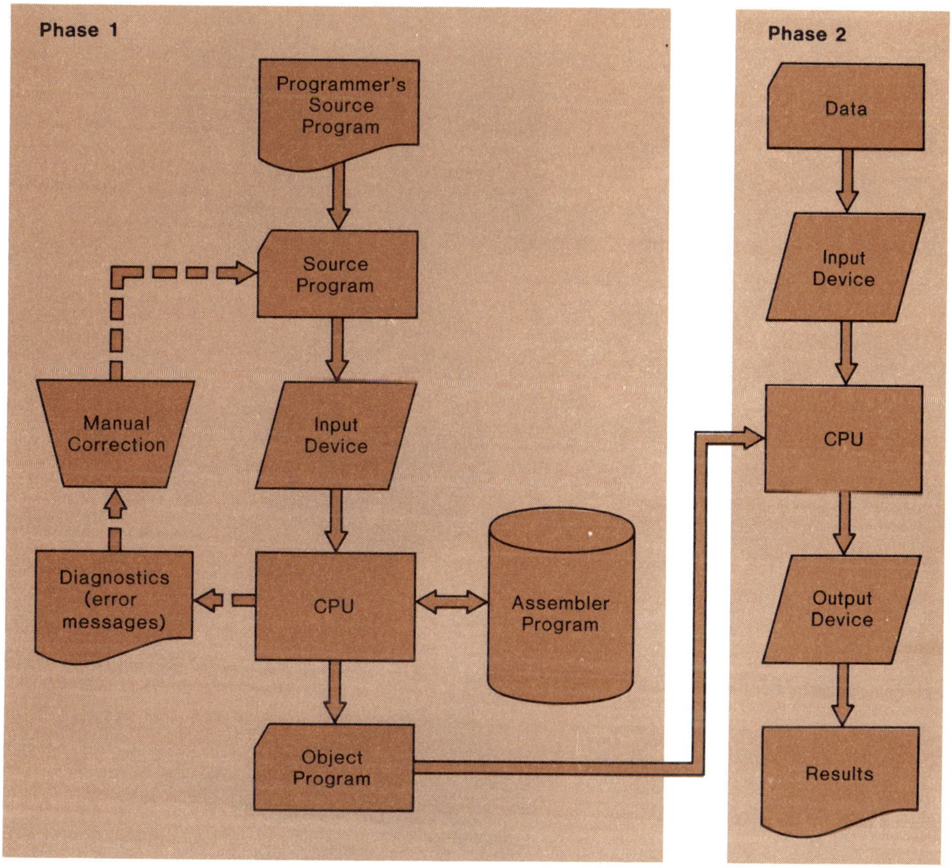

as the *object program.* This program is then available to instruct the computer which operations to perform in order to process the application that the program represents. The object program can be retained in storage and/or written on an output device (e.g., punched, printed, or recorded on magnetic tape). Thereafter, the object program (not the source program) will be used for computer processing. This saves computer time, as the translation has to take place only once (when the program is originally written) and is not required each time the program is to be used (see Exhibit 10–4).

In addition to generating the object program, the assembler provides an error-message list. This list can detect errors (referred to as *diagnostics*) that occur because of violation of syntax (the grammatical correctness) of the instruction structure; instructions that are out of sequence and illogical; references to nonexistent parts of the program; and illegal mnemonic operation codes. The assembler generates a list of the errors, and the list helps the programmer correct the source program. The assembler will not generate an object program until all errors in the source program have been corrected. Then, once the object program is available, it can be put into operation—that is, the program can be used to process data and generate results.

HIGHER-LEVEL PROGRAMMING LANGUAGES

Higher-level languages permit the programmer to concentrate on the problem (or procedure) and not be overly concerned with hardware details. In fact, the programmer often does not know very much about the computer itself and how it operates. Some programmers may come into direct contact with the computer equipment only rarely.

Higher-level programming languages are relatively independent of any specific computer model. A program written in a higher-level language is said to be universal; that is, the program can be used on virtually any computer, with minor modifications. Of course, there are some obvious constraints; for instance, there must be sufficient storage to handle the particular application.

Programs in higher-level language tend to be much more like normal communication (e.g., English sentences and algebraic equations) than either assembly-language programs or machine-language programs are. Also, the higher-level-language program is usually much more compact than an assembly-language or machine-language program. This is because a single instruction in a program written in higher-level language may be equivalent to as many as ten or more assembly-language or machine-language instructions.* These characteristics (similarity to normal communications, and compactness) tend to increase the programmer's productivity and to clarify the documentation of computer applications.

Here is a comparative example of an instruction.

	Operation Code	*First Operand*	*Second Operand*
Machine-level instruction	21	10000	11050
Assembly-level instruction	A	REG	OVT

The higher-level instruction equivalent might take on one of the following forms:

ADD REGULAR-PAY, OVERTIME-PAY GIVING GROSS-PAY, or
PAY = REGPAY + OVTPAY

In higher-level programming languages, the process of translating programs is called *compiling*. A compiler, which the computer manufacturer normally provides, can take a single instruction written in a higher-level programming language and generate one or more related machine-level instructions. The compiler also assigns

* This is sometimes called "macro-instructions."

Exhibit 10–5 Use of Compiler-Language Program

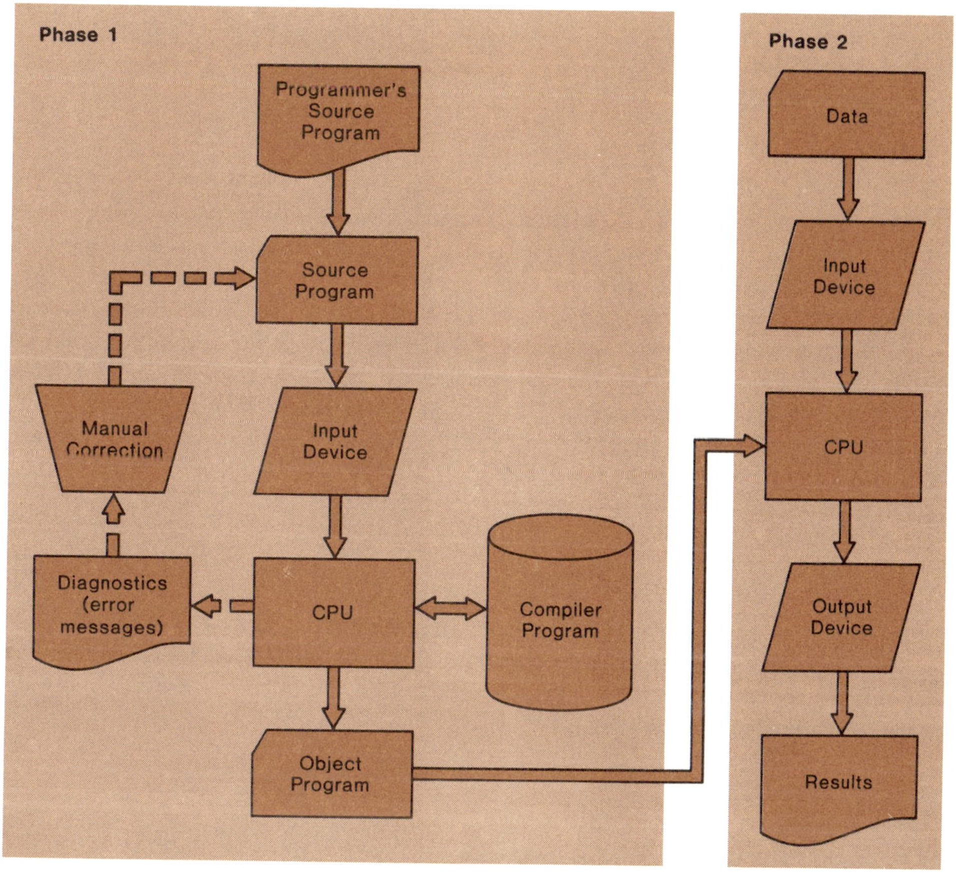

storage locations to data and instructions, which relieves the programmer of this tedious detail.

Like assemblers, compilers provide auxiliary functions that help the programmer correct and document a program. For example, in the translation process, the compiler detects common errors in language use and prints an error list to alert the programmer.

A disadvantage of compilers is that some take longer to translate a program than assemblers* do to translate an equivalent program. In addition, some object programs that are generated from higher-level source programs are less efficient than those generated from assembler programs or those written directly in machine language. Also, since some programmers who use higher-level languages do not know the details of computer hardware and machine language, they can have difficulty with some

* However, experience has revealed that some assemblers are slower than high-level compilers.

debugging problems (even higher-level language programs must be translated to machine language before execution can begin).

Exhibit 10–5 illustrates the compilation process (note its similarity with the assembling process).

Some of the more frequently used higher-level programming languages are now identified and discussed.

COBOL

COBOL (*CO*mmon *B*usiness-*O*riented *L*anguage) is the widest-used higher-level business-programming language. One reason is that it has achieved nation-wide standardization; practically all computer models have a COBOL compiler available. COBOL was developed under the aegis of the American National Standards Institute (or ANSI, a private organization that serves as a focal point for developing common standards for industry), with the cooperation of the U.S. government, computer manufacturers, professional societies, and computer users. As the words that COBOL stands for suggest, this compiler has particular capability for business-related applications (e.g., payroll, accounting, and sales).

RPG

RPG (*R*eport *P*rogram *G*enerator) is used fairly widely for relatively simple applications in which routine business reports need to be generated. RPG has gained particular acceptance among smaller-computer users because the programming involved is relatively straightforward.

FORTRAN

FORTRAN (*For*mula *Tran*slation) is one of the earliest higher-level programming languages (it was developed by IBM in about 1954). Today, it still remains one of the widest-used languages. Although it was developed primarily for the scientific-type user, it has also been utilized for certain business applications.

ALGOL

ALGOL (*Algo*rithmic *L*anguage) was intended as an improvement (if not replacement) for FORTRAN as a scientific language. Although it has achieved considerable support in European computer-circles, particularly for scientific applications, it has not achieved wide acceptance in the United States (primarily because FORTRAN was already so widely used).

PL/1

PL/1 (*P*rogramming *L*anguage *1*) was developed in recent years by IBM, with the idea of incorporating the best features of COBOL and FORTRAN and, thus, providing a single language that was efficient for writing either business or scientific programs. However, PL/1 is utilized primarily by certain IBM-computer users, and it has not achieved the wide acceptance that was originally forecast.

BASIC

BASIC (*B*asic *A*ll-purpose *S*ymbolic *I*nstruction *C*ode) was developed at Dartmouth College as a simple instructional tool to teach fundamental programming concepts and to facilitate the educational use of computers. Since then, it has become widely used as a time-sharing language (making on-line inquiries of the computer and getting back responses), particularly in educational institutions.

APL

APL (*A P*rogramming *L*anguage) is most often used with time-sharing computers, as BASIC is; however, APL is the more complex and powerful programming language. Since it is a mathematics-oriented language, it tends to find greatest application for scientific applications. There is some expectation that wider use will be made of APL in the future.

SELECTING A PROGRAMMING LANGUAGE

Of course, all computers are provided with a machine language; normally, an assembler language is provided also.

However, the computer manufacturer does not provide all computer models with all of the wider-used higher-level programming languages. Generally, the larger the computer, the more comprehensive the software support by the computer manufacturer. Some of the smaller computers have limited software-support available from the manufacturers. Using organizations sometimes buy or lease software from software organizations; or, if they have talented programming staffs, they may develop their own software.

In selecting a programming language, one of the important constraints to consider is the availability of a particular compiler with the computer model in the using organization. Another consideration is the cost of using a specific language. As indicated, it usually costs more to write a program in machine or assembler language than it does to develop a comparable program in higher-level language. On the other hand, it usually costs more to translate and execute higher-level language programs.

Another consideration is the nature of the application. For instance, a business application is more likely to be programmed in COBOL, while a scientific application is more likely to be programmed in a language such as FORTRAN or APL. Also, unless the existing staff is trained in additional languages, its programming competence will partly dictate which languages can be used and which cannot. Some organizations find it helpful to standardize on one or two programming languages so that they don't end up with a maze of programs that are written in many different languages.

Summary

The term "software" covers all programs, including those general ones written by the computer manufacturers as well as those written by the individual using organization. The latter are referred to as "applications software" (or programs), while the former are called "systems software" (or programs).

Three broad classes of programming languages are used to write programs: machine-level, assembly-level, and higher-level. The higher-level programming languages are of greatest interest, because they are most easily used by people.

There are several widely used higher-level programming languages: COBOL, RPG, FORTRAN, PL/1, BASIC, APL, and ALGOL.

Terms to Learn

Programmer
Systems software
Applications software
Software
Language
Machine-level programming language
Assembly-level programming language
Label
Translation
Assembler
Diagnostic
Source program
Object program
Higher-level programming language
Compiling
COBOL
RPG
FORTRAN
PL/1
BASIC
APL
ALGOL

Review Questions

1. Define *software.* How does it differ from *hardware?*
2. Discuss *machine-level programming languages.*

3. Discuss *assembly-level programming languages*. How do they differ from machine-level programming languages?
4. Discuss *higher-level programming languages*. How do they differ from assembly-level programming languages?
5. Briefly, identify *COBOL, RPG, BASIC*, and *FORTRAN*.
6. How would you select a *specific programming language* to use in your organization's computer department? Might you recommend the use of several languages? If "yes," why?

TOPIC 2—SPECIAL ISSUES ABOUT SOFTWARE

OPERATING SYSTEMS

To use the computer system most effectively, there must be as little manual operation or intervention as possible, since the inherent slowness of such acts will be inefficient.

Instead of a computer being controlled manually, most modern computers use advanced software (supplied by the computer manufacturer), called *operating systems*, to direct the computer's coordination and control. As the name operating system (OS) suggests, this software was designed to help the computer operators—i.e., those people who actually operate the hardware. The operating system is a complex of systems programs written in machine-level language. It comes in different versions, depending on the amount of storage and on the number of devices to be controlled, among other factors. For instance, IBM provides a DOS (*D*isk *O*perating *S*ystem) and a TOS (*T*ape *O*perating *S*ystem) and an OS (full *O*perating *S*ystem).

An operating system consists of two basic types of programs: a supervisor program, and a collection of other programs (translators, service/utility programs, and applications programs) that are under the control of the supervisor* (see Exhibit 10–6).

Supervisor Program

In an operating system, the supervisor module is the software that directs and coordinates all other modules of the operating system; that is, it *supervises* the computer system. The supervisor is sometimes called the "monitor," the "executive," the "controller," or the "nucleus."

Among the specific tasks of the supervisor are:

1. Scheduling the sequence of jobs to be run, taking into account such factors as job priority, availability of input and output devices, and storage.

* Assume a primary storage of 64,000 storage locations. The supervisor may take 8,000 storage locations, leaving 56,000 for other purposes. If a payroll program is called in from secondary storage and requires 24,000 positions, that will leave 32,000 positions for other purposes. When the payroll program has been executed, control again goes to the supervisor, which then loads the next program into primary storage.

Exhibit 10–6 The Operating System in Storage

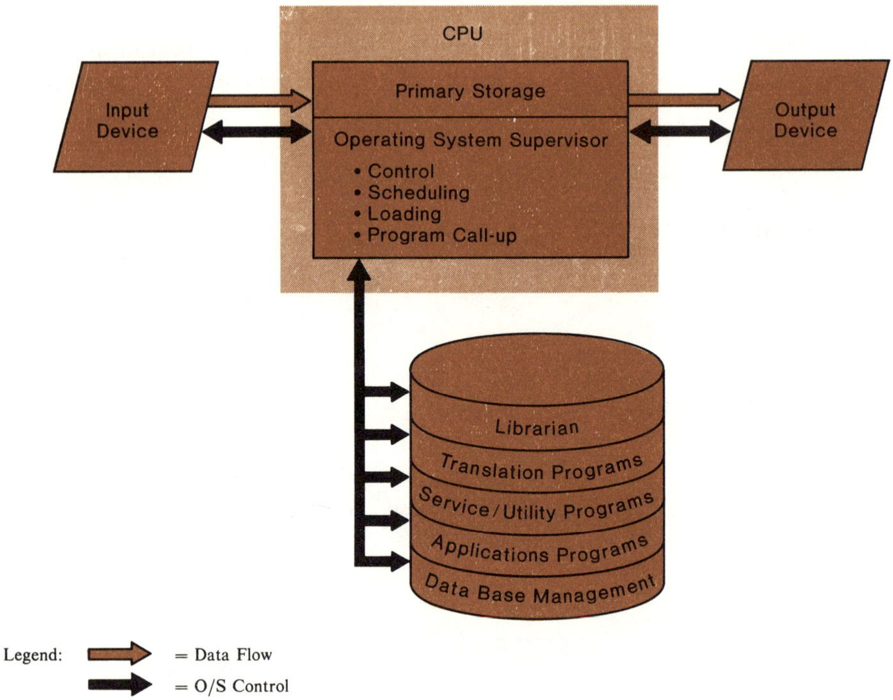

2. Controlling the system; for instance, to cause input and output devices to be activated.
3. Loading programs and data files into computer storage from an input device or from the system library in secondary storage.

The supervisor itself (or those parts of it that are to be used) must be resident in primary storage.* An example is the program-load subroutine, which is needed to bring the proper program into primary storage. Other portions of the supervisor may be stored in the system library, usually on a direct-access storage device, and—under control of the supervisor—can be moved to primary storage when needed. When the subroutine is no longer needed, it can be moved back to secondary storage and be replaced with something else (e.g., another subroutine, another program, or other data).

The supervisor itself gets into primary storage by means of an initial program

* The supervisor usually remains in the primary storage and may occupy a considerable amount of the available space and thus reduce space available for applications programs of the user.

loader (IPL), which is a very small program that can be loaded into primary storage manually (e.g., through the console keyboard). By setting certain controls on the computer console and then pressing the console load key, the operator causes the IPL program to be transferred to predetermined primary-storage locations.

This is a machine function, not a programmed function. No instructions are executed during the process of loading the IPL. Once the IPL program is loaded, control of the computer systems passes to it. That is, the computer begins executing IPL instructions. The small IPL program has one very important function: it locates and loads the supervisor from the system residence device (e.g., magnetic-disk secondary storage). After the supervisor is loaded into primary storage, control of the computer passes to it. This means that the computer will be executing supervisor instructions. Now that the IPL's function is completed, it can be overlaid by another program or data. Two important routines in the supervisor are its load program (which loads all other programs) and the job-control program.*

System Library

There is a librarian subroutine—a set of service programs under control of the supervisor—that facilitates the cataloging routines in maintaining, servicing, and organizing all system-library programs that are maintained in secondary storage. Among the main collections of programs in such a system library are:

1. *Language translators,* including assemblers and compilers such as COBOL, FORTRAN, and BASIC.
2. *Service or utility programs,* which perform standardized operations such as sorting and merging routines, converting one medium to another (e.g., punched cards to magnetic tape), providing input/output control systems (IOCS),† etc.
3. *Applications programs and subroutines,*‡ which can include such things as payroll, sales analysis, and inventory updating.
4. *Sophisticated software,* such as a data-base management system.

Because storage is both limited (even in large-scale computers) and costly, only programs that are used frequently or that must be available for on-line inquiries and response should be kept in the system library. Those programs that are not used frequently or that are not needed for on-line purposes are best kept in off-line files so that they don't tie up on-line secondary storage. When these programs are to be used, they can be loaded into the system through an input device.

* As we will see shortly, this subroutine carries out the function of interfacing with all jobs fed to the computer.

† The IOCS lets the programmer write a simple macro instruction to specify input/output operations (e.g., GET). The software will not only generate all the needed detailed machine-language instructions but also will keep track of input/output-device addresses, filled and available storage areas, and so on.

‡ Programming is simplified and made more economic by the use of precoded library routines which can be called into primary storage from secondary storage as needed. This eliminates the need to have repetitious segments in many programs. A standard subroutine may be called in and linked with numerous programs.

Job-Control Cards

The operating system is directed by user-prepared *job-control cards* that communicate with the supervisor's job-control subroutine. These job-control cards indicate what function is to be performed. For example, suppose that a source program written in COBOL is to be translated. A typical day's activities can consist of a mix of types of jobs: compiling a COBOL program; compiling a FORTRAN program; executing the payroll program; and so on. Rather than handling each job individually, the computer operator or programmer prepares a series of job-control cards, which are instructions to the operating system's control programs (see Exhibit 10–7). As the first job-control card is read, it effectively indicates to the control program that a COBOL program is to be compiled. The COBOL compiler, stored on disk, is brought into primary storage; and translation of the COBOL source-program begins. An object program may be created, or the program may be executed immediately (assuming that it has been debugged), depending on the specifications placed in the job-control cards. When this job has been completed, the next job-control card is read and indicates that a FORTRAN program is to be compiled. The FORTRAN compiler, stored on disk, is brought into primary storage. Now, execution of this job begins. When it is completed, the last job-control card is read. It indicates that an applications program (previously translated into an object program) is to be executed. Through the control program, the payroll program is transferred from the disk to primary storage and is executed (i.e., prepare the payroll register, payroll checks, etc.).

Thus, control cards allow all operations to be performed automatically, as one continuous job stream, with a minimum of operator intervention. However, the computer operator still must perform certain tasks (e.g., changing the paper forms on the printer).

A more explicit view of control cards is shown in Exhibit 10–8. The job-control cards for a given purpose depend on a number of factors, such as the specific operating system environment, options desired, and type of file used. For example, the minimum job-control cards required to compile a program written in COBOL would be as follows:

1. // JOB. This job card assigns a name to the source program (in this case, "STUDENT").
2. // EXEC COBOL. This card causes the COBOL compiler to be loaded from the secondary-storage device and to be executed. COBOL is the name given to the COBOL compiler stored in the library of programs on the secondary-storage device.
3. Source Deck. The actual source program, written by the programmer, is inserted after the first two control cards.
4. /*. This control card indicates "end-of-file" to the control program; that is, the end of the source deck has been reached.
5. /&. This control card signifies the end of the job.

Exhibit 10–7 Job-Control Cards and a Job Stream

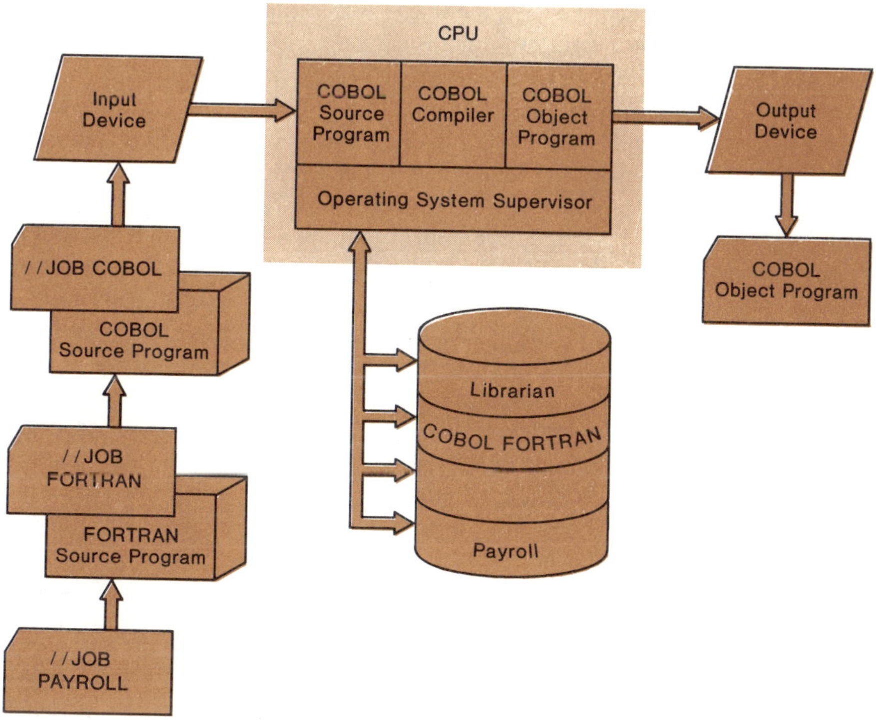

Exhibit 10–8 Card Setup for Compiling a COBOL Program

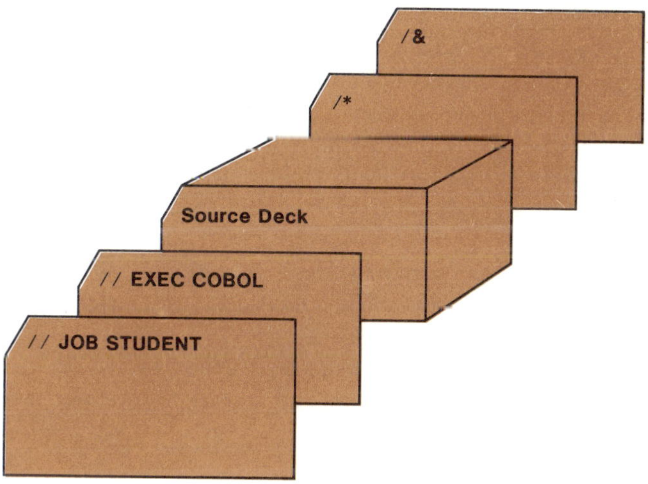

Multiprogramming

In order to utilize the computer more effectively, a technique known as *multiprogramming* has been developed. This is a module that is available in an operating system that handles scheduling. Multiprogramming is defined as the execution of two or more programs that both reside in primary storage.

Since the CPU can execute only one instruction at a time, it cannot simultaneously execute instructions from two or more programs. However, it can execute instructions from one program, then from a second program, then from the first program again, and so on. This type of processing is referred to as "concurrent execution." This is desirable because input and output operations are much slower than internal CPU operations are. If only one program is being processed, the CPU is often idle while it waits for an input/output operation to be completed. However, in a multiprogramming environment, the CPU can execute one program's instructions while a second program is waiting for I/O operations to take place.*

In one system of multiprogramming, storage is allocated for each program. The areas of primary storage allocated for individual programs are called "partitions." Each partition must have some form of storage protection and priority—*protection* to ensure that a program in one partition will not accidentally write over and destroy the instructions of another partition, and *priority* (when two or more programs are residing in primary storage) because both programs will need access to the CPU's facilities (e.g., the arithmetic and logic section). A system of priority—some method that will determine which program will have first call on the computer's facilities—is normally determined by locating the programs in specific partitions.

Programs that have the highest priority normally are stored in an area called the "foreground partition." Programs with the lowest priority are stored in an area called the "background partition" (see Exhibit 10–9).

Data-Base Management Systems (DBMS)

As Chapter 8 indicated, there is a trend towards the use of integrated data-bases. Such files usually require software, known as a data-base management system, to handle the complex data-structures and file organizations. Integrated data-bases and direct-access storage devices that permit on-line inquiry and response require comprehensive software that facilitates storage, retrieval, and updating. Specifically, such software provides for definition and creation of the files and data bases, the maintenance of indexes, and for file security.

In using a data-base management system, the user simply writes macro commands that specify the data-management operation to be performed. The software system takes care of the details of execution.

A data-base management system usually is accompanied by a simple query language, which allows persons who are not familiar with computer programming to

* Refer to Chapter 7, "Input and Output Devices," which discusses overlapping.

Exhibit 10–9 Allocation of Primary Storage in Multiprogramming Environment

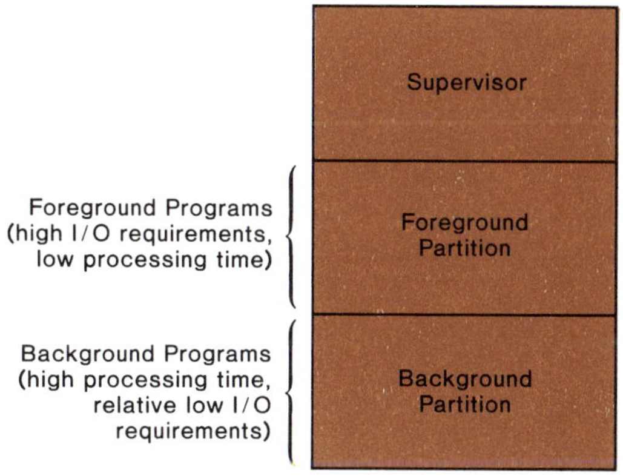

have a dialogue (or conversation) with the computer. For example, a personnel manager at a data terminal might enter the following type of message:

QUERY PERSONNEL FILE
LIST EMPLOYEES WITH SALARIES OVER $25,000
COUNT NUMBER
COUNT NUMBER OF MALES
COUNT NUMBER OF FEMALES

This type of query would cause the computer to list the names (and employee numbers, if desired) of employees earning more than $25,000 a year. It would also tally the number of males making more than $25,000 and the number of females, as well as providing an overall total. The information could be displayed on a CRT or be printed out. Such query languages obviously encourage more managers to utilize the computer's data base and provide more rapid service than methods that require all such requests to be sent for handling through computer technicians. In essence, the technical middleman is eliminated.

MICROPROGRAMMING (FIRMWARE)

Microprogramming can be considered as an intermediate step between hardware and software. Although microprograms are really computer programs (software), they are stored in the ROM (*R*ead-*O*nly *M*emory) hardware. A microprocessor can read instructions stored in its ROM, but it cannot write into memory. In a sense, this involves a computer within a computer. This is particularly useful for minicomputers, which are intended to be inexpensive. Rather than building computers with a wide range of operations (instruction set), many of these computers have a limited instruction set. However, they are built so that a user can have different sets of modules (boards) inserted (or removed from) the computer. These modules are called microprogramming (or firmware). This option gives the user flexibility in selecting the optional instruction set needed for the particular organization.

Summary

Modern computers are complex, and despite declining costs for computer power, computers remain a substantial cost for an organization. Systems software has been continually improved to make the computer operate more efficiently. Of particular interest is the operating system (a master program). This software package automatically performs many functions that formerly were handled by human operators in prior-generation computers. The operating system contains a number of modules that have different functions (e.g., supervisor program and system librarian).

Terms to Learn

Operating system
Supervisor program
IPL
System library
IOCS
Control card
Job-control card
Job-control routine
Multiprogramming
Data-base management system (DBMS)
Microprogramming
Firmware
Macrocommands
Query language
Conversational mode
Background partition
Foreground partition

Review Questions

1. What is an *operating system,* and what function does it perform?
2. Discuss what the *supervisor program* does. How does the *IPL* function?
3. What is in a *system library?* Where is the system library stored?
4. What use is made of *control cards?*
5. Define *multiprogramming.*
6. What is *microprogramming?*
7. What is a *macro command?*
8. Describe *data-base management system.*

Computer A. microseconds - discount price - for purchase now -
Computer B. fourth gener- - ation - bubble memory - for rent or lease.
Computer C. built by new firm - nanoseconds many spec- -ial features.
Computer D. distributed data processing - fifth generation - two year delivery date.
Computer E. picoseconds - new programming language - debug me.

CHAPTER 11

PREPARING A COMPUTER PROGRAM

Exhibit 11-1 A Program Flowchart to Determine Arithmetic Mean

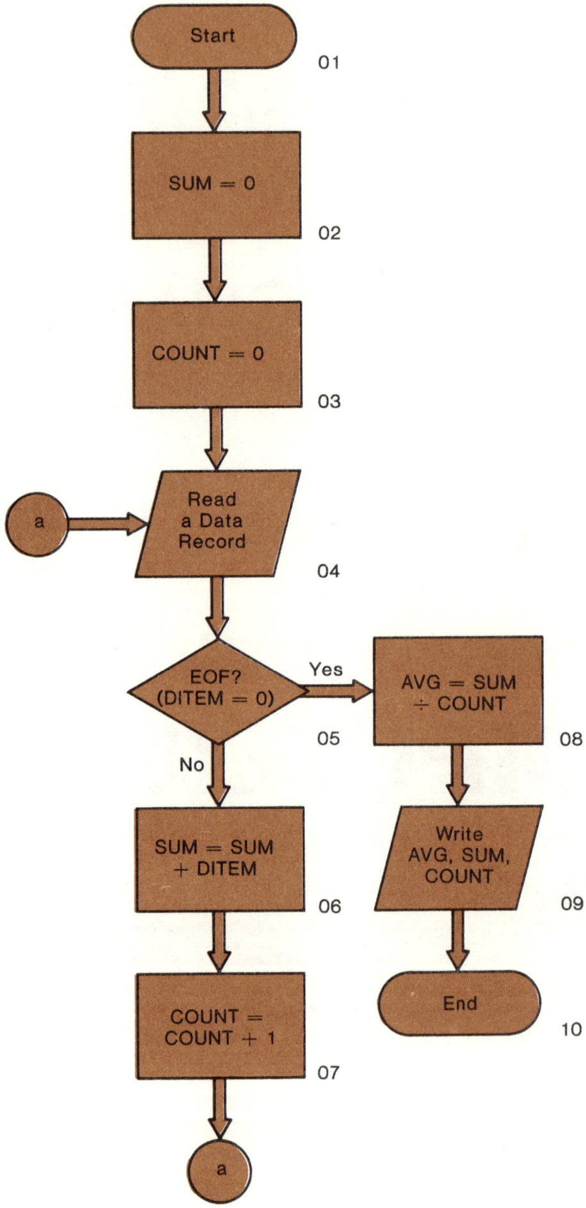

Note: This flowchart, a duplicate of the chart presented in Chapter 9, is presented here for convenience purpose.

TOPIC 1—AN OVERVIEW OF PROGRAMMING

AN INTRODUCTION TO COMPUTER PROGRAMMING: A COMPARISON OF FORTRAN AND BASIC PROGRAMS

Chapter 9 presented an example of a *program flowchart* depicting the logic for computing the arithmetic mean (simple average) for a group of figures. Exhibit 11–1 is a duplicate of that same program flowchart. If you need a refresher, go back to Chapter 9 and reread the description of the program flowchart for computing averages.

Using such a flowchart as a guide, the programmer can prepare a computer program. Exhibit 11–2 shows how the program would appear in the *FORTRAN* program-

Exhibit 11–2 The Average Program in FORTRAN

Program:

```
C THE AVERAGE PROGRAM IN FORTRAN
   10 SUM=0.0
   20 COUNT=0.0
  300 READ (5,30, END = 80) DITEM
   30 FORMAT(F4.0)
C EVERY READ OR WRITE INSTRUCTION MUST HAVE A
C CROSS-REFERENCED FORMAT
C STATEMENT WHICH DESCRIBES THE TYPE OF DATA AND
C ITS WIDTH
   50 SUM=SUM+DITEM
   60 COUNT=COUNT + 1
   70 GO TO 300
   80 AVG=SUM/COUNT
   90 WRITE(6,100) AVG, COUNT
  100-FORMAT  ( '1', '  AVERAGE =  ', F5.0,
     -  '  COUNT =  ', F5.0)
      WRITE (6,77)
   77 FORMAT ('1')
  110 STOP
      END
```

Output:

```
AVERAGE =     34.  COUNT =      5.
```

ming language. Exhibit 11–3 shows how the program would appear in the *BASIC* programming language.

In studying the program flowchart and the two computer programs, notice that the programs follow the general logical pattern of the flowchart.* In comparing the two computer programs, notice some similarities, as well as dissimilarities, between the two programming languages. The dissimilarities exist because each language is unique; but in spite of the dissimilarities, both the FORTRAN and BASIC programs will produce the same results for a given problem. In our example, the programs calculate a simple average for a string of input data: 50, 20, 10, 60, 30. Even though the programs are somewhat different, both generate output indicating that the average is "34."

To understand one of the differences between the two programming languages, look at the *variable names* in the programs.

FORTRAN Variable Names	*BASIC Variable Names*
SUM	S
COUNT	C
DITEM....................	D
AVG	A

The FORTRAN language allows variable names to have up to six characters,† while the BASIC language only allows variable names to have one or two characters. Thus, the FORTRAN variable names are more descriptive of the data fields than the terse variable names that can be used in the BASIC language.

The FORTRAN program contains fourteen instructions‡ (see the left-hand numbers 1 through 14). The unnumbered lines are strictly for informational purposes; they begin with a letter "C," which stands for "Comments." Similarly, the BASIC program also contains lines that are strictly for informational purposes. In BASIC, such *nonexecutable* parts of programs begin with the characters "REM," which stand for "REMarks."

Table 11–1 presents a side-by-side comparison of the FORTRAN and BASIC programs. The study of both this material and the accompanying description of the instructions should give you a deeper understanding of the nature and structure of program instructions, and of how they can be interpreted by both the computer and people.

A more detailed explanation of the programming process will be given later in this chapter, after this simple programming example.

* The programs presented may vary slightly from the explicit logic of the flowchart. Such variations are due to a combination of a programmer's individual approach in writing his/her program and the uniqueness of each programming language. The main objective, of course, is to develop a computer program that will generate the correct results. It is less important whether the program technically adheres to some minute standard that does not affect the final results.

† The number of characters permitted in a variable name may differ among various versions of FORTRAN (e.g., FORTRAN II, FORTRAN IV) and the FORTRAN compilers of the different computer manufacturers.

‡ The terms *instruction* and *statement* are considered interchangeable, for our purposes.

Table 11–1

A Comparison of FORTRAN and BASIC Programs

FORTRAN Program*	BASIC Program*	Description of Instructions
10 SUM=0.0	100 LET S = 0	Sets a storage location to zero.
20 COUNT=0.0	110 LET C = 0	Sets a storage location to zero.
300 READ (5,30, END = 80) DITEM 30 FORMAT(F4.0)	120 INPUT D	Causes input data to be read. FORTRAN instruction also provides for end-of-file branch.
	130 IF D = 0 THEN 200	BASIC instruction provides for end-of-file branch.
50 SUM=SUM+DITEM	140 LET S = S + D	Summation of the values of a data field.
60 COUNT=COUNT + 1	150 LET C = C + 1	Causes a counter to be incremented by "1."
70 GO TO 300	160 GOTO 120	A loop to cause the next record to be read.
80 AVG=SUM/COUNT	200 A = S / C	At end-of-file, the arithmetic average is computed.
90 WRITE(6,100) AVG, COUNT 100 FORMAT ('1', 'AVERAGE = ', F5.0, 'COUNT = ', F5.0)	210 PRINT 220 PRINT 'AVERAGE = ', A 230 PRINT 'COUNT = ', C	Causes the output of the results: the computed average and the count of the number of data records.
WRITE (6,77) 77 FORMAT ('1')		FORTRAN instruction causes output paper to align to a new page for printing.
110 STOP END	240 END	The termination of the program processing.

* The nonexecutable "C" (Comments) and "REM" (REMarks) lines have been dropped for purposes of this comparison.

The number before each instruction or statement (i.e., statement number) is assigned by the programmer. In BASIC, each instruction *must be* assigned a number, and they *must be* in ascending sequence order. In FORTRAN only *certain instructions* must have a statement number; the numbers *do not* have to be in ascending sequence order.

PROGRAMMING STEPS

As Chapter 9 mentioned, it is the systems person who develops the overall blueprint for the planned computer application. This development includes specifications for output,

Exhibit 11–3 The Average Program in BASIC

Program:

```
 10 REM -- THE AVERAGE PROGRAM IN BASIC
 20 REM -- THE PROGRAM CLOSELY FOLLOWS THE FLOWCHART
 30 REM -- EXCEPT BASIC RESTRICTS VARIABLE NAMES TO
 40 REM -- TWO CHARACTERS.
 50 REM -- S = SUM, C = COUNT, D = DITEM, A = AVG
100 LET S = 0
110 LET C = 0
120 INPUT D
130 IF D = 0 THEN 200
140 LET S = S + D
150 LET C = C + 1
160 GOTO 120
200 A = S / C
210 PRINT
220 PRINT 'AVERAGE = ', A
230 PRINT 'COUNT   = ', C
240 END
```

Output:

```
AVERAGE =          34
COUNT   =          5
```

files, input, and processing. The programmer uses the specifications, flowcharts, decision tables, and so forth as a guide for writing the computer program.*

Exhibit 11–4 indicates some of the major steps in the programming effort. These steps are not necessarily accomplished in strict sequential order. For instance, preparation of files and input may take place as the program is being tested and debugged; documentation of the system is usually a cumulative effort during the systems and programming efforts; and so on.

* As earlier chapters have mentioned, some applications may be completely handled by one individual who performs both the systems work and the programming. Some people argue that this is best, since it gives the person a sense of doing a complete job; others argue that specialization is needed because of the growing sophistication of systems work and programming. Still others say that the systems and programming tasks must be separated in order to have a check-and-balance approach that may prevent collusion in manipulating data-processing records.

Another factor is the practical need to assign several programmers to do sections (subroutines) of a very large program.

Exhibit 11–4 Steps in the Programming of an Application

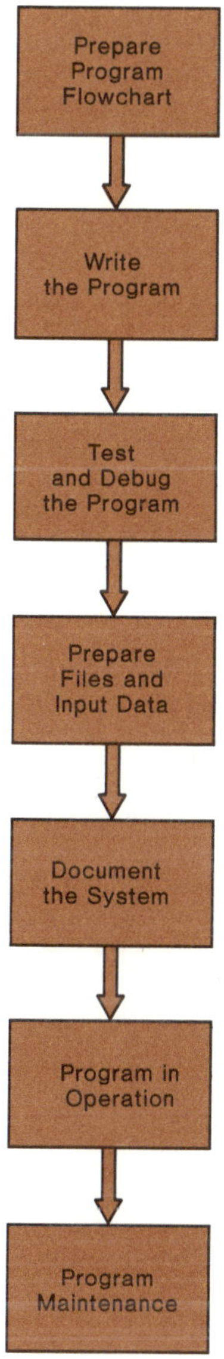

Such assignment of effort is needed if such large programs are to be completed within a reasonable time. A program that one programmer can write in twelve months presumably can be written in about three months if four programmers are assigned to the effort.

If the programmer is experienced, the systems person may provide only general systems guidelines. However, if the programmer is relatively inexperienced, the systems person will likely provide detailed systems guidelines, leaving only a minimum of discretion to the programmer.

Summary

Programming involves using a special language to code the instructions that the computer is to follow. The programmer uses systems specifications (i.e., input and output specifications) and flowcharts as guidelines in developing a program.

Certain specific steps are required for a successful programming effort: preparing a program flowchart; writing the program; testing and debugging the program; preparing files and input data; documenting the system; getting the program into operation; and maintaining the program.

Terms to Learn

FORTRAN
BASIC
Program flowchart
Variable name
Statement
Statement number
Nonexecutable statement

Review Questions

1. Contrast some of the features of *FORTRAN* and *BASIC* programming languages. How are they similar? How are they different?
2. Suppose that someone wanted to compute the standard deviation as well as the mean (average). Suggest how the program *flowchart* (Exhibit 11–1) would have to be modified to accomplish this additional goal. Draw the revised flowchart.
3. How would the *standard deviation routine,* developed in Question 2, be built into the FORTRAN and BASIC programs (Exhibits 11–2 and 11–3)?
4. Which language, FORTRAN or BASIC, seems *simpler* to you? Why?
5. Suggest how the average program might be used for processing *actual data.* Think in terms of data from real-life situations—in a college, office, bank, department store, etc.
6. Create some test data, and trace them through the various symbols in the program flowchart (Exhibit 11–1). What are the results? (In essence, by doing this, you are assuming the role of the computer.)
7. Discuss the *programming steps* that should be followed in a programmer's work.
8. How does the programmer interface with the *systems person?* How does the programmer interface with the *end user* (the person who will use the output generated by the program being prepared)?

Exhibit 11–5 General Systems Flowchart for Payroll Application

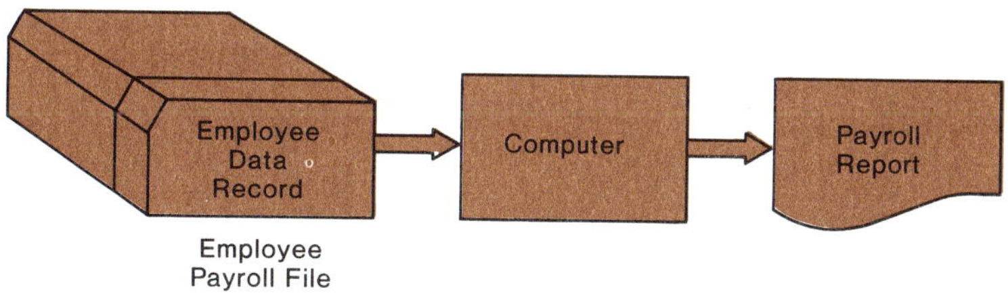

TOPIC 2—A CASE EXAMPLE OF PROGRAMMING

PREPARE THE PROGRAM FLOWCHART

Chapter 9 discussed the technique of flowcharting. The programmer prepares a program flowchart from the systems flowchart and other specifications provided by the systems analyst. While the systems flowchart may have little to do with the specifics of computer processing, the program flowchart must deal directly with the underlying details of computer processing. Thus, the programmer must have a sound technical background in such specifics.

Let's assume a simple computer application involving payroll (see Exhibit 11–5). The general objective is to take an employee payroll file, which is on punched cards, and to generate a weekly payroll report (or register).

Input and Output Specifications

Each employee record, in the employee payroll file, has specifications as indicated in Table 11–2. The organization has an indeterminate number of employees. The report output specifications are indicated in Exhibit 11–6. The *print chart* is used to plan the layout of a report. The form provides for 136 horizontal *print positions* (some printers have more and some have fewer print positions) and 68 vertical lines of print (which is standard depth, although it is possible to have longer or shorter reports). The print chart is helpful in determining where headings should be printed on the page (i.e., in which specific print positions), and how the actual data should be formatted underneath the respective headings. The data format indicates how a line of data (one line representing an individual employee) would appear; the Xs merely indicate that real data will be substituted when actual printing takes place. For instance, under the

Table 11–2

Specifications of Employee Record

Data Field	Columns*
Employee Name	1–15
Blank	16–19
Hours Worked	20, 21
Blank	22–24
Hourly Rate of Pay †	25–27
Blank	28–80

Note: Each employee will be represented by one punched card, and each card will be in the format specified above.

The *blanks* between fields (e.g., columns 16–19) are not needed. That is, it is possible to have data fields immediately adjacent to each other. For instance, the Hours Worked field could have started in column 16. However, for our illustration we have decided to leave blanks between each data field.

heading "HOURS WORKED," the number of hours will be printed in print positions 21 and 22. If an employee worked 44 hours, that number would be printed in print positions 21 and 22.

Computational Specifications

Besides the input and output specifications, other facts relevant to the application are:

1. If an employee works more than forty hours in a week, he/she is paid for such overtime hours at a rate of one and a half times the normal hourly rate.
2. For purposes of this illustration, we will assume the following rates‡ for deductions from gross wage:

Federal income tax, 6.27%
State income tax, 1.75%
Social security tax, 6.13%
Retirement (pension) deduction, 6%

* The field columns conform to those used for the FORTRAN program presented later in this chapter.

† The Hourly Rate of Pay field (columns 25–27) is a three-digit field. Thus, the maximum figure that could be recorded in that field would be 999. However, an assumed decimal point would exist and be positioned as follows: 9.99. It is highly unlikely that any employee would be paid 999 dollars an hour! The assumed decimal point is handled either through a format statement or through programming.

‡ In actual practice, tables are stored in the computer, for deductions such as federal income tax. The actual rate for the deduction is based on salary bracket (i.e., the higher the bracket, the higher the rate) and the number of dependents claimed by the individual.

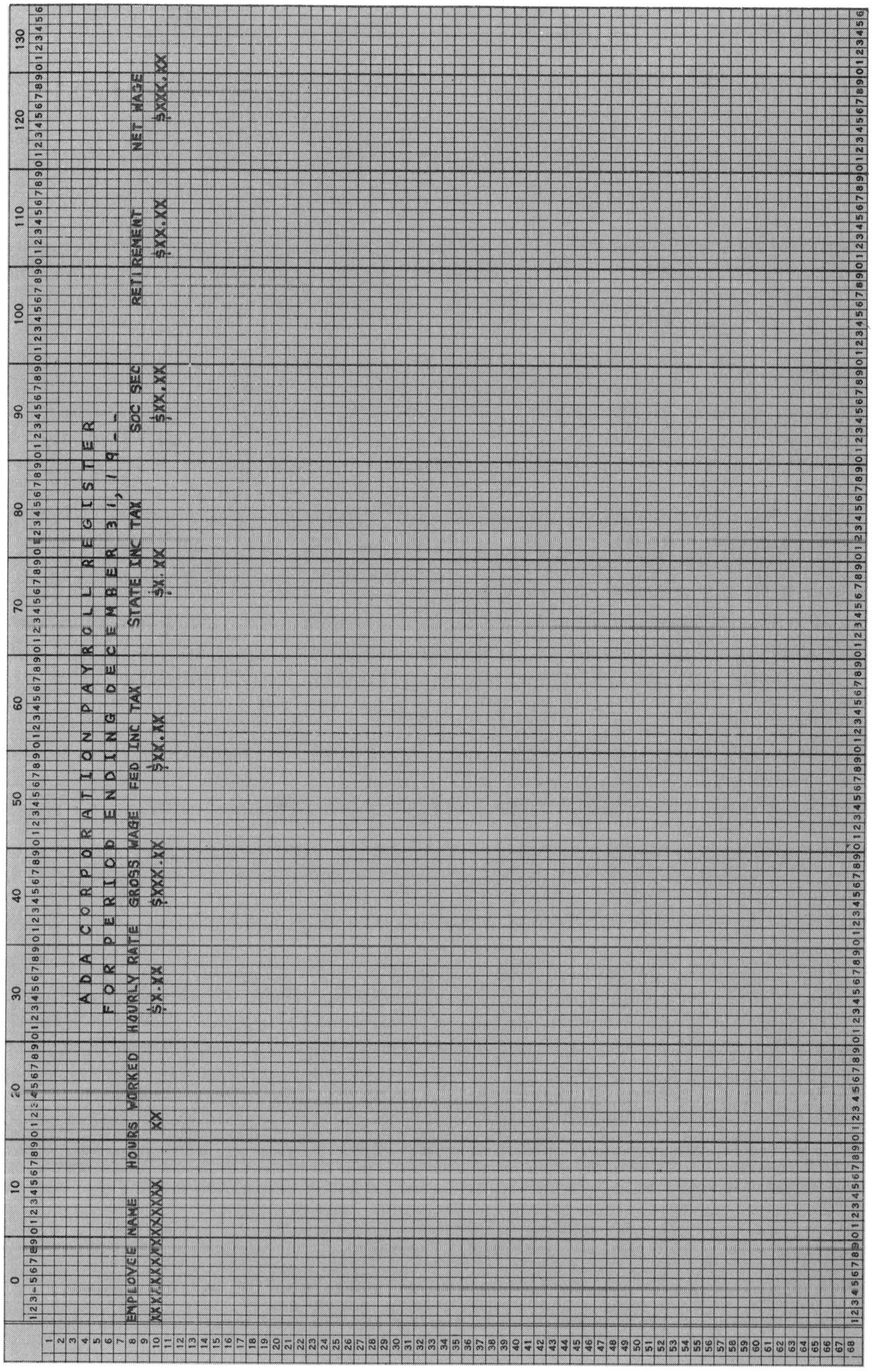

Exhibit 11–6 Printer Layout Chart

Program Flowchart

Once the programmer knows the facts that the systems analyst has supplied, he/she can develop a program flowchart. An example of such a flowchart is presented in Exhibit 11–7. Let's briefly discuss each *symbol* in the program flowchart.*

Symbol 01. The writing (printing) of the headings on the payroll report is accomplished. In this application, these headings include company and report name, and date, and also identify the content of each field of the output: "EMPLOYEE NAME," "HOURS WORKED," "HOURLY RATE," etc. Without such headings, the user would find the report's numeric content awkward to read and understand.

Symbol 02. An employee's data record is read, and the data in the record is transferred to the CPU. The data in each input record are: the name of employee, the number of hours worked in the week, and the employee's hourly rate of pay.

Symbol 03. If there is an *end-of-file indication,* computer control branches to Symbol 15. Otherwise, *computer control* passes to Symbol 04.

Symbol 04. This decision symbol involves checking the employee's data record (specifically, the number of hours worked in the week) to determine whether overtime hours are involved. In this illustration, hours in excess of forty hours are considered to be overtime hours. This test for overtime hours can be accomplished by either of two logical approaches:

1. Is the number of hours worked greater than forty (>40)? If the answer is "yes," the difference between the number of hours worked and forty would give the overtime hours. If the answer is "no," the number of hours worked would be regular hours.
2. Is the number of hours worked forty or less ($\leqq 40$)? If the answer is "yes," the number of hours worked would be regular hours. If the answer is "no," the difference between the number of hours worked and forty would give the overtime hours.

   If overtime hours are involved, the next step is represented by Symbol 05. If no overtime hours are involved, the branch (transfer of control) is to Symbol 08. In the latter instance, the overtime subroutine is automatically bypassed by the branch.

Symbol 05. The overtime hours, logically checked in the prior step, are explicitly computed (overtime hours = hours worked minus forty).

Symbol 06. The overtime wage (in money terms) is computed by multiplying the

* There are three versions of the Payroll Program—one each in FORTRAN, COBOL, and RPG. For illustrative purposes, we have used the FORTRAN program in developing the flowchart. If we wanted to use COBOL or RPG, the logic of the flowchart would be somewhat different, according to the idiom of the language in question. Also, there are slight discrepancies (due to programmer preferences) among the three programs; for instance, there are minor differences in the spacing of the output of the printer. It is important to appreciate that, despite these differences, the essential results (i.e., a correct payroll) are generated by each of the three programs.

Exhibit 11–7 Program Flowchart for Payroll Application

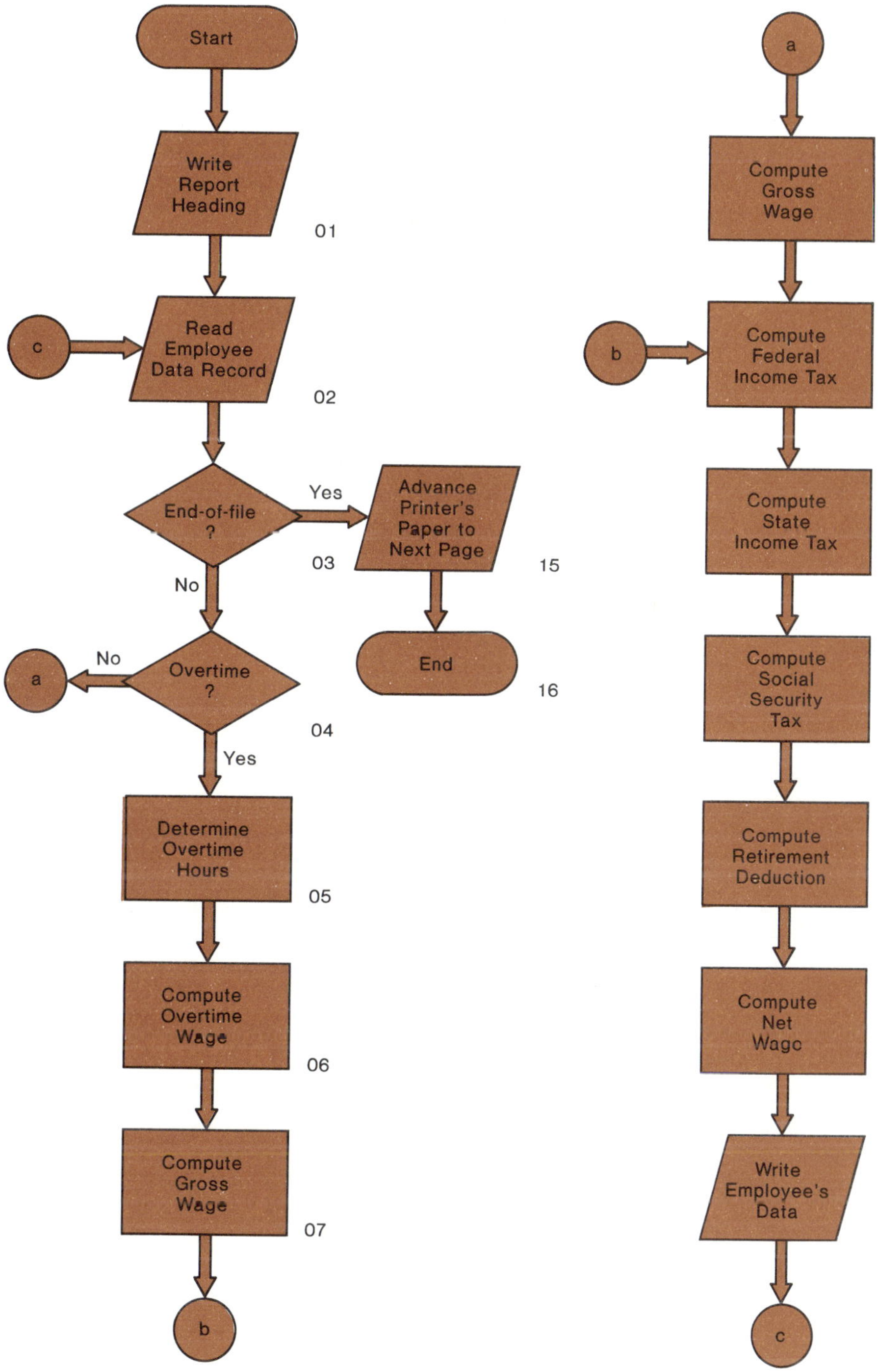

overtime hours by the hourly rate of pay by 1.5. (Recall that overtime pay, in this case, is one and a half times the normal hourly rate.)

Symbol 07. The employee's gross wage is computed by multiplying the normal hourly rate by forty hours, and adding the overtime pay (computed in the previous step).

Note that control is transferred to Symbol 09; this is accomplished in the flowchart by use of a connector: ⓑ. Symbol 08 is skipped for those employees with overtime because that step is only needed for employees who did not work overtime.

Symbol 08. This step involves computing the gross wage of the employees who did not work any overtime. For such employees, the number of hours worked is simply multiplied by the hourly rate, which results in the gross wage. (Note that transfer to Symbol 08 was from Symbol 04—the decision step that identified those employees without any overtime hours.)

Symbol 09. All employees' records, whether the employees had overtime or not, proceed through this and all succeeding steps in the flowchart. Symbol 09 represents the computing of federal income tax deduction (gross pay multiplied by an assumed rate of 6.27%).

Symbol 10. State income tax is computed (gross pay multiplied by an assumed 1.75%).

Symbol 11. Social security tax is computed (gross pay multiplied by an assumed 6.13%).

Symbol 12. The retirement deduction is computed (gross pay multiplied by an assumed 6%).

Symbol 13. The net wage to be paid to the employee is computed by subtracting all deductions from the gross wage. The total amount to be deducted from the gross wage is the sum of: federal income tax; state income tax; social security tax; and retirement amount.

Symbol 14. Since all necessary computations have been made for the individual employee by the computer, the results are now written (printed). The printed data include: the employee's name; hours worked; hourly rate of pay; gross wage; federal income tax deduction; state income tax deduction; social security tax deduction; retirement amount deduction; and net wage.

After the printing takes place, the connector ⓒ creates a loop that returns control to Symbol 02.

When the end-of-file condition is finally reached, after processing all data records the computer control eventually branches to Symbol 15.

Symbol 15. This symbol merely indicates that, since the payroll register report has been completed, the printer's paper should be automatically advanced to a clean sheet of paper. This gets the printer ready for the next print job.

Symbol 16. Since the payroll job is completed, this symbol explicitly indicates that the job has ended.

WRITE THE PROGRAM

Required Programming Aids

After the programmer has prepared a program flowchart, and after it has been checked carefully by the programmer (and perhaps by others, such as the systems analyst and the programmer's supervisor), the programmer can write the program. Using the program flowchart as a "road map," he/she writes the *code** of the program on *coding forms*. The coding form facilitates the recording of neat, readable programs, which is helpful when the program is key punched or keyed in for direct entry to the computer. See Exhibit 11–8 for examples of blank program-coding forms.†

Of course, to have a successful experience, the programmer must have a sound knowledge of the programming language being used. For instance, the programmer must know:

1. What operation codes are available for use with the particular language.
2. Constraints on the programmer, regarding assigning labels or variable names to files and data fields.
3. Proper use of *syntax* (grammar) in writing instructions. Each programming language has a set of rules for coding instructions, and these must be followed meticulously.

The Program Code

Exhibits 11–9 and 11–10 present a FORTRAN version of a computer program written on coding forms.‡ The program was developed by closely following the program flowchart in Exhibit 11–7. Even persons who are unfamiliar with the technicalities of the FORTRAN programming language will be able to perceive a definite relationship between the FORTRAN program and the program flowchart, and the output and input specifications for the payroll register problem discussed previously.

Each line in the program is numbered for ease of identification (see columns

* The writing of a program is frequently referred to as coding. This act of program coding should not be confused with the previous use of the word code: CPU codes (i.e., binary), I/O codes (e.g., Hollerith code), and so on. The word code has several meanings, depending on which context it is used in, in the computer field.

† Coding forms usually are not used with the BASIC language, since that language is interactive. That is, the individual writes the program by directly keying it in on the keyboard of a data terminal. The program can be forwarded, via the terminal, to the computer's storage and/or written out on the terminal's printer or cathode-ray tube. Procedures for using a time-sharing data terminal are presented in Appendix C.

‡ The FORTRAN version was presented rather than either the COBOL or RPG version because the FORTRAN program is considerably more condensed than comparable programs written in the other two languages.

Exhibit 11–8 Some Widely Used Program-Coding Forms

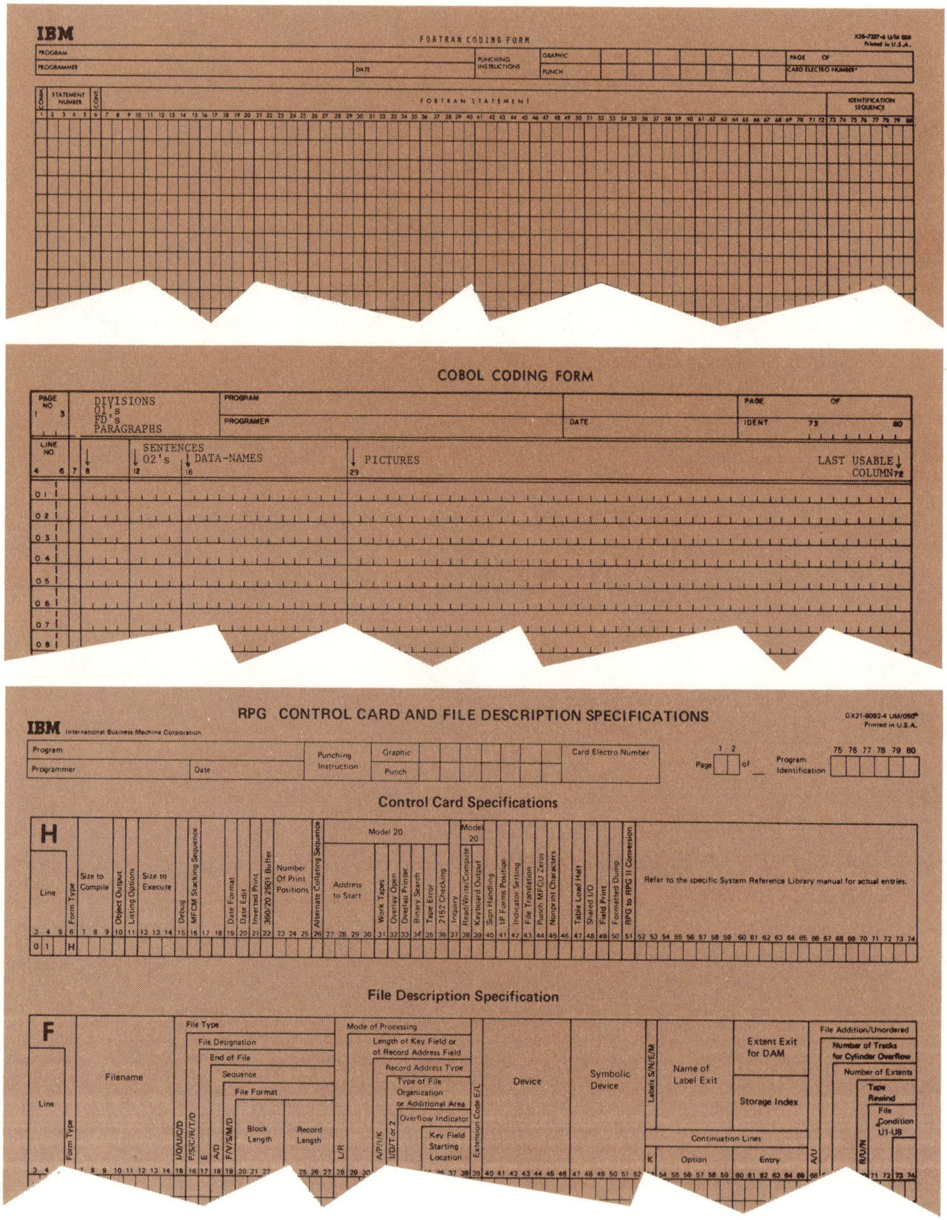

Exhibit 11–9 FORTRAN Computer Program

IBM FORTRAN CODING FORM

PROGRAM: ADA PAYROLL REGISTER — PROGRAMMER: D.S. BECKER — PUNCHING INSTRUCTIONS: GRAPHIC O Ø; PUNCH 11-6 O — PAGE 1 OF 2

```
C    THIS PROGRAM CALCULATES THE WEEKLY WAGES OF THE EMPLOYEES OF THE ADA COMPANY
      WRITE (6,8)
    8 FORMAT ('1', 33X, 'A D A  C O R P O R A T I O N  P A Y R O L L  R
     -E G I S T E R')
      WRITE (6,9)
    9 FORMAT ('Ø',32X,'F O R  P E R I O D  E N D I N G  D E C E M B E R
     - 3 1,  1 9 - -')
      WRITE (6,1Ø)
   1Ø FORMAT ('Ø', 'EMPLOYEE NAME', 3X, 'HOURS WORKED', 2X, 'HOURLY RATE
     -', 2X,'GROSS WAGE', 2X,'FED INC TAX',6X, 'STATE INC TAX'
     -, 7X, 'SOC SEC',     6X, 'RETIREMENT', 6X, 'NET WAGE')
      OWAGE = Ø.Ø
   11 READ (5,12,END = 999)  NAME1, NAME2, NAME3, NAME4, IHRS,HRRATE
   12 FORMAT ( 3A4,A3, T2Ø, I2, T25, F3.2)
      IF (IHRS .LT. 41) GO TO 13
      IOHRS =  IHRS - 4Ø
      OWAGE = (IOHRS * HRRATE * 1.5)
      GRWAGE  =  HRRATE * 4Ø + OWAGE
      GO TO 14
   13 GRWAGE =  IHRS *  HRRATE
   14 FIT    =  GRWAGE  * .Ø627
      SIT    =  GRWAGE  * .Ø175
      SST    =  GRWAGE  * .Ø613
      RETIRE =  GRWAGE  * .Ø6
```

Exhibit 11–10 FORTRAN Computer Program (Continuation of Exhibit 11–9)

IBM FORTRAN CODING FORM

PROGRAM: ADA PAYROLL REGISTER — PROGRAMMER: D.S. BECKER — PAGE 2 OF 2

```
      WAGNET   =  GRWAGE - (FIT + SIT + SST + RETIRE)
      WRITE  (6,5) NAME1,NAME2,NAME3,NAME4,IHRS,HRRATE,GRWAGE,FIT,SIT,
     -SST,RETIRE,WAGNET
    5 FORMAT ('Ø',3A4,A3,5X, I2, 1ØX, '$', F4.2, 6X, '$', F6.2,  7X, '$'
     -,F5.2,12X, '$',  F4.2,13X, '$', F5.2, 11X, '$', F5.2,9X, '$',
     -F6.2)
      GO TO 11
  999 WRITE (6,1ØØØ)
 1ØØØ FORMAT ('1')
      STOP
      END
```

73–80, "Identification Sequence"). To help you correlate the flowchart and the program, a cross-indexed listing is presented below:

Program Flowchart Symbol	*Related FORTRAN Statement(s) (Identification Sequence lines)*
01 Write Report Headings	1 through 10
Set variable OWAGE to zero	11
02 Read Employee Data Record	12, 13
03 End-of-File?	12*
04 Overtime?	14
05 Determine Overtime Hours†	15
06 Compute Overtime Wage	16
07 Compute Gross Wage (for employee with overtime)	17
ⓑ Connector By-passing Symbol 08 and Passing Control to Symbol 09	18
08 Compute Gross Wage (for employee without overtime)	19
09 Compute Federal Income Tax	20
10 Compute State Income Tax	21
11 Compute Social Security Tax	22
12 Compute Retirement Deduction	23
13 Compute Net Wage	24
14 Write Employee's Data	25 through 29
ⓒ Connector Creating a Loop to Symbol 02 (to read the next data record)	30
15 Advances Printer's Paper to Next Page (when end of file is reached)	31, 32
16 End	33, 34

Preparation of Source Deck, Compilation, and Program Lists

After the program has been written on coding forms, the *source deck* is created by key punching a punched card for each line of the coding sheets. Sometimes these cards, which constitute the source program, are verified for accuracy. As with data, it is also

* The end-of-file indicator is built into the READ instruction. "END = 999" means "go to statement number 999 at end-of-file processing." Statement number 999 begins the end-of-file routine. If the answer is "yes" (i.e., it is end of file), control passes to Symbol 15 in the flowchart or statement number 999 in the program. If the answer is "no" (i.e., it is not end of file), control passes to Symbol 04 in the flowchart or the next sequential instruction in the program.

† If no overtime is involved, connector ⓐ passes control to Symbol 08; if overtime is involved, control is passed to Symbol 05.

Exhibit 11–11 FORTRAN Program Listing

```
$JCB
C  THIS PROGRAM CALCULATES THE WEEKLY WAGES OF THE EMPLOYEES OF THE ADA COMPANY
       WRITE (6,8)
     8 FCRMAT ('1', 33X, 'A D A  C C R P O R A T I C N  P A Y R O L L  R
      -E G I S T E R')
       WRITE (6,9)
     9 FCRMAT ('0',32X,'F O R  P E R I C D  E N D I N G  D E C E M B E R
      -  3 1,  1 9 - -')
       WRITE (6,10)
    10 FCRMAT ('0', 'EMPLCYEE NAME', 3X, 'HCURS WORKED', 2X, 'HOURLY RATE
      -', 2X,'GRCSS WAGE', 2X,'FEC INC TAX',6X, 'STATE INC TAX'
      -, 7X, 'SCC SEC',     6X, 'RETIREMENT', 6X, 'NET WAGE')
       CWAGE = C.0
    11 READ (5,12,END = 999)  NAME1, NAME2, NAME3, NAME4, IHRS,HRRATE
    12 FCRMAT ( 3A4,A3, T20, I2, T25, F3.2)
       IF (IHRS .LT. 41) GO TO 13
       ICHRS =  IHRS - 40
       CWAGE = (ICHRS * HRRATE * 1.5)
       GRWAGE  =  HRRATE * 40 + CWAGE
       GC TC 14
    13 GRWAGE =  IHRS *  HRRATE
    14 FIT    =  GRWAGE  * .0627
       SIT    =  GRWAGE  * .0175
       SST    =  GRWAGE  * .0613
       RETIRE =  GRWAGE  * .06
       WAGNET   =  GRWAGE - (FIT + SIT + SST +RETIRE)
       WRITE  (6,5) NAME1,NAME2,NAME3,NAME4,IHRS,HRRATE,GRWAGE,FIT,SIT,
      -SST,RETIRE,WAGNET
     5 FCRMAT ('0',3A4,A3,5X, I2, 10X, '$', F4.2, 6X, '$', F6.2,  7X, '$'
      -,F5.2,12X, '$',  F4.2,13X, '$', F5.2, 11X, '$', F5.2,9X, '$',
      -F6.2)
        GC TC 11
   999 WRITE (6,1000)
  1000 FCRMAT ('1')
       STOP
       END

$DATA
```

Exhibit 11–12 Output from FORTRAN Program

A D A C O R P O R A T I O N P A Y R O L L R E G I S T E R

F O R P E R I O D E N D I N G D E C E M B E R 3 1, 1 9 - -

EMPLOYEE NAME	HOURS WORKED	HOURLY RATE	GROSS WAGE	FED INC TAX	STATE INC TAX	SOC SEC	RETIREMENT	NET WAGE
BECKER	16	$8.75	$140.00	$ 8.78	$2.45	$ 8.58	$ 8.40	$111.79
WHITE	20	$5.55	$111.00	$ 6.96	$1.94	$ 6.80	$ 6.66	$ 88.63
CHAN	39	$4.65	$181.35	$11.37	$3.17	$11.12	$10.88	$144.81
SINGLETON	5	$3.25	$ 16.25	$ 1.02	$0.28	$ 1.00	$ 0.97	$ 12.98
EDWARDS	46	$9.00	$441.00	$27.65	$7.72	$27.03	$26.46	$352.14
SMITH	40	$5.00	$200.00	$12.54	$3.50	$12.26	$12.00	$159.70
STONE	40	$5.00	$200.00	$12.54	$3.50	$12.26	$12.00	$159.70
THOMAS	46	$9.00	$441.00	$27.65	$7.72	$27.03	$26.46	$352.14
SANCHEZ	42	$8.20	$352.60	$22.11	$6.17	$21.61	$21.16	$281.55
DAVIS	6	$8.75	$ 52.50	$ 3.29	$0.92	$ 3.22	$ 3.15	$ 41.92

Exhibit 11–13 COBOL Program Listing

```
$JOB  WATBOL  BECKER

00101  IDENTIFICATION DIVISION.
00102  PROGRAM-ID. WAGES.
00103  AUTHOR. D. BECKER.
00104  INSTALLATION. ADA COMPUTER.
00105  DATE-WRITTEN. 5/16/78.
00106  DATE-COMPILED.  TUE, JUN. 20, 1978.
00107  SECURITY. THIS PROGRAM SHOULD NOT LEAVE COMPUTER CENTER.
00108  REMARKS.  THIS PROGRAM CALCULATES THE WEEKLY WAGES OF FULL-TIME
00109          EMPLOYEES OF THE ADA COMPANY.
00110  ENVIRONMENT DIVISION.
00111  CONFIGURATION SECTION.
00112  SOURCE-COMPUTER. IBM-370.
00113  OBJECT-COMPUTER. IBM-370.
00114  SPECIAL-NAMES.
00115      C01 IS TOP-OF-PAGE.
00116  INPUT-OUTPUT SECTION.
       FILE-CONTROL.
00117      SELECT EMPLOYEE-RECORDS-FILE ASSIGN TO  UR-S-SYSIN.
00118      SELECT EMPLOYEE-PAYROLL-FILE ASSIGN TO  UR-S-SYSPRINT.
00201  DATA DIVISION.
00202  FILE SECTION.
00203  FD  EMPLOYEE-RECORDS-FILE
00204      LABEL RECORD IS OMITTED
00205      DATA RECORD IS CARD-RECORD.
00206  01  CARD-RECORD.
00207      03  EMPLOYEE-NAME              PIC     A(15).
00208      03  FILLER                     PIC     X(4).
00209      03  HOURS-WORKED               PIC     99.
00210      03  FILLER                     PIC     XXX.
00211      03  HOURLY-RATE                PIC     9V99.
00212      03  FILLER                     PIC     X(53).
00213  FD  EMPLOYEE-PAYROLL-FILE
00214      LABEL RECORD IS OMITTED
00215      DATA  RECORD IS PAYROLL-RECORD.
00216  01  PAYROLL-RECORD.
00217      03  FILLER                     PIC     X.
00218      03  EMPLOYEE-NAME-OUT          PIC     A(15).
00219      03  FILLER                     PIC     X(5).
00220      03  HOURS-WORKED-OUT           PIC     Z9.
00221      03  FILLER                     PIC     X(8).
00222      03  HOURLY-RATE-OUT            PIC     $9.99.
00223      03  FILLER                     PIC     X(8).
00224      03  GROSS-WAGE-OUT             PIC     $$$$.99.
00301      03  FILLER                     PIC     X(09).
00302      03  FEDERAL-INC-TAX-OUT        PIC     $$$.99.
00303      03  FILLER                     PIC     X(10).
00304      03  STATE-INC-TAX-OUT          PIC     $$$.99.
00305      03  FILLER                     PIC     X(06).
00306      03  SOC-SEC-TAX-OUT            PIC     $$$.99.
00307      03  FILLER                     PIC     X(7).
00308      03  RETIREMENT-OUT             PIC     $$$$.99.
00309      03  FILLER                     PIC     X(3).
00310      03  NET-WAGE-OUT               PIC     $$$$$.99.
00311      03  FILLER                     PIC     X(02).
00314  WORKING-STORAGE SECTION.
00315  77      GROSS-WAGE                 PIC     999V99

  00316  77      OVERTIME-HOURS             PIC     99.
  00317  77      OVERTIME-RATE              PIC     99V99.
  00318  77      OVERTIME-WAGE              PIC     999V99.
1 00319  77      FED-INCOME-TAX-RATE        PIC     V9999   VALUE   .0627.
  00320  77      FEDERAL-INCOME-TAX         PIC     99V99.
2 00321  77      ST-INCOME-TAX-RATE         PIC     V9999   VALUE   .0175.
3 00322  77      SOC-SECURITY-TAX-RATE      PIC     V9999   VALUE   .0613.
  00323  77      STATE-INCOME-TAX           PIC     99V99.
  00324  77      SOCIAL-SECURITY-TAX        PIC     99V99.
4        77      RETIREMENT-RATE            PIC     V99     VALUE   .06.
  00402  77      RETIREMENT                 PIC     99V99.
  00404  01  COLUMN-HDG.
```

```
5     CC405        C3  FILLER              PIC     X       VALUE   SPACES.
6     CC4C6        C3  FILLER          PIC X(13)    VALUE    'EMPLCYEE NAME'.
7     CC407        C3  FILLER          PIC X(2)     VALUE    SPACES.
8     CC408        C3  FILLER          PIC X(12)    VALUE    'HCURS WCRKED'.
9     CC409        C3  FILLER          PIC X        VALUE    SPACES.
10    CC410        C3  FILLER          PIC X(11)    VALUE    'HCURLY RATE'.
11    CC411        C3  FILLER          PIC X(2)     VALUE    SPACES.
12    CC412        C3  FILLER          PIC X(1C)    VALUE    'GRCSS WAGE'.
13    CC413        C3  FILLER          PIC X(5)     VALUE    SPACES.
14    CC414        C3  FILLER          PIC X(12)    VALUE    'FED INC TAX'.
15    CC415        C3  FILLER          PIC X(4)     VALUE    SPACES.
16    CC416        C3  FILLER          PIC X(13)    VALUE    'STATE INC TAX'.
17    CC417        C3  FILLER          PIC X(3)     VALUE    SPACES.
18    CC418        C3  FILLER          PIC X(7)     VALUE    'SCC SEC'.
19    CC419        C3  FILLER          PIC X(3)     VALUE    SPACES.
20    CC420        C3  FILLER          PIC X(1C)    VALUE    'RETIREMENT'.
21    CC421        C3  FILLER          PIC XX       VALUE    SPACES.
22    CC422        C3  FILLER          PIC X(8)     VALUE    'NET WAGE'.
      CC431   C1   REPCRT-HDG-1.
23    CC432        C3  FILLER          PIC X(29)    VALUE    SPACES.
24    CC433        C3  FILLER          PIC X(6C)    VALUE    'A D A  C C R P C R A
      CC434 -      ' T I C N   P A Y R C L L   R E G I S T E R'.
      CC437   C1   REPCRT-HDG-2.
25    CC4372       C3  FILLER                PIC X(26)     VALUE SPACES.
26    CC438        C3  FILLER          PIC X(63)    VALUE    'F C R   P E R I C D
      CC439 -      'E N D I N G   D E C E M B E R   3 1,   1 9 - -'.
27    CC501   PRCCEDURE DIVISICN.
      CC502   CO2-START.
28    CC503        CPEN    INPUT   EMPLCYEE-RECCRDS-FILE
      CC504                CUTPUT  EMPLCYEE-PAYRCLL-FILE.
      CC505   C1C-HEADING.
29    CC506        MCVE REPCRT-HDG-1 TC PAYRCLL-RECCRD.
30    CC507        WRITE PAYRCLL-RECCRD AFTER ADVANCING TCP-CF-PAGE.
31    CC5071       MCVE REPCRT-HDG-2 TC PAYRCLL-RECCRD.
32    CC5072       WRITE PAYRCLL-RECCRD AFTER ADVANCING 2  LINES.
33    CC5073       MCVE CCLUMN-HDG    TC PAYRCLL-RECCRD.
34    CC5074       WRITE PAYRCLL-RECCRD AFTER ADVANCING 2  LINES.
      CC508   C5C-READ.
35    CC509        MCVE ZERCS TC CVERTIME-WAGE.
36    CC510        MCVE SPACES TC PAYRCLL-RECCRD.
37    CC511        READ EMPLCYEE-RECCRDS-FILE AT END GC TC 9CC-FINISH-RUN.
39    CC512        MCVE EMPLCYEE-NAME       TC       EMPLCYEE-NAME-CUT.
40    CC513        MCVE HCURS-WCRKED        TC       HCURS-WCRKED-CUT.
41    CC514        MCVE HCURLY-RATE         TC       HOURLY-RATE-CUT.
42    CC515        IF  HCURS-WCRKED LESS THAN 41 GC TC 1CC-NO-OVERTIME.
      CC5155* CALCULATE CVERTIME HCURS-RATE-WAGES


44    CC516        CCMPUTE CVERTIME-HCURS  = HOURS-WCRKED - 4C.
45    CC517        CCMPUTE CVERTIME-RATE   = 1.5  * HCURLY-RATE.
46    CC518        CCMPUTE CVERTIME-WAGE   = CVERTIME-HCURS * CVERTIME-RATE.
47    CC519        MCVE 4C TC HCURS-WCRKED.
      CC520 * CALCULATE REGULAR GRCSS WAGE TAXES AND NET
      CC601   1CC-NC-CVERTIME.
48    CC602        CCMPUTE GRCSS-WAGE       = HCURS-WCRKED * HCURLY-RATE.
49    CC603        ADD CVERTIME-WAGE TC GRCSS-WAGE.
50    CC604        CCMPUTE FEDERAL-INCCME-TAX = GRCSS-WAGE *
                                              FED-INCCME-TAX-RATE.
51    CC606        CCMPUTE STATE-INCCME-TAX = GRCSS-WAGE * ST-INCCME-TAX-RATE.
52    CC607        CCMPUTE SOCIAL-SECURITY-TAX = GROSS-WAGE *
      CC608                                     SCC-SECURITY-TAX-RATE.
53    CC609        CCMPUTE RETIREMENT = GROSS-WAGE * RETIREMENT-RATE.
54                 CCMPUTE NET-WAGE-CUT = GRCSS-WAGE - FEDERAL-INCCME-TAX
                           STATE-INCCME-TAX - SOCIAL-SECURITY-TAX - RETIREMENT.
55    CC614        MCVE  GRCSS-WAGE     TC       GRCSS-WAGE-CUT.
56    CC615        MCVE  FEDERAL-INCOME-TAX TC FEDERAL-INC-TAX-OUT.
57    CC616        MCVE  STATE-INCCME-TAX TC   STATE-INC-TAX-CUT.
58    CC617        MCVE  SOCIAL-SECURITY-TAX TC  SCC-SEC-TAX-CUT.
59    CC618        MCVE  RETIREMENT TC RETIREMENT-CUT.
60    CC620        WRITE  PAYRCLL-RECCRD AFTER  ADVANCING 2 LINES.
61    CC621        GC TC 050 READ.
      CC622   9CC-FINISH-RUN.
62    CC6225       MCVE SPACES TC PAYRCLL-RECCRD.
63    CC6226       WRITE PAYRCLL-RECCRD AFTER ADVANCING TCP-CF-PAGE.
64    CC623        CLCSE   EMPLCYEE-RECCRDS-FILE   EMPLCYEE-PAYRCLL-FILE.
65    CC624        STCP RUN.
```

Exhibit 11-14 Output from COBOL Program

A D A   C C R P O R A T I O N   P A Y R C L L   R E G I S T E R

F O R   P E R I O D   E N D I N G   D E C E M B E R   3 1,   1 9 - -

EMPLCYEE NAME	HCURS WCRKED	HOURLY RATE	GROSS WAGE	FED INC TAX	STATE INC TAX	SOC SEC	RETIREMENT	NET WAGE
BECKER	16	$8.75	$140.00	$8.77	$2.45	$8.58	$8.40	$111.80
WHITE	20	$5.55	$111.00	$6.95	$1.94	$6.80	$6.66	$88.65
CHAN	39	$4.65	$181.35	$11.37	$3.17	$11.11	$10.88	$144.82
SINGLETON	5	$3.25	$16.25	$1.01	$.28	$.99	$.97	$13.00
EDWARDS	46	$9.00	$441.00	$27.65	$7.71	$27.03	$26.46	$352.15
SMITH	40	$5.00	$200.00	$12.54	$3.50	$12.26	$12.00	$159.70
STONE	40	$5.00	$200.00	$12.54	$3.50	$12.26	$12.00	$159.70
THOMAS	46	$9.00	$441.00	$27.65	$7.71	$27.03	$26.46	$352.15
SANCHEZ	42	$8.20	$352.60	$22.10	$6.17	$21.61	$21.15	$281.57
DAVIS	6	$8.75	$52.50	$3.29	$.91	$3.21	$3.15	$41.94

Exhibit 11-15 RPG Program Listing

```
       H
01 020 FCARDIN  IP  F  80  80             READ40 SYSIPT
01 030 FPRINT   O   F 132 132     OF      PRINTERSYSLST
01 040 F* COMMENT-THE-ABOVE ENTRIES ASSIGN  INPUT-OUTPUT FILES
02 010 ICARDIN  AA  35  20NC
02 020 I                                      1  15 NAME
02 030 I                                     20  210HOURS
02 040 I                                     25  272RATE
02 060 I*COMMENT-THE INPUT FIELDS FOR THE TIME CARD RECORD ARE DEFINED
02 065 I        BB  36
02 070 C   35                Z-ADDO        OVERT   52
02 080 C   35                Z-ADDO        OTIME   20
03 010 C   35      HOURS     COMP 40                    4545CHECK FOR OVER
03 020 C      45             GOTO END                       TIME,GO TO
03 050 C   35N45   HOURS     SUB  40       OTIME   20       REGULAR PAY IF
03 060 C   35N45   OTIME     MULT 1.5      OVERT   52       HOURS UNER 40.
03 070 C   35N45   RATE      MULT OVERT    OVERT            OTHERWISE FIND
03 080 C           END       TAG                            OVERTIME
03 090 C   35 45   RATE      MULT HOURS    GROSS   62
03 098 C   35N45   RATE      MULT 40       GROSS
03 100 C   35N45   GROSS     ADD  OVERT    GROSS
03 110 C   35      GROSS     MULT .0627    INCTAX  52H
03 120 C*COMMENT-           COMPUTE GROSS,OVERTIME PAY AND FEDERAL TAX
03 130 C   35      GROSS     MULT .0175    STTAX   52H
03 140 C   35      GROSS     MULT .0613    SOCSEC  52H
03 150 C   35      GROSS     MULT .06      RETIRE  52H
03 155 C*COMMENT-            COMPUTE NET PAY BY SUBTRACTING DEDUCTICNS
03 160 C   35      GROSS     SUB  INCTAX   NETPAY  62
03 170 C   35      NETPAY    SUB  STTAX    NETPAY
03 180 C   35      NETPAY    SUB  SOCSEC   NETPAY
03 190 C   35      NETPAY    SUB  RETIRE   NETPAY
03 31  CPRINT   H  201    1P
03 32  C       OR         OF
03 33  C                                 57 'A D A  C O R P O R A T I'
03 35  C                                 82 'O N  P A Y R O L L  R E '
03 37  C                                 93 'G I S T E R'
03 39  C        H  2      1P
03 40  C       OR         OF
03 41  C                                 55 'F O R  P E R I O D  E N '
03 42  C                                 79 'D I N G  D E C E M B E R'
03 43  C                                 94 '  3 1,  1 9 - -'
04 01  C        H  3      1P
04 02  C       OR         OF
04 03  C                                 19 'EMPLOYEE NAME'
04 04  C                                 36 'HOURS WORKED'
04 05  C                                 50 'HOURLY RATE'
04 06  C                                 63 'GROSS WAGE'
04 07  C                                 76 'FED INC TAX'
04 08  C                                 91 'STATE INC TAX'
04 09  C                                100 'SOC SEC'
```

```
04 10  C                                  112 'RETIREMENT'
04 11  C                                  124 'NET WAGE'
04 12  C        D  2     35
04 13  C                          NAME         21
04 14  C                          HOURS  Z     30
04 15  C                          RATE         47 '$0.  '
05 01  C                          GROSS  B     63 '   , $C.  '
05 02  C                          INCTAX B     74 '   $0.  '
05 03  C                          STTAX  B     88 '   $C.  '
05 04  C                          SOCSEC B     99 '   $C.  '
05 05  C                          RETIRE B    112 '   $0.  '
05 06  C                          NETPAY B    124 '    $C.  '
```

SYMBOL TABLES

RESULTING INDICATORS

ADDRESS RI	ACCRESS RI	ACCRESS RI	ACCRESS RI	ACCRESS RI	ACCRESS RI	ACCRESS RI
000004 U1	000005 U2	000006 U3	00C007 U4	000008 U5	0CC009 U6	CC000A U7
0CCC0B U8	C00011 OF	000014 1P	00C015 LR	0CC016 00	CCC039 35	CCC03A 36
0CC043 45	C0007A LO	000085 H0	00C086 H1	0CC087 H2	CCC088 H3	C00089 H4
00008A H5	CC008B H6	00008C H7	00008D H8	0CC08E H9		

FIELD NAMES

ADDRESS FIELD	ACCRESS FIELD	ACCRESS FIELD	ACCRESS FIELD	ACCRESS FIELD
00012C NAME	00013B HOURS	00013D RATE	CC0128 END	00013F CVERT
C00142 CTIME	000144 GROSS	000148 INCTAX	CCC14B STTAX	C0014E SCCSEC
C00151 RETIRE	C00154 NETPAY			

LITERALS

ADDRESS LITERAL	ACCRESS LITERAL	ADDRESS LITERAL
C00158 0	0C0159 40	CC015B 1.5
00015D .0627	000160 .0175	000163 .0613
000166 .06	000168 A D A C O R P O R A T I	000180 O N P A Y R O L L R E
000198 G I S T E R	CC01A3 F O R P E R I O D E N	CC01B8 D I N G D E C E M B E R
0001D3 3 1, 1 9 - -	0001E2 EMPLOYEE NAME	0001EF HOURS WORKED
0001FB HOURLY RATE	000206 GROSS WAGE	000210 FED INC TAX
C0021B STATE INC TAX	000228 SOC SEC	C0022F RETIREMENT
000239 NET WAGE	000241 /.--	000247 --,--/.--
000251 ----/.--		

Exhibit 11–16 Output from RPG Program

A D A C O R P O R A T I O N P A Y R O L L R E G I S T E R

F O R P E R I O D E N D I N G D E C E M B E R 3 1, 1 9 - -

EMPLOYEE NAME	HOURS WORKED	HOURLY RATE	GROSS WAGE	FED INC TAX	STATE INC TAX	SOC SEC	RETIREMENT	NET WAGE
BECKER	16	$8.75	$140.00	$8.78	$2.45	$8.58	$8.40	$111.79
WHITE	20	$5.55	$111.00	$6.96	$1.94	$6.80	$6.66	$88.64
CHAN	39	$4.65	$181.35	$11.37	$3.17	$11.12	$10.88	$144.81
SINGLETON	5	$3.25	$16.25	$1.02	$.28	$1.00	$.98	$12.97
EDWARDS	46	$9.00	$441.00	$27.65	$7.72	$27.03	$26.46	$352.14
SMITH	40	$5.00	$200.00	$12.54	$3.50	$12.26	$12.00	$159.70
STONE	40	$5.00	$200.00	$12.54	$3.50	$12.26	$12.00	$159.70
THOMAS	46	$9.00	$441.00	$27.65	$7.72	$27.03	$26.46	$352.14
SANCHEZ	42	$8.20	$352.60	$22.11	$6.17	$21.61	$21.16	$281.55
DAVIS	6	$8.75	$52.50	$3.29	$.92	$3.22	$3.15	$41.92

possible to enter the source deck directly into the computer; as the person keys in the data on a keyboard, the source program is sent directly to the computer's storage. This source deck, with appropriate *job-control cards,** can then be submitted to the computer for *compilation.*

Assuming that the program has been processed by computer for compilation, the computer can provide a *listing* of the source program. Examples of such compiled program listings (with output) follow. Exhibits 11–11 and 11–12 show the FORTRAN program listing and output. Exhibits 11–13 and 11–14 present the COBOL program listing and output. Exhibits 11–15 and 11–16 are program listings and output in RPG language.

At the end of each program listing, some actual test results appear in the desired output format. This output generally conforms to the output specifications set in Exhibit 11–6.†

TEST AND DEBUG THE PROGRAM

Types of Errors

It is unusual, except in simple programs, for a new program to be free of errors ("bugs," in computer terminology). Such errors are of two main categories:

Syntax Errors. These are of the type that violate the rules of the programming language used. The programmer must correct such errors, since the compiler will refuse to generate a machine-level (object) program until the source program is free from violations of the rules of the programming language.

A few examples of syntax errors follow:

1. Assume that a field is labelled RATE. In an instruction for computation, the following appears:

   INTEREST = PRINCIPLE * RT

   The computer would have no way of knowing that the RATE field and RT are, in fact, the same (assuming that the programmer inadvertently recorded RT instead of RATE).

2. In some languages, the labels (variable names or words) that the programmer assigns to data fields must be restricted to a certain number of characters (e.g., no more than six characters). Thus, if the programmer identifies a field as PRINCIPLE, this identification would result in an error, since PRINCIPLE contains more than six characters.

3. Assume that a programmer has assigned a field a width of eight digits, and that the

* See Chapter 10 for a refresher about the use of job-control cards.

† The COBOL program results in output that in some cases (e.g., net wage of $41.94) is a few pennies different from the calculations of the FORTRAN and RPG programs. This occurs because of the particular *rounding technique* that the programmer who developed the respective programs used.

logic of the program involves moving a ten-digit figure to the field. Since a ten-digit figure cannot fit into an eight-digit field, an error condition would result.

4. A programming language has certain reserved words (e.g., words to be used for only specific purposes, such as operation codes). MOVE might be such a reserved word. If the programmer uses such reserved words to identify or label a data field, a syntax error results.
5. Punctuation in instructions is very important. A misplaced period, comma, or bracket can result in a syntax error.

Logic Errors. Such errors do not necessarily violate any rules of the programming language, but they do result in a program that may execute without solving the intended problem.

A few examples of logic errors are as follows:

1. Assume that it is desired to compute the interest on principle (interest equals principle multiplied by rate), but that the programmer wrote the instruction as follows:

   $$\text{INT} = \text{PRINC} + \text{RATE}$$

   Obviously, by adding (instead of multiplying) the principle and rate, nonsensical results will occur.
2. Two data fields may be in the computer's storage: GROSS (for gross pay of employee) and NET (for net pay of employee). If the programmer inverts the data, they will be printed out under the wrong report heading.

GROSS PAY	NET PAY
$100.00	$120.00

3. Assume that there is a string of data fields that are to be added: A, B, C, D, E, F. If the programmer mistakenly includes an unintended field in the addition, instead of one that was intended, the computer will carry out the computation.

   $$X = A + B + C + D + E + G$$

   Obviously, wrong results will creep into the output reports.

Subtle errors in logic can remain undetected for long periods of time, particularly if the errors are spurious and occur somewhat randomly. (See Exhibit 11–17.)

Chapter 12, "Controls and Computer Systems," suggests a series of approaches that will help minimize error conditions in a computer installation.

Desk Checking

Programmers are encouraged to check their programs carefully, for syntax errors and logic errors, at the coding stage—before the computer translates the source deck to an object deck.

Exhibit 11–17 Murphy's Law Applied to Programming

Definition	A "working" program is one that has only unobserved bugs.
Law	Every nontrivial program has at least one bug.
Corollary I	A sufficient condition for program triviality is that it has no bugs.
Corollary II	At least one bug will be observed after the author leaves the organization.
Law II	The subtlest bugs cause the greatest damage or problems.
Corollary I	A subtle bug will modify storage, thereby masquerading as some other problem.
Law III	Bugs will appear in one part of a working program when another "unrelated" part is modified.
Law IV	*Lulled into Security Law.* A "debugged" program that crashed will wipe out source files on storage devices when there is the least available backup.
Law V	A hardware failure will cause systems software to crash, and the CE (computer company's customer engineer) will blame the programmers.
Law VI	A system software crash will cause hardware to act strangely, and the programmers will blame the CE.
Law VII	The documented interfaces between standard software modules will have undocumented quirks.
Law VIII	The probability of a hardware failure disappearing is inversely proportional to the distance between the computer and the CE.
Law IX	Murphy designed the computer in your organization.
Law X	(O'Shea's law) Murphy was an optimist.

Note: For those who may be in doubt, Murphy's law states that if anything can go wrong, it will, and always at the most inconvenient time.

Debugging a program on the computer can be time-consuming. Programmers who use this approach may have to submit their source deck time and time again before they are able to eliminate all errors from the program. Obviously, this can waste expensive computer time.

During desk checking, it is often desirable to have the programmer simulate the computer and try to visualize how the program would handle actual data if the program were being executed by the computer. For instance, let's assume two hypothetical data records and trace how those records would be processed through the program flowchart for the payroll application (see Exhibit 11–7). The assumed input data is as follows:

Employee Name	*Hours Worked*	*Hourly Rate of Pay ($)*
Edwards	46	9.00
Becker	16	8.75

If each of these data records is traced through the logic of the program flowchart, the programmer can learn the result of each operation and can probably notice any illogical steps. For the above data, the programmer can ascertain what the output will be for the two employees:

	Edwards		*Becker*	
Gross Wage	$441.00 (40 hours at $9.00; 6 hours at $13.50)		$140.00 (16 hours at $8.75)	
Federal Income Tax (6.27% of Gross Wage)	$ 27.65	= $88.86	$ 8.78	= $28.21
State Income Tax (1.75% of Gross Wage)	$ 7.72		$ 2.45	
Social Security Tax (6.13% of Gross Wage)	$ 27.03		$ 8.58	
Retirement Deduction (6% of Gross Wage)	$ 26.46		$ 8.40	
Net Wage (Gross Wage less Deductions)	$352.14		$111.79	

Compiler Checking

After the program has been desk checked, it is then key punched and submitted for translation. The compiler will identify any syntax error on an error listing (sometimes referred to as a diagnostic listing), and provide a printout of the source program.*

The programmer uses the error listing generated by the computer, and corrects the syntax errors; the source deck is resubmitted until an error-free compilation has taken place. Again, the compiler will not generate an object program until syntax errors are removed from the source program.

Run with Test Data

When the above steps have been completed and the object program has been generated (as explained in Chapter 10), the programmer should conduct several *trial runs,* on the computer, by using hypothetical or representative test data. The programmer should determine in advance what results should be expected from the test data.

* Exhibits 11–11, 11–13, and 11–15 did not contain any errors on program listings.

Exhibit 11–18 Content of Documentation

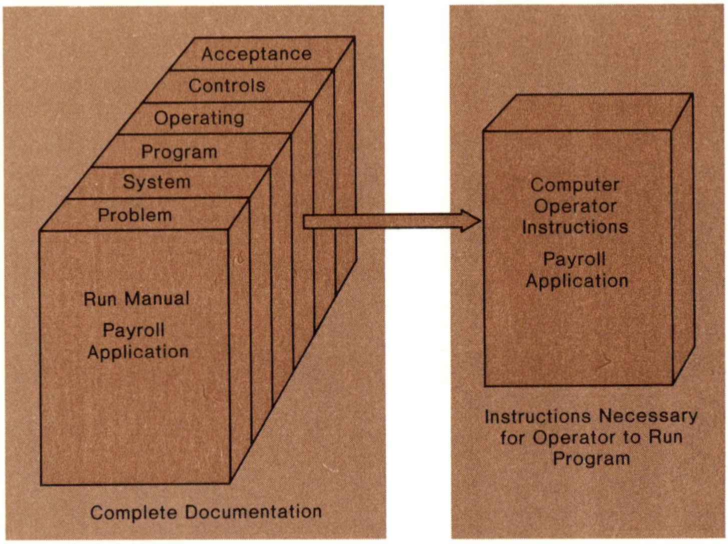

The test data should include all important variations in input data, including data with errors. This will test the program's handling of error conditions (no error subroutines have been provided in our simple payroll example). Also, all the various paths in the processing logic of the program should be tested. Some "checked-out" programs that have produced correct output for months and even years, have produced erroneous output when they encountered a previously unused condition or path.

Diagnostic Procedures

Sometimes a program does not run correctly, but the logical errors in the program are difficult to find. When this happens, as it often does in complex programs, a variety of diagnostic procedures may be used, depending on the programming language and compiler being used.

A common diagnostic procedure uses a program called a *trace routine.* This prints out the results of key processing steps in the program being tested—steps like the value of selected variables and the indication of various paths taken in the program.

Sometimes it is desirable to obtain a storage dump (a map that indicates the content of storage) when the program "hangs up" during a test run. The programmer can then study the listing to get possible clues about the cause of the program's problems. However, when a high-level language is being used, such a memory dump is usually not necessary.

PREPARE FILES AND INPUT DATA

In addition to preparing a program, input data and files must be converted to machine-readable media.

In business applications, this step can be time-consuming and costly, as some input data and files can be huge. Obviously, the input data and files must conform to the format specifications indicated in the computer program.

Even if the program is free of errors, inaccurate input data and files can cause the computer to generate inaccurate results. Consequently, such data and files should be subject to verification before processing.

Programs that are new typically are run in *parallel* with the old method for a short time (e.g., one or two cycles) to compare results of the new system with the old one. While such parallel processing of two systems can be expensive, experience has shown it to be an excellent safeguard against overconfidence in a new system. An immediate cutover to a new system, which is subject to some unexpected breakdowns, can cause considerable chaos in an organization.

DOCUMENT THE SYSTEM

The programmer, in collaboration with the systems analyst, proceeds with *documentation.* Documentation consists of gathering together, in reference manuals, all relevant documents and records that describe the computer application.

While this phase of a project is a vital one, it is often neglected in many computer departments because: accurate documentation can require painstaking effort; it is often difficult to update; and frequently the analyst and programmer are assigned a new project, leaving them little or no time to document the just-completed effort.

Documentation is important because it provides a coherent explanation about the application. This sort of explanation is often required by supervisors, users, computer operators, and analysts and programmers who may have to learn about the intricacies of the application or who may have to modify the program.

Two of the more important documents in the package are:

1. *Run Manual.* Among the sections of this type of manual are: problem definition; systems description; program description; operating instructions for computer operators; and controls for the application.
2. *Computer Operator Instructions.* This is part of the more complete run manual. Such instructions are sometimes called a console run book, and should contain all guidelines necessary for running the job on the hardware. Types of coverage include: program description and listing; punched-card layouts; key punch instructions; description of master and transaction files to be used; computer console switch settings; and console messages and halts (see Exhibit 11–18).

The documentation should be reviewed by a supervisor, and permanent copies should be placed in a secure location for access by authorized personnel.

PROGRAM IN OPERATION

Once the program has been debugged of errors and has been tested and proven acceptable, it can, when desired, be loaded into the computer, along with the required data to be processed. The documentation package guides the computer operators, control clerks, and others in handling the application.

The computer operations supervisor prepares a production schedule showing when the job is to be run. When that time arrives, the operator takes steps to accomplish the task (e.g., prepares necessary control cards, loads the necessary files on the proper devices, has the program loaded, and inserts the proper form paper into the printer). The program is then run. After it is acccomplished, the operator may have to remove certain files and return them to off-line storage, remove or change the paper in the printer, or perform other steps. The running time for the job usually is noted automatically by the operating system (the computer has an internal clock). The times are summarized, by job and date, for review by management. See Chapter 14, "Management of a Computer Department," for other relevant comments.

The control clerk performs various checks on the output before dispatching it to the proper parties. See Chapter 12, "Controls and Computer Systems," for comments about this phase.

PROGRAM MAINTENANCE

Program maintenance involves updating programs for necessary changes.

Programs tend to be dynamic, and most of them are subject to periodic revisions; some programs are subject to frequent modifications. Sometimes, when revisions are extensive, an organization considers completely reprogramming the job instead.

Some organizations assign specific programmers to the task of program maintenance.

When changes are made in programs, these changes should also be reflected in the documentation package.

Summary

This part of Chapter 11 provided a step-by-step description of the work a programmer performs in coping with an actual programming assignment. This should provide some degree of deeper understanding of the actual work behind the programming steps outlined in Exhibit 11–4. The meaning behind the preparation of a program flowchart, the writing of a program, and the other steps involved should now be much clearer.

Terms to Learn

Print chart
Print position
Blank field
Report heading
Program flowchart symbol
Branch
Computer control
End-of-file indicator
Program code
Coding form
Syntax
COBOL
RPG
FORTRAN statement
Identification sequence
Source deck
Program compilation
Program list
Rounding
Job-control card
Test and debug
Syntax error
Logic error
Object deck
Desk checking
Compiler checking
Computer run
Diagnostic procedure
Trace routine
Parallel run
Documentation
Run manual
Computer operator instruction
Operational program
Program maintenance

Review Questions

1. Discuss the need for systems design, including the *flowchart, input and output specifications, computational specifications,* etc. Why are they needed prior to actually programming a job?
2. Are *blank fields* required between fields that contain actual data?
3. Describe the structure and use of a *printer layout chart*. What is the likely result of not using such a chart?
4. Describe, in your own words, what is intended by the *symbols* of the flowchart presented in Exhibit 11–7.
5. Identify a simple computer job, such as computing students' grade averages. Identify the *input and output specifications* and the *computational specifications,* and draw a program flowchart to handle the problem.
6. Describe, in your own words, what is involved in the actual *coding* of a program. What *aids* does a programmer require?
7. Describe the structure and use of a *program coding form*. What is the likely result of not using such a chart when preparing a FORTRAN, COBOL, or RPG program?

8. Why do the coding forms of FORTRAN, COBOL, and RPG all *differ* in structure?
9. In your own words, discuss how the *FORTRAN program* (Exhibits 11–9 and 11–10) relates to the *flowchart* (Exhibit 11–7).
10. Discuss the *program compilation procedure.*
11. What is a *program list,* and of what value is it?
12. Study the FORTRAN, COBOL, and RPG program lists (Exhibits 11–11 through 11–16). Generally, what are some of the *differences* and *similarities* that you observe?
13. How can three different programs, such as those identified in Question 12, all generate substantially the *same* results?
14. Give examples of *syntax errors* and *logic errors.*
15. Describe how *desk checking* and *compiler checking* eliminate program errors. Will compiler checking discover all logic errors?
16. What is the significance of testing a new program with an *array* of data? Why not test the complete data file rather than using only limited sample data?
17. Why is the preparation of *data files* and *input data* sometimes as time-consuming as the actual preparation of the computer program itself?
18. Why is it desirable to have *parallel runs* instead of immediately cutting over to a new computer program? If a program has been tested and debugged, shouldn't it be perfect? Why duplicate costs by running two systems for a period of time?
19. Describe what is involved in *documentation,* and indicate why documentation is important in the computer field.
20. Who is responsible for the actual *production runs* of a computer program?
21. What is *program maintenance,* and why is it important? Identify several specific examples of things that may require program maintenance on, say, a payroll program.

ADDENDUM: RUNNING A COMPUTER PROGRAM

Once a program is compiled into the object language, it must be loaded into computer storage in order for it to be run. Then the computer must be directed to the first instruction in the program. From that point on, the program can be executed automatically. Typically, there are two approaches for loading a program and transferring control to the first instruction of a program. One approach is to use the computer console; this, however, is a slow process. The second approach is to place the process under the control of the operating system (discussed in Chapter 10).

Computer Console*

The computer console contains a control panel, with which the operator monitors the action of the computer. The console may be physically part of the CPU, or it may be a separate unit. A low-volume I/O device, such as a typewriter, is usually associated with the console. The console's typewriter, panel lights, dials, and switches are used to:

- Manually instruct the computer.
- Display the status of the CPU and the I/O devices.
- Alter the operation of the computer equipment.
- Display the status of storage and/or registers.
- Alter the contents of storage and/or registers.
- Diagnose equipment malfunctions.
- Provide programmed messages to the console operator.

For example, the console typewriter may be instructed by a program in storage to type a message such as: "TYPE TODAY'S DATE IN FORMAT SS-OO-PP". The operator may be required to type in the date (e.g., 02-19-80), and only then will the program proceed. The console typewriter can also give instructions and error messages. Sometimes manual intervention, to change the running of a program, is handled through the console typewriter.

Loading a Program

When the source program is compiled, the result is a machine-language program. Each instruction must be assigned a separate storage location. Such an assignment can be made in two ways:

- *Absolute assignment.* The compiler assigns a specific memory location to each instruction. When the program is loaded into storage, the same instruction will always be placed in the same location.
- *Relative assigment.* The instructions are given relative addresses rather than being assigned to specific locations. The assignment is performed when the program is loaded into storage, and therefore the location used may vary from one use to the next.

In either case, an address is associated with each instruction. Instructions will not automatically place themselves in the designated storage locations. There must be a procedure for taking each instruction and placing it in the specified location. A load program accomplishes this task. The load program may be a separate program that must be in memory in order to read and store the program to be loaded, or a load routine may be part of each program to be loaded. In the latter case, a bootstrap

* Consoles were discussed in Chapter 7.

technique is employed. The first instruction entered into memory loads the next one, which loads a third one, and so on. A special load button on the console is usually available to read the first record into storage to start the bootstrap operation.

Initiating the Program

As its last step, the load program will usually transfer control to the operating program just loaded. The starting address may be a standard one used by all programs (e.g., location 000000), or it may be completely variable. The load program may set up a pause and give the operator a message. Then he/she must press "run" for the program to start, or else the program may automatically begin without further human intervention.

The console also provides some means for specifying a starting address and transferring control to it. This is required in order to allow the operator to start or restart a program at a point other than the beginning. Branching may be done through console switches, dials, or the console typewriter.

When loading and starting the computer, the operator must also prepare the I/O units. The printer must be loaded with paper forms, magnetic disks and tapes must be mounted, and all units must have their "on" switches activated. If the equipment and switches are not properly set, the program may report an error condition on the console typewriter.

TOPIC 3—NEW DEVELOPMENTS IN PROGRAMMING

MODULAR AND STRUCTURED PROGRAMMING*

To simplify matters, the sample payroll program used in this chapter has been kept purposely elementary. But in reality, a payroll is considerably more complex. For instance, we have used a single income tax rate of 6.27%. In practice, a payroll application uses a federal income tax table containing many tax rates, depending on number of dependents and salary level. Also, social security tax is computed at a standard rate, but only up to a maximum figure. Moreover, some payrolls have numerous other deductions aside from the ones identified in the simple example.

Even a common application like payroll can get quite complex if we try to handle the entire problem as one huge problem. To simplify the task, there is a trend toward designing a series of separate program modules (*subprograms*) tied together by a control module (or *mainline*) rather than trying to write a single monolithic program. This approach is a key element of modular programming (or structured programming). A related idea is the *top-down approach;* this means that a general approach is used first, and then details are introduced gradually, layer by layer. In other words, the top-down approach does not encourage people to immediately attack the minute

* Modular and structured programming are generally used together. Structured programming involves the use of only a limited number of flowchart symbols (in practice, three) to develop a flowchart. In particular, the "GO TO" step is almost completely eliminated or used in a restricted way.

Exhibit 11–19 An Example of a Structured Program-Flowchart

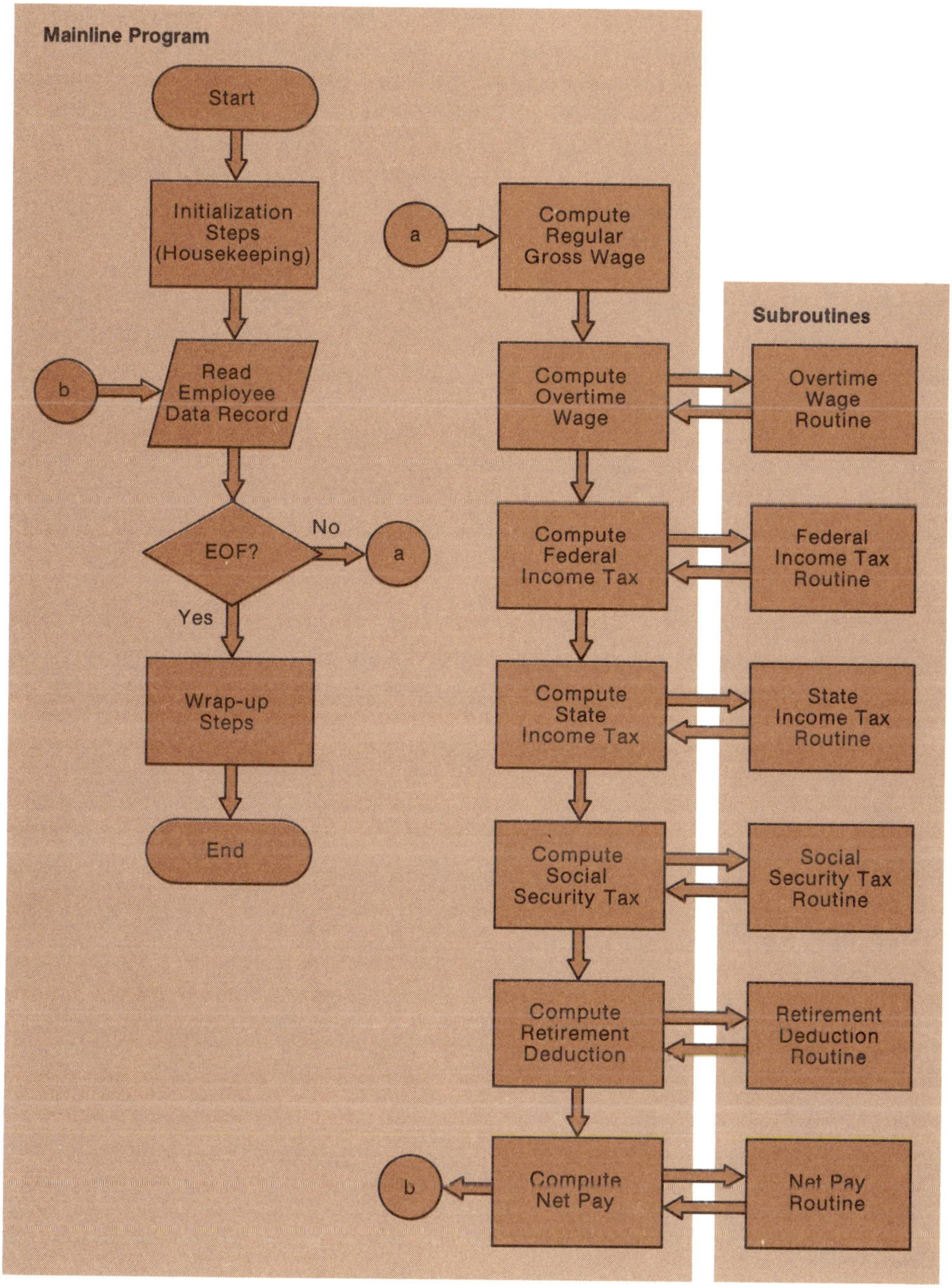

details of a problem, but to move from generality to specificity. This is consistent with the systems approaches discussed in Chapters 1 and 2, and also with the systems design and analysis techniques explored in Chapter 9.

A flowchart depicting a program designed along modular lines is shown in Exhibit 11–19. Note that the mainline program has few actual computations. Rather, it has links to modules for computational details: control passes to the respective module for computation and then returns to the mainline. A considerable amount of the details have been removed from the mainline program.

Some of the advantages of modular programming are that: several programmers can program the modules concurrently; a generally used function can be programmed once as a module and used by all programs needing this function; modules can be stored in secondary storage and brought into primary storage as needed, thus saving storage space; if a change is required, only those modules affected need be modified; and testing is made easier, since small modules can be tested individually as they are completed.

While the ideas behind modular and structured programming have been used for some time, recently they have been given more attention and wider use, as programming costs rise more rapidly than other costs (e.g., hardware).

Summary

Computer programming is a dynamic area. Programming languages and aids are being improved, and new approaches are sometimes introduced. There has been increased interest in the use of modular and structured programming to improve the effectiveness and efficiency of programming efforts.

Terms to Learn

Modular programming
Structured programming
Module
Subprogram
Mainline program
Control module
Top-down approach

Review Questions

1. Investigate and find out the details of how to compute the *social security tax deduction.* What is the maximum (or cut-off point) amount of wages/salary subject to this deduction?
2. How would you *flowchart* the information developed in Question 1? Develop a subroutine and then suggest how it might be integrated with the flowchart in Exhibit 11–7.
3. Discuss the significance of *modular* and *structured programming.* Why do you think these concepts are growing in popularity and use?
4. Contrast the *structured flowchart* (Exhibit 11–19) with the *prior flowchart* (Exhibit 11–7). What are the advantages of a structured program flowchart?

A.D.A. CRT
ECONOMY
1980 1985 1990
My answer is displayed on my C.R.T.
The probability that I am accurate is 90%
Please give the forecast in constant dollars using base year 1976...
What is the state of economy going to be in 1990?
What is the degree of certainty of your forecast?
AGENDA
1. ECONOMY
2. MOVE
FUNDS

CHAPTER 12

CONTROLS AND COMPUTER SYSTEMS

Objectives

Chapter 12 explores a vital but too often neglected area of computer work: computer controls. Computer users should institute effective controls for computer systems because the computer's very power can, when uncontrolled, cause organizations severe problems and losses. A computer system has potentials for high-magnitude errors, fraud, etc., unless an effective control system prevents such undesirable happenings.

THE NEED FOR CONTROL

Since the computer department produces vital information that affects the organization's operations and decisions, quality control* is needed within the department. If the computer produces inaccurate information, poor management decisions and organizational ineffectiveness† can result. Inadequate controls can also invite fraudulence, which may involve many thousands of dollars.

Since quality control has a cost affiliated with it, a balance must be reached between undercontrolling and overcontrolling. The nature of an application often suggests the degree of control necessary. For instance, a vital application (e.g., payroll) that is involved with disbursement of company funds needs more control than a statistical study, which may need to be only approximately accurate to be useful.

Computer controls are somewhat different from the controls that are maintained in an environment where most work is performed by people. The computer is extremely fast and performs its work electronically (this work is largely invisible to humans). Frequently, managers and employees do not understand the computer program and processing. If any errors exist in the program or data files, the computer will try to process the files in any case; consequently, the output can be misleading, and the user may not be aware that he/she is using incorrect information.

It is important for the systems designers and computer programmers to be aware of the kinds of controls they can and should build into computer applications rather than to make after-the-fact discoveries of errors in the completed computer-work. By

* An application that is 100 percent controlled would require an elaborate and costly control procedure. On the other hand, an application without any controls could result in numerous errors, faulty information, etc., creating problems and penalties (i.e., costs) for the organization. Generally, an organization must seek some compromise between these two extreme positions on controls.

† There are some dramatic examples of the impact of errors. Several years ago at Cape Kennedy, a rocket rose majestically from its launch pad and headed toward Venus. But following lift-off, it began to wobble uncontrollably and had to be destroyed after only five minutes of flight. A minor error in a program resulted in the destruction of $18.5 million worth of space equipment. Other examples of such errors and problems are presented in Chapter 16.

Exhibit 12–1 Control Points for a Computer System

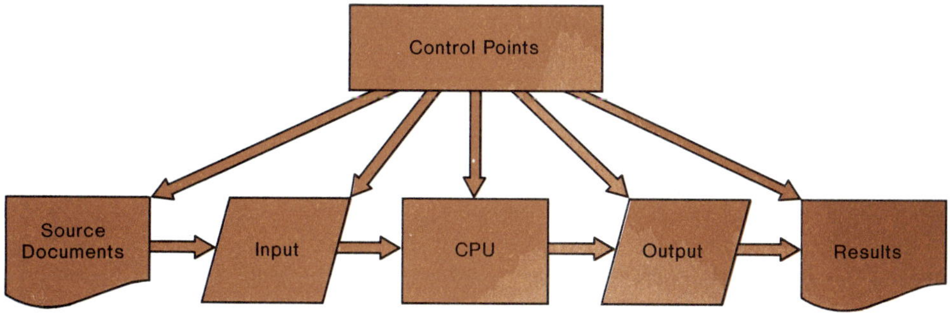

designing and programming applications with appropriate, built-in controls, the frequency of errors and complaints can be greatly reduced.*

Exhibit 12–1 shows the framework of control for a computer system in an organization.

SOURCES OF ERRORS IN COMPUTER SYSTEMS

Errors in computer systems may arise from several sources. The primary causes of errors are:

1. *Inaccurate input data.* Inaccurate data may originate when the recording on source documents is faulty, or when machine-readable media or direct-entry input are prepared.
2. *Illogical systems and programs.* Systems analysts and programmers may design and develop computer programs that work but do not solve the intended problems (e.g., an algorithm that performs the multiplication function when it should be performing the addition function).
3. *Manual mishandling.* The employees working in the computer department may mishandle data or program files. For instance, if a few punched cards are missing from a file, the computer processing can result in substantial inaccuracies.
4. *Machine malfunctioning.* A slight malfunctioning of any hardware component can cause aberrations in computer operations and affect the accuracy of processing and output.

* Chapter 16, "Computer and Society Issues," deals with some related topics, including paperwork pollution, the computer and privacy, and the computer and its use for criminal purposes.

5. *Software malfunctioning.* Software, some of which the computer manufacturer provides, may not be thoroughly debugged and tested. Using organizations can often discover errors that can be traced to software (including such sophisticated software as compilers, operating systems, and packaged programs). Other errors may go undetected, and the consequences can be harmful to the organization.

COMMUNICATION BARRIERS CREATE CONTROL PROBLEMS

In general, one chief source of many of the foregoing problems is a breakdown in communication. The technical nature of computers often impedes meaningful communication between technicians and users; the user may not know how to identify computer errors, while the computer technician may not be sensitive to the user's needs. Ultimately, the user blames the computer technician if something goes wrong, and of course the computer technician blames the user.

First, users need to have some familiarity with the computer's capabilities and limitations so that they can deal intelligently with computer technicians. Next, computer technicians should be trained to be aware of the users' needs, and applications should be designed and programmed for such user service.

Computer applications should be designed and programmed on a team basis, so that both users and computer technicians take on joint responsibility. Adequate attention to and review of systems analysis and design material, computer programs, and related documentation can greatly ensure that computer applications will meet the intended purposes.*

THE COMPUTER CONTROL SECTION

In many computer departments, a special control section is established.† This section is staffed by control clerks who are responsible for monitoring data processing from origination on source documents through computer output (see Exhibit 12–2). Some examples of the control section's functions include:

1. Logging in source documents and maintaining clerically prepared control totals.
2. Checking whether input data, in machine-readable form, agree with source-document controls.
3. Tracking progress of data-processing work through the computer department.

* Chapter 9, "Systems Analysis, Design, and Applications," and Chapter 14, "Management of a Computer Department," discuss a number of related topics.

† Chapter 14 discusses the organization and operation of a computer department, including the control section. The control section of a computer department should be distinguished from the control section of the CPU (discussed in Chapter 4). The CPU's control section is part of its engineered hardware, and it performs automatic control procedures. The computer department's control section performs control functions external to the computer.

Exhibit 12–2 Some Functions of the Control Section

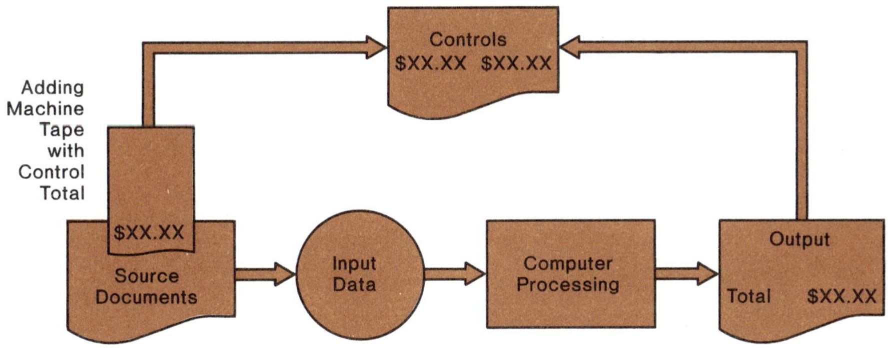

Note: Control total for source documents should tally with total of output results.

4. Ensuring output quality and maintaining an output log.
5. Supervision and distribution of output to authorized persons.
6. Handling complaints from users and following through on corrections needed.
7. Maintaining complaints and error logs.

A properly functioning control section can help maintain high levels of accuracy in a computer department.

TYPES OF CONTROL TECHNIQUES*

There are a number of specific control techniques. Some of them are described here (see also Exhibit 12–3).

Input and Output Controls

Since input data usually involve considerable amount of human recording, and since people are prone to making mistakes, a great many errors emanate from this human source. Of course, it is desirable to discover such errors and to correct them before they enter the actual production runs (e.g., the updating of master files or the generation of output reports or checks). There is a very true saying in the computer field: garbage in, garbage out (GIGO).

* Chapter 14 deals with the topic of management control in a computer department. Management control emphasizes broader overall controls rather than specific technical controls, such as those that are built into computer applications.

Exhibit 12–3 Some Examples of Computer Controls

Input and Output Controls

- Procedure Controls
- Prenumbered Forms
- Proper Authorization
- Verification
- Control Totals
- Validation/Edit Runs

Programmed Controls

- Testing and Debugging
- Check Digits
- File Labels
- Condition Tests

Hardware Controls

Physical Controls over Programs and Files

Procedure Control. The standardization of clerical practices and well-designed source and input forms set procedural guidelines for the creation of data. For example, a source document may have a series of nine boxes for account number. This constrains the clerk completing the forms from erroneously recording a ten-digit number for account number. Some computer departments make a practice of clerically reviewing key fields on source documents before the data are converted into machine-readable data.

Prenumbered Forms. Important forms (e.g., authorization for payment of bills, or checks) usually are prenumbered to protect against unauthorized use. All such forms, even those that are damaged or cancelled, must be accounted for. Also, sometimes an individual outside the computer department maintains physical control over the forms (e.g., checks) and only releases forms for use at the time the specific job is to be run on the computer.

Proper Authorization. There should be established procedures for authorizing data-processing transactions. For instance, source documents should require some kind of authorization (e.g., signature of officer) before they are accepted for processing in the computer department. If direct entry of data into the computer is involved, the data-terminal user should have some method of signifying that he/she is an authorized computer user. This may involve assigning computer users and jobs unique identifying codes. Under such a system, if the person does not have the key code, the computer will not permit entry on the computer.

Also, there should be a procedure to ensure that output is issued only to authorized individuals. Before output is released, it should be reviewed for completeness and agreement with manual controls, as well as screened for any obvious errors.

Verification. Verification can be performed on data that have been converted to machine-readable form. For instance, after cards have been punched, an off-line machine known as a "verifier" can be used to check the accuracy of the original punching. Using the verifier to obtain punched-card verification involves a complete repetition of the keying-in process. The machine automatically compares the second keying in of data with the original data that were punched in the card. If there is a discrepancy, an indicator alerts the operator of the inaccuracy.

Control Totals. Control totals are a basic method of error control to determine whether or not all items in a batch of work have been processed. Usually, control totals are established before the data are entered into the computer. Such totals might be:

1. Total amount fields (e.g., total hours worked).
2. A record count (e.g., the number of employees on the payroll).
3. Hash totals, which are not typically added for data fields. The total is relevant only to control; it does not serve any other useful purpose (e.g., total of all employee numbers).

Control totals prepared prior to computer processing are often compared to the control totals that the computer generates during processing. If the two totals agree, at least this means that the computer has processed everything it was fed as input, and that certain fields of computer output agree with manual controls. If there are disagreements, the reasons for the discrepancies must be traced; this is usually a manual audit task.

Validation/Edit Runs. Before data are used in updating files or other processing, a separate input validation or editing run can test them for errors as much as possible. For instance, the machine-readable input data may be run through the computer with a separate validation/editing program, which scrutinizes the input data and prints out messages if any input data do not meet certain preset standards. Some of the conditions that may be reported are: a transaction record does not have a matching master record; a numeric field has alphabetic data in it; or duplicate records exist.

Programmed Controls

Computer programs can be designed to automatically perform a variety of procedures to ensure accuracy of data processing. The foregoing discussion of "control totals" and "validation/edit runs" involves programming controls that are used in connection with input and output.

Testing and Debugging. Of course, all programs should be thoroughly tested and debugged to ensure that: all illogical errors have been eliminated; the instructions adhere to the programming language's standards; the program properly handles input data and files; and the program generates output that satisfies the users' needs.

Check Digits. The use of a check digit can ensure the accuracy of a key number, such as an account number, customer number, or employee number. A check digit is determined by performing some arithmetic operation on the number in such a way that the errors that typically occur in transcribing a number are detected. As an example of a simple check-digit procedure, consider the following:

1. Start with a number without a check digit:	57648
2. Take every other digit and multiply these by two:	10 12 16
3. Sum the digits in the resulting numbers, plus the digits not multiplied:	1 + 0 + 7 + 1 + 2 + 4 + 1 + 6 = 22
4. Subtract the sum from the next higher number ending in zero:	30 minus 22 = 8
5. Add check digit to number. Thus, the number becomes:	576488

A check-digit procedure is not completely error-proof. It merely tends to ensure that the number's integrity is maintained through data-processing steps. Input devices and/or the computer can check the key number for the check digit automatically.

File Labels. File labels are used (e.g., for magnetic tape, magnetic disk) at the beginning and end of each file to ensure that the proper file is used and that the entire file has been processed. A typical header label at the beginning of a file may contain such information as: name of file; date the file was created; and file identification number. A typical trailer label at the end of a file may contain such information as: number of records in the file; control totals for particular fields in the records; and end-of-file indicator.

Condition Tests. Once the data enter the computer, they can be subjected to various programmed tests to establish the reasonableness of the data. Here are some examples of such checking:

1. If there is only a limited number of valid codes (e.g., sex code for male or female), the code being processed can be checked to see whether it is one of the valid codes.

2. Data fields that are intended to be numeric fields can be checked to ensure that no invalid characters are in a location. Similarly, alphabetic fields can be tested to determine the existence of invalid numeric characters in a location.
3. If a number should be a specified number of characters in width, or if a numeric field should always be a positive or negative, tests may be made on those conditions.
4. Records that should have a certain number of data fields can be tested to make sure that all the data fields are represented.
5. In sequential files, the records can be checked to make sure that they are in the proper ascending or descending sequence.
6. When applicable, two files can be checked to ensure that there is a transaction record for every record in a master file, or a master file record for each record in a transaction file.
7. Reasonableness tests can be performed to assure that the data fall between certain upper and lower limits. For example, an organization may know that no employee earns less than $5.00 an hour or more than $15.00 an hour. These parameters can be built into the payroll program to ensure that no employee is paid less than the lower limit or more than the upper limit.
8. It is frequently possible to check computer data-processing in the same way that the manual method of cross-footing is used in accounting. In this method, individual fields are totaled independently; then a crossfooting total is developed from the totals. For example, in a payroll application, the totals are developed for gross pay, for each of the deduction items (e.g., income tax), and for net pay. Then the total net pay is recomputed by taking the total for gross pay and deducting the totals for each of the deduction items. If this cross-footing does not yield figures identical to the columnar total for net pay, there has been some error in processing. A simple example of cross-footing follows:

	Employee Number		*Gross Pay*	*Deductions*	*Net Pay*
	123456789		$10,000	$2,000	$ 8,000
	373178902		8,000	1,000	7,000
	780582340		12,000	3,000	9,000
hash total	1277218031	Totals	$30,000	$6,000	$24,000
		Cross-foot proof:	$30,000 minus $6,000 equals $24,000		

9. The computer can be programmed to automatically recalculate figures for the control total fields to determine whether the computer control totals agree with those established manually at the input stage. (For example, does the machine-readable transaction file, when processed by computer, have control totals that equal the batch totals maintained manually by the control clerk?)

10. A checkpoint procedure is part of many programs. This involves automatically performing checks on controls to determine whether or not processing has been performed correctly up to that point. Checkpoint procedures segment a long job into a series of small jobs; thus, if a problem is discovered, it is restricted to only a part of the overall job. This can localize errors and prevent entire jobs from having to be redone. In addition, there are restart procedures that permit the entire computer system to go back to a specified point in a procedure (this is usually a checkpoint). For instance, the restart procedure may automatically restore main storage to its status at the preceding checkpoint (e.g., having the same data in memory). The checkpoint and restart procedures let the computer discard incorrect parts of jobs and save jobs affected by power failure or machine malfunction, as well as interrupt one job to execute others.

Hardware and Software Controls

The computer manufacturers build certain features into the hardware and software that provide for control. Although it is true that computers are largely electronic and highly reliable, they can malfunction and cause inaccuracies to appear in data-processing operations. Some of the causes for deterioration in computer reliability include: extremes of heat or humidity; power disturbances; dust, mishandling of equipment; and normal wear. Computers should have periodic preventive maintenance (for large computers, this may be necessary daily) to detect equipment problems and correct them before they affect processing accuracy. Maintenance engineers use sophisticated testing equipment (e.g., oscilloscopes) and software packages to check out the hardware's functioning. Input and output units and peripheral devices are at least partly mechanical, and consequently may be subject to more operating problems than the electronic CPU. Failures can be traced not only to the hardware but also to such things as warped punched cards and magnetic tape defects. Equipment controls usually are based on the concept of redundancy. These controls all involve a separate repeating operation, which provides a double check on a previous operation. Here are two examples:

1. One type of equipment control involves checking bits for odd or even parity. If the computer operates on even parity, for instance, each character in the CPU must be represented by an even number of bits or else the computer will automatically sense problems in the bit patterns (i.e., bits are either being added or dropped, and thus incorrect data are resulting) and signal the operator.
2. Another type of equipment control is to have the same process performed twice, and then to compare the results of the two operations. Any difference between the first operation and the second will signal an error. For instance, most punched-card readers have two read stations. A punched card is read twice and compared for agreement before the data on the card are transmitted to the CPU. Some arithmetic units of the CPU perform each calculation twice and compare results before assum-

ing that the results are accurate. If this dual process turns up inconsistencies, a signal is given to the operator.

Even though vendors do their own software testing (e.g., on a new-version operating system), they partially depend on users' reports of software problems to refine complex software. After finding bugs in such software, the manufacturer advises all known affected computer installations, and eventually new versions of the software are introduced.

CONTROL OVER COMPUTER PROGRAMS AND FILES

Computer programs and files are valuable information resources of the organization. Without them, an organization can be paralyzed. One can imagine what would happen if an organization's payroll, accounts receivables, and inventory programs and files were destroyed. A number of special controls can be used to protect programs and files.

1. Generally, there should be some separation of duties, so that no one individual has total responsibility for a computer application. In a large organization, it is normal that separate individuals have responsibility for the systems work, computer programming, and computer operations. This creates a check-and-balance system that prevents one person from manipulating programs and files.
2. Managers should review systems design and programming work, to make certain that the computer application operates as per the specifications. In particular, the computer application should be reviewed for adequacy of input, processing, and output controls. This implies that management should ensure that there is appropriate documentation for each computer application, and that there are procedural safeguards over changes in programs, files, and documentation.
3. Sometimes it is desirable to involve the internal auditing staff in the design, programming, and testing of computer applications. The auditing staff should be competent to suggest procedures for input controls, processing controls, and output controls. Some auditing staffs maintain copies of sensitive computer programs and documentation, and they may periodically test the computer application to determine whether any errors or fraud is apparent.
4. Physical safeguards are necessary to prevent harm to programs and files, and indeed to the entire computer operation. Such safeguards must take into account fire, floods, and security against access by unauthorized individuals. Thus, environmental conditions for the computer, as well as for related programs and files, must be given careful planning. Such conditions include: special air conditioning and humidity control; adequate power and electrical wiring; sprinkler and alarm systems; and fireproof files and cabinets. Some organizations maintain duplicates of vital programs and files in a location other than the computer facility. Insurance should be part of a computer installation's protection plan. This insurance may

provide for coverage of risks from fire, flood, etc. If data-processing work is being performed for others, it might be well to consider liability insurance for suits due to nonperformance of work.

5. The computer department can use procedural controls to minimize the possibility that an operator's error will cause the destruction of a data file or program. There are magnetic-tape protection rings that prevent a tape from being written on, thus preventing the data written on the tape from being unintentionally destroyed. The ring must be removed or inserted (depending on the computer manufacturer) before the tape can be written on. Also, each file and program should have an external label that clearly indicates the content of and other pertinent information about the file and program. Within a computer facility, a specific individual may be responsible for maintaining a logging system to control all off-line copies of data files and programs. When an authorized person wishes a file or program, it is signed out to him or her.

6. Retention and reconstruction procedures are also important. The retention period of data files and reports should be specified. The period of retention varies, depending on organizational policy, legal and accounting requirements, etc. Files should not be destroyed until current processing has proven to be in balance. Further, there should be a plan for reconstruction of files, in case the files are unexpectedly destroyed.

7. Applications should provide for audit trails that permit an auditor to trace through a transaction from point of origination (e.g., source document), through processing, to output.

   In a magnetic-tape system, this means retaining magnetic tapes for a period of time (see Exhibit 12–4). For instance, the transaction and master tapes might be retained for two or three cycles. If three cycles are involved, the earliest tape is referred to as the "grandfather tape," the next-earliest tape as the "father tape," and the current tape as the "son tape." By saving the tapes, it is relatively easy to reconstruct data events as they occurred.

   In direct-access files (e.g., magnetic disk), it is more difficult and complex to maintain audit trails. One approach (albeit a slow and costly one) is to periodically "dump" (record) the files from the disk to a tape or a printout. This approach must be considered, since updating a direct-access master record usually involves writing over (or destroying) the "old" data.

   Without planned audit-trail procedures, it is difficult if not impossible to reconstruct records to determine "what went wrong, where, and why."

Summary

Various controls are needed for the computer to produce accurate and useful information. Without adequate controls, the computer can generate voluminous information that may at best be somewhat inaccurate, and may at worst be completely useless. An

Exhibit 12–4 Retention of Magnetic-Tape Files

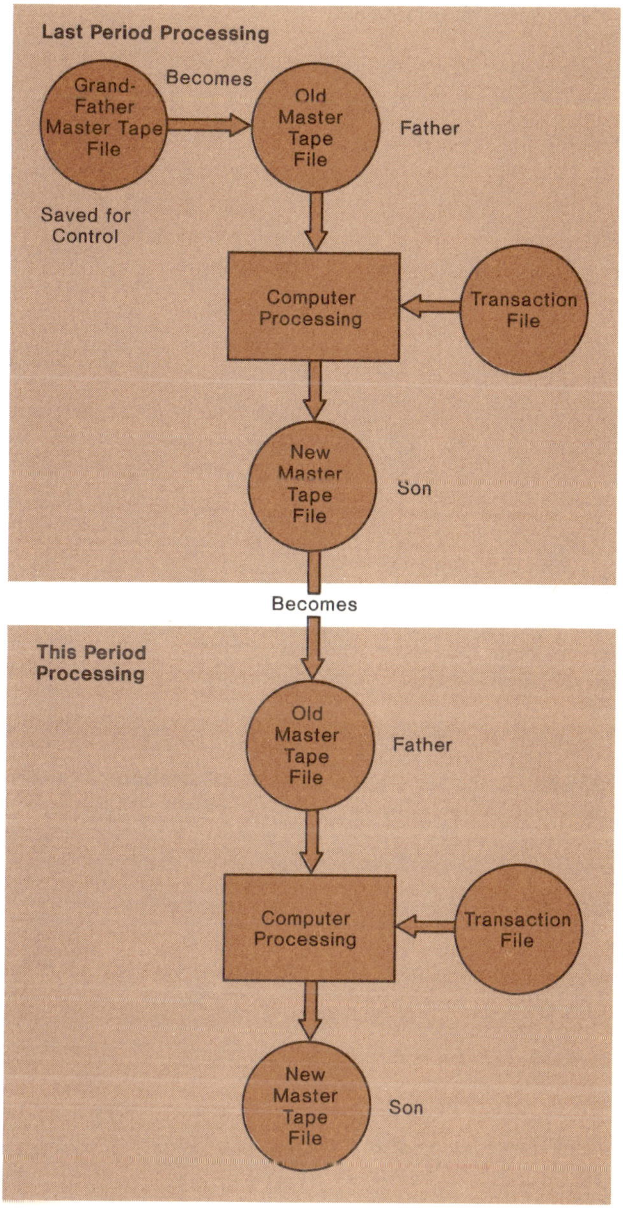

organization must seek a balance between the cost of controls and the need for accurate and useful information.

Some controls are maintained external to the computer. Other controls can be built into the application's program; and still others are built into hardware and software by the computer manufacturer.

Terms to Learn

Control
Computer-related errors
Control section in computer department
Control techniques
Procedure control
Prenumbered forms
Proper authorization
Verification
Control total
Hash total
Record count
Validation/edit run
Testing and debugging
Check digit
File label
Condition test
Hardware control
Retention and reconstruction procedure
"Grandfather" tape
"Father" tape
"Son" tape
Audit trail
Disk dump

Review Questions

1. Discuss the particular need for *good control* in computer systems.
2. How do *computer controls* differ from *noncomputer controls?*
3. Identify some of the primary sources of *errors* in computer systems.
4. How can *communication barriers* between computer professionals and laypersons create control difficulties?
5. What are the functions of the *computer department's control section?*
6. Identify and explain several *input* and *output controls.*
7. Distinguish between *hash totals* and *record counts.*
8. Discuss several *programmed controls.*
9. Using the guidelines given in this chapter, what would the *check digit* be for the number 1733?
10. Give several examples of *condition tests.*

11. What types of *hardware controls* are supplied by the computer manufacturers?
12. Describe a good *control approach* to protecting the integrity and security of the organization's computer programs and files.
13. Discuss the *audit aspects* of control.

SECTION V

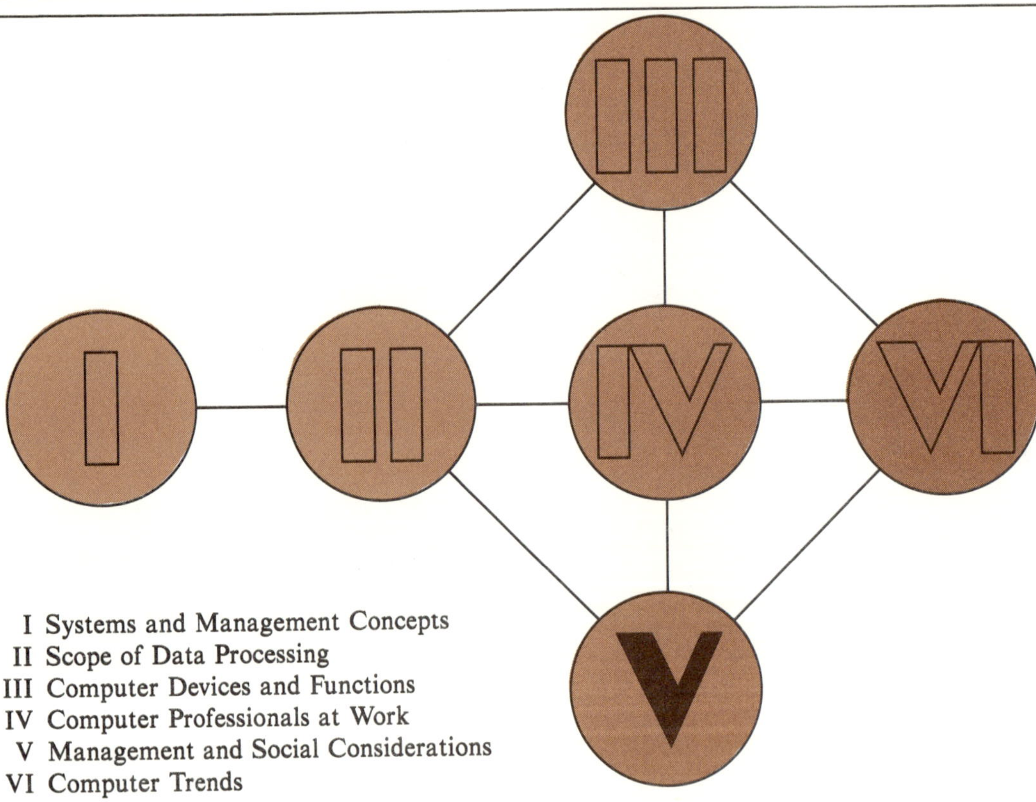

I Systems and Management Concepts
II Scope of Data Processing
III Computer Devices and Functions
IV Computer Professionals at Work
V Management and Social Considerations
VI Computer Trends

MANAGEMENT AND SOCIAL CONSIDERATIONS

The basic principle of the humanistic management method is that, in spite of the bigness of the enterprises, centralized planning, and cybernation, the individual participant asserts himself toward the managers, circumstances, and machines, and ceases to be a powerless particle which has no active part in the process. Only by such affirmation of his will can the energies of the individual be liberated and his mental balance be restored.

ERICH FROMM

The future manager will find the computer as much a fact of life as children today find the telephone. . . . The computer is a tool of liberation if used correctly. Otherwise, you become its servant. It should liberate you from being chained to operations and to your desk and enable you to have time for people and for the outside, where the results are.

PETER DRUCKER

Only highly skilled need apply.
Control unit
Hal Computer
Pal Computer
Sal Computer
Line up here for unemployed benefits.
unemployed
Retraining for new skills.

CHAPTER 13

EVALUATING AND INSTALLING COMPUTERS

Objectives

Chapter 13 provides guidelines by which to evaluate computer alternatives. There are many different computers on the market, and the manager needs some framework for deciding how to compare the computers and how to select the "best" one for his/her organization. Once the decision is made, managerial decisions are needed to make sure that the organization can effectively use the computer, after it has been delivered and installed. This chapter provides guidelines for the installation of a computer.

COST OF A COMPUTER FACILITY

Installing a computer is a major commitment; and whether it is a first computer or an existing one is being upgraded, the decision should be made only after careful analysis. The computer itself should be installed according to a plan and with due regard for its impact on people and the organization. The specific steps of evaluating and installing a computer should be tailored to suit the needs of the individual organization.

The computer is priced unit by unit, and each CPU may have many extra features attached—which are, of course, additional cost options.* Consequently, the same computer, as configured by two different users, may vary considerably in cost. The following figures are general guidelines:

	Mini-computer	*Small Computer*	*Medium Computer*	*Large Computer*
Cost of purchase†	under $60,000	$60,000 to 250,000	$250,000 to 1,000,000	$1,000,000 to 10,000,000
Monthly rental†	under $1,200	$1,200 to 5,000	$5,000 to 20,000	$20,000 and over

The cost of the computer itself is only a fraction of the cost of the computer facility. In the earlier days of computers, the hardware cost constituted about half of the total cost of running the computer department. However, in recent years this

* Previously, the cost or rental of a computer included a complete service, including software support. However, there has been a trend towards "unbundling," which ultimately means that the user pays separately for hardware, software, training, etc.

† This book uses a fifty-month basis to convert purchase price to a monthly rental cost. In practice, computer vendors use a considerable range in making such conversions.

Even if an organization purchases its computer, it usually amortizes (or depreciates) the investment over the life of the equipment, and as a consequence writes off the cost on a monthly or yearly basis.

hardware-cost figure has been between 30 and 40 percent. The relative cost of hardware has been declining while the cost of personnel has been increasing. As a guideline, the continuing costs of the department, after a computer has been installed, may be distributed approximately as follows:

Monthly Cost Items	*Percentage of Total Cost*
Hardware costs	35
Systems analysis and design, and programming	30
Operations of Computer Department	35

The startup costs necessary to get a computer installed, tested, and ready for operation will vary, depending on circumstances. It is not unusual for this cost to be approximately the equivalent of one year's anticipated monthly costs. For instance, assume that a small computer rents for $3,000 a month. The following costs may be calculated:

Monthly Cost Items	*Monthly Cost*	*Percentage of Total Cost*
Hardware costs	$3,000	35
Systems analysis and design, and programming	2,572	30
Operations of Computer Department	3,000	35
Total cost per month	$8,572	100

From the foregoing data, we can estimate that the startup costs will be about $102,000 ($8,572 times 12 months). It is obvious that one-time preparation costs can be a significant outlay for an organization.

TIME REQUIREMENT FOR INSTALLING A COMPUTER

Installing a computer usually requires many months of preparation before it is ready for operation. Experience indicates that it may take from twelve to twenty-four months from the point when a computer's feasibility is first investigated to the point when it has been installed and is operating satisfactorily.

In some instances, the total elapsed time may be reduced by performing some of the tasks simultaneously, in parallel fashion, rather than one after another. In any case, even under ideal conditions, a year is probably a minimum period of preparation time. Indeed, complex computers may require lead time of from two to three years, since such computers are manufactured to order.

Exhibit 13–1 illustrates the use of a bar graph* to plan required tasks and activities over a time horizon (in this case, over a twenty-four-month period) for preparing for installation of a computer.

* This is sometimes referred to as a "Gantt chart." The name Gantt is derived from a management practitioner who developed the charting technique.

Exhibit 13–1 Example of Planning for a Computer

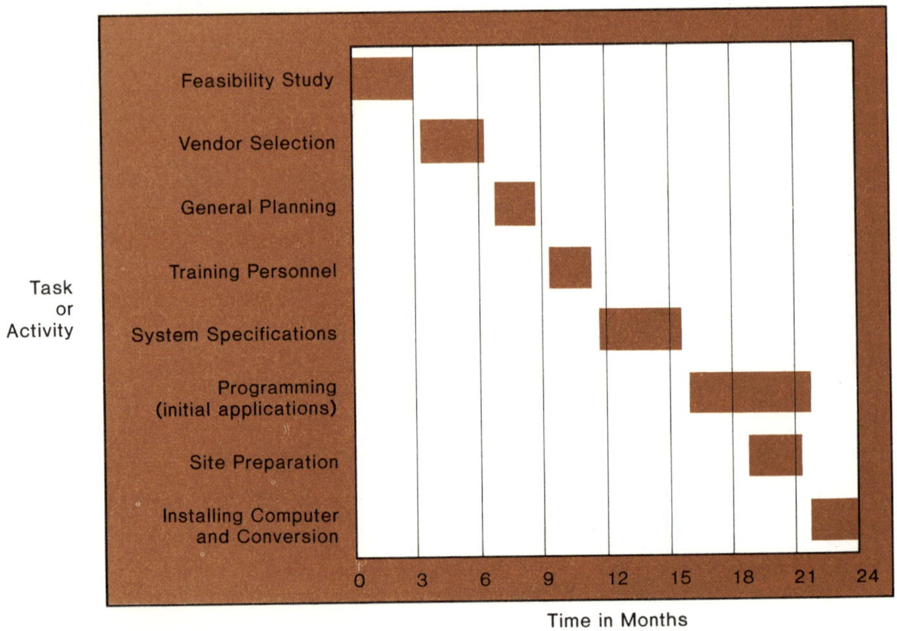

EVALUATING A COMPUTER

Data-processing costs usually are substantial in organizations like government offices, insurance companies, banks, and department stores. A large part of the overhead cost of organizations that manufacture a product or render a service relates to paperwork. Potentially, therefore, there is great leverage for improving (rather than eliminating—which in some instances laws may prevent) data processing and thus achieving cost reductions and performance improvement (i.e., profits). Organizations have viewed computers as one method of either reducing or at least containing costs.

Data processing can also affect the quality of the product and services rendered to customers. For instance, customers want quick and accurate information about products and services. If the organization cannot fulfill the customer's needs, or if the paperwork is inaccurate (e.g., improper billing), customers may be dissatisfied and both customers and revenues may be lost. Thus, the computer's role in improving a data-processing system can enhance sales and revenue.

More intangibly, the computer can affect the management of the organization. To some extent, managers are dependent on good information for their decisions. Inaccurate information or lack of information can reduce management effectiveness and result in bad decisions.

Exhibit 13–2 Some Reasons for Computerizing

Expense Reducing Objectives

- Reduce Clerical Expense
- Reduce Supervisory and Managerial Expense
- Reduce Equipment Expense
- Reduce Space and Other Overhead Expense
- Reduce Supplies Expense
- Reduce Inventory Carrying Expense

Revenue Improving Objectives

- Shorten Processing Time
- Provide More Accurate Information
- Provide More Useful Information
- Improve Operating Control
- Improve Customer Service

Other Objectives

- Establish Prestige and Modern Image
- Competitive Necessity
- Cope with Labor Shortages
- Prepare Required Government Reports

Exhibit 13–2 suggests some objectives that are relevant when computer alternatives are being considered.

Economics of Computer Systems

The economics of getting a first computer or upgrading an existing computer must be carefully considered and should be a key point in making a decision. Exhibit 13–3 illustrates the breakeven type of analysis, which can be helpful in making such a decision.

As the volume and complexity of data processing increases, the need for additional employees grows proportionately, as does the cost of doing the work. In fact, labor cost may increase more, relatively, than the work volume because of bureaucratic red tape in large organizations and of the scarcity of skilled employees. Less-skilled workers are often relatively unproductive.

Exhibit 13–3 The Economics of Switching to a Computer System

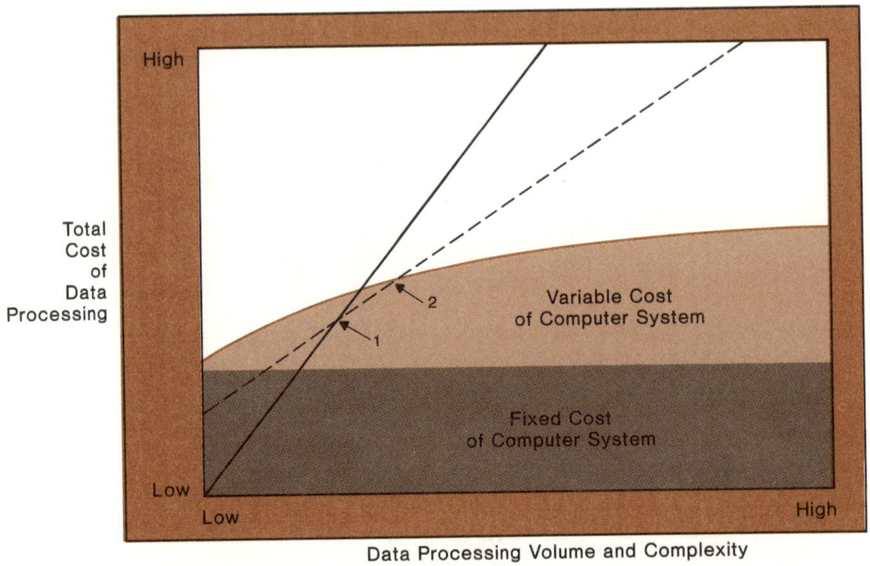

Legend: ——— = Manual System
– – – = Mechanical System
——— = Electronic Computer System

Note: Fixed cost would include such things as the cost of the computer hardware and software, while variable cost changes with volume and includes labor and supplies.

At some point, it becomes economic to obtain equipment that has a certain fixed cost, rather than to merely hire additional workers to do the work. A large degree of productivity gains are due to investment in equipment (labor-saving and -facilitating devices) that can greatly increase the output per individual employee.

Point 1 on the chart (Exhibit 13–3) indicates where the organization's total cost will be less if it uses a mechanical system for any additional data-processing work. Point 2 indicates the juncture at which the organization should consider switching to a computer system. While the manual and mechanical systems have significant increases in total cost when volume gets high, the computer system absorbs high volumes of work with only modest increases in total cost. This confirms that the per unit cost of data processing is potentially much lower when a computer is used to do the work.

INVESTIGATING COMPUTERS

Generally, the appraisal of a computer (see Exhibit 13–4) consists of the following steps, which usually are carried out or supervised by a study group: conducting a

Exhibit 13–4 Computer Selection Dilemma

Table 13–1
Cost/Benefit Analysis of a Computer

	Details	Totals
Estimated Initial Cost of a New Computer		
Cost of Site Preparation	$XXXX	
Systems and Programming Work for Initial Applications	XXXX	
Cost of Training, Etc.	XXXX	
Total One-Time Costs		$XXXX
Annual Estimated Operating Costs		
Hardware Rental Costs	$XXXX	
Personnel	XXXX	
Supplies, Power, Etc.	XXXX	
Total Recurring Costs		$XXXX
Annual Savings (Annual Costs of Current System Minus Annual Costs of New System) Estimated		$XXXX
Estimated Rate of Return		XX%
Other Intangible Benefits (List and Describe):		

feasibility study; preparing computer specifications; obtaining proposals from computer manufacturers; and making a selection from among the proposals.

Usually, it is best to form a representative committee or task force to handle the feasibility study. The committee consists of management personnel who represent the business' main functions (e.g., accounting and marketing), plus individuals who are knowledgeable about computers. The management personnel serve an important purpose: they help to identify the array of applications that might be computerized.

The Feasibility Study

The purpose of the feasibility study is to: investigate the present systems; evaluate the possible application of computer methods (as well as noncomputer methods); select a tentative system; evaluate the cost and benefits of the proposed system; and evaluate the impact of the proposed system on the organization and personnel.

A feasibility study is conducted similarly to that described in Chapter 9, "Systems Analysis and Design." However, it is usually conducted on a very broad basis, rather than being focused on one particular application.

In the course of its investigation, the feasibility study team conducts interviews, collects and studies forms, and analyzes current procedures, frequently using the approaches of the systems analyst. When enough data have been collected, an attempt is made to conceptualize the improved systems design. Invariably, this effort must focus on such specifics as:

Table 13–2

Estimated Rate of Return on Computer Acquisition

Year	Column 1 Effects on Cash Flow of Computer Acquisition	Column 2 10% Discount Factors	Column 3 Present Value of Cash Flow
1	$−100,000	0.9091	$−90,910
2	− 75,000	0.8264	−61,980
3	− 25,000	0.7513	−18,782
4	+ 50,000	0.6830	+34,150
5	+100,000	0.6209	+62,090
6	+150,000	0.5645	+85,675
Totals	$+100,000		$+10,243

1. What output information is required or desired?
2. What types of files and input data will be required?
3. What processing steps will be needed to generate the output information?
4. What volumes of work are involved?
5. How frequently must the work be processed?

Since the feasibility study usually covers many applications (e.g., accounting, marketing, manufacturing, and personnel), the effort can take many months of analyses and design.

One of the feasibility study's major objectives is to estimate the financial impact on the organization (see Table 13–1 for an example). Of course, at the feasibility stage any figures are only estimates, because specific hardware has not yet been selected.

The costs associated with the computer should be compared with how else that money could be used. Assume, for instance, that the organization can earn a 10 percent return on its money by investing it in securities. Thus, the computer should generate a rate of return at least equal to 10 percent. If it does not, there is a serious question as to whether the computer should be acquired.

Assume that a financial analysis for a six-year period is made of the flow of costs and savings related to the proposed computer acquisition (see Table 13–2). Column 1 reflects the net costs and savings year by year. The first three years show that costs will exceed savings, while the last three years indicate that savings will exceed costs in those years. Column 2 shows the present value* of $1 in years 1, 2, 3, 4, 5, and 6, when the

* Present value recognizes the fact that near-term money is worth more than future money. Present-value tables are available to facilitate calculations. See Robert N. Anthony, *Management Accounting* (Homewood, Illinois: Richard D. Irwin, Inc.) and Billy E. Goetz, *Quantitative Methods: A Survey and Guide for Managers* (New York: McGraw-Hill Book Company).

required rate of return is 10 percent. At the end of year 1, 10 percent interest on \$0.9091 is \$0.0909; thus, the present value (\$0.9091) plus the interest (\$0.0909) gives \$1 at the end of a year. Column 3 is the product of column 1 multiplied by column 2. The time-adjusted rate of return on investment would be exactly 10 percent if the total of column 3 were zero. A negative total would mean that the 10 percent return cannot be expected. In the example in Table 13–2, the estimated return is found to exceed 10 percent; thus, management can seriously consider going ahead with plans to acquire the computer.

The results of the feasibility study, with the study team's recommendations, are presented in report form to management for consideration. If management approves the recommendations, then the next step is to prepare specifications for vendors.

Computer Specifications

The computer specifications, drawn from the feasibility study, define what is to be accomplished by the computer. The primary use of the specifications is to give guidelines to computer manufacturers who may wish to submit proposals to the organizations.

The following will be among the contents of such specifications:

- *General:* Description of the organization; current system; and selection process to be used in choosing a computer.
- *Applications* (the following should be specified for each application): Systems design description; output specifications; file and input specifications; frequency and volumes of processing; and systems flowcharts.
- *Hardware/Software:* Hardware features required; software required; support required from vendor; delivery time required for hardware and software; and cost constraints.

Proposals from Vendors

The underlying idea is that the organization will measure the vendors' proposals against the organization's specifications.

Each vendor is provided with a copy of the specifications, and the organization should establish rules for submitting proposals. For instance, the vendors might be advised that proposals must be submitted no later than ninety days from a certain date. During this period, members of the organization will usually confer with vendors to clarify the content of the specifications.

When the proposals are ready, the manufacturer's representative usually has an opportunity to make a presentation before the study group and/or management. The proposal is a response to the organization's specifications, and it usually contains such things as: proposed hardware configuration; cost of proposed hardware; software availability, support available to customers; contract terms; and performance of the proposed hardware for the customer's applications.

After the proposals have been received from all the vendors, the organization's staff can analyze them.

Exhibit 13–5 Some Computer-Selection Factors

Economic Factors

- Cost Comparisons
- Return on Investment

Hardware Factors

- Hardware Performance, Capacity, and Price
- Extent of Modularity and Compatibility
- Number and Accessibility of Back-up Facilities
- Certainty of Delivery Date
- Probable Life of Proposed Hardware

Software Factors

- Programming Languages Available
- Efficiency of Available Software
- Availability of Packaged Programs and User Groups
- Certainty of Delivery Date for Promised Software

Service Factors

- Facilities Provided by Manufacturer for Checking New Programs
- Training Availability
- Programming Assistance
- Conversion Assistance
- Maintenance

Reputation of Manufacturer

- Financial Stability
- Performance with Other Users

Selecting a Proposal

In selecting from among the various proposals, the organization should have already established the criteria to be used in judging the proposals, and should have assigned them weights.

Exhibit 13–5 suggests some of the factors that can be used in evaluating proposals and in establishing a formula for making the best selection for a particular organization.

The feasibility study team should not unquestioningly accept the contents of the vendors' proposals. Hardware timing estimates, in particular, are often optimistic. The ideal (or maximum) equipment speeds are attained infrequently, and some realistic estimate is required. If possible, it is desirable to make *test runs* (sometimes referred to as "benchmarks") on the vendor's computer to determine actual performance. Extrapolating test runs to the organization's total volume of work can provide some reasonable estimate of the ***throughput*** time needed to process all work on the proposed computer. The throughput estimate should not only take into account an average work volume, but also peak volume periods.

Aside from relative cost, a major question is whether or not a particular computer will do the organization's work in the time required, and whether it is sufficiently flexible to absorb more work in the future. Thus, modularity (a computer that can be made more powerful by the addition of equipment options) and a compatible family of computers (which allows the user to move easily from a smaller computer to increasingly larger ones) are important.

Software is another important consideration, since a computer without proper software can lead to higher programming and operating costs for the computer user. As with hardware, it is desirable to test the vendor-provided software prior to selecting a particular computer.

When the evaluation has been completed, the feasibility study team issues a recommendation to management. Assuming that management agrees with this recommendation, a contract is negotiated with the selected manufacturer. While there are standard contracts, some points are open for negotiation. For example, the assistance to be provided by the manufacturer (e.g., technical support, or hours of free test-time) is usually a variable that is worked out at contract time.

CONVERTING TO A COMPUTER

Rarely is a computer delivered shortly after the order has been signed; usually it takes at least several months, and sometimes as long as two or three years. The organization should plan the installation date on the basis of its own readiness for delivery, rather than agreeing to set the date for the manufacturer's convenience. The lead time is necessary to accomplish preparatory tasks, including: training; site preparation; and detailed systems and programming work for initial applications.

The computer manufacturer typically provides the initial training of staff in programming and in hardware operation. The vendor usually provides manuals and other instructional materials.

Most computers require special site preparation. These requirements are related to electrical power, air conditioning, humidity control, and other factors. A site-planning engineer from the vendor is usually available for assistance.

The first applications to be run on the computer should be programmed, tested, and debugged before the hardware is delivered. The vendor usually provides computer time at the manufacturer's test facilities for these purposes. In addition, all master files, required forms, and so forth must be ready at the time the computer is delivered.

When converting from one computer to another, various methods are used to ease the problem of rewriting programs (which could be a huge job, since some installations have hundreds or even thousands of existing programs). These methods include:

1. *Emulation.* This is an extra-cost hardware feature that executes the instructions of the old computer on the new one by interpreting each old instruction into its new-instruction equivalent. However, programs do not run as fast under emulation as they do when they are rewritten in the language of the new computer.
2. *Simulation.* Simulation performs the same function as the emulator, except that it is a software rather than a hardware feature. Simulation consists of a program that interprets each instruction and executes the equivalent instructions in the new machine. Simulation is generally slower than emulation.
3. *Conversion Routines.* This software, provided by the manufacturer, produces source programs for the new computer from the old computer's source program.

Some applications may be reprogrammed immediately; others may be emulated or simulated until they can be reprogrammed.

When the computer is delivered, a determination should be made which applications will be cut over immediately and which will be processed in parallel. Parallel processing involves running the application under both the old method and new method until the new system is proven to be completely satisfactory.

There are computer user organizations that are useful sources of information for the user. These organizations are operated by the participating users of the same computer (e.g., all IBM small-computer business users). Among their activities are sharing information related to problems and new ideas about the hardware and software; exerting pressure on the manufacturer to improve hardware and software; and suggesting data-processing standards.

POST-INSTALLATION REVIEW

In preparing for a computer, cost and benefit estimates are made. But too often it happens that cost savings are overestimated and benefits are not as great as forecasted.

Thus, a post-installation review is desirable to detect such variations and determine what measures might be taken to improve performance.

If it is known in advance of the feasibility study that a post-installation review will take place, all concerned are likely to be more scrupulous in carrying out their tasks.

FINANCING THE USE OF COMPUTERS

There are three major approaches to financing the use of computers: renting or leasing from the manufacturer;* purchasing the computer; or leasing it from an independent leasing firm.

Rental from the Manufacturer

This is the most common financing method. The rental price includes maintenance for using each piece of hardware. There are differences in the rental agreements that different manufacturers use, but the most common agreement calls for a base rental for 176 hours of actual use per month. This represents an 8-hour shift per day for an average month of 22 working days. Hours above 176 are usually charged at a lower rate (e.g., 30 percent of the implied hourly rate for the first 176 hours).

The user can most often cancel a standard rental agreement on fairly short notice (usually about two or three months). Manufacturers offer reduced rental rates for companies that are willing to sign binding, long-term leases (three to five years) for the hardware. Users may also rent the hardware, with options to purchase.

The major advantages of renting are: the absence of a large capital outlay; the manufacturer's assumption of all maintenance of hardware; and the removal of the risk of hardware obsolescence. Of course, the latter risk is not entirely removed, since the user has large amounts of funds invested in such things as site preparation, employee training, and systems and programming work that may be partly "lost" if the computer is replaced by a different manufacturer's computer.

The major disadvantage of renting a computer is the higher total cost. Manufacturers generally base rentals on a five-year life for the hardware, but modern computers are more likely to have productive "lives" of closer to eight or nine years.

Purchase from the Manufacturer

The major incentive for purchasing a computer is the savings to be had over the life of the equipment. There is also a tax advantage because of an investment credit provision of the income tax law. On the other hand, the problem with purchasing is that the purchaser assumes risks related to obsolescence, hardware reliability, and maintenance of the hardware. An organization may either arrange for a separate contract for maintenance of the equipment, or, if the computer department is large, hire maintenance personnel of its own.

* There is a thin line of demarcation between renting and leasing. Technically, a lease suggests a formal contract, while renting may or may not involve a formal contract period. In practice, a contract is normal when a user agrees to use a vendor's computer. In this sense, the terms "rent" and "lease" are almost interchangeable for our purpose.

A rule of thumb is that a computer with a forecasted useful life of more than five years should be purchased rather than rented. However, in any specific case, the breakeven point is dependent on such factors as the number of shifts that the hardware will be used.

Leasing from Third-Party Organization

A company that has examined the obsolescence and reliability problems and has concluded that purchase is the best alternative may not have funds available; or, perhaps, using the funds for purchasing computers will restrict future sources of funds. Under these circumstances, the possibility of leasing from an independent leasing company should be examined.

A lease typically provides for the purchase by a leasing company of the specific equipment configuration that the user desires. The leasing company then leases it to the user. Lease agreements vary, but usually they have provisions such as the following:

1. The user agrees to lease for a minimum period, say five years, with purchase and trade-in options.
2. The lease payment includes a maintenance contract and other charges.
3. There is no additional charge for second- or third-shift operations (except perhaps some additional maintenance charges).
4. After the minimum period, the lease charges drop to a lower rate.

If the lease is terminated before the minimum period is up, the user must pay a termination charge. This sometimes takes the form of a guaranteed sale price. The lease payments and termination payments amortize the cost of the equipment. These provisions apply to a "full payout" lease. A less common form is the equity lease, which has higher payments but no termination penalty. In both cases, the user obtains the investment credit tax benefit, just as if the equipment had been purchased.

Alternatives Available to Users

The increase in competition within the computer industry has given rise to increased contract negotiations, which have put organizations in a better position to arrange an attractive purchase or rental (lease) agreement with computer manufacturers or leasing companies. There is a substantial market for so-called second-hand computers. These prior-generation computers can usually be obtained at substantial discount prices—which, in certain circumstances, can be very attractive.

COMPUTER MAINTENANCE*

In order to protect against interruption of computer service, hardware requires regular maintenance. In large installations, preventive maintenance may be carried out each day at a specific time that is allotted for this purpose. If so, maintenance personnel may be assigned to the installation on a full-time basis. Smaller installations, on the other hand, may be given maintenance checks once a week, or be on an "on-call" basis, obtaining maintenance only if the customer reports hardware malfunctioning.

Preventive maintenance involves identifying and replacing components that are likely to fail, and keeping mechanical parts properly adjusted. The modular design of electronic circuits usually means that within a few minutes, a faulty module can be removed and replaced.

Some organizations have two similar computers to ensure backup if one fails. However, unless the backup computer can be kept productively busy, this is a costly approach. More often, a user is aware of alternative outside backup facilities. These may be at a data-processing service center, a facility of the computer manufacturer, or an installation of another user who has a similar computer configuration.

COMPUTER SERVICE CENTERS

If an organization can benefit from computer processing but cannot justify spending money on keeping its own computer, a data-processing service center may be the answer. These service centers, located in most cities, are businesses that provide data-processing service to clients on a fee basis. This service is available either on an as-needed basis or on a continuing-contract basis.

Even if an organization has its own computer, it may still use such service centers to handle periodic overloads.

When planning to use a computer service center, it is important for an organization to determine such things as: who will handle the preparation of the input data; where the data files will be stored; and who will prepare needed programs and perform program maintenance. Also, security of information and programs, schedules to ensure availability of results when needed, and method of charging for the service must be resolved.

The use of a data-processing service center shifts many of the computer problems that come with on-site computers to the service center. On the other hand, using a service center makes the organization dependent on a second party that is less familiar and dedicated to the organization's needs.

* If the user rents the computer from the manufacturer, the manufacturer usually maintains its equipment. If a user purchases the computer, the user may maintain the equipment, or contract with the computer manufacturer or another organization to render maintenance services.

Summary

The cost of a computer is usually substantial. Consequently, it is important to use good management practices when considering a first computer or when replacing an existing computer. In fact, the computer hardware is only the tip of the iceberg as far as costs are involved; nonhardware costs may be as much as 65 percent or higher of total costs of a computer facility. Also, the startup, one-time costs of computerizing can be substantial.

Planning is required for a computer, since there are many tasks to be performed before a computer should be installed and can be placed in productive operation. Part of the planning includes carefully appraising the available computer alternatives by objectively determining what work is to be done by the computer and which computer can do the work best. Converting to a computer can require particularly careful control, because unexpected problems can arise during such a major change. After the cutover to a computer, there should be a postmortem follow-up to determine whether the computer is performing up to original expectations.

Special topics of importance are: financing the computer (i.e., renting, purchasing, or leasing); maintaining the computer; and using computer service centers.

Terms to Learn

Purchase price of a computer
Rental cost of a computer
Unbundling
Feasibility study
Breakeven point
Variable cost
Fixed cost
Computer specification
Proposals from vendors
Test run (benchmark)
Throughput
Conversion
Site preparation
Emulation
Simulation
Conversion routine
Parallel processing
Backup computer
Post-installation review
Leasing a computer
Computer maintenance
Computer service center

Review Questions

1. Discuss the relative costs, in a computer department, of *hardware, systems work* and *programming,* and the *operations* of the computer department.

2. Why do you think that *people-related costs* and *software costs* are rising, while *hardware costs* are (relatively speaking) declining?
3. If your organization were planning for its first computer, what words of advice would you give your boss about the *one-time costs* of computerizing?
4. Refer to Exhibit 13–1, and discuss the importance of *planning* for a computer.
5. What kinds of *objectives* can be established in connection with computer planning? Identify some *tangible* objectives and some *intangible* objectives.
6. What are the steps in conducting a *feasibility study?* How is a feasibility study similar to systems analysis and design work?
7. How would you select a *computer alternative* from among several proposals submitted by different computer vendors?
8. After selecting a computer, what work must be accomplished *prior to delivery* of the computer?
9. Discuss *emulation, simulation,* and *conversion routines* when switching from one computer to another.
10. What is the significance of *parallel processing* during conversion to a computer?
11. Why would you wish to have a *post-installation review* after the computer was installed?
12. Discuss financing alternatives: *renting, purchasing,* or *leasing* a computer. What are the advantages and disadvantages of each?
13. Who is responsible for the *maintenance* of the computer?
14. Why might it sometimes be better to use an *outside computer service center* to do data processing, rather than using one's own computer?

More reports
Paper
Pollution
Facts
Memos
Reports
Errors

CHAPTER 14

MANAGEMENT OF A COMPUTER DEPARTMENT

Objectives

Good management and organization concepts and practices are important in a computer department. These concepts and practices were originally identified in Chapter 2; and now, in Chapter 14, they are explained in terms of the computer function. This chapter also explores the importance of planning, organizing, control standards, and actuating (staff) as they pertain to the computer department. Lastly, the role of top management in the computer function is discussed.

BACKGROUND ON MANAGEMENT RESPONSIBILITIES AND TASKS

Chapter 2 explored important concepts and practices related to management and organization structure. These ideas were developed early in the book to stress that the computer professional must understand the needs of business organizations and their managers.

Such management and organizational concepts and practices apply, of course, to the internal practices of the computer department itself. Usually, a computer facility is a significant budget item.* Moreover, it serves a vital service function for many other parts of the organization. Consequently, mismanaging the computer department can seriously affect the success of other departments—and indeed of the entire enterprise.

In Chapter 2, we discussed the management functions: planning, organizing, control, and actuating (leading). Clearly, the management of the computer department must also carry out such functions. For instance:

1. The many technological developments in the computer industry require the organization to plan well into the future, so that it will not be handicapped with inadequate computer resources. Computer plans should be coordinated with the organization's other plans (e.g., financial planning and market planning) so that they will not be out of phase with the organization's overall planning and goals.
2. The human resources, hardware, software, and other resources of the computer department must be allocated so that waste is minimized and productivity is maximized in the computer department.
3. There must be accountability, as well as a method of determining that the computer department is performing its work according to high standards. Such control

* It is not unusual for the computer department to account for from 1 to 5 percent or more of an organization's total budget. Some large billion-dollar (yearly sales or revenue) organizations have multi-million-dollar expenditures for computers and related data-processing.

information should be available to responsible managers who can take any corrective actions needed.

4. The leaders in the computer department must actuate computer professionals. This is a difficult task, since such people are often quite individualistic and independent.

COMPUTER-RELATED PLANNING

As computer technology has advanced and as applications have grown in size and complexity, the job of managing an organization's computer activities has become more intricate and difficult. To keep on top of this problem, computer resources and applications must be planned formally. The horizon may span from two to ten years, and only by such planning can an orderly and professional approach to computers be achieved. Overall planning must consider such problems as:

1. Technological change in equipment and programming options, and appraisal of cost and performance.
2. Improvement in existing computer applications, and identification of new application opportunities.
3. Manpower needs and training requirements to achieve the computer department's goals.
4. Implications of plans, in situations where scarce resources must be allocated prudently.
5. Contingency plans in case of disaster; provision for security; and so forth.
6. The likely impact of computer plans on other parts of the organization, employees, and others.

Because of such considerations and of the substantial commitments to computers there is a growing need for professional management in computer departments.

ORGANIZATIONAL STRUCTURE OF THE COMPUTER DEPARTMENT

No matter what the organizational structure of a computer department may be, the mission of the installation must be clear. Consequently, one of the first requirements is that the objectives, scope of service, and means of service be formalized and made known throughout the organization.

For instance, in a large organization it is important to specify whether the corporate headquarter's computer department services only the headquarter's offices, or whether it has some responsibility for computer matters in the company's operating divisions. Most computer departments operate as a closed shop, which means that only

Exhibit 14–1 Organizational Structure for Small Computer-Department

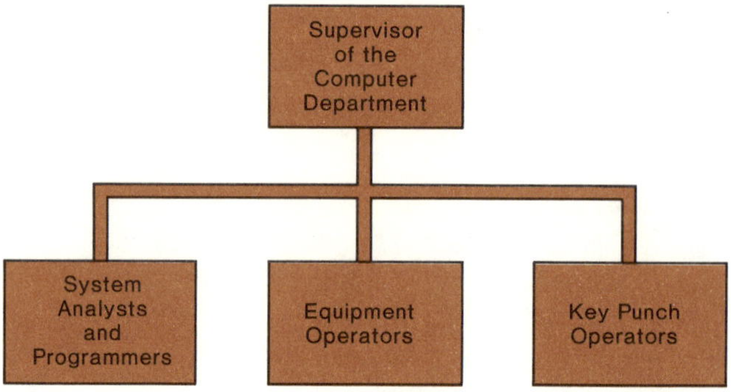

Exhibit 14–2 Organizational Structure for Large Computer-Department

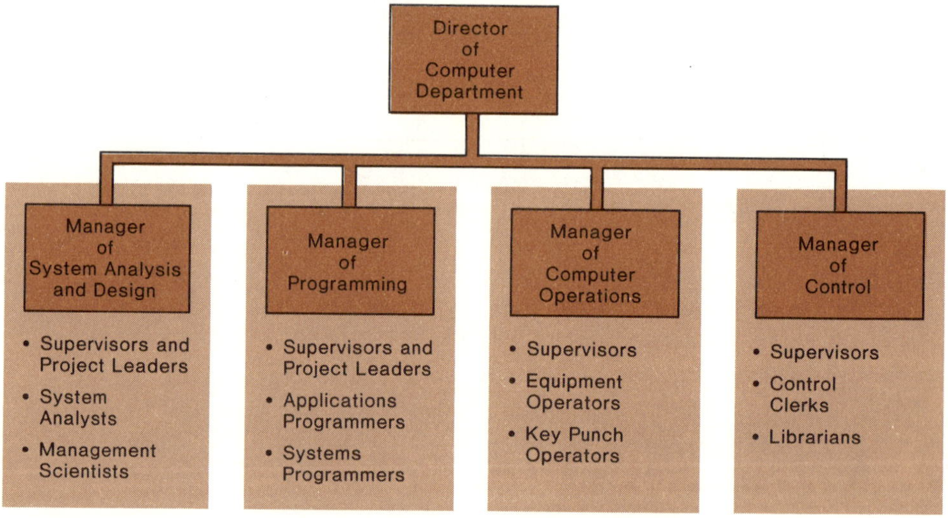

trained computer personnel are allowed inside the computer facility to operate the equipment. However, some computer departments operate as an open shop, permitting each user to have access to the equipment. The computer department's mission must be identified in terms of broad policies like these, if a computer department is to be managed effectively.

The specific organizational structure of the computer department depends on such factors as: size of the organization; degree of geographical dispersion; and degree

Exhibit 14–3 Organizational Structure for Multiple Computer-Units

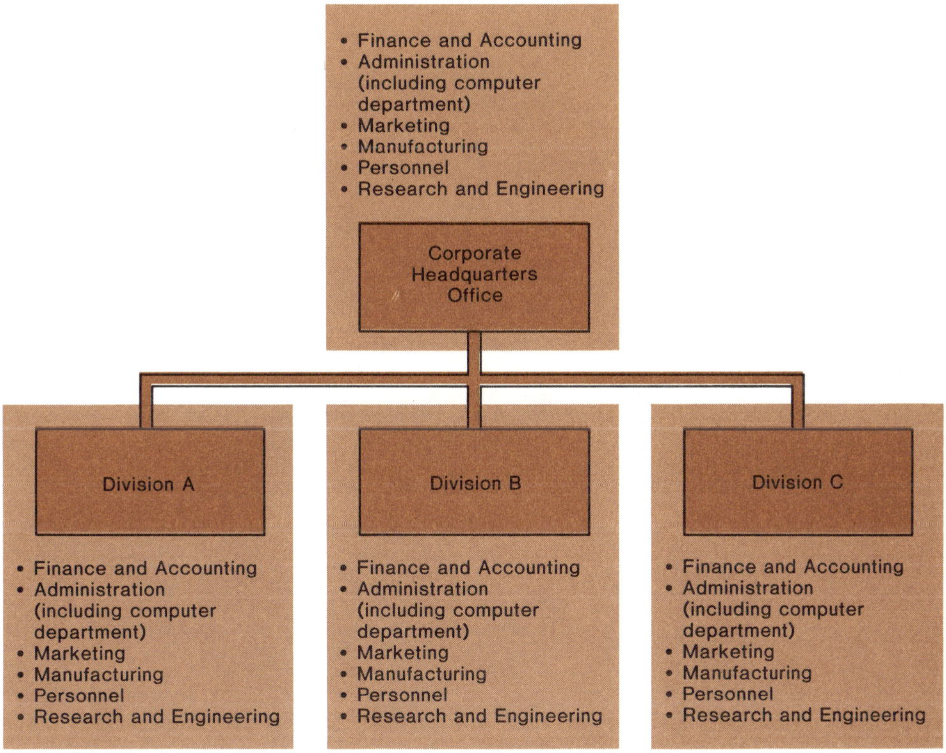

of delegation of authority. Several organizational charts are presented to illustrate the variety of approaches used.

Exhibit 14–1 illustrates a simple organizational structure that is suitable for a small computer-installation employing only several individuals in the computer department. In such an installation, there might be only one person doing all the systems analysis, design, and programming. In a small installation, it is not unusual for the supervisor to perform some of the subordinate functions, such as operating equipment.

Exhibit 14–2 illustrates an organization chart for a larger computer facility that may employ dozens, or even hundreds, of people. In such an installation there are, of course, more levels (director, managers, supervisors and project leaders, etc.) than there are in a small facility. Also, specialization tends to increase as an installation becomes larger. Although one person may perform all the systems and programming work in a small installation, in a very large computer department, analysts and programmers may be specialized by areas. For instance, some programmers may work only on applications programs, others only on systems programs, and still others only on the maintenance of programs. And systems analysts may specialize in particular

Exhibit 14–4 Traditional Reporting Relationship of Computer Department

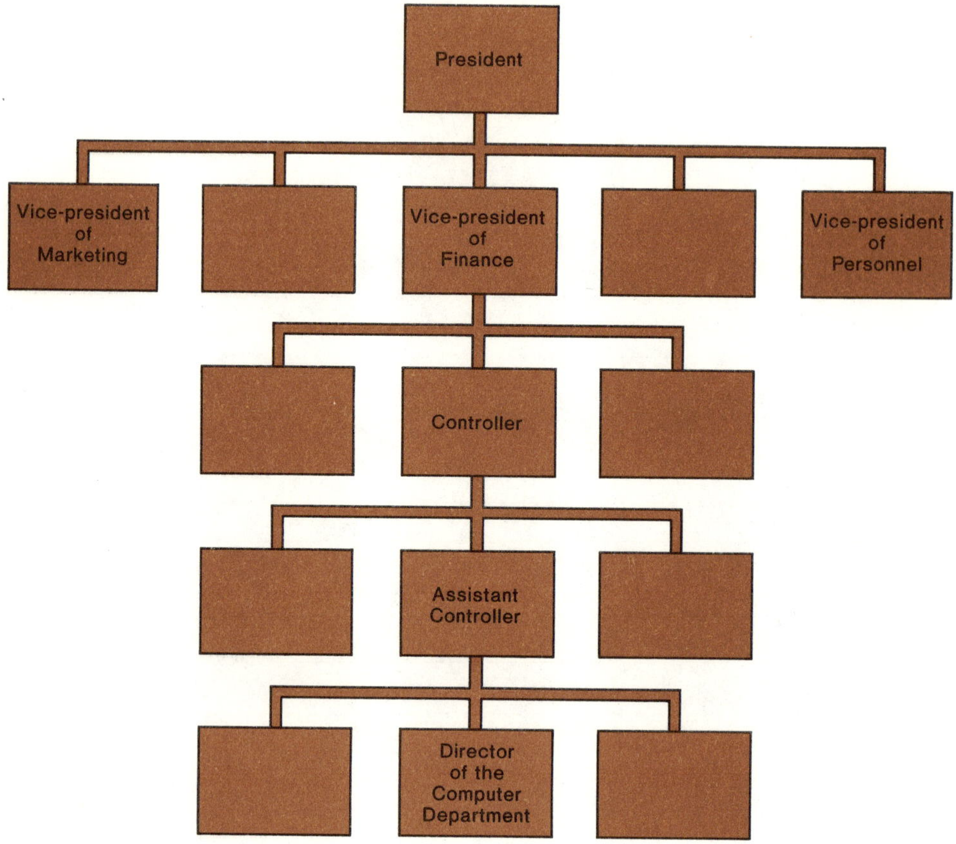

functional areas (e.g., accounting systems, marketing systems, or manufacturing systems).

Large enterprises that have several divisions, and those organizations that operate in numerous foreign nations, often decentralize computer units in various parts of the company. The computer department that services the headquarters' offices frequently must offer guidance to the decentralized computer units (see Exhibit 14–3).

The advent of data communication and minicomputers has propelled some organizations in the direction of decentralized or distributed data-processing. This means that if it is economically justified, any unit of the organization can have its own computer power rather than depending on a central-computer facility. Thus, even in a single location, various users may have their own computer rather than sharing a common, larger computer. Other organizations think that this approach may be wasteful, and claim that central-computer services are more economical because of scale-of-operation. There are successful and unsuccessful examples of both approaches.

Exhibit 14–5 Modern Trend for Reporting Relationship of Computer Department

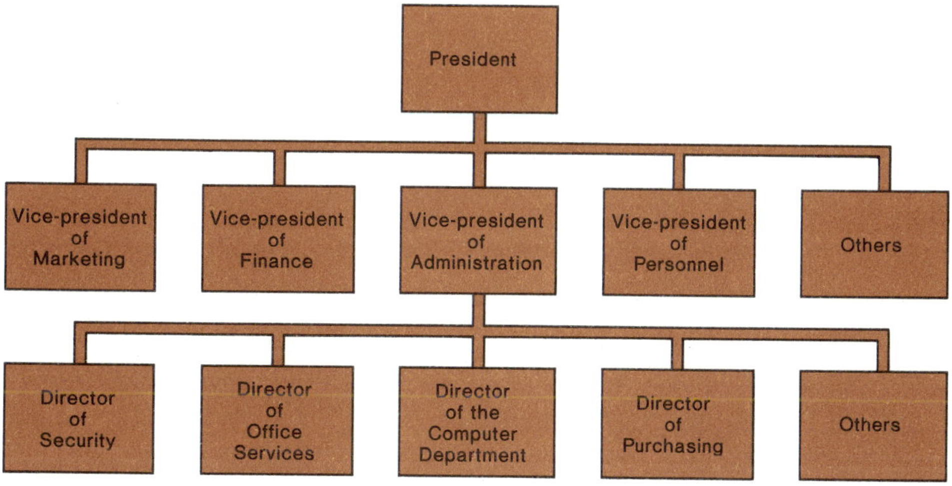

In any case, it is desirable to coordinate among computer installations so that the organization has some degree of standardization and interchange of computer programs, hardware, and staffs. Further, coordination is needed to effectively negotiate with computer, software, and supply vendors.

Traditionally, the computer used for business data-processing was under the direction of the financial executive, who usually reported to an Assistant Controller. Today, this probably is still the most prevalent situation (see Exhibit 14–4). Also, in the past, organizations with substantial engineering and scientific staffs usually provided separate computer facilities for such technical functions.

But now, the trend toward placing the computer resource under an independent administrative executive (e.g., vice president or administration) is increasing (see Exhibit 14–5). This is because such a move encourages the organization's diverse functional areas (e.g., marketing and manufacturing) to utilize computer services. When the computer function is under the financial executive, most applications tend to be of an accounting nature. This tendency can impede other functional areas from utilizing the computer. Furthermore, since many modern computers can now handle both business data-processing computer applications and scientific computer applications, separate computers for business jobs and for scientific jobs are unnecessary. The problem of parochialism that arose when the computer was within the jurisdiction of a single functional department was further compounded by its having, in many cases, to report to a relatively low management level (e.g., assistant controller). However, experience has shown that the manager who is in direct charge of the computer resource should report to someone of top-management stature, if the computer is to be used most effectively. This facilitates the acceptance of the computer department's mission. Frequently, the mission requires change—which is resisted unless it is backed by top management. In addition, a vice president's independent administrative status helps traditional departmental barriers (necessary in some applications—e.g., management information systems) to be crossed.

STAFFING OF THE COMPUTER DEPARTMENT*

Staffing for the computer function is one of an organization's most challenging personnel activities. This is true for a number of reasons:

1. The demand for well-trained and highly experienced computer personnel (particularly systems analysts and programmers) continues to exceed the available supply.
2. Computer technicians have demonstrated a pattern of high mobility. The turnover rate of systems analysts and programmers, as well as of computer-management personnel, is likely to remain relatively high.
3. Developments in the high-technology computer industry necessitate constant attention, lest the computer staff become obsolete. This requires an active training and education program.
4. The foregoing points underscore the necessity of being sensitive to morale in computer departments, and of doing everything possible to maintain and improve motivation and loyalty.

Job descriptions should be available, identifying the work performed and classified in the computer department. While the titles may vary among computer installations, the following abbreviated descriptions are indicative of the more common computer-oriented positions.†

Title	*Description*
Director or Manager	Managerial personnel are charged with the responsibility of effectively directing organizational resources (e.g., human resources, hardware resources, and software resources). Such personnel are usually seasoned in business, as well as being competent in technical matters. Of course, managerial personnel must be able to provide leadership to the computer staff and to work effectively with other personnel in the organization. Usually, such positions require the incumbent to have at least a college degree, more frequently a master's degree, and even sometimes a doctorate.

* In Chapter 4, we briefly sketched the human resources required in a computer department.

† As mentioned earlier, some of the above positions are not mutually exclusive. For instance, in some organizations the same individual performs the functions of the systems analyst and programmer. Also, each occupation has career ladder steps, for example: Senior Systems Analyst, Systems Analyst, Junior Systems Analyst, and Trainee Analyst.

Systems Analyst	The systems person analyzes existing procedures, activities, organizational structures, etc.; develops improved and new procedures, activities, organizational structures, etc.; and designs and guides implementation of improved and new systems. The analyst prepares the specifications that the programmer uses. Increasingly, systems analysts are expected to be college educated.
Management Scientist	The management scientist performs many of the same functions as the systems analyst; however, the management scientist requires sophisticated mathematical skills (e.g., development of mathematical models). Almost invariably, such personnel are college educated (with specializations in mathematics, engineering, operations research), and many have advanced degrees.
Computer Programmer	The computer programmer is skilled in one or more computer-programming languages. He/she converts the systems design of the systems analyst or management scientist into instructions that the computer can understand. The programmer is responsible for making certain that the program operates properly. As with systems analysts, programmers are increasingly expected to have college educations.
Computer Operator	The computer operator is trained to operate the various pieces of equipment comprising the computer system, including off-line devices. The operator may interact with the computer via the computer console. The computer operator feeds operational programs written by the computer programmers to the computer (along with data and files). Normally, these jobs do not require college education.
Data-Preparation Operator	The data-preparation operator is trained to operate typewriter-like devices that either create machine-readable data for feeding to the computer, or that involves direct entry to the computer. These are considered clerical-level jobs, and they do not require college education.
Control Clerks	Control clerks maintain human control over input data and computer output in order to maximize the accuracy and integrity of the computer system's operations. The higher-level control positions might call for college education (e.g., accounting), although high-school education may suffice for most of the jobs.

Aside from the technical staffs of a computer department, there are usually various supporting administrative and clerical employees (e.g., receptionists and secretaries).

A Balanced Staff

Attaining a balanced computer-staff can present a dilemma, particularly since there has been a long-standing shortage of highly qualified systems analysts and programmers. Usually, an organization needs particularly heavy computer support during peak periods (e.g., when getting a new computer or when converting from one computer to another). To cope with such conditions, some organizations have developed large staffs and then had to face the problem of reducing the staff, or of reassigning the people to marginal projects or other parts of the enterprise.

Some organizations supplement their own staffs with outside assistance. A growing number of service and consulting firms offer clients a wide variety of computer-related capabilities. These firms take on assignments on a fixed-fee basis if the job is well defined, or otherwise on a daily or even hourly basis. The disadvantages of the outside-service approach are: that the company loses real supervisory control; that the apparent cost is high; and that, once the outside contractor has completed the job and departed, the company partially loses the insights it had gained. On the other hand, the use of an outside contractor has some distinct advantages: the organization does not have to commit itself to a large internal staff; new perspectives are brought to the problem area; highly specialized experts can be obtained; independent judgment can be expected; and the organization's staff may be stimulated by the outside influence.

Recruitment

Sources of trained people are: computer manufacturers; employment agencies and executive recruiters (some of which now specialize in computer personnel); professional and technical societies (e.g., Association for Systems Management, Association for Computing Machinery, Data Processing Management Association); technical training institutes; and universities and colleges. Merely scanning the "Help Wanted" advertisements in newspapers and journals underscores the large demand that exists for computer-oriented personnel. Some organizations prefer to train internal personnel about computer techniques, rather than to recruit computer specialists from outside the firm. The advantage of this approach is that the internal employees have some familiarity with the organization's policies and procedures. However, it is important to make sure that such employees have the aptitude for computer work. Top-level skills in systems work and programming require years of practical experience and education.

Aside from the obvious attractions of salary, benefits, and location, computer professionals want organizations to have:

1. A *professional reputation* for leadership in computer use.

2. *Outstanding computer staffs* from whom they can learn, thereby upgrading their own skills.
3. *Modern computer equipment* that challenges the individual's technical ability.
4. *Stimulating computer plans and projects* that will result in interesting assignments.
5. An *active and continuing training effort* so that the staff can keep up with changes in the field.
6. *Adequate promotional paths.*
7. An *organizational environment* that provides acceptance of change and of the computer department's mission.

Selection

There is a wide range of quality among computer personnel. The systems analysts and programmers who not only have excellent command over the techniques of their field but who also understand the realities of organizations' operations and the relevance of the social system are relatively rare. The majority of computer practitioners offer a command of some narrow aspect of computer technology (e.g., ability to code in COBOL language) and have only a limited understanding of the organization's operations and social system.

Careful selection is needed to match the computer department's real staffing needs with the people available in the market. It is as unrewarding to hire a superior analyst for a mundane task as it is to hire an average or mediocre analyst for a complex assignment. The ability to select personnel can be refined in the following ways:

1. *Multiple interviews,* and *evaluation* of applicants by several individuals.
2. Careful *reference checks* from responsible persons who know the applicant's technical capabilities, past performance, and organizational loyalties.
3. Use of *aptitude tests* or related examinations.
4. Assessment of *academic work.*
5. Solution of short, simulated *computer problems* by applicants.

From the applicant's side, the organization should be as candid as possible about the realities of the job being offered. Too often, people who take positions have mistaken ideas about the position, the opportunities, the limitations, and the organization involved.

Most of the research that's been done about how to select computer personnel has been devoted to designing or validating tests to predict how well a programmer will succeed. Apparently, the successful programmer needs to have: above-average intelligence; a logical mind; analytical ability; and an almost-compulsive need for accuracy in detail. Also important are the ability to work under pressure and to work with people.

Several widely used tests for computer technicians are available, including: Computer Programmer Aptitude Test Battery; General Aptitude Test Battery (GATB); and Watson-Glaser Critical Thinking Appraisal.

Several professional organizations (e.g., Association for Computing Machinery and Data Processing Management Association) have developed a method for testing and certifying computer personnel. To do this, an Institute for Certification of Computer Personnel (ICCP) has been established. The Educational Testing Service (ETS) has also established tests to determine the level of computer comprehension. These tests increasingly are being used by colleges and universities, where, in some cases, students must exhibit some basic competency in computer use.

Tests are obviously valuable as an initial screening device for applicants. However, if an employer wishes to know how useful any given test is for selecting potential computer personnel for his/her own organization, the instrument planned for use within the organization must be validated.*

Evaluation

Many organizations have had difficulty not only in selecting computer professionals and technicians, but also in evaluating them. The performance appraisal is ideal when the criteria (or demands of the job) can be objectively rated and clearly understood by the employee, and when the results of supervisory ratings are openly communicated at the end of each rating period. This appraisal requires three sets of information: what the worker does on the job (the job description); the standards required (management expectations); and finally, how well the worker attains the standards set (performance appraisal). Too often, management's expectations are neither clear nor formalized, and this vagueness causes appraisal decisions to be arbitrary and inconsistent.

One of the chief evaluation methods is a results-oriented review of personnel's work. Adherence to work schedules and customer satisfaction with work performed are, of course, two key criteria of work well performed.

Education for Computer Professionals

Increasingly, even students in high schools and even in some elementary schools, as well as those in colleges and universities, are being given some background in computers. Some education is very broad (e.g., "Computers and Society"), while other training is very specific and utilitarian (e.g., "Programming in the COBOL Language"). Increasingly, students are expected to have computer proficiency in order to be admitted to some institutions and specialized schools (e.g., graduate schools of business). Computer training has long been thought necessary in certain fields, such as mathematics, engineering, science, education, and business. Even in those fields where

* Because of relatively recent equal employment opportunity and affirmative action laws, many people have become apprehensive about the meaningfulness (and indeed the legality) of tests that have not been exposed to validity and reliability checks.

the computer was once felt to be inapplicable, interest is growing. Such fields include medicine, social sciences, and law.

Since college education is so readily available to the general population, most computer professionals (systems analysts, programmers, and management scientists) are expected to have one or more degrees in order to compete in the field. The analytical nature of the work, the ability to communicate with managers and others about business problems, and the ability to absorb the ever-expanding computer technology demand that such personnel be above average in skill and background.

Up until recently, computer professionals had a wide variety of educational backgrounds (e.g., college and university educated persons had specializations in mathematics, engineering, business administration, psychology, and music). However, the last several years have seen a trend toward establishing specializations in computers. A degree in computer sciences amounts to the technical/scientific path, while computer data-processing or some similar designation is the business specialization. In the future, a greater percentage of computer practitioners probably will be drawn from the programs that award degrees in a computer specialization. The Association for Computing Machinery (probably the most prestigious professional society in the computer field) has developed a series of model educational programs for colleges and universities. These models suggest the curriculum for both computer science and computer data-processing.

In addition to having a background in formal education, computer practitioners must keep abreast of the developments in computer technology. There are various technical training programs for this purpose, including: courses offered by computer vendors; seminars conducted by professional societies; continuing education extensions of colleges and universities; and journals and periodicals (including programmed instruction material). An individual can use the latter material as an independent study or as part of one of the identified training programs.

STANDARDS IN THE COMPUTER DEPARTMENT

One of the most effective management techniques is the use of procedure and performance standards. *Procedure standards* refer to procedures that indicate the way a job should be done. *Performance standards* state the amount and quality of work to be expected.

Procedural Standards

Procedural standards should be established to clearly define how each job is to be done. For instance, a standards manual describes the organization's guidelines for: specific flowcharting conventions to be used; preferred programming techniques; testing and debugging requirements; and documentation methods to be used.

Such standards: provide a discipline for computer personnel; reduce training difficulties; simplify review by supervision; minimize the impact of personnel turnover; and provide a more objective basis for performance evaluation.

If a programmer is allowed to program, test, debug, and document a program in his/her own individual fashion, it would probably be difficult to review the work; and if the programmer left the employ of the organization, it would be difficult for another programmer to pick up the work. Also, computer operators probably would have trouble following operating instructions if each set had its own nonstandard terminology, formats, and so on.

The standards manual should be comprehensive and should cover all the main functions of the computer department, such as systems, programming, operations, and control. Some broadly recognized standards are available in the computer field. As an example, the American National Standards Institute (ANSI) has developed specific conventions—for instance, for flowcharting and programming. These conventions have been adopted fairly widely (sometimes with modification) in large computer-installations in private industry, government, and elsewhere. In addition, there is even an international-level effort to gain acceptance for computer-related standards among the many different nations of the world.

Performance Standards

Performance standards are helpful: in evaluating performance; in assigning and scheduling work; and in controlling costs related to systems and programming effort, and use of equipment.

"Equipment standards" should specify the amount of time the equipment should be available for setup, production, scheduled maintenance, and unscheduled maintenance. "Production time" is the time available in which to run jobs. Based on the equipment's speed, it is possible to estimate the volume of work that the equipment can handle in a given period of time. Realistic timings rather than rated speeds must be used, since provision has to be made for such factors as manual handling time and possible error stops. Based on work priorities, jobs can be scheduled on the various pieces of equipment.

Periodic reports should be available, indicating the effective utilization* of all equipment in the computer department. This should help reveal both underutilized equipment and overutilization conditions that may identify the need for equipment upgrading, improved scheduling, etc. (See Table 14–1 for an illustration of such utilization reporting. An explanation might be required where utilization was only 64 percent.)

Each program should be reviewed and evaluated to determine whether it is efficient. Although some programs accomplish the work accurately, because of the way in which they are written either they waste the computer's costly storage or they

* Effective utilization levels will differ, depending upon type of computer system, applications, etc. Most well-run computers are utilized between 70 to 90 percent of the available time. Some slack is desirable to provide a cushion for the unexpected.

Table 14–1
Example of Hardware Utilization Reporting

Tasks	Actual Monthly Computer Use Hours	Percentage of Use
Setup Time	7	4
Production Runs	80	46
Maintenance, Scheduled	4	2
Maintenance, Unscheduled	2	1
Testing and Debugging	20	11
Total Hours Used	113	64
Unused Hours	63	36
Total Available Time*	176	100

* Assumes a one shift operation

take an inordinate amount of computer-processing time. A skilled computer supervisor can evaluate the computer program and identify inefficiently written routines. An inefficient program that is used frequently can cost the organization thousands of dollars by unnecessarily tying up the computer. Similarly, software that is provided by computer manufacturers and software vendors should be appraised carefully. Two software packages accomplishing the same task may have remarkably different operating efficiencies in terms of memory used and time taken to carry out the tasks.

Where possible, performance standards should be set for all technical personnel. It is easy to set standards for key punch operators; for instance, they may be expected to key punch a certain number of columns per hour, and to have only a maximum number of errors in the punching. However, it is more difficult to set standards for systems analysts, since they are working with relatively nonroutine problems. Although some attempt has been made to provide guidelines—that require programmers to write a certain number of instructions per hour—this has met with only modest success, because some programming tasks are trivial while others are extremely complex.

Nevertheless, the computer manager or supervisor should set a schedule for each project assigned to a systems analyst or programmer. Such schedules often are worked out after consultation with the analyst and/or programmer. At that point, the agreed-on schedule becomes a standard, which the systems analyst and programmer try to meet. If they do not meet the schedule, they must explain the delay or come up with a revised schedule. Exhibit 14–6 presents a simple example of such a technique. It shows that the systems analysis and design effort were completed before schedule, while the programming and documentation effort took more time than assigned by schedule.

Exhibit 14–6 Example of Project-Control Schedules

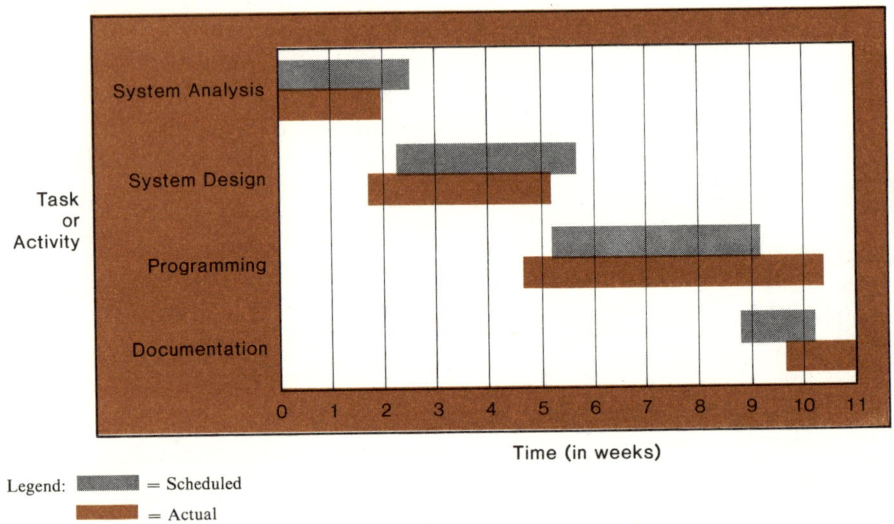

MANAGEMENT AUDIT OF THE COMPUTER DEPARTMENT

The very nature of the computer's operation makes periodic and continuing management audits essential. The computer department influences many sections of the company; is characterized by rapid technological developments and high staff turnover rates; and has been the location of frauds.

Table 14–2
An Example of a Management Control Report

	Budget	%	Actual	%	Variance*
Hardware Cost	$ 3,000	30	$ 3,000	26	—
Systems Analysis and Design	2,000	20	2,500	22	Over $ 500
Programming	1,500	15	2,400	21	Over $ 900
Computer Operations	2,500	25	2,400	21	Under $ 100
Other	1,000	10	1,200	10	Over $ 200
Totals	$10,000	100	$11,500	100	Over $1,500

* Explanations should be provided for variances.

A continuing or periodic management audit requires that the computer department's performance be evaluated by objective criteria, such as: plans versus actual performance; chargeouts to using departments; user satisfaction with the service of the computer department; employee turnover rates; comparison of indexes (e.g., computer costs relative to total revenue, and computer costs per employee) with other computer facilities; and effective utilization and efficiency of computer equipment.

One example of a management control report, presented in Table 14–2, shows the budget variances of the computer department. These variations must be explained and justified by the management of the computer department.

TOP-MANAGEMENT INVOLVEMENT

In view of the importance of the computer and its potential impact on the organization, there is a need for high-level management to be involved in the overall goal-setting and appraisal of the computer function. Experience indicates that lack of top-management involvement often results in ineffective computer operations and use.

An organization's top managers should understand: broad computer concepts; the value of the newer management information-systems approaches; the impact of computer systems on the organization and people; and how to evaluate the computer function. Top management should be sufficiently knowledgeable to provide general leadership to the computer staff. Only such top-level participation can ensure that the computer will be used in a way that is consistent with overall organizational policy and goals.

Summary

Good management and organization practices should be applied in the internal affairs of a computer department. Too often, a computer department wishes to improve the state of affairs in other parts of the organization, while its own "shop" may be in disarray. (Refer back to Chapter 2, which surveyed important concepts and practices of management and organization.)

The dynamic nature of computers requires planning on the computer manager's part. There are a number of ways to organize the computer department's resources, and such factors as the size of the organization will influence the approach used. Increasingly, the computer function is reporting to a member of top management; and the function is assigned so that it can service any and all units of the organization. Concurrently, the distributed data-processing trend places computer power wherever it is needed in the organization.

In a computer department, staffing presents a major challenge because of the shortage of highly qualified computer professionals. Special considerations include: maintenance of a balanced staff; recruitment tactics; selection methods; evaluation procedures; and the education and training of staff.

For purposes of control, procedural and performance standards are important. Procedural standards indicate how things should be done. Performance standards provide the basis for determining how well things were done.

Because the computer department is so vital, top management should be involved in the goals, plans, and overall control of the computer department.

Terms to Learn

Balanced staff
Recruitment
Selection
Computer aptitude test
Validity
Staff evaluation
Computer education
Degree in computer science
Degree in computer data-processing
Procedural standards
Performance standards
Equipment utilization
Project control
Management audit
Control report

Review Questions

1. Discuss the following statement: "Computer professionals have promoted good management and organization practices with their clients, but they do not practice what they preach."
2. Why may it be more important for the boss of the computer department to be a good manager than to be a good technician?
3. "A lack of planning can cause particular havoc with an organization's computer effort." Discuss this statement.
4. Contrast the likely differences in the organizational structure of a *small computer department* with that of a very large enterprise.
5. Contrast the organizational structure of an organization that has a highly *centralized* computer department with one that has *decentralized* computer units in many parts of the organization. What are the pros and cons of both approaches?
6. Why is the *staffing problem* in a computer department a particularly difficult one?
7. Describe the main *occupational paths* available in a large computer department. What are the educational requirements for each?
8. Identify several specific *procedural standards* that might be used in a computer department.

9. Identify several *performance standards* that might be used in a computer department.

10. Describe how a *management audit* of a computer department might be conducted.

11. Discuss the following statement: "Without top management interest and involvement, a computer effort is probably destined to be mediocre and/or concentrate on relatively trivial problems."

Computer invasion of privacy
JOHN W. DOE
PRIVATE
Report on John W. Doe
Failed Physics in College....
Fired from job 10 years ago....
12 Traffic Violations...
Drug arrest at 17...
decisions...
no loan.
reject job application...
etc...

CHAPTER 15

MANAGEMENT INFORMATION SYSTEMS

Objectives

Chapter 15 gives an overview of the ways in which managers can use the computer, and explores some of the challenges and opportunities of computer-based management information systems. It is likely that, more and more, management will use the computer for management-level purposes.

THE EMERGENCE OF MANAGEMENT INFORMATION SYSTEMS

Underlying Concepts of Information Systems

An information system is a method of using reports to abstractly represent the actual events and conditions related to an organization. An organization has certain physical and human resource inputs, and in a processing system these are used to generate product or service outputs for the market. The information system reports on these occurrences of the organization.

A *management information system (MIS)* can be defined as an assemblage of data (e.g., facts and opinions) that are processed (e.g., summarized, categorized, or projected) in such a way that they result in intelligence (i.e., information) that management can use to make decisions, and that the organization can use to attain its goals.

This book focuses on computerized information systems, although an information system may also be handled by manual and/or mechanical methods.

Data-Processing and Information Systems

Traditionally, computers have been used for basic data-processing jobs, which, while they affected the organization's operations, were largely not directly significant to management. Such applications included preparing payroll checks and billing customers. Although these basic data-processing applications are important, and although in many organizations they have been computerized, increasingly the focus is on applications that do have direct managerial implications.

Very small organizations, like the neighborhood retail store, may function well with an informal information system; in this type of system, the information may be stored in the mind of the owner and on scraps of paper. Even in such cases, however, government regulations (e.g., tax records are required) necessitate some kind of formal recordkeeping and reporting. As an organization grows in size and diversity, informal information systems no longer suffice. Lack of organized information and improper communication can cause organizational breakdowns.

Exhibit 15–1 Contrast of Data Processing and MIS

Data Processing Frequently Has the Following Characteristics:

- Routine
- Procedurized
- Accounting Oriented
- Internal Data
- Mechanistic
- Basic Computations
- Historical or Current Data
- Precision Recording

Examples of Data Processing

- Payroll
- Man-Job Matching
- Labor Cost Accounting

MIS Frequently Has the Following Characteristics:

- Nonroutine and Novel
- Difficult to Procedurize
- Extends Beyond Accounting
- External as Well as Internal Data
- Requires Human Judgement
- Complex Computations
- Predictive
- Estimates

Examples of MIS

- Collective Bargaining Strategy
- Manpower Forecasting
- Human Resource Accounting

Larger organizations must have some kind of formal information system, which provides a basis for making decisions related to planning, organizing, controlling, and actuating the enterprise. An information system is a major method of communicating among humans in an organization, and links those humans with the external environment. In addition to the formal information system, each organization has an informal information system, based on personal contacts, the "grapevine," and so on.

Traditionally, management information has not received high priority. At best, it usually has represented a relatively loose amalgamation of data and reports without any overall consistent pattern. Invariably, such information is generated only to fulfill basic accounting and legal requirements, and thus does little to support management decision making. Exhibit 15–1 contrasts the routine data-processing characteristics that prevail in many organizations with the emerging MIS approach.

The sheer volume and complexity of information patterns in today's society have revealed the inadequacies of traditional approaches to information. Such inadequacies include: information overload; irrelevant information; untimely information; and inaccurate information. Such limitations can cause decision making to be based on arbitrariness, inadequate analyses, and uninformed judgment.

Growing Interest in MIS

There are a number of reasons why management has a growing interest in information systems:

1. Today, less time is available between the moment when a problem is presented to management, and the moment when a solution is needed. The complexity of organizations, as well as the sheer volume and size of problems, requires information systems that can facilitate sound and timely decision making.
2. Changed public attitudes towards organizations and authority create need for information systems. The executive must be able to respond more sensitively to the inquiries and requests of various active members of the public—for instance, government, consumer groups, stockholders, researchers, and investigatory units.
3. Increasingly, organizations are staffed with sophisticated, better-educated people whose work is related to higher-technology processes (e.g., research and development, science-oriented organizations, automation and computer systems, and market research). Executives must be able to provide leadership for such human resources, including assessing their activities and information.
4. Many organizations have gained experience with computers, and to some extent have established the basic data-processing elements that permit advancement towards an MIS.
5. The computer hardware and software that are needed to handle MIS-level approaches are available now, in contrast with just several years ago.

The Importance of Information for Decision Making

All managers perform the functions of planning, organizing, controlling, and actuating with a view to using the organization's resources in the best way possible. The success of any organization is determined by how well its leaders perform those activities. And how well those functions are carried out is dependent, in part, on how well the managers' information needs are being met. Each function involves decision making, and decision making must be supported by information that is accurate, timely, complete, concise, and relevant. If a manager's information does not possess these characteristics, the quality of his/her decisions will probably suffer, and the organization will not attain the success it might otherwise have had.

Exhibit 15–2 suggests: that quality information, in the hands of those who can effectively use it, will support good decisions; that good decisions will lead to effective performance of managerial functions; and that effective managerial performance will lead to successful attainment of organizational goals.

The specific information required by a particular manager includes information needed to:

1. Establish, evaluate, and adjust goals;

Exhibit 15–2 The Importance of Information to an Organization

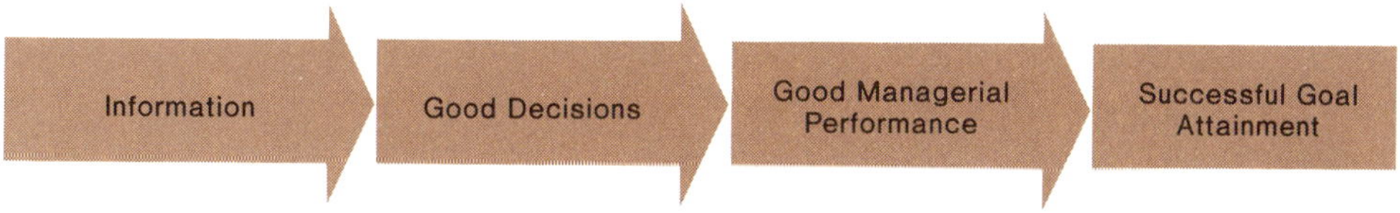

2. Develop plans and standards to initiate action;
3. Measure actual performance and take appropriate action when performance varies from the plans and standards; and
4. Assess achievements.

Here is a related guideline, which can help determine the information needed by a particular manager.

1. Identification of those factors that determine the success of the manager's contribution to organizational goals;
2. Determination of how these critical factors can be measured;
3. Establishment of quantifiable measurements that indicate success, for each critical factor; and
4. Identification of the information needed to ensure achievement of the success measurements.

Each day, numerous management decisions may be required. Each decision process can be viewed as a transformation of information inputs into decision outputs. Thus, the designer of an information system must concern himself or herself with three aspects of the decision process:

1. The *information inputs* for the decision.
2. The *decision process*.
3. The *decision outputs* and how they result in action.

Preparing inputs and outputs permits considerable formalizing; and formalizing the decision process usually requires that a mathematical decision model be developed, which represents the decision's significant characteristics. The transformation of inputs into outputs is usually expressed symbolically, as a series of mathematical equations in a computer program.

It is fairly easy to formalize routine decisions. However, nonroutine decisions, which are qualitative and subjective rather than quantitative, are much harder to formalize. In such circumstances, the formal system may be, at best, a limited aid to the human decision maker. Nevertheless, the continued advances in computer technology and MIS techniques are constantly making heretofore unmanageable problems more manageable.

An Example of a Management Information Report

Table 15–1 presents a simple example that compares data-processing information with MIS. The data-processing report is a straightforward, traditional listing of expenses by department, with a total that indicates the expenses for the period. However, this report is of little value to a manager, who cannot judge what the figures mean unless he/she has other sources of information. Are the figures good indicators? Are they bad indicators?

In contrast, the management information report gives the manager rational and helpful information that can sharpen his/her analysis and decisions. The manager can quickly ascertain that, for the period, Departments A and C have expenses in excess of their budgets. Also, it is apparent that Department B is operating under budget. The manager can find out why Department A has exceeded its cost objectives by $2,000, which is a substantial variance (25 percent).

He/she might even want to find out how Department B is able to operate effectively while $1,000 under budget for expenses. On the surface, this condition appears to be a favorable development; however, suppose that the saving is because a critical position in the department cannot be filled? In that case, the "favorable" variance may actually hide an *un*favorable condition.

Table 15–1

A Comparison of Data-Processing and Management Information

Data-Processing Report		Management Information Report				
ADA Corporation Expenses		ADA Corporation Budget/Expenses				
Department	$	Department	Budget $	Expenses $	$ Variance	% Variance
A	10,000	A	8,000	10,000	(2,000)	(25)
B	15,000	B	16,000	15,000	1,000	6.2
C	1,100	C	1,000	1,100	(100)	(10)
Total	$26,100	Total	$25,000	$26,100	$(1,100)	(4.4)

Note: Variances in brackets signify unfavorable situations.

As Table 15–1 shows, the management information report stimulates thinking and managerial action.

COMPUTER-BASED MIS

Recent technology has created the potential for significant improvements in MIS. This potential has aroused considerable interest about computer-based MIS, although widespread implementation of such systems still seems largely in the future.

The computer's features that make an MIS more feasible are:

- Accurate and rapid processing of data.
- Vast storage and prompt retrievability of information.
- Performance of computations and logical operations with very high reliability.

Without the computer, sophisticated and even unsophisticated information systems would be difficult to attain in today's complex organizations. Such organizations may deal with data in the following kinds of magnitudes:

- Thousands, tens of thousands, or hundreds of thousands of employees.
- Many hundreds, thousands, or even millions of customers or clients.
- Numerous vendors.
- Thousands, tens of thousands, or hundreds of thousands of stockholders.
- Numerous facilities, equipment, inventories, resources, etc., in many different locations.
- Thousands or even millions of different records and reports.

An effective information system should have certain characteristics that permit:

1. *Selection* of information that is relevant to particular situations (management by exception), thus preventing either an excess or scarcity of information.
2. *Comparison* of current information, with plans (feedback) to discover deviations and, if needed, trigger corrective action.
3. *Immediate access* to information to support management decisions in unpredictable situations.
4. *Delivery* of information in a timely fashion to facilitate decision making.
5. *Horizontal and vertical dissemination* of needed information so that all affected persons will be informed properly.

Exhibit 15–3 depicts the management information systems concept. A planned data-base constitutes the foundation of the MIS. The data base contains not only rigorously selected and defined data elements that represent the organization's activities, but also pertinent external inputs. Considerable care is given to making sure that the data elements, which, collectively make up the data base, are accurate, consistent, and

Exhibit 15–3 Management Information Systems Concept

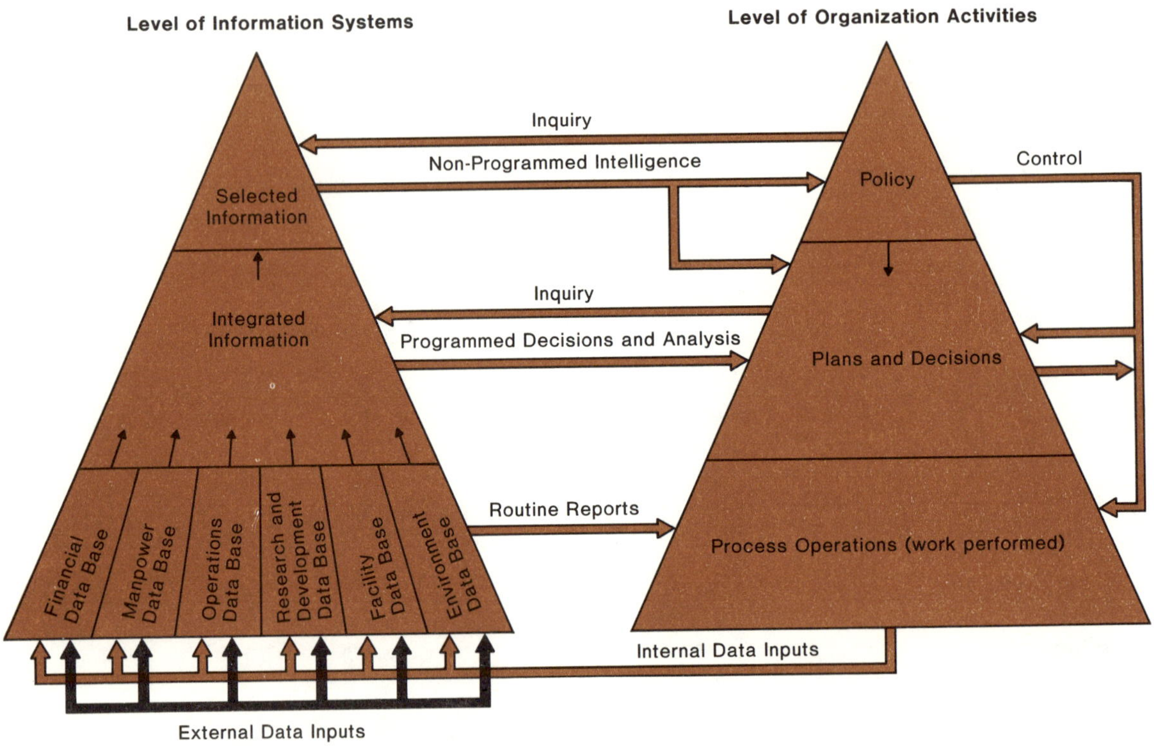

up to date. In essence, the data base is a supra-file, with flexibility, quick retrievability, and expandability. The data elements in the data base can be combined and manipulated to provide any combination of integrated information. The integrated information can be filtered on the basis of any set of rules, resulting in selected information. The levels of the MIS are planned so that they are responsive to the levels of responsibility in the organization.

What information is needed? All managers need to understand the organization's purpose—that is, its policies, plans, and goals. But beyond these basic requirements, the question of what information is needed can be addressed only in broad, general terms, because managers and organizations differ in the ways in which they view and use information. Also, information needs vary, depending on the organizational level of the managerial job. Supervisors at working levels need information so that they can make practical, day-to-day operating decisions. Middle managers often are required to assess integrated information, and to develop short-range tactical plans for their areas of responsibility. At the top levels, information is needed to support long-range, strategical planning and to set organizational policy.

MANAGEMENT SCIENCE IN MIS

Management science (or operations research) is a discipline that can make MIS more sophisticated. Management science, which involves extensive computations, has developed along with the computer; in fact, the computational power provided by the computer has actualized management science approaches that previously had been only impractical theories.

Without the modern computer, it would be difficult (if not impossible) to perform the mathematics necessary for some classes of problems. Mathematical problems with several linear equations often are difficult to solve by noncomputer methods. If nonlinear equations are involved, the problem often truly cannot be solved without a computer. Management science applications can involve up to hundreds or thousands of variables and interrelated computations.

In addition to relying on the computational power of the computer, the management science techniques depend on an information system to provide the data elements identified by the known variables. Without such data, the elegant mathematical formulae would be inoperative.

Management science involves:

1. Constructing mathematical, economic, and statistical descriptions or models of decision and control problems to treat situations of complexity and uncertainty.
2. Analyzing the relationships that determine the probable future consequences of decision choices, and devising appropriate measures of effectiveness in order to evaluate the relative merit of alternative actions.

Here are some examples of how management science can be used in various areas of an organization:

Purchasing. *Management science can be used to develop rules for buying raw materials whose prices either are stable or vary.*

Production. *Management science can be used to aid in the design and site selection of plants, to determine: how many plants of what size and mix capabilities are required; to what extent they should be automated, and how; and what number and types of different kinds of equipment should be installed.*

Marketing. *Management science has been used to determine where distribution points should be located, how large they should be, how much they should stock of what, and whom they should supply. Also, it has been used to determine how large a sales budget should be and how the budget should be allocated to direct selling, sales promotion, and advertising.*

Research and Development. *The management science approach can be applied in determining what the budget for research and development should be, how this should be divided between basic and applied research, and which projects should be supported.*

Exhibit 15–4 A Simple Example of a Network for a Project

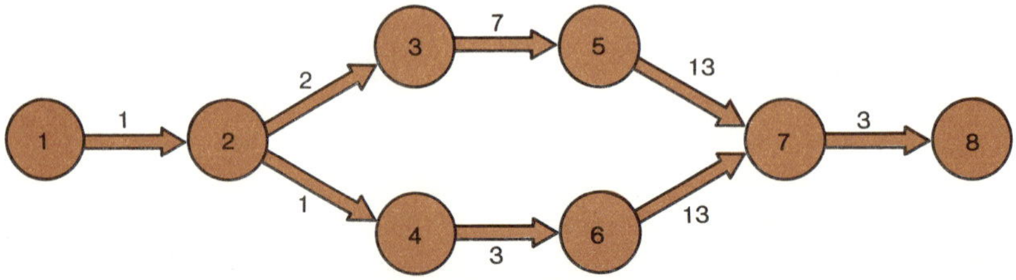

Event	Activity Description	Most Likely Time to Complete Activity (in days)	Required Preceeding Event Completion
1	Start	None	None
2	Plan the Project	1	1
3	Staff the Project	2	2
4	Order Equipment	1	2
5	Train the Staff	7	3
6	Transport the Equipment	3	4
7	Assemble Equipment	13	5, 6
8	Test Equipment	3	7

Legend: ⬤ = Event
➡ = Activity

Personnel. *Management science has been employed to determine: what mix of age and skills among workers is most desirable; what causes accidents, and how they can and should be prevented; and what causes absenteeism and labor turnover, and how they can be minimized.*

Finance and Accounting. *Management science has been used to design accounting and auditing procedures that minimize the sum of the cost of the procedure and error.*

A number of quantitative aids have had particular management significance: network analysis; mathematical programming; and simulation.

Network Analysis

Both PERT (*P*rogram *E*valuation and *R*eview *T*echnique) and CPM (*C*ritical *P*ath *M*ethod) are network models that are used to plan, schedule, and control complex projects. The following general procedure is used to set up a network model:

1. All activities to be performed in a project must be identified.
2. The sequence of each activity must be determined (i.e., it must be known which events* have to be completed prior to the start of a further activity).
3. The time interval required to complete each activity must be estimated.
4. The longest sequence of events in the project must be identified. The sum of the individual activity times in this sequence becomes the "total project time," and this sequence of activities is known as the "critical path."

Exhibit 15–4 presents a very simple network. There are two paths through this network:

- The path through events 1, 2, 3, 5, 7, and 8 takes twenty-six days.
- The path through events 1, 2, 4, 6, 7, and 8 takes twenty-one days.

Thus, the critical path is the first one; as things now stand, it will take twenty-six days to complete the project.

The network permits the manager to decide whether he/she wishes to shift or to add more resources to reduce the time of the critical path, and thus reduce the total project time. Improving the completion time often involves some sacrifice in additional costs. In any case, the network is a valuable method that can be used to help in planning and controlling complex projects.

Mathematical Programming

The purpose of mathematical programming is to find the best strategy from among a large number of options. Most mathematical programming involves the use of *linear programming*. Linear-programming (not to be confused with computer programming) models are used to find the best combination of limited resources to achieve a specified objective (typically, to maximize profit or minimize cost). One important class of linear-programming applications is in blending operations, where the objective is often to minimize the cost involved in producing a given amount of blended product. For example, cattle feed may be a mixture of minerals, grains, and fish and meat products. Since the prices of these ingredients are subject to change, the least expensive blend required to achieve specified nutritional levels is subject to variation. Linear programming can help quickly determine the correct blend to use in order to minimize cost and yet meet product specifications.

In addition to blending, linear programming is being used for such diverse purposes as scheduling manpower, selecting media for advertising purposes, and determining minimum transportation costs from given supply points to specified points of delivery.

* An "event" simply indicates the point at which a specific activity is completed.

Simulation*

Simulation resembles scientific experimentation in that managers can evaluate proposed decisions by using mathematical models. Simulation can help determine what is likely to happen when certain decisions are made under particular conditions. Simulation is a trial-and-error problem-solving approach, since both decisions and conditions can be modified.

For example, simulation models can help managers decide whether or not to expand by acquiring a new plant. Such models have to deal with complicating variables like facts and assumptions about: the present and potential size of the total market; the organization's present and potential share of this total market; the selling prices of the product; and the investment required to achieve various production levels.

Simulation models also are used to improve inventory management. The problem of managing inventories is complicated, because different organizational units have conflicting desires, and what is best for one department may not be best for the entire organization. For instance, the purchasing, production, and sales departments often prefer to have large quantities of inventory on hand; on the other hand, the finance department usually takes a more conservative approach for various reasons (e.g., it doesn't want to tie up funds or increase the storage expense). Simulated inventory techniques can enable the organization to experiment with various alternatives, and thus to arrive at more profitable inventory policies.

Several conditions have kept management science from being more widely adopted. First, it is usually a costly endeavor: high-priced management scientists are needed; mathematical models can take many man-years to develop; often, extensive data must be collected to be processed by the mathematical model; and such models require considerable computer time. Second, some of the management science efforts, in the past, have been expensive theoretical exercises, applying to the real world in only a limited fashion.

COMPUTERS AND DECISION MAKING

While most computer time is still assigned to routine data-processing work, increasingly the computer is being planned (if not used) for higher-level assignments. However, it still has almost unlimited potential for assisting management.

Table 15–2 indicates that routine, repetitive decisions have been programmed. These decisions include such things as automatic determination of when to replenish inventory, and in what quantity, and selection of vendor(s) to supply needed material. Nonprogrammed decisions are difficult to structure and standardize; most of them are thus still made by humans. Examples of nonprogrammed decisions might include determining the impact of political and sociological changes on the business. The com-

* As Chapter 13 indicated, simulation can be used to make one computer act like a different computer when executing a program.

Table 15–2
Decision-Making Paradigm

Types of Decisions	Decision-Making Techniques	
	Traditional	Modern
Programmed Routine, Repetitive Decisions	Habit, Clerical Routine, Organizational Structure	Computers, Management Science
Nonprogrammed One-Shot, Ill-Structured, Novel Policy Decisions	Judgment, Intuition, Creativity, Rules of Thumb	Heuristics, Interactive Computers, Artificial Intelligence

This chart is adapted from various works of Herbert Simon.

puter can perform analyses that provide background information for nonprogrammed decisions, but eventually it is human beings who must appraise the information, and who must factor in subjective and qualitative elements.

Table 15–3 indicates some of the major kinds of changes that are induced by computer technology. Such changes involve new patterns for executives and organizations. As Table 15–3 suggests, the computer supplants or supplements the activities of human beings.

Table 15–3
The Computer's Increased Role in Organizations

Noncomputer Era	Computer Era
Human Memory and Files	Data Banks
Manual Search and Human Recall	Information Storage and Retrieval
Specialization and Simplification to Cope with Volume, Complexity, and Distances	Integration via General Systems in Order to Consider All Vital Factors
Written Policies and Procedures, Habits and Traditions, Executive Interpretation	Automated Systems with Feedback for Control and Correction
Executive Review	Preprogrammed Selection of Exceptions for Attention and Disposition
Executive Judgment and Intuition About Complex and Creative Matters	Testing via Models and Simulation
Human Forecasting and Best Estimates	Quantification via Econometrics, Mathematical Programming, and Network Analysis
Rules of Thumb and Subjective Evaluation and Discontinuous Control	Augmented Standards and Continuous Control

Exhibit 15–5 The Expanding Frontier for Computerization

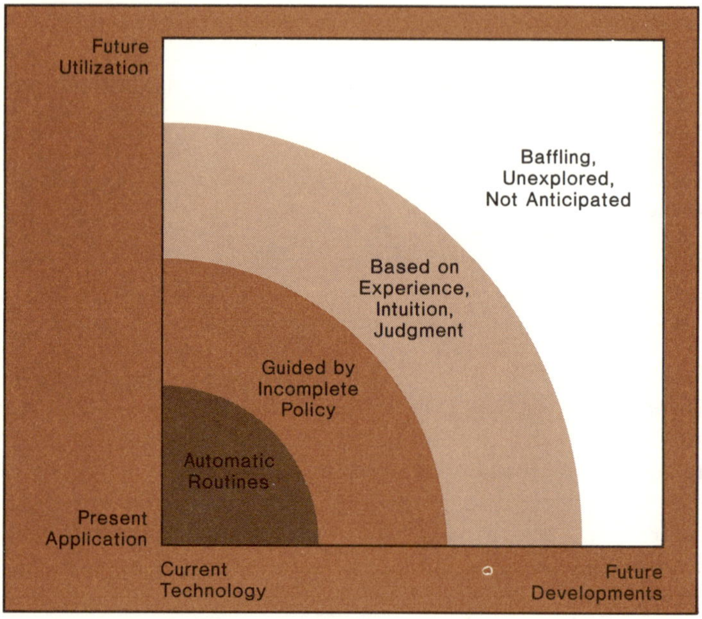

Note: This chart is adapted from various works of Jay Forrester.

However, managers needn't be overly worried about whether they will be replaced by computers. Instead, they should be concerned with whether they can sufficiently structure current decision making so that the computer can handle it. Moreover, since the manager will seek new problems, he/she must be able to adapt to a greater fluidity in his/her work. When such problems are sufficiently structured, the computer is likely to best handle many of them. This moves the point of managerial decisions into the future, for the manager must define decision rules, rather than make the actual decisions.

Managers will be motivated to seek new challenges in uncharted areas that will not be susceptible to computerization for some time. This search will tend to increase management's sophistication, and to create a demand for increasingly higher-skilled managers.

Exhibit 15–5 depicts this tendency: a constantly expanding frontier of knowledge moves away from the precisely defined routines (which are or can be automated) to the newly identified problems, or to those that have not yet been identified or even imagined.

Nowadays, *artificial intelligence* is being researched. This approach would have the computer perform functions that are normally considered human (e.g., learning, adapting, reasoning, self-correcting, and improving). Artificial intelligence requires a *heuristic* program that handles a problem by the trial-and-error approach. Most conventional programs are deterministic, in that they simply execute a preset series of routines. Obviously, this is inadequate for higher-level decisions that cannot be precisely defined in advance.

MAN-MACHINE SYSTEMS

Since future generations of managers will be familiar with the computer as a normal tool, they will use it much more extensively than today's managers do (see Exhibit 15–6). Future managers will also make wider use of *interactive computer systems,* employing a data terminal that is connected to a computer to explore alternatives and to obtain information in response to queries. Interactive computer systems combine human strengths (e.g., recognizing subtle patterns, associating, learning, original thinking, and inductive reasoning) with computer strengths (e.g., ability to handle mass data; speed; reliability; and accuracy). This approach can increase the manager's ability to explore numerous opportunities rapidly and efficiently—a clumsy and slow process when implemented by humans alone.

Exhibit 15–7 is a schematic model of an interactive man-machine decision-making system. It allows a manager to raise a host of "what if" questions about his/her organization and to receive quick answers that show the impact of the proposed change on the financial condition, work schedule, manpower planning, and other performance aspects. The program calls on specified logic from the software for the problem at hand, using pertinent information from a bank of general and specific data. The program utilizes rapid computations from the computer. In a few moments, the effects of the proposed change are displayed for the manager's inspection and use. The new information may then lead to a managerial decision, or to further questions about additional alternatives.

Management science models and computers can enable many factors to be considered at the same time; indeed, systems of several hundred variables are not infeasible. On the other hand, it is difficult for humans to handle problems where as many (or, seen in terms of the computer's ability, as few) as five factors are considered simultaneously. Moreover, the computer's calculations can be made so quickly that various alternatives can be tested in scores of computer runs. Therefore, tremendously complex problems, which before could be solved only by the manager's judgments, estimates, and intuition, can now be examined quantitatively.

Exhibit 15–6 Man-Machine System

Exhibit 15–7 Interactive Decision Making

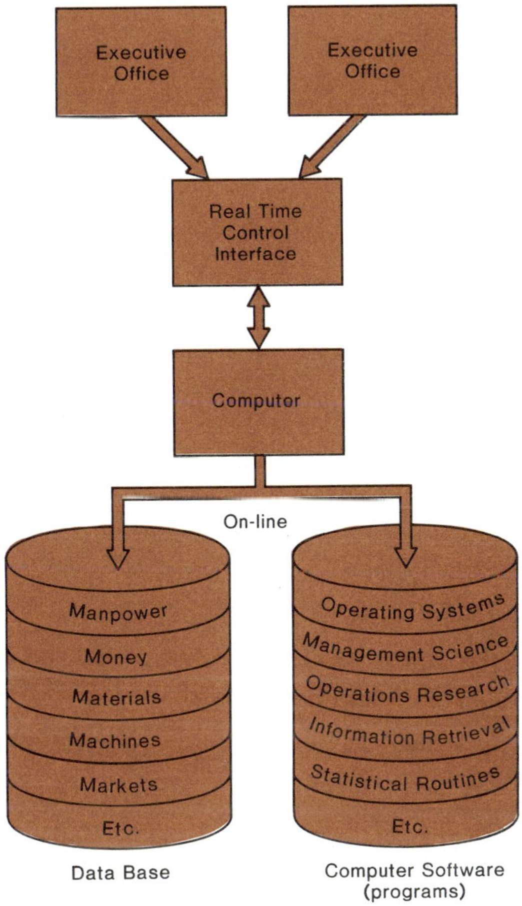

CENTRALIZATION/DECENTRALIZATION

The computer's tremendous capacity encourages some degree of centralization of computer processing and preparation of information. Such centralization encompasses various functions that previously were performed in many splintered departments. Obviously, some degree of standardization and coordination must be reached. Increased centralization of information processing is probably a trend, but increased centralization of decision making is probably not. In fact, since the computer can free managers of many day-to-day problems that formerly took much of their time, the computer can encourage decentralization of decision making. Managers can access the computer, via a data terminal, to deal with higher-level problems. And minicomputers and on-line data terminals have opened up a new concept of distributed data-processing (which, in essence, returns at least part of the computer power to the point of the user). This counteracts the trend towards centralization.

Computerized information systems frequently involve a power struggle, since they tend to shift the locus of physical location and control over vital information, thereby disrupting the balance of political power among various groups. Consequently, optimal MIS may be difficult to attain; more likely, some compromise will be necessary.

PLANNING AND IMPLEMENTING MIS

The planning and implementation of MIS can be time-consuming, costly, and complex. Since information, like any other product, has cost associated with it, its value must outweigh its cost, if it is to be justified. Sometimes organizations spend millions of dollars on information, and yet barely understand the real costs and benefits.

Planning MIS

Ideally, MIS should be designed for the entire organization, so that all subsystems are integrated. This will ensure that the overall system will function in the best interest of the organization as a whole.

While an overall MIS design is desirable, the actual implementation can proceed by subsystems, since it would probably be impractical to implement all MIS subsystems simultaneously. MIS planning should be a continuing effort, since organizations and information should be responsive to change. While there are some general MIS principles that are useful in most organizations, specific MIS design must suit the individual organization.

The complexity of a comprehensive computer-based information system is accounted for by a number of factors:

1. Typically, it deals with very large quantities of input data. The collection of data and error-protection methods are expensive, and they affect many data-originating units of an organization.
2. Large volumes of data must be maintained more or less permanently in data files, and there must be a method of linking related data.
3. A variety of computer programs must be written to provide for the desired output and performance of the MIS.
4. Computer programs and their output are intimately linked to an organization's practices and management style. This linkage reduces the extent to which standardized procedures can be transferred from one organization to another.

5. On-going operations must continue, thus necessitating that the conversion from an existing system to a new one be done carefully (often over the course of one or more years).
6. Many parts of the system must tie together into an integrated whole.
7. The efforts of many persons must be closely coordinated over a considerable period of time.

Flexibility and open-endedness are needed in such systems, since it is difficult to anticipate all changes, all needs of users, and all specific ways in which technology will evolve.

Implementing MIS

The implementation of an MIS assumes that the managers are sufficiently familiar with it to use it meaningfully in making decisions. This assumption implies that management development and training constitute a vital part of the MIS effort. However, although MIS can be a substantial aid to decision making, it does not supplant human judgment. Furthermore, the formal MIS should be only part of the information flow that will influence managerial decision making. For the rest, the manager will have to consider such things as: discussions with superiors, colleagues, and subordinates; sensory impressions of human situations; and intuitive and creative insights. Although some of these factors are not a part of the formal MIS they may be just as important in the decision-making process.

Designing a management information system requires that the manager's information needs be determined on the basis of his/her responsibilities, authorities, and relationships. Since the decisions that managers make largely define the kinds of information required, such decisions set the parameters of the system itself. Since this is the case, the managers should be involved in identifying decision patterns when the MIS is designed. Some decisions, particularly at the higher levels of management, are difficult to anticipate, since they are novel, usually are not repeated, and sometimes are based more on qualitative than on quantitative factors.

Why are computerized information systems retarded in many organizations? Here are some reasons: managers' lack of familiarity with computers; shortage of competent analysts and programmers; policies and procedures that impede the integration of data; and lack of coordination among units of the organization. Until these barriers are resolved satisfactorily, MIS will probably not advance notably.

Summary

While computers have been used primarily for relatively routine data-processing, there is significant interest in sophisticated management information systems. Some organizations have made notable advances towards MIS, which is computer-based.

Modern management can view the computer as an aid for improving its own functions and actions. In the past, management let technicians determine which applications would be processed by computer. An MIS approach constitutes a much greater technical and intellectual challenge than computerizing routine data-processing applications does. In particular, a better definition of management's decision-making process is needed; however, this is difficult to attain, since some decisions are not structured well. But because management science techniques use higher mathematics, they are helpful in this area. As newer-generation managers rise up the organizational ladder, they can be expected to have a comfortable, interactive relation with the computer. Such managers will consider the computer a routine but powerful tool to improve their decision making.

Designing and developing an MIS requires considerable professional attention in the planning and implementation stages.

Terms to Learn

Information system
Management information system (MIS)
Computer-based MIS
Management science
Operations research (OR)
Network analysis
Mathematical programming
Simulation
Programmed decision
Nonprogrammed decision
Artificial intelligence
Deterministic program
Heuristic program
Man-machine system
Interactive computer system

Review Questions

1. Define *management information system.*
2. Contrast an organization that uses its computer for *data processing* with another organization that uses its computer for *information systems.*
3. Why haven't more organizations developed comprehensive *computer-based MIS?*
4. What organizational and technical factors now make it timely for organizations to develop computer-based MIS?
5. Why are younger managers more likely than older ones to have an interest in computer-based MIS?
6. How can the *quality* and *timeliness* of information affect the decisions of management, and thus affect organizational profits, sales, etc.?
7. Discuss the characteristics of *programmed decisions* and *nonprogrammed decisions.* Why is it difficult to computerize nonprogrammed decisions?

8. What are some of the *characteristics* that should exist in an information system?
9. How do the information needs differ at different levels of management (i.e., top management, middle management, supervision)?
10. Define *management science* (operations research).
11. Describe some of the *practical application* uses of management science.
12. How might an organization use *network analysis, mathematical programming,* and *simulation?*
13. How is the computer likely to change the nature of management?
14. Discuss the relative merits of a *centralized* information system versus a *decentralized* approach to information systems.
15. Discuss some of the *planning* and *implementing challenges* connected with MIS.

Computer
Crimes...
"Doctored info"
Corporation
rip-offs'...
False data...
Hidden losses...
Fact/figure
manipulation...
$$$ bilking...
Figure juggling...

CHAPTER 16

COMPUTER AND SOCIETY ISSUES

Objectives

Chapter 16 explores some of the broad social issues that are related to computers. These include the ways computers affect employees, consumers, and citizens. Government and public interest groups are studying the computer, and as a result there will probably be more and more legislation that will affect both the computer industry and computer users.

SCOPE OF THE SOCIAL CHALLENGE

We can begin to sense the vast dimensions of the computer and data-processing challenges by considering a few U.S. statistics:*

- Approximately 45,000,000 individuals do white-collar work that involves paperwork.
- About 100,000,000 checks clear through the banking system each day.
- An estimated 500,000,000 telephone calls are made each day, which triggers paperwork (e.g., billing).
- Something like 100,000,000,000 pieces of mail are handled each year by the U.S. Postal System.

It is within the framework of such staggering statistics that the computer functions.

A number of provocative social issues are entangled with the development, use, and future of computers. As society becomes increasingly dependent on technology and machines, there may be accompanying trends that can be considered dehumanizing. However, in the multifaceted social system, dehumanization stems from many causes. For instance, family life is less stable than it was in the past; mobility of individuals is increasing; loyalty to God, country, home, and job (by historical standards) seems to be diminishing; and large-scale impersonal organizations influence much of our lives.

The computer—an inanimate device—causes discomfort to those people who prefer to interact with humans. The programmed computer is tireless, persistent, and rapid. As a result, a human being can feel futile, fearful, and harassed when interacting with a computer system. As currently designed, computer-paced work is often unsympathetic to individualistic human characteristics, since it treats all people with impersonal objectivity and uniformity.

The very publicity about the computer's power, potential and indispensability can make individuals and groups who are affected by it feel inadequate.

* These statistics were derived from the U.S. Statistical Abstracts, and are representative of the late 1970s.

The computer remains a mysterious, if not a threatening, device to a large number of people. Sometimes the computer is viewed as a composite of the demonic and the divine, as some of the terms used to refer to it illustrate: the "giant brain," the "monster," the "black box." Perhaps one of the fundamental reasons behind the computer's public image involves the permeating yet obscure role it has in our lives. People often are expected to adjust to the computer system, rather than vice versa. While it's true that people often are adaptable, if the adaptation is coerced and if it disturbs the preferred human system, resentment often occurs.

HUMAN BEINGS AND COMPUTERS

There are similarities between the overall functions of a human being and a computer (see Exhibit 16–1). As humans, we can perform the following functions:

1. *Input.* We absorb data from our environment and experiences through our sensory perceptions (i.e., sight, hearing, smell, touch, and taste).
2. *Storage.* We store the data we have perceived. The storage may be in the memory cells of our brain and/or in external files (e.g., notebooks).
3. *Process.* At intervals, we may manipulate the data we have in storage according to some conscious logical order or through some subconscious process.
4. *Output.* When appropriate, we can retrieve something from storage and send messages (via spoken words, written words, gesticulations, actions, etc.) to the external world.

Carl Sagan, the noted writer about human development, has described the marvel of the human brain.* He mentions that the brain, which weighs about three pounds, may have about ten billion switching elements called neurons, and that an average neuron may have between 1,000 and 10,000 links (synapses) with adjacent neurons. This means that the brain may have 10^{13} linkages! Sagan indicates that there are electrical microcircuits in the brain that are more sophisticated than those in electronic computers; they are about 1/10,000 of a centimeter.

According to Sagan, over a 60-year life a person may have committed to memory some 200 billion bits of data. The brain, he says, is ten thousand times more densely packed with information than the computer is. In other words, if the computer were to hold the information contained in a human brain, it would have to be about ten thousand times larger in volume than the human brain. However, modern electronic computers are capable of processing information at a rate of 10^{16} to 10^{17} bits per second, compared to the brain's peak rate, which is ten billion times slower. In spite of the relative slowness of the human brain, Sagan says, one must marvel at the brain, since it still can do so many significant tasks so much better than the best computer. In this

* See Carl Sagan, *The Dragons of Eden* (New York: Random House, 1977); and Carl Sagan and I. S. Shklovskii, *Intelligent Life in the Universe* (San Francisco: Holden-Day, Inc., 1966).

Exhibit 16–1 The Human Brain

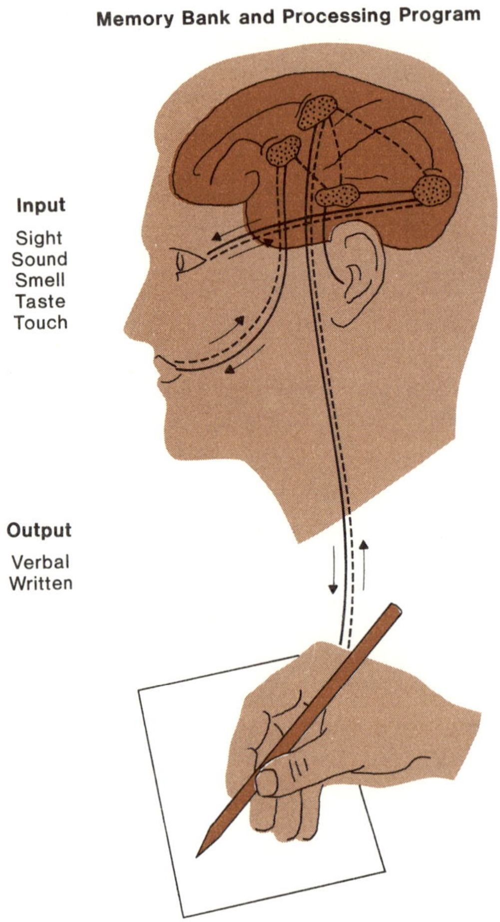

area, we find such acts as painting a beautiful picture, writing a creative story, expressing feelings of tenderness for others, and inventing new things for society (e.g., the computer!). While a person can do anything a computer can do (albeit much slower), a computer cannot do everything a human being can do. A person is best suited to thinking, reasoning, and creating; a computer is best adapted to calculating, manipulating, comparing, and following minute instructions.

THE COMPUTER AND WORK

Throughout history, the introduction of tools has undoubtedly caused some dislocation in employment and the nature of work. The spear and bow and arrow changed the hunters' approach to pursuing game. The wheel considerably altered human methods of transporting and hauling goods. The mechanical machines of the Industrial Revolution shifted considerable portions of the heavy workload from people to machines, as well as increasing productivity and mass production. In more recent years, we have witnessed a surge of new devices that create a constantly changing work environment; chief among them, perhaps, is the electronic computer, which touches the life of almost every citizen.

As Chapter 3 indicated, many causes contributed to the development of data-processing technology. One reason includes the rapidly growing number of white-collar (office) workers and their demands for increasing salary (partly mandated by minimum-wage laws). United States statistics indicate that about half the employees are classified as white collar; to a large extent, all these people deal with paperwork. Organizations undoubtedly are looking for ways to stem the tide of steadily increasing administrative costs.

It is difficult to isolate and establish the specific impact of computers and automation on such factors as unemployment and productivity, because other variables also are operating (e.g., social attitudes about work; shifts in organizational goals; the rise of new industries and products and the decline of others; and modification in life styles and consumer demands).

One analysis indicates that the computer has had little effect on our overall employment levels (see Exhibit 16–2). This exhibit shows that during the 1950s, 1960s, and early 1970s, unemployment ranged from 4 to 6 percent. Most experts attributed the recession that began in the mid-1970s to such factors as the energy crisis, which pushed the unemployment rate up to around 7 percent. However, during this same period, employment in the data-processing industry showed unparalleled growth. Today, there are even fewer jobs for unskilled laborers but expanded opportunities for skilled and professional persons.

Nevertheless, automation and computerization clearly have influenced the composition and distribution of work, as menial tasks and even some higher-order activities are absorbed by machinery. A now almost-classic example is that of the General Motors' Lordstown plant:

> *General Motors' Lordstown, Ohio plant was constructed to have the most modern and efficient assembly line and equipment. However, there has been continuing employee discontent, as well as product problems, since the plant was built. This has been partly attributed to the fact that the employees were considered robot-like extensions of the plant's automated machines. Mechanistic systems like this require workers to be moron-like in an age (even during economic recessions and unemployment) when most workers not only are better educated and more liberated, but also they react against meaningless and unchallenging work.*

Exhibit 16–2 United States Unemployment Patterns and the Growth of Jobs in Data Processing

Unemployment Rates in the United States

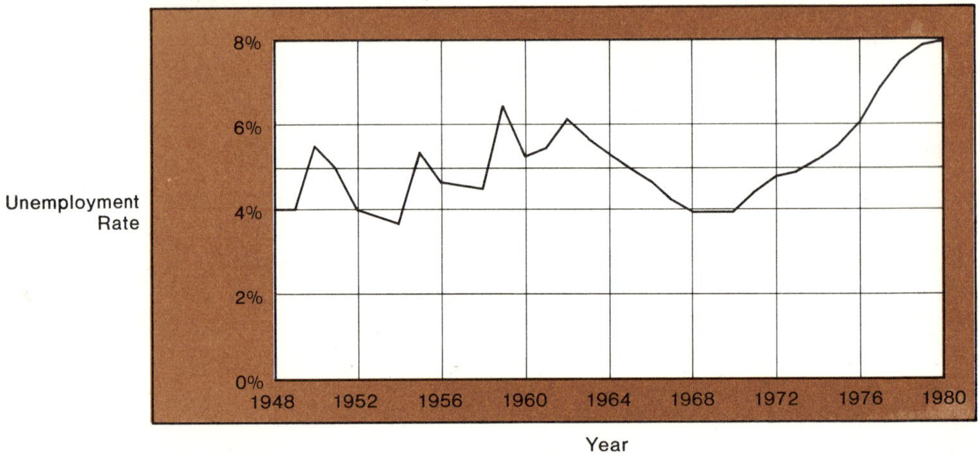

Employees in the Data Processing Industry

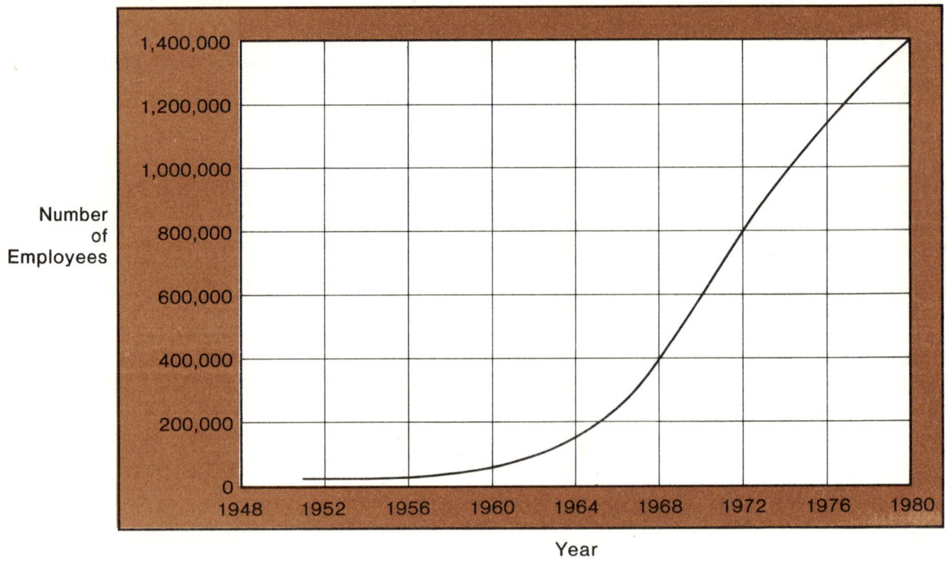

The dilemmas that occurred in the manufacturing plant have an analogue in the office. It can be said that the computer has turned administrative and office work into a "paperwork factory."

> *Budget analysts who formerly did a complete job of preparing budget forecasts were reduced to almost blindly placing numbers in certain boxes on preprinted forms. The data then were punched by key punch operators (who, to a large extent, did not understand the data they were key punching), and finally the computer did all of the computations, analyses, and printed the reports. What was once the team effort of proud, enthusiastic, and dedicated employees who supplied management with valuable reports now became a highly automated, dull, and repetitious activity. The budget analysts could derive little job satisfaction from their new, mundane duties. The computer had absorbed all the interesting work. Errors crept into the computerized system because of its sheer monolithic size and its lack of human involvement in and understanding about the computer process.*

While, in many cases, automation in the factory has no connection with automation in the office, eventually these two major components of a manufacturing organization will have to be linked, if complete integration is to take place. What happens in the plant (e.g., use of materials and supplies; expenditure of labor; and inspection for quality and flaws in products) obviously has a direct relation to many administrative activities (e.g., inventory records; manpower planning; financial statements; and customer complaints).

Computerization and automation promise: to rid people of work that is toilsome and demeaning; to produce more and better products without increasing the work force; and to make available new services that otherwise would be classified only as visionary (such as instant dial-up information retrieval) everyday realities.

The threat, of course, of automation and computerization is layoffs and unemployment. However, the extent to which automation and computers significantly reduce employment is debatable. Some observers believe that the threat of automation and computerization has been greatly exaggerated; that both automation and computerization are being introduced gradually; and that, where introduced, they do not appreciably decrease the need for workers, although they may change the nature of the jobs available. Numerous reasons—primarily automation and computerization, but also the fact that in a competitive economy, the more efficient survive—explain why many, if not most, of our industries can increase production while holding relatively constant, or even decreasing, the size of their labor forces. Thus far, the net result has not been massive unemployment, but shifts in work and a general reduction in hours worked, instead. Of course, automation and computers affect some positions more intensively than others (e.g., they would more greatly affect the clerk or factory worker doing repetitive jobs than they would service workers who render personal services to people, or professional-type employees).

Although blue-collar and white-collar workers are the most obvious individuals to be affected by automation and computerization (see Exhibit 16–3), managers and

Exhibit 16–3 Impact of the Computer on Jobs

professional people also are influenced by the new technology. Here are a few examples:

- *The computer is being used in the health and medical field (for such things as diagnostics) to relieve the shortage of staff and to extend vital services to the public.*
- *The computer is making legal searches, which reduces the need for law clerks to do the work.*
- *The computer can perform financial and investment analyses, and perhaps relieve high-priced financial and investment analysts from such duties.*

Research indicates that clerical, nonclerical, and even management personnel resist computerization substantially. The reasons for the opposition include: threats to economic security; threats to status or power; increased job complexity; uncertainty and unfamiliarity; changed interpersonal relations; changed superior-subordinate relationships; and increased rigidity or time pressures. In a sense, the computer paces and controls the work in offices in the same way that the assembly line and conveyor belt paces work in a factory.

- *A bank teller was immobilized by an uncooperative computer terminal, which would not post deposits or withdrawals, or calculate interest. The queue of bank customers became longer and more aggravated, and the teller was subjected to verbal abuse. It is not known whether such happenings result in loss of deposits.*
- *An executive was unable to fulfill the president's request and issue a vital report on time, because the computer was "down." In such situations, critical decisions can be delayed or made without needed information.*
- *The breakdown of a stock exchange's computer prevented any transactions from being processed for many hours, thus disrupting the entire financial community and individual investors' plans.*

To some degree, the essentiality of humans is diminished when powerful automation and computer equipment absorb vast segments of work processing, decision making, and even control itself. While on the surface such systems may seem to improve efficiency, overall organizational effectiveness may actually be reduced. Employees' loyalty, morale, and motivation may deteriorate as the employees sense that they are being viewed as replaceable components who happen to service the needs of a monstrous equipment system. The U.S. Postal Service illustrates this:

Despite increasing automation, the U.S. Postal Service seems to be more erratic and more costly to the public. Millions of dollars are spent on automation equipment, and thousands of postal workers have been displaced; yet neither service nor costs have been favorably affected. And employee morale in the postal system is reported to be in serious decline.

There are some organizations that develop systems that are adapted to the needs of people, rather than requiring people to adapt to the system. For example, in an IBM plant in Amsterdam, the production process has been decentralized and placed in the hands of small groups of employees who make their own decisions on such things as production, engineering, quality control, and materials handling. In the United States, companies such as American Telephone and Telegraph Company have been using *job-enrichment techniques* to try to give workers in both plants and offices more dignity and responsibility. These techniques are incorporated in systems design efforts. Unfortunately, examples like these are still too limited in number.

To date, there are no clear-cut guides that indicate the degree to which an application should be computerized or automated. Too often, computer practitioners have interpreted this lack of guideline as a license to automate or computerize everything possible, as long as cost advantage and benefits to justify the investment are obtained. The human factors of systems work have been severely neglected. Computer vendors (when they develop hardware and software) and users (when they design applications) give too little attention to the best balance of assignments between employees and equipment. There is little attempt to structure work and provide an environment that is interesting, motivating, and challenging to employees. The result is often disillusionment and cynicism towards automation, computers, and those technicians who design systems and operate equipment.

The broader economic consideration of whether automation and computers cause unemployment is a moot issue. Some people claim that full employment would be a certainty if work for people, rather than work for machines, were considered more fully. Others feel that technological developments (e.g., computers) are equivalent to progress, and that overall societal progress is more important than some dislocations in work.

THE COMPUTER AND PAPERWORK POLLUTION

Complex societies and organizations like ours are recordkeeping societies and organizations. Paperwork is required for communication, legal, reference, and decision purposes. The massive increase in paperwork (see Exhibit 16–4) simply makes it necessary for machines and computers to do a considerable part of the paperwork processing. It is unlikely that organizations and societies could continue to function without such paperwork-facilitating machines and computers.

Yet, we see a constantly exploding volume of paperwork and therefore we might ask the question, "Is all the paperwork necessary or desirable?"

Distressed by the growth of government paperwork, Congress created a commission (Commission on Federal Paperwork) to study the onerous problem. The commis-

Exhibit 16–4 The Computer and Paperwork Pollution

sion has compiled some formidable figures. Something like $100 billion a year of taxpayers' money is used to pay the bills for federal paper-shuffling.* About half this cost is absorbed by businesses that must fill out forms, and the other half is the cost of the government's printing, processing, and filing requirements. If one included the paperwork of state and local governments, in addition to the federal government, the total paperwork cost of all government might well be about $200 billion a year! And the problem seems to keep on growing.

The computer's enormous capacity and speed, its printers, and related copying and reproducing equipment create data pollution. Citizens are bombarded by junk mail, generated by computer-processed mailing lists that marketers appear to use indiscriminately. Managers and employees are saturated with seemingly endless reports (many of which are unclear to the person who is not computer-oriented), which add to the paperwork pollution that abounds in most offices. Useless reports often clutter files, desks, window sills, and other storage spaces; and this paperwork avalanche undoubtedly interferes with more productive activities.

Computer errors also plague people—including management, consumers, and employees. Here are a few so-called "horror stories":

- *A young pneumonia patient received a bill from a hospital computer that charged him not only for his chest ailment but also for delivery room nursery costs—alleging that he had given birth to a baby girl.*
- *One man gave twenty magazine subscriptions to friends as gifts, but the donor got all the magazines, while his friends got all the bills.*
- *One of the largest stockholders of a billion-dollar industrial organization had the name of Alfred A. Smit. The computer misprinted one of his dividend checks, so that his last name formed a four-letter obscene word.*
- *Mary and John Doe are alive and well, and therefore were justifiably surprised to receive a computer-generated notice of their respective deaths from the local Social Security and Blue Cross offices.*
- *You just know I. B. Gone will never pay his tax bill. The computer-printed tax bill was mailed to the correct address, but the addressee has been dead for over forty years!*

Few individuals have been fortunate enough not to receive computer-generated bills that were either indecipherable or just plain incorrect. Most people find it difficult, if not impossible, to obtain prompt clarification or correction of such computer-created bills. The inflexibility of many computer applications makes them unable to cope with exception cases or inquiries. For instance, merchandise is often returned by mail after the computer-generated bills for the original purchases have been mailed.

* This means that U.S. citizens are paying about $500 per person for federal government paperwork.

When payment is not received within the stated time, the account is flagged as delinquent, and service charges may be added. Sometimes a comedy of errors results whereby returned merchandise is not recorded as a credit but as an additional charge.

In a specific case, a lawsuit for $100,000 was filed against a major chain of department stores. When the complainant returned merchandise that he had purchased costing $16.78, his account was again charged, instead of being credited. He complained to a store representative, but in spite of assurance that correction would be made, another entry caused still another incorrect charge. After several months of trying to get the account straightened out, he closed his account and returned his credit card. Then he began to receive letters from a collection agency. In all, the customer received forty-two different statements, past-due notices, and letters from collection agencies and attorneys—when, in fact, he owed the company no money at all. Finally, he filed a suit for damages as a way of alerting the company that its system was malfunctioning.

The Federal Truth in Lending Act gives the customer some protection against billing mistakes or bills that are in dispute. It is difficult to attribute such errors to a particular cause; each occurrence requires a careful audit before blame can be fixed. Often it is true that many errors can be traced to human fallibility (e.g., key punching the wrong data), poorly designed computer applications, and inadequate controls. However, other errors may occur because the computer hardware and software that the vendor supplied are malfunctioning.

If such nuisance errors occur in relatively simple data-processing like billing, the manager should be concerned: the computer could supply him/her with faulty information, which then would be used for vital decision making (e.g., selecting among alternative investment opportunities). Even more dramatically, recall the president in the movie, *Dr. Strangelove,* trying futilely to countermand the computer-controlled order for the U.S. military to launch an unwarranted air strike against Russia. Here is yet another such example:

A state policeman radioed an inquiry about the license plate of a speeding automobile to the police computer information system. The computer relayed back the message that the automobile was stolen. The policeman stopped the vehicle, and, because the driver reached into his pocket, shot and killed the driver. The policeman feared the driver was reaching for a weapon; but actually the driver was reaching for his driver's license. He had been driving fast to get to a hospital where his father was gravely ill. After the killing, a complete check revealed that the dead man was the legitimate owner of the vehicle—which, indeed, had been stolen several months ago. However, the car had been recovered and returned to the owner but the police records on the computer were not yet updated to include the recovery of the car!

Exhibit 16–5 The Computer and Privacy

THE COMPUTER AND PRIVACY

Continuing technological improvements in computers have made large-scale data files economically and technically feasible. Data that once were scattered, unintegrated, and uneconomical to collect, store, retrieve, and analyze can now become centralized, integrated, and relatively inexpensive. Because of this development, government's and business' need for improved information must be balanced by the individual's protection against invasion of privacy, as well as against other potential misuses of such concentrated information (e.g., "big-brother-type snooping"—see Exhibit 16–5).

Thus, the computer joins the ranks of those technical developments that have the potential to attack the individual's right to privacy: polygraphing, personality testing, truth drugs, wire tapping devices, and drugs and brain surgery (both of which can manipulate an individual's personality).

It would seem that the First Amendment of the American Constitution, which guarantees our rights to freedom of speech, press, and association, was intended to have a corollary: that we also have the right *not* to communicate. This means that we have the right to choose whom to communicate with, and the terms on which to communicate.

Computer files have been misused in many ways. Here are only a few examples:

- *Credit bureaus have massive files of data on many millions of people. Although there is some evidence that the data in such files can be inaccurate or out of date, nevertheless, the files are used to determine whether a person will be granted a needed loan or offered a job with an organization. Faulty data may seriously affect an individual's well being.*
- *Business organizations and government have sub rosa means of circumventing various laws against discrimination on the basis of race, sex, age, etc. Employee and potential employee records may contain special codes that permit the organization to automatically bypass "undesirables" for certain positions.*
- *The government itself has used data banks to harass citizens who have differing political views (e.g., leftists) or social mores (e.g., hippies).*

Some years back, a national data bank, which would have integrated and expanded the government's scattered data-files, was in the planning stage. Had this bank actually been established, it might have integrated such diverse data on citizens as: income tax; social security; military service; criminal; welfare; and education. However, a master plan for this monolithic data bank was increasingly opposed, as the concern grew over the misuse of information in some government agencies (e.g., the Central Intelligence Agency, the Federal Bureau of Investigation, and the Internal Revenue Service), and as the Watergate Affair unfolded and exploded. Indeed, legislation developed to restrain both government and business from setting up such computer data-banks.

- The Consumer Credit Protection Act, as amended in 1971, gives the consumer the right of access, and the right to challenge credit information collected by credit agencies.
- The Privacy Act of 1974 imposes restraints on federal departments and agencies in order to prevent them from misusing or compromising data concerning individuals.
- The Family Educational Rights and Privacy Act of 1974 (Buckley Amendment) restricts the release of data from files in federal agencies and educational institutions to persons who have a clear "right to know."
- The proposed Bill 1984,* considered by Congress, would extend the Privacy Act of 1974 to the private sector as well as to state- and local-government bodies.
- A number of states have passed their own laws protecting their citizens' privacy, and additional states have legislation in various stages of development.

Within the next several years, such laws are likely to affect almost every organization that maintains records on employees or customers. Consequently, all organizations would do well to assess their files and output related to personnel and customers carefully. Do employees and customers have the right to fully inspect their records and make corrections, and to be informed whenever data about them are released to any person or organization? Obviously, the increased concern about privacy is forcing systems analysts and programmers to pay more attention to the integrity and control aspects of their systems and programs.

THE COMPUTER AND ELECTRONIC TRANSFER OF FUNDS (ETF)†

Our check-oriented and credit-oriented society generates an enormous amount of paperwork. Exhibit 16–6 illustrates the movement of a check through the Federal Reserve System. Here, a check may take six to eight days to clear through the system. Both the volume of paperwork created and the time delays make the system inefficient.

Proposals have been made to develop a so-called "checkless" society; some authorities go even further, suggesting a "cashless" society as well. In such a society, each person would have a machine-readable universal identification card to use instead of cash or a check (see Exhibit 16–7). In order for such a system to function broadly, electronic computer files would have to be available for most individuals in our society.

When an individual made a purchase (except for small convenience items like newspapers), the person's identification card would be machine read at the point of sale (POS), and data about the transaction (i.e., customer's identification number; store number; product identification number; and dollar amount of the purchase)

* This bill is most appropriately numbered, since George Orwell's novel *1984* forecasted a society that monitored virtually every phase of a person's life.

† The U.S. Postal Service may soon start an electronic mail service. In this system, a person would bring his/her letter to a post office, where it would be transmitted by satellite to the distant post office of the addressee. Supposedly, this would ensure one-day delivery; and it has been claimed that the cost of electronic mail delivery could be significantly reduced, compared to conventional truck, railroad, and air delivery service.

Exhibit 16–6 The Existing Check-Oriented Society

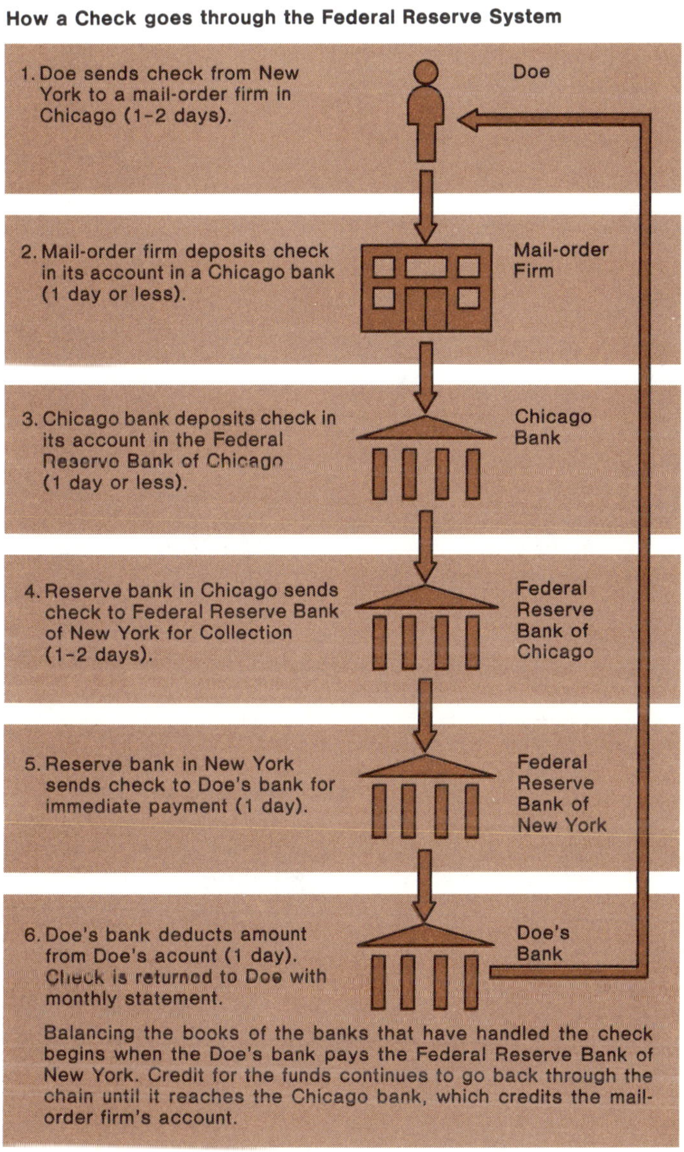

would be transmitted through the system electronically. The data would be used not only to update the department store's record (e.g., inventory and sales) but also to update the customer's record in his/her bank. That is, funds could be transferred electronically from the customer's bank account, and recorded in the department

Exhibit 16–7 The Electronic Transfer of Funds

store's bank account, thus significantly reducing paperwork requirements. This approach would keep data records and money transfers up to date. Currently, there is a time lag; usually, billing is generated once a month, and then several days lapse before a check clears through the banking system.

Some current examples of this approach exist. In addition, there are some related, limited approaches. For example:

- Banks now provide electronic banking terminals (or pushbutton banking) that allow bank customers to withdraw or deposit moneys during any hours (evenings, weekends, and holidays).
- For some years, large businesses have submitted income tax and social security data to the Federal Internal Revenue Service via magnetic tape.
- Some businesses' payrolls are automatically forwarded to employees' bank accounts, and therefore no payroll checks are needed. The federal government has also begun this service for some of its disbursements (e.g., social security checks are eliminated by depositing funds directly into the person's bank account).

Aside from the sheer cost of a checkless/cashless society, the individual's privacy would be risked. It is possible for the banks and the federal government (through the Federal Reserve Bank) to monitor the electronic data, to infer information about the individual's buying habits, financial records, and so forth, and to track the individual's physical movements, etc.

THE COMPUTER AND CRIME

Safeguards must be built into the computer's activities. In a number of ways, the computer breaks down conventional manual means of control. This breakdown can open avenues for illegal acts that would employ the computer as an electronic accomplice in crime (see Exhibit 16–8).

To some extent, computerization has encouraged the centralization of data-processing records. Paperwork that once was performed by people in a variety of offices (e.g., accounting, payroll, personnel, and purchasing) is now largely processed in a single physical location: the computer department. This has weakened the inherent check-and-balance protection that exists when different departments and individuals perform different phases of an overall job. Centralizing the control of information under one authority can encourage people to manipulate records.

When work is placed on a computer, many of the conventional visual records are modified—indeed, some no longer exist. In a computer, considerable amount of data may be stored and processed in electronic form; such records are invisible to human eyes. Thus, traditional procedures (often involving visual audits) for catching problem areas no longer are as effective in computer applications. Moreover, computer technicians design computer applications and programs that frequently mystify managers and auditors who don't understand computer technology. To an extent, the organization is at the mercy of the computer technocrats.

Exhibit 16–8 Computer Crimes

The complexity of the computer and its mysterious image have encouraged some employees who *are* knowledgeable about computer techniques to misuse their specialized skills. More and more, we hear about computer-related crimes. The U.S. National Bureau of Standards estimated that recent losses due to computer-related fraud have exceeded $200 million per year—and this figure may be low, since a huge subterranean layer of undetected or unreported computer crimes is likely. Some examples:

- *The chief teller of a large bank in New York City stole $1.5 million from the bank over a period of three years. The teller had used the computer to assist him in shuffling money back and forth among accounts, so that any account could be made to look normal when necessary—for instance, when interest was due. He chose to steal only from accounts with very little activity so that the chance of someone noticing an error would be small. If, however, an account holder noticed a discrepancy and complained, the problem would be reported directly to the embezzler himself, since he was the chief teller. He could then make a rapid adjustment by "borrowing" from another account to correct the one being questioned. Actually, a fortuitous event caused the discovery of his crime: the investigation of a bookmaking betting operation, where the chief teller was placing bets as high as thirty thousand dollars a day.*

- *Some employees of a large insurance company, including members of top management, used computers to extensively falsify the company's records. Computer records were created for which no real insurance policies existed. Of the 97,000 policies the company claimed to have in force—more than three billion dollars' worth—two-thirds were false. A secret code associated with each policy enabled those in on the deception to distinguish the real policies from the fake ones; but to anyone else, they all appeared to be sound insurance policies. These policies were then sold to other insurance companies (this is a fairly common practice known as "reinsurance"). The company that first writes the policy gets immediate cash for it, and the buying company then collects the periodic premiums from the policyholders and pays whatever benefits accrue. When auditors asked to see the paperwork behind any of these fictional policies, they were put off for a few hours. This allowed sufficient time to fabricate the applications, the doctor's certificates, etc., and to submit them for inspection. If the auditor wanted further verification and wrote the policyholder directly, the address given turned out to be the home address of some member of the staff who was in on the fraud. Occasionally, of course (and with statistical regularity), one of the fictional policyholders had to "die." Those responsible for the fraud then collected the additional benefit of the insurance payment. The fraud was finally discovered when an ex-employee decided to reveal the entire situation—which, of course, precipitated the crash of the company as well as criminal action against those involved in the fraud.*

- *A young man occasionally rummaged through the trash cans outside the offices of a telephone company for discarded equipment he might be able to use. One day he found records that revealed the codes and procedures for ordering equipment from the company's warehouses. It only required keying in the necessary codes via touch-tone telephone. The young man was able to order all the equipment he wanted, using the codes he had found. He opened up a shop as a supplier of specialized electronic equipment, all of which he got just by picking up his phone and ordering from the telephone company's computer. One of the young man's partners revealed the scheme to authorities. After the young man was released from jail, he went into business as a computer-security expert, advising organizations on how to improve the design of their computer systems to make them more tamper-proof.*

It is disturbing that crimes like these often escape discovery when monitored by normal controls and are identified only by chance events. A report of the Systems Accountability Control Project of the Institute of Internal Auditors indicates a substantial deficiency of auditing procedures in the search for fraud in computer applications. The computer can do things faster and better, and this seems to apply to the use of the computer for criminal purposes. The Stanford Research Institute has indicated that the national average for all bank frauds was $19,000, while the average for computer-aided bank frauds was about $500,000, or a ratio of almost 25 to 1. If this continues, computer users may be facing the same type of insurance crisis as other professionals (e.g., physicians, lawyers) who are concerned with malpractice, because protection from fraud and errors may become prohibitively expensive. In addition, white-collar crime is often given very lenient penalties (if any) in our criminal justice system. In effect, this can encourage the continuation and growth of such crime; the rewards may be greater than any prospective penalty, even if the criminal is caught.

There is even concern that organized crime might employ computers, for instance, to help their gamesmanship in gambling activities, and to improve their master plans for robberies.

Summary

Despite its pervasiveness in society, the computer remains somewhat mysterious to many people.

It has affected people's work greatly; if we include plant automation among the computerized activities, the impact has been enormous. People disagree as to whether this impact has been favorable, unfavorable, or somewhere in between. Generally, the feeling is that the use of such equipment tends to increase productivity, permit growth without comparable increases in work force, and create new types of jobs. On the other hand, computers and automation, at minimum, have tended to cause changes in the nature of some work, and to eliminate some jobs. Not many organizations, probably, have given enough attention to using the computer to make work more rewarding to workers.

Paperwork pollution has increased enormously, along with modern computing and reproducing machinery. This pollution includes the sheer volume of paperwork, as well as the number of errors and unclear data in the paperwork.

The computer's great power has increased the concern that the computer might be used to invade people's privacy and rights.

Some developments suggest that we are heading towards a society that uses electronics to transfer funds; this would mean that money and checks would eventually become almost artifacts.

An increasing number of reports indicate that the computer is becoming a favorite aid of the white-collar criminal.

These major social issues indicate (even if from a somewhat negative vantage point) the enormity of the impact computers are having on each individual and on modern civilization as a whole.

Terms to Learn

Automation
Job enrichment
Paperwork pollution
Privacy
Electronic transfer of funds (ETF)

Review Questions

1. Computers have been in existence since the 1950s. Why is there still some apprehension and confusion about them?
2. Defend the statement that "computers bring more benefits than harm to workers."
3. Argue for the statement that "computers, as currently used, have greatly harmed many workers and occupations."
4. Try to envision how computers might be used to enhance the work of:
   a. A blue-collar worker;
   b. A white-collar worker;
   c. A professional technician; *and*
   d. A manager.
5. How might the *paperwork pollution* generated by computer and reproducing equipment be abated?
6. What are the laws that give *protection* to the individual against *invasion of his/her privacy* by computerized systems?
7. Describe the *electronic transfer of funds* that may occur in the future, and how it would work if you purchased some item (say an automobile).
8. What steps can management take to *protect* against the *manipulation of the computer's records* that might result in losses due to fraud or embezzlement?
9. Discuss whether, on the whole, the computer has made a positive or a negative contribution to the progress of society.

SECTION VI

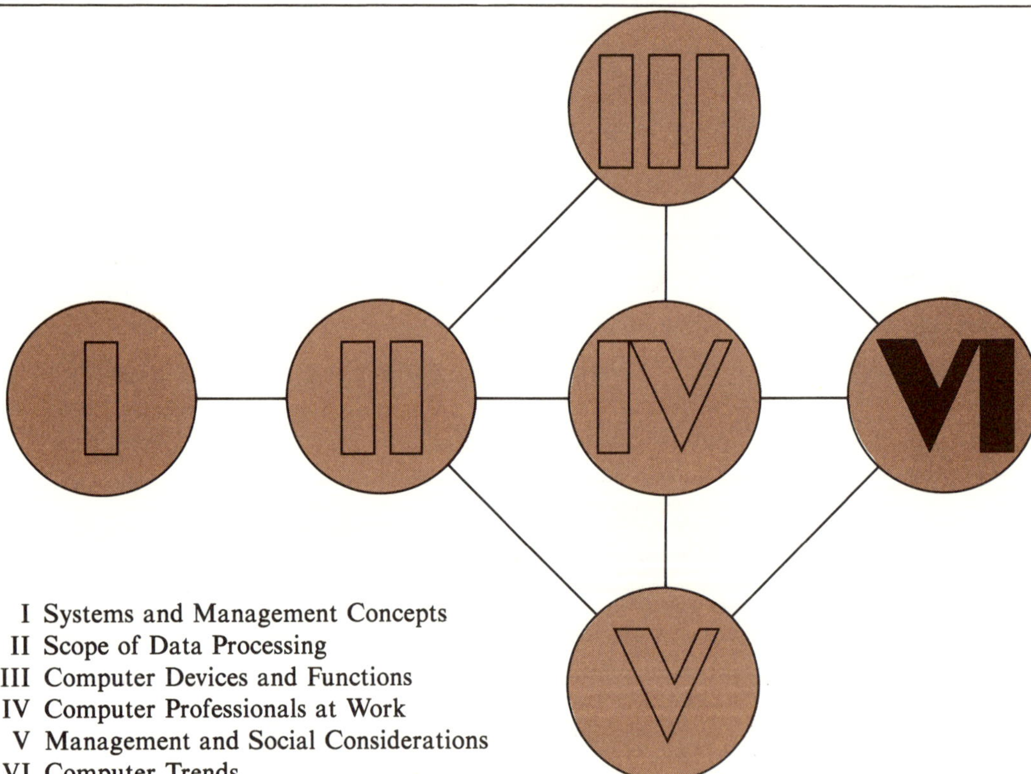

I Systems and Management Concepts
II Scope of Data Processing
III Computer Devices and Functions
IV Computer Professionals at Work
V Management and Social Considerations
VI Computer Trends

COMPUTER TRENDS

Mankind is poised midway between the gods and the beasts.

PLOTINUS

He was not running or cheering any longer. He was back in the Ministry of Love, with everything forgiven, his soul white as snow. . . . He had won the victory over himself. He loved Big Brother.

GEORGE ORWELL

. . . The electric age of servomechanisms suddenly releases man from the mechanical and specialist servitude of the preceding machine age. . . . We are suddenly threatened with a liberation that taxes our inner resources of self-employment and imaginative participation in society. This would seem to be a fate that calls men to the role of artist in society. . . . with electricity and automation, the technology of fragmented processes suddenly fused with the human dialogue and need for over-all consideration of human unity. . . . Men are suddenly nomadic gatherers of knowledge, nomadic as never before, informed as never before, free from fragmentary specialism as never before—but also involved in the total social process as never before; since with electricity we extend our central nervous system globally, instantly interrelating every human experience.

MARSHALL MCLUHAN

A.D.A. Corp.
Warehouse
A.D.A. Corp. Shipping
A.D.A. Corp
Billing
ADA
DRESS
SALE
DRESS
B
TV
MOVIES
TV
BUYS
TV
CLASSES
Mrs. Consumer
T&W BANKING
COMPUTER AID

CHAPTER 17

COMPUTER TRENDS

GENERAL TRENDS

The computer industry has grown extraordinarily since its beginning in the 1950s. Now it looms as one of the largest industries in the United States. Gradually, the computer is widening its scope; increasingly, it is affecting the entire world.

The computer industry is likely to double in dollar volume every five years. Total user spending of data processing in the United States is likely to rise from about 2 percent of the gross national product in the 1970s to more than 10 percent in the 1990s (or from about $100 per capita in the 1970s to more than $1,200 per capita in the 1990s).

Chapter 17* discusses some of the computer-related technical developments that are likely in the future, and forecasts how these developments are apt to affect business and society.

TECHNICAL TRENDS

Here are some of the computer-related technical trends that are anticipated (see also Exhibit 17–1):

1. Computers are becoming more powerful and less expensive. This trend is expected to continue. One study indicated that the CPUs of fifth-generation computers will be more than 100 times more effective (in terms of both cost and performance) than the CPUs of first-generation computers. Modern computers are becoming increasingly miniaturized, fast, and able to hold more data.
2. Computer power may well become available in much the same way that electricity and telephone services are today. A very large-scale central computer, servicing numerous users, can make data banks available that no individual organization can feasibly maintain.
3. The information explosion will cause the government, libraries, organizations, and other institutions to use new methods of computer storage to relieve the mountains of traditional paperwork, journals, books, and so on.
4. Integrated computer-communication networks will emerge that will speed up data processing, permit decisions to be made on a more timely basis, and eliminate considerable paperwork between organizations and among the units of an organization.
5. Computers will become continually easier to use. Programming languages will become more versatile, while allowing the user to use natural language (i.e., English) when communicating with the computer.
6. Organizations already using the computer will begin to use it largely for high-level management decision-making purposes.

* Refer back to Chapters 3, 15, and 16 for a discussion of related material.

Exhibit 17–1 Some Computer Systems Trends

Hardware

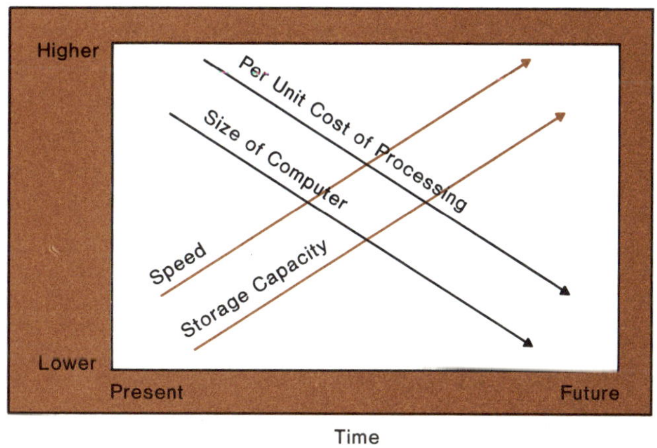

Systems and Programming

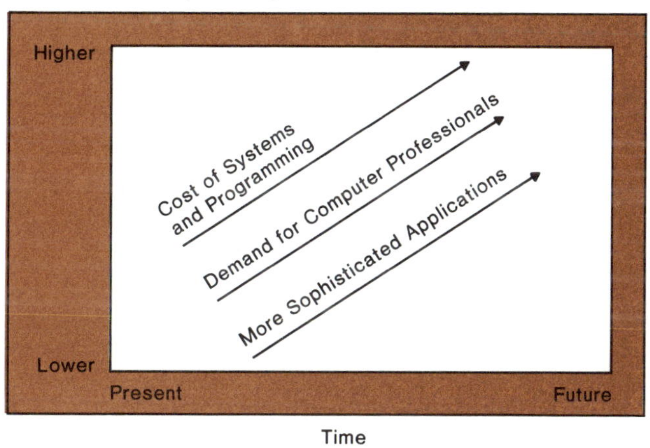

7. There will be vast libraries of application packages for specific functional areas and industries. These packages will eliminate the need to duplicate individual applications. Such packages are particularly important for the growing number of small business and individual users that may not have programming facilities.
8. There will be an interface between the computer and automation in manufacturing facilities, office word-processing, laboratory instrumentation, etc. This will make for a more integrated system in organizations.

9. There will be input and output breakthroughs, including devices that will reliably and economically handle typewritten and handwritten input, spoken communication between people and computers, and pictorial images and graphics.
10. Research on the potential of implanting a computer memory in humans will progress. Such an implanted memory could store many millions of characters of data, and be "on call" by the human being's brain. For instance, a lawyer could have an implant containing all relevant legal precedents so that they could be rapidly retrieved when needed.
11. Distributed data-processing and computer education are spreading knowledge about computer use. By the 1990s, the majority of workers will in some way be affected by computers. There will be substantial, continued demand for computer technicians, particularly systems analysts, programmers, maintenance and repair specialists. Only the health-services field will have comparable growth in demand for workers.
12. While the cost of computer hardware is declining, the relative costs of software and staffing are increasing. Thus, a prime focus will be on how to use hardware and software to increase the productivity of computer technicians and the end-users.

These technical trends will influence the future patterns of management and society. We will now consider what some of these patterns may be.

MANAGEMENT AND SOCIAL TRENDS

Even though computers have had their limitations and caused some disappointments, the impact of the computer cannot be minimized. Some of the possible future developments (see also Exhibit 17–2) include:

1. A substantial part of work may eventually be done at home, using a data terminal that is linked by communications lines to the employer's or to a computer utility's central computer. It is not difficult to imagine many occupations that are adaptable to this return to working at home: for instance, staff experts; accountants; lawyers; designers; etc.
2. The consumer may shop and order goods via the telephone or a combination television-catalog-computer data terminal, which is linked by communications lines to the major retail warehouses. People will be able to select the category of merchandise to be displayed (in color) on a giant television screen in their home. When the consumer is ready to order, he/she will simply depress a few keys to immediately send a message about the order to the retail outlet.
3. Because personal computers will be inexpensive, individuals and families will use them for such things as: monitoring use of energy (e.g., electricity and heat) and security systems (e.g., fire and burglary); on-the-spot health checkups (e.g., pulse

Exhibit 17–2 A Personal Computer

and temperature); preparing diversified and healthy menus; and balancing checkbooks and preparing income tax statements.

4. Students can receive much of their schooling at home, using a combined television-computer data terminal, which will serve as their private tutor. Such a device can provide almost complete flexibility in terms of curriculum selection. However, the need for human teachers will not be eliminated completely.
5. The nation's financial system will be largely handled by electronic computers and communications lines. Little if any conventional money or checks will be used. When a person makes a purchase, the proper bank account can be instantaneously charged at the time of the transaction. This will eliminate not only the need for current billing paperwork but also delays in collection.
6. It may become less expensive and faster to send mail and messages electronically than via conventional mail. Also, word-processing machines are being used more widely, making the routine preparation and handling of correspondence, reports, etc., more efficient.
7. Instantaneous communication, computation, and information will permit governments to function in a potentially more democratic fashion. Collectively and individually, the citizens can make their opinions known and thus influence government decision making more directly. The town hall concept of total citizen participation will again become feasible, and the need for remote representative government could recede.

If these predictions come to pass, the home and family will regain much of their recently diminished importance. The fruition of these predictions can also significantly reduce the extensive social problems related to transportation congestion, the air pollution from automobile exhausts, the vast sums expended for highways, and the great waste of time and resources involved in going to and from work, shopping areas, and schools.

Of course, such predictions create other problems. What would happen to the office buildings in cities if most administrative and other work were performed from home? Would the multi-billion-dollar shopping centers, with their enormous parking areas, become new "ghost" areas if most shopping were done from the comfort of one's own home? Would banks largely become electronic services if the bulk of money transfers involved electronic payments and receipts? And if so, would the numerous bank branches, with their large clerical staffs, be needed?

If children can be educated better at home than at school, what happens to our fantastic investment in school plant and equipment facilities? If educational material can be taped for reuse, how will this affect the large number of teachers?

Some experts even go further than these forecasts. For instance, one of them*

* "Toward an Intelligence Beyond Man's," *Time*, February 20, 1978, p. 59.

suggests that:

> *In another 15 years or so—two more generations of computer evolution, in the jargon of the technologists—we will see the computer as an emergent form of life. . . . We are still in control, but the capabilities of computers are increasing at a fantastic rate, while raw human intelligence is changing slowly, if at all. . . . In the 1990s, when the sixth generation appears, the compactness and reasoning power of an intelligence built out of silicon will begin to match that of the human brain. . . . Computer intelligence is growing by leaps and bounds, with no natural limit in sight. But human evolution is a nearly finished chapter in the history of life. The human brain has not changed, at least in gross size, in the past 100,000 years, and while the organization of the brain may have improved in that period, the amount of information and wiring that can be crammed into a cranium of fixed size is limited.*

Some social scientists express grave concerns about some of these trends. They ask such questions as:

- Will humans become too dependent on computers and thus weaken our capacities to do arithmetic, analyze problems, etc.?
- If we can do most of our work, shopping, studying, and so on in the home, will this create an environment of isolation, and psychological problems?
- Will computer technology, as it continues to permeate our society, accelerate the problems related to unemployment? Modern technology has already indicated the obsolescence of most unskilled workers and farmers. Will semiskilled workers, office workers, and even some skilled workers be next?
- Can the human race become, at some point, subservient to computers?

Such developments suggest that the computer will have a substantial impact on our society, and on the ways in which businesses, government, and other organizations operate. In light of this, progressive managers—in making their overall plans and decisions—will do well to carefully consider the broader implications of computers.

Summary

The computer industry will continue to have a dynamic future. More computer power will become available to users at lower cost.

As the computer permeates all sizes of organizations, including small enterprises and even the home, it will substantially affect the conduct of business and government as well as the style of life in the nation.

The computer is becoming as essential to work and personal life as such aids as the telephone and television set.

Terms to Learn

Computer utility
Integrated computer-communication network
Natural language
Computer implant
Personal computer

Review Questions

1. Discuss the *future growth prospects* of the computer industry. Where is the major growth likely to take place (e.g., in what industries, in what geographical areas, in what job occupations)?
2. Identify some of the likely *computer trends for hardware and software* over the next decade or two.
3. Discuss how the hardware and software trends are likely to affect *business enterprises, government,* and even *individuals.*
4. How has the computer affected you as an *individual?* How is it likely to affect you in the future?
5. What do you think are the *most vital challenges to society* posed by the computer over the next two decades?
6. What is the responsibility of the *businessman* regarding computer trends? What is the responsibility of the *government leader* regarding computer trends? What can the *individual citizen* (or groups of citizens) do about influencing the impact of computer trends?

The best invest-
-ments are...
Your general
health is good...
but more exercise
and vitamin B
supplement would
help. Your golf
game can be
improved by...
How should I invest
my $100,000 in
cash?
How is my
general health?
How can I
break par on
the golf
course?

APPENDICES

APPENDIX A

Number Systems

Chapter 5 explored the nature and use of the binary representation that the computer's CPU uses.* Appendix A will cover number systems.

The four number systems that are relevant are as follows:

Name of Number System	*Base*†	*Absolute Values*
Decimal	10	0, 1, 2, 3, 4, 5, 6, 7, 8, 9
Binary	2	0, 1
Octal	8	0, 1, 2, 3, 4, 5, 6, 7
Hexadecimal	16	0 through 9; A, B, C, D, E, F

The latter two systems (octal and hexadecimal) are of interest mostly to the computer technician.

BACKGROUND ON NUMBER SYSTEMS

We tend to take the decimal system for granted because we have used it for so long.

Possibly the earliest numeration system consisted of additive marks (e.g., 𝍸 ||) to

* Since the binary number system was covered in Chapter 5, this appendix will only cover the decimal, octal, and hexadecimal number systems.

† A number's base is indicated as a subscript, as follows: $(n)_{10}$ for decimal; $(n)_2$ for binary; $(n)_8$ for octal; and $(n)_{16}$ for hexadecimal. Without a subscript, technically speaking, the number "10" is of uncertain value. By everyday convention we assume it to be a decimal "ten," but it might be a binary "one, zero," or a hexadecimal or octal "one, zero." A decimal ten is more correctly recorded as $(10)_{10}$. A binary "10" is more correctly recorded as $(10)_2$, which has, of course, a value of decimal two (this was discussed in Chapter 5). By convention, however, the absence of a subscript usually indicates the use of a base-ten number.

represent such things as possessions, number of animals, etc. Each symbol (stroke) represented the same value, regardless of the position it occupied in the number.

Until the sixth century, Europeans used Roman numerals (e.g., VII), which evolved from the additive marks. However, to say the least, Roman numerals were inconvenient for performing mathematical calculations.

The decimal system is believed to have been invented by Hindu mathematicians. The Arabs are known to have used it around the seventh century A.D., and through them it reached Western Europe about 300 years later. But it was not until around the 1600s that the decimal system was used fairly widely in Western civilization. A big factor in its advancement was the development of positional numbering systems, a necessary ingredient of which is a digit representing zero (0). The recognition of the zero represented a major advance in human knowledge of arithmetic. In such systems there are a limited number of symbols, and the symbols represent different values according to the position they occupy in the number (e.g., while 5 = V, 51 does not equal VI because the meaning of 5 has changed with the change in its position).

There is nothing sacred about the decimal (base-10) system. The only reason that it was originally developed and has become so widely used is that people happen to have ten fingers. Other systems have been created in history. For example, the Babylonians had a base-60 system, and the Mayans had a base-20 system.

DECIMAL SYSTEM

In the attempt to understand CPU codes, it will help if we refresh our minds about our own decimal system and the meaning of our positional notation.

Each numeric symbol has a fixed value that is one digit higher than the symbol immediately preceding it, in the progression from the smallest to the largest number: 0, 1, 2, 3, 4, 5, 6, 7, 8, 9. When several positions are used, the value is dependent upon the relative position of the digits as well as on the digit values themselves. In any system of numbers, the digit position on the extreme right has the smallest value and is known as the low-order position (i.e., the least significant digit). The increase in value of each digit position depends upon the base (or radix) of the number system. Each number system is identified by its base, which indicates the number of digits used in the system. The decimal system with a base of 10 uses the ten different digits, 0 through 9. The highest number to be represented by a single digit is one less than the base.

Characteristic of all numbering systems is the positional numbering system. Thus, in the decimal numbering system, each digital position is assigned a value equal to a power of 10. These positions of the decimal system are commonly called (from right to left): units; tens; hundreds; thousands; etc. The following table lists some values of powers of 10.

Exponential Value* of Positions	10^6	10^5	10^4	10^3	10^2	10^1	10^0
Integer Value of Position	1,000,000	100,000	10,000	1,000	100	10	1

The values positioned to the left of the least significant digit increases by powers of 10. For example, the decimal 3,692 really means:

10^3	10^2	10^1	10^0
1,000	100	10	1
3	6	9	2

$2 \times 1 = 2$
$9 \times 10 = 90$
$6 \times 100 = 600$
$3 \times 1{,}000 = 3{,}000$
$(3{,}692)_{10}$

This may also be expressed as follows:

$$3{,}692 = 3 \times 10^3 + 6 \times 10^2 + 9 \times 10^1 + 2 \times 10^0$$

The decimal number in each digital position is multiplied by its respective digital-position value. The products added together form the total.

In the decimal number 3,692, the right-most digit (2) has the smallest value and is considered the least significant digit, while the left-most digit (3) has the highest value and is considered the most significant digit.

An important rule is that any base to the zero power equals 1 (thus, $2^0 = 1$, $8^0 = 1$, $16^0 = 1$, etc.). This rules applies to any positional numbering system. Indeed, all the general rules described above (i.e., about positional power, exponentiation, etc.) apply to all numbering systems, regardless of base.

OCTAL SYSTEM

Chapter 5 indicated how the pure binary system or modified versions of it (BCD, EBCDIC) are used in the computer's CPU to represent data.

While such data representations are fine for the CPU, they frequently are unwieldly for humans to handle. If the computer programmer or operator had to write down a set of, say, thirty-two bits, the chances for human error would be great. This is illustrated by the following example of a thirty-two bit set expressed in binary and the corresponding octal and hexadecimal shorthand used by programmers and operators:

* An exponent is used to denote a number that is raised to a specified power. That is, an exponent of 2 indicates a number raised to the second power, or a number multiplied by itself. For example: $4^2 = 4 \times 4 = 16$; $4^3 = 4 \times 4 \times 4 = 64$.

Binary	10010111101000110111011101110111
Octal	2 2 7 5 0 6 7 3 5 6 7
Hexadecimal	9 7 A 3 7 7 7 7

Obviously, using either octal or hexadecimal notation to describe the underlying binary digits is less error-prone and more efficient for humans. When a computer uses one of these number systems for operator or programmer purposes, the computer messages regarding the instructions and data stored in memory are in that notation rather than in binary form. Many of the computer console displays on the operator's panel may show a light for each binary digit, but the lights are marked off in groups of three or four bits so that the operator can read them off in octal or hexadecimal notation.

Because of the simple relationship between binary and octal numbers, both can be converted from one system to the other by means of inspection. The base or radix of the octal system is eight, which means that the largest possible digit is 7 (0, 1, 2, 3, 4, 5, 6, 7). There is no 8 or 9 in the octal number system. Converting from binary to octal is rather simple, since one octal position is equivalent to three binary positions. Here are the octal bit equivalents:

Octal Number	*Bit Equivalents*			
	4	2	1	(bit values)
0	0	0	0	
1	0	0	1	
2	0	1	0	
3	0	1	1	
4	1	0	0	
5	1	0	1	
6	1	1	0	
7	1	1	1	

Any binary number can be converted to octal by grouping the bits in 3s, starting at the right-most bit and then reconverting each group into its octal equivalent. For example, the following binary number is converted to octal: 1 1 0 0 1 0 1 0

011	*001*	*010*	
3	1	2	equals 312 octal equivalent

Similarly, it is simple to convert octal numbers to binary equivalents. For instance, take the octal number 431:

4	*3*	*1*	
100	011	001	equals 100011001 binary equivalent

If one wants to convert octal numbers to decimal values, that can be done easily. First, convert the octal number to binary; then convert the binary number to decimal. For instance, the number $(431)_8$ would result in the following decimal value:

2^8	2^7	2^6	2^5	2^4	2^3	2^2	2^1	2^0
256	128	64	32	16	8	4	2	1

$$
\begin{aligned}
1 \times 1 &= 1 \\
1 \times 8 &= 8 \\
1 \times 16 &= 16 \\
1 \times 256 &= \underline{256} \\
& \quad (281)_{10}
\end{aligned}
$$

Let us analyze the octal numbering system in another way. The decimal, or base-10, number system gives values to each position in factors of 10:

Exponential Value of Positions	. . .	10^3	10^2	10^1	10^0
Integer Value of Position	. . .	1000	100	10	1

The binary, or base-2, numbering system gives value to each position in factors of 2:

Exponential Value of Positions	. . .	2^3	2^2	2^1	2^0
Integer Value of Position	. . .	8	4	2	1

The octal, or base-8, numbering system gives value to each position in factors of 8:

Exponential Value of Positions	. . .	8^3	8^2	8^1	8^0
Integer Value of Position	. . .	512	64	8	1

Thus, we can determine the decimal equivalent of an octal number by multiplying the positional values by the corresponding digits and adding the results. For example, let us again look at the octal number 431:

8^2	8^1	8^0
64	8	1
4	3	1

$$1 \times 1 = 1$$
$$3 \times 8 = 24$$
$$4 \times 64 = 256$$
$$(281)_{10}$$

To find the octal equivalent of a decimal number, we again use the remainder method, this time dividing by the base 8. For instance, let us determine the octal equivalent of $(281)_{10}$:

	Remainder
0	4
$8\overline{)4}$	3
$8\overline{)35}$	1
$8\overline{)281}$	

Resultant octal number, read from top to bottom $(431)_8$

In converting from decimal to binary, there will probably be fewer errors if one first converts to octal (which requires one-third fewer divisions than if one converts directly to binary) and then substitutes the proper group of three bits for each octal digit.

While the preceding discussion has centered on converting pure binary (base-2) and pure octal (base-8) numbers, we may also use octal as a shorthand for a binary representation of coded data. In general we only do this for codes whose length is evenly divisible by three, since we do not want an octal digit to overlap two code groups. Thus, a computer that uses the standard BCD code would use octal as a shorthand for both pure binary and binary coded data.

HEXADECIMAL SYSTEM

The hexadecimal system (hex for short), like the octal system, is simply a shorthand method of expressing the binary bit patterns within a computer. Each hexadecimal digit stands for four bits. Hexadecimal means sixteen, and the system requires sixteen symbols to represent the possible values. It uses the ten decimal digits (0 through 9), plus the letters A, B, C, D, E, and F. The hexadecimal bit equivalents are:

Decimal Number	*Hexadecimal Character*	*Bit Equivalents*				
		8	4	2	1	(bit values)
0	0	0	0	0	0	
1	1	0	0	0	1	
2	2	0	0	1	0	
3	3	0	0	1	1	
4	4	0	1	0	0	
5	5	0	1	0	1	
6	6	0	1	1	0	
7	7	0	1	1	1	
8	8	1	0	0	0	
9	9	1	0	0	1	
10	A	1	0	1	0	
11	B	1	0	1	1	
12	C	1	1	0	0	
13	D	1	1	0	1	
14	E	1	1	1	0	
15	F	1	1	1	1	

To convert a binary number to its hexadecimal equivalent, one only needs to divide the number into groups of four binary digits, starting from the right, and replace each group of four by the hexadecimal equivalent. For example, the following binary number is converted to hexadecimal: 11001010

1100	*1010*	
C	A	equals CA hexadecimal equivalent

Again, the following binary number is converted to hexadecimal: 011011010011

0110	*1101*	*0011*	
6	D	3	equals 6D3 hexadecimal equivalent

Similarly, it is simple to convert hexadecimal numbers to binary equivalents. For instance, take the hexadecimal number 7B8:

7	*B*	*8*	
0111	1011	1000	equals 011110111000 binary equivalent

If one wants to convert hexadecimal numbers to decimal values, that can be done easily. First, convert the hexadecimal number to binary; then convert the binary number to decimal. For instance, hexadecimal number 7B8 would result in a decimal value as follows:

2^{11}	2^{10}	2^9	2^8	2^7	2^6	2^5	2^4	2^3	2^2	2^1	2^0
2048	1024	512	256	128	64	32	16	8	4	2	1
0	1	1	1	1	0	1	1	1	0	0	0

$$
\begin{aligned}
1 \times 8 &= 8\\
1 \times 16 &= 16\\
1 \times 32 &= 32\\
1 \times 128 &= 128\\
1 \times 256 &= 256\\
1 \times 512 &= 512\\
1 \times 1024 &= \underline{1024}\\
&\quad (1976)_{10}
\end{aligned}
$$

Since the hexadecimal system has a base of 16, each positional value can be expressed as a power of 16:

. . .	16^3	16^2	16^1	16^0
. . .	4096	256	16	1

Thus, we can determine the decimal equivalent of a hexadecimal number by multiplying the positional values by the corresponding digits and adding the results. For example, let's look at the hexadecimal number 10:

16^1	16^0
16	1
1	0

$$
\begin{aligned}
0 \times 1 &= 0\\
1 \times 16 &= \underline{16}\\
&\quad (16)_{10}
\end{aligned}
$$

Let's assume that the hexadecimal digits AF are to be converted to decimal equivalents:

16^1	16^0
16	1
A	F

$$
\begin{aligned}
15 \times 1 &= 15\\
10 \times 16 &= \underline{160}\\
&\quad (175)_{10}
\end{aligned}
$$

It is true that hexadecimal-to-decimal conversion can be accomplished by using expanded notation. But because it is difficult to remember or to mentally compute the values of 16^4, 16^5, etc., hexadecimal-to-decimal conversion tables are available (see Exhibit A–1). The table can be used to quickly convert hexadecimal FA9C4D to a decimal equivalent. Notice that the position (place value) of each hexadecimal digit in the number being converted corresponds to the position of the X below each column. In other words, the first (left-most) digit of FA9C4D (the F) is in the sixth column from the right (or X00000). All the equivalent values must be added to obtain the final decimal result.

Hexadecimal Number	*Table Column Code*		*Decimal Number*
FA9C4D			
	F00000	=	15,728,640
	A0000	=	655,360
	9000	=	36,864
	C00	=	3,072
	40	=	64
	D	=	13
			$(16{,}424{,}013)_{10}$

This indicates the shorthand nature of hexadecimal. In the above example, six characters in hexadecimal represent an eight-digit decimal number.

Exhibit A–1 Hexadecimal to Decimal Conversion Table

Hex	Decimal							
0	0	0	0	0	0	0	0	0
1	268,435,456	16,777,216	1,048,576	65,536	4,096	256	16	1
2	536,870,912	33,554,432	2,097,152	131,072	8,192	512	32	2
3	805,306,368	50,331,648	3,145,728	196,608	12,288	768	48	3
4	1,073,741,824	67,108,864	4,194,304	262,144	16,384	1,024	64	4
5	1,342,177,280	83,886,080	5,242,880	327,680	20,480	1,280	80	5
6	1,610,612,736	100,663,296	6,291,456	393,216	24,576	1,536	96	6
7	1,879,048,192	117,440,512	7,340,032	458,752	28,672	1,792	112	7
8	2,147,483,648	134,217,728	8,388,608	524,288	32,768	2,048	128	8
9	2,415,919,104	150,994,944	9,437,184	589,824	36,864	2,304	144	9
A	2,684,354,560	167,772,160	10,485,760	655,360	40,960	2,560	160	10
B	2,952,790,016	184,549,376	11,534,336	720,896	45,056	2,816	176	11
C	3,221,225,472	201,326,592	12,582,912	786,432	49,152	3,072	192	12
D	3,489,660,928	218,103,808	13,631,488	851,968	53,248	3,328	208	13
E	3,758,096,384	234,881,024	14,680,064	917,504	57,344	3,584	224	14
F	4,026,531,840	251,658,240	15,728,640	983,040	61,440	3,840	240	15
	X0000000	X000000	X00000	X0000	X000	X00	X0	X
Column	8	7	6	5	4	3	2	1

To find the hexadecimal equivalent of a decimal number, we again use the remainder method by dividing by 16. For instance, let's determine the hexadecimal equivalent of the decimal 281:

	Remainder
0	1
16)1	1
16)17	9
16)281	

Resultant hexadecimal number, read from top to bottom $(119)_{16}$

As another example, let's convert decimal 382 to hexadecimal:

	Remainder
0	1
16)1	7
16)23	14 − E
16)382	

Resultant hexadecimal number, read from top to bottom $(17E)_{16}$

However, since we normally do not do short division by 16 unless we have learned all the multiples up through 9 of 16, the above may not be too practical. As a solution, there is another method of converting from decimal to hexadecimal. It may seem circuitous, but it avoids the problem of dividing by 16 and minimizes errors. In this method, one converts from decimal to octal, then from octal to binary, and then from binary to hexadecimal.

As with octal, we may use hexadecimal as a shorthand for binary whether the binary is a base-2 representation or a code. In the latter case, we use hexadecimal as a shorthand only if the code length is evenly divisible by 4, such as EBCDIC, since we do not want the hex digits to overlap two code groups.

Let us assume that the character T is stored in primary storage in EBCDIC code. It would be stored as a byte as follows:

Zone				*Numeric*			
8	4	2	1	8	4	2	1
1	1	1	0	0	0	1	1

The hexadecimal printout would not be "T" but rather "E3." This is because hexadecimal handles each four bits separately. It would interpret 0011 as equivalent to a hexadecimal "3," and interpret 1110 as a hexadecimal "E."

Let us assume that the binary equivalent of the decimal 8 is stored as a byte in EBCDIC code. It would be stored as follows:

Exhibit A–2 Hex Equivalent of EBCDIC

Character	EBCDIC Bit Configuration	Hex
	1100 0000	C0
A	1100 0001	C1
B	1100 0010	C2
C	1100 0011	C3
D	1100 0100	C4
E	1100 0101	C5
F	1100 0110	C6
G	1100 0111	C7
H	1100 1000	C8
I	1100 1001	C9
	1101 0000	D0
J	1101 0001	D1
K	1101 0010	D2
L	1101 0011	D3
M	1101 0100	D4
N	1101 0101	D5
O	1101 0110	D6
P	1101 0111	D7
Q	1101 1000	D8
R	1101 1001	D9
	1110 0000	E0
	1110 0001	E1
S	1110 0010	E2
T	1110 0011	E3
U	1110 0100	E4
V	1110 0101	E5
W	1110 0110	E6
X	1110 0111	E7
Y	1110 1000	E8
Z	1110 1001	E9
0	1111 0000	F0
1	1111 0001	F1
2	1111 0010	F2
3	1111 0011	F3
4	1111 0100	F4
5	1111 0101	F5
6	1111 0110	F6
7	1111 0111	F7
8	1111 1000	F8
9	1111 1001	F9

Exhibit A–3 Printout of Storage

0027E0	D5D640D5	C1D4C540	FF150007	FA00292E	0A0407F1	6A0028C2	00002868	000036E8
002810	00002890	00006FFF	00002800	00006FCC	FFFFFF34	00002858	000027F0	00004140
002840	00000000	00000000	00000000	00000000	00000000	00000000	00008000	08000000
002870	00002974	00002938	02002974	20000050	47000000	47000000	00000000	00000000
0028A0	00002B48	08900909	00002904	00000000	07004700	00000000	090029C4	20000050
0028D0	00002890	0A02D24F	A102A152	5810A20E	58F10010	45EF000C	5810A212	58F10010
002900	A103A0B2	D213A115	A0B7D203	A133A0CB	D204A145	A0D45810	A20E58F1	001045EF
002930	A1A6A216	47F0A026	D24FA102	A1A8F321	A123A1A6	96F0A125	F363A143	A1A296F0
002960	4110A206	4500A0AE	00002858	00002890	0A020A0E	F1F2F3F5	F6C2D6D3	E3404040
002990	F6404040	4040F5F2	52187F40	40404040	40404040	40404040	40404040	40404040
0029C0	40404040	40F1F2F3	F5F64040	40404040	40404040	404040C2	D6D3E340	40404040
0029F0	40404040	40F2F1F5	F6404040	40404040	40404040	404040F5	F2F1F8F7	40404040
002A20	40404040	40404040	40404040	C4C5E2C3	D9C9D7E3	C9D6D540	40404040	40404040
002A50	40404040	404040C1	D4D6E4D5	E3404040	40404040	0000000C	000CE3C8	C540D5E4
002A80	D6C3C5E2	E2C5C440	C9E24040	40404040	40404040	E3C8C540	E3D6E3C1	D340C1D4
002AB0	40404040	40404040	404007FE	615C0000	5B5BC2D6	D7C5D540	5B5BC2C3	D3D6E2C5
002AE0	0A320000	0A320000	47F0F01A	0A320000	C9D1C3C6	E9C9E9F3	F3F20A00	91801002
002B10	10044780	F04858E0	F0609140	10024780	F01A58E0	101C07FE	D501F05C	E0004770
002B40	BA0028F4	0A320000	0A320000	0A320000	0A320000	47F0F01A	C9D1C4C6	E9E9E9E9
002B70	00000000	00000000	00000000	00000000	00000000	00000000	00000000	00000000
006FE0	00000000	00000000	00000000	00000000	00000000	00000000	00000000	00000000

Zone				*Numeric*			
8	4	2	1	8	4	2	1
1	1	1	1	1	0	0	0

In a hexadecimal printout, the "8" would be printed as "F8." The 1000 would be interpreted as a hexadecimal "8," and the 1111 as a hexadecimal "F."

Since each hexadecimal digit is used to represent four binary digits, two hexadecimal digits are needed to represent one byte or eight bits or one EBCDIC character. Exhibit A–2 presents a table summarizing the hex equivalent to EBCDIC.

Since reference to storage locations or bytes on a computer printout takes the form of hexadecimal notation, the computer technician should be familiar with the hexadecimal number system. Exhibit A–3 illustrates such a printout of storage. Without knowledge of hexadecimal, the computer technician would find the printout meaningless.

APPENDIX B

Procedures for Key Punching

While direct entry is expanding in use, considerable use is still made of the off-line key punch to prepare source decks for programs and to generate initial data-files. We will discuss the operation of the IBM 029 key punch, which is one of the most widely used models.* (A picture of the machine appears as Exhibit 7–33 in Chapter 7.) Exhibit B–1 is a schematic of the key punch machine.

The key punch can be operated strictly manually, or it may be made more automatic by a program control card.

Exhibit B–2 displays how the keyboard of the key punch machine looks.† Some of the relevant functional keys are discussed below.

Functional Keys

- *NUMERIC* (numeric shift). This key places the keyboard into a numeric shift or mode for as long as it is held down. (The key is depressed to allow the punching of numbers in an alphabetic field.)
- *ALPHA* (alphabetic shift). The ALPHA key places the keyboard into an alphabetic shift or mode; when not using a program control card, the key punch stays in this mode unless the NUMERIC shift key is depressed. (The ALPHA shift key must be depressed to allow the punching of alphabetic letters in a numeric field.)

* Another widely used key punch, the IBM 026, has a slightly different keyboard, and a few Hollerith codes are printed as different characters compared to the IBM 029. However, the basic ideas in this appendix apply to all key punch machines.

† The keyboard of the key punch is very similar to that of the typewriter. Of course, some of the functional keys are different, and the results are different: a key punch machine produces a punched card rather than a typed letter or document.

Exhibit B–1 Schematic of Key Punch Machine

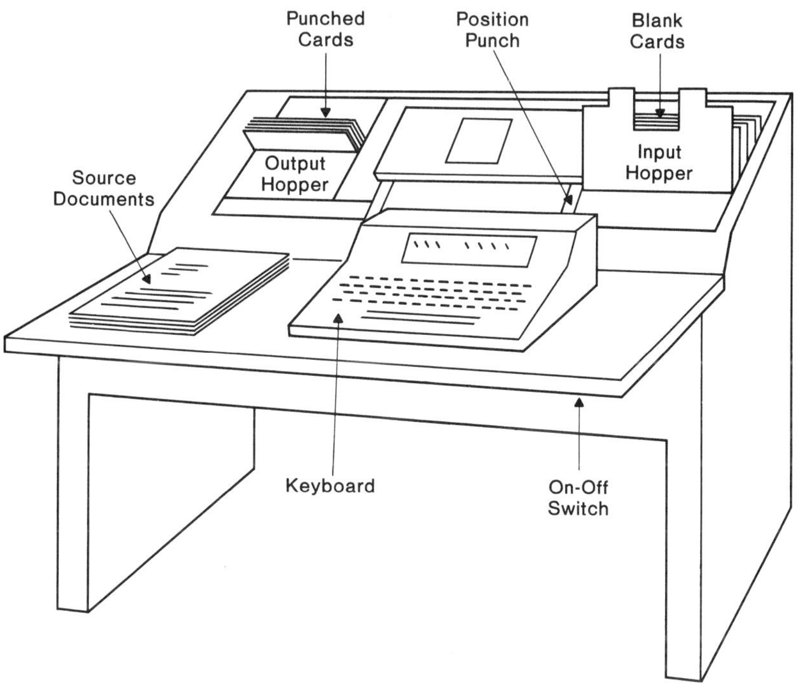

- *DUP* (duplicate). The DUP key allows data from the card at the reading position to be duplicated into the card at the punching position.
- *REL* (release). Depressing the REL key causes the cards at the punching and reading stations to be sent to the next station automatically.
- *FEED* (card feed). When depressed and held, the FEED key will cause two cards to be fed from the hopper of the key punch. If a card is already registered at the punching position, it is inoperative.
- *REG* (register). This key is used when cards are fed manually into the punching or reading stations and the card hopper is not utilized. Depression of this key registers the cards at the punching and reading stations.

Exhibit B–3 shows the feed mechanism part of the key punch machine; this mechanism is located directly over the keyboard.

Exhibit B–2 Keyboard of Key Punch Machine

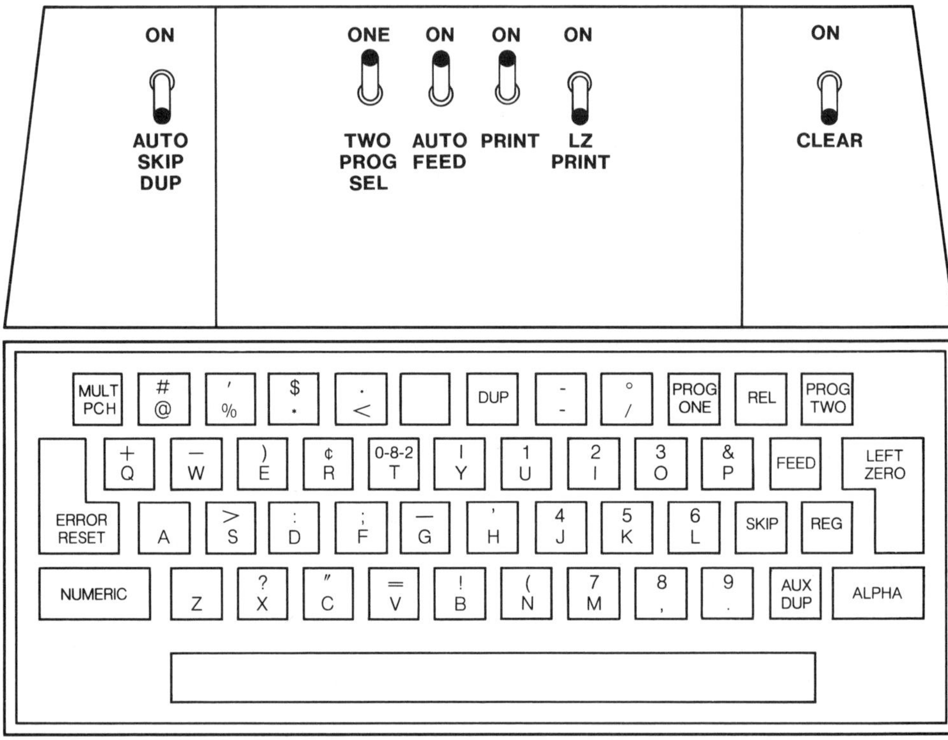

Manual Operation of the Key Punch

Normal use of the key punch in the manual mode is as follows:

1. Set the switches located above the keyboard, so that AUTO FEED and PRINT are on and AUTO SKIP DUP and LZ PRINT are off. The position of the other switches doesn't matter.
2. If not already on, turn on the power switch that is located below the desk-like surface of the key punch.
3. Make sure that there are blank cards in the input hopper at the upper right-hand side of the machine.
4. Depress the FEED key twice. This will feed two cards into the feed mechanism and place one of them at the punching station.

Exhibit B–3 Feed Mechanism of Key Punch Machine

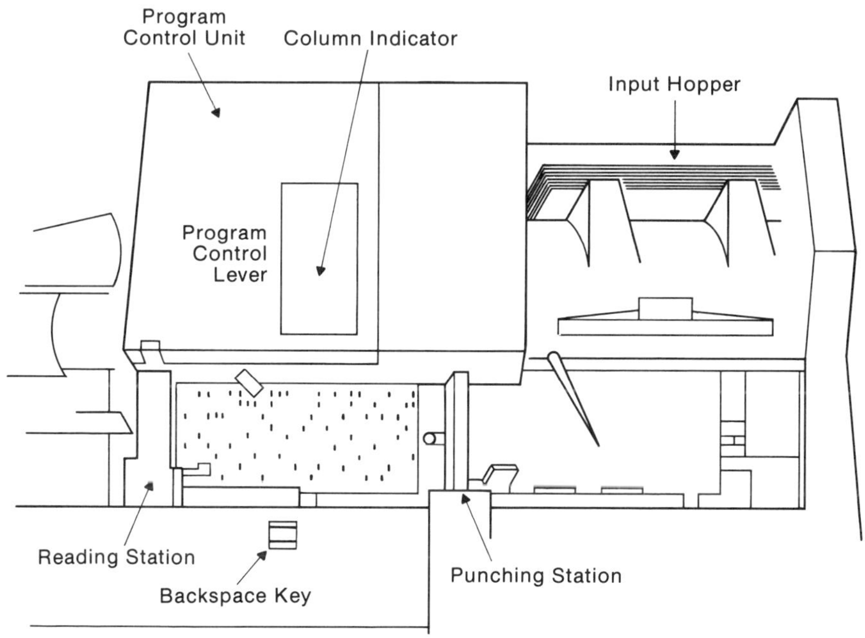

5. Key in the appropriate data. The column indicator keeps the operator informed of the next column to be punched. As with a typewriter, the space bar is used to skip spaces (columns) that are to be left blank. The keyboard keys are normally in alphabetic shift; if numbers or other upper-shift characters are to be punched, the NUMERIC key must be used.
6. When all desired data have been punched, depress the REL key, which will move the punched card to the next station. Then the next blank card can be punched, and so on.
7. When all cards have been punched, push the CLEAR switch to the ON position; this will clear the reading and punching stations of any cards. All cards will be automatically placed in the stacker.

The DUP key can be used to duplicate the data from one card to the next card; the key is depressed for the columns to be duplicated.

The backspace key can be used to move back one column at a time if, for instance, the operator has forgotten to punch something into a bypassed column of a card.

Exhibit B–4 Illustration of a Program Card

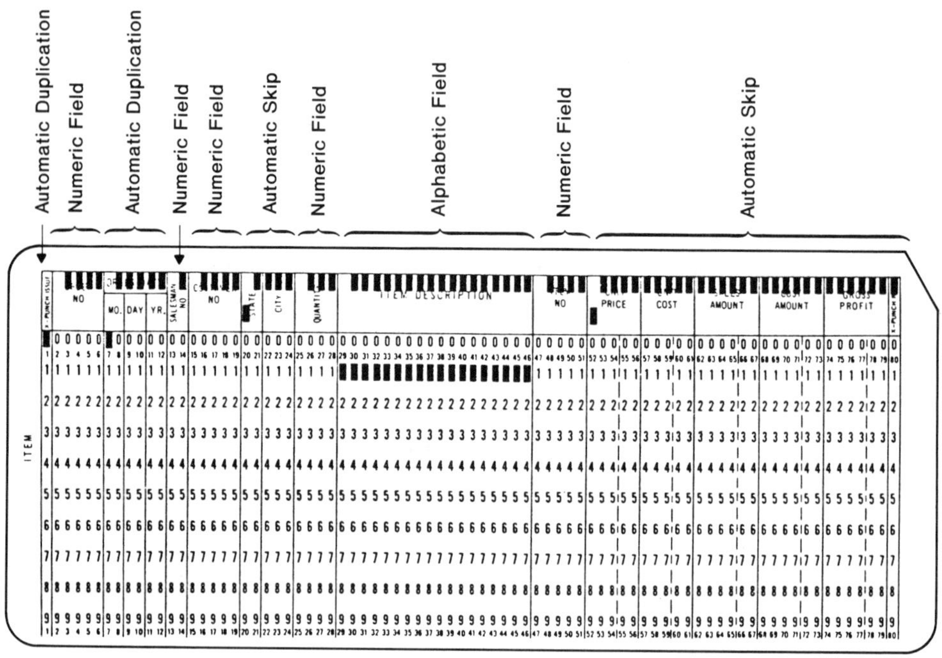

Program Control Operation

The program control unit of the key punch can speed up key punching by making the steps of duplication automatic, skipping columns, and shifting.

The key punch operator must punch a program card. These are the available codes:

Code	*Functions To Be Performed*
Blank	Initiates beginning of a field to be punched manually with numeric data.
0	Initiates automatic duplication.
1	Initiates beginning of a field to be punched manually with alphabetic data.
11	Initiates automatic skipping.
12	Defines the length of a numeric field.
A	Defines the length of an alphabetic field.

Exhibit B–5 Program Control Unit of Key Punch Machine

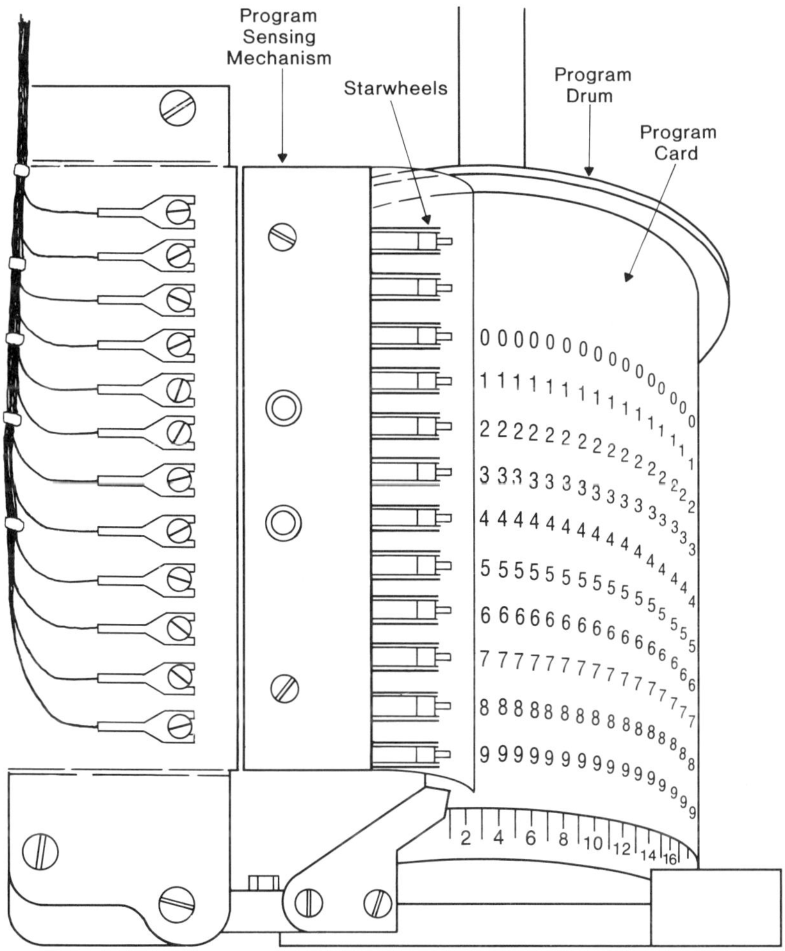

Of course, to punch a program card, the operator must know the application (e.g., which columns are to be skipped, and which fields are alphabetic and which are numeric). Exhibit B–4 illustrates a program card for a particular application.

Before the program drum is removed from the program control unit (see Exhibit B–5), the starwheels must be lifted off the drum. This is done by flipping the program control lever to the right. After putting the program card in place on the drum, the drum must be securely locked into position so that it will rotate properly in the program control unit. The starwheels should remain in the "up" position. The starwheels in the program sensing mechanism detect the punches in the program card; these punches indicate to the machine the automatic functions that are to take place, and the key punch operates accordingly.

To engage the drum, turn the program control lever on; to disengage the drum, turn the lever off.

When using the program control feature, turn the AUTO SKIP DUP switch, as well as the AUTO FEED and PRINT switches, on. Also, set the PRO SEL (program select) switch to ONE.

Two additional switches can be mentioned: when LZ PRINT (leading zeros) is in the OFF position, it will suppress the printing of leading zeroes in a field (thus, the figure will be printed at the top of the card as 100 rather than as 000100). The MULT PCH (multiple punch) key is used in those unusual instances when a punch combination is desired in a particular column and a normal key cannot provide the appropriate punches. The multiple punch key keeps the card from advancing, allowing three keys to punch in one column.

Because of the sensitive mechanism of the program control drum, the novice should obtain personal instruction when first using the program control feature.

APPENDIX C

Procedures for Using a Time-Sharing Data Terminal

A time-sharing data terminal permits the user to have direct entry to a computer in the on-line mode. This means that the user can access a remote computer by picking up a telephone attached to the data terminal and dialing the computer.

There are numerous types of on-line data terminals. To show how the user uses time-sharing services, we will describe one fairly widely used terminal—the teletype machine. This is quite similar to an electric typewriting machine. The operator of the machine can key in certain messages that can be transmitted to the remote computer, and the computer can send printed messages back to the teletype machine. Punched-paper tape can also be used as input/output on the teletype machine.

The Keyboard

Exhibit C–1 presents the keyboard of the teletype machine (Model 33). There are other model machines; their keys and buttons may be somewhat different.

Operation of the Data Terminal

Let's assume that Joe Doe wishes to solve a business problem quickly. He turns to his teletype machine, presses a button marked ORIG, and dials the computer's phone number. The computer types a message on the data terminal, in effect saying, "I am here waiting to serve you." Then the computer causes the terminal to type out:

USER NUMBER—

Joe types in his assigned number, which authorizes use of the computer.

USER NUMBER—X99999

Next, the computer needs to know which computer programming language Joe intends to use. Let's assume that Joe wishes to use the BASIC programming language. The computer's message and Joe's answer would look like this:

SYSTEM—BASIC

Then the computer wants to know whether Joe intends to write a new program or to use one he has already written, used, and saved. Let's assume that he intends to write a new program. The computer types and Joe replies:

NEW OR OLD—NEW

The computer now requests a name for the new program. Each program must have a unique name so that it can be distinguished from all other programs in the particular computer's storage. Let's assume that Joe assigns the name PAYROLL to his program.

NEW PROBLEM NAME—PAYROLL

Finally, the computer types:

READY

Now Joe may begin typing his program on the keyboard. If he makes a mistake along the way that violates the rules of the BASIC programming language, the computer will print a message telling him, and giving him a chance to correct it. Finally, when Joe has keyed in the entire program and it has been entered into the

Exhibit C–1 Keyboard of Teletype Machine

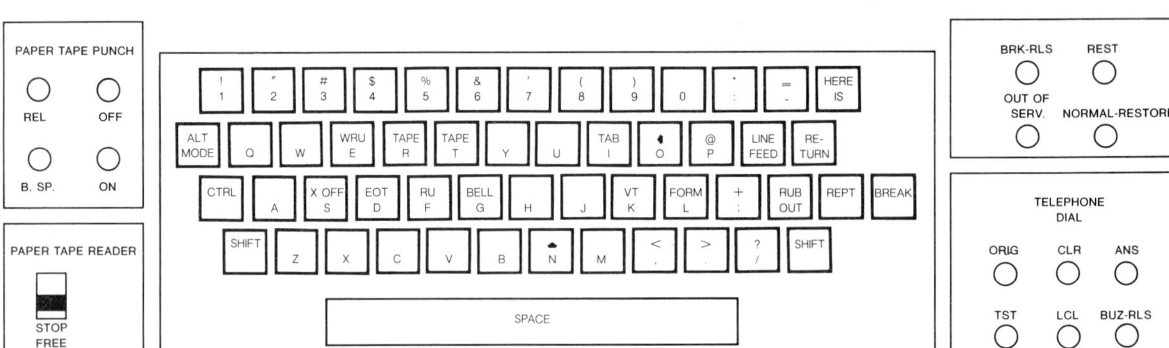

computer's storage, he types:

RUN

Data have been entered, via the keyboard, along with the program. Typing RUN causes the computer to solve the problem. Under control of the computer, answers are typed immediately following the word RUN.

After Joe has received his answers, he may want to save the program so that he can use it again another day. In order to do this, he types:

SAVE

The computer then stores the program for future use. Now Joe can sign off by typing:

BYE

Now suppose that Joe Doe is faced with the necessity of solving the same problem the following week. Again, he can access the teletype machine, dial up the computer, and converse with it as follows:

USER NUMBER—X99999
SYSTEM—BASIC
NEW OR OLD—OLD
OLD PROBLEM NAME—PAYROLL
READY.

The computer types the word READY, indicating that it has retrieved the user's program and has made it available to him. If Joe wants to, he can now change parts of the program or enter new data. After the problem has been run, Joe simply types:

BYE

He does not have to type SAVE again; the computer will retain the program until Joe no longer wants the program in computer storage. When he wishes to remove the program from the computer, he can type:

UNSAVE

This example covers only the fundamentals of data terminal use. The student should consult with an informed individual about the types of data terminals that may exist in his/her organization, and receive personal guidance before attempting to use the terminals.

APPENDIX D

Sources of Further Information

LEARNING MORE ABOUT COMPUTERS

For those individuals who want more information about the computer and related fields, there are a number of professional societies, publications, and other organizations that are good sources. Some are listed below.

Professional Societies

The following organizations are professional societies that, in most cases, offer membership provisions, conduct conferences, and publish journals. Some of the societies have special student-membership rates.

- American Federation of Information Processing Societies* (AFIPS), Montvale, New Jersey 07645
- Association for Educational Data Systems (AEDS), Washington, D.C. 20004
- Association for Systems Management (ASM), Cleveland, Ohio 44138
- Association of Computing Machinery (ACM), New York, New York 10036
- British Computer Society (BCS), London, England
- Canadian Information Processing Society (CIPS), Toronto, Canada
- Data Processing Management Association (DPMA), Park Ridge, Illinois 60068
- Institute of Electrical & Electronics Engineers (IEEE), New York, New York 10017
- International Federation for Information Processing* (IFIP), Geneva, Switzerland
- Society for Management Information Systems (SMIS), Chicago, Illinois 60601

* These two groups are not open to individual membership, but rather are umbrella organizations that have the various societies as members.

Publications

There are numerous journals and other publications about computers.

Rather than listing selected books, the author suggests that the reader refer to the annual January listing of computer books published by "Computing Newsletter," University of Colorado, Colorado Springs, Colorado 80907. By obtaining the most recent edition of the "Newsletter," the reader can have access to an updated list of several hundred books that have been classified by topic (e.g., programming languages, systems analysis, and accounting applications).

Aside from the many books about computers that are available, there are a number of journals, including:

Weekly:

- *Computerworld,* Newton, Massachusetts 02120
- *EDP Weekly,* Washington, D.C. 20004

Semi-Monthly:

- *EDP Industry Report,* Newtonville, Massachusetts 02160

Quarterly:

- *Computer Characteristics Review,* Lexington, Massachusetts 02173

Monthly:

- *Association for Computing Machinery Journal,* New York, New York 10036
- *Communications of ACM,* New York, New York 10036
- *Computer Decisions,* Philadelphia, Pennsylvania 19101
- *Computer Journal,* London, England
- *Computers and People,* Newtonville, Massachusetts 02160
- *Computing Newsletter,* University of Colorado, Colorado Springs, Colorado 80907
- *Computing Reviews of ACM,* New York, New York 10036
- *Computing Surveys of ACM,* New York, New York 10036
- *Data Processing Digest,* Los Angeles, California 90045
- *Data Management,* Park Ridge, Illinois 60068
- *Datamation,* Greenwich, Connecticut 06830
- *EDP Analyzer,* Vista, California 92083
- *Infosystems,* Wheaten, Illinois 60187
- *Journal of Systems Management,* Cleveland, Ohio 44138
- *Management Datamatics,* Leyden, Netherlands

Certificate in Data Processing

In order to improve the professional status of the computer field, a number of professional societies have sponsored a certificate in data processing. To qualify for certification, the applicant must take an examination that covers the following areas: data-processing equipment; computer programming and software; principles of management; quantitative methods; and systems analysis and design.

Information about the certification and examination can be obtained from: Institute for Certification of Computer Professionals, 304 East 45th Street, New York, New York 10017.

Standards in the Computer Field

To promote desirable standardization relative to computer hardware, software, programming, and systems techniques, considerable cooperative effort takes place among computer manufacturers and other vendors, as well as among computer users.

In particular, the reader is referred to:

- American National Standards Institute
  1430 Broadway
  New York, New York 10018
- Business Equipment Manufacturers Association
  1828 L Street, N.W.
  Washington, D.C. 20036

Publications are available about standards for such things as: magnetic tape; punched cards; FORTRAN; COBOL; documentation; flowcharts; terminology and glossary; and data communications.

The federal government has been a leader in the effort to achieve standardization, chiefly through the National Bureau of Standards, U.S. Department of Commerce, Washington, D.C. 20036.

User Groups

Computer users who have similar types of computers have organizations that serve as clearinghouses for experiences with computers. For instance, many users of IBM computers belong to an organization known as SHARE. Users of other manufacturers' equipment have similar user groups. These groups can be a rich source of information about a particular computer's performance, programming problems, and computer applications. Such groups also influence the computer manufacturers by informing them of users' needs. The reader can identify the user groups by contacting the appropriate computer manufacturers.

Computer Vendors

Some representative computer vendors are identified below:

Computer Systems:

- Burroughs Corporation, Detroit, Michigan 48232
- Control Data Corporation, Minneapolis, Minnesota 55440
- Digital Equipment Corporation, Maynard, Massachusetts 01754
- Hewlett Packard Corporation, Cupertino, California 95014
- Honeywell Corporation, Wellesley Hills, Massachusetts 02181
- IBM Corporation, Armonk, New York 10514
- National Cash Register Company, Dayton, Ohio 45400
- UNIVAC Division, Sperry Rand Corporation, Blue Bell, Pennsylvania 19422

Peripheral Equipment:

- Mohawk Data Sciences Corporation, Herkimer, New York 13350
- Sanders Associates, Inc., Nashua, New Hampshire 03060
- Friden Division, Singer Company, San Leandro, California 94577
- Varian Data Machines, Newport Beach, California 92660
- Wang Laboratories, Inc., Tewksbury, Massachusetts 01876

Software Packages:

- Applied Data Research, Inc., Princeton, New Jersey 08540
- Boole & Babbage, Inc., Sunnyvale, California 94086
- Comress, Inc., Rockville, Maryland 20850
- Informatics Co., Canoga Park, California 91304
- Information Science Inc., Montvale, New Jersey 07645
- Management Science America, Atlanta, Georgia 30304
- University Computing Company, Dallas, Texas 75247

GLOSSARY

GLOSSARY

Because some of the technical terms used in this text are not included in many standard dictionaries, and because others have particular definitions, this glossary has been developed.

Several glossaries that are used widely in the computer field have been used as sources. These include:

1. *American National Standard Vocabulary for Information Processing,* American National Standards Institute.
2. *A Data Processing Glossary,* IBM Corporation.
3. *Vocabulary of Information Processing,* International Federation for Information Processing.

The glossary in this text was developed partially from the above sources, which the author sometimes adapted and supplemented with his own definitions to make it consistent with the text.

Abacus. An early computing device on which numbers are represented by a pattern of a series of beads on a number of strings.

Absolute address. A specific address that is permanently assigned by the equipment designer to a storage location.

Access mechanism. A part of a disk storage unit that is used to contain one or more access arms having reading and writing heads.

Access method. Any of the techniques available to the user for transferring data between primary storage and an input/output device. The basic methods are sequential access and direct access.

Access time. The time interval between (1) the instant when data are called for from a storage device and the instant delivery begins; or (2) the instant when data are requested to be stored and the instant when storage is started.

Accumulator. A register in which the result of an arithmetic or a logical operation is developed.

Accuracy. The computer's ability to process data and generate results that are reliable and error-free.

Acronym. A word formed from a few letters of the words in a name, term, or phrase. For example, "bit" is an acronym formed from *bi*nary digi*t*; COBOL is formed from *Co*mmon *B*usiness *O*riented *L*anguage.

Action entry. The lower-right quadrant of a decision table. It specifies the action to be taken.

Action stub. The lower-left quadrant of a decision table. It lists every possible action that can be taken.

Actuating. A manager's ability to demonstrate leadership by having people carry out necessary duties.

Adaptive system. A system that adapts to conditions.

Address. A name, label, or number that identifies a particular location in storage or device.

Address register. A register that contains the address of a storage location or device.

Addressable storage. Storage such as a magnetic disk or magnetic drum, each location of which is addressable, in contrast to nonaddressable storage such as magnetic tape and punched cards.

Addressing technique. One of the several addressing techniques: indexed sequential; randomizing; etc.

Aiken, Howard. Developer of the MARK computer, the first modern computer. Since his was considered to be a mechanical computer, it predates the electronic computer.

ALGOL (*Algo*rithmic *L*anguage). A higher-level programming language used for mathematical problems.

Algorithm. A set of well-defined rules for solving a problem in a finite number of operations.

Alphabetic data. Data that is composed exclusively of the letters of the alphabet and the blank.

Alphameric. Pertaining to a character set that includes both alphabetic characters, numeric characters, and, usually, special characters such as punctuation marks.

Analog computer. A computer that operates on data in the form of continuously variable physical quantities, such as electrical voltages and temperatures.

APL (*A*lgebraic *P*rogramming *L*anguage). A high-level mathematical programming language that is particularly useful in interactive mode.

Application program. A program that performs a user function.

Argument. The known reference factor necessary to find the desired item (function) in a table.

Arithmetic and logic unit. The portion of a central processing unit in which arithmetic and logical operations are performed.

Array. An organized collection of data in which the argument is positioned before the function.

Artificial intelligence. Refers to attempts to use the computer as a learning instrument.

ASCII (*A*merican National *S*tandard *C*ode for *I*nformation *I*nterchange). A standard code, using a coded character set consisting of seven-bit coded characters (eight bits, including the parity check), that is used for data interchange involving computers and communications equipment.

Assemble. To prepare a machine language program from a symbolic language program. Absolute operation codes and addresses are substituted for symbolic operation codes and addresses.

Assembler. A computer program that assembles.

Assembler language. The source language for an assembler.

Asynchronous. Refers to events without regular time relationship. For instance, in reference to program execution, it means unexpected or unpredictable instruction sequence.

Atanasoff, John V. Developer of an electronic computer that is considered the first nonmechanical computer.

Audit trail. A means for identifying the actions performed on data by tracing the data on a source document to an output such as a report, or tracing an output to the source items from which it was derived.

Automation. Usually, the use of automated equipment in a manufacturing (as opposed to an office) environment.

Auxiliary storage. See secondary storage.

Babbage, Charles. A computer pioneer who developed computer-like machines in the mid-1800s.

Background partition. The area of a multiprogramming system holding lower-priority programs, which are executed only when higher-priority programs are not using the system.

Backup. A procedure, technique, or hardware intended to be used in an emergency to help substitute for lost or destroyed data or to keep a system running.

Bandwidth. In data transmission, it refers to the frequency range that can be accommodated by a transmission line, which in turn determines the rate at which data can be transmitted.

Base. In a number system, the base is the value that indicates how many absolute values are used in the system. For example, the binary system has base 2, octal has base 8, and hexadecimal has base 16.

BASIC (*B*eginners *A*ll-purpose *S*ymbolic *I*nstruction *C*ode). A high-level programming language used in a time-sharing environment.

Batch processing. The grouping of data prior to processing. Pertains to the sequential input of data or computer programs.

Baud. A unit of measuring speed in communications. For instance, one baud equals one bit per second in a series of binary signals.

Benchmark. An application or a mix of instructions that are used in evaluating the performance of a particular computer as compared to other computers.

Binary. The representation of data by only two possible conditions (combinations of 1 and 0). Components that have only two stable states.

Binary coded decimal (BCD). A six-bit code (seven bits, including the parity check) in which unique combinations of two zone bits and four numeric bits represent specific data characters.

Binary system. A numeration system using the digits 0 and 1 and having a base of 2. For example, the binary numeral 1001 means $(1 \times 2^3) + (0 \times 2^2) + (0 \times 2^1) + (1 \times 2^0)$, which is equivalent to the decimal numeral 9.

Bit (*bi*nary digi*t*). The symbol 0 or 1 in the representation of a value in binary notation.

Block. A group of characters, fields, or records, handled as a unit.

Blocking. Combining two or more records into one common block.

Blocking factor. The number of logical records in a single physical record or block.

Boundaries. The constraints set to delimit a system.

Branch. Alternative paths emanating from a decision step.

Breakeven point. The point at which the total cost of a fixed cost alternative and the total cost of a variable cost alternative are equal.

Broadband. See wideband.

Buffer. A storage area used to collect data. Use of a buffer compensates for differences in rates of data flow or times of occurrence of events when transmitting data from one device to another.

Bug. An error in a program or an equipment fault.

Burster. An off-line device that automatically separates continuous-form paper.

Burst mode. Transfer of all the data in one record from an input device to primary storage, or all the data in one area of storage to an output device, in one operation.

Business application. Such computer applications usually have relatively simple calculations (compared to scientific applications) and a large volume of data. Examples include payroll, accounting, and marketing statistics.

Byte. A fixed number of adjacent bits that are operated on as a unit. Commonly, a byte is a group of eight adjacent bits and can represent one alphameric character or two digits.

Byte mode. Transfer of one byte of data to or from primary storage in one operation.

Calculate. To compute.

Calculator. A data processor that is especially suitable for performing arithmetic operations that require frequent intervention by a human operator.

Card column. A single vertical line of punch positions of a punched card.

Card punch. A device to record data in cards by punching holes in the cards to represent characters.

Card reader. A device that senses and translates the holes in punched cards into internal code.

Card row. A single horizontal line of punch positions of a punched card.

Cartridge. See cassette.

Cashless-checkless society. The society we will have when the electronic transfer of funds eliminates the need for cash and checks.

Cassette. A small, self-contained magnetic tape used for storing data.

Cathode ray tube (CRT). A device that presents data in visual form on a television-like screen.

CBMIS (*C*omputer-*B*ased *M*anagement *I*nformation *S*ystem). A management information system that substantially uses computers.

Centralized data-processing. A system that consists of a central computer facility. All data are transmitted to the central computer for processing, and results of processing data and inquiries are transmitted to users.

Central processing unit (CPU). The unit of a computer that is the heart of the computer system. It contains the following: arithmetic/logic section; control section; and primary storage. The CPU contains the circuits controlling the interpretation and execution of instructions.

Chaining. See pointer.

Channel. (1) A path for transmitting input data to the CPU or transmitting output data from the CPU; (2) The portion of a storage medium that is accessible to a given reading or writing station (e.g., track or band); or (3) In communication, a means of transmission.

Character. A letter, digit, or special symbol that is used to represent data.

Character-addressable. Pertaining to a computer that performs operations on variable-length words. Each character, if desired, is addressable.

Check bit. See parity bit.

Checkpoint. A place in a routine where a check, or a recording of data for restart purposes, is performed.

Classify. To group data by specific classifications.

COBOL (*Co*mmon *B*usiness *O*riented *L*anguage). A high-level programming language designed primarily for business data-processing.

Code. (1) A set of unambiguous rules specifying the way in which data may be represented; or (2) The human programmers' steps in writing instructions (i.e., to code the program).

Code conversion. Conversion from one code to another, e.g., from Hollerith code to EBCDIC.

Coding. The act of writing program instructions.

Collate. See merge.

Communicate and coordinate. The act, on the part of management, of sharing two-way information with other interested persons.

Communication link. See data communication.

Communication service. Services offered by common carriers like the telephone company.

Communications control unit (CCU). In a data-communications system, the CCU is the means by which the CPU communicates with various I/O devices. The CCU is connected to the CPU by means of data channels that coordinate the flow of data into and out of the computer.

Compatibility. The ability to handle programs and data from one computer system on another computer system without modification.

Compile. To prepare a machine-language program from a computer program that is written in a high-level language.

Compiler program. A program that compiles programs written in a high-level language to produce machine-language programs.

Computer. Equipment that can process data without requiring intervention by a human operator during the run.

Computer configuration. The particular array of computer equipment required to make up a specific computer for a user.

Computer data-processing. To process data with a computer.

Computer generation. A generation is established when new technology tends to make existing computers obsolete.

Computer implant. The implant of a miniature computer in the human body (this trend is forecasted for the future).

Computer industry. The organizations that manufacture, market, and offer services related to computers.

Computer network. A complex consisting of two or more interconnected computers.

Computer operator. An individual who operates a computer.

Computer output microfilm (COM). Microfilm that is produced by the use of a COM device. A COM device displays data on a CRT screen, and the data is exposed to microfilm. Output is a microfilm copy of the data, either in roll or microfiche form. The computer produces an index to locate the proper roll and frame for a given output.

Computer program. See program.

Computer service center. An organization that offers computer time to users either on a job basis or hourly basis.

Computer system. The hardware, software, and people that must function together so that a computer can actually process data and generate information.

Computer word. A sequence of bits or characters that are moved, used in operations, and stored as a unit.

Condition entry. The upper-right quadrant of a decision table. It indicates all the possible combinations of conditions listed in the condition stub.

Condition stub. The upper-left quadrant of a decision table. It indicates the conditions related to a particular problem.

Conditional branch. An instruction that may or may not cause a transfer from the normal sequence of instruction execution, depending upon the result of some operation, the contents of some register, or the setting of some indicator.

Connector symbol. A small circle that is used to connect two parts of a flowchart.

Console. The part of a computer that is used for communication between the human operator and the computer.

Constant. A fixed or invariable value or data item.

Continuous form. Forms, used by computer printers, which are continuous. The forms are perforated for separation after printing has taken place.

Control. To effectively direct an operation so that it stays within desired limits.

Control card. See job-control card.

Control field. See key field.

Control panel. (1) A manually set plugboard that is used to control the operation of equipment. Such plugboards are mostly used with off-line electromechanical punched-card equipment and some peripherals. (2) A part of the computer console that contains manual controls.

Control program. See supervisor.

Control report. A management report indicating actual performance in terms of the stated goals.

Control section of computer department. A staff that maintains external controls to assure the integrity of the work in the computer department.

Control total. A sum of the numbers in a specified field. By determining the control total repetitively during processing steps, any discrepancy from the total indicates that an error has occurred.

Control unit of CPU. The part of the CPU that retrieves instructions in proper sequence; interprets each instruction; and signals the arithmetic/logic unit and other parts of the computer, in accordance with this interpretation.

Control unit of I/O. A device functioning between the central processing unit and one or more input/output devices to perform such functions as buffering, code conversion, and error checking during input/output operations.

Conversational mode. On-line interaction between the user and the computer, with a dialogue taking place.

Conversion. The changeover from one system to another system.

Core. See magnetic core.

Cost per unit of data processing. Total cost of a job, divided by some factor (such as number of items processed).

Counter. An adder, in the CPU, that automatically adds an amount (e.g., 1) each time through a cycle.

CPU-bound. A program or a computer system that is restricted or limited by the speed of the CPU.

Critical path method (CPM). See network analysis.

Crossfoot check. A system check in which various results computed during processing are summed and compared to an inclusive total.

Cycle. One iteration or loop through a set of logical steps.

Cycle time. The interval between the call for and delivery of data from a storage device.

Cylinder. All tracks accessible at one setting of the access mechanism of a direct-access storage device.

Data. A representation of facts, concepts, or instructions in a formalized manner suitable for communication, interpretation, or processing by human or automatic means.

Data base. A comprehensive collection of files of data.

Data-base management (DBM). A general term that collectively describes those functions of the control program that provide access to data, enforce data-storage conventions, and regulate the use of input/output devices.

Data collection. The step of bringing data from one or more points to a central point.

Data communication. The transmission of data from one point to another.

Data entry. Introducing data into a data-processing system.

Data field. See field.

Data file. See file.

Data format. See data organization.

Data hierarchy. The range of data from the smallest (a bit) to the most encompassing (a data base).

Data manipulation. The variety of data processing, such as moving, sorting, merging, and editing data.

Data organization. A systematic method of structuring or visualizing data.

Data-preparation device. A device that takes source data and makes the original recording for a data-processing system. Such devices include key punches and key-to-tape machines.

Data processing. The execution of a systematic sequence of operations performed on data.

Data-processing method. Alternative methods of processing data include manual methods, mechanical methods, and electronic (computer) methods.

Data-processing steps. The individual tasks required to accomplish the work of processing data.

Data record. See record.

Data representation. The representation of normal data in some type of coded form, such as EBCDIC.

Data set. A device that performs the modulation and demodulation necessary to provide compatibility between data-processing devices and communications facilities.

Data structure. See data organization.

Data terminal. A terminal for entering data.

Data-transfer rate. The amount of data that can be transferred from one device to another in a given period of time.

Data transmission. See data communication.

Deblocking. Separating blocked data into individual logical records.

Debug. To detect, locate, and remove mistakes from a routine, or malfunctions from a computer.

Decimal number system. Our number system, which is a base-ten system that uses the digits 0, 1, 2, 3, 4, 5, 6, 7, 8, 9.

Decision. The act of deciding among alternative courses.

Decision table. A table of all contingencies that are to be considered in a description of a problem, together with the actions to be taken.

Decollator. An off-line device that removes interspersed carbon paper from multiple-copy continuous forms.

Demodulation. The process of converting tones to a direct-current (DC) signal. The conversion process is performed by a data set.

Density. The number of bits in a given area of a recording medium.

Desk checking. Checking a program manually before it is prepared for submission to a computer.

Destructive read-in. A reading process that destroys, or replaces, any data that were previously in the location. The new data read-in replaces the previous data.

Deterministic program. A program that has a set algorithm for solving problems.

Devices. See hardware.

Diagnostic. Computer output that is designed to provide the programmer with information of maximum utility and convenience in checking out programs.

Dialed service. In data transmission, the intermittent use of communication facilities. When a message is to be transmitted, the user dials the destination number (either a computer or remote terminal), just as for a telephone call. With dialed service, the user must compete with other users for an available line, and a busy signal is possible at any given time. The user is charged only for the time used, and rates depend on the time of day, day of the week, and distance involved.

Digit. A symbol that represents one of the non-negative integers smaller than the radix.

Digital computer. Basically, a counting device that operates on discrete or discontinuous data or numbers. A digital computer performs sequences of arithmetical and logical operations, not only on data but also on its own program.

Direct-access file. Pertaining to the process of obtaining data from, or placing data into, storage where the time required for such access is independent of the location of the data most recently obtained or placed in storage.

Direct entry. A system that is oriented toward direct entry of data from a keyboard.

Direct-relation addressing. Occurs in a direct-access system, when the key field's number is the same as the absolute address of the location where the record is stored.

Disk dump. The process of periodically recording on a printer the storage content of a disk.

Disk pack. A stack of magnetic disks that are removable from the disk device.

Diskette. A small disk pack.

Distributed data-processing. Decentralized data-processing.

Documentation. The collection of documents on a given subject.

Document-handling device. Paper-handling equipment, such as magnetic character-recognition and optical character-recognition devices.

Downtime. The length of time a computer is inoperative due to a malfunction.

Duplex. See full duplex.

EBCDIC (*E*xtended *B*inary *C*oded *D*ecimal *E*xchange *C*ode). An eight-bit code (nine bits, including the parity check) in which unique combinations of four zone bits and four numeric bits represent specific data characters.

Eckert, J. Prosper. The developer, along with John W. Mauchly, of ENIAC, one of the first electronic computers. Eckert and Mauchly drew on the work of John V. Atanasoff in their developments.

Edit. To modify the form or format of data. For example, inserting or deleting characters like dollar signs, decimal points, or leading zeros; or rearranging data items.

Edit run. A computer run that is run to discover any mistakes in data.

EDSAC (*E*lectronic *D*elayed *S*torage *A*utomatic *C*omputer). The first electronic computer to use the stored program concept.

Effective address. See absolute address.

Electromechanical punched-card equipment. Pertains to conventional punched-card equipment (not computers) that generally are directed by wired control panels and that process punched-card records.

Electronic. The use of electricity in such a way that few if any moving parts are involved; rapid speeds are the result.

Electronic data-processing (EDP). Data processing performed largely by electronic equipment, particularly by electronic digital computers.

Electronic transfer of funds (ETF). The automatic, electronic transfer of monetary transactions, replacing paperwork and checks, among consumers, vendors, and banks.

Electronically erase. A characteristic of magnetic storage whereby new data that are brought into a location automatically replace the previous data in that location.

Elementary item. A data item or field containing no subordinate items. In other words, elementary items are data items or fields that are not subdivided.

Emulator. A device, usually used in conjunction with special programmed routines, that enables one computer to execute machine-language instructions intended for another computer dissimilar in design, without prior translation.

ENIAC (*E*lectronic *N*umerical *I*ntegrator *A*nd *C*alculator). One of the first electronic computers. ENIAC was designed by John W. Mauchly and J. Prosper Eckert.

EOF (*e*nd-*o*f-*f*ile). An indicator that alerts the computer that the end of a file has been reached.

Equipment. See hardware.

Equipment utilization. The extent of use of equipment in a given period of time, compared with the total time available.

E-time (execution time). The time required to perform the operations specified by an instruction.

Execution. The act of carrying out an instruction or performing a routine.

Execution cycle. See E-time.

External storage. A storage device or medium outside the computer that can store data in a form acceptable to the computer. External storage consists of punched cards, magnetic tape, and documents encoded with magnetic ink characters or optical characters.

"Father" tape. Usually, a master tape from a previous processing period that was used to generate a "son" tape. The "father" tape is retained for backup purposes.

Feasibility study. The process of evaluating the relative cost and benefits of a particular course of action (e.g., switching to a more powerful computer).

Feedback. The part of a closed loop system that automatically brings back information about the condition being controlled.

Field. In a record, a specified area used for a particular category of data.

Fifth-generation computer. The computer that is anticipated in the 1980s.

File. A collection of related records treated as a unit.

File label. See label.

File maintenance. The activity of keeping a file up to date by adding, changing, or deleting data.

File organization. The physical arrangement of records on a data-storage device.

File processing. Creating, utilizing, or maintaining files.

File ring. A small plastic ring that can be inserted into the back of a reel of magnetic tape. When the ring is in place, the tape can be used for output; without the ring, the tape is limited to input operations only.

File size. The number of records in a file.

Firmware. Electronic circuits, typically arranged in the form of a card or a board, which can easily be added to or deleted from a computer's electronics.

First-generation computer. In the period 1951–1958, a computer that utilized vacuum tube components.

Fixed cost. A cost that remains the same for all levels of activity.

Fixed field-length. Setting a standard fixed length for each respective field in the records in a file.

Fixed record-length. Setting a standard fixed length for each record in a particular file.

Fixed word-length. A computer word in which there is always a constant number of positions. The size of a fixed word depends on the particular computer.

Floppy disk. A small disk, with relatively limited storage capacity, that often is used on a minicomputer or an intelligent data terminal.

Flowchart. A graphic representation, to define, analyze, or solve a problem, in which symbols are used to represent operations, data flow, equipment, etc.

Foreground partition. The partition in a multiprogramming system containing the high-priority application programs.

FORTRAN (*FOR*mula *TRAN*slating system). A high-level programming language that is primarily intended for use in mathematical problems.

Fourth-generation computer. In the period 1971–1980, a computer that considerably improved on the third-generation computers.

Full duplex. In communications, a simultaneous two-way independent transmission in both directions.

Functions of management. See management functions.

Functions of organization. See organization functions.

Gantt chart. The predecessor to network analysis, in which the representation of tasks and their relationship is shown via a time scale.

General-purpose computer. A computer that is designed to handle a wide variety of problems.

"Grandfather" tape. An old master tape. It provides backup for both the "father" and "son" tapes.

Group item. An item that is further subdivided.

Half duplex. In communications, pertaining to an alternate, one-way-at-a-time, independent transmission.

Hardware. Physical equipment, in contrast to software or method of use. Hardware may include mechanical, magnetic, electrical, or electronic devices.

Hash total. An account, total, or tally of items in certain fields, used for control of input, processing, and output operations. The total that is useful for control purposes has no other usefulness.

Heuristic program. A problem-solving method in which solutions are discovered by evaluating the progress made toward the end result. A directed trial-and-error approach.

Hexadecimal number system. A numeration system having a base of 16 and using the symbols 0, 1, 2, 3, 4, 5, 6, 7, 8, 9, A, B, C, D, E, F.

Hierarchy of information. See data hierarchy.

High-level language. The programming languages that are relatively free of the limitations of a specific computer. These languages are COBOL, FORTRAN, RPG, and BASIC.

High-order position. Pertaining to the digit or digits of a numeral that have most significance. For example, in the number 3179, the high-order digit is 3.

Hollerith code. A code that is used widely for representing data on standard eighty-column punched cards.

Hollerith, Herman. Developer of the first punched-card data processing systems in the late 1800s.

Host processor. In a data-communication system, there may be several computers; often, a large central computer, known as the host computer, performs the major data-processing tasks.

Housekeeping. Pertaining to operations in a program or system that do not contribute directly to the solution of a particular problem but are essential processing functions. For example, housekeeping could involve checking labels and determining whether all input/output devices are attached to a system and readied for processing.

Hybrid computer. A combination analog and digital computer.

Index. An ordered reference list of the contents of a file or document, together with keys or reference notations for identifying or locating those contents.

Indexed sequential. A file organization technique in which data are placed on a file in sequence and an index is maintained, thus allowing both sequential and direct access. This technique is designed to be used exclusively on magnetic disk.

Information. The meaning that a human assigns to data, using the known conventions used in their representation.

Information system. See management information system.

Information utility. A business concern that offers numerous computing facilities (including computer time and programming) for sale or lease.

Initialize. To establish an initial value for a counter.

Initial program load (IPL). The procedure that causes the initial part of an operating system or other program to be loaded, enabling the system to proceed under its own control.

Input. Pertaining to a device, process, or channel involved in the insertion of data or states, or to the data or states involved.

Input device. The device or collective set of devices used for conveying data into another device.

Input/output (I/O). Pertaining to either input or output, or to both.

Input/output control system (IOCS). A standard set of programming routines designed to initiate and control the input and output operations required for a user's applications program.

Instruction. A statement that specifies an operation and the values or locations of its operands.

Instruction address register. See address register.

Instruction counter. See counter.

Instruction cycle. See I-time.

Instruction modification. See program modification.

Instruction register. Temporary storage location that contains the instruction to be processed.

Instruction set. The set of operations that can be represented in a given operation code.

Integrated circuit. A complete, complex electronic circuit that is capable of performing all the functions of a conventional circuit containing numerous transistors, diodes, capacitors, and/or resistors, all of whose component parts are fabricated and assembled in a single integrated process.

Integrated data-base. A data base whose parts are linked or otherwise integrated.

Integration. Linking all related parts of a system.

Intelligent terminal. A terminal with some logical capability.

Interactive computer system. See conversational mode.

Interblock gap. On magnetic tape, the distance between the end of one block and the beginning of the next one.

Interface. A shared boundary.

Internal data transfer. See move.

Internal storage unit. See primary storage.

Interpreter. A computer program that translates and executes each source language statement before it translates and executes the next one.

Interrecord gap (IRG). On magnetic tape, the distance between the end of one record and the beginning of the next one.

Interrupt. A signal, condition, or event that causes normal processing operations to be suspended temporarily.

I/O. See input/output.

I/O-bound. A program or computer system which is restricted or limited in processing speed by its I/O devices.

Item. See field.

I-time (instruction time). The time required to move an instruction from primary storage to the address and operation code registers; that is, the time required to set up circuit paths necessary for instruction execution.

Job. A specified group of tasks prescribed as a unit of work for a computer.

Job-control card. A statement in an input job stream that is used to identify the job or describe its requirements to the operating system.

Job-control language. The set of statements used to direct operating system programs that control processing.

Job-control routine. An operating system program that reads job-control statements describing work to be performed by the computer.

K. (1) An abbreviation for the prefix *kilo;* i.e., 1000 in decimal notation; or (2) When referring to computer storage capacity, K refers to 1024 in decimal notation.

Key. One or more characters within an item of data that are used to identify it or control its use.

Key field. A field that serves as a key.

Key punch. A keyboard-actuated device that punches holes, representing data, in a card.

Key-to-disk. Hardware designed to transfer the data that were entered via a keyboard to a magnetic disk.

Key-to-tape. Hardware designed to transfer the data that were entered via a keyboard to a magnetic tape.

Key transformation. A scheme, usually mathematical, which is utilized to determine a number that is used as the address of a record.

Keyboard terminal. A terminal through which data can be entered into a data-processing system by means of a typewriter-like keyboard.

Label. (1) One or more characters used to identify a statement or an item of data in a computer program; or (2) A header or leader on a reel of magnetic tape or on magnetic disk containing information identifying the content stored thereon.

Language. A defined set of symbols, conventions, and rules used to write a program.

Language processor. A program that accepts a symbolic or high-level language (source language) program as input, and produces a machine-language (object language) program as output.

Large-size computer. A powerful computer that usually costs over $1,000,000. Some super computers may cost more than $10,000,000.

Latency. See rotational delay.

Leased computer. In contrast with a computer that is purchased, a leased computer is leased or rented, usually for a contracted period of time.

Leased line. A communication line intended for the use of a single customer.

Left-hand justified. To begin recording data at the left-most position of a location, leaving excess space to the right unused.

Leibnitz, Gottfried Wilhelm. Developer of an early mechanical calculator in the 1600s.

Librarian. A set of operating system service programs that maintain, service, and organize all system libraries.

Library. A collection of related files.

Limit check. A test of specified fields of records or of computed totals to determine whether certain pre-established limits have been exceeded.

Linear programming. The analysis of problems in which a linear function of a number of variables is to be maximized (or minimized) when those variables are subject to a number of linear constraints.

Link. To join anything together.

Linkage editor. A program that produces a load module by: transforming object modules into a format that is acceptable to fetch; combining separately produced object modules and previously processed load modules into a single load module; resolving symbolic cross references among them; replacing, deleting, and adding control sections automatically on request; and providing overlay facilities for modules requesting them.

List. A data structure in which logical records are connected by means of pointers.

Load. To read a program into primary storage so that it can be executed.

Load module. (1) The output of the linkage editor; or (2) A program whose format is suitable for loading into main storage for execution.

Loadpoint marker. On magnetic tape, a reflective strip, visible to the operator, marking the beginning of the area of the tape that is actually used to store data.

Location. In a computer, an addressable area in primary or secondary storage where a unit of data may be stored or retrieved.

Logic. The science that deals with the principles of correct or reliable inferences.

Logic errors. Errors in the logic of a particular program.

Logical file. A complete set of related records for a specific area or purpose that may occupy a fraction or all of a physical file, or may require more than one physical file.

Logical record. A collection of items, independent of their physical environment. Portions of the same logical record may be located in different physical records.

Logical test. This involves examining a condition to determine what operations shall take place. Logical tests may include: testing which of two numbers is larger; determining which key code is on a record; and ascertaining whether there is a negative condition.

Longitudinal record check. A parity check performed on the bits in each track of a block of recorded data on magnetic tape or paper tape.

Loop. A sequence of instructions that is executed repeatedly until a termination condition prevails.

Low-order position. The position of the digit or digits of a numeral that have least significance. For example, in the number 3179, the low-order digit is 9.

Machine cycle. The basic operating cycle of a CPU, during which a single instruction is fetched, decoded, and executed.

Machine-level language. A language in which there is a one-to-one correspondence between source program statements and operations to be performed by the computer.

Machine-readable. Pertaining to the characteristic of being able to be sensed or read by a device, usually by a device that has been designed and built specifically to perform the reading or sensing function. Thus data on tape, cards, drums, disks, and other media are machine-readable.

Macro instruction. One statement in a source program that is replaced by a number of equivalent instructions in an object program.

Magnetic core. A tiny magnetic ring, made of a material such as iron, which can be selectively magnetized to represent data.

Magnetic disk. A flat, circular plate with magnetic surfaces on which data can be written by selective magnetization of portions of its surfaces.

Magnetic-disk device. Equipment that handles the magnetic disk medium.

Magnetic drum. A cylinder with a magnetic surface on which data can be written by selective magnetization of portions of the surface.

Magnetic-drum device. Equipment that houses the magnetic drum.

Magnetic ink. An ink containing particles of a magnetic substance that is detectable by magnetic sensors.

Magnetic-ink character-recognition device (MICR). The machine reading of characters printed with magnetic ink.

Magnetic tape. A tape with a magnetic surface on which data can be written by selective magnetization of portions of the surface.

Magnetic-tape device. Equipment that handles magnetic-tape media.

Main memory. See primary storage.

Main storage. See primary storage.

Mainframe. See central processing unit.

Mainline. The primary path of logical flow through a program.

Maintenance. Any activity intended to eliminate faults or to keep hardware or software in satisfactory working condition.

Management actions. The managerial actions of decision making and communication/coordination.

Management audit. A managerial assessment of the condition of a unit of the business.

Management by exception. The management principle that is concerned with exceptional conditions; that is, when actual results differ from objectives. When results occur within a normal range, they need not be reported to management.

Management by objectives (MBO). To establish objectives to be achieved, and then to periodically compare results with the original goals.

Management functions. The managerial functions of planning, organizing, actuating, and controlling.

Management information system (MIS). A system that generates information useful for management functions and actions.

Management science. The use of higher mathematics to solve systems problems.

Man-machine system. A system that is designed to effectively distribute the effort between humans and machines.

Manual data-processing. Data processing by manual means.

MARK. The first modern computer, developed by Howard Aiken.

Mass storage. See secondary storage.

Master file. A file that is either relatively permanent, or that is treated as an authority in a particular job.

Master-file update. The process of maintaining a master file.

Mathematical programming. One of the techniques used in management science to solve problems. In particular, it deals with linear programming.

Mauchly, John W. The developer, along with J. Prosper Eckert, of ENIAC, one of the first electronic computers. Eckert and Mauchly drew on the work of John V. Atanasoff in their developments.

Mechanical data-processing. Processing data with mechanical equipment such as electromechanical punched-card equipment, in contrast with electronic computers.

Medium. The material on which data is recorded; for example, magnetic tape or punched cards.

Medium-size computer. A computer that usually costs between $250,000 and $1,000,000.

Memory. See storage.

Merge. To form a single sequenced file by combining two or more similarly sequenced files.

Message switching. The process of transferring messages among various communication media to ensure accurate transmission from the correct source to the correct destination.

Method. See data-processing method.

Microcomputer. A very small computer; often, a special-purpose or single-function computer on a single chip.

Microfilm. In lieu of paper, a medium that permits data to be recorded on film in greatly reduced size.

Microfilm device. Equipment that handles the microfilm medium.

Micro-instructions. A set of basic subcommands that are built into the computer and translated by hardware into machine commands. These commands are in a special read-only storage unit of the computer.

Microprocessor. See microcomputer.

Microprogramming. See micro instructions.

Microsecond. One millionth of one second.

Millisecond. One thousandth of one second.

Minicomputer. A small computer costing under $60,000; some cost under $1,000.

Mnemonic code. A symbol chosen to assist the human memory; e.g., an abbreviation such as "MPY" (standing for multiply).

Model. A representation of a system; an outline of the major parts of a system in relation to other parts.

Modem. See data set.

Modularity. The ability to increase the power of a computer by adding components to it.

Modular program flowcharting. A technique of representing, on successively more detailed levels of flowcharts, the processing steps required in a program.

Modular programming. A program that is written as a series of separate but linked blocks of logic.

Modulation. The process of converting a direct current (DC) signal into tones for transmission via communications links. The conversion process is performed by a data set.

Module. A separate and distinct (yet integral) part of a system that can be compiled independently.

Monitor. See supervisor.

Monolithic integrated circuit. See integrated circuits.

Move. The movement of data from one location to another.

Multiplex. To interleave or simultaneously transmit two or more messages on a single channel.

Multiplexor channel. A data channel that multiplexes or overlaps the operation of two or more low-speed I/O devices. It uses the byte mode.

Multiprocessing. A technique for executing two or more sequences of instructions simultaneously in a single computer system, generally by using more than one central processing unit.

Multiprogramming. A technique for handling two or more independent programs at the same time by loading them into primary storage and executing their instructions concurrently.

Nanosecond. One billionth of one second.

Narrowband. Facilities capable of transmitting data at relatively slow rates for applications with low volumes of data.

Natural language. Language approximating the language that people use in everyday life.

Network. (1) A complex consisting of two or more interconnected computers, or (2) A series of points interconnected by communication channels.

Network analysis. A graphic method for defining and interrelating on a time scale the jobs and events that take place to accomplish desired objectives. The interdependency of tasks establishes a network in which the longest path through the network is the critical path that determines the duration of the overall project.

Noise. (1) Any disturbance that tends to interfere with the normal operation of a device or system, or (2) Random variations of one or more characteristics of any entity, such as voltage, current, or data.

Nonaddressable storage. Storage that is not addressable, such as punched cards and magnetic tape.

Nondestructive read-out. A reading process that does not destroy or change the data in the source.

Nonoverlapped processing. A technique whereby reading, writing, and internal processing can occur only in a serial manner.

Nonprogrammable decisions. Decisions (usually of top management) that are not susceptible to programming.

Nucleus. See supervisor.

Number system. A number representation system such as the decimal system (base 10) or the binary system (base 2).

Numeric bit. In a binary system, the group of bits that is assigned the task of recording numeric data.

Numeric data. Data consisting exclusively of digits, with decimal point permitted; data whose individual digits are written in the positional notation of some number system.

Numeric punch. A punch in any one of the rows 0 through 9 on a punched card.

Object code. Output from a compiler or assembler that is itself executable machine code, or is suitable for processing to produce executable machine code.

Object deck. An object program in punched-card form.

Object language. The form of an output from a translation process.

Object program. A program expressed in an object language; generally, a machine-language program that can be executed by a particular computer.

Objectives. The goals that are set to provide a purpose for the organization, and to establish a basis for measuring performance.

Octal number system. Pertaining to a numeration system with a base of 8 and using the digits 0, 1, 2, 3, 4, 5, 6, 7.

Off-line. Pertaining to equipment that is not under control of the central processing unit.

On-line. (1) Pertaining to equipment or devices that are under control of the central processing unit; or (2) Pertaining to a user's ability to interact with a computer.

Operand. That which is operated upon. An operand is usually identified by an address part of an instruction.

Operating system. Software that controls the execution of computer programs and that may provide scheduling, debugging, input/output control, accounting, compilation, storage assignment, data management, and related services.

Operation. (1) The act of obtaining a result from one or more operands in accordance with a rule that specifies the result for any permissible combination of operands; (2) The act specified by a single machine-language instruction; or (3) A program step executed by the computer (for example, addition or multiplication).

Operation code (opcode). A code that represents specific operations.

Operation code register. A register that contains the operation-code portion of a machine-language instruction, during interpretation and execution of that instruction.

Operations research. See management science.

Operator. In a compiler language, a symbol that represents an operation to be performed, such as + for addition or * for multiplication.

Operator, computer. The person who operates a computer.

Optical character recognition (OCR). The machine identification of printed characters, through the use of light-sensitive devices.

Organization functions. Among the traditional functions of an organization are accounting and finance, marketing, manufacturing, and personnel.

Organization structure. The way an enterprise is organized for the purpose of carrying out its mission.

Output. Pertaining to a device, process, or channel involved in an output process, or to the data or states involved.

Output device. The device or collective set of devices used for conveying data out of another device.

Overlapped processing. A process in which the typical cycle (i.e., read, process, and write) is performed simultaneously. The total cycle time is determined by the event that takes the most time to perform (either read time, or write time, or processing time).

Overlay. To transfer segments of a program from auxiliary storage to primary storage locations that presently are occupied by data or instructions that are no longer needed.

Packed decimal. A decimal format in EBCDIC in which the zone portions of numerical digits are removed and two decimal digits are packed into each eight-bit set. The sign of the number is stored in the right-most portion of the character string.

Page. A fixed-length portion of a program or data that can be transferred between main memory and a secondary storage device on a virtual memory system. Also, a fixed-length portion of a program that can be loaded into main memory and can be addressed independently of the rest of the program.

Paper tape. An input/output medium on which data can be recorded as a pattern on punched holes.

Paper-tape device. Equipment that handles the paper-tape medium.

Parallel operation. Pertaining to the simultaneous processing of individual parts of a whole, such as the bits of a character or the characters of a word, using separate facilities for the parts.

Parallel processing tests. Processing the new system and the old system, with the same input and time period, to verify that the new system meets standards satisfactorily.

Parity bit. A check bit appended to an array of binary digits to make the sum of all the binary digits, including the check bit, always odd or always even.

Parity check. A check to determine whether the number of 1 bits in a bit pattern is either even or odd.

Partition. A portion of a computer's primary memory that is set aside to hold a single program in a fixed partition memory management system.

Pascal, Blaise. Developer of the first mechanical adding machine in the 1600s.

Payback analysis. An analysis to determine the period of time necessary to recover the costs on an investment or project.

Peripheral equipment. In a data-processing system, any unit of equipment, distinct from the central processing unit, which may provide the system with outside communication.

Personal computing. A hobby concerned with the building and use of small, personal computers.

PERT (*P*rogram *E*valuation and *R*eview *T*echnique). See network analysis.

Physical file. A physical unit, such as a reel of magnetic tape.

Physical record. A single block of data as transferred between an I/O device and primary storage; it may contain several logical records.

Picosecond. One billionth of one second.

PL/1 (*P*rogramming *L*anguage *1*). A high-level programming language designed to handle both business and scientific problems.

Pointer. A link between two records.

Point-of-sale device (POS). A device that is used to input sales data at the time when a sale is executed.

Polling. A technique by which each of the terminals sharing a communications line is periodically interrogated to determine whether it requires servicing. The multiplexor or control station sends a poll that, in effect, asks the terminal, "Do you have anything to transmit?"

Port. A connection point for a communication line on a front-end device or a control unit.

Positional value. See base.

Precision. The degree of discrimination used when describing a quantity. For example, a two-digit decimal numeral discriminates among 100 possibilities.

Prenumbered forms. Forms that are prenumbered (such as checks) for purposes of control; that is, to account for every form.

Present value. An analysis that takes into account the time value of money. Present value is the current equivalent value of future dollars, discounted back from a specified future date to the present date at a given rate of compound interest.

Primary storage. The general-purpose storage that is part of the CPU. Primary storage holds the program and data that are currently in use at any one time.

Print chart. A structured, preprinted form used to plan the way in which output is to appear. Systems people and programmers prepare such a chart prior to coding a program.

Printer. An output device that prints human-readable characters.

Priority. Assigned status or ranking. For example, in a multiprogramming environment, a foreground program has higher priority than a background program.

Privacy. Making information available only to proper individuals; also, the techniques of keeping such information private.

Private line. See leased line.

Problem definition. The first step in the program development or systems analysis process; concerned with determining, in general terms, what must be done.

Procedure. A sequence of steps performed to solve a problem.

Procedure-oriented language. See high-level language.

Process-bound. See CPU-bound.

Process operation. A systematic sequence of operations to produce a specified result.

Processing. (1) Executing instructions; or (2) Converting data into information.

Processing program. A program that is not a control program; includes language processors, service programs, and user-written applications programs.

Program. A sequence of instructions that directs the computer to perform a specific series of operations.

Program card. On a key punch, a control card used to allow portions of the card to be punched or skipped automatically.

Program coding form. A structured, preprinted form used to facilitate proper coding of a program by programmers.

Program flowchart. A flowchart that uses specific symbols to graphically depict the order of the steps planned for a program.

Program maintenance. To periodically update a program to make it have continuing usefulness.

Program modification. The computer's ability not only to process data, but also to act on its own program by treating the program as data and thereby modifying the program's instructions when such modification is desired.

Programmer. A person who is involved in designing, writing, and testing computer programs.

Programming language. A language used in writing programs to direct processing steps carried out by a computer.

Project control. A method to control the work of systems and programming personnel working on a project. Objectives are set for each job, and progress is compared to determine fidelity to objectives.

Proof figure. An additional item of data carried in a record specifically for use in system-check procedures. For example, if 10 is selected as a constant for use in computing a proof figure and 6 is the input value, then 4 is the proof figure (10 minus 6).

Punched card. A card that is punched with a pattern of holes representing data.

Punched-card column. A vertical punching area. In a standard punched card, there are eighty columns, and each column can contain the code representing one character.

Punched-card device. Equipment that handles the punched-card medium.

Punched-card punch. A device that punches holes, representing data, into cards.

Punched-card reader. A device that reads the data punched on cards.

Punched-card row. A horizontal punching area. In a standard eighty-column punched card, there are twelve such rows.

Purchased computer. In contrast to leased (or rented) computers, the buying outright of a computer, usually from a computer manufacturer.

Pure binary. See binary system.

Query language. A programming language that makes it relatively simple for any person to engage in a conversational mode with a computer.

Radix. In positional representation, that integer by which the significance of the digit place must be multiplied to give the significance of the next higher-digit place. For example, in decimal notation the radix of each place is ten; in binary code, the radix is two.

Random access. See direct access.

Random processing. To process data as they appear, with no attempt to batch or reorganize them.

Randomize. To compute relative record numbers from actual keys, via any of a number of mathematical techniques.

Rate of speed. A method of measuring the amount of work that can be accomplished in a given period of time.

Read. In computer terms, to read is the same as to input something into a system.

Read-only storage (ROS). A type of storage into which data cannot be written during program execution, and thus generally containing nonalterable data and instructions.

Read/write head. The mechanism that writes data to or reads data from a magnetic recording medium.

Real memory. A computer's actual main memory, which is directly addressable by the CPU.

Real time. (1) Pertaining to the actual time during which a physical process transpires; or (2) Pertaining to the performance of a computation during the actual time that the related physical process transpires, in order that the results of the computation can be used in guiding the physical process.

Reasonableness check. A means of verifying data to ensure that they do not exceed the limit prescribed by reason.

Record. A collection of related items of data fields that are treated as a unit. A complete set of records form a file.

Record count. A tally of the number of records in a group (e.g., batch or file) that were accumulated prior to or during processing for control purposes.

Redundancy. The repetition of data in two or more places.

Reel. A single spool of magnetic tape.

Register. A device capable of storing a specified amount of data, such as one word. Such registers are usually nonaddressable.

Remote device. A device connected to a computer via communication lines.

Remote job entry (RJE). Entering jobs into the regular batch-processing job stream from a remote facility.

Resources. An organization's resources include physical resources, financial resources, and human resources.

Response time. In the case of an inquiry or receipt of message by addressee, the elapsed time between the generation of a message at a terminal and the receipt of a reply.

Retention and reconstruction procedure. Determining how long records and files should be retained, and how records and files can be reestablished, if there is need to do so.

Return on investment. An analysis to determine the expected return on monies invested. This return is derived by dividing income by the cost of an investment.

Right-hand justified. To position data in the right-most area of a location, thus leaving any excess space to the left blank or unused.

Rotational delay. The time required for the desired record to rotate under the read/write heads, once they have been positioned over the proper track on a disk or drum.

Rounding. Deleting or setting to zero the least significant digit or digits of a numeral, and adjusting the part retained in accordance with established rules.

Routine. A sequence of instructions to control the computer as it performs a particular process.

RPG (*R*eport *P*rogram *G*enerator). A business-oriented, high-level programming language designed to support the generation of business reports.

Run. Execution of one or more routines with little or no operator intervention, whereby the computer performs a series of prescribed operations on a given set of data.

Run manual. A documentation manual designed to explain the details of operating a computer during the execution of a particular program.

Scheduling. Determining the sequence in which programs will be loaded and/or executed.

Scientific application. Such computer applications usually have sophisticated mathematical calculations, and, relative to business applications, a small volume of data.

Secondary storage. Storage that is on-line and supplements primary storage.

Second-generation computer. In the period 1958–1964, a computer that utilized solid-state components.

Sector. A portion of a track (from a magnetic disk) whose shape is similar to a slice of pie. Each track is divided equally into sectors, each of which may have its own distinct address.

Seek time. The time required to move the read/write head mechanism of a direct-access device to a desired position.

Segment. To divide a computer program into parts so that the program can be executed without the entire program being in internal storage at any one time.

Selector channel. A data channel that handles high-speed I/O devices. It uses the burst mode.

Semiconductor memory. Memory composed of semiconductor components or integrated circuits.

Sequential file. A file of records organized in a fixed sequence; for example, a file of punched cards or tape.

Sequential-file processing. Processing records in a file in fixed sequence.

Serial operations. Pertaining to the sequential processing of individual parts of a whole, such as the bits of a character or the characters of a word, using the same facilities for successive parts.

Service bureau. See computer service center.

Service programs. Programs that are used in the maintenance and operation of the computer and in the preparation of programs rather than for the solution of specific problems. Examples are linkage editor, librarian, sort/merge, and utility routines.

Significant digit. A digit that contributes to the accuracy or precision of a numeral. The number of significant digits is counted beginning with the left-most (or most significant) digit and ending with the right-most (or least significant) one.

Simplex. Data transmission in one direction at a time.

Simulate. To represent the functioning of one system by another; for instance, a mathematical model can simulate a business system.

Site preparation. The work necessary to prepare a facility for a computer. Such work may include the installation of air conditioning, humidity control, and adequate electrical power.

Small-size computer. Computers that usually cost between $60,000 and $250,000.

Software. A set of programs, procedures, and associated documentation concerned with the operation of a data-processing system.

Solid state. Pertaining to electronic components whose operation depends on the control of electric or magnetic phenomena in solids. Examples are transistors, crystal diodes, and ferrite cores.

"Son" tape. A master tape that is generated from a "father" tape and a transaction tape.

Sort. To arrange data in sequence, according to specific rules.

Source code. Program statements written in a source language.

Source deck. A source module in punched-card form.

Source document. A document containing source data.

Source language. The form of an input to a translation process.

Source program. A program written in a source language, such as COBOL, FORTRAN, or BASIC, for input to a compiler, generator, or an assembler.

Special character. A character that is neither a letter of the alphabet nor a digit. Examples are commas, semicolons, dollar signs, and decimal points.

Special-purpose computer. A computer engineered to carry out special functions, in contrast with a general-purpose computer which is useful for many purposes.

Specifications. The standards for a system, including input, processing, and output.

Spooling. Moving data from a slow I/O device to a high-speed I/O device prior to moving them into primary storage. This helps minimize the speed disparity between the computer and the I/O. On output, the order of data movement is reversed.

Stacked job processing. The same as batch processing.

Stand-alone computer. A computer, in one location, which is not linked with any other computer.

Standards. The level of expectation against which performance will be measured.

Statement. In computer programming, a meaningful expression or generalized instruction in a source language.

Storage. (1) Pertaining to a device into which data can be entered, in which they can be held, and from which they can be retrieved at a later time; or (2) Any device that can store data.

Storage capacity. The maximum amount of data that can be contained in a particular storage device.

Storage protection. A technique that is applied to prevent unauthorized reading or writing of data in a particular area of storage.

Stored program. A series of instructions placed in a computer's primary storage to control the computer.

Stored program computer. A computer than can perform operations under control of internally stored instructions.

Structured programming. Planning and implementing a program as a series of linked logical modules, paying special attention to documentation, testability, and program clarity in order to simplify program debugging and maintenance.

Subprogram. A part of a larger program that can be compiled independently.

Subroutine. A routine that can be part of another routine.

Subsystem. A subdivision of a broader system.

Summarizing. Accumulating totals from a number of input records for later output.

Supervisor. A routine or routines executed in response to a requirement for altering or interrupting the flow of operation through the central processing unit, or for performance of input/output operations; therefore, the medium through which the use of resources is coordinated and the flow of operations through the central processing unit is maintained. A control routine that is executed in the supervisor state.

Symbol. An entity that represents something else by reason of relationship, convention, definition, or association.

Symbolic address. An address that is expressed in symbols convenient to the programmer and is translated into an absolute address before it is interpreted by the computer.

Synchronous. Occurring concurrently, and with a regular or predictable time relationship.

Synergism. The concept that the whole is equal to more than the sum of the parts.

Synonym. A record whose computed or randomized relative record number is identical to that of a different record.

Syntax error. An error in the usage of the programming language utilized.

System. (1) An assemby of methods, procedures, or techniques united by regulated interaction to form an organized whole; or (2) An organized collection of humans, machines, and methods required to accomplish a set of specific functions.

System check. A check on the overall performance of a computer system. Examples are record counts and control totals.

System flowchart. A flowchart that uses specific symbols to graphically depict the steps in a system. The systems flowchart is not limited to computer operations, but also covers manual and mechanical steps. The systems flowchart is prepared prior to preparing a program flowchart.

System library. See library.

System loader. A resident routine of the supervisor that loads all programs (other than the supervisor itself and the initial program loader) into main storage.

System model. See model.

System residence device. An auxiliary storage unit on which operating system programs are stored so that they can be loaded into primary storage at appropriate times.

Systems analysis. The analysis of an activity to determine precisely what must be accomplished and how to accomplish it.

Systems analyst. A person who practices systems analysis, analyzing systems from a broad point of view.

Systems design. The specification of the standards for a system.

System software. Programs or routines that belong to the entire system rather than to any single programmer, and that usually perform a support function.

Systems study. The initial phase of the system cycle, which documents organization history, external environment, and objectives and policies, and delineates a master plan.

Systems tests. Actually running applications on the complete system, using actual or test data, and analyzing the results to determine a system's accuracy, capability, and adequacy.

Table. An organized collection of data, usually arranged in an array, in which each item in the array is uniquely identifiable by some label or by its relative position. Items in a table are easy to locate or identify, and thus provide a ready reference.

Tape ring. See file ring.

Telecommunications. See data communication.

Teleprocessing. See data communication.

Terminal. (1) A point in a system or communication network at which data can enter or leave; (2) A piece of hardware designed to be placed at the terminal of a communication network for the purpose of entering or obtaining data; or (3) A symbol, used in flowcharting, which indicates the beginning and end of the chart.

Testing. The process of ensuring that an implemented program or system actually solves the problem that it is intended to solve.

Third-generation computer. In the period 1964–1971, a computer that utilized monolithic integrated circuits.

Throughput. A measure of system efficiency; the rate at which work can be handled by a system.

Time sharing. Pertaining to the interleaved use of the time of a device. In particular, an on-line system in which many users share availability of a remote central computer.

Top-down approach. Solving problems by starting with a broad, total system point of view and gradually introducing details, layer by layer, until a solution is obtained.

Total system. An organized grouping of all related systems.

Tracing routine. A routine that provides documentation of specified events and the sequence in which those events occur during execution of a program.

Track. The portion of a moving storage-medium, such as a drum, tape, or disk, that is accessible to a given read/write-head position.

Transaction. A single input record or a single query.

Transaction file. A file containing relatively transient information; for example, records of individual transactions occurring during a specific period of time.

Transfer rate. The amount of data that a device can send to another piece of equipment in a given period of time.

Transistor. Part of the electronic components of many modern computers. Transistors replaced the vacuum tubes used in earlier computers.

Translator. A routine, program, or device capable of directing the translation or transformation of statements or their equivalent codes in one language to equivalent statements or their equivalent codes in another language.

Transmission mode. Simplex, half duplex, and full duplex communication channels.

Turnaround. The elapsed time between submission of a job to a computer center and the return of results.

Unbundling. For pricing purposes, the separation of equipment costs and other costs (e.g., software and training). This allows the user to select only those things desired, and to pay for only those.

Unconditional branch. An instruction that always causes a transfer from the normal sequence of instruction execution.

Unit record. A punched card containing one complete record.

UNIVAC I. The first commercially available electronic computer.

Universal product code (UPC). Codes used primarily on retail products (e.g., canned and boxed goods) to identify the item automatically at the checkout counter. The codes appear mostly in the form of bars.

Utility program. A routine in support of a computer; for example, an input/output diagnostic, tracing, or monitoring routine.

Validation run. See edit run.

Validity. To determine the accuracy of something.

Variable. A quantity that can assume any of a given set of values.

Variable cost. A cost that varies with activity.

Variable field-length. Setting variable-length field sizes, depending on need, for the fields of a record in a file.

Variable name. A programmer-assigned label that may identify both a data field and a storage location.

Variable record-length. Setting variable-length record sizes, depending on need, for the records in a file.

Variable word-length. A computer word in which the number of characters in a given word is variable and subject to the discretion of the programmer. Each character is addressable, which permits control of word lengths.

Verification. The act of verifying.

Verify. To determine whether a transcription of data or other operation has been accomplished accurately.

Virtual storage. Memory space on a secondary-storage device that is used to hold programs and data on a virtual memory system. Instructions and data must be transferred from this virtual memory into real memory, prior to execution or processing.

Virtual storage access method. An access method or file organization in which data are stored on a secondary device in fixed-length segments or pages, and transferred into real memory such as program pages or segments on a virtual memory system.

Voiceband. In data transmission, the voiceband is used to denote a channel suitable for transmission of speech or data.

Voice-response unit. A unit that permits audio response. That is, an inquiry is made to the computer, usually by means of a keyboard. The computer transmits the response to an audio response unit that contains a magnetic drum. The unit selects words and phrases from a prerecorded vocabulary stored on the drum, and forms a verbal response.

Volatility. On data files, a measure of the frequency of additions to or deletions from the file.

von Neumann, John. The individual who was largely responsible for developing the ideas of the stored program concept, and the use of the binary system for modern computers.

Wideband channel. A communication channel capable of carrying data at a rate higher than a voice-grade channel.

Word. A character string or bit string considered as an entity.

Word-addressable. Pertaining to a computer that performs operations on fixed word lengths.

Word processing. The automation of the office, particularly by recording words (e.g., letters and reports) on some storage medium so that selective corrections and changes can be made, and so that the storage device can generate the desired documents very rapidly.

Write. In the computer field, to record output.

Zone bit. In EBCDIC, four of the eight bits used to represent a character are referred to as zone bits. The zone bits, in combination with numeric bits, form codes to represent characters.

Zoned decimal. A decimal representation in EBCDIC in which each character is encoded as an eight-bit character, utilizing both the zone and numeric bits for each character. For numbers, the zone bits represent the sign of the number; that is, a bit pattern of 1111 in the zone portion represents an unsigned number; 1100 represents a positive number; and 1101 represents a negative number.

Zone punch. A 12, 11, or 0 punch on a punched card.

INDEX

A

B

C

D

E

F

G

H

I

N

O

P

R

S

T